The Gift of Reading
The Houston
Graduate Chapter
Swing Phi Swing Social Fellowship, Inc.®

AF769805

Perpetrating the Holocaust

Perpetrating the Holocaust

Leaders, Enablers, and Collaborators

PAUL R. BARTROP AND EVE E. GRIMM

[redacted]

ABC-CLIO™

An Imprint of ABC-CLIO, LLC
Santa Barbara, California • Denver, Colorado

Copyright © 2019 by ABC-CLIO, LLC

All rights reserved. No part of this publication may be reproduced, stored in a retrieval system, or transmitted, in any form or by any means, electronic, mechanical, photocopying, recording, or otherwise, except for the inclusion of brief quotations in a review, without prior permission in writing from the publisher.

Library of Congress Cataloging-in-Publication Data

Names: Bartrop, Paul R. (Paul Robert), 1955– author. | Grimm, Eve E., author.
Title: Perpetrating the Holocaust : leaders, enablers, and collaborators / Paul R. Bartrop and Eve E. Grimm.
Description: Santa Barbara, California : ABC-CLIO, [2019] | Includes bibliographical references and index.
Identifiers: LCCN 2018033514 (print) | LCCN 2018034234 (ebook) | ISBN 9781440858970 (eBook) | ISBN 9781440858963 (hardcopy : alk. paper)
Subjects: LCSH: Holocaust, Jewish (1939–1945)—Encyclopedias. | War criminals—Germany—Biography. | World War, 1939–1945—Collaborationists—Biography. | Crimes against humanity—Germany—Biography. | Germany—Biography.
Classification: LCC D804.25 (ebook) | LCC D804.25 .B37 2019 (print) | DDC 940.53/1803—dc23
LC record available at https://lccn.loc.gov/2018033514

ISBN: 978-1-4408-5896-3 (print)
978-1-4408-5897-0 (ebook)

23 22 21 20 19 1 2 3 4 5

This book is also available as an eBook.

ABC-CLIO
An Imprint of ABC-CLIO, LLC

ABC-CLIO, LLC
147 Castilian Drive
Santa Barbara, California 93117
www.abc-clio.com

This book is printed on acid-free paper ∞

Manufactured in the United States of America

Every reasonable effort has been made to trace the owners of copyright materials in this book, but in some instances this has proven impossible. The editors and publishers will be glad to receive information leading to more complete acknowledgments in subsequent printings of the book and in the meantime extend their apologies for any omissions.

*To those who refused to yield to the perpetrators and
to the memory of those unable to*

All humans are human, and there are no humans more human than others.

—Romeo Dallaire, UN Force Commander,
Rwanda, 1993–1994

Contents

List of Entries

List of Primary Source Documents

Nazi Abbreviations Used in the Text

BdM	*Bund deutscher Mädel*: League of German Girls
DAF	*Deutsche Arbeitsfront*: German Labor Front
Gestapo	*Geheime Staatspolizei*: Secret State Police
HJ	*Hitlerjugend*: Hitler Youth
HSSPF	*Höherer SS- und Polizeiführer*: Higher SS and Police Leader
Kripo	*Kriminalpolizei*: Criminal Police
NSDAP	*Nationalsozialistische Deutsche Arbeiterpartei*: National Socialist German Workers' Party
NS-Frauenschaft	*Nationalsozialistische Frauenschaft*: National Socialist Women's League
Orpo	*Ordnungspolizei*: Order Police
RSHA	*Reichssicherheitshauptamt*: Reich Main Security Office
RuSHA	*Rasse- und Siedlungshauptamt der SS*: SS Race and Settlement Main Office
SA	*Sturmabteilung*: Storm Detachments
SD	*Sicherheitsdienst*: Security Service
SiPo	*Sicherheitspolizei*: Security Police
SS	*Schutzstaffel*: Protection Squad
SS-HA	*SS-Hauptamt*: SS Main Office
T-4	*Aktion T-4*, from Tiergartenstrasse 4: the Nazi euthanasia program
WVHA	*SS-Wirtschafts- und Verwaltungshauptamt*: SS Main Economic and Administrative Office

SS Ranks Compared with the U.S. Army

Officer Ranks

SS-Reichsführer	None
SS-Oberstgruppenführer	General
SS-Obergruppenführer	Lieutenant General
SS-Gruppenführer	Major General
SS-Brigadeführer	Brigadier General
SS-Oberführer	None
SS-Standartenführer	Colonel
SS-Obersturmbannführer	Lieutenant Colonel
SS-Sturmbannführer	Major
SS-Hauptsturmführer	Captain
SS-Obersturmführer	First Lieutenant
SS-Untersturmführer	Second Lieutenant

NonCommissioned Officer Ranks

SS-Sturmscharführer	Sergeant Major
SS-Hauptscharführer	Master Sergeant
SS-Oberscharführer	Sergeant First Class
SS-Scharführer	Staff Sergeant
SS-Unterscharführer	Sergeant
SS-Rottenführer	Corporal

Preface

In 2016, one of the authors of this book, Paul R. Bartrop, produced a volume entitled *Resisting the Holocaust: Upstanders, Partisans, and Survivors*. It was a book about people who said no to the attempt by National Socialist Germany, between 1933 and 1945, to disenfranchise, dehumanize, and ultimately destroy the Jewish people of Europe. Those who said no did so in a wide variety of ways and for a plethora of reasons. If we were to group them all together, we would inevitably find ourselves using a single word—"resistance"—to describe their activities.

After the book's appearance, it took little time to realize that a second volume examining those who committed the crimes of the Holocaust would have to be written. It would be the darkness that so illuminated the light generated by the resistance book—the yin, so to speak, of the first book's yang. And given the uncertain times characterizing the second half of this century's second decade, such a book was considered both timely and necessary, if only for the reason that more and more people are demanding to know why such acts as the Nazis perpetrated took place—and what this means for our world today.

The Holocaust was the most horrific crime any group of people ever perpetrated against another. It spoke of a human dream: how, in the Nazi view, humanity could be perfected. In attempting to reach this perfection, the Nazis concluded that it was necessary to eliminate those they considered to be an impediment to achieving this goal—the Jews. In the Nazi view, they acted with the best of intentions and to guarantee the future of the "Aryan" people. Their Jewish victims, on the other hand, possessed neither a present nor a future, other than as a people who until now had avoided their intended (and inevitable) fate. As the Holocaust's perpetrators, the Nazis planned, perpetrated, and presided over that fate. They were committed, for reasons clear to them, to realizing the dream of achieving racial and national homogeneity for the German people, a pure society comprised only of others like themselves, a place representing the closest possible approximation to human perfection. The deeds carried out by those perpetrating the Holocaust were vicious, violent, inhumane, and, from the perspective of Western morality at least, utterly wrong.

That said, this work does not attempt to judge or assess the behavior of those it discusses, but merely to tell their story in summary form and to allow the unfolding narrative of each to encourage readers to draw their own conclusions. In that sense, this is not meant as the last word on each subject but rather as an introduction to each of those whose biographies are narrated here. We have not sought to ask why people behaved in certain ways, and to the best of our ability, we have refrained from making judgments about their behavior. Some, indeed, we consider to be morally repugnant, but in all instances, we have done our best not to let our bias show.

This is, therefore, a reference work designed to assist others in their own research. It is not an examination of ethical behavior as such, although the actions of all those here could serve as a manual of how not behave in any given situation.

When we began our hunt for perpetrators of the Holocaust, we thought that the process would be relatively easy. It took us no time at all to find a seed list of major perpetrators, but this only fed our desire to dig deeper. We began looking for others to add to the list. Sometimes it was through sheer accident or luck that we found names that had been little studied up until now. In other instances, dealing with one name led inevitably to uncovering another—just as with the layers of an onion, we kept peeling back without ever reaching a central core. The process of discovery continued right up to the very last days. Long after we thought the phase of writing the entries was finished, we found ourselves still adding one or two or three names to the list and then writing up their stories.

As we found, however, choosing the people to feature here was actually no easy task, and the list could easily have been extended into the thousands. In addition, our selections were conditioned by our preference for examples representative of the wide range of perpetrator activities that could have been, and were, undertaken. For every person included here, there were dozens more we could have added.

This presented an added problem: space. We simply could not include every leader, enabler, or collaborator who had an involvement in the Holocaust, as the amount of space permitted by the publishing process would not allow for this in a single volume. More is the pity; practical considerations have led to many people being omitted, although this can count as a positive for students and researchers seeking to undertake their own projects. The field, in many respects, remains wide open.

Tens of thousands of perpetrators, of all kinds and in all locations, deserve their place in a book of this kind, and as authors, we frequently faced a dilemma as to whom to leave out. It is our hope, therefore, that readers will appreciate that those profiled here are but a sample of an otherwise-enormous range of human beings who, for one reason or another, chose to follow Adolf Hitler in his search for German glory and destructive plans for the Jews of Europe. Those not appearing in these pages were no less dishonorable or murderous than those who are.

That said, it is our hope that the entries we have included here provide a profile of Holocaust perpetrators that is broad enough to enable readers to derive some measure of understanding regarding the men and women who chose to commit this enormous crime. We hope, in this context, that the examples we have included will be sufficiently illustrative of a cohort that is thousands of times greater in expanse than the current volume suggests.

The entries have been organized in such a way as to provide maximum accessibility for readers. It is a straightforward alphabetical listing, by last name, of a variety of Holocaust perpetrators, whether those who led the process, those who made it happen, or those who collaborated. To assist readers where cross-references occur, we have placed figures in **bold** when they appear in the entries of others featured in the volume.

In writing this work, we have employed a wide range of sources, ranging from books and documentaries to a massive range of Internet sites that could not be listed even if we were to try. Often while researching a person's life, we had to consult up to 30 or more sites only to find three or four key facts. Sometimes, despite all efforts, some data simply could not be found. On other occasions, we were lucky and hit the information mother lode after consulting only five or six sites. In every case, however, we would only consider a piece of data legitimate after corroboration from two or more sources independent of each other. Internet sites are notorious for the extent to which they lift the work of one or two generic sites and then just keep replicating the same information uncritically again and again. It is our hope that the standards of corroboration we have applied have dealt with the issue satisfactorily and eliminated the worst excesses of inexactitude.

A further note of explanation is needed. Europe in the 1930s and 1940s was a continent in flux; countries and regions changed borders, and towns and cities often changed names. To preserve the contemporaneity of the situations under examination, we have preserved the names of the localities by which they were best known within the context of the Holocaust (e.g., Vilna) with their modern renditions in parenthesis alongside (Vilnius). Our hope is that this will enhance clarity for modern readers and cut through what might otherwise be a confusion of names.

The extensive bibliography has been designed as more than just a list of relevant books and articles. In most of the titles listed, the name of at least one of the perpetrators has been added in **bold**, to better enable readers to locate pertinent works on the perpetrator and the events in which he or she participated.

Finally, mention should be made of two additional lists that accompany the volume. First, a listing of abbreviations of Nazi terms, as used in the text, has been included to assist readers and not crowd the text. Also, rather than replicate the equivalence of SS and U.S. military ranks, we have provided a list with these details. Within the text itself, only the SS ranks have been included.

As this project developed, we were fortunate to receive encouragement and support from several people who now deserve our public thanks. Florida Gulf Coast University (FGCU) is a vibrant center of educational excellence, which presented many opportunities for us to develop and extend our thoughts regarding those listed in this work. The associate vice president of research and dean of graduate studies, Dr. T. C. Yih, and the dean of the College of Arts and Sciences, Dr. Robert Gregerson, have been steadfast in the confidence they have shown us as we worked through this often-difficult project. Dean Gregerson, furthermore, found funds to help hire a graduate assistant, Taylor Neff, who helped us with researching some of the people featured here.

The library staff at FGCU have assisted in numerous ways throughout the project and deserve our deep respect and gratitude.

Throughout the writing of this book, we have been fortunate to have a remarkable editor at ABC-CLIO who has shown complete faith in the project from its inception. We are pleased to express our appreciation to Padraic (Pat) Carlin for his help, ideas, and forbearance. The book would not have appeared without his assistance.

Introduction

One day in November 1944, several children arrived at Auschwitz. We do not know from where they came or what their names were. They were Jewish children. As the truck slowed, one little boy holding an apple jumped off. His intention was not to run away; in his youthful excitement, he wanted simply to be first off the truck so that he could eat his apple. One of the SS men standing nearby, **Wilhelm Boger**, saw the boy next to the truck, enjoying himself. Suddenly Boger went over to the boy, grabbed his legs, and smashed his head against the wall. Then he calmly picked up the apple and went back to his office. About an hour later, a prisoner who had seen the boy's murder was called to the office to assist in a translation issue. There, he saw Boger eating the child's apple.[1]

American sociologist and Holocaust survivor Fred E. Katz notes that Boger's gruesome killing of this innocent child for the apple had a theatrical quality to it: "He ate the apple in front of a witness to the murderous deed. It was no accident that Boger ate the apple when the witness was there to see it. He was *flaunting* his evil."[2]

For that little boy, Boger's act was the supreme example in his short life of the Nazi new order. We do not know what experiences the child had already lived through, but there is no doubt that at that moment, in those circumstances, SS officer Boger embodied the full horror of the Holocaust.

Questions about the Holocaust

Ever since revelations about the Holocaust first came to light, questions have abounded regarding the nature of those who perpetrated what was unquestionably the greatest criminal act of deliberate mass murder in history. Did the killers not possess a conscience? Were they all psychopaths? What type of society was the Germany that could plan and carry out this massive criminal act?

To address these and other questions, many studies have been made of those whose actions describe them as perpetrators of the Holocaust, looking at the phenomenon from a variety of perspectives. When all such studies are taken into consideration, however, certain facts remain constant—the primary one being that the so-called Final Solution of the Jewish Question (*Endlösung der Judenfrage*) was a massive state project at the heart of Nazi wartime race and population policy. When it comes to assessing responsibility for any crime, the key question is, who did it? In the case of the Holocaust, that figure runs into hundreds of thousands.

In the first place, it must be remembered that it was a *Nazi* government from *Germany* that was responsible for the Holocaust. Antisemitism was embedded directly into the DNA of Nazism and featured prominently in the party platform of 1920.[3] There was always a compulsion to eliminate Jews from German life, although it is important to realize that Nazism did not automatically equate with genocidal mass murder. This was an aspiration that developed over time, as did the techniques—and the expertise—to achieve it.[4]

When the destructive phase of the Nazi assault on the Jews was initiated, no other country had developed racial policies as radical as those of Nazi Germany. The destruction of the Jewish people was never the policy of any other European country or government, and those who led the destruction were German Nazis. **Adolf Hitler**, as head of the Nazi government, was its prime mover. His views of the Jews as an "eternal race enemy," coupled with his notions of inclusivity and exclusivity relating to the German *Volk*, could leave no one with any illusions as to his preferences.[5]

He could not, however, have achieved his aims relative to the Jews, or anything else, without the willing, and often-enthusiastic, support of others around him. The head of the SS, **Heinrich Himmler**, and those in charge of the security services, **Reinhard Heydrich** and **Kurt Daluege**, created a tyrannical police state founded on issues of race, control, and violence. And the SS (*Schutzstaffel*) itself, an organization that began as Hitler's personal bodyguard but mutated into one of the most powerful organizations in Nazi Germany, was the foremost agency of security, surveillance, and terror both within Germany and, later, throughout German-occupied Europe. Not only were members of the SS the most important actors in the destruction of the Jews of Europe but also the entire project was entrusted to Himmler and Heydrich and run as an SS campaign.

How Many Killers?

In view of that, it must be said that fully hundreds of thousands of people were directly involved in carrying out the Final Solution. The political leaders of the Third Reich were of course those who desired the entire operation, but the organizers and killers came from a variety of Nazi organizations. These were the praetorian guards of mass murder, forming the essential personnel running the extermination camps, operating the mobile killing units (*Einsatzgruppen*), and administering the whole program.

In a remarkable documentary made in 2005, Danish filmmaker Ove Nyholm sought to learn the motivations of mass murderers at a time of war. Interviewing Serbian killers from the Yugoslav wars of the 1990s, he showed how such people, through their actions, acquired ancestors—the SS murderers of the Holocaust. He was, he said, attempting to plumb the depths of heartlessness. Quoting one of the *Einsatzgruppen* killers who was confronted by a victim just before being gunned down in a pit killing, Nyholm reached what he considered to be the quintessential justification of genocide. "You must die," the SS officer said, "so that we might live."[6]

Upon further reflection, Nyholm sought to ascertain the full extent of the killing culture: the density, in real world terms, of the murder cohort when charted on a map of Germany. He took the figure of 107,000 files relating to alleged Nazi war criminals held in the archives of the Central Office of the State Justice Administrations for the Investigation of National Socialist Crimes (*Zentrale Stelle der Landesjustizverwaltungen zur Aufklärung nationalsozialistischer Verbrechen*), in Ludwigsburg, Germany. Calculating the ratio of war criminals in relation to the total geographical area of the country (including lakes, mountains, and forests), he found an average of 2.4 perpetrators per square kilometer. "Seen from street level," he concluded, "that's less than 700 meters between each one; 688 meters, to be precise."[7]

Leaders: Who Did It?

This shocking figure tells only part of the story, for there were many thousands of others involved for whom files were not kept. SS and police commanders, together with those commanding the *Einsatzgruppen*, directed the clearing of ghettos and villages, the concentration of inhabitants in open spaces, and then the systematic shooting of men, women, and children in the killing fields of the occupied Soviet Union. In occupied Poland, SS leaders established factories of death, killing centers equipped with gas chambers that enabled mass murder to take place as if on an assembly line.

And it was not only members of the SS and police who were actively enmeshed in the implementation of the Final Solution. Until a short time ago, the German army had, for several decades, projected the image that it was not directly caught up in the killing of Jews; its sole responsibility was always (so the argument went) one of military combat. More recent scholarship, however, has shown conclusively that the Wehrmacht made its contribution to the Final Solution in the Soviet Union and that the SS was far from alone.[8] This involvement, it must be added, sometimes extended to the highest levels of the military, while letters and photographs sent home by frontline German soldiers often documented atrocities—either those they had witnessed or those in which they had themselves taken part.

Perhaps the most important agent of death was the SS, formed in 1923 as a specialized unit of 50 men to act as Hitler's personal bodyguard. After Hitler's failed putsch of November 11, 1923, the SS was banned, but it was reconstituted under the leadership of Heinrich Himmler as a racially elite unit in 1929. The inspiration for his restructure might have come from Himmler's own Roman Catholic upbringing and his admiration for the military-style discipline and obedience of the Jesuit order.[9] Himmler conceived of a paramilitary organization consisting of members of high moral caliber, honesty, and decency who would be committed to the Nazi vision and agenda and thoroughly antisemitic in orientation. Its infamous black uniform and *Totenkopf*, or "Death's Head," insignias were introduced in 1932. By 1933, it was a force of more than 200,000 men.[10] Under Himmler's guidance, the SS not only developed the Nazi concentration camp system but also took responsibility for staffing the camps, instituting the discipline policies within them, and planning how best to exploit the prisoners as slave labor.[11]

From the summer of 1941 onward, the SS took control of the annihilation of Europe's Jews, first through the *Einsatzgruppen* and then, after 1942, through the extermination camps located in Poland. Thus, those primarily responsible for the murder of European Jewry in the various slave labor, concentration, and death camps came from the ranks of the SS. After the war, at the International Military Tribunal at Nuremberg, the SS was formally declared a criminal organization and compulsorily disbanded. Himmler committed suicide on May 23, 1945, but the overwhelming majority of SS members were never brought to trial. A very large proportion, in fact, lived out full lives and died in their beds, some at an advanced age.

Many Nazis of high rank (although not Hitler or **Hermann Göring**, for long the second most powerful man in the Third Reich), as well as many members of the SS, were well educated. **Josef Goebbels** held a PhD from the University of Heidelberg; **Heinrich Himmler** studied agronomy at the Munich *Technische Hochschule* (now the University of Technology, Munich); **Hans Frank**, appointed governor-general of occupied Poland, was a lawyer, as were a majority of the 15 attendees at the Wannsee Conference in January 1942. **Alfred Rosenberg**, the Nazi Party's leading race ideologue, possessed a PhD in engineering from a university in prerevolutionary Russia. Three out of the four commanders of the *Einsatzgruppen* operating in the Soviet Union had earned doctorates, and the list goes on. These were all part of a genocidal project that formed a central platform of the Nazi state.

It is remarkable, moreover, how frequently many of the actual killers on the ground encountered each other throughout the war. Schooled in murder during the early days of the Nazi movement, they became experts in their craft, and as experienced specialists, they could often be found close by to each other—at meetings, in the camps, or in their numerous deployments. Indeed, often they succeeded each other in a range of different assignments.

While an immediate response to the question of who the perpetrators of the Holocaust were might settle on the person of Adolf Hitler, it must always be borne in mind that within Nazi Germany, all sectors of society played their role in planning, facilitating, and executing the Final Solution.

Enablers: Who Made It Possible?

If the leaders of the Holocaust and their followers in the vanguard of the genocide can be considered under the heading of "who did it?" then those we can term "enablers" could comfortably fall into the category of "who made it possible?" A broad cross section of German society fits under this classification, which was top heavy with well-educated professionals: bankers, professors, doctors, journalists, transport workers, engineers, judges, authors, teachers, lawyers, and civil servants. The range of those who aided and abetted the killers was as wide ranging as the German social fabric itself. Carrying out the Final Solution required cooperation from people in all walks of life and was far from being just an SS or military project. Not everyone was necessarily aware of the full extent of the role they were playing, but all fitted into the bigger picture, and few questioned what the logical outcome of their actions could be.

Among the leaders in the corporate world were the owners and managers of major industrial and commercial enterprises who sought to profit from Nazi programs of Aryanization, persecution, and, indeed, extermination of the Jews. Many of the major German corporations were running short of labor to carry out the day-to-day work in which they were engaged; they did not hesitate to use slave labor, even from concentration camp inmates who were being worked to death under extraordinarily brutal conditions. Nor could many of these same corporations resist theft—of ideas, premises, artwork, and client lists—from Jewish (or formerly Jewish) companies. The actions of the German corporate sector deserve scrutiny, and in some cases, the motives and behavior of individuals relating to the Holocaust have been examined here. A comprehensive treatment, however, still awaits its author.

After the war, it was recognized that many people involved in the murder process had volunteered eagerly to be part of it. Others, however, always saw themselves as simply obeying orders, such as several members of Reserve Police Battalion 101, a unit of 500 middle-aged, lower- and lower-middle-class family men from Hamburg, who were drafted into the so-called Order Police and were active in murdering up to 38,000 men, women, and children in Eastern Europe in 1942 and 1943. A variety of hypotheses can be proffered regarding their behavior: wartime brutalization, racism, segmentation and routinization of their tasks, careerism, obedience to authority and orders, ideological indoctrination, conformity, quasi-military status, and a sense of elitism. No single explanation, however, provides an all-embracing answer, and this can be extrapolated beyond this single unit.[12]

Moreover, throughout Nazi-occupied Europe, many others enjoyed the power Nazi authority gave them. Some also exploited the situation for personal gain. While leaders can be classified under the heading of "who did it?" and enablers under that of "who made it possible?" collaborators in other lands certainly earned the caption "who helped?"

Collaborators: Who Helped?

Non-German collaborators were to be found in every country, and the Nazis relied upon them to carry out their terrible acts against individuals and communities across Europe. Further, one did not have to be a German to be a Nazi. This was made clear through the experiences Jews had with the Arrow Cross Party in Hungary, the Hlinka Guard in Slovakia, antisemitic Poles who denounced Jews to their German occupiers, Vichy French officials and police, Ukrainian collaborators who often dominated the guard detachment in the extermination camps, and so on. Each state responded differently to the Nazi extermination program, with significant variations in the level of cooperation.[13]

The Nazis, moreover, traded on local animosities and prejudices when it came to the question of collaboration. They were happy for the French to do their dirty work for them; indeed, the Vichy regime hastened to act against its Jews before being required to by the Nazi occupiers. In Croatia, homegrown excesses were so extreme that the Nazis invited their Croat allies to tone down the vehemence of their actions. Romanian brutality against Jews in the occupied Crimea shocked

German observers. And in Latvia and Lithuania, the Nazis sought to deflect responsibility for their antisemitic activities by arranging for native collaborators to undertake pogroms on their behalf.

The term "quisling," meaning a person who collaborates with an enemy occupying force (or, more broadly, a synonym for the word "traitor"), originated in the person of **Vidkun Quisling**, the main Norwegian collaborator with the occupying Germans. There were a variety of such people in the countries occupied by the Nazis, particularly in France, Belgium, and the Netherlands in Western Europe and in Ukraine and the Baltic States in Eastern Europe. The countries allied with Germany also played their part in the destruction of the Jews, notably Romania, Hungary, Slovakia, and Croatia. Italy introduced antisemitic laws in November 1938, although these were never embraced by the Italian population at large.

In many of the countries that might be considered German satellites—whether occupied or allied—a variety of auxiliary forces were brought into the anti-Jewish project, and in some cases, their actions were the equal (at least) of Nazi barbarities. The degree to which collaborators supported, facilitated, or were accessories to the Holocaust varied. Some people took part enthusiastically in killing operations, and some enlisted in the Waffen-SS for active service due to strongly held convictions about Nazi ideology.[14] Indeed, full Waffen-SS divisions—French, Croatian, Danish, Norwegian, Bosnian, Latvian, Dutch, Ukrainian, Belgian, and many others—were created in lands occupied by the Nazis and then deployed to fight on behalf of Nazi Germany. Collectively, these numbered in the hundreds of thousands, adding enormously to the pool of available manpower from whom the Germans could draw. Other collaborators acted from additional motives, which could be monetary, careerist, or based in a fear of retribution. From time to time, genuinely held opportunistic motives surfaced; on other occasions, collaborators were prompted to act in especially violent ways owing to unmet sociopathological needs.

In short, the Holocaust was visited upon the Jews of Europe by a wide variety of messengers, whether Germans or not.

The Holocaust and Its Perpetrators

This book looks at just a bare handful of these people. Most are men from Germany and Austria; some are women; some are collaborators from other countries. All were motivated by a longing to destroy a Jewish presence in Europe (if not the whole world), and all possessed the ability to choose between life and death, between participation and avoidance.

It was this that separated them from Jews who shared in the killing process—those singled out, for example, as members of the Jewish Councils (*Judenräte*) or Jewish police in ghettos or *kapos* in the concentration camps. For them, life choices did not exist, and in that sense, they could not be viewed as complicit. In most cases, they did not even have control over their daily activities. They certainly had no control over the time, place, or manner of their death, and they were both persecuted by the Nazis and punished by other Jews owing to their involvement.

The Holocaust was a period in which the most revolting mass atrocities were committed by humans against other humans. Who were the perpetrators of these crimes? For the mother forced to choose between two children on the ramp at Auschwitz, it was that Nazi soldier forcing the choice; for the adolescent girl torn from the embrace of her little sister because she was old enough to work while the younger girl was not, it was an SS officer; for the old man beaten to death by the roadside by a Nazi soldier because he couldn't move fast enough when ordered to, it was a Nazi soldier; and for the newlyweds who were forced into the squalor of the ghetto where the bride watched her husband die of starvation and disease only to die herself immediately afterward, the Holocaust was represented by those who had brought them into this condition. Elsewhere, local variants of all these scenarios were played out. Some had extensive support; some did not.

But everywhere, regardless of the level of enthusiasm from leaders, enablers, or collaborators, Jews were always vulnerable to discrimination, denunciation, deportation, and, ultimately, extermination. As Rabbi Hugo Gryn, a survivor of Auschwitz, Sachsenhausen, and Mauthausen, recalled about the Holocaust, "It was the most terrible revelation about the principle of evil. . . . We were its victims, and we know who the perpetrators were. And Europe, it seems to me, was a bystander. And this is the essence of the tragedy."[15]

Notes

1. Bernd Naumann. *Auschwitz: A Report on the Proceedings against Robert Karl, Ludwig Mulka and Others before the Court at Frankfurt*. New York: Praeger, 1996, p. 133; quoted in Fred E. Katz. *Ordinary People and Extraordinary Evil: A Report on the Beguilings of Evil*. Albany, NY: State University of New York Press, 1993, p. 88.
2. Ibid.
3. See Document 1, this volume.
4. In an otherwise extensive literature, see especially Karl A. Schleunes. *The Twisted Road to Auschwitz: Nazi Policy toward German Jews, 1933–1939*. Urbana, IL: University of Illinois Press, 1970; and Christopher R. Browning. *The Origins of the Final Solution: The Evolution of Nazi Jewish Policy, September 1939–March 1942*. Lincoln, NE: University of Nebraska Press, 2004. Browning has also written some useful essays on this topic in *Fateful Months: Essays on the Emergence of the Final Solution*. New York: Holmes and Meier, 1985.
5. The libraries of books written about Hitler over the past 80 years have all had something to say about his attitude toward the Jews, and this is not the place for a detailed excursus into Hitlerania. One very good study (with an excellent accompanying bibliography) is Richard Weikart. *Hitler's Ethic: The Nazi Pursuit of Evolutionary Progress*. New York: Palgrave Macmillan, 2009. Indispensable in this context is Ian Kershaw. *Hitler, the Germans, and the Final Solution*. New Haven: Yale University Press, 2008. Two other useful works are Philippe Burrin. *Hitler and the Jews: The Genesis of the Holocaust*. London: Edward Arnold, 1994; and Gerald Fleming. *Hitler and the Final Solution*. London: Hamish Hamilton, 1985.
6. *Anatomy of Evil (Ondskabens anatomi)*, Angel Films, dir. Ove Nyholm, prod. Janne Giese, 2005.
7. Ibid.

8. Wehrmacht involvement in the Holocaust has been demonstrated in a number of key studies. See, for example, Omer Bartov. *The Eastern Front, 1941–45, German Troops, and the Barbarisation of Warfare*. New York: Palgrave Macmillan, 1986; Omer Bartov. *Hitler's Army: Soldiers, Nazis, and War in the Third Reich*. New York: Oxford University Press, 1991; Jeff Rutherford. *Combat and Genocide on the Eastern Front: The German Infantry's War, 1941–1944*. Cambridge: Cambridge University Press, 2014; and Geoffrey P. Megargee. *War of Annihilation: Combat and Genocide on the Eastern Front, 1941*. Lanham, MD: Rowman and Littlefield, 2005.
9. A definitive biography of Himmler can be found in Peter Longerich. *Heinrich Himmler*. Oxford: Oxford University Press, 2012.
10. The most recent history of the SS is Adrian Weale. *Army of Evil: A History of the SS*. New York: NAL Caliber, 2012. For the intellectual underpinnings of the SS, see also Christian Ingrao. *Believe and Destroy: Intellectuals in the SS War Machine*. Cambridge: Polity, 2013.
11. Two recent studies on the SS and the camps are essential. For the early Nazi period, see Kim Wünschmann. *Before Auschwitz: Jewish Prisoners in the Prewar Concentration Camps*. Cambridge, MA: Harvard University Press, 2015; and for an overall history of the camps, see the magisterial study by Nikolaus Wachsmann. *KL: A History of the Nazi Concentration Camps*. New York: Farrar, Straus and Giroux, 2015. A very useful set of essays can be found in Jane Caplan and Nikolaus Wachsmann (eds.). *Concentration Camps in Nazi Germany: The New Histories*. London: Routledge, 2010.
12. For a pioneering closer examination of the Reserve Police Battalions, see the celebrated study by Christopher Browning. *Ordinary Men: Reserve Police Battalion 101 and the Final Solution in Poland*. New York: HarperCollins, 1992. Guenter Lewy has recently examined some of the other Reserve Police Battalions; see his *Perpetrators: The World of the Holocaust Killers*. New York: Oxford University Press, 2017.
13. A vast amount of literature exists on collaboration during the Third Reich. Excellent short histories can be found in Rab Bennett. *Under the Shadow of the Swastika: The Moral Dilemmas of Resistance and Collaboration in Hitler's Europe*. New York: New York University Press, 1999; and István Deák. *Europe on Trial: The Story of Collaboration, Resistance, and Retribution during World War II*. Boulder, CO: Westview Press, 2015.
14. See, for example, Christopher Hale. *Hitler's Foreign Executioners: Europe's Dirty Secret*. Stroud, UK: The History Press, 2011.
15. Rabbi Hugo Gryn, in *Auschwitz and the Allies*, BBC Films, prod. Rex Bloomstein, 1982.

A

ABETZ, OTTO (1903–1958)

Otto Abetz was the German ambassador to Vichy France during World War II. Abetz was born on March 26, 1903, in Schwetzingen, Baden-Württemberg. His father, an estate manager, died when Abetz was only 13. Matriculating in Karlsruhe, he became an art and biology teacher at a girls' school, and with an interest in French culture, he founded a Franco-German cultural youth group, the Sohlberg Circle, consisting of a hundred German and French youth from all walks of life.

Abetz joined the Hitler Youth, befriending **Joachim von Ribbentrop**, and pledged allegiance to the Nazi Party in 1931. In 1932, he married his French secretary, Susanne de Bruyker, and in 1934, the Sohlberg Circle transformed into the Franco-German Committee.

Abetz joined the German Foreign Office in 1935 as a French expert. He only joined the Nazi Party in 1937, the same year he applied for the German Foreign Service. In the latter capacity, as a German representative in Paris, he attended the Munich Conference in September 1938.

In June 1939, Abetz was forced to leave France owing to agitation from the French fascist Cagoulard movement. This was for allegedly bribing two French newspaper editors to publish pro-German articles and for allegedly bribing French foreign minister Georges Bonnet.

Abetz worked as a translator on **Adolf Hitler**'s team during the invasion of Poland in September 1939. Returning to France in June 1940, Abetz was assigned by Ribbentrop to the German Embassy in Paris, a post he held until July 1944. He was given responsibility for handling political matters in both the occupied and unoccupied zones of France, providing counsel to the German military and the administration of the Paris police. Because there was never a peace treaty between Germany and France—only an armistice—Abetz was not formally accredited as ambassador, but he acted with the full powers of one. In May 1941, he negotiated the Paris Protocols to expand German access to French military facilities.

In August 1940, Abetz was named ambassador to the Vichy government of Philippe Pétain, a position he held for four years. He worked and resided in Paris rather than Vichy and visited the collaborationist capital when he had to deal with Pétain's government in person. Pétain and his representatives, on the other hand, were not authorized to journey to Paris.

Following a directive from Hitler dated June 30, 1940, Ribbentrop assigned Abetz the project of "safeguarding" all objects of art, public, private, and especially Jewish owned. Abetz informed the Wehrmacht that the embassy had been "charged with the seizure of French works of art . . . and with the listing and seizure of works owned by Jews." Pétain's government protested in late October but could not stop the German plunder; by the end of October 1940, so much confiscated material had accumulated at the Louvre that the embassy had to rent outbuildings to house the items prior to their transportation by train to Berlin. Many of the stolen pieces were hung in Abetz's residence, as well as inside Ribbentrop's Foreign Office.

Abetz presented a German cultural face to the French by establishing the German Institute in late 1940. Thirty thousand people signed up for the institute's German language courses, but the concerts featuring Germany's best musicians, including Herbert von Karajan and the Berlin Philharmonic Orchestra, were much more popular.

Abetz was also head of the French fifth columnists through a special unit established by Ribbentrop. His primary objective was to secure complete collaboration from the French through negotiations with Prime Minister **Pierre Laval** and Admiral François Darlan. In 1942, Abetz was appointed as *SS-Brigadeführer*.

Abetz himself held antisemitic beliefs, which was one of the reasons he was recruited, personally, by Adolf Hitler. It was he who proposed deporting stateless Jews to France's unoccupied zone and from there to extermination camps in the East. He took a large role in the deportation of both foreign Jewish refugees and French-born Jews, especially after Germany occupied southern France in the fall of 1942. On July 2, 1942, Abetz advocated in a telegram for the deportation of 40,000 Jews from France to Auschwitz, claiming that all measures should be taken to remove them within both the occupied and unoccupied zones.

Following the occupation of Vichy on November 11, 1942, Abetz was ordered back to Germany for a year, as his political rivals in the Foreign Ministry were displeased with the influence he had accrued while in France. In 1943, he returned and was reinstated as ambassador in Paris. With the advance of the Allies following the Normandy landings of June 6, 1944, and the resulting retreat of German troops, Abetz fled with Pétain to Sigmaringen, Germany. Dismissed as German ambassador, he retired to his villa in Baden-Baden with his collection of stolen art, gold, and money. He then attempted to go into hiding, but on October 25, 1945, he was arrested in Todtmoos and sent to Paris for trial by a military tribunal.

Abetz denied participating in the murder of French Jews, even though he was aware of the Final Solution while it was happening. In July 1949, he was convicted by a French court for crimes against humanity, especially for his part in the deportation of French Jews from Drancy to Nazi extermination camps. Sentenced to 20 years' imprisonment, he was released on April 17, 1954, from Loos prison, having served only 5 years.

Abetz and his wife died together on May 5, 1958, in Langenfeld, on the Cologne-Ruhr motorway, when his car ran off the road and caught fire. Rumor has it that the car he was driving, which had recent steering damage, was provided to him by a Frenchman as an act of revenge.

AL-HUSSEINI, HAJ AMIN (1895–1974)

Mohammed Amin al-Husseini was a Palestinian Arab nationalist and Muslim leader in what was to become Mandated Palestine. He was born in Jerusalem in 1895, the son of Mufti Tahhir al-Husseini and scion of a family of wealthy landowners claiming direct descent from the grandson of the Prophet. He received his education in an Islamic school; an Ottoman school, where he learned Turkish; and a Catholic school, where he learned French. Sent to Cairo for his higher education, he studied Islamic jurisprudence at Al-Azhar University and then at the Cairo Institute for Propagation and Guidance. He went on to the College of Literature at Cairo University and then the Ottoman School for Administrators in Istanbul, which trained future leaders of the Ottoman Empire. In 1913 he made pilgrimage to Mecca, earning his honorific "Haj."

Mohammed Amin al-Husseini was a Palestinian Arab nationalist and mufti of Jerusalem in Mandatory Palestine before and during World War II. A passionate antisemite, he became a key ally of Adolf Hitler in endorsing the annihilation of Europe's Jews, at the same time vetoing attempts to rescue Jews (particularly Jewish children) and trying to convince the Nazis to bomb Tel Aviv and Jerusalem. (Hulton Archive/Keystone/Getty Images)

At the outbreak of World War I in 1914, he joined the Ottoman army as an artillery officer assigned to Izmir. After the war, he moved to Damascus as a supporter of the Arab Kingdom of Syria, but with the collapse of Hashemite rule in Damascus, he moved back to Jerusalem.

On the death of the mufti of Jerusalem on March 21, 1921, elections were held to choose a successor. Although al-Husseini only came fourth in the votes, the British governor, Sir Herbert Samuel, appointed al-Husseini as the new grand mufti in order to maintain the balance of power between the rival elite Husseini and Nashashibi clans.

Al-Husseini's preaching of anti-Jewish hatred led to him making a speech on August 23, 1929, which generated riots that killed 133 Jews and wounded 339 more. As a demonstration of his authority, he later played a role in pacifying rioters and reestablishing order.

On March 31, 1933, al-Husseini met with the German consul general in Jerusalem, who advised Berlin that the mufti was an excellent ally in Palestine. He identified that the mufti aimed to terminate Jewish settlement in Palestine and saw that a holy war of Islam, in alliance with Nazi Germany, would remove the Jewish problem everywhere.

In 1936, the Peel Commission arrived in Palestine to investigate the establishment of a two-state solution for the mandate. Arab anger against the proposal resulted in riots against Jews breaking out in Jaffa on April 19, 1936. Before and after these riots, which continued through to 1939, al-Husseini was establishing Nazi connections, and later he indicated that without funding from Germany, the riots could never have been engineered.

By 1937, al-Husseini oversaw a youth group, the Holy Jihad, inspired by the Hitler Youth. British police tried to arrest al-Husseini in July 1937 for his part in the Arab rebellion, but he managed to escape to the sanctuary in the Muslim area on top of the Temple Mount.

Al-Husseini's lobbying in response to the 1936–1939 Arab Revolt resulted in the British white paper of May 17, 1939, approved by the House of Commons on May 23, 1939. It called for the establishment of a Jewish national home in an independent Palestinian state within 10 years, rejecting the creation of a Jewish state and the partitioning of Palestine. It also limited Jewish immigration to 75,000 for 5 years. Additional immigration was to be determined by the Arab majority. This created huge problems for Jews because of their increasing suffering in Nazi Germany since 1933 and the Evian Conference's failure to find a resolution to the settlement of Jewish refugees.

In a letter of June 21, 1939, to **Adolf Hitler**, al-Husseini wrote of Arab readiness to rise against the common enemy, Anglo-Jewry, and once war broke out, he went to Iraq and set up his base of operations there on October 13, 1939. On April 3, 1941, he attempted a takeover of the Iraqi government with Nazi support. In the resultant pogrom, 600 Bagdadi Jews were killed, 911 Jewish houses were destroyed, and 586 Jewish businesses ransacked. When Britain suppressed the takeover, al-Husseini blamed the failure of the Nazi takeover on the Jews.

On July 22, 1941, al-Husseini fled to Teheran. After the Allied occupation of Iran on October 8, 1941, and the new Persian government of Shah Mohammad Reza Pahlavi severed diplomatic relations with the Axis powers, al-Husseini was taken under Italian protection and smuggled through Turkey to Italy in an operation organized by Italian military intelligence. He arrived in Rome on October 10, 1941.

He then began serious discussions with the fascist regime of Benito Mussolini. He secured an agreement with the Italians that in return for Axis recognition of a fascist Arab state encompassing Iraq, Syria, Palestine, and Transjordan, he would agree to support the war against Britain. The Italian foreign ministry also urged Mussolini to grant al-Husseini 1 million lire.

Over the next few days, al-Husseini drafted a proposed statement of an Arab-Axis cooperative effort by which the Axis powers would recognize the right of the Arabs to deal with Jewish elements in Palestine and approve the elimination of the Jewish National Homeland in Palestine. Mussolini approved the declaration and sent it to the German Embassy in Rome. Al-Husseini was invited to Berlin as a guest of the Nazi regime, which gave him a luxurious home on a fashionable street, a full staff of servants, a chauffeured Mercedes, and a monthly stipend of $10,000. He remained headquartered in Berlin until May 1945. Then on November 28, 1941, he met with Adolf Hitler, concluding afterward that Nazis and Arabs were engaged in the same struggle to exterminate the Jews.

From the mid-1930s, al-Husseini had been friends with the SS officer **Adolf Eichmann**. When he visited Eichmann's office at the end of 1941 or the beginning of 1942, he was briefed on the Nazis' Final Solution. His involvement with the Holocaust saw him allegedly visit Auschwitz and Majdanek; he was on close terms with Auschwitz commandant **Rudolf Hoess** and the commandants of Mauthausen, Theriesenstadt, and Bergen-Belsen. He also organized antisemitic Arab radio propaganda, espionage in the Middle East, and the establishment of the Arab Legion and the Arab Brigade, Muslim military units that fought for the Nazis. He had at his disposal six radio stations (Berlin, Zeissen, Bari, Rome, Tokyo, and Athens), from which he urged Muslims to kill Jews everywhere.

As early as January 1941, the mufti traveled to Bosnia to convince Islamic leaders that a Muslim Waffen-SS division would bring honor and glory to Muslims, claiming that they shared four principles: family, order, the leader, and faith. As many as 100,000 Muslim fighters were thereby recruited and fought for the Nazis.

In January 1942, al-Husseini discussed with German leaders the formation of a German-Arab military unit, and on May 3, 1942, he sought from the Italian and German governments another declaration supporting, among other things, the liquidation of the Jewish national home in Palestine. In consultation with the mufti, Eichmann had created an *Einsatzgruppe Ägypten* (*Einsatzgruppe* Egypt), ready to disembark for Palestine.

In July 1942, al-Husseini and the Iraqi Rashid Ali broadcast that it was the duty of Egyptian Muslims to kill the Jews before the Jews killed them, as the Jews were preparing to violate their women, kill their children, and destroy them completely. On December 11, 1942, the mufti urged Arab Muslims to "martyrdom" as allies with the Nazis, as "the spilled blood of martyrs is the water of life."

In late 1942, *SS-Reichsführer* **Heinrich Himmler** gave his permission for 10,000 Jewish children to be transferred from Poland to the concentration camp at Theresienstadt, with the eventual aim of allowing them to go to Palestine in exchange for German civilian prisoners. The plan was abandoned, however, because of al-Husseini's protests. In all likelihood, these children were murdered subsequently in Auschwitz.

In a speech delivered to the SS on January 11, 1944, SS leader Heinrich Himmler argued that the bond between Nazism and Islam was built on enduring common values. Inspired by his words, the Waffen-SS Handschar Division went into action in February 1944. The division played a major role in rendering the Balkans *Judenrein* (Jew-free) in the winter of 1943 to 1944, cutting a path of destruction across the Balkans that encompassed a large number of Catholic parishes, churches, and shrines and that resulted in the deaths of thousands of Catholics as well as all Jews they could find. By the end of the war, al-Husseini's fanatical soldiers had killed over 90 percent of the Jews in Bosnia.

In the spring of 1943, al-Husseini learned of negotiations between Germany's Axis partners with Britain, Switzerland, and the International Red Cross to transport 4,000 Jewish children to safety in Palestine. Al-Husseini sought to prevent the rescue operations with protests directed at the Germans and Italians, as well as at the governments of Hungary, Romania, and Bulgaria. Demanding that the operations be scuttled, he suggested that the children be sent to Poland, where they would be subject to "stricter control" (exterminated). They were duly sent to a concentration camp, meeting al-Husseini's demand that they be killed in Poland rather than transported to Palestine.

In September 1943, intense negotiations to rescue another 500 Jewish children from the Arbe concentration camp in Italy collapsed due to an objection from al-Husseini, who blocked their departure to Turkey because they would end up in Palestine.

In 1943, al-Husseini organized a chemical attack on Tel Aviv, but the five parachutists sent on the mission were captured near Jericho before they could complete their task. Their equipment, found by the British, consisted of submachine guns, dynamite, radio equipment, £5,000 cash, a duplicating machine, a German-Arabic dictionary, and enough toxin to kill 250,000 people by poisoning water.

The mufti also tried to convince the Nazis to bomb Tel Aviv and Jerusalem. Concerned over the turning tide of war, he wrote to Himmler on June 5, 1944, and July 27, 1944, asking him to do all he could to complete the extermination of the Jews.

After the war, Britain, France, and the United States refused to prosecute the mufti as a war criminal, even though Yugoslavia had placed him on a list of war criminals. He attempted to obtain asylum in Switzerland, but his request was refused. Taken into custody by French occupying troops at Konstanz on May 5, 1945, he was transferred to the Paris region on May 19 and put under house arrest. French authorities hoped that his presence could lead to an improvement in France's status in the Arab world and accorded him special detention conditions and other benefits as a result. Satisfied with his situation in France, al-Husseini stayed for a full year.

He arrived in Egypt on June 20, 1946, where King Farouk provided him with sanctuary. Even with the fall of Farouk and the rise of Gamal Abdel-Nasser as head of Egypt in 1952, al-Husseini remained safe. His last public appearance came in 1962, when he delivered a speech to the World Islamic Congress. He used this final opportunity to address the world to call for the ethnic cleansing of the Jews.

The grand mufti of Jerusalem, Haj Amin al-Husseini, died in Beirut, Lebanon, in 1974.

ANTONESCU, ION (1882–1946)

Romanian marshal and dictator Ion Antonescu was born into a Romanian Orthodox military family in Pitesti on June 14, 1882. During his childhood, his father divorced his mother to marry a woman who was a Jewish convert to Romanian Orthodox Christianity. This breakup was traumatic for the young Antonescu, and he disliked his stepmother, identifying her as a femme fatale who had destroyed his parents' happy marriage.

Antonescu graduated as a captain from Romanian military schools in Craiova in 1902 and Iaşi in 1904. A cavalry lieutenant during the 1907 Peasant Revolt, he fought in the Second Balkan War (June 16, 1913–July 18, 1913). Romania entered World War I in 1916 on the side of France, Britain, and Russia, and Antonescu served as an operations officer. From 1922 to 1927, he was Romanian military attaché in Paris, Brussels, and London. In 1923, he married Rachel Mendel, a

Ion Antonescu, dictator of Romania from 1940 until August 1944, meets with Hermann Göring in Vienna in 1941. Antonescu's fascist regime was responsible for the death of more than 250,000 Romanian and Ukrainian Jews and Roma as a result of its "Romanization" policies, despite the country's refusal to formally join with Germany in pursuing the latter's Final Solution. (Library of Congress)

Jewish woman, whom he divorced in 1926. He was married to Maria Antonescu from 1928 until his death in 1946. Antonescu was chief of the army general staff in 1933 and 1934.

Antonescu was an anticommunist and antisemite who favored British and French political influence and was never a Germanophile. He monitored closely both the flourishing of the Third Reich and the looming threat of the Soviet Union, and he pragmatically favored political association with Germany. Named minister of defense in 1937, he protested King Carol II's establishment of the Royal Dictatorship and his suppression of the fascistic Legion of Saint Michael (the Iron Guard). Antonescu defended the Iron Guard's leaders in court, was ousted from government and briefly jailed, and was sent into a kind of internal exile to Kishinev (Chişinău) near the Soviet border.

From June to September 1940, one-third of Romanian territory was partitioned between the Soviet Union, Hungary, and Bulgaria. The area occupied by the Soviet Union (Bessarabia) was ceded to Hungary in the summer of 1940. On September 4, 1940, King Carol appointed Antonescu as prime minister with absolute powers, prior to the king abdicating under pressure in favor of his 19-year-old son, Michael. Antonescu's title, conducator, was the Romanian equivalent of duce or führer, and he used his broad powers to oust the Iron Guard from government in January 1941.

In June 1941, he assigned 14 Romanian divisions to Germany's invasion of the Soviet Union, Operation Barbarossa. As a reward for reclaiming Romanian lands from the Soviets, Antonescu was proclaimed marshal by the young King Michael on August 23, 1941, during which time he continued to supply the German war effort with troops in exchange for German military favors. Ultimately, Romania lost substantially more men in the war on the Eastern Front than did Italy, while at home Antonescu struggled to control Germany's appetite for Romania's oil and agricultural bounty.

On Romania's Jewish question, Antonescu preferred his own solution to anything dictated by Berlin. He employed policies that officially allowed Jews to emigrate in exchange for payment, or they would face deportation to Romanian-administered work camps in the Ukrainian region of Transnistria. He sent tens of thousands of Jews to their death in Transnistria, and yet he refused to send other Romanian Jews to the death camps in Poland.

Nonetheless, Antonescu's regime was responsible for the deaths of more than 250,000 Romanian and Ukrainian Jews and Roma as a result of its "Romanization" policies during 1940 to 1944, despite the country's refusal to join formally with Germany in pursuing the latter's Final Solution. Although he was unquestionably an antisemite, ironically more Jews survived under his rule than in any other country within Axis Europe.

Antonescu was deposed by King Michael on August 23, 1944, and turned over to the occupying Soviet forces. His trial for war crimes, held in Bucharest across the period May 4 to 17, 1946, led to his conviction and execution on June 1, 1946.

ARĀJS, VIKTORS (1910–1988)

Viktors Arājs was a Latvian collaborator who participated in the Holocaust during the German occupation of Latvia and Belarus as leader of the *Arājs Kommando*, a unit that murdered about 26,000 Latvian Jews.

Viktors Bernhard Arājs was born on January 13, 1910, in Baldone, Latvia. His father was a blacksmith, and his mother came from a well-off Baltic German family. Arājs attended *Jelgava Gymnasium*, which he left in 1930 to undertake his national service in the Latvian army. In 1932, he commenced studying law at the University of Latvia, in Riga. He joined the student fraternity *Lettonia*, which helped him obtain employment with the Latvian police, and he remained there until he left the service in 1938. Arājs completed his law degree in 1941.

When war between Germany and the Soviet Union began on June 22, 1941, the Red Army retreated from Riga. **Franz Walter Stahlecker**, head of the SiPo and *Einsatzgruppe A*, needed Latvian militia cooperation when conducting pogroms so that locals could be identified with *Aktions* against the Jews rather than such measures being viewed as wholly German. Stahlecker had already found such assistance in Lithuania through **Algirdas Klimaitis**; now he sought a Latvian collaborator. A Latvian translator, Hans Dressler, whom Arājs had known in high school and during his army service, introduced Arājs to Stahlecker.

On July 2, 1941, Stahlecker ordered Arājs to instigate a pogrom that had to appear as if it were Latvian in origin, spontaneous, and not associated with the German occupiers. Arājs had earlier taken over an empty police post at 19 Valdemāra Street and had started organizing recruits from his student fraternity and *Pērkonkrusts* (Thunder Cross), an ultranationalist, anti-German, and antisemitic political party.

On July 4, 1941, the Germans placed a recruitment notice in the German-controlled Latvian language newspaper *Tēvija* (*Fatherland*), stating, "all patriotic Latvians, *Pērkonkrusts* members, Students, Officers, Militiamen, and Citizens, who are ready to actively take part in the cleansing of our country of undesirable elements" should enroll themselves at the office of the Security Group at 19 Valdemara Street. *Pērkonkrusts* members, as it turned out, were banned from participating after August 25, 1941, due to what the Germans considered to be an unacceptable level of nationalism.

On July 4, 1941, the Security Group Arājs, known generally as the *Arājs Kommando*, consisted of some 500 volunteers. They started their *Aktion* by trapping some 20 Jews in the Riga Synagogue on Gogola Street. There, the Jews were burned alive while hand grenades were thrown through the windows; any who attempted to break out were shot down by Arājs's adjutant, Herberts Cukurs. Stahlecker filmed and photographed the scene as evidence that the first spontaneous executions of Jews and communists in Latvia were carried out by locals.

After these initial murders, the remainder of the Riga Jews were rounded up and put into ghettos. To make room for the anticipated arrival of German Jews, the remaining Jews in Riga were taken from the ghetto to the Rumbula forest between November 30 and December 8, 1941, and shot. The *Arājs Kommando* was involved extensively in these mass shootings. It is estimated that they killed at least 26,000 Jews, Roma, and other "undesirables," first in Latvia and then in Belarus.

The *Arājs Kommando* was also notorious for its ill-treatment of women. It was known that Viktors Arājs raped a Jewish woman, Zelma Shepshelovitz, during the war; her evidence later served a vital part in his trial.

As the war progressed, Arājs was upgraded to police major in 1942 and then, in 1943, to *SS-Sturmbannführer*. Before the Soviets returned, *Aktions* resulted in all Jews under 18 years or over 30 years of age being shot, with the 18- to 30-year-olds being moved to the Stutthof concentration camp. Overall, during the Nazi occupation of Latvia, some 90,000 people were killed in Latvia, including 70,000 Jews and 20,000 Roma.

Until 1949, Arājs, whose paramilitary group was involved in so many killings in Latvia, was held in a British internment camp in Germany. He worked as a driver for the British armed forces under the military government in Delmenhorst and then in the British Zone of Occupation. With assistance from the Latvian government in exile in London, he took on the alias of Victor (Viktors) Zeibots, working in Frankfurt am Main as an assistant at a printing company.

On December 21, 1979, Arājs was found guilty in the State Court of Hamburg. On December 8, 1941, the court determined that he had conducted the Jews of the greater Riga ghetto to their deaths by the mass shootings in the Rumbula forest. For his participation in the murder of 13,000 people, he was sentenced to life imprisonment. He died on January 13, 1988, in Kassel, Germany, imprisoned in solitary confinement.

Arājs's adjutant, Herberts Cukurs, was accused of involvement in several killings; in his defense, he claimed that he had worked as head of vehicle maintenance in Arājs's unit. After the war, he moved to South America and was assassinated by Mossad agents in 1965. Another Latvian involved in the *Arājs Kommando* killings, Kārlis Lobe, fled to Sweden and remained there until his death in 1985. Yet another Latvian involved in the *Arājs Kommando*, Konrāds Kalējs, lived in Denmark after the war, then in Australia, and afterward in the United States. In 1984, after attempting to reenter the United States, Kalējs was deported to Australia. The Latvian government opened proceedings against Kalējs in 2000, which were delayed by his ill health. He died in Melbourne in 2001; in a final interview on Australian television, Kalējs admitted his involvement in the killings in Latvia.

B

BACH-ZELEWSKI, ERICH VON DEM (1899–1972)

Erich von dem Bach-Zelewski was a senior SS commander who took charge of "bandit fighting" against partisans and others (mostly civilians) designated as a danger to Nazi rule in occupied Eastern Europe. In August 1944, he was instrumental in the suppression of the Warsaw Uprising.

Erich Julius Eberhard von Zelewski was born on March 1, 1899, in Lauenberg (Lębork), Pomerania, to insurance inspector Otto Jan von Zelewski and his wife Elżbieta, of Kashubian gentry background. In 1933, Erich added "von dem Bach" to his surname, and in November 1941, he removed "Zelewski" because of its Polish-sounding origin.

Zelewski's impoverished father died on April 12, 1911, when his son was just 12 years old. Upon Zelewski's completion of school in 1914, his uncle persuaded him to join the military, and on November 9, 1914, he enlisted in the German army. He served throughout World War I, was wounded twice, and earned the Iron Cross First and Second Class. In 1916, aged 17, he was commissioned as a second lieutenant.

After the war, Zelewski served in a *Freikorps* against Polish Silesian rebels. He served as a Reichswehr officer until 1924, when he left the army and returned to his farm in Düringshof (Bogdaniec). He later evinced shame that his three sisters had each married a Jewish man and claimed that this had forced him to leave the army.

He enrolled in and then served with the border guards (*Grenzschutz*) between 1924 and 1930. On October 23, 1925, he legally changed his surname to von dem Bach-Zelewski.

In 1930, he left the *Grenzschutz* and joined the Nazi Party. He became a member of the SS in 1931 and attained the rank of *SS-Brigadeführer* in late 1933. He served as a member of the Reichstag representing Breslau (Wrocław) from 1932 to 1944. After a quarrel with his SS staff officer, Anton von Hohberg und Buchwald, Bach-Zelewski had him killed during the Röhm Putsch on July 2, 1934.

From 1934 on, Bach-Zelewski led SS units, initially in East Prussia and after 1936 in Silesia. In 1937, he was higher SS and police leader (*Höherer SS- und Polizeiführer*, or HSSPF) in Silesia.

In November 1939, after the German occupation of Poland, *SS-Reichsführer* **Heinrich Himmler** offered Bach-Zelewski the role of strengthening *Deutschtum* (German influence) in Silesia, with responsibility for mass resettlement and the confiscation of Polish private property. By August 1940, as part of *Aktion Saybusch*, some 18,000 to 20,000 Poles from Żywiec County were forced to leave their homes.

Because Bach-Zelewski's actions had created overcrowded prisons, his assistant, *SS-Oberführer* Arpad Wigand, had to find a new location for prisoners. As a result, a concentration camp was created and sited in former Austrian cavalry barracks at Auschwitz (Oświęcim). The first transport arrived there on June 14, 1940, and two weeks later, Bach-Zelewski personally visited the camp.

Later, during Operation Barbarossa, Bach-Zelewski served as HSSPF in occupied Belarus. In 1941, he became a general of the Waffen-SS and was involved in action on the Eastern Front until the end of 1942. During this period, he took part in many atrocities; from July to September 1941, he oversaw the extermination of Jews in Riga and Minsk at the hands of *Einsatzgruppe B*, led by **Arthur Nebe**, while also visiting other sites of mass killings, such as Białystok, Grodno, Baranovichi, Mogilev, and Pinsk. He regularly cabled headquarters on the extermination progress; for example, a message on August 22, 1941, stated, "Thus the figure in my area now exceeds the thirty thousand mark."

While in a Berlin hospital to treat "intestinal ailments" in February 1942, Bach-Zelewski experienced "hallucinations connected with the shooting of Jews." Before returning to duty in July, he asked Himmler for reassignment to antipartisan duty. Accordingly, through 1943, he took command of antipartisan units on the central front, a special command created by **Adolf Hitler**. Bach-Zelewski was the only HSSPF in the occupied Soviet territories to retain full authority over the police after **Hans-Adolf Prützmann** and **Friedrich Jeckeln** lost their authority to the civil administration.

Sometime in June 1943, Himmler announced the creation of bandit-fighting formations (*Bandenkampfverbände*), with Bach-Zelewski named as commander. Once the Wehrmacht had secured territorial objectives, the *Bandenkampfverbände* then ensured the security of communications facilities, roads, railways, and waterways, followed by rural communities and agricultural and forestry resources. The SS oversaw the collection of the harvest, deemed critical to strategic operations. Any Jews or communists in the area were killed. Under Bach-Zelewski, the formations murdered 35,000 civilians in Riga and more than 200,000 in Belarus and eastern Poland. His methods produced a high civilian death toll but relatively minor military gains. After an operation was completed, any military presence was removed, and partisan groups would then resume where they had left off.

In July 1943, Bach-Zelewski took command of all antipartisan actions in Belgium, Belarus, France, the General Government, the Netherlands, Norway, Ukraine, Yugoslavia, and other areas. His major focus of his activities, however, remained confined to Belarus and adjacent parts of Russia.

On August 2, 1944, Bach-Zelewski took charge of all German troops fighting the Polish Home Army of General Tadeusz Bór-Komorowski during the Warsaw Uprising. The German forces were made up of 17,000 men, including the Dirlewanger Brigade of convicted criminals. Units under Bach-Zelewski's command killed approximately 200,000 civilians, more than 65,000 in mass executions.

Warsaw was destroyed in the process. During the campaign to reduce the city, the Woła massacre occurred—a brutal act of systematic killing by German troops of between 40,000 and 50,000 people in the Woła district of Warsaw. On September 30, 1944, Bach-Zelewski was awarded the Knight's Cross of the Iron Cross for his actions in Warsaw.

With the end of the war, Bach-Zelewski hid and tried to leave Germany, but on August 1, 1945, he was arrested by U.S. military police. In return for testifying at Nuremberg against his former superiors, Bach-Zelewski was never indicted for war crimes, nor was he extradited to Poland or the USSR. He left prison in 1949.

In 1958, however, Bach-Zelewski was convicted of killing Anton von Hohberg und Buchwald during the Night of the Long Knives back in 1934 and was sentenced to four and a half years' imprisonment. In 1961, he was arrested again and tried for the murder of six German communists in 1933. He was convicted and sentenced to an additional 10 years in home detention. Neither indictment mentioned his wartime role in Poland and the Soviet Union or his participation in the Holocaust, although he openly accused himself as being a mass murderer.

Bach-Zelewski gave evidence for **Adolf Eichmann**'s defense in Israel in May 1961, to the effect that operations in Russia and parts of Poland were not subject to the orders of Eichmann's office nor was Eichmann able to give orders to the officers in charge of these units.

Bach-Zelewski died in a Munich prison on March 8, 1972, a week after his 73rd birthday.

BARBIE, KLAUS (1913–1991)

Klaus Barbie, the infamous "Butcher of Lyon," was head of the Gestapo in Lyon, France, and earned a reputation for his sadism and brutality during World War II.

Nikolaus Klaus Barbie was born into a Roman Catholic family on October 25, 1913, in Bad Godesberg, Germany. His parents were both teachers, and he attended the school where his father taught until moving to a boarding school in Trier in 1923. The family joined him there in 1925. In 1933, Barbie's brother and his abusive, alcoholic father both died, which thwarted Barbie's plans to study theology or enter academia. Unemployed, he was drafted into the Nazi labor service (*Reichsarbeitsdienst*); membership was compulsory for all young German men and women. A strong nationalist, Barbie joined the local Hitler Youth group in April 1933. In September 1935, he joined the *Sicherheitsdienst* (SD, security service) branch of the SS.

With the outbreak of war in 1939, Barbie rose quickly in the SD. In May 1940, he was sent to the SD office in The Hague, Netherlands. There, his main task was to arrest Jews and German political refugees who fled to the Netherlands, and he organized and participated in mass arrests and deportations of Jews. After his promotion to *SS-Obersturmführer*, Barbie returned to Germany to be trained in counterinsurgency work. In November 1942, he was sent to Dijon, and after German forces took over Vichy France, he was deployed to Lyon as head of the local Gestapo, in charge of 25 officers. His operational area covered Lyon, the Jura and Hautes-Alpes police departments, and Grenoble.

In Lyon, Barbie became renowned for his brutal policies aimed at French resistance fighters and Jews. He personally tortured prisoners—men, women, and children—and has since been blamed directly for the deaths of 4,000 people. Barbie also oversaw the deportation of Jews to the death camps in the East. In April 1944, he ordered the residents of the Jewish children's home at Izieu to be transported to Auschwitz. Forty-one children, aged 3 to 11, were gassed.

Barbie's postwar notoriety came primarily from the arrest and death by torture of Jean Moulin, the highest-ranking member of the French Resistance. Hot needles were shoved under Jean Moulin's fingernails. His knuckles were broken by catching them in a door hinge and slamming the door until the knuckles broke. His handcuffs were screwed so tightly that they broke through the bones of his wrists. Moulin would not talk; he was whipped and beaten until his face was an unrecognizable pulp. Unconscious and mute, he was shown to other resistance leaders being interrogated at Gestapo headquarters; this was the last time Moulin was seen alive. For this work, Barbie was awarded the First Class Iron Cross with Swords, with the decoration presented by **Adolf Hitler** himself.

As American forces approached Lyon in August 1944, Barbie ordered the execution of 120 prisoners. Fleeing the city, he later returned to execute 20 former collaborators. After the war, he was recruited by the Western Allies. Initially he worked until 1947 for the British. He was later protected and employed by American intelligence agents because of his "police skills" and anticommunist zeal in being able to infiltrate communist cells in the German Communist Party. In 1949, France requested that Barbie be extradited to stand trial for his crimes. With American assistance in stalling and bureaucratic red tape, Barbie had time to flee to Bolivia with his family in 1951. Assuming the name Klaus Altmann, he remained unidentified for 20 years.

In 1971, Nazi hunters Beate and Serge Klarsfeld succeeded in locating Barbie, but at this time, he enjoyed the protection of Bolivia's right-wing government. After long negotiations and pressure from France's socialist government, it was only in February 1983 that the newly elected Bolivian government of Hernán Siles Zuazo arrested and extradited Barbie to France to stand trial.

In 1984, Barbie was notified that he was to be tried for crimes committed while in charge of the Gestapo in Lyon between 1942 and 1944. Many of the charges were dropped due to new laws protecting people accused of crimes under the Vichy regime and in French Algeria.

On May 11, 1987, however, Barbie's trial in Lyon commenced, a jury trial before the Rhône *Cour d'assises*. The trial was filmed because of its historical value. The lead defense attorney, Jacques Vergès, argued that Barbie's actions were no worse than the ordinary actions of colonialists worldwide and that his trial was selective prosecution. During his trial, Barbie stated, "When I stand before the throne of God, I shall be judged innocent." Overall, he was held responsible for some 26,000 killings. Found guilty on July 4, 1987, he was sentenced to life imprisonment for crimes against humanity. On September 25, 1991, at the age of 77, he died in prison in Lyon of leukemia.

BATZ, RUDOLF (1903–1961)

Rudolf Batz was an SS officer who commanded *Einsatzkommando* 2 in the Baltic and was therefore one of those responsible for the mass murder of Jews in the Baltic States (particularly Latvia) between July 1 and November 4, 1941.

Batz was born in Bad Langensalza, Thuringia, on November 10, 1903. He graduated from school in March 1922 and studied law at the Universities of Munich and Göttingen, graduating in 1934. In the meantime, on May 1, 1933, he joined the Nazi Party. On December 10, 1935, he joined the SS and was assigned to the legal department at Gestapo headquarters in Berlin. In June 1936, he became a deputy Gestapo leader in Breslau (Wrocław), and from the beginning of October the same year, he also served as a political adviser to the government in Breslau. Moving to Linz, Austria, in mid-July 1939, he took charge of the Gestapo there, prior to a further transfer to the state police headquarters in Hanover in December 1939. In 1940, he was promoted to the rank of *SS-Sturmbannführer*, rising to *Obersturmbannführer* in 1942.

Although based in Hanover, Batz also received temporary assignments outside Germany. In mid-October 1940, he was sent to The Hague, in the occupied Netherlands, where he served in a security policing function; this lasted until early January 1941. Then in November 1941, he was appointed to command *Einsatzkommando* 2 (EK2) in *Einsatzgruppe A*. There were four *Einsatzgruppen* (mobile killing squads), comprising around 3,000 men, divided into several *Einsatzkommandos*. Their task was to exterminate Jews, Polish intellectuals, Roma, communists, and other "enemies of the Reich" behind the advancing German combat troops.

EK2 comprised about 40 men. After the start of Operation Barbarossa in the summer of 1941, EK2 was given responsibility for the mass murder of Jews in the Baltic States. Batz's second in command, Gerhard Freitag, would later testify that Batz presided over the planning and execution of Jewish men, women, and children. In August 1941, Batz and Freitag reported to *SS-Brigadeführer* **Franz Walter Stahlecker** (the head of *Einsatzgruppe A*) that they and their men had exceeded the death toll by up to two or three times that of other units, who were not pulling their weight in the murder process.

During his time with EK2, Batz retained his office in Hannover, but in September 1943, he was sent to Kraków to command the Security Police and Security Service there. In this role, his task was to suppress the Polish resistance movement; where he could, he also organized the deportation of Jews to extermination camps. Two months later, however, in November, he returned to Hanover as head of the Gestapo. Here, he organized the deportation of Jews from the city and its adjacent region. The first transport from Hanover was sent to Riga.

At the beginning of 1945, Batz was transferred to Dortmund as Gestapo head. At this stage of the war, his main role was the control and punishment of forced laborers and anti-Nazi resisters. Under his command, hundreds were murdered.

With the end of the war, Batz assumed a false identity. Married and the father of three children, he lived undetected for 15 years in the Federal Republic of

Germany. On November 11, 1960, however, he was arrested and charged with crimes against humanity over his involvement in the mass murder of Jews in Latvia. While in custody awaiting trial, he committed suicide in his prison cell on February 8, 1961.

BAUER, ERICH (1900–1980)

Erich Bauer was an *SS-Oberscharführer* at the Sobibór death camp. He was renowned as one of the worst murderers operating in the gas chamber, where he was known as the *Gasmeister.*

Hermann Erich Bauer was born in Berlin on March 26, 1900. During World War I, he served as a soldier in the German army before being captured by the French and living out the conflict as a prisoner of war. With the ascent to office of the Nazis in 1933, Bauer, at that time a tram conductor, joined the Nazi Party and the SA. In 1940, he began working with the *Aktion T-4* euthanasia program, learning how to kill through the introduction of lethal injections and gas those with physical and/or psychological disabilities. At the start, he was assigned duties as a driver, but he moved into other areas of the process as he gained experience and knowledge of the program.

Early in 1942, Bauer received a new assignment when he was transferred to occupied Poland and the Lublin district, under the command of *SS- und Polizeiführer* **Odilo Globocnik**. In April 1942, he was deployed to the death camp at Sobibór and given the SS rank of *Oberscharführer*. He was to remain at Sobibór for the next 19 months, until the camp was closed in December 1943.

Given his experience in the T-4 program, Bauer was placed in charge of gassing procedures in Lager III at Sobibór, while he still drove trucks from time to time. Cruel and uncouth, he was generally remembered as a heavy drinker who cared little for his personal appearance and was frequently unkempt while on duty. He was naturally sadistic toward those under his command and often whipped, beat, and shot at the prisoners. He also kept attack dogs, trained to target the prisoners upon command. As gassings were taking place, he was usually seen on the roof checking the progress of the extermination procedure. It was from this that he picked up the nickname *Badmeister* (Bath Master); after the war, other survivors remembered he was also called *Gasmeister* (Gas Master).

Because of his brutality and unpredictability, the prisoner underground identified Bauer as one of the first who would have to be eliminated in the event of any uprising. As things turned out, when the uprising took place on October 14, 1943, Bauer was not present; he had gone to nearby Chełm to search for supplies. Returning sooner than expected, however, Bauer found that another *SS-Oberscharführer*, Rudolf Beckmann, had already been killed. Bauer opened fire at the two Jewish prisoners unloading his van, and the uprising began in earnest. The result would ultimately see 11 SS officers killed, the camp guards overpowered, the armory seized, and the inmates bursting through the wire and making a break for the forest outside. About 300 out of the 600 inmates managed to escape, with about 60 surviving to see the end of the war.

Within days of the uprising, **Heinrich Himmler** ordered the Sobibór site closed, the remaining prisoners killed or sent to other death camps, and the guards redeployed. The killing apparatus was to be dismantled, and the site was to be planted with trees.

Bauer was sent to other duties, and when the war ended in 1945, he was arrested by American forces in Austria. Imprisoned through the following year, he was released during 1946 and sent to his native Berlin to clear up debris left by the massive bombing the city had suffered in the last year of the war.

Two former Sobibór prisoners, Samuel Lerer and Esther Raab, recognized him in 1949; he was rearrested and sent for trial in 1950. Despite his protestations of innocence during the trial, Bauer's claims to have been only a truck driver did not convince any of those in the courtroom. On May 8, 1950, he was sentenced to death for crimes against humanity, a sentence commuted to life imprisonment, owing to the fact that the Federal Republic of Germany had since abolished the death penalty.

Over the next 21 years of his custody in Berlin's Alt-Moabit Prison, Bauer spoke publicly about his time at Sobibór, admitting his involvement in the mass murders with words such as "I cannot exclude any member of the Sobibór camp staff of taking part in the extermination operation" and "Each of us had at some point carried out every camp duty in Sobibór."

Erich Bauer died while still serving his sentence in Berlin's Tegel prison on February 4, 1980.

BECHER, KURT (1909–1995)

Kurt Becher was chief of the Economic Department of the SS Command in Hungary during the German occupation in 1944. In this capacity, he negotiated with the Hungarian Jewish community in the failed Blood for Goods initiative, the acquisition of the massive Manfred Weiss industrial complex at Csepel, and the Kasztner train.

Kurt Andreas Ernst Becher was born to a wealthy equestrian family on September 12, 1906, in Hamburg. After completing his education, he worked in a Hamburg food store as a clerk from 1928 until the outbreak of World War II. He was a competent horse breeder and rider, and after the Nazi seizure of power by **Adolf Hitler** in 1933, Becher joined the *Reiter-SS* (the SS cavalry regiment) in 1934.

In 1937, Becher became a member of the NSDAP. From 1939 on, he was in the *SS- Totenkopfverbände* first equestrian unit in Poland. This infamous unit was used in Warsaw and in the war against the Soviet Union after 1941 to fight guerillas. In the fight against resistance fighters in the Pripet Marshes (Belarus), standing orders read that "Every partisan is to be shot. Jews are to be deemed partisans." During this early phase of the Final Solution, about 14,000 Jews were murdered by Becher's unit. His promotions were rapid. From *SS-Obersturmführer*, he was promoted to *SS-Hauptsturmführer* in mid-March 1942, and then he was transferred to the SS leadership office. In 1944, Becher was promoted twice: first to *SS-Sturmbannführer* on January 30 and then to *SS-Obersturmbannführer* in October. That same year, he was awarded the German Cross in Gold.

In the spring of 1944, Becher headed the Waffen-SS Equipment Branch, reporting to **Oswald Pohl**. Following the German invasion of Hungary in March 1944, Pohl, acting on orders from **Heinrich Himmler**, sent Becher to Hungary to acquire 20,000 horses and other war material for the Wehrmacht and the Waffen-SS.

Becher played a crucial part in taking control of the massive Manfred Weiss armaments firm at Csepel. Although owned by a Jewish family, it was under majority Aryan control by that family's non-Jewish members. Both Himmler and **Hermann Göring** were interested in this enterprise, with its 20,000 workers, coal mines, munitions, and Messerschmitt engine plants. Germany could not appropriate Hungary's industrial plants, as treaty obligations meant that Germany was not to violate Hungary's sovereignty; accordingly, negotiations took place between Becher and Ferenc Chorin, representing the Weiss family, over how to proceed.

The agreement reached was mixed. In return for the purchase for 3 million Reichmarks of the Aryan 51 percent controlling share, the SS would permit 46 members of the Weiss family to leave Hungary, taking some of their valuables and foreign currency. Nine of the 46 family members would be held as hostages until the agreement was signed, and the remainder would be given safe passage to neutral Portugal and Switzerland. The nine hostages were to follow on May 17, 1944, the date when the transaction was to be completed. The deal was signed on May 17, 1944.

The 51 percent controlling interest was to be administered by Becher's holding company for 25 years, and then it would be returned to the Aryan branch of family. Becher and the SS would get 5 percent of the gross income for their service as trustees. This agreement was approved by both Himmler and Adolf Hitler, but it upset Göring, the German Foreign Office, and Döme Sztójay's Hungarian government, as it removed this massive valuable enterprise from their control.

Becher was also appointed by **Adolf Eichmann** to head negotiations with Rezső (Rudolf) Kasztner and the Jewish Relief and Rescue Committee of Budapest for ransoming 15,000 Hungarian Jews incarcerated in Bergen-Belsen and their transfer to Switzerland.

On April 25, 1944, Eichmann summoned Rescue Committee member Joel Brand and offered a deal under which the Nazis would "sell" 1 million Jews in exchange for certain goods to be obtained from outside Hungary. In this Blood for Goods scheme, the Jews would not be permitted to remain in Hungary but would be delivered, via Germany, upon receipt of certain goods. Britain called Brand to a meeting in Cairo, imprisoned him in a military prison, and interrogated him for several days.

The mission failed, however, on three grounds. First, the Allies saw this offer as Germany obtaining war material from the Allies; second, the USSR could interpret these discussions as the Western Allies jointly negotiating with the enemy and ignoring the Russians; and third, Germany would use a rejection of the proposal as justification for extreme measures against the Jews. On June 15, 1944, Britain formally briefed the Soviet Union of the proposition, and the USSR immediately vetoed it. On July 19, 1944, the BBC picked up the story and stressed that the "monstrous offer" of the Germans to barter Jews for munitions was a loathsome attempt to blackmail and sow suspicion among the Allies. Kasztner and Joel Brand's wife, Hansi, were imprisoned in Hungary when Brand failed to return promptly.

On June 14, 1944, Kasztner was informed by Eichmann that he was willing to allow 30,000 Hungarian Jews to be held in Austria as a demonstration of his goodwill. In return, he demanded an immediate payment of 5 million Swiss francs. Eichmann's offer was based on the instructions he had received from **Ernst Kaltenbrunner**, head of the RHSA, who was desperate for slave labor to service Austrian industries. The selection of which Jews would be chosen as slave labor was left up to the Jewish leadership. From June 25 to 28, 1944, several transports of approximately 20,000 Jews were directed to Strasshof, a concentration camp near Vienna. About 75 percent of them survived the war.

Kasztner then resumed negotiations with Eichmann to save more Jews. Following discussions with **Dieter Wisliceny**, Eichmann agreed to allow a special group from Kolozsvár (Cluj) to come to Budapest. Kasztner could not resist the chance to save his family, friends, and most deserving members of the Kolozsvár community, and 338 were taken to Budapest on June 10, 1944. The Jewish Relief and Rescue Committee had to pay Germany a general figure of 5 million Swiss francs, plus 1,000 more for every individual to be included in the transport. About 150 places were "sold" to wealthy individuals. The valuables were delivered to the SS in three suitcases and received by Becher, and the transport left Budapest on June 30, 1944, with 1,684 Jews on board. Certain prominent persons were included, together with many friends and relatives of Relief and Rescue Committee members. They arrived in Bergen-Belsen on July 8, 1944, and were given privileged status.

Kasztner depended on Becher to transport the chosen Hungarian Jews from Bergen-Belsen to Switzerland, in what came to be called the Kasztner Transport. With the approval of Himmler, Becher also met with the head of the American Jewish Joint Distribution Committee in Switzerland, Saly Mayer, and the War Refugee Board representative, Roswell McClelland, on November 4, 1944. Becher regarded the meeting as highly important, as McClelland represented President Franklin D. Roosevelt. At this meeting, Becher also confirmed that the SS had by now annihilated the Slovakian Jews.

In January 1945, Himmler appointed Becher as special Reich commissioner for all concentration camps. Then on March 11, 1945, he empowered Becher to arrange with **Josef Kramer**, the commandant of Bergen-Belsen, a cease-fire between the advancing British army and German forces nearby. The camp was surrendered to the British on April 15, 1945.

Becher was arrested by the Allies in May 1945 and imprisoned at Nuremberg, but he was released owing to Kasztner's intercession on his behalf.

Becher collected large sums of money, jewelry, and precious metals as the war came to an end. Almost all of this came from Hungarian Jews and was estimated at around 8.6 million Swiss francs in what became known as the Becher Deposit. It was alleged that Becher hid this plunder before he was captured, but another explanation is that it was purloined by U.S. troops.

Becher became a prosperous businessman in Bremen and headed the Bremen Stock Exchange with a reported $30 million, making him one of the wealthiest men in West Germany in 1960. He was the president of many corporations, including the *Cologne-Handel Gesellschaft*, which did extensive business with the Israeli government.

Becher came to public attention once again in 1961, when he served as a witness for the prosecution during the Jerusalem trial of **Adolf Eichmann**. Becher provided his testimony from his home in Germany, because he was unwilling to travel to Israel itself.

On August 8, 1995, age 86, Becher died in Bremen, reportedly a wealthy man, without ever having to stand trial in court for his deeds.

BECKER-FREYSENG, HERMANN (1910–1961)

Hermann Becker-Freyseng was a German physician who became a medical adviser to the Luftwaffe and participated in medical experiments on Dachau concentration camp internees before and during World War II.

Becker-Freyseng was born in Ludwigshafen, Germany, on July 18, 1910. He graduated as a medical doctor from the University of Berlin in 1935. The following year, he was given the rank of captain in the Medical Service and was posted to the Department of Aviation Medicine. His first important research was his work with Hans-Georg Clamman in 1938 on the physical effects of pure oxygen. Becker-Freyseng became an expert on the effects of high-altitude, low-pressure conditions on human beings.

In 1938, he joined the Nazi Party. Hubertus Strughold, a physiologist and prominent medical researcher who served as chief of aeromedical research for the Luftwaffe, engaged Becker-Freyseng to work in his human-experimentation program. This began a connection in which Becker-Freyseng's colleagues came to hold him in high esteem. He conducted over 100 experiments on himself, some of which drove him to unconsciousness and the brink of death.

Becker-Freyseng's key area of experimentation was low-pressure-chamber research. The Department of Aviation Medicine was established in 1936, with Becker-Freyseng initially just attached before he was promoted to coordinator.

Becker-Freyseng's work in Nazi concentration camps became infamous. He both conducted and supervised several experiments involving unwilling prisoners. Experiments undertaken by him or under his supervision—in particular, the various low-pressure chambers designed to mimic the effects of high-altitude experiments—were performed on inmates of Dachau concentration camp. These often resulted in fatalities. Other experiments recorded the effects of extremely cold temperatures on the human body. One of Becker-Freyseng's more sinister experiments involved forcing 40 internees to drink salt water to measure their bodies' reactions. Some also had salt water injected directly into their bloodstreams. The subjects were then subjected to liver biopsies without the benefit of anesthesia to measure that organ's reaction to the salt water. All subjects of the experiment died.

At the end of World War II in 1945, Becker-Freyseng was taken into custody by U.S. occupation authorities and put on trial for his medical experiments. In 1946, at the Doctors' Trial, he was found guilty of war crimes and crimes against humanity and sentenced to 20 years in prison. In 1946, however, Becker-Freyseng's name was on a list with other German doctors, scientists, and engineers as part of Operation Paperclip, a joint British-American operation conducted with the objective of seizing Germany's top scientists and technologists and transporting them back to Allied countries. Operation Paperclip aimed to prevent these persons from working for the Soviets during the early Cold War period.

Becker-Freyseng was given responsibility for collecting and publishing the research undertaken by him and his colleagues. The resulting book, *German Aviation Medicine: World War II*, appeared just after Becker-Freyseng began his prison sentence. He was diagnosed with multiple sclerosis in 1960 and died on August 27, 1961, in Heidelberg, Germany.

BERGER, GOTTLOB (1896–1975)

Gottlob Berger was a senior Nazi official responsible for SS recruiting during World War II. A zealous antisemite, he was a champion of the Final Solution.

Gottlob Christian Berger was born on July 16, 1896, at Gerstetten, Württemberg, one of eight children of sawmill owners Johannes and Christine Berger. Educated in Nuertingen between 1910 and 1914, he became a physical education teacher. He served in the German army from the start of World War I, was wounded four times, and was awarded the Iron Cross First Class. In 1919, as a first lieutenant, he was discharged as 70 percent disabled. He had three brothers, two of whom died in the trenches of World War I and the other was executed in the United States in September 1918 on a charge of espionage.

Upon demobilization, Berger returned to teaching, but he had trouble adjusting to civilian life. Between 1919 and 1921, he was a leader of the *Einwohnerwehr* (Citizens' Defense) militia in North Württemberg. This was a far-right paramilitary organization operating throughout Weimar Germany, established with the goal of defending the country against the possibility of a communist takeover. While engaged in this activity, Berger maintained his gymnastic and physical education interests, and in 1921, now qualified as a sports trainer, he married his fiancée, Maria. Together they would raise a family of four children.

Berger joined the Nazi Party in 1922, and in the spring of 1923, he started a local SA group in his hometown of Gerstetten. After the failed 1923 Beer Hall Putsch and the ban on the NSDAP, he worked as a teacher near Tübingen. He rejoined the Nazi Party in the late 1920s, and in 1931, he joined the SA.

After the Nazi seizure of power in January 1933, Berger led operations involving the roundup of political "undesirables" and Jews. In July 1934, he began work with the head of SA training, **Friedrich-Wilhelm Krüger**. In 1936, on Krüger's recommendation, Berger was recruited into the *Allgemeine-SS* by **Heinrich Himmler**. This saw Berger first assigned as head of regional SS physical education; he was soon transferred to Himmler's staff as leader of the sports office. In 1938, Himmler appointed Berger to the SS Main Office (*SS-Hauptamt*, or SS-HA, the central command office of the SS), to head up recruitment.

Berger set the Waffen-SS on a sound basis. His recruiting methods allowed the Waffen-SS to sidestep Wehrmacht controls over conscription. With the onset of war, he managed to extend Waffen-SS recruiting to "Germanic" volunteers from Scandinavia and Western Europe. From here, he recruited *Volksdeutsche* (ethnic Germans) from outside the Reich. Others would follow in succeeding years.

Berger sponsored and shielded his friend **Oskar Dirlewanger**, whom he placed in charge of a unit of convicts that later perpetrated war crimes. Berger's recruiting methods upset senior officers of the Wehrmacht and the Waffen-SS, but by the end of the war, the latter had grown to an impressive total of 38 divisions.

Within the SS, Berger was known as one of Himmler's "Twelve Apostles," nicknamed *der Allmächtige Gottlob* ("the Almighty Gottlob," a play on "Almighty God"), for his closeness to the *Reichsführer* and because he was one of 12 leading Nazis who dabbled in *Völkish* spirituality.

Berger ran the SS-HA office in Berlin from 1940 and was heavily involved in activities relating to "Eastern Territories." The year 1942 saw the publication of the pamphlet *Der Untermensch* (*The Sub-Human*), which Berger coauthored with Himmler. It was written to assist soldiers after the start of Operation Barbarossa in June 1941 and described those the Nazis were in the process of conquering as spiritually and mentally lower than animals.

On March 6, 1942, Himmler transferred to Berger the responsibility of recruiting more Waffen-SS divisions, together with police units and guard battalions, along with the establishment, leadership, and training of various SS units in other parts of Europe.

On July 28, 1942, Himmler wrote to Berger that **Adolf Hitler** had given him instructions that the occupied eastern territories must become free of Jews and that Himmler was to be personally responsible for this task.

On August 10, 1942, while continuing in his role as chief of the SS-HA, Berger was selected to be chief of political operations in the occupied eastern territories. This appointment, which lasted until January 1945, enabled the SS to incapacitate any resistance to SS domination in Eastern Europe. Berger now proposed a plan to kidnap and enslave 50,000 Eastern European children between the ages of 10 and 14, under the codename *Heuaktion* (Operation Hay Harvesting). On June 14, 1944, **Alfred Rosenberg** issued orders implementing Berger's idea, and the plan was carried out.

Berger was also present when Himmler spoke, on October 4, 1943, to a secret meeting of SS officers in Posen (Poznań), in occupied Poland, that Germany was exterminating the Jews.

On July 20, 1944, Berger was given responsibility for the administration of German prisoner-of-war camps. Following the failed attempt on Hitler's life that same day, the Führer turned to Himmler to head the Replacement Army (*Ersatzheer*), providing fill-in troops for the combat divisions of the regular army. Himmler quickly delegated his responsibility over the prisoner-of-war camps to Berger, who, in turn, allowed the camps to continue as they were, with the same staff and procedures.

In August 1944, Berger was deployed to serve as military commander of German troops in Slovakia dealing with the Slovak National Uprising. The Slovakian government had until now been procrastinating over the deportation of Slovak Jews, and when Himmler nominated **Hermann Höfle** as the officer to suppress the revolt, Berger relinquished the role of military commander on September 19, 1944. Deportations of Jews then resumed, and between September 1944 and March 1945, 11 transports deported 8,000 Slovak Jews to Auschwitz, another 2,700 to Sachsenhausen, and 1,600 to Terezín (Theresienstadt).

Berger was then appointed as one of two chiefs of staff to organize the *Volkssturm* (Home Guard) in Germany. In the final months of the war, he commanded German forces in the Bavarian Alps, which included remnants of several of the Waffen-SS units he had helped recruit. He surrendered to U.S. troops near Berchtesgaden and was promptly arrested.

Berger was put on trial in the Ministries Trial at Nuremberg in 1947. He claimed that he knew nothing about the Final Solution until after the war, even though it was proved that he had been present at Himmler's 1943 Posen speech. Berger's defense counsel attempted to mitigate Berger's actions by claiming that the Cold War bore strong parallels to the Nazi fight against "Jews and Bolsheviks" and that it was possible that the United States would soon have to fight the Soviet Union. Berger, for his part, displayed no remorse for his actions.

In 1949, Berger was convicted for war crimes and crimes against humanity, atrocities, and offences committed against civilian populations. His conviction included being involved with the *SS-Sonderkommando Dirlewanger*, being a conscious participant in the concentration camp program, conscripting nationals of other countries, transporting Hungarian Jews to concentration camps, and recruiting concentration camp guards. He was also convicted under the charge of using child and youth slave labor, including the *Heuaktion*.

Given credit for the nearly 4 years during which he had been in custody awaiting trial, Berger was sentenced to 25 years in prison. On January 31, 1951, his sentence was commuted to 10 years' imprisonment on the dual grounds that he had intervened to save the lives of Allied officers and men who were due for execution and that he had saved 21 *Prominente* prisoners from Colditz, including Viscount Lascelles and the Master of Elphinstone (both nephews of King George VI), and Giles Romilly, a nephew of British prime minister Winston Churchill. Berger arranged for them to be evacuated from Colditz and transported south, where they were handed over to advancing U.S. Army troops.

Gottlob Berger was released from Landsberg prison in December 1951 after serving six and a half years. He died at the age of 77 in his hometown of Gerstetten on January 5, 1975.

BEST, WERNER (1903–1989)

Dr. Karl Rudolf Werner Best was a German jurist, police chief, *SS-Obergruppenführer*, and Nazi Party leader from Darmstadt, Hesse. As a leading constitutional theoretician and jurist in the Third Reich, he gave respectability and legitimacy to the political police and the concentration camps. He considered that as long as the Gestapo was carrying out the will of the Führer, it was acting legally.

Best was born on July 10, 1903, in Darmstadt. In 1912, his parents moved to Dortmund and then to Mainz, where he completed his education. His father, a senior postmaster, was killed during the first few days of World War I. After the war, Best founded the first local group of the German National Youth League and became active in the Mainz group of the German National People's Party. In his involvement with the German youth movement, Best was inspired by its return to nature, its Germanic legends, and its *Völkish* worldview.

From 1921 to 1925, he studied law at Frankfurt am Main, Freiburg, Giessen, and Heidelberg, where he received his doctorate in 1927. In 1929, he was appointed a judge in Hesse but was forced to resign when the so-called Boxheim documents were found in his possession. The documents bearing Best's signature set out a blueprint for a Nazi putsch and the subsequent execution of political opponents. The disclosure of the Boxheim documents embarrassed **Adolf Hitler** at a time when he was seeking power by legal means. Despite this, Best was made police commissioner for Hesse in March 1933, and by July 1933, he was appointed governor.

Over the next six years, Best advanced rapidly, becoming chief legal adviser to the Gestapo and chief of the Bureau of the Secret State Police at the Reich Ministry of the Interior. He helped the Gestapo destroy much of the old Weimar legal system and showed them how to use orders for preventive detention without judicial checks.

In 1934, Hitler decided that his internal opposition in the party had to be eliminated. On June 30, 1934, the SS and Gestapo acted in coordinated mass arrests against Ernst Röhm and the SA in a purge that became known as the Night of the Long Knives. Best was sent to Munich to arrest SA members in the southern part of Germany, and at this time up to 200 people were killed.

By 1935, Best was **Reinhard Heydrich**'s closest collaborator in building up the Gestapo and the Security Service (SD). Then in April 1936, he assumed a leading role in ideological training for the Gestapo. Using biological metaphors, he described the role of the Gestapo and the political police as fighting "disease" in the national body; among the implied sicknesses were communists, Freemasons, and the churches. Above and behind all these stood the Jews.

On September 27, 1939, the security agencies of the Reich were folded into the new Reich Main Security Office (*Reichssicherheitshauptamt*, or RSHA), which was placed under Heydrich's control. Best was made head of Department I: Administration and Legal, dealing with legal and personnel issues relating to the SS and security police. Heydrich and **Heinrich Himmler** relied on Best to develop and explain legally the activities against enemies of the state and in relation to Nazi Jewish policy. In this capacity, he was charged after the war with complicity in the murder of thousands of Jews and Polish intellectuals.

As a Himmler favorite, Best was being groomed for the very top of the SS, but an internal power struggle saw him dismissed by Reinhard Heydrich in 1939. He left the RHSA on June 12, 1940. He then served for two years as civil administrator in occupied France, involved in fighting the French Resistance and in the deportation of Jews, and in this time period he was nicknamed the "Butcher of Paris."

In November 1942, Best was appointed the Third Reich's supreme power in Denmark. In this role, he supervised civilian affairs. He kept this position until the end of the war in May 1945, even after the German military had assumed direct control over the administration of the country on August 29, 1943.

As a response to an increase in sabotage attacks in 1943, Best was instructed by Berlin to deliver a statement to the Danish resistance by eliminating the country's Jewish population. With limited German troops at his disposal and fearing a civil uprising if he deported 8,000 Danish Jews to certain death, he went about fulfilling Hitler's order to the letter, although not in the spirit the führer intended.

Best's urgent and repeated requests for additional SS battalions were not met. During the time in question, from September through early October 1943, all available SS troops had been deployed by Heinrich Himmler to Italy, where they were needed to shore up Benito Mussolini's puppet regime, and thus could not be spared for Denmark.

Best knew that unless he could mount a swift roundup with surgical precision, requiring ruthless and massive SS involvement, his future career would be in jeopardy. He therefore sent his naval attaché, Georg Duckwitz, to Sweden to arrange safe passage and accommodation for Denmark's Jews, and then Best himself walked into a Jewish tailor's shop in Copenhagen and warned the tailor and his family that a roundup of the Jews was imminent and told them to flee. The word then spread quickly through the Jewish community.

Almost all Danish Jews survived the Final Solution by escaping to Sweden, ferried over at night by the boats of their non-Jewish Danish neighbors. Only 477 out of more than 7,000 Danish Jews were finally rounded up by German troops, who were forbidden by Best to break into Jewish apartments. Half-Jews were let go, and patrols were not especially vigilant.

It is arguable that Best undermined the Final Solution outcome not out of an altruistic desire to save human life but out of a pragmatic need to maintain a stable status quo in occupied Denmark and to preserve the Reich's influence. His success depended on the willingness of the Danish people to save their Jewish neighbors—to refuse to see them as anything but fellow Danes. That, in the end, is perhaps the true miracle of the Danish rescue.

To avoid the deportation of Danes to German concentration camps, the permanent secretary of the ministry of foreign affairs, Nils Svenningsen, proposed in January 1944 the establishment of an internment camp within Denmark. Best accepted this proposal but on the condition that the camp should be built close to the German border. Frøslev prison camp was opened in August 1944. In deliberations on May 3, 1945, when preparing for the impending German defeat, Best then fought to avoid implementation of a scorched earth policy in Denmark.

After the war, Best testified as a witness at the International Military Tribunal at Nuremberg and was later extradited to Denmark. In 1948, he was sentenced to death by a Danish court, but his sentence was reduced to five years in prison (of which four years had already been served). This created outrage among the Danish

McCullough Jr. High Library

public, and the Supreme Court changed the sentence to 12 years. Best was granted a clemency release in August 1951.

He then returned to West Germany, working for a time in a solicitor's office and then as a lawyer for Stinnes & Co., one of the largest German trading concerns. In 1958, he was fined 70,000 deutsche marks by a German denazification court for his past actions as a leading SS officer, and in March 1969, Best was held in detention while new investigations were carried out concerning his responsibility for mass murder. He was released in August 1969 on medical grounds, although the accusations were not withdrawn.

In 1972, he was charged again when further war crimes allegations arose, but he was found medically unfit to stand trial and was released. After that, he became part of a network that helped former Nazis. He died on June 23, 1989, in Mülheim.

BIEBOW, HANS (1902–1947)

Hans Biebow was the Nazi chief administrator of the Łódź ghetto in Poland, principally responsible for organizing deportations of Jews from there to the Chełmno extermination camp. During his time at Łódź, the Jewish population of the ghetto disintegrated from 200,000 to less than 1,000. As head of the ghetto's *Judenrat* (Jewish Council), Mordechai Chaim Rumkowski had a close, though subordinate, relationship with Biebow and reported directly to him.

Biebow was born on December 18, 1902, in Bremen, Germany, the son of an insurance company director. He graduated from secondary school and commenced work at his father's district branch of the Stuttgart Insurance Company. That was far from successful, however, as the insurance industry had fared badly in the economic circumstances of the 1920s crash and there was little work available. After working in several jobs in the food industry, he started his own small business in Bremen in the coffee trade.

Following the German invasion of Poland on September 1, 1939, the Nazis created ghettos in major cities in which they forced the Jews to live. One of the largest of these ghettos was in Łódź. Biebow, who was recognized as a skilled administrator by his Nazi Party superiors, became the overseer of the ghetto after it was established in April 1940. Initially, he was put in charge of food stocks but was soon made head of the ghetto government.

It was in this capacity that Biebow realized that the ghetto could make a profit for the Germans. He saw an opportunity to benefit from the establishment of over 100 factories and workshops manned by Jewish slave labor to produce goods for the German war effort. Establishing and leading a German staff of some 250 people, Biebow's transformation of the ghetto into something more akin to a slave labor camp managed to forestall its liquidation until the summer of 1944.

Biebow was not alone in his conviction that producing goods needed by the German army was the best way for the ghetto to avoid liquidation. Mordecai Chaim Rumkowski, the head of the Łódź ghetto *Judenrat*, was also convinced that producing needed goods was the only way for the Jews entrapped in the ghetto to survive. Thus, Biebow and Rumkowski had similar goals for a high level of productivity from the ghetto and seemed to have a good working relationship as a result. Rumkowski and the Jewish Council established 117 different workshops that used the Jews as slave labor to help manufacture military equipment for the German front lines. The strategy of running the ghetto as a support for the German army was successful, in that Łódź was the last ghetto in Poland to be liquidated.

Biebow derived significant personal wealth from his unfettered exploitation of slave labor and expropriation of Jewish valuables and property. The Jews were promised food and medical supplies in return for their work in the workshops, but his policy of food distribution was the direct cause of widespread starvation. The quality and quantity were less than minimal, and often large portions were completely spoiled. Ration cards for food were quickly put into effect on June 2, 1940, and by December 1940, all provisions were rationed. Allegedly, Biebow pocketed much of the money allocated to buying enough food, leading tens of thousands of Jews to die from some combination of mass starvation, overcrowding, exposure to the elements, arbitrary shootings and beatings, and disease that was the inevitable result of horrid sanitary conditions.

Biebow brought that same enthusiasm to his task of arranging and transporting thousands of Jews from the ghetto to the Chełmno and Auschwitz extermination camps, even as he was trying to keep ghetto production going for as long as possible. He was ruthlessly efficient and saw that his orders to transport Jews to their death were carried out without delay and unhampered by moral concerns. He also organized the collection of personal possessions and clothing of Jewish victims at Chełmno to be warehoused and eventually sent to Germany.

When it became apparent that Germany was going to lose the war, **Adolf Hitler** called up German men capable of fighting. This increased the need for trained workers, even if Jewish, and so the factories in the Łódź ghetto continued turning out needed goods and equipment. Yet deportations continued, and the ghetto was completely liquidated by August 1944.

Biebow escaped into hiding in Germany in 1945, but he was recognized by a ghetto survivor in Bremen and subsequently arrested. At his trial from April 23 to April 30, 1947, he was found guilty on all counts and was executed by hanging in Łódź on June 23, 1947.

BIERKAMP, WALTHER (1901–1945)

Born in Hamburg on December 17, 1901, Walther Bierkamp was a lawyer who headed the SiPo and SD in Düsseldorf and who commanded *Einsatzgruppe D* for a full year across 1942 and 1943.

During 1919 and 1921, Bierkamp was a member of Hamburg's far-right nationalist *Freikorps Bahrenfeld* and an active participant in the Kapp Putsch of 1921. He studied law in Göttingen and Hamburg, passing the first state examination in 1924 and the second in 1928. He joined the civil service, where he started as *Oberregierungsrat* (senior entry-level lawyer). Over time, he became head of the Criminal

Investigation Department in Hamburg, and as a public prosecutor, he joined the NSDAP on December 1, 1932. In February 1937, he became chief of Hamburg's Kripo, and then on April 1, 1939, he entered the SS.

On February 15, 1941, Bierkamp was named inspector of the SiPo and the SD in Düsseldorf, a position he held until September 1941, when his responsibilities were compounded by a move to Paris and he was given the same offices for Belgium and Northern France. He remained on station as *Höherer SS-* and *Polizeiführer* (higher SS and police leader, or HSSPF) and held all offices until April 1942. On May 3, 1942, he was promoted to *SS-Oberführer* and was released on June 24, 1942, before accepting his next command.

On June 30, 1942, Bierkamp relieved **Otto Ohlendorf** as commander of *Einsatzgruppe D* in southern Ukraine and Crimea. When the 11th Army began its summer offensive toward the Caucasus, *Einsatzgruppe D* moved in behind it. In August, the first major action took place against Jews in the region. Gas vans were employed against children from orphanages in Krasnodar and Yeysk as well as residents of Pyatigorsk. Then on August 21 to 22, 500 people were murdered in the Krasnodar Forest, followed by the inhabitants of Mineralnyje Wody on September 1, and the Jews of Yessentuki and Kislovodsk on September 9 to 10. In all, the campaign realized a death toll of more than 6,000 Jews.

By January 4 to 5, 1943, Jewish survivors in the region, who had lived long enough to be used as slave labor, were murdered in Kislovodsk; by then, the number of Jewish victims had grown to about 10,000. In May 1943, to accompany the start of the German army's summer offensive, *Einsatzgruppe D* was renamed *Kampfgruppe Bierkamp* (Bierkamp Combat Group) in honor of their commander. This name was kept for a short time until June 15, 1943, when upon his return from *Einsatzgruppe* duties, Bierkamp was sent to Kraków as HSSPF for the *Generalgouvernement*.

As the war situation deteriorated and the Soviets began to advance of Poland, Bierkamp saw that drastic measures would need to be taken if the remaining Jews in the *Generalgouvernement* were not to fall into Russian hands. Thus, in addition to overseeing the final "cleansing" of the Jews of Kraków, he issued a decree on July 20, 1944, ordering that Jews working at forced labor in the arms industry be immediately transported to death camps. If this was not possible, he demanded that they "will be liquidated on the spot, and their corpses will have to be eliminated by incineration, blasting or by other means." On November 9, 1944, Bierkamp received his final promotion, to *SS-Brigadeführer* and police major general.

In this capacity, he was sent to command police and security services in Stuttgart until February 20, 1945, when he was sent as HSSPF to Breslau (Wrocław), where he took over on March 17, 1945. With the further advance of the Russians, the territory he was controlling was largely overrun; although by his title, he remained HSSPF Southwest until mid-April 1945. From April 14, 1945, until the war's end, Bierkamp was stationed in Hamburg.

On the night of May 15 to 16, 1945, Walther Bierkamp committed suicide in Scharbeutz, a municipality in Schleswig-Holstein not far from the city of Lübeck.

BIKKER, HERBERTUS (1915–2008)

Herbertus Bikker was a Dutch member of the Waffen-SS who served as a prison guard at Camp Erika near Ommen from June 19, 1941, until April 11, 1945.

He was born into a large farming family on July 15, 1915, in Wijngaarden, the Netherlands. His mother died when he was six years old. His father gave him a strict education, but as he had to help on the farm, he only completed primary school. Prior to World War II, he became a member of the *Nationaal-Socialistische Beweging in Nederland* (National Socialist Movement in the Netherlands, or NSB), and in early 1940, Bikker was imprisoned by the Dutch police for security reasons. After the German occupation of the Netherlands, he was released.

In 1941, with the start of Operation Barbarossa, Bikker enlisted as a Dutch volunteer in the Waffen-SS and served on the Eastern Front. When wounded, he was discharged from further military service and returned to the Netherlands.

Between July 1942 and May 1943, Bikker was put in charge of the Control Commando, which ran Kamp Erika. By 1943, he had recovered from his war wounds, and as a member of the *Ordnungspolizei* (uniformed Nazi police), he served in Nijmegen, Tiel, and Maastricht. In August 1944, he returned to Kamp Erika. A later report, by Jan Meulink for the Ministry of Justice, stated that Bikker abused his prisoners; Meulink noted that witnesses described him as "a plague, by the way he hit prisoners, mistreated with a carabiner, or stamped" on them, crippling healthy inmates. For his actions in hunting down resistance fighters and for his brutal behavior toward inmates, he was known as the "Butcher of Omman." He was responsible for the murder of 27-year-old Dutch resistance fighter Jan Houtman, who was killed on November 17, 1944, and the death of another resistance fighter, Herman Meijer, on October 12, 1944.

On May 10, 1945, Bikker was arrested by the Dutch army, but he escaped and worked with a farmer until discovered in late 1945. In June 1949, he received the death penalty for his crimes as a guard in Kamp Erika, including torture, deportation, and treason, as well as two murders. The punishment was converted to life imprisonment on December 7, 1949.

On December 26, 1952, Bikker, along with several other criminals, escaped from the Dome Prison in Breda, and that night they crossed the border into West Germany, where they reported to the police. The next day a German district court judge fined them 10 deutsche marks for illegal crossing. Under a decree from 1943, foreign members of the Waffen-SS automatically received German nationality, and as Germany did not extradite its own nationals, Bikker, with German citizenship, fell outside the grasp of Dutch justice.

In 1957, Bikker was summoned to appear before a Dortmund court, but the case was discontinued due to "lack of evidence." Dutch courts were reluctant to hand over their evidence to German courts, because they distrusted the many former Nazi judges who had continued in their posts after the fall of the Third Reich. Bikker allegedly also received assistance in Germany from former SS members who were once again occupying influential positions.

In 1972, Bikker threatened the Dutch investigative journalist Ben Herbergs with an ax in a barn behind Bikker's home in Hagen, Westphalia. Herbergs had located Bikker in Germany after a political uproar had arisen in the Netherlands about the freeing of other Nazi war criminals. Bikker had agreed to a "short conversation from fellow countryman to fellow countryman" with the Dutch reporter and a German photographer, and he spoke frankly about his work and his illegal family visits to the Netherlands. When he discovered a tape-recording device with loose microphone cable, Bikker flew into a rage; he grabbed heavy tools and an ax and barred the access door, but the Dutch reporting team escaped.

For decades, prosecutors sought Bikker's return. In 1994, a Dutch journalist and Nazi hunter, Jack Koistra, traced Bikker to his residence in Hagen. After this was reported on Dutch television, the Dutch minister of justice sought Bikker's immediate extradition; this was again rejected by German authorities. In November 1995, German and Dutch members of anti-fascist groups, together with a few surviving resistance fighters, protested outside Bikker's home, shouting that "Herbertus Bikker is a murderer." The demonstrators were fined for demonstrating without a permit.

Stern editors Werner Schmitz and Albert Eikenaar noted the way this demonstration was handled, and it was due to their investigative journalism that Bikker again came before the courts. But it was Bikker's own boast, in a 1997 interview with Schmitz, of having shot Jan Houtman that started a lawsuit against him. Describing the events on November 17, 1944, Bikker told Schmitz that he gave Houtman "the final shot." After the publication of the *Stern* interview in 1997, chief prosecutor Ulrich Maass from the Nazi crimes central office began investigations at the state attorney's office in Dortmund.

It took another six years before the case commenced. In the meantime, some of the eyewitnesses to Jan Houtman's murder had died. Houtman's widow had also died three years earlier. But an important witness, who had already provided written evidence five years previously, was able to appear at the district court in Hagen on October 10, 2003, to testify.

On September 8, 2003, in the German district court of Hagen, almost 59 years after Jan Houtman's murder, the trial of the now 88-year-old Herbertus Bikker opened. He stood accused of shooting Houtman to death on November 17, 1944. The indictment read that Houtman had been injured trying to escape a labor camp and was lying on the floor of a nearby barn when Bikker caught up with him, pulled out his pistol, and shot Houtman saying, "And now a good death." Bikker's only chance to evade prosecution and trial was to claim diminished responsibility due to illness. When a doctor attested that Bikker was medically fit to stand trial, his case came to court. However, after Bikker had a breakdown and fainted in court, neurologists advised against him standing trial due to illness. For that reason, the hearing was adjourned on February 2, 2004.

Bikker lived in Hagen as a pensioner until his death on November 1, 2008, in Haspe, Germany. His passing was not announced until April 2009.

The trial shed light on the brutal occupation of the Netherlands by **Adolf Hitler**'s National Socialist regime and the terrible consequences resistance fighters suffered at the hands of both the military secret service and their Dutch collaborators. That so much time elapsed before Bikker was obliged to stand trial showed the diffident attitude of German authorities to those responsible for Nazi crimes.

BINZ, DOROTHEA (1920–1947)

Dorothea Binz was a prison guard at Ravensbrück concentration camp during World War II, where she gained a reputation as one of the most brutal women within the Nazi system.

Dorothea "Theodora" Binz was born on March 16, 1920, in Gross-Dölln, Brandenburg, to a German middle-class family. The middle daughter of Walter Binz, she attended school until she was 15, missing much schooling along the way due to tuberculosis. Upon leaving school, she worked for a while as a kitchen aide and then as a housekeeper, which she is reputed to have hated.

Physically, she had beautiful blond hair and blue eyes, the ideal of the Nazi woman. Binz joined the *Bund deutscher Mädel* (League of German Girls, or BdM), the female counterpart of the Hitler Youth (*Hitlerjugend*), and became influenced by Nazi doctrine. She wanted to join the SS and applied for a job as a kitchen hand in the women's camp at Ravensbrück in August 1939. On September 1, 1939, she was sent to Ravensbrück to undergo training as a guard. During her time there, at least 50,000 women died.

The senior officers under whom Binz served included Emma Anna Maria Zimmer, Johanna Langefeld, **Maria Mandl**, and Anna Klein-Plaubel. At times, she worked with Dr. **Herta Oberheuser** and the Polish prisoners (nicknamed "the rabbits") at Ravensbrück in various parts of the camp, including the kitchen and the laundry. After 1942, she oversaw the training of new guards at Ravensbrück. In August 1943, she was promoted to deputy chief wardress. As a member of the command staff between 1943 and 1945, she directed training and assigned duties to over 100 female guards and introduced training for recruits destined for other concentration camps, such as Buchenwald and Auschwitz-Birkenau. Binz reportedly trained some of the cruelest female guards in the system, including Ruth Closius-Neudeck and **Irma Grese**.

Binz supposedly supervised the bunker where women prisoners were tortured and killed. She earned the reputation of being sadistic and of being extremely cruel. Smashing heads and shooting or maltreating prisoners for no apparent reason (and often for no reason at all) became a daily occurrence; it appears that she fully enjoyed her abuse of power. She would walk through the camp with a whip in one hand and her leashed German shepherd dog in the other. She could kick a prisoner to death with her heavy boots or choose to have the prisoner executed, and she was especially cruel to Soviet prisoners of war, whom she dubbed "Russian pigs." Binz maintained a special truck to take prisoners to the gallows and took pleasure in watching their death.

While at Ravensbrück, she had an affair with a young married SS officer, Edmund Bräuning, and their favorite pastimes included "romantic" walks through the camp, arm in arm or hand in hand, as they showed amusement at seeing women who were flogged. Stripped prisoners went to Ravensbrück's "bunker"—torture cells—where they were handed over to Binz and her junior officers. Camp survivors testified how Binz and her team regularly tortured prisoners by immersing them in ice-cold water.

As the Allies advanced in 1945, Ravensbrück was evacuated. Survivors were sent on a death march, from which Binz fled, but she was caught by British troops in Hamburg on May 3, 1945. She was imprisoned for a time in Recklinghausen, a subcamp of Buchenwald, until she was tried with other SS and camp personnel by a British court at the Ravensbrück War Crimes Trials. She was convicted of perpetrating war crimes and sentenced to death by hanging. On May 2, 1947, the sentence was carried out in the prison of Hameln by British hangman Albert Pierrepoint. To avoid any signs of martyrdom, the bodies of Binz and the others were buried in the Hamelin prison yard. In 1954, the bodies were reburied in holy ground at Am Wehl Cemetery. Originally the graves had iron crosses placed over them, but after a succession of visits from neo-Nazis, all 200 crosses were removed on March 3, 1986. The graveyard is now a grass field.

BLOBEL, PAUL (1894–1951)

Paul Blobel was an SS commander who led *Sonderkommando 4a* (a part of *Einstazgruppe* C), which became notorious for the mass murder in 1941 of 33,771 Jews in Babi Yar, a ravine near Kiev, Ukraine.

He was born on August 13, 1894, in Potsdam, near Berlin, the son of a craftsman. He qualified as a stonemason and carpenter. In World War I, he served in an engineering unit, was awarded the Iron Cross First Class, and in 1918 rose to the rank of staff sergeant.

After demobilization, Blobel studied construction between 1919 and 1920, and from 1921 to 1924, he was employed by various firms as an architect. He opened his own architectural practice in 1924, but because of the Weimar Republic's economic crisis, he received no new work and lived on a social security allowance between 1930 and 1933. By December 1, 1931, Blobel had joined the Nazi Party, the SA, and the SS. In 1933, he joined the Düsseldorf police force, and in June 1934, he was recruited into **Reinhard Heydrich**'s SD. On January 30, 1941, he was promoted as chief of the SD in Salzburg, with the rank of *SS-Standartenführer*.

During the German invasion of the Soviet Union in June 1941, Blobel took command of *Sonderkommando 4a* of *Einsatzgruppe C*, then active in Ukraine. *Einsatzgruppe C* was under the control of **Otto Rasch**. The role of the *Einsatzgruppen* (mobile killing units) was to follow troops of the Wehrmacht as they advanced into Ukraine; they were tasked with eliminating political and racial "enemies" of the Third Reich.

Blobel was primarily responsible for carrying out the notorious massacre of 33,771 Kiev Jews at the Babi Yar ravine in Kiev. In August 1941, in Belaya Tserkov, some 50 miles south of Kiev, all adult Jews were murdered by Blobel's unit. Execution of the children was suspended by a junior officer, Helmuth Groscurth, who

Paul Blobel was an SS commander who led *Sonderkommando 4a*, which became notorious for the mass murder in 1941 of 33,771 Jews at Babi Yar, a ravine near Kiev, Ukraine. Here, Blobel pleads not guilty during the *Einsatzgruppen* trial at Nuremberg in 1947. At the left of the photo is another indicted SS commander, Franz Six. (Chronos Dokumentarfilm GmbH/ullstein bild via Getty Images)

drafted a report in which he wrote that the execution of women and children "did not differ in any way from the atrocities perpetrated by the enemy."

His superior officer was Walther von Reichenau, whose position on such matters would be encapsulated on October 10, 1941, in what became known as the Severity Order. Reichenau's order asserted that German soldiers "must learn fully to appreciate the necessity for the severe but just retribution that must be meted out to the subhuman species of Jewry." The order paved the way for mass murder of Jews in areas coming under his command, and the expectation was that all Jews would from this point onward be either summarily shot or handed over to the *Einsatzgruppen*. He thus rejected Groscurth's concerns and stated that the argument should never have been written down in the first place. Blobel and his assistant, August Häfner, had already told Groscurth that execution of the children had to continue. An argument then arose between Blobel and Häfner about who should carry out their murder; Häfner said his troops had their own children and should not be forced to carry out this cruel act. He suggested that von Reichenau's Ukrainian field militia should execute the children, which they did.

Shortly after the children of Belya Tserkov had been executed, Blobel and his *Sonderkommando* arrived in Kiev. The Soviet security service (NKVD) had bombed the city center during the battle for control of the city, and as a result, many German soldiers had died. In reprisal, Blobel determined that the Kiev Jews would be exterminated, even though they—mainly the elderly, women, and children—could in no way be blamed for the bombing. On September 29, 1941, all Jews were ordered to congregate and told that they would be deported to labor camps. Instead, they were shot into in a ravine at Babi Yar, northwest of the city. In his progress report dated October 7, 1941, Blobel reported the execution of 33,771 Jews there.

Following the mass murder at Babi Yar, a gas van was made available to Blobel's *Sonderkommando*. *Einsatzgruppe C* was issued at least five gas vans and gave two to *Sonderkommando 4a*, two to *Einsatzkommando* 6, and one to *Einsatzkommando* 5. From June 1941 to the end of 1943, 59,018 people were murdered by *Sonderkommando 4a*, although after January 13, 1942, this was no longer done under Blobel's command. He was removed by his successor, *SS-Oberführer* Erwin Weinmann, who had him transferred to Berlin for disciplinary reasons (probably related to Blobel's excessive drinking). Once there, he was not given an immediate assignment and was placed under the supervision of the Gestapo chief **Heinrich Müller**.

During 1942, *SS-Reichsführer* **Heinrich Himmler** decided that the buried remains of Jews and other victims of the *Einsatzgruppen* had to be cleared away. The same had to be done with victims of the extermination camps who had not been cremated but buried in mass graves. Reinhard Heydrich was charged with this operation, and in 1942, he met with Blobel to discuss the nature of the operation that now had to take place. Blobel's commission was suspended by Heydrich's death on June 4, 1942, but later that month, he was officially ordered by Heinrich Müller to take charge of the operation, which was top secret and codenamed *Aktion 1005*.

Before the exhumations could be started, a suitable method had to be found for destroying the corpses. The place chosen for trials was Chełmno, the first death camp, which had been operating since the end of 1941. *Aktion 1005* would take place by disinterring and cremating the bodies in wood fires in open pits. The bones were crushed in a special machine, and the ashes and any remaining bone fragments were buried in the graves from where the corpses had originally been exhumed. With a suitable method now found for erasing the traces of mass extermination easily and efficiently, the operation could begin in earnest and was carried out by *Sonderkommando 1005*—a special unit of about 20 men, members of the SS, SiPo, and other police forces under Blobel's command.

Blobel's last role in the Third Reich was commanding *Einsatzgruppe Iltis*, a unit consisting of two *Einsatzkommandos* tasked with fighting partisans on the Austro-Yugoslav border. Several of his men had already served under him in *Sonderkommando 1005*; after the war, he alleged that he himself had not been active as leader of *Einsatzgruppe Iltis*, as he had fallen ill in 1944 (his drinking had developed into alcoholism) and been confined to a sanatorium from February to April.

At the beginning of May 1945, Blobel was apprehended by the Americans. Placed on trial at Nuremberg, he protested his innocence, but he was nonetheless found guilty of crimes against humanity, war crimes, and membership of illegal organizations. He was sentenced to death. During the trial, he showed no remorse and only allowed expressions of compassion for the perpetrators who had been tasked with this dirty work. He was executed by hanging in Landsberg Prison on June 7, 1951.

BLOME, KURT (1894–1969)

A high-ranking Nazi doctor and research scientist, Kurt Blome controlled unethical medical experiments on concentration camp prisoners. Captured by U.S. forces, he was acquitted at the Doctors' Trial in 1947 and worked with U.S. scientists to impart his knowledge of bacteriological warfare and biological weapons from these experiments.

He was born in Bielefeld, Germany, on January 31, 1894, and graduated from high school in Dortmund. He moved to Rostock in early 1914 to study medicine at the University of Göttingen. On April 1, 1914, he began his compulsory military service with the Mecklenburg Fusilier Regiment "Kaiser Wilhelm" No. 90. During World War I, he was promoted to the rank of lieutenant. Wounded in March 1918, Blome ended the war as a patient in a Bremen hospital.

From 1918 to 1919, he continued his medical studies in Münster and Giessen and became a member of the *Freikorps* in Rostock. In 1920, he was actively involved in the so-called Kapp Putsch, in which he was wounded. He passed his medical examination in 1920 in Rostock, and in 1921, he was awarded a doctor of medicine degree at Rostock for his work on the behavior of bacteria.

Blome joined the NSDAP in 1922. In November 1923, after the party had been banned following **Adolf Hitler**'s abortive putsch, he was dismissed by the University of Rostock owing to his Nazi activities. From 1924 to 1934, he then led a medical practice as a specialist for skin and sex diseases.

In 1934, Blome became director of the Office of Public Health in Mecklenburg-Lübeck. The same year he was appointed to the main office for public health in Berlin as commissioner for the exemption provisions of the Nuremberg Laws. He was later appointed as head of medical training for the Third Reich in January 1935. On February 8, 1936, Blome became a member of the Reich Committee for the Protection of German Blood, and from April 20, 1939, he was deputy head of the Office for National Health.

His appointment on April 30, 1943, as head of the Central Institute for Cancer Research in Nesselstedt near Posen was a camouflage for his work on biological weapons. Blome was also appointed as a member of the *Blitzforschung* ("lightning research") working group, which was preparing for biological warfare. An expert on the development of biological weapons, Blome had a long-standing interest in the military use of carcinogenic substances and cancer-causing viruses. He worked on methods for the storage and dispersal of biological agents, like plague, cholera, anthrax, and typhoid, and later he confessed to have infected concentration camp prisoners at Dachau with bubonic plague to test vaccines. Blome was an expert in aerosol dispersants and the transmission of malaria to humans. At Auschwitz, he sprayed nerve agents like Tabun and Sarin from aircraft on prisoners.

In March 1945, Blome fled from Posen (Poznań) just ahead of the Red Army. He was unable to destroy the evidence of his experiments, however, which is why so much is known about them. On May 17, 1945, with the defeat of Germany, Blome was arrested in Munich by American military personnel. He was subsequently tried at the Doctors' Trial in 1947 on charges of practicing euthanasia and conducting experiments on humans. Inexplicably, he was acquitted; it was rumored that he was saved by American intervention. Two months after his Nuremberg acquittal, Blome was transferred to the United States, where he was interviewed at Camp David, Maryland, about biological warfare.

In 1951, Blome was hired by the U.S. Army Chemical Corps under Project 63 to work on chemical warfare. Although his file did not mention his trial at Nuremberg, Blome was denied a visa to work in the United States. He was, however, employed at the European Command Intelligence Center at Oberursel, West Germany, where he worked on chemical warfare projects. Blome also conducted research on cancer.

Blome's fate is unclear, with two different possible endings. Most biographies state that he was eventually arrested by French authorities, convicted of war crimes, and sentenced to 20 years in prison. Other reports state that he was not arrested or charged with war crimes again after his acquittal at the Nuremberg Doctors' Trial in 1947 and that he continued to practice medicine in West Germany, as a free man who never paid for his crimes. It has also been suggested that he was active in politics as a member of the right-wing Germany Party. All accounts agree, however, that Blome died in Dortmund on October 10, 1969, aged 75.

BLUME, WALTER (1906–1974)

Walter Blume was a midranking SS commander and leader of *Sonderkommando 7a*, part of *Einsatzgruppe B*. The unit perpetrated the killing of thousands of Jews in Belarus and Russia. Blume was also responsible for the deportation of over 46,000 Greek Jews to Auschwitz.

He was born on July 23, 1906, in Dortmund, into a Protestant family. His father was a schoolteacher with a doctorate in law. The younger Blume studied law in Bonn, Jena, and Münster; passed the bar examination; and received his doctorate in law from Erlangen University in April 1933. On March 1, 1933, he became head of the political section of the Dortmund court, where he worked as a state judicial state examiner and assistant judge.

In 1933, Blume joined the SA on March 1 and the NSDAP on May 1. On April 11, 1935, he became a member of the SS and joined the Reich Main Security Office (RSHA), working in the Prussian Secret Police.

Four years later, in December 1939, Blume was appointed as director of staff in the Berlin Gestapo, serving in Halle, Hanover, and Berlin until 1941. In March 1941, he was summoned to Düben, Saxony, where he was tasked with reorganizing the *Einsatzgruppen* ready for action in the forthcoming campaigns in the Soviet Union.

In May 1941, he took command of *Sonderkommando 7a* of *Einsatzgruppe B* (under overall command of **Arthur Nebe**). The head of the SD, **Reinhard Heydrich**, instructed Blume that he and his unit were tasked with wiping out Jews in the areas to be occupied. *Einsatzkommando 7a* was sent to Vitebsk (Belarus) and part of western Russia (Klintsy, Nevel, and Smolensk). In completing the *Aktions* that followed, Blume later reported that he had exterminated 24,000 Jews. On August 17, 1941, Blume left *Sonderkommando 7a* and was succeeded by Eugen Steimle. For the next two years, he took charge of the Gestapo office in Düsseldorf.

In 1942, Blume was promoted to *SS-Standartenführer* and sent to Greece as commander in charge of the Security Police (*Sicherheitspolizei*, or SiPo) in Athens. He increased the office staff and requisitioned city buildings in the center of Athens as locations in which to undertake interrogation (often by torture), and he directed the exclusion, concentration, and ultimately the expulsion of the Greek Jews. He also set up the Haidari concentration camp, which operated from September 1943 until it was shut down in September 1944. It was the largest and most notorious of some 20 camps set up by the Nazis in Greece.

In August 1943, Blume, under the direction of **Adolf Eichmann** and together with **Dieter Wisliceny** and Anton Burger (an *SS-Obersturmführer* and soon-to-be commandant at the Terezín concentration camp), organized the deportation of 46,000 Jews from the cities of Athens, Ioannina, Corfu, Rhodes, and Kos to Auschwitz-Birkenau. By October 18, 1943, Blume headed the SiPo and SD in Athens. At the end of 1944, he returned to Berlin.

With the German surrender in 1945, he was taken prisoner in Salzburg, Austria.

In April 1948, Walter Blume was a defendant at the Nuremberg *Einsatzgruppen* trial. The indictment claimed that he was directly responsible for the murder of 996 people between June and August 1941. He was not indicted for the crimes committed in Greece, including his involvement in the deportation of the Greek Jews. He was sentenced to death by U.S. Military Court II. In 1951, the Advisory Board on Clemency for War Criminals, run by U.S. high commissioner to Germany John J. McCloy, reduced Blume's death sentence to 25 years. In 1955, Blume was released from Bavaria's Landsberg prison.

After 1957, Blume ran a business in the Ruhr Valley. He remarried in 1958 and had six children.

Ten years later after the first trial, the Bremen public prosecutor's office investigated Blume, Anton Burger, and Friedrich Linnemann (Blume's assistant in Athens during the deportations). Despite the serious nature of the charges against them, a decision was made on January 29, 1971, not to proceed with any charges.

Walter Blume died on November 13, 1974, in Dortmund, aged 68.

BOGER, WILHELM (1906–1977)

Wilhelm Boger, known to some as the "Tiger of Auschwitz," was a German police commissioner and concentration camp supervisor. He was notorious for the nature of the crimes he committed at Auschwitz.

Wilhelm Friedrich Boger was born on December 19, 1906, in Zuffenhausen near Stuttgart. In 1922, he completed his formal schooling and joined the National Socialist youth movement (later named Hitler Youth) the same year. From 1922 to 1925, he worked as an apprentice, and in 1925, he took a clerical job at the Stuttgart office of the National German Commercial Employees' Association. Until the end of 1929, Boger was in the Artaman League, an organization that aimed to replace universal military service with voluntary agricultural service. He joined the NSDAP in 1929 and the SS in 1930. He married for the first time in 1931.

Boger lost his job in the spring of 1932. On March 5, 1933, as a member of the SS, he was called up to serve in the auxiliary police at Friedrichshafen, and on July 1, 1933, he was transferred to the Stuttgart political police. In October 1933, Boger moved into Friedrichshafen's political police force, and from 1936 to 1937, he attended police training school. After passing his examination, he was appointed as a police commissioner, despite a 1936 conviction for mistreating a prisoner during an interrogation.

When Germany invaded Poland in September 1939, Boger was transferred to the state police office at Zichenau. Three weeks later, he was commissioned to set up and supervise the border police station in Ostrolenka, Poland.

In 1940, Boger transferred to the Second SS Police Engineer unit, and after a brief training period, he was sent to the front, where he served until he was wounded in action in March 1942.

After his recovery, Boger was sent to Auschwitz and assigned to the Political Department, which represented the RSHA in the camp. Its chief duties were to receive and keep records on prisoners, maintain camp security, combat internal resistance, and conduct interrogations.

From December 23, 1943, until the evacuation of the camp in January 1945, he led the section dealing with investigations and interrogations. He was known for his cruelty and carried the reputation with pride. To assist with interrogations, he invented what became known as the Boger swing, a particularly vicious instrument of torture that resulted in ever-increasing levels of suffering as a prisoner's flesh would be flayed with each successive incorrect or unacceptable response during questioning. Employing this method, Boger was able to obtain a high confession rate from his victims.

In the last days of January 1945, with the help of *SS-Untersturmführer* Hans Schurz and other colleagues including **Pery Broad**, he took a truck loaded with incriminating files to Buchenwald. He then worked at Nordhausen, where he resumed his activity in the political service, supervising 5,000 prisoners on an evacuation march to Ravensbrück.

With the end of the war, he fled to Ludwigsburg, where his parents lived. He was arrested there in June 1945 by the American military police. In November 1946, he was due to be extradited to Poland for trial but escaped from custody. From 1948 until mid-1949, he worked as a farmhand near Stuttgart. In July 1949, he was rearrested and imprisoned in Lüneburg until August but was soon released. From late 1949, he was employed under his own name at the Heinkel aircraft factory in his hometown of Zuffenhausen. He was arrested again in October 1958 by the Stuttgart denazification court, which found him to be a rational, well-schooled police commissioner and civil servant, and not brutal at all. Passing his denazification tribunal, he was once more released.

In 1959, he was arrested one further time, and on this occasion, Boger was charged for war crimes committed while he was at Auschwitz. On August 20, 1965, he was indicted at the Frankfurt Auschwitz Trial for aiding and abetting in the murder of Jews. After testimony was heard from a series of eyewitnesses, he was finally sentenced to life imprisonment for murder in at least 5 cases, collective murder in at least 109 others, and shared assistance for collective murder.

Boger died at the age of 70 in Bietigheim-Bissingen prison, Baden-Württemberg, on April 3, 1977.

BORMANN, JUANA (1893–1945)

Juana Bormann was a Nazi concentration camp guard noted for her brutality shown toward the prisoners over whom she exercised authority.

She was born on September 10, 1893, in Birkenfelde, East Prussia. While not much has been recorded about her early life, it is known that she was a deeply religious Catholic woman who had at one time considered the life of a missionary. During the 1930s, however, she gave up this possibility to join the SS. To make more money, she enlisted as a civilian employee at Lichtenburg, the first women's concentration camp, on March 1, 1938. At first, she worked in the kitchens. When the new women's camp at Ravensbrück was opened in May 1939, she, together with the rest of the staff and prisoners from Lichtenberg, was transferred there.

At Ravensbrück, she was appointed as an *Aufseherin*, or overseer—in reality, a camp guard. In March 1942, she was transferred to Auschwitz (main camp), before being sent on to the extermination complex at Birkenau in October that year. Here, she worked alongside, and sometimes under the direction of, her supervisors, who included **Maria Mandl** and **Irma Grese**.

Known for her cruelty, Bormann was notorious for beating prisoners and turning loose her dogs on them; indeed, she was nicknamed the "woman with the dogs." At least two deaths were recorded due to mauling, and it was said that one of her favorite diversions was unleashing her German shepherd dog (by some accounts, an Irish wolfhound) on the prisoners. All, it was noted, were afraid of Bormann and did their best to avoid her.

One of the many subcamps of Auschwitz was established at Hindenburg (Zabrze), where a private enterprise belonging to the *Vereinigte Oberschlesische Hüttenwerke AG* (United Upper Silesian Steelworks AG) received permission to operate. At the beginning of August 1944, a transport of about 350 women prisoners, most of them Polish Jews, arrived from Birkenau at the subcamp that had been built there. Bormann was sent as a guard, under commandant *SS-Unterscharführer* Adolf Taube. In January 1945, the camp was evacuated, and the prisoners were marched on foot to Gleiwitz (Gliwice). Bormann was sent back to Ravensbrück, before moving on to Bergen-Belsen in March. Her new commandant was **Josef Kramer**, and she was reunited with Irma Grese and another guard with whom she had previously served, **Elisabeth Volkenrath**.

On April 15, 1945, Bergen-Belsen was liberated by British troops, and most of the camp personnel, including Bormann, were arrested. After being interrogated, she was remanded to a prison in the nearby town of Celle to await trial. The Belsen Trial, which took place between September 17 and November 17, 1945, was conducted by the British army in Lüneburg. Bormann was charged on various counts dating back to her time at Auschwitz, with witnesses testifying that she assisted in selecting prisoners to be sent to the gas chambers as well as for experiments with **Josef Mengele** and another Auschwitz doctor, Fritz Klein. She denied all charges, admitting only to slapping prisoners with her hand for disciplinary reasons.

In evidence, she told the court that she was a single woman and related her history of work in the concentration camps. Upon being asked about her involvement in the selection process for gassing, she replied that she had never attended selections and was only present at morning and evening roll calls. She admitted that she had a dog at Belsen, but she said that this was a pet rather than a camp guard dog and that she never set it against prisoners. Asked whether she had ever tried to leave the SS, she replied that she had applied in writing to do so in 1943 but that her application had been turned down.

Juana Bormann was found guilty of violating the laws and customs of war for her actions at Auschwitz and Belsen and was sentenced to death by hanging, along with Grese and Volkenrath. She was transferred to Hameln jail on December 9, 1945, to await execution. The hangings were set for Thursday, December 13, 1945. Volkenrath's was first, followed by Grese and then Bormann. Albert Pierrepoint, the British executioner, chronicled that at 52 years of age, she looked "old and haggard" as she "limped down the corridor" toward the gallows. Her last recorded words were "I have my feelings." She was buried in the jail's courtyard until 1954, when her body and those of the others were moved to the Am Wehl cemetery in Hameln. All the graves were (and remain) unmarked.

BORMANN, MARTIN (1900–1945)

Martin Bormann was a close friend and the private secretary of **Adolf Hitler**, and by the end of World War II, he had become the second most powerful man in Germany.

Martin Ludwig Bormann was born on June 17, 1900, in Wegelben near Halberstadt, one of five children of a former Prussian regimental sergeant major who later became a postal worker. Bormann had a poor relationship with his strict father. Educated at a Lutheran school, Bormann dropped out to work on a farming estate in Mecklenburg. He volunteered to serve in the German army during the last few months of World War I, joining the 55th Field Artillery Regiment, although he never saw action.

In 1922, while working as manager of a large estate, Bormann joined the *Freikorps Rossbach* in Mecklenburg. Here he befriended and fought alongside **Rudolf Hoess**, who, many years later, became commandant of Auschwitz concentration camp.

The so-called Feme murders were politically motivated murders committed in 1919 to 1923 by the German far right against political opponents. German nationalist Albert Leo Schlageter was executed by the French occupation forces in the Ruhr, and Walther Kadow (Bormann's former elementary school teacher) was suspected of having betrayed Schlageter to the French. In May 1923, Hoess, with Bormann as his accomplice, brutally murdered Kadow. In 1924, Hoess was sentenced to 10 years imprisonment and Martin Bormann to 1 year for their part in the murder.

Martin Bormann was a close friend and the private secretary of Adolf Hitler. By the end of World War II he had become the second most powerful man in Germany after the Führer. He followed Nazi ideology with the utmost brutality and remained at Hitler's side right through to the end of the war. Afterward he disappeared, never to face justice. It was later concluded that he took his own life a week after Hitler committed suicide in 1945. (Library of Congress)

In July 1926, after his early release, Bormann saw Hitler for the first time and was immediately impressed by him. Bormann joined the National Socialists, becoming head of the Nazi regional press in Thuringia in 1926. From 1928 to 1930, Bormann held posts in the SA Supreme Command.

On September 2, 1929, Bormann married 19-year-old Gerda Buch, whose father, **Walter Buch**, served as a chairman of the Nazi Party Court; Hitler served as a witness at their wedding. Martin and Gerda Bormann had 10 children, of whom a daughter died shortly after childbirth. Bormann also had a lover, the actress Manja Behrens, with whom he spent more time than with his own family.

In October 1933, Bormann became a *Reichsleiter* ("Reich Leader") of the NSDAP. A month later, he was elected as a Nazi delegate to the Reichstag. The Adolf Hitler Contribution to the German Economy, organized by Bormann in 1933, brought money from employers into the party coffers, and Bormann demonstrated his financial skills. In 1933, Hitler entrusted him with the administration of his own finances, which brought him access to Hitler himself and to the close circle around him.

From July 1933 until 1941, Bormann was the chief of cabinet in the Office of the Deputy führer, Rudolf Hess, acting as his personal secretary and right-hand man. The powers of Hess's staff were constantly extended. Its principal task was to assert the will of the party over the state apparatus. This meant control of legislative activity, influence over appointments, and regular interference at state and party political levels. After Hess's flight to Britain in May 1941, Bormann was appointed to succeed him, and he became head of the Party Chancellery at age 40. He had the authority of a Reich minister, but his actual power exceeded his formal positions in the party and state apparatus. Bormann's rise to power was based on his administrative and financial abilities, his unscrupulousness and intrigues, and his unconditional loyalty to Hitler.

In 1942, Bormann became Hitler's secretary and was given the post of deputy führer. He controlled all the papers and people Hitler saw, and he wielded a growing influence on government policy. He took charge of all of Hitler's paper work, appointments, and personal finances. Hitler came to have complete trust in Bormann and the view of reality he presented. During one meeting, Hitler was said to have screamed, "To win this war, I need Bormann!"

People whose access to Hitler Bormann controlled included **Josef Goebbels**, **Hermann Göring**, **Heinrich Himmler**, **Albert Speer**, and **Joachim von Ribbentrop**. As Hitler rarely left the headquarters, his judgments were invariably wrong during the final stages of the war.

Bormann pursued the aims and the ideology of Nazism with the utmost brutality. He pushed through the exclusion of the Christian churches from public life, and he favored extremely harsh treatment of the Slav population in the territories occupied by German troops and an intensification of the antisemitic measures of the Nazi state. He advocated extremely harsh, radical measures when it came to the treatment of Jews, of the conquered eastern peoples, and of prisoners of war. He signed a decree on October 9, 1942, which prescribed that "the permanent elimination of the Jews from the territories of Greater Germany can no longer be carried out by emigration but by the use of ruthless force in the special camps of the East." Bormann's further decree, signed by him on July 1, 1943, gave **Adolf Eichmann** absolute power over Jews, confirming the exclusive jurisdiction of the SS in this area.

Bormann remained at Hitler's side right up to the latter's suicide and pursued to the end—although with decreasing success—the implementation of Hitler's orders, including the destruction of Germany's remaining infrastructure. When it became clear that Germany was losing the war, Bormann attempted on May 2, 1945, to break through the lines of the Red Army with Hitler's driver and four others. They moved underground in small groups to Friedrichstrasse station, emerging to find Berlin in flames and Soviet shells exploding around them.

Bormann's fate remained unclear for a long time. In October 1946, the International Military Tribunal in Nuremberg condemned him to death in absentia. Despite frequent reports that Bormann had survived, the search for him proved fruitless. It was rumored for many years that Bormann had flown to Argentina.

On December 8, 1972, near the site of the *Führerbunker* in Berlin, construction workers uncovered human remains. Albert Krummnow, a postal official, came forward and informed the authorities that he had buried two bodies, one of which was Bormann's, on May 8, 1945. Fragments of glass found in one of the men's jawbones indicated that they committed suicide via cyanide capsules. DNA testing in 1988 later found the remains to be compatible with that of Bormann's son. It was confirmed that Bormann had committed suicide on May 2, 1945, aged 44, in

Berlin. His remains were cremated, and in 1999, Martin Bormann Jr. was permitted to scatter his father's ashes in the Baltic Sea outside German territorial limits. The cremation and burial cost the German government $4,700.

BOSS, HUGO (1885–1948)

Hugo Boss was a German clothing manufacturer whose enterprise embraced the Nazi period and, in more recent times, has become a global fashion house.

Born in the small Württemberg town of Metzingen on July 8, 1885, Boss was the youngest of five children in the family of Heinrich and Luise (née Münzenmayer) Boss, owners of a lingerie and linen shop. After a routine upbringing for a young middle-class German of the time, he assumed control of the store in 1908, the same year he was married. After serving in World War I, Boss established his own clothing company in Metzingen in 1923, followed by a clothes factory the following year. This produced shirts, jackets, work wear, sportswear, and raincoats.

One of Boss's earliest clients was Rudolf Born, a textiles distributor. He contracted Boss to produce some brown shirts for a small but growing political group known as the National Socialist Party; this was, of course, the nascent Nazi Party, which would assume office in January 1933. Boss himself at this time was relatively apolitical; he produced clothes for a variety of clients, including other political parties, the police, and the postal service.

With the onset of the Depression, Germany's economic climate deteriorated and then collapsed, and Boss was forced into bankruptcy. In 1931, he reached an agreement with his creditors that enabled him to start his business and found that he had an ally in the Nazis. On April 1, 1931, he joined the Nazi Party as member number 508,889 and became a sponsor of the SS. Over time, his economic situation improved.

Boss's reasons for becoming a Nazi, it appears, were twofold: as a businessman, it made good commercial sense to align himself with a growing political party that seemed likely to take power at some time in the future; and, given the economic and social turmoil in which Germany found itself, Boss saw Hitler as the only man able to regenerate the country.

The design of Nazi uniforms eventually saw the involvement of the Hugo Boss company, and the all-black outfit of the SS, introduced in the fall of 1932, was designed by artist and *SS-Oberführer* Professor Karl Diebitsch and a graphic designer, Walter Heck. It has often been asserted that the black SS uniform was designed by Boss himself, but this was not the case. However, the Hugo Boss company did produce the uniforms, together with the brown shirts of the SA and the uniforms of the Hitler Youth. In 1934, Boss claimed that he had been supplying the Nazis with uniforms since 1924, but it is more likely that he became entrenched in this role in 1928, when he received the status of official supplier to the Nazi movement.

In 1938, Boss had his best year to date and became a supplier of uniforms to the German army. Yet in 1940, Boss was employing only 250 workers; he was successful but not yet a major provider to the Nazi state. The outbreak of war in September 1939 changed this.

By 1941, his sales and profits had skyrocketed, but this came at a price. Like most private manufacturers in Germany, Boss found it hard to find employees during the war, and unable to fill his factories with workers, he was obliged to use prisoners of war and forced laborers from countries occupied by the Nazis. During the war, Boss used 140 such workers, swelled by 40 French prisoners of war from 1940 onward. Conditions in Boss's factory were considered by all to be appalling; the barracks were pestilential, food was inadequate and of poor quality, and medical facilities for the workers were practically nonexistent. Evidence exists to the effect that managers and foremen were enthusiastic Nazis.

With the end of the war in 1945, Boss was subjected to the process of denazification, whereby he was tried for his complicity in the Nazi state. His early Nazi Party membership now counted against him, as did his financial support of the SS and his supplying of uniforms for both the various Nazi Party organizations and the German army. He was denounced as a war profiteer and classified as an activist member of the party and "beneficiary of National Socialism." In 1946, he was fined and forbidden to vote as a German citizen or to run a business. Upon appeal, Boss was retried and reclassified; he now became a "follower of National Socialism" (*Mitläufer*) rather than an activist, and his penalties were reduced.

Hugo Boss died on the night of August 8 to 9, 1948. While his company survived to become one of the leading fashion houses in the world today, there remains a stigma attached to the company owing to its association with the Third Reich.

BOTHE, HERTA (1921–2000)

Herta Bothe was a concentration camp guard infamous for her brutality toward her prisoners at Ravensbrück, Stutthof, Auschwitz, and Bergen-Belsen.

Born in Teterow, Mecklenburg-Schwerin, on January 8, 1921, she was the daughter of a woodworker. Before the outbreak of war in September 1939, she worked briefly as a nurse while a member of the Nazi *Bund deutscher Mädel* (League of German Girls) youth organization. In September 1942, Bothe joined the Nazi concentration camp corps as an *SS-Aufseherin* (overseer) in the women's camp at Ravensbrück. After a period of training, she was sent to the camp at Stutthof, where she was soon nicknamed the "Sadist of Stutthof," having quickly acquired a reputation as one who beat prisoners without mercy.

Bothe's career as a guard saw her transferred through several different deployments, notably Stutthof's female subcamp, Bromberg-Ost, where she was sent in July 1944. Here, she would often beat sick or weak prisoners without mercy or would otherwise engage in sadistic tortures (including shooting) of those carrying heavy food containers from the camp kitchen.

On January 21, 1945, Bothe received orders to move to Auschwitz to assist with the camp's evacuation of prisoners away from the advancing Red Army. She was to accompany what became a death march of female prisoners and to head toward the camp at Bergen-Belsen in northwestern Germany. She arrived in late

February 1945, and in March, she was put in charge of 60 prisoners undertaking woodcutting duties.

Bergen-Belsen was liberated and then occupied by British troops on April 15, 1945, but the enormous carnage accompanying the end of the war saw chaos, overcrowding, and general horror pervading the camp. On the day of the liberation, the British found approximately 60,985 survivors; there were some 10,000 unburied dead who lay where they had fallen in the compound and another 15,000 who succumbed to disease and starvation after the British arrived.

In an attempt to help clean up the camp, thus trying to save the lives of those remaining, the British camp administration forced the captured Nazi guard detachments to carry the corpses of Jewish dead and deposit them into mass graves. Bothe expressed a defiant show of anger at this order, as she feared contamination and exposure to disease—especially typhus, which had been running rampant through the camp and taking thousands of lives. The anger of the British in setting the captured Nazi guards to work in gathering the dead as a matter of punishment was apparent to all, and most of the dead were simply piled up in what became mountains of putrescent flesh, prior to being shoved unceremoniously into giant pits dug by British army bulldozers.

After completion of this grisly task, Bothe was placed under formal arrest and taken to a jail at Celle to await trial for war crimes. The subsequent Belsen Trial took place in nearby Lüneburg, with SS men and women who had been apprehended at the time of the liberation and afterward as defendants. At her trial, Bothe was charged on two separate counts: mistreatment of prisoners at Bergen-Belsen and mistreatment of prisoners at Auschwitz. She admitted to striking inmates for camp violations but maintained that she never killed anyone or used anything other than her hands to strike the prisoners. She failed to convince the military tribunal, was convicted, and was sentenced to 10 years in prison for using a pistol on prisoners.

However, on December 22, 1951, after serving six years of her sentence, she was granted an early release on the ground of clemency from the British government. She then retreated into anonymity and lived for the next half century in Germany under the name Lange, dying at the age of 79 on March 16, 2000.

BOTHMANN, HANS (1911–1946)

SS-Hauptsturmführer Hans Bothmann was commandant of the Chełmno extermination camp from 1942 until its liquidation and leader of the *SS-Sonderkommando Bothmann*, which conducted the extermination of Jews from the Łódź ghetto and other places.

Hans Johann Bothmann was born in Dittmarschen, Holstein on November 11, 1911, to farmer Hermann Bothmann and his wife Dora. He attended primary school in Lohe, middle school in Bad Segeberg, and high school in Neibüll. In 1932, Bothmann joined the Hitler Youth, and by 1933, he was a member of the SS. Soon afterward, Bothmann worked full-time with the Gestapo office in Berlin and was promoted in 1937 to *Kriminalkommissar* (detective inspector) in the detective unit there. Bothmann, 28 years old at the time of the German invasion of Poland in September 1939 and recently promoted to *SS-Hauptsturmführer*, was transferred to the state police headquarters in Posen (Poznań), an area of Poland annexed to Germany.

Bothmann replaced *SS-Hauptsturmführer* **Herbert Lange** as commandant of the Chełmno death camp in March 1942 and served there until mid-April 1943. Prompted by two incidents in March and April 1942, Bothmann made substantial changes to the camp's killing methods. First, one of the gas vans being used to murder Jews broke down on the highway while conveying victims to their death; soon after that, another van exploded while the driver was revving its engine at the loading ramp. Bothmann worked to ensure that such incidents would not recur and introduced "efficiencies" into the killing procedure.

Ultimately, until transports of Jews to Chełmno were discontinued in late March 1943, the camp was credited with the murder of at least 180,000 Jews under Bothmann's administration.

After Chełmno was dissolved in mid-April 1943, all members of Bothmann's unit took special leave in April 1943. The 85 members of *SS Sonderkommando X* then chose to serve in Yugoslavia under Bothmann in a reconstituted *Sonderkommando Bothmann*. They were used in antipartisan campaigns as an auxiliary military-police force (*Feldgendarmerie*) and incurred significant losses.

In mid-February 1944, *SS-Reichsführer* **Heinrich Himmler** and Governor **Arthur Greiser** decided to reduce the number of Jews in the Łódź ghetto and to keep only the minimum number of Jews needed for the defense industry.

In April 1944, Bothmann was recalled from Croatia to become commandant of Chełmno death camp a second time. The purpose was to oversee the final reduction of the Łódź ghetto; thus, 7,176 Jewish men, women, and children were transported from Łódź to the reactivated Chełmno in 10 rail transports between June 23 and July 14, 1944. They were murdered in gas vans. Once the murder process was completed, transports to Chełmno ceased from the end of August 1944.

In early 1944, with the tide of war turning against Germany, many senior Nazis, especially Higher SS and Police Leader (*Höherer SS- und Polizeiführer*, or HSSPF) for the Wartheland **Wilhelm Koppe**, expressed concern to Himmler that there remained at Chełmno many buried corpses needing to be exhumed and cremated and that all evidence of the murders carried out there had to be expunged. Himmler sent Bothmann back to Chełmno one more time with orders to dig up the bodies and leave no evidence of the killings. The resultant *Aktion 1005* was carried out in July and August 1944, with any Jews remaining in the vicinity used to clear up all traces of the camp. When Soviet troops captured Łódź, Bothmann and his men shot dead the last surviving Jewish workers during the night of January 17 to 18, 1945.

Bothmann and his unit fled west just before the arrival of the Soviets. The unit was dissolved, and its members were allocated to various police departments. In February 1945, Bothmann headed the border police commissariat in Flensburg, in Schleswig. With the end of the war, he was taken into British custody, but on April 4, 1946, he committed suicide by hanging himself in prison not far from Flensburg, in Heide.

BOUHLER, PHILIPP (1899–1945)

Philipp Bouhler was a high-ranking Nazi official who implemented *Aktion T-4*, the so-called euthanasia program for those who were mentally ill, the disabled, and the inmates of hospitals and nursing homes deemed "unworthy" of Nazi society. With **Heinrich Himmler**, Bouhler also developed *Aktion 14f13*, which killed between 15,000 and 20,000 concentration camp prisoners.

Philipp Bouhler was born on September 11, 1899, in Munich, the son of Emil Bouhler, a retired colonel. Between 1912 and 1916, he was a cadet, and from July 6, 1916, he served in the Bavarian Fusiliers Regiment, fought in World War I, and was badly wounded.

From 1919 to 1920, he studied philosophy for four semesters at the University of Munich before joining the staff of the *Völkischer Beobachter* ("People's Observer") in 1921. In July 1922, he joined the National Socialist Party, and by 1925, Bouhler was the party's business manager, a post he held until 1936.

On March 5, 1933, after the Nazi seizure of power, Bouhler joined the Reichstag, representing Westphalia. On April 20, 1933, he joined the SS; he was promoted to *SS-Obergruppenführer* on January 30, 1936.

On August 29, 1934, Bouhler was appointed president of the Munich police. However, he never took up the position, because that September he was chosen to head **Adolf Hitler**'s new chancellery, a post specially created for party business. Bouhler stayed in that position until April 23, 1945. The office was responsible for all correspondence for Hitler, which included private and internal communications as well as responding to public inquiries.

Bouhler was also chairman of the Official Party Inspection Commission for the Protection of National Socialist Literature. This commission determined which writings were suitable for release into Nazi society and which were not approved and should be censored or removed.

On October 18, 1935, the Nazi government, with the assistance of **Karl Brandt**, passed the Law for the Protection of the Hereditary Health of the German People. The Nazis had declared that Germany was in severe danger of *Volkstod* (death of a people, nation, or race), and this law set up the model under which Nazi doctors could take the life of those deemed to be "life unworthy of life" (*Lebensunwertes Leben*).

In August 1939, the Reich Committee for the Scientific Registration of Serious Hereditary and Congenitally Based Diseases was established. Brandt and Bouhler were put in charge of the program of euthanasia employed to deal with the incurably insane or the physically handicapped, a program that Hitler said would result in the "racial integrity of the German people."

From 1939 onward, Bouhler was responsible for *Aktion T-4*, the program named after its headquarters on Tiergassestrasse 4, Berlin, which began in the fall of 1939. At first, mandatory sterilization formed an important part of the Nazi plan of racial purification, and those who were deemed to have hereditary "weaknesses" became its victims. No one knows how many people were sterilized, with estimates ranging anywhere from 200,000 to 350,000 people.

The first person to die via the T-4 program was one Gerhard Kretschmar, a child born on February 29, 1939. His parents, who lived in Saxony, petitioned Hitler for Gerhard to be "put to sleep," as he was born blind, mentally retarded, and without one leg and part of one arm. Carbon monoxide gas was selected as the means of death, and after this, several asylums were equipped with gas chambers. The first killing center was Schloss Hartheim in Upper Austria, and once the program got underway, between October 1939 and August 1941, *Aktion T-4* killed over 70,000 people.

The program was carried out secretly, but over time, the public became aware of the killings. This led to legal action. In the summer of 1940, Lothar Kreyssig, a judge in Brandenburg, lodged a complaint against Bouhler for murder. Bouhler met the minister of justice, **Franz Gürtner**, several times, and on August 27, 1940, he sent Gürtner a copy of Hitler's note of September 5, 1940, directing Bouhler to instigate T-4. Yet religious communities opposed the murder of people with physical, emotional, or mental disabilities, and public disapproval was very strong. In response and on Hitler's orders, *Aktion T-4* was suspended on August 24, 1941. In practice, murders in health care institutions continued, by systematic malnutrition and overdose of drugs.

As World War II progressed, the euthanasia program, now called *Aktion 14f13*, was used to murder people believed to be biologically inferior, such as Jews, Poles, Russians, and Roma. The scheme operated under the Inspectorate of Concentration Camps and the office of the *SS-Reichsführer*, under the codename *Sonderbehandlung 14f13*. The combination of numbers and letters was derived from the SS record-keeping system. *Sonderbehandlung* (special handling) was the euphemism for murder. The final step was the mass killing, mostly of Jews, in the extermination camps themselves.

Beginning in 1942, Bouhler's influence in the NSDAP started to wane, and by 1944, many of the functions of his office were absorbed by the Party Chancellery under **Martin Bormann**.

On April 23, 1945, on orders of Adolf Hitler, Bouhler was arrested in Berchtesgaden by the SS and stripped of all his functions. He was released on May 1, 1945, after Hitler had committed suicide. Captured by American troops on May 9, 1945, Bouhler committed suicide with cyanide on May 19, 1945, in an American prison camp in Zell am See, Austria.

BOUSQUET, RENÉ (1909–1993)

René Bousquet, a French collaborator, was secretary-general of the Vichy French police in the government of **Pierre Laval** from April 18, 1942, to December 31, 1943. In this capacity, he organized the notorious roundup at the *Velodrome d'Hiver* (Winter Velodrome, or Vel' d'Hiv) on July 16 to 17, 1942. Here, more than 13,000 Jews were arrested by French police, handed over to the Germans, and then deported to the East.

He was born in Montauban into the family of a French notary on May 11, 1909, and earned a bachelor's degree in law from Toulouse. In March 1930, he

René Bousquet was secretary general of the Vichy French police in the government of Pierre Laval between April 1942 and December 1943. On July 16–17, 1942, Bousquet oversaw the mass arrest of all foreign Jews in Paris, in what became known as the Vel' d'Hiv roundup. In this image Bousquet (center) is shown inspecting a guard of honor alongside the prefect of police, Amédée Bussière. (Keystone-France\Gamma-Rapho via Getty Images)

was awarded the *Légion d'Honneur* for saving dozens of people from drowning in a flood. Because of this heroism, Bousquet was put in charge of the reconstruction of the disaster departments of the south.

In 1931, at the age of 22, he was deputy chief of staff to the undersecretary of state for the interior in the first Laval government, where he became a close associate. He served as chief of staff for several ministers, and in May 1936, Bousquet was named assistant bureau chief of the Interior Ministry with responsibility over the national security files, which classified 5 million French and 2 million foreigners as "suspects" or "undesirables." These files were important later in the identification of foreign Jews during the Vel' d'Hiv roundup.

In 1939, prior to the outbreak of World War II, Bosquet became secretary-general of the Marne department. In May 1940, following the Armistice in which France surrendered to Germany and agreed to occupation, Marshal Philippe Pétain, head of the collaborationist Vichy regime, appointed Bousquet prefect of the Marne. In this capacity, he managed to spare the Marne from economic colonization by Nazi Germany, and while certain prisoners of war escaped, in November 1941, he collaborated with the Rheims police in the denunciation, arrest, and handover to the Germans of communist militants.

In early 1942, Bosquet was twice offered the Ministry of Agriculture but refused on both occasions. On April 18, 1942, as the SS was taking over security duties in the Occupied Zone from the Wehrmacht, Laval appointed Bousquet secretary-general of police in the Ministry of the Interior, giving Bousquet permanent credentials to sign on behalf of the head of state. As such, he took a leading role in the police collaboration between Vichy and the German occupation. Bousquet concentrated all police services under his personal authority.

Bosquet met with **Reinhard Heydrich** of the SD on May 6, 1942, and obtained consent from the SS to transfer another 5,000 Jews from the transit camp at Drancy to the extermination camps in the East.

Laval, Bosquet, and Louis Darquier, commissioner for Jewish affairs, entered into discussions with their Nazi counterparts—Heydrich; **Carl Oberg**, head of the SS in France; and *SS-Reichsführer* **Heinrich Himmler**—about the status of Jews in France. After consultation with Laval, Bousquet agreed to have his personnel serve the occupation forces in arresting the foreign Jews in Vichy and to have his personnel participate in the roundup of Jews throughout the rest of France. The forces the Germans had in France were limited; without this cooperation, they could not have carried out these actions.

On July 16 to 17, 1942, Bousquet ordered the mass arrest of all foreign Jews in Paris, in what became known as the Vel' d'Hiv Roundup (*La Rafle*). Approximately 13,000 Jews were arrested, sent to Drancy, and then deported to Auschwitz, where most were murdered. During Bousquet's term as secretary-general, the majority of the approximately 76,000 Jews to be deported from France were arrested.

Senior SS and Police Leader Carl Oberg oversaw the German police in France, and Bousquet negotiated with him the Oberg-Bousquet accords, presented to all regional prefects on August 8, 1942. The agreement formally recognized the autonomy of the French police and gendarmerie and said that the French police would not be compelled to provide hostages or to hand their prisoners over to German services. The final text of the agreement laid down as a principle that the French police would not be called upon by the services of the SS commander to designate hostages and that those arrested would in no case be subject to reprisals by the German authorities. Thus, French nationals guilty of political offenses or ordinary offenses (though not those directed against occupation forces) would be punished by the authorities in accordance with French law. The agreement mentioned "communists" and "saboteurs," but it did not refer to Jews. In breach of this agreement, three days later, the Germans demanded that the French hand over 93 hostages, who were shot in retaliation for the murder of 8 Germans.

The fall and winter of 1942 to 1943, coinciding with the beginning of Allied victories over the Axis forces, marked a turning point in Vichy's attitude toward the deportation of Jews. Laval now refused to participate in the Franco-German collective raids, and in March 1943, Bousquet requested that the French no longer take part in the deportations of French Jews. In April, the Germans requested that the French police participate in two transports of 2,000 Jews (including 1,500 native French Jews) to Leguay. In response, Bousquet said that the French security forces wished to be exempted from participating. Between April and June, the deportations were halted.

Oberg and Bousquet signed a new agreement on April 2, 1942, under which the French police "promised to defend the order against the attacks of the Jews, Communists, and other enemies," while the Germans promised not to force the French to take hostages and to no longer to intervene in "strictly French" police affairs. From this period, the Vichy police, although still very active against the communist resistance, moderated their actions in the hunt for the French Jews.

In 1943, Bousquet protected some members of the resistance who were threatened with arrest, including future French president François Mitterrand, who had run a network of escaped prisoners, and had sabotaged certain operations mounted against the maquis, and released detained persons.

At the end of 1943, Bousquet, who had agreed to collaborate in the arrest of communist "terrorists" and foreign Jews claimed by no country, rebelled as soon as he was asked to "strike without discrimination." In November 1943, the German authorities wanted to consult the lists of Israelites established by the prefecture. Bousquet, who was losing the confidence of Carl Oberg and knew that he was leaving, wrote in response,

> For the police and the French administration the fact of being an Israelite does not constitute a presumption of responsibility, neither in political matters nor in matters of common law. It cannot even entail an aggravation of this responsibility, insofar as a Jew is prosecuted for a crime or an offense punishable by our criminal law. On the other hand, the German ordinances concern only the occupied zone. The attitude of the French administration cannot therefore be different from what it is.

In December 1943, under pressure from the Germans, Bousquet resigned his position. On December 20, he burned his archives to complicate the work of his successor, Joseph Darnand, who replaced him on December 31. During the 20 months of Bousquet's presence at the head of the police (April 1942 to December 1943), 60,000 Jews were deported, while under Darnand's 8 months (January to August 1944), another 15,000 to 16,000 were deported.

On June 9, 1944, just before the liberation, Bousquet was arrested by the Germans and sent under house arrest to a villa in Bavaria. He was released in April 1945 by the American forces. In May 1945, he returned to France, where he was jailed at the Fresnes prison from May 17, 1945, to July 1, 1948. Laval, with whom he was always close, was also imprisoned at Fresnes. Bousquet helped Laval prepare for his trial, and on the eve of Laval's execution, Bousquet spent part of the night with him.

In 1949, René Bousquet was the last Frenchman to be tried by the High Court of Justice. The Cold War loomed large, as did the problems of reconstruction. French conscience lacked morality about the Holocaust; the Jewish community was much more concerned with its painful memories rather than with demanding justice for the crimes perpetrated against it. The postwar media focus on the roundups of the summer of 1942 was, therefore, limited. At the end of a three-day trial, René Bousquet was acquitted of the charge "against the interests of national defense" but was "convicted of the crime of national unworthiness," which was automatically found for all those people who participated in the Vichy government. He was sentenced to the minimum sentence of "five years of national degradation." This was lifted immediately, however, on the ground that he had "actively and sustainably participated in the Resistance against the occupier."

After his conviction, like other Vichy officials, Bousquet could not join the French civil service. Instead, he enjoyed a successful career at the *Banque de l'Indochine* and in newspapers. He met with François Mitterrand through Jean-Paul Martin, Bousquet's former collaborator in Vichy. On January 17, 1958, the *Conseil d'État* amnestied him.

In 1974, Bousquet supported and helped finance Mitterrand for the presidential election against Valéry Giscard d'Estaing. Bousquet was also acquainted with numerous other political and cultural figures. On October 28, 1978, Louis Darquier, the former Vichy commissioner for Jewish affairs and now an old man living in Spain, gave an interview in *L'Express* revealing the extent of Bousquet's involvement in the mass deportation of Jews.

From 1986 onward, when the accusations against Bousquet became consistent, encounters between Bousquet and Mitterand became less frequent. A judicial investigation was conducted, and Mitterrand was accused of intervening in the proceedings to restrain it. The Paris public prosecutor's office decided to dismiss Bousquet before a Court of Justice had been closed, which aroused public ire. Mitterrand was specifically targeted when the lawyers of the mission of the International Federation of Human Rights Leagues made the claim that "there is a political decision at the highest level not to advance the Bousquet case."

These words gave a decisive boost to the efforts of French lawyer and Nazi hunter Serge Klarsfeld to bring some responsible Vichy French officials to justice, in formal recognition of Vichy's complicity in the deportation of Jews from France. In 1989, Serge Klarsfeld filed a complaint against Bousquet for crimes against humanity, for the deportation of 194 children from six departments of the south of France. After eight years of investigation and numerous delay tactics, Bousquet was indicted in 1991.

On June 8, 1993, a few weeks before his trial was to begin, Bousquet was shot dead at his home by 51-year-old Christian Didier. Consequently, Bousquet never stood trial for his wartime actions. Didier pleaded not guilty to murder, as he claimed that the killing was justified by Bousquet's wartime crimes. Ruled sane, Didier was tried and convicted of murder and sentenced to 10 years in prison. If the trial against Bousquet had proceeded, it would have been the first against a French citizen for crimes against humanity committed during the war years and probably also the first trial of the crimes of the Vichy government.

BRACK, VIKTOR (1904–1948)

Viktor Brack was the organizer of the euthanasia program known as *Aktion T-4*, under which over 70,000 Germans and Austrians with disabilities were murdered. He later became one of the men responsible for gassing Jews in Nazi concentration camps.

Viktor Hermann Brack, the son of a German medical practitioner, was born on November 9, 1904, in Haaren (modern-day Aachen), Germany. After studying economics at a Munich university, he befriended **Heinrich Himmler**, for whom he worked for a time as chauffeur. Brack enlisted in an SA regiment in 1923, and in 1929, he became a member of the NSDAP and joined the SS. In 1932, he took a staff position at Nazi Party headquarters in Munich. He was promoted to the rank of *SS-Sturmbannführer* in the SS in 1935, and in 1936, notwithstanding his lack of prior medical or scientific experience, he became chief of Office 2 in the führer's chancellery and chief liaison officer with the health ministry in Berlin. Office 2 handled matters concerning the Reich ministries, armed forces, the Nazi Party, clemency petitions, and complaints received by the führer from all parts of Germany.

In late 1939, Brack was tasked by his superior officer, **Philip Bouhler**, with implementing the Nazi euthanasia program, known as *Aktion T-4*. This implemented early-20th-century ideas of eugenics and of improving the race by not allowing disabled or mentally ill people to reproduce. In December 1939, Brack delegated to August Becker the task of arranging gas-killing operations of mentally ill patients and other people whom the Nazis deemed "life unworthy of life"; this program resulted in the murder of tens of thousands of Germans and Austrians with disabilities. Brack himself personally interviewed and selected personnel for the euthanasia establishments, from those involved in cremating the corpses all the way through to cleaners. On November 9, 1940, Brack was promoted to *SS-Oberführer*.

Persecution of the Jews had become a fixed Nazi policy very soon after the outbreak of World War II, and by 1941, that had become the Final Solution. The agencies organized to implement *Aktion T-4* were used for this operation. Because of the urgent need for laborers in Germany, it was decided not to kill Jews who were able to work but to sterilize them. Accordingly, Himmler instructed Brack to research from physicians involved in *Aktion T-4* how to sterilize persons without the victim's knowledge.

In March 1941, Brack forwarded to Himmler his signed report on the results of experiments concerning the sterilization of human beings by means of X-rays. Brack advocated a two-part system. The first part simply referred to the mass gassing of internees unable to work; the second, aimed at "useful" laborers, would introduce forced sterilization to prisoners so that they would not be able to reproduce. Forced sterilization was carried out mainly through the use of massive doses of radiation aimed at prisoners' reproductive organs. In some cases, male prisoners were physically castrated. As many as 4,000 prisoners per day were sterilized between late 1943 and early 1945.

In 1942, Brack joined the Waffen-SS, and during the late summer of that year, he was ordered to active duty, where he remained until the end of the war.

After the defeat of Germany, on May 20, 1945, Brack was taken into custody by U.S. counterintelligence officers. He was charged with various crimes against humanity and defended himself in the Doctors' Trial, which began in late 1946 in Nuremberg. Found guilty in 1947, he was sentenced to death. Brack was hanged on June 2, 1948, in Landsberg Prison.

BRADFISCH, OTTO (1903–1994)

Otto Bradfisch was an economist and a political scientist, jurist, *SS-Obersturmbannführer*, leader of *Einsatzkommando 8* of *Einsatzgruppe B* of the SiPo and the SD, and commander of the Security Police in the Łódź ghetto and Potsdam.

Bradfisch, the son of food trader Karl Bradfisch, was born on May 10, 1903, in Zweibrücken, in the Rhineland. He attended primary school in Kaiserslautern and then completed his schooling at the local school in 1922. Studying economics at the universities of Freiburg, Leipzig, and Heidelberg, he graduated in 1926 from Austria's University of Innsbruck with a doctorate in politics. On January 1, 1931, he joined the NSDAP.

Due to the unreliable economy, Bradfisch then studied law to increase his job opportunities. After studying at the universities of Erlangen and Munich, he passed his first (February 17, 1932) and second (October 9, 1935) state legal examinations. While studying at Munich University, he worked as the acting local NSDAP group leader. He then worked as an assessor in Upper Bavaria's government until he became a government assistant in the Bavarian Ministry of the Interior.

In 1936, Bradfisch left the Evangelical Church. He applied to serve in the Gestapo, and on March 3, 1937, he became its deputy head in Saarbrücken. In 1938, he entered the SS and was appointed as an *SS-Sturmbannführer*. From November 4, 1938, to the spring of 1941, he served on the local council in Neustadt an der Weinstrasse, until he was selected to serve in Russia and given command of an *Einztaszkommando*.

Just prior to Operation Barbarossa on June 22, 1941, a briefing occurred in Pretzsch, in which senior SS leaders from the Reich Security Main Office, including **Reinhard Heydrich** and **Heinrich Müller**, were present. The leaders of the *Einsatzgruppen*, staff officers, and commanders of the *Einsatzkommandos* attended. Heydrich announced the imminent invasion of the Soviet Union and reported that the *Einsatzgruppen* had been tasked to carry out "special treatment" (i.e., killing) of potential adversaries, which included Jews, communist functionaries, saboteurs, assassins, agitators, and the like, who would advance in the wake of the army in order to pacify the occupied population. According to Heydrich, **Adolf Hitler** had himself issued this extermination order. There was an agreement between the Wehrmacht and the SS on the division of responsibilities between the *Einsatzgruppen* and army units.

From 1941 until the end of March 1942, Bradfisch was head of *Einsatzkommando 8* (EK 8) of *Einsatzgruppe B*, headed by *SS-Brigadeführer* **Arthur Nebe**, and the SD, directing the shooting of more than 60,000 people. From Warsaw, EK 8 marched first to Białystok, where it arrived in late June or early July 1941, and remained for about a week. In carrying out the extermination order, EK 8 shot and killed Jews in areas across the demarcation line established in 1939 between the German Reich and the Soviet Union. To find Jews, some members of EK 8 surrounded villages or streets, while others rounded up victims from their homes. All were either transported immediately to previously prepared shooting sites, or held in schools or factory buildings until the next day, or shot a few days later. Old and sick people unable to walk were shot in or around their homes.

The mass shooting took place outside the villages. Natural crevasses, abandoned army positions, and mass graves dug by the victims themselves functioned as execution sites. The victims were unloaded from the trucks and thrust toward the pits. First, they handed over their valuables and clothing, and then they had to lie facedown in the pit. They were then shot in the back of the head. Occasionally, victims had to stand at the edge of the pit in order to be shot into the pits.

During the first weeks of the Russian campaign, men between the ages of 18 and 65 years were killed, while women and children were initially spared. In Białystok, EK 8 arrived at the end of June or the beginning of July 1941, where it carried out two shootings in which Jewish men were killed; at one such site, at least 800 men were shot in a forest. EK 8 reported that on July 13, 1941, in Białystok, 215 Jewish and communist functionaries were shot and that executions continued after then at about the same rate.

After this, EK 8 moved further eastward to Baranowicze (Baranavichy) to continue its "elimination work" over the next fortnight. The unit ran at least two *Aktionen* against the resident Jewish population, initially shooting around 100 Jewish men; by July 24, 1941, at least 381 Jewish male deaths had been reported. Bradfisch supervised and directed at least one of these actions, and the preparation and execution of both executions were at his order.

EK 8 arrived in Minsk in the second half of July, where it remained until the end of August. At the shooting in Minsk, EK 8 began to kill men and women of all ages as well as children. During July and August 1941, the unit carried out at least seven further shootings in which women and children were among the victims. *SS-Reichsführer* **Heinrich Himmler** was present at one of these mass executions, in which at least 300 Jews were killed, following which he stated to the members of EK 8 and police reservists that the order to exterminate the Jews in Eastern Europe came directly from the führer and must be carried out. He saw the annihilation of the Jewish population as his historic task. The massacre at which Himmler was present saw Bradfisch himself give the order to shoot.

On September 9, 1941, EK 8 reached the suburbs of Borisov and Orsha, Mogilev, where Bradfisch led EK 8 in at least eight mass shootings, killing at least 4,100 Jewish men, women, and children, as well as Russian prisoners of war. Bradfisch then engaged a White Ruthenian militia unit to support a major action in Mogilev. After this, EK 8 reported that the ghetto site in Mogilev was now available to the city administration, since Mogilev was virtually free of Jews.

In November 1941, Bradfisch ordered and led EK 8 in a major *Aktion* against the Bobruisk Jewish population, in which a total of at least 5,000 men, women, and children were shot. He reported subsequently that Bobruisk and its surrounds were free of Jews.

By December 1941, the German offensive against Moscow had halted. While EK 8 was originally intended for security-police duties in what would have been an occupied Moscow, the unit now settled in Mogilev.

In April 1942, Bradfisch was transferred to Łódź as head of the state police station, a position he held until 1945. In August 1943, he was appointed acting mayor of Łódź. From here, he was responsible for the deportation of around 100,000 Jews to the extermination camps at Chełmno and Auschwitz.

During the last months of the war, Bradfisch was the higher SS and police leader (*Höherer SS- und Polizeiführer*, or HSSPF) in Potsdam. In mid-January 1945, he fled westward, as the German authorities abandoned Łódź before the advancing Red Army. He abandoned his unit and acquired an army identity document (*Wehrmachtssoldbuch*) that had been issued to a corporal, Karl Evers. As Karl Evers, he was captured by the Americans, handed over to the British, and released in August 1945.

After his release, Bradfisch, still operating as Karl Evers, at first worked in agriculture and then in mining. After 1953, he resumed working under his own name and was employed selling insurance until he was arrested on April 21, 1958, based on a warrant issued by the district court of Heilbronn. On July 22, 1961, he was convicted in the Munich District Court of the murder of 15,000 people and was subsequently jailed.

In October 1967, Bradfisch's sentence was reduced for health reasons, and on July 21, 1969, he was discharged from prison. He then lived in Munich and died at the age of 91, on June 22, 1994.

BRANDT, KARL (1904–1948)

Karl Brandt was a German physician and SS officer who served as Adolf Hitler's personal physician and participated in the *Aktion T-4* program, which systematically murdered handicapped and mentally challenged individuals and others deemed "unworthy of life."

He was born into the family of a Prussian army officer in Mühlhausen, in the then-German Alsace-Lorraine, on January 8, 1904. Receiving his degree in medicine from the University of Freiburg in 1928, as a doctor, he specialized in head and spinal injuries. In 1932, Brandt joined the Nazi Party, and in 1933, he became a member of the SA.

In August 1933, **Adolf Hitler**'s niece, Geli Raubal, and his adjutant, Wilhelm Brückner, were hurt in a car crash. Brandt, working as a doctor in Upper Bavaria, was summoned to help them; he made such a good impression that he was asked to be one of Hitler's personal physicians. By 1934, Brandt was a member of Hitler's inner circle at Berchtesgaden. Brandt was made a major general in the Waffen-SS and was appointed Reich commissioner for health and sanitation; his free access to Hitler, more than any administrative role, was the source of Brandt's power. Brandt became an adherent of "racial hygiene" policies, which were based on the premise that medical professionals could remove hereditary and other defects from a nation or racial group. Brandt was both a believer in eugenics and a career-minded opportunist.

In 1939, a request from a German family for the mercy killing of their severely handicapped child became the pretext for the initiation of the Nazi euthanasia program. Brandt and **Philipp Bouhler**, head of Hitler's chancellery, were placed in charge of its planning and execution. They received a rare explicit authorization from Hitler allowing them to "grant mercy deaths" to "incurable" patients as of September 1, 1939. Brandt and Bouhler then implemented *Aktion T-4*, which saw the mass murder of mentally ill and handicapped German adults and children. There were two separate euthanasia programs: one, dating back to the spring of 1939, dealt with infants and toddlers up to three who had physical deformities; a second program included mentally disabled children and adults. Brandt had a hand in both.

On October 6, 1939, Hitler ordered Brandt to "relieve through death" those mentally ill individuals who could not "take any conscious part in life." Hitler backdated his signature to September 1, 1939, in order to highlight the order's connection to the war; his logic was that the life of every dead soldier should be balanced by taking the life of a person "unworthy of life." While the child euthanasia program murdered its victims through lethal overdoses of medication, adult patients were removed from their home institutions and transferred to six designated euthanasia, or killing, centers throughout Germany, where they were murdered in specially designed gas chambers. By the end of January 1941, about 70,000 mentally ill adult patients had been gassed. Public concern about the program persisted until Hitler "suspended" it in August 1941, but Brandt soon expanded it in 1941 to include other nationalities. In the summer of 1942, the effort resumed in a more decentralized format and saw the murder both of children and of adult patients through means of lethal overdose and starvation.

As euthanasia slowed, its specialists brought their expertise in killing to the extermination of the Jews. Some of Brandt's workers in the T-4 program were sent to Riga and Lublin to help in the construction of gas vans, as well as to other parts of occupied Poland in 1942 to assist **Odilo Globocnik** establish the *Aktion Reinhard* death camps of Bełżec, Sobibór, and Treblinka. In 1941, T-4 physicians transferred 15,000 to 20,000 concentration camp prisoners from several camps to killing centers, where they were gassed in *Aktion 14f13*.

Brandt was also behind a program of enforced abortions for women classed as "genetically defective." This included those who were physically or mentally disabled. Additionally, Brandt pushed forward a program of enforced sterilization, and he conducted medical experiments to see which method of sterilization was most effective in terms of the number of people who could be sterilized at one go.

By 1942, Brandt became chief of medicine and health for the Third Reich and was the most powerful medical practitioner in Germany. He administered not just the euthanasia program but also other Nazi medical undertakings, including a range of human experimentation projects on concentration camp inmates. Correspondence between Brandt, Himmler, and **Oswald Pohl**, head of the SS Economic and Administrative Office (WVHA), clearly demonstrates that Brandt knew of, initiated, and supported these unethical medical experiments in concentration camps.

Brandt sought further control over the medical profession and health-related services before falling out of favor with Hitler in 1944. Hitler was furious when he learned that Brandt had moved his wife and son out of Berlin and toward Allied lines in the West, something Brandt had done in the expectation that they would be in a "better" zone of occupation rather than in one occupied by the Soviet Union. Hitler accused him of defeatism and ordered that he should face a court-martial on the charge of treason. Brandt was then arrested for allegedly planning to surrender to the Allies. Although Brandt escaped his Nazi death sentence, he was arrested by the British on May 23, 1945.

As the leading Nazi doctor and because of his involvement in so many unethical medical enterprises, Brandt was the focus of prosecutors at the Nuremberg Doctors' Trial, which began in December 1946. He was found guilty of war crimes, crimes against humanity, and membership in a criminal organization (the SS). He and six other colleagues were executed by hanging on June 2, 1948, at Landsberg Prison.

BROAD, PERY (1921–1993)

Pery (sometimes Perry) Broad was a guard active at Auschwitz between April 1942 and 1945, working as a translator and stenographer in the Political Department (*Politische Abteilung*). His report on the conditions he observed at Auschwitz served as evidence in subsequent trials of former Auschwitz officials.

Pery Broad was born on April 25, 1921, in Rio de Janeiro, Brazil, to a German mother and a Brazilian businessman. When Broad was five years old, his mother took him to Berlin, where he attended school. In 1931, he was an early member of the Hitler Youth. As he grew to maturity, the educated and well-read Broad learned music and spoke several languages fluently. He studied at the Technical College of Berlin until December 1941.

In 1941, Broad entered the SS and then volunteered for the Waffen-SS as a foreigner. He had offered to serve in the army, but because of a medical disability (extreme myopia), he was demobilized in 1942 and sent to Auschwitz, initially to work on security details. Broad later was transferred to the *Politische Abteilung*, in the investigation and interrogation service.

He served at Auschwitz until the dissolution of the camp in January 1945. After the camp's evacuation, he undertook service for two months at Dora-Mittelbau, near Nordhausen, until he was assigned to guard duties during death marches of prisoners in advance of liberation by Allied armies.

He was captured by British troops on May 6, 1945. As a prisoner of war interned in the Gorleben detention center in Lower Saxony, Broad voluntarily wrote a long and detailed memoir on what he witnessed at Auschwitz, which became known as the Broad Report. In the report, which he gave to the Secret Intelligence Service, Broad related very precisely the functioning of the gas chambers. In December 1945, much of the report was included in a courtroom affidavit.

As an informant, Broad was separated from other German prisoners, and much use was made of his testimony; when former Auschwitz camp staff were on trial at Bergen-Belsen, his detailed statements were also used in the tribunal held there. In addition, Broad testified for the prosecution at the Tesch trial in March 1 to 8, 1946, when **Bruno Tesch**, a German chemist and coinventor of Zyklon B, together with company director Karl Weinbacher, were convicted and sentenced to death for the supply of Zyklon B used for the purpose of mass murder.

Broad was released from British captivity in 1947 and then worked as a clerical employee at a sawmill on the River Örtze in Munster, as well as with other private companies.

On April 30, 1959, he was arrested in connection with the investigation for the first Auschwitz Trial, but at the end of 1960, Broad was released on bail. He was then arrested a second time, in November 1964, as a defendant in the Frankfurt Auschwitz Trials. He was charged with complicity in joint murder on at least 22 separate occasions, 2 involving the murder of at least 1,000 inmates. He now made a radical turnaround; unlike in his report, he acted like all the other defendants. He denied the crimes, did not choose to remember anything, and spoke no words of remorse. Yet when presented with his own records in the courtroom, Broad was unable to deny his presence at the selection ramp or in the infamous Block 11. Witnesses gave damning evidence against him. Broad was found guilty of supervising selections at Birkenau and of participating in interrogations, torture, and executions. On August 19, 1965, he was sentenced to four years' imprisonment at hard labor.

In 1965, the Auschwitz State Museum published the Broad Report. It is interesting that his involvement in the liquidation of the so-called Gypsy camp at Auschwitz-Birkenau had been secondary to the main proceedings at Frankfurt and had not been relevant to the verdict. While a separate review of Broad's role in liquidation of the Gypsy camp was promised by the Hessian minister of justice, Lauritz Lauritzen, this never happened.

In February 1966, Broad was released from custody, as his pretrial detention was credited to the sentence. He was thus released based on time served. After release from prison, Broad lived quietly and died on November 28, 1993, in Düsseldorf.

BRUNNER, ALOIS (1912–2010)

Alois Brunner, an Austrian SS officer and assistant to **Adolf Eichmann**, was responsible for deporting over 100,000 European Jews to ghettos and concentration camps in Eastern Europe. He ran the Drancy transit camp outside Paris from June 1943 to August 1944, during which time over 25,500 people were deported.

Alois Brunner was born on April 8, 1912, in Nádkút Vas, Austria-Hungary (modern-day Rohrbrunn, Austria) to Joseph Brunner and Ann Kruise. He joined the Austrian Nazi Party in May 1931 at the age of 16 and the SA in 1932. In 1933, he relocated to Germany and served five years in the Austrian Legion. With the Nazi annexation of Austria in 1938, Brunner served in a number of minor posts prior to volunteering for the SS in 1938. After joining the SS in 1938, he was reassigned to the staff of the *Zentralstelle* (the Central Office for Jewish Emigration) in Vienna; there, he helped Eichmann develop the Vienna Model, a plan to rob and force the emigration of Jews from Austria. He also worked closely with Eichmann on the Nisko Plan, a proposed Jewish reservation in Nisko, Poland.

Brunner rose to the rank of *SS-Hauptsturmführer* (captain) and served Eichmann as his personal secretary, later describing Brunner as his "right-hand man." Then, Brunner became the director of the *Zentralstelle*.

In April 1939, Brunner was sent to the new Protectorate of Bohemia and Moravia to speed up the emigration of Czech Jews. After war broke out in September 1939, he organized the deportation of over 1,500 Viennese Jews to Nisko in October 1939. Over time, he directed the removal of 56,000 Austrian Jews, and his success in Vienna earned him a further promotion. In October 1942, he was transferred to Berlin to implement the Vienna Model there.

Brunner became Eichmann's favorite troubleshooter. He sent the entire Jewish population of Salonika, Greece—some 43,000 strong—to death camps in the East in the space of less than two months. In July 1943, as commandant of Drancy, he oversaw the transport of 25,500 Jews to Auschwitz. Brunner took special delight in the arrest and deportation of children.

In September 1944, Brunner participated in the arrest and transport of 14,000 Slovakian Jews.

There are different stories as to Brunner's fate immediately after World War II. He was sought after and had some narrow escapes from the Allies. It is rumored that shortly after the war, he was employed by Reinhard Gehlen and the U.S. Central Intelligence Agency. Gehlen, **Adolf Hitler**'s top anti-Soviet spy, surrendered to the Americans and offered them his services, which the CIA accepted, enabling Gehlen to reestablish his spy organization. Here, he enlisted thousands of Gestapo, Wehrmacht, and SS veterans.

Brunner was sentenced to death in absentia in France in 1953 for crimes against humanity, and in 1954, a new lawsuit was filed there based on his sending children to Auschwitz.

He fled West Germany in 1954. First, he went to Egypt, where he was allegedly recruited by former Nazi Otto Skorzeny into another CIA program designed to train the Egyptian secret service. He subsequently relocated to Syria, where he became a government adviser and remained under the protection of the Syrian government until his death. Brunner was believed to have lived in Damascus under the alias of Dr. Georg Fischer. He was reportedly given asylum, a generous salary, and protection by the ruling Ba'ath Party in exchange for his advice on effective torture and interrogation techniques used by the Germans in World War II.

Brunner was the object of many manhunts and investigations over the years by different groups, including the Simon Wiesenthal Center, Serge and Beate Klarsfeld, and others. He lost an eye and then the fingers of his left hand as a result of letter bombs sent to him in 1961, possibly by the Israeli Mossad.

When the Austrian news magazine *Bunte* interviewed him in 1985, Brunner was unrepentant and said his one regret was that he had not murdered more Jews. In a separate 1987 telephone interview, he told the *Chicago Sun-Times*, "The Jews deserved to die. I have no regrets. If I had the chance I would do it again."

The government of Syria under Hafez el-Assad came close to extraditing him to East Germany, before this plan was halted by the fall of the Berlin Wall in November 1989. Starting in the 1990s and continuing for two decades, there was periodic media speculation about Brunner's exact whereabouts and his possible demise. Germany applied for his extradition from Syria in 1987, and in 1991, the

European Parliament voted to condemn Syria for continuing to harbor him. However, German journalists visiting Syria in the 1990s reported Brunner to be living at the Meridian Hotel in Damascus.

In December 1999, unconfirmed reports surfaced that he had died in 1996 and was buried in a Damascus cemetery. In 2000, rumors circulated that Poland was preparing to seek his extradition. Brunner was last seen alive in 2001 in Syria. In July 2013, sketchy rumors emerged that he might still be alive in Syria. Finally, in November 2014, the Simon Wiesenthal Center reported that Brunner had died in Syria in 2010 and that he was buried somewhere in Damascus. The news of his death was received from a credible former German secret service agent who confirmed rumors about Brunner's death.

BUCH, WALTER (1883–1949)

Walter Buch was a jurist holding the rank of *SS-Obergruppenführer* during the Nazi era. He was also **Martin Bormann**'s father-in-law. During denazification proceedings in 1949, Buch was classified as a major offender (*Hauptschuldiger*).

Walter Hans Buch was born on October 24, 1883, in Bruchsal, Baden. His father, Hermann Buch, an eminent jurist, was senate president of the Supreme Court of Baden. From 1890 to 1902, Buch attended school at Bruchsal and Konstanz, and in 1902, he enrolled as a career soldier in the Sixth Infantry Regiment in Konstanz. In 1908, he married and had two daughters and two sons.

Buch fought in World War I as an officer, attaining promotions as the war lengthened. From September 1918, he worked in the Prussian War Ministry in Berlin until on November 20, 1918, he was discharged with the rank of major.

From 1919 to 1922, Buch was a member of the *Deutschnationale Volkspartei*, Weimar Germany's major conservative and nationalist party. He was the leader of the *Deutschvölkischer Schutz- und Trutzbund* in Baden, an organization founded in Bamberg in February 1919 to fight Judaism. He remained leader until it was banned by the state government.

In March 1920, Buch met **Adolf Hitler** for the first time and was inspired by the meeting. After this, he occasionally exchanged letters with Hitler, monitoring his works through word of mouth and newspapers. On December 9, 1922, Buch became a member of the NSDAP, and on January 1, 1923, he joined the SA. Between August 1923 and 1924, he organized the Franconian SA in Nuremberg.

In mid-1923, after Hermann Ehrhardt quarreled with Ernst Röhm and Adolf Hitler, 8 SA members formed the Hitler Shock Troop (*Stosstrupp-Hitler*) to protect Hitler . This small unit, forerunner to the SS, never comprised more than 20 members and included Buch. From this foundation, he became a high-ranking honorary leader of the SS.

Buch participated in the failed Beer Hall Putsch in Munich on November 8 to 9, 1923, and returned to Munich within four days of the coup. Sent by **Hermann Göring** (who had fled to Innsbruck) to bolster the cohesion of the party troops, Buch established ties with the now-outlawed SA groups.

With the banning of the party, Buch became a wine merchant in Munich. He maintained regular contact between the imprisoned Hitler and the exiled leadership until Hitler's release and the reestablishment of the party on February 20, 1925. Until January 1, 1928, Buch led and organized the SA in Upper Bavaria.

On November 27, 1927, Buch became chairman of the *Untersuchungs- und Schlichtungs-Ausschuss* (Inquiry and Mediation Board, or USCHLA), an internal party disciplinary body that became to the party what the Gestapo was for Germany as a whole. Acting as the party's secret police force, the board was feared among the party's followers. Buch ruled on internal party disputes, spied on party members, and put them under pressure if they strayed from the party line. There was no appeal against board judgments, other than directly to Hitler. Buch built up a powerful, independent secret-police organization within the party and engaged in surveillance of other political organizations in and outside of Germany.

On May 20, 1928, Buch was one of the 12 elected NSDAP members in the Reichstag, where he remained until 1945. Between June 1930 and October 1931, he led the party's youth leadership, and until 1933, he was editor in chief of the *Völkischer Beobachter*.

On September 2, 1929, Buch's eldest daughter, Gerda, married Martin Bormann, with Adolf Hitler and Rudolf Hess as witnesses.

During the Röhm Putsch of June 30, 1934, Buch played a leading part and was present at the arrest of Ernst Röhm by Hitler. It was Buch who directed the SS unit that shot the leading SA men in the Stadelheim Prison courtyard. As a reward for having given Röhm's murder the outward appearance of legality, Buch was appointed supreme party judge and *SS-Gruppenführer* on November 9, 1934.

Buch was responsible for legalizing party members' excesses during the *Kristallnacht* of November 9 to 10, 1938; he declared that those responsible for the more than 100 Jewish deaths had only been following orders. His own entrenched antisemitism saw no need to question those who had given these orders, considering that Jews were literally "not humans." In an article in *Deutsche Justiz* dated October 21, 1938, Buch wrote, "The Jew is not a human being. He is an appearance of putrescence. Just as the fission-fungus cannot permeate wood until it is rotting, so the Jew was able to creep into the German people, to bring on disaster, only after the German nation . . . had begun to rot from within."

On November 9, 1941, Hitler dismissed Gauleiter Josef Wagner from all his offices after his wife opposed the marriage of their daughter to an SS man. A party court chaired by Walter Buch ruled on February 6, 1942, that Wagner had not caused any damage to the party and could remain in the party. Hitler annulled that decision, however, and threw Wagner out of the NSDAP. For his defiance, Hitler ruled that Buch would henceforth be required to have all his decisions signed by his son-in-law Martin Bormann.

On April 30, 1945, American troops captured Buch and imprisoned him from May to August 1945. American interrogators questioned him about the whereabouts of Martin Bormann, but to no avail. Buch then gave evidence as a witness at the Nuremberg trials. Buch's daughter Gerda died of cancer in March 1946.

In August 1948, Buch was sentenced to five years of forced labor and confiscation of all his property. Upon appeal, the Munich denazification court confirmed the finding that Buch was a major offender (*Hauptschuldiger*) but reduced his sentence from five years to three and a half years. He was released based on time served.

Six weeks later, on November 12, 1949, Buch committed suicide by slitting his wrists and throwing himself into Bavaria's Ammersee.

BÜHLER, JOSEF (1904–1948)

Josef Bühler was a Nazi officer who served as state secretary and deputy governor to the German-controlled General Government in Kraków, Poland, during World War II. He actively participated in the imposition of Nazi Germany's Final Solution of the Jewish Question.

Bühler was born on February 16, 1904, in Bad Waldsee, Germany, into a Catholic family of 12 children. His father was a baker. After completing high school, in 1922, Bühler commenced the study of law at the University of Munich. He joined the NSDAP in 1922 and participated in the attempted Nazi putsch in Munich on November 8 to 9, 1923.

From 1930 to 1932, he worked in the Munich law firm of **Hans Frank**, a legal adviser to **Adolf Hitler** and the Nazi Party. Bühler graduated from university in Berlin in 1932 with a doctorate in law, and from 1932, he worked as a district judge in the Bavarian Ministry of Justice. From October 1934, he was an administrator to the Munich Court. In 1935, he became the chief of the Prosecutors Division of the Reich Justice Ministry. In 1938, Hans Frank, now Reich minister without portfolio, placed Bühler in charge of Frank's cabinet office.

After the German invasion of Poland on September 1, 1939, Hans Frank was appointed governor-general of occupied Poland, and Bühler accompanied him to Kraków. From November 1939, Bühler managed the governor-general's office; after March 1940, he served as Frank's secretary of state, and he was appointed to the honorary rank of *SS-Brigadeführer* by SS chief **Heinrich Himmler**.

Already on November 24, 1939, Bühler gave the so-called special commissioner for the capture and protection of art and cultural treasures, Kajetan Mühlmann, the necessary funds for art theft. Bühler then took part in two conferences, on May 16, 1940, and May 20, 1940, in preparation for the Extraordinary Pacification Action, which aimed to wipe out any resistance from the Polish intelligentsia. In a special circular dated January 12, 1942, Bühler instructed the district governors that they were not to exercise their right of pardon against those Jews who had been sentenced to death for escaping from the ghetto.

On January 20, 1942, Bühler represented the governor-general's office at the Wannsee Conference in Berlin, during which leading Nazi bureaucrats and others discussed the imposition of the Final Solution. Bühler stated to the other conference attendees that he wanted "a speedy solution of the Jewish question" in the General Government and that action was to be carried out as quickly as possible. He urged **Reinhard Heydrich**, who ran the conference, to begin the Final

Solution in the General Government, where "no transport problems" existed. In 1942, Bühler participated in the ethnic cleansing of Poles in what became known as *Aktion Zamość*, in which German police and the military expelled 116,000 Polish men and women in just a few months from the Zamość region to make way for projected German settlements. This involved, among other things, the abduction and deportation of Poles to Germany for forced labor.

On January 18, 1945, Bühler fled from Kraków. He was arrested on May 30, 1945, by the Americans and was interned in the Nuremberg witness jail. On April 23, 1946, he testified on Hans Frank's behalf before the International Military Tribunal at Nuremberg. Bühler and Frank had attempted to hold the SS leader **Friedrich-Wilhelm Krüger**, who had committed suicide in American captivity on May 10, 1945, responsible for the crimes in Poland and to blame everything else on Himmler.

After his witness hearing, Bühler was extradited to Poland in May 1946 in accordance with the Moscow Declaration, which required that "the National Socialist criminals were to be transferred to the place of their crimes." Between June 17, 1948, and July 5, 1948, Bühler was tried by the Supreme National Tribunal of Poland in Kraków for crimes against humanity. He was found guilty on July 10, 1948, and was sentenced to death and the forfeiture of all property. Bühler was executed by hanging in Kraków on August 22, 1948.

C

CONTI, LEONARDO (1900–1945)

Leonardo Conti was a Swiss German physician who served as the Reich health leader in Nazi Germany. As an *SS-Obergruppenführer*, he was the most senior medical practitioner in Nazi Germany. Involved in the infamous *Aktion T-4* euthanasia program, he oversaw the murder of many Germans who were deemed to be of "unsound mind."

Leonardo Ambrogio Giorgio Giovanni Conti was born on August 24, 1900, in Lugano, Switzerland, to a Swiss Italian father, Silvio, and a German mother, Nanna. His parents divorced in 1903. Nanna Conti would later become the Reich midwifery leader under the Nazis. In 1915, Conti received German citizenship, and in 1918, he completed his examinations at the Friedrich-Wilhelms high school in Berlin. He then volunteered as a gunner in a Küstrin artillery regiment. In 1918, he cofounded the antisemitic *Kampfbund Deutscher Volksbund* and was highly responsive to the *völkisch* movement that became popular in Weimar Germany.

From 1919 to 1923, Conti studied medicine in Berlin and Erlangen, and together with his brother, Silvio Conti, he became active in the nationalist student movement. In 1919, he joined the DNVP (German National People's Party) and participated in the 1920 Kapp Putsch against the Weimar Republic.

Having passed his state examination in 1923, he joined the National Socialist SA (*Sturmabteilung*) and became its first physician. In 1925, Conti received his doctorate on facial soft tissue surgery and published *Über Weichteilplastik im Gesicht (About Soft Tissue Plastic in the Face)*, a book about facial plastic surgery. On August 22, 1925, he married Elfriede, who was a member of the NSDAP, and they had four children together.

After a medical internship and a volunteer assistant position, he worked as a general practitioner and pediatrician in Berlin between October 1925 and February 13, 1933. In December 1927, he joined the NSDAP. In 1928, he organized the structure of the medical service for the SA, and Conti, together with **Martin Bormann** and Gerhard Wagner, developed the Aid Organization for the Wounded. In 1929, he cofounded the National Socialist German Doctors' League (*Nationalsocialisticher Deutscher Ärtzebund*, or NSDÄB), on whose board he served from 1931.

As senior physician east of the Berlin SA, Conti treated the SA leader Horst Wessel, who had been injured during fighting with communists, from January 14, 1930, until his death a few weeks later, on February 23. That same year, Conti moved from the SA to the SS and headed the medical services supporting the annual Nuremberg Party Rally.

In 1931, Conti joined the Berlin Medical Association, and in May 1932, he was elected as a member of the Prussian Parliament, where he served as a deputy until its dissolution in the fall of 1933. On February 13, 1933, Conti, as a party "old fighter," was appointed by **Hermann Göring** to the Prussian Ministry of Interior as commissioner for special purposes. On April 9, 1933, he was expelled temporarily from the SS, only to be reinstated the following month, on May 12, 1933.

After **Adolf Hitler** became chancellor, Conti volunteered to serve for the Reich Ministry of the Interior. In February 1934, he headed up the Main Office of Public Health of the NSDAP in Berlin. On April 12, 1934, he was appointed by Hermann Göring to the Prussian State Council.

In 1936, Conti took command of the medical health services for the Berlin Olympic Games, and in 1937, he was elected to the presidency of the International Federation of Sports Medicine. In addition, in 1936, Conti lectured on public health at the University of Berlin.

On January 30, 1938, Conti became an *SS-Brigadeführer*, and in September 1938, he was appointed as secretary of state in the Reich Ministry of the Interior. He also took over the NSDAP Main Office for Public Health, where he initiated, among other things, the establishment of the *Reichsvollkornbrot* (rich whole-wheat bread) committee. Behind this was the National Socialist idea that the "people's body" must be strengthened to achieve greater work, higher fertility, and better combat power. From 1939, Conti was the Reich medical officer, head of the Main Office of Public Health, and remained head of the NSDÄB.

Leonardo Conti was a staunch promoter of a public medical administration strongly controlled by the Nazi state. Under his leadership, local health offices were further expanded to allow for a genetic control and selection of the population so that "weak" elements were removed for the improvement of the German race. "Racial hygiene" was a lethal part of the Nazi philosophy. Conti shared responsibility, with *SS-Obergruppenführer* **Phillipp Bouhler** and *SS-Gruppenführer* **Karl Brandt**, for the forced sterilization program, racially motivated forced abortions, and ultimately the *Aktion T-4* program. Conti's participation in human experiments, such as with typhus at the Buchenwald concentration camp, is also undisputed.

This euthanasia program was the basis for later programs of mass murder during the Holocaust and in other contexts. Many of the SS staff involved in these murders developed their lethal methods during the *Aktion T-4* program overseen by Conti. Victims were deceived in the same way as in *Aktion T-4*, using very elaborate means to convince them that no harm was intended.

In August 1941, Conti once more became a member of the Reichstag. On April 20, 1944, he was promoted to *SS-Obergruppenführer*. He was closely involved in forensic investigations into the Katyn Forest massacre of Polish military officers in the Soviet Union and received a detailed report, known as the Katyn Commission, from an international team of experts. In August 1944, he resigned as Reich health leader, and on January 17, 1945, he was appointed as an honorary professor in Munich. Another appointment as honorary professor at the State Academy for the public health service in Berlin followed on March 3, 1945.

On May 19, 1945, after Germany's surrender, Conti was arrested. He was investigated for his involvement with the euthanasia program and would have been brought before the International Military Tribunal as part of the Doctors' Trial for his involvement in *Aktion T-4*. However, on October 6, 1945, over a year before the trial began, Leonardo Conti hanged himself in his Nuremberg cell.

CSATÁRY, LÁSZLÓ (1915–2013)

László Csatáry, a Hungarian, was convicted in absentia as a Nazi war criminal in 1948 by a Czechoslovak court and sentenced to death, but he escaped, fled to asylum in Canada, and later fled to Budapest, dying at the age of 98 without ever facing trial.

Csatáry was born on March 4, 1915, in the small town of Mány, Hungary (then part of the Austro-Hungarian Empire). He became a policeman, and in 1944, after the German invasion of the country, he collaborated as the Royal Hungarian Police commandant in charge of the Jewish ghetto in Kassa (Košice, Slovakia). In this capacity, Csatáry organized the deportation of over 15,500 Jews to Auschwitz, where practically all of them perished.

Reports have surfaced of Csatáry's extreme cruelty to inmates and the demonstrable pleasure he took in it. Among other things, he was accused of having physically brutalized Jews in detention, beating them with his hands and a dog whip.

After he was sentenced to death in 1948, Csatáry escaped to Canada and sought asylum there, justifying his request on the ground that he sought sanctuary from the Hungarian communist regime. Living under an assumed identity, he worked as an art dealer in Montreal, where he became a Canadian citizen in 1955. Thereafter he led a peaceful and quiet life until 1997, when his war history was drawn to the notice of Canadian authorities. Csatáry's Canadian citizenship was revoked for lying on his citizenship application, and while the Canadian government was preparing his deportation, Csatáry fled Canada in late 1997.

Based on a tip received by the Simon Wiesenthal Center in September 2011, Csatáry was located in Budapest, Hungary, in 2012. In the summer of that year, his address was revealed by reporters, and on July 18, 2012, he was taken into custody for questioning by Hungarian authorities and indicted for war crimes. On July 30, 2012, the Slovak justice minister, Tomáš Borec, announced that Slovakia was ready to bring a prosecution case against Csatáry and requested that Hungary extradite him. Czechoslovakia had abolished the death penalty in 1990, and so on March 28, 2013, the Slovak County Court in Košice changed the 1948 verdict in Csatáry's case from the death penalty to life imprisonment.

In August 2012, the Budapest Prosecutor's Office decided not to proceed with the charges, on the basis that further research had revealed that Csatáry was not in Kassa at the time and lacked the rank to organize the transports. In January 2013, however, Slovak police found a witness to corroborate other charges relating to the deportation from May 1944 of 15,700 Jews from Kassa. On July 8, 2013, a Budapest higher court adjourned the case, stating that Csatáry had already been sentenced for the crimes included in the proceedings, in former Czechoslovakia, in 1948.

Csatáry remained in Budapest and died there from pneumonia, on August 10, 2013, aged 98. He never faced trial.

D

DALUEGE, KURT (1897–1946)

Kurt Daluege was head of Nazi Germany's uniformed *Ordnungspolizei* (Orpo), which became involved in the murders of Soviet Jews from 1940 onward. After the assassination of **Reinhard Heydrich** in 1942, he served as deputy protector of Bohemia and Moravia.

Kurt Max Franz Daluege was born on September 15, 1897, in Kreuzburg, Upper Silesia, the son of a Prussian civil servant. He completed high school in 1916 and joined the German army. In October 1917, he commenced officer training, but he was severely wounded in combat in the head and shoulder. Hospitalized and declared 25 percent disabled, he was decorated for bravery.

From 1918 to 1921, Daluege took part in an Upper Silesia militia unit fighting Polish irregulars. After working briefly in Berlin as a factory hand, he studied civil engineering at the Technical University of Berlin between 1921 and 1924, graduating as an engineer. During 1922, he served in the *Freikorps Rossbach*, and in 1923, he became a member of Berlin's *Teuto-Rugia*, a German American fraternity. Also in 1923, Daluege joined the NSDAP.

From 1924, he organized *Berlin Frontbann*, a front organization for the SA, since both the SA and NSDAP were then banned in Prussia. In March 1926, he openly joined and became leader of Berlin's SA. He rejoined the NSDAP once it was reinstated, becoming **Joseph Goebbels**'s deputy gauleiter in Berlin.

On October 16, 1926, Daluege married Käthe Schwarz. In 1937, they adopted a son, after which Käthe had three biological children. Between 1927 and 1933, Daluege was department head of a construction firm.

In July 1930, Daluege resigned from the SA and joined the SS with the rank of *SS-Oberführer*, as **Adolf Hitler** had tasked him to scrutinize the SA and political opponents within the party. The next month when Berlin SA leader Walter Stennes's men attacked the Berlin NSDAP headquarters in what became known as the Stennes Revolt, Daluege's unit overpowered the attack. In an open letter thanking Daluege for his service, Adolf Hitler declared, "SS man, your honor is loyalty," which became the motto thereafter adopted by the SS.

In November 1932, Daluege was elected to the Reichstag, a seat he retained until 1945. In May 1933, **Hermann Göring** moved him into the Prussian Interior Ministry, where he took charge of the regular police force. In this capacity, he purged the force of "social democratic" elements and filled it with SS men.

Daluege played a key role in the notorious Night of the Long Knives, during which Ernst Röhm and many leaders of the SA were purged between June 30 and July 2, 1934. This neutralized the SA and shifted power within the NSDAP to the SS.

Kurt Daluege, chief of Nazi Germany's uniformed *SS Ordnungspolizei* (Orpo), offers a salute during a march in Munich in 1938. Later he became an integral element in the regime's plans to "cleanse" the Soviet Union of Jews and communists after Operation Barbarossa in the summer of 1941. (Hugo Jaeger/Timepix/The LIFE Picture Collection/Getty Images)

After this, Daluege was assigned by Göring to reorganize the SA throughout north Germany. In August 1934, *SS-Reichsführer* **Heinrich Himmler** promoted Daluege to *SS-Obergruppenführer*.

By November 1934, Daluege's authority covered all German uniformed police. He commanded municipal police forces, the rural gendarmerie, traffic police, the coast guard, the railway police, the postal protection service, fire brigades, the air-raid services, the emergency technical service, the broadcasting police, the factory protection police, building regulations enforcement, and the commercial police.

Despite a heart attack in 1936, Daluege became Himmler's deputy as German chief of police and head of the Orpo, which he commanded until 1943.

In 1936, the entire German police force was reorganized; administrative functions were now under the actual control of Himmler's SS. There were two main branches: under Heydrich were the political police (Gestapo) and the criminal police dealing with nonpolitical crimes (Kripo), and under Daluege was the Orpo, which covered the municipal police, the rural police, and the community police.

By 1938, Daleuge had over 62,000 police officers under his command. With the indication that enlisting in Orpo might be an alternative to regular military service, by mid-1940, this had risen to 244,500. As it turned out, many Orpo units were transferred into the regular army, as they had become an essential source of manpower for holding down occupied Europe. Daluege also established a unit of police officers responsible for the suppression of internal revolt.

Daluege was an integral element in the Nazi plans to "cleanse" the Soviet Union after Operation Barbarossa. At Hitler's command, this war was to be considered a war against Bolsheviks and Jews, and Daluege's police battalions were told to pursue their tasks ruthlessly. During the summer of 1941, mass shootings were frequent all over the occupied territories, and Daluege was present at several. In one, a mass execution of 4,435 Jews took place at the hands of the 307th Police Battalion, near Brest-Litovsk.

In mid-July 1941, a second *Aktion* at Białystok, which was nearly 50 percent Jewish, was instigated from the highest SS levels. **Erich von dem Bach-Zalewski**, Kurt Daluege, and Heinrich Himmler had met shortly before it commenced. On July 9, 1941, Daluege congratulated his troops for participating in the defeat of Bolshevism, and on July 12, male Jews between the ages of 17 and 45 were brought to a sports stadium. A day later they were taken to antitank ditches, and by the end of the *Aktion*, about 3,000 Jews had been killed.

Shortly afterward, on September 1, 1941, Daluege attended another mass execution of Jews near Minsk, in occupied Belarus. In October 1941, he signed deportation orders for Jews from Germany, Austria, and the Protectorate of Bohemia and Moravia to Riga and Minsk.

The direct involvement of the Orpo was pervasive. The massacre in Minsk occurred immediately after Daluege met with Bach-Zalewski in that city, and it was obvious that Daluege was inciting, not forbidding, involvement of the Orpo in these massacres.

Daluege then authorized a new role for the Orpo: they would guard transports organized by Heydrich's SD. Between the fall of 1941 and the spring of 1945, hundreds of deportation trains took German, Czech, and Austrian Jews to death camps and ghettos in the East, together with many additional transports from Hungary, the Netherlands, Slovakia, France, Belgium, Greece, Italy, Bulgaria, and Croatia—a vast number under the control of Daluege's Orpo.

When Governor **Hans Frank** in occupied Poland failed to take sufficient action after Reinhard Heydrich was assassinated in May 1942, Hitler and Himmler sent Daluege to Prague to become deputy protector of Bohemia and Moravia (and acting protector in all but name). In June 1942, he ordered the villages of Lidice and Ležáky razed to the ground in reprisal for Heydrich's assassination. The destruction of Lidice saw the murder of all 173 male inhabitants, with the village's 198 women and children deported to Ravensbrück.

Daluege then attended a conference on July 7, 1942, organized by Himmler. This discussed an extension of *Aktion Reinhard*, the Nazi secret plan for the mass murder of Polish Jews in the General Government. Named for the assassinated Heydrich, it was in some respects a revenge *Aktion* but also the ultimate phase of the previously decided Final Solution.

Daluege acted as deputy protector of Bohemia and Moravia from 1942 until May 1943, when he suffered a massive heart attack; he resigned in August 1943 and took no further part in the war.

In May 1945, Daluege was arrested by British troops in Lübeck. He was interned in Luxembourg and then tried at Nuremberg as a major war criminal. In September 1946, after being extradited to Czechoslovakia, he was tried for crimes against humanity committed in the Protectorate. Throughout his trial, he was unrepentant, claiming that he was beloved by "three million policemen," only following Hitler's orders, and had a clear conscience. He was convicted on all charges and sentenced to death on October 23, 1946. Aged 48, Daluege was hanged in Pankrác prison in Prague the next day.

DANNECKER, THEODOR (1913–1945)

Theodor Dannecker was an SS captain who administered the Final Solution in several countries during the Holocaust, including overseeing the arrest of Jews by French police during the Vel' d'Hiv roundup that resulted in the deportation of more than 13,000 Jews to Auschwitz, where most were murdered.

Dannecker was born in Tübingen, Germany, on March 27, 1913. His father, who ran a menswear business, died in November 1918, leaving two sons: five-year-old Theodor and his older brother. Theodor attended the High School of Commerce in Reutlingen and commenced an apprenticeship in Stuttgart in 1930, curtailing this after only a few months when his mother died. He ran his family business as a textile dealer for two years after her death, until he joined the Nazi Party and the SS in 1932.

Dannecker joined an SS special combat support unit in 1934, and in 1935, he joined the *Sicherheitsdienst* (SD), the intelligence service of the SS and the Nazi Party. In March 1937, he joined the staff of *SS-Obersturmbannführer* **Adolf Eichmann** at the *Judenreferat* (Department of Jewish Affairs) in the SD's main office in Berlin, where Dannecker was put in charge of the section controlling assimilated Jews.

In 1938, Dannecker helped create the Central Office for Jewish Emigration in Vienna. Following the German invasion of Poland on September 1, 1939, he helped set up the Lublin Reservation, a concentration camp compound near the borders of Lublin and Nisko, designed by the SS to resettle Poland's Jews. In the spring of 1940, Dannecker created a system for Jewish emigration in Prague like that in Vienna.

In September 1940, given Dannecker's expertise with assimilated Jews, Eichmann chose him to direct the Jewish Affairs Department in Paris. Dannecker headed its French bureau and *Judenreferat*, receiving his orders directly from Eichmann, although he was placed under the authority of Helmut Knochen, a senior commander of the Security Police and SD in Paris. Knochen was responsible for rounding up French Jews and deporting them to concentration camps. The task of deportation enabled Dannecker to oversee the names of the French Jews who were arrested in May and August 1941. He formulated the regulations for the deportations of native-born French Jews and Jewish immigrants, referred to as "stateless Jews."

Dannecker claimed credit for being the first to propose continuous Jewish deportations from France to the East and constantly pressured the Vichy authorities to take more active antisemitic measures. Xavier Vallat, the coordinator of Jewish Affairs in Vichy responsible for launching and implementing France's anti-Jewish legislation, created the Union of French Jews in late 1941 on Dannecker's initiative. The two men clashed over Dannecker's extreme antisemitism and Vallat's unwillingness to be subservient to the Nazis.

On July 10, 1942, Dannecker telexed Eichmann about the coming roundup of French Jews to occur at the *Vélodrome d'Hiver* (Vel' d'Hiv) stadium in Paris, prior to their deportation to Drancy and eventually Auschwitz. Dannecker said the raid would be from July 16 to 18, conducted by the French police, and include about 4,000 children in the arrests. The French police agreed to collaborate and organize the roundup under German control. Jean Leguay, of the National Police in Vichy, and **René Bousquet**, the Vichy police secretary-general, agreed to negotiate with Dannecker. However, the French police, not the Germans, ran the whole roundup operation.

Dannecker's ongoing differences with Knochen and Vallat over his extreme views on Jewish deportations, together with his unwillingness to collaborate with Vichy authorities, became a management problem. In early August 1942, following the roundup of Jews in Paris, Dannecker was recalled to Berlin for abuse of power and misuse of his position. SS officer Heinz Röthke took over the Paris branch from Dannecker.

In January 1943, Dannecker was transferred to Eichmann's office in Sofia, Bulgaria, where he continued to oversee deportations and implement the Final Solution there in all the Bulgarian territories. During March 1943, Dannecker arranged for 11,343 Jews to be deported from the German-occupied Bulgarian-annexed territories of Greece and Yugoslavia to Auschwitz and Treblinka. Only 12 are known to have survived.

Dannecker's attempt to deport Jews with Bulgarian citizenship from old Bulgaria, a collaborationist ally, failed due to widespread opposition led by King Boris III, supported by the heads of the Bulgarian Orthodox Church, metropolitan bishops Stephan from Sofia and Kiril from Plovdiv, and vice president of the parliament, Dimitar Peshev.

In October 1943, he was posted to Verona, Italy, as commissioner for Jewish Affairs. Prior to the German occupation of Italy, Benito Mussolini refused to turn over Jews to the Nazis except those in areas annexed or occupied by the Italians in the Balkans. Between September 1943 and January 1944, when Italy surrendered to the Allies and Germans occupied Italy, Dannecker deported Italian Jews. He was responsible for the transport of 1,259 Jews from Rome to Auschwitz.

After Germany occupied Hungary, Dannecker and the Hungarian establishment deported more than a half a million Hungarian Jews between early 1944 and summer of 1944.

Under the tutelage of Adolf Eichmann, Dannecker developed into one of the SS's most ruthless and experienced experts on the Jewish question, and his involvement in the genocide of European Jewry was one of primary responsibility. Dannecker became Jewish commissary for Italy in October 1944, remaining with the Eichmann commando to the end of the war.

Arrested by Allied troops at the end of the war, Dannecker committed suicide in an American prison camp in Bad Tölz on December 10, 1945.

DIRLEWANGER, OSKAR (1895–1945)

Oskar Dirlewanger commanded the infamous Nazi SS Dirlewanger Brigade during World War II. His name and that of the unit are closely linked to wanton SS war crimes.

Dirlewanger was born on September 26, 1895, into a middle-class family in Würzburg, northern Bavaria. In 1913, at the age of 18, he enlisted in the German army and received a commission as lieutenant. He fought as a machine gunner on the Western Front, where he met **Gottlob Berger**, who later became head of the SS Main Office (SS-HA). Dirlewanger was wounded six times, leaving him partially disabled, and was awarded the Iron Cross First and Second Class.

After experiencing the violence of the Western Front, Dirlewanger was described in a postwar police report as being "a mentally unstable, violent fanatic and alcoholic, who had the habit of erupting into violence under the influence of drugs." Unable to adapt to peace, he joined the *Freikorps* paramilitary militia and created an armed formation of students, a militia called the Württemberg Highway Watch. They deployed to the town of Sangerhausen, which had been occupied by communists. Many years later, in 1935, Dirlewanger was made an honorary citizen of Sangerhausen and was celebrated as its "liberator from the Red terrorists."

In 1922, Dirlewanger was awarded a doctorate in political science from Goethe University, Frankfurt. He joined the Nazi Party in 1923, just two years after it was formed. The fact that he had been in trouble with the law for possessing a firearm illegally and "anti-Semitic incitement" aided his standing in the party. From 1928 to 1931, Dirlewanger was an executive director of a textile factory in Erfurt (owned, ironically, by a Jewish family), and although he renounced active service in the SA, he supported it financially.

By 1932, Dirlewanger held a senior office in the SA, but in 1934, he was convicted and sentenced to two years imprisonment in Dachau prison for the statutory rape of a 14-year-old girl from the League of German Girls (BdM). He lost his job, his professional title, and all military honors, and he was expelled from the NSDAP.

Upon his release, Dirlewanger was reinstated in the SS general reserve through the auspices of his former army comrade Gottlob Berger. He then volunteered to join the German Condor Legion in Spain, fighting for General Franco from 1936 until 1939 against the leftist Republican government. He was wounded three times and awarded military honors for, among other things, the death of 15 Republicans.

Returning to Germany, Dirlewanger found preparations for the Nazi invasion of Poland well underway. Owing to Berger's lobbying with *SS-Reichsführer* **Heinrich Himmler**, Dirlewanger rejoined the SS and was made a lieutenant in the Waffen-SS. His doctorate was also restored by the University of Frankfurt.

In 1940, Dirlewanger was tasked with creating his own unit and formed *SS-Sonderkommando Dirlewanger*, initially from a few convicted poachers as well as conventional soldiers. Later members would be German convicts and concentration camp criminal prisoners. Both Hitler and Himmler considered that by using ex-convicts in policing, bullying, and terrorizing the populace of their newly conquered lands, they would instill order through fear.

Initially the unit carried out security duties in German-occupied Poland, where Dirlewanger was commandant of a labor camp at Stary Dzików. Here, and in the nearby Lublin ghetto, he was accused of committing sadistic cruelties, including injecting strychnine into naked young Jewish female prisoners to watch them die in convulsions.

After investigating these reports of abuse and cruelty, the SS Court Main Office (*Hauptamt SS-Gericht*) sought to investigate Dirlewanger and to ensure that the unit was under control. The allegations of atrocities were investigated by SS judge Georg Konrad Morgen, who found Dirlewanger guilty of murder, corruption, and race defilement (having sex with racially unacceptable people). Berger and Himmler were little concerned; Dirlewanger was instead simply relocated, while Judge Morgen was punished for his findings.

Berger and Himmler needed units such as the Dirlewanger Brigade to keep "subhumanity" under control. **Odilo Globocnik** wrote to Himmler that Dirlewanger, in charge of the Jewish camp of Dzików, was an excellent leader.

In summer 1941, Dirlewanger directed his unit to supervise the Polish Jewish population forced to slave labor in the construction of military facilities along the River Bug. In autumn, the unit was involved in pacification of the Lublin region and was thus directly involved in the violent removal of thousands of villagers from around Lublin to make room for ethnic Germans. This area would later serve as the site for a Waffen-SS concentration camp.

At the beginning of 1942, the unit was assigned to "antibandit" operations, fighting Soviet partisans in Belarus. Now designated as a "volunteer" formation, Dirlewanger's men brutalized partisans, suspected collaborators, or anyone who got in their way, and engaged in looting, raping, and extortion. Allegedly, a favorite method was to herd the local population of a suspected "bandit" village into a barn, set the barn on fire, and then machine-gun anyone who sought to break free from the flames. Civilians were used from time to time as human shields or marched over minefields. Dirlewanger and his force raped and tortured young women and slaughtered Jews in Belarus beginning in 1942. Overall, it is estimated that the Dirlewanger Brigade killed at least 30,000 Belarusian (and likely many more) civilians. Himmler, aware of Dirlewanger's deeds, awarded him the German Cross in Gold on December 5, 1943, in recognition of his unit's actions.

All antipartisan activities were committed to paper in the form of written reports, and after one two-day operation, Dirlewanger reported taking 33 bunkers, killing 386 "bandits" and 294 "bandit suspects." Further, it was reported that the unit "harvested" 3 men, 30 women, 117 horses, 248 children, 140 sheep, 14 pigs, and 120 tons of food. In Operation Swamp Fever, during September 1942, the brigade reported killing 8,350 Jews, 389 "bandits," and 1,274 "bandit suspects."

By August 1944, the Dirlewanger unit was a full battalion, made up of criminals, court-martialed SS troops, and even former political prisoners. As the Red Army advanced west, though, many in the unit unsurprisingly defected to the Russians. In mid-1944, when the Germans were being driven out of Belarus, Dirlewanger's Brigade suffered heavy losses in rearguard fights against Soviet regulars. Reconstructed as a storm brigade, the unit was used to suppress the Warsaw Uprising in the summer of 1944. Dirlewanger participated in the Woła massacre; together with police units, the brigade rounded up and shot around 40,000 civilians in just two days of mayhem, torture, and atrocities. Despite this, Dirlewanger's unit suffered severe casualties in Warsaw, losing massive numbers in only two months of fighting.

Dirlewanger received his final promotion, to the rank of *SS-Oberführer*, on August 15, 1944. In October 1944, he was awarded the Knight's Cross of the Iron Cross, and the same month, he led his men to put down the Slovak National Uprising, eventually being posted to Hungary and eastern Germany to fight the advancing Red Army.

In February 1945, the unit was expanded and redesignated as an SS grenadier division. That same month, Dirlewanger was shot in the chest while fighting against the invading Soviet forces near Guben in Brandenburg and sent to the rear. It was his 12th and final war injury.

On April 22, 1945, Dirlewanger went into hiding. By the end of the war, he had overseen and personally taken part in the torture, rape, and murder of many thousands of civilians in Germany, Belarus, and Poland, all under the guise of eliminating "bandits" behind the front line.

He was arrested by French occupation authorities on June 1, 1945, near the town of Altshausen in Upper Swabia. After this, his fate becomes cloudy. The exact cause of his death is unknown, which over time has led to speculation. His death certificate, issued by French authorities, shows him to have died on June 7, 1945, of natural causes. However, a Luftwaffe lieutenant named Anton Füssinger later claimed he was Dirlewanger's cell mate and said that he witnessed Dirlewanger being gravely beaten by Polish guards in French service on the night of June 4 to 5, 1945, resulting in his death. No one, however, confirmed any of Füssinger's statements. The lack of corroborating evidence led to even more rumors after the war ended, and there were many presumed sightings of Dirlewanger around the world over the years.

Rumors and tabloid stories persisted, suggesting that Dirlewanger had escaped and lived on, including one popular story of Dirlewanger serving with the French Foreign Legion in Vietnam during the First Indochina War and later defecting to Egypt to join Gamal Abdel Nasser's army (in another variation, to Syria). In response, the Department of Public Prosecution in Ravensburg arranged the exhumation of Dirlewanger's corpse to confirm his identity in November 1960. The place of his burial was suppressed.

DOLP, HERMANN (1889–1944?)

Hermann Dolp was born on September 12, 1889, in Türkheim, Bavaria. After service in World War I, he joined one of the many right-wing paramilitary *Freikorps* units active in Bavaria, and as an early adherent to the ideas of **Adolf Hitler**, he became one of the initial SA street fighters; as such, he served time in prison for beating up political opponents. In November 1923, he took part in the Beer Hall Putsch. Entering the National Socialist Party in 1928, he joined the SS in October 1929 as an unpaid *Untersturmführer*. In September 1930, he was promoted to *SS-Standartenführer*, commanding Hitler's protection squad in Munich.

In late 1933, he was sent to assist in organizing the construction and further development of Dachau concentration camp (which had opened in March of that year), and he remained there through the summer of 1934. From January

1935 onward, he served as an officer at SS headquarters, and in August 1939, he was sent to Sachsenhausen concentration camp, not far from Berlin, as garrison commander.

Married and the father of four children, Dolp was a good organizer although not highly endowed with intellect. He had a weakness for alcohol, which he consumed in large quantities. After the German attack on Poland in September 1939, he was given command of local ethnic German paramilitary units there and then headed the Gestapo in Kalisch (Kalisz). It was here that his drinking got him into trouble. On November 1, 1939, he was caught drunk trying to rape a young Polish woman, who happened to be the girlfriend of another German official. The case was investigated at the order of the inspector of concentration camps, **Theodor Eicke**, and Dolp was arrested on January 9, 1940. He was tried before an SS court on February 4, 1940, found guilty, and militarily degraded. He was demoted to *SS-Sturmbannführer*, removed from Sachsenhausen, and forbidden from touching alcohol for two years. On February 8, 1940, *SS-Reichsführer* **Heinrich Himmler** wrote to Dolp and pointed out expressly that any disregarding of the alcohol ban would result in him being drummed out of the SS.

By mid-February 1940, Dolp was transferred to the command of SS chief of the Lublin District, **Odilo Globocnik**, the primary architect of the Holocaust in German-occupied Poland. One of Dolp's first tasks was to accompany a march of Jewish forced laborers to work in the city of Biała Podlaska, during which hundreds of Jews died. Globocnik then placed him in charge of organizing the construction of a labor camp on Lipowa Street, Lublin. In the late spring of 1940, Globocnik sent Dolp to supervise the installation of trench-work defenses along the border with the Soviet-occupied part of Poland. It was in this context that he set up forced-labor camps around Bełżec, prior to the establishment of a death camp there in late 1941.

Keen to redeem his reputation, Dolp threw himself into his task with zeal and saw that his orders were carried out ruthlessly. At Bełżec, he was assisted by Franz Bartetzko, the commandant of another forced-labor camp, Trawniki. Dolp was notorious for his cruelty, even sadism, toward the prisoners, as well as his corruption; prisoners assigned to camp workshops were forced to produce everyday items such as clothes and shoes at Dolp's command, after which he was known to sell them on the black market.

After the German attack on the Soviet Union in June 1941, Globocnik sent Dolp as his SS and police (*SS- und Polizeiführer*, or SSPF) representative in Minsk and Mogilev in the occupied Soviet Union, working in the construction of police and SS bases. He remained in the region until May 1942, after which he was sent from May 1942 to August 1943 to serve as commandant of a prisoner-of-war camp at Osen-Elsfjiord, Norway, also overseeing Norwegian forced-labor camps. Until February 1944, he served at SS headquarters in Berlin, following which he became a battalion commander of the Latvian 19th Waffen-SS Grenadier Division. Reestablishing his former rank, on June 21, 1944, he was promoted to *SS-Obersturmbannführer* and Waffen-SS *Obersturmbannführer*.

Hermann Dolp was reported as missing in action, believed killed, in Romania late 1944. His body was never found.

E

EBERL, IRMFRIED (1910–1948)

SS-Obersturmführer Irmfried Eberl was an Austrian psychiatrist and medical director of the *Aktion T-4* euthanasia institutes in Brandenburg and Bernburg. In 1942, he was transferred from *Aktion T-4* to construct and run the Treblinka extermination camp, where he worked from July 11, 1942, until his dismissal on August 26, 1942.

Eberl was born on September 8, 1910, in Bregenz, Austria, the son of Franz Josef Eberl, an engineer and commercial inspector attached to the Technical University in Vienna, and his wife Theresia. Both parents were strong right-wing nationalists.

While still studying medicine at Innsbruck University, Eberl was radicalized in the student fraternity *Germania*, and on December 8, 1931, he joined the Nazi Party. He graduated as a physician in 1933 and earned his medical doctorate in 1934. Trained and practicing as a psychiatrist, Eberl strongly supported the Nazi policy of the mass murder of people with mental disorders as "life unworthy of life" (*Lebensunwertes Leben*).

Eberl worked as an intern between February 20, 1935, and March 8, 1936, but because of his Nazi activities, he could not obtain a government job in Austria. In 1936, he went to Germany and completed several internships, and then during 1937 to 1938, he became a research fellow in Berlin's Main Health Office under the Reich medical leader, **Leonardo Conti**.

On February 1, 1940, at the age of 29, Eberl became the medical director of the T-4 killing center at Brandenburg an der Havel, which was an integral part of the *Aktion T-4* euthanasia program. In a designated killing room, the first trial gassing of around 20 men took place by carbon monoxide poisoning. Eberl was present on this occasion. After this and up to October 1940, some 9,000 people were murdered at Brandenburg. On most occasions, it was the prison doctors who turned on the gas, a task from which Eberl was not exempt. In the fall of 1941, Eberl took over the directorship of the same unit at Bernburg euthanasia center.

After a public outcry against *Aktion T-4* forced its abandonment, the Nazi leadership made the decision to use personnel from the program to murder much large numbers of people in Poland, using variations of the methods used in the T-4 killings. Eberl was among these "specialists," sent first to the extermination camp at Chełmno, followed by assignment to Lublin in January 1942. In both settings, he used his T-4 expertise in killing.

In the spring of 1942, Eberl saw service in the occupied Soviet Union, and in June, he was appointed to construct the death camp at Treblinka and take over its operation. On July 11, 1942, he became the first commandant of Treblinka as part of *Aktion Reinhard*. With the start of the liquidation of the Warsaw ghetto that summer, he hoped to be able to exceed all death counts elsewhere.

At the beginning of August 1942, **Odilo Globocnik**, the SS police leader for Lublin and head of *Aktion Reinhard*, appointed **Christian Wirth**, the first commandant of Bełżec death camp, as inspector of the *Aktion Reinhard* camps. In August 1942, Wirth and Globocnik came to inspect Treblinka and were shocked by what they saw. Dead bodies were everywhere, and conditions in the camp were chaotic. Within days, on August 26, Wirth dismissed Eberl. There were several grounds for the dismissal: not disposing the thousands of bodies effectively; not killing people in an efficient and timely enough manner; and not properly concealing the murders from the local community, as the stench from decomposing bodies was able to be smelled 10 kilometers from the camp.

It was alleged that the problems at Treblinka were caused solely by Eberl's poor management, but there were other problems as well. The gas chambers were operated by a set of diesel engines, which broke down when overworked. Also, there were wildly unrealistic expectations as to Treblinka's ability to "process" the vast number of prisoners being sent to the camp in an ever-increasing number of transports. Wirth took temporary command of Treblinka himself, until **Franz Stangl**, the commandant of Sobibór, was transferred there in September 1942.

There was one further reason for Eberl's dismissal. He had, it was alleged, been part of a criminal ring at the camp that stole the possessions of those they had murdered and then sent them back to their cronies at the Reich Chancellery in Berlin. As plunder was considered property of the state, its appropriation had been expressly forbidden by *SS-Reichsführer* **Heinrich Himmler**, on the basis that such property should have been contributed to the German war effort. Suggestions were made that Eberl gave his true loyalty to Globocnik—who would have preferred the corrupt millions in stolen money to go to him instead—and that this was the real reason for Eberl being fired.

In mid-September 1942, Eberl returned to Bernburg euthanasia center, where he was responsible for further killings in *Aktion 14f13*. From 1944 onward, he served with the Wehrmacht as a military doctor in France, and in April 1945, he was captured by the Americans, who released him in July of that year.

With the war over, Eberl settled back into civilian life as a physician under his own name in Blaubeuren, near Ulm. His wife Ruth died in 1944, and Eberl remarried and had a son in 1947. During the processing of his application for establishment as a general practitioner during the denazification process, the court looked at his work in Bernburg. In January 1948, he was arrested on the charge that he had "insidiously and cruelly killed people as murderers for low motives." Interestingly, he was not charged as one of main perpetrators and key figures in the *Aktion T-4* or *Aktion Reinhard* campaigns or for his role as commandant of Treblinka.

Five weeks after he had been remanded in custody, he committed suicide on February 16, 1948.

EICHMANN, ADOLF (1906–1962)

Adolf Eichmann is one of history's most notorious figures. As Nazi Germany's head of the Gestapo's Department IV B4, he planned and carried out the Nazis' so-called Final Solution—the murder of 6 million Jews in what would become known as the Holocaust.

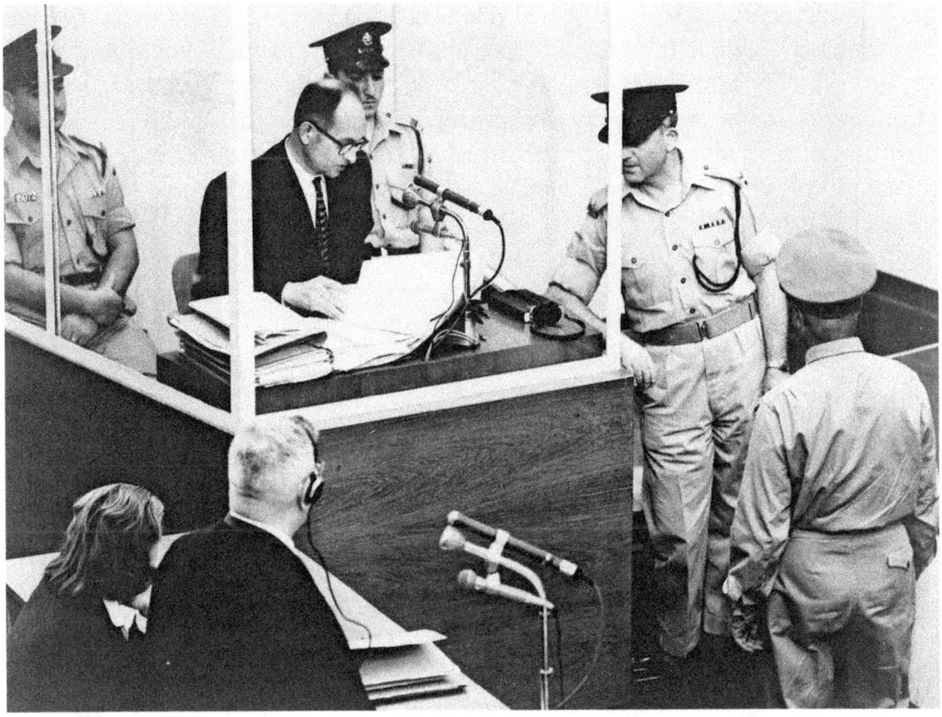

Adolf Eichmann was the head of the Gestapo's Department IV B4, in which he planned and carried out the Nazis' Final Solution of the Jewish Question. Arguably one of the most notorious of all Nazis involved in perpetrating the Holocaust, he is shown here standing trial for crimes against humanity in Jerusalem, Israel, in 1961. (Library of Congress)

Otto Adolf Eichmann was born on March 19, 1906, in Solingen, Germany, near Cologne. He was born into a strongly nationalistic, Calvinist, middle-class Protestant family. His father was an active member of the Evangelical Church, as was Otto Eichmann until 1937. In 1914, the family moved to Linz, Austria, where Eichmann failed to complete his engineering studies. In 1916, Eichmann's mother died, and his father remarried.

In his early life, Eichmann enrolled in the *Wandervogel* youth movement, which had strongly nationalistic ideas about the German homeland. Later, after World War I, he joined the Linz branch of the *Heimschutz,* a paramilitary association of army veterans. After working for a mining company his father owned, he took a sales position with an American company, Vacuum Oil, where he worked from 1927 until 1933. While there, he learned how to identify prime sites at communication junctions, to timetable tasks, to organize deliveries, and to market products.

On April 1, 1932, at the instigation of the son of one of his father's business associates, **Ernst Kaltenbrunner**, Eichmann joined the Austrian Nazi Party and then the Austrian SS. After Eichmann lost his job in 1933, the party was outlawed, and Kaltenbrunner arranged for Eichmann to go to Germany, where he attended an SS training center. He was then sent for further training to an exiled Austrian SS unit for 14 months, before being posted to Dachau concentration camp. In September 1934, he joined the Security Service (SD) of the SS, headed by **Reinhard Heydrich**. Eichmann first worked on files concerning members of the Freemasons, who were also persecuted by the Nazis, but he quickly became an expert on Jewish matters. By the start of 1935, he was the official responsible for all so-called Jewish questions at the Berlin head office of the SD, specializing in collecting information on prominent Jews and the Zionist movement. He learned some Hebrew and Yiddish, and as head of the Scientific Museum of Jewish Affairs of the SD, he briefly visited Palestine in 1937 to explore the possibilities of Jews being transported there from Nazi Germany, which the Nazis encouraged through violence and economic pressure.

After Germany's *Anschluss* with Austria, *SS-Reichsführer* **Heinrich Himmler** chose Eichmann to head the Central Office for Jewish Emigration in Vienna. Eichmann used this to extort Jews who were frantically seeking to escape the Third Reich.

In 1939, Heydrich appointed Eichmann head of the newly created Gestapo Section IV B4 in Berlin, responsible for implementing Jewish policy throughout German-occupied countries during World War II. With the outbreak of war in September 1939, Eichmann directed that Jews be concentrated in ghettos in major cities with the expectation that they would be transported later, either farther east or overseas. He planned initially for a Jewish enclave at Nisko in southeastern Poland, and after early German victories in Western Europe in the summer of 1940, he proposed that Jews be sent either to Nisko or to the island of Madagascar. Neither plan, however, was carried out.

Once Germany attacked the Soviet Union in the summer of 1941, Nazi Jewish policy changed from emigration to extermination. Eichmann sent special killing squads of SS (*Einsatzgruppen*) to begin murdering East European Jews who fell under Nazi control. Even this was not efficient enough, as the troops carrying out these murders were often badly affected by the killings. As a result, on January 20, 1942, Eichmann and Heydrich organized the Wannsee Conference, in which leading Nazi bureaucrats and others discussed the best way to coordinate the mass extermination of all 11 million Jews deemed to be living at Europe at that time. Eichmann served as Heydrich's secretary at the meeting and prepared the minutes. The resultant policy saw the creation of a system of death camps that would process, rob, gas, and cremate tens of thousands of human beings every day.

Eichmann and his staff personally oversaw the massive logistical operation of rounding up, transporting, murdering, and disposing of millions of Jews through the death camps, where the victims were gassed. Seeing himself as an efficient bureaucrat, he complained constantly about delays caused by the lack of zeal in some of the occupied zones. With the German invasion of Hungary in March 1944, Eichmann oversaw the deportation of most of Hungary's Jews. Most were sent to Auschwitz, where around 80 to 90 percent were murdered. The Hungarian transports stopped in July 1944. By that time, 437,000 of Hungary's 725,000 Jews had been killed.

Eichmann continued the work unabated during the final months of the war, when transport and other military resources were desperately needed for the defense of the Third Reich. Toward the end of the war, Eichmann famously said that he would "leap laughing into the grave because the feeling that he had five million people on his conscience would be for him a source of extraordinary satisfaction."

With the end of the war in 1945, Eichmann was arrested and imprisoned by U.S. forces, but he escaped, hiding for a time in Germany. In 1950, he used the Vatican ratline to escape to Argentina, where German expatriates were made to feel welcome. In 1952, he was joined there by his family, and by the mid-1950s, he settled in Buenos Aires, where he worked as a foreman in the local Mercedes-Benz factory.

Revelations from the Nuremberg war crimes trials made Eichmann the most notorious Nazi still at large. Nazi hunters were determined to bring him to justice. In 1959, the Israeli intelligence service, Mossad, learned that Eichmann was living in Buenos Aires under the assumed name of Ricardo Klement. After months of planning, in May 1960, Mossad agents kidnapped, drugged, and smuggled him back to Israel. Despite protests from leading U.S. papers as well as the Argentine government about the breach of Argentine sovereignty, Eichmann went on trial as a war criminal in Jerusalem in 1961.

He was charged on 15 counts: 8 for crimes against the Jewish people, 4 for crimes against other groups, and 1 each for membership in the SS, the SD, and the Gestapo, all of which had been declared illegal organizations at Nuremberg. During his four-month televised trial in the summer of 1961, more than 100 witnesses testified against him. He sat inside a bulletproof-glass booth in the courtroom and did not deny the facts.

Like the other Nazis who preceded him at Nuremberg, he simply claimed he was following orders. He testified, "It was my misfortune to become entangled in these atrocities. However, these misdeeds did not happen according to my wishes. It was not my wish to slay people. The guilt for the mass murder is solely that of the political leaders." The court found him guilty on all 15 counts and sentenced him to death on December 15, 1961. Eichmann was hanged at Israel's Ramleh Prison on May 31, 1962.

EICKE, THEODOR (1892–1843)

Theodor Eicke was integral in establishing concentration camps in Germany, was in charge of the Dachau concentration camp, and headed the SS *Totenkopf* (Death's Head) division of the Waffen-SS.

The son of a stationmaster and the youngest of 11 children, Eicke was born in Hudingen (Hampont) in Alsace-Lorraine (then Germany) on October 17, 1892. At 17, he dropped out of high school. He fought in World War I, rose to subpaymaster, and received the Iron Cross First and Second Class for bravery.

In 1919, Eicke returned to his studies, but lack of money forced him to drop out once more. He served in a local *Freikorps* before entering the police force in Thuringia. In 1920, Eicke qualified as an inspector. He was later briefly employed by the security police, criminal police, and the police administration in Ludwigshafen on the Rhine. However, he lost these positions because of his participation in many violent antigovernment demonstrations. In 1923, Eicke was hired by I. G. Farben as a commercial executive, with responsibility for antiespionage measures.

Theodor Eicke was integral in establishing concentration camps in Germany, as well as heading the third SS Panzer Division *Totenkopf* ("Death's Head") of the Waffen-SS. He was commandant of the Dachau concentration camp in 1933 and 1934, during which he established a regularized form of administration that became known as the Dachau Model and was applied to camps throughout the Third Reich. (ullstein bild/ Getty Images)

Eicke's view of the Weimar Republic was closely aligned with that of the Nazi Party, of which he became a member in 1928. At the same time, he joined the SA, transferring to the SS on July 29, 1930. Eicke rose quickly because he recruited new members and enlarged the SS in Bavaria. In 1931, **Heinrich Himmler** promoted Eicke to the rank of SS colonel.

In early 1932, he was dismissed from I. G. Farben when he was caught in Bavaria preparing bomb attacks on political enemies; for this, he received a two-year prison sentence in July 1932. It was after his dismissal from I. G. Farben that Eicke's full-time service with the SS began. Due to protection received from **Franz Gürtner** (later Nazi minister of justice), Eicke fled to Italy on Himmler's orders. In Italy, at Lake Garda, Eicke ran Himmler's "terrorist training camp for Austrian Nazis," returning to Germany in 1933, less than three months after **Adolf Hitler's** ascent to office.

Following a quarrel with the politician Josef Bürckel, who declared him to be "a dangerous lunatic," Eicke was arrested, placed in a mental asylum for some months, and struck off the SS rolls, but he was released and reconfirmed in his old rank on June 26, 1933.

In March 1933, Himmler established Dachau, describing it as the first concentration camp for political prisoners. Upon Eicke's release from the asylum, Himmler appointed him as the new commandant at Dachau, after the first commandant, *SS-Sturmbannführer* Hilmar Wäckerle, had permitted the murder of several detainees under the guise of "punishment." Eicke served as commandant in 1933 and 1934, setting up regularized concentration camp rules and cautioning guards that they faced discipline if they showed any mercy to the inmates. Dachau's SS motto that "tolerance is a sign of weakness" became a model for the German concentration camp system overall. Eicke's new guarding provisions included rigid obedience to orders as well as tight discipline and punishment regulations for detainees. Prisoners and guards were put into uniforms; the guards' uniforms had a special Death's Head insignia on their collars, from which they took their title as the Death's Head (*Totenkopfverbande*) units. This new administrative system for Dachau was known as *SS-System Eicke* or *Dachauerschule*. In some quarters, it became known as the Dachau Model.

On July 1, 1934, Eicke and a subordinate took a leading role in the Night of the Long Knives, when they shot and killed storm troop (SA) leader Ernst Röhm. Eicke was promoted to inspector of concentration camps and leader of SS guard formations between 1934 and 1939, and the *Dachauershule* rules were standardized throughout all concentration camps in the Reich. Eicke also organized the expansion of the Death's Head units into the Obeybayern, Brandenburg, and Thuringian regiments, and he set up the SS Death's Head for service in Poland in World War II.

In November 1939, Eicke commanded the first *SS-Totenkopf* division (a motorized unit and one of three original Waffen-SS divisions) and personally led it into combat in both France and the Soviet Union. Bloodthirsty, zealous, and aggressively antisemitic, Eicke molded his Death's Head division to his own character, and it went on to become one of the most effective German formations on the Eastern Front. During the war, Eicke's division became known for brutality and war crimes, including the murder of 97 British POWs in Le Paradis, France, in 1940; the murder of captured Soviet soldiers; and the plundering and pillaging of several Soviet villages as part of Army Group North's invasion of the Soviet Union during Operation Barbarossa.

On February 26, 1943, Eicke died when the aircraft in which he was flying was shot down behind Soviet lines in Michailovka, Ukraine.

F

FISCHER, EUGEN (1874–1967)

Eugen Fischer was a German professor of medicine, anthropology, and eugenics, and a member of the Nazi Party, whose ideas on eugenics formed the basis Nuremberg Laws of 1935 and the justification for *Aktion T-4*. His ideas helped to underpin Nazi attitudes of racial superiority.

He was born to a conservative Catholic family on July 5, 1874, in Karlsruhe, southwest Germany. He attended the *Berthold-Gymnasium* in Freiburg, and then he studied medicine and natural sciences at Freiburg University. In 1900, he qualified to teach anatomy and anthropology. Fischer was appointed to professorships at the Universities of Würzburg and Freiburg, and by 1906, he had won the Parisian Anthropological Society's prestigious Broca Award for studies he had conducted on the skull width of Papuans from New Guinea.

In 1908, Fischer undertook a research expedition to study the Rehobother Basters in the German colony of South West Africa, to demonstrate the validity of the Mendelian heredity theory in man. The territory had been taken over by Germany in 1885, and the colonists treated the local Herero and Nama peoples very badly. In 1904, the Herero revolted, and by the time the Germans put down the revolt in 1907, 80 percent of the Herero and 50 percent of the Nama had been murdered. The Rehobother Basters, a mixed-race people from Hottentot women and white male colonists, had settled in the village of Rehoboth in the center of South West Africa.

Fischer concluded that the Basters were racially inferior because of the traits inherited from their nonwhite ancestors. His study also conducted unethical experiments on the Nama and Herero populations. His work concluded with a call to prevent a "mixed race" by the prohibition of mixed marriages such as those he had studied, arguing that the offspring should not continue to reproduce. His deeply flawed and unscientific research was accepted, and his recommendations were followed; by 1912, interracial marriage was prohibited throughout the German colonies. In 1913, Fischer published his field study results under the title *The Rehobother Bastards and the Problem of Miscegenation among Humans*; this was the background for later racial debates and scientific support for the Nuremberg Laws.

Fischer became a leader in eugenics, the political and social movement that sought to improve society by preventing births of "inferior" groups while promoting births of "superior" people. He was appointed professor of anatomy and director of the Anatomical Institute in Freiburg in 1918. In 1921, he and two colleagues (Erwin Baur and Fritz Lenz) published *The Principles of Human Heredity*, a text that became a yardstick in the field of eugenics. In 1924, a copy was presented to

Adolf Hitler, who was in Landsberg Prison for his failed overthrow of the Bavarian government. Hitler embraced Fischer's theories, incorporating them into his manifesto, *Mein Kampf*.

In 1927, Fischer took over as director of anthropology in the newly created Kaiser Wilhelm Institute of Anthropology, Human Heredity, and Eugenics (KWI) in Berlin. At the same time, Otmar Freiherr von Verschuer was appointed as director of the Department of Human Genetics. After the Nazis came to power in 1933, Fischer taught Nazi "racial hygiene" to SS doctors, an elite corps implementing racial policy. The KWI became integral to the development of Nazi biological racism.

In 1933, Fischer signed the Loyalty Oath of German Professors to Adolf Hitler and the National Socialist state, and Hitler appointed him rector of the Frederick William University of Berlin (now Humboldt University).

In 1935, Fischer and his colleagues from KWI and the German Ministry of the Interior discussed the issue of about 600 children in Nazi Germany who were descended from white German mothers and French African soldiers who had been deployed to the Rhineland as a result of the 1919 Versailles Treaty after World War I. Fischer's work on mixed races in South West Africa was discussed, and Fischer advocated drastic measures to prevent the destruction of the superior Aryan race of pure-blooded Germans. In 1937, his call to sterilize these mixed-race children was implemented, and the children were brought into custody. While most were involuntarily sterilized, some were also sent for medical experimentation, and many died from these surgical procedures and subsequent infections.

Fischer put forth his view that natural reproduction was subject to economic constraints and that, for the health of the nation and the future, a "rationalization of births" was necessary. The Hadamar Clinic, a mental hospital in Hadamar, Germany, was used by the Nazi government as the site of *Aktion T-4*, the Nazi euthanasia program for the "incurably sick," which was strongly associated with eugenics and the racial-hygiene theories put forward by Lenz and Fischer and by its director, Otmar von Verschuer.

In June 1939, Fischer spoke to Ruhr coal magnates regarding the forthcoming war. To promote the goals of Nazism, he emphasized the danger of Jews and Africans, and he called for the magnates' support to protect the purity of the German race.

Fischer officially joined the Nazi Party in 1940. He developed the physical descriptions used to dictate racial origins, creating the so-called Fischer-Saller scale. He and his team experimented on Roma and African Germans, taking blood and measuring skulls to find scientific validation for his theories. In 1940, Fischer decided to publish a book on his personal antisemitic philosophy. To supplement the text with images, he sent his assistant to the newly established Łódź ghetto to photograph the Jewish residents there.

As Germany continued the mass murder of Jews during the invasion of the Soviet Union through the late summer and spring of 1941, Fischer was the guest speaker at the inaugural meeting of the Institute for Research on the Jewish Question. The agenda focused on the annihilation of European Jews, and the discussions concluded that the "total solution to the Jewish question" was extermination through forced labor.

Fischer retired as rector of the Frederick William University of Berlin in 1942. Shortly afterward, he received a huge grant to study twins and to determine the importance of heredity over environment. He appointed his protégé, von Verschuer, to lead the study. Newly appointed as director at KWI, Verschuer engaged his former graduate student **Josef Mengele** to continue the twin research. Mengele was sent to Auschwitz-Birkenau in May 1943 and there conducted pseudoscientific experiments on Jewish and Roma twins and dwarves.

In June 1944, Fischer chaired the Anti-Jewish Congress in Kraków, Poland.

Shortly after the war ended, Fischer was denazified; he returned to Freiberg University, and in 1952, he was appointed honorary president of the German Anthropological Society. He was not prosecuted as a war criminal. To avoid publicizing German medical atrocities and the public finding that the entire medical community could no longer be trusted, the Nuremberg Doctors' Trial presented medical researchers as having been "perverted" by the manipulative control of the SS and as poisoned by Nazism. It was also alleged that the human experiments were so ill conceived as not to be worthy of the status of science. Therefore, it was concluded that the ties of the German medical community—especially those at Kaiser Wilhelm Institutes—were not in any way associated with the death camps. The SS and medical personnel, such as Mengele, who were directly involved with the death camps were identified as those most responsible for the atrocities of National Socialism.

After the war, Eugen Fischer completed his memoirs, which concealed his role as the justifier of the genocidal program of the Third Reich. He died in Freiburg, on July 9, 1967.

FRANK, HANS (1900–1946)

Hans Frank, a German lawyer who worked for the Nazi Party during the 1920s and 1930s and became **Adolf Hitler's** personal lawyer, served as governor-general of occupied Poland and later earned the nickname the "Butcher of Poland."

Hans Michael Frank was born on May 23, 1900, in Karlsruhe, to Karl and Magdalena Frank. After completing high school, in 1917, he enlisted in the German army, too late to experience extensive combat. In 1919 and 1920, he served in the occultist Thule Society, a rightist group focused on ancient German culture. Frank also served also in the *Freikorps* under Franz Ritter von Epp, which battled communists and other "enemies of Germany." From this base, Frank took part in the defeat by the *Freikorps* of the communist Munich Republic on May 3, 1919.

In 1919, together with other members of the Thule Society, he joined the German Workers' Party (DAP), which soon mutated into the NSDAP. In September 1923, Frank became a member of the *Sturmabteilung* (SA); a month later, he joined the NSDAP. Frank took part in the Beer Hall Putsch of November 1923, an unsuccessful coup intended to serve the same function as Benito Mussolini's March on Rome. When this failed, Frank fled to Austria, returning in Munich in 1924, after the Bavarian government shelved pending charges upon Adolf Hitler's imprisonment in Landsberg Prison.

Frank had been studying law and passed his final state examination in 1926. He quickly developed an important profile in the NSDAP because of his legal skills and commitment to party ideals. In 1928, he founded the National Association of German Jurists, with himself as president. As the Nazis rose to power, he became Adolf Hitler's personal legal adviser. He also served as the party's lawyer, representing it in over 2,400 cases. In September to October 1930, he served as the defense attorney at the court-martial in Leipzig of three army officers charged with membership in the NSDAP. The trial was a media sensation. Hitler testified in person; the defense successfully put the Weimar Republic itself on trial. Many army officers were sympathetic to the NSDAP as a result.

Also in 1930, Frank was elected to the Reichstag. After Hitler's ascent to office as chancellor on January 30, 1933, Frank was appointed minister of justice for Bavaria, at the same time becoming president of the Academy of German Law. Frank's adherence to the law and its proper implementation found him initially at odds with Hitler, as Frank opposed not only the extrajudicial murders at Dachau concentration camp but, more importantly, Hitler's elimination of rivals, including Ernst Röhm, during the Night of the Long Knives, from June 30 to July 2, 1934.

Germany invaded Poland on September 1, 1939, and the country was split into three sectors. The western third was annexed directly to the Third Reich, and the eastern third was taken by the Soviet Union. The central third, of roughly 90,000 square kilometers, was made into the *Generalgouvernement*, a semi-independent administrative unit. On October 26, 1939, following the end of the invasion of Poland, Hans Frank was appointed governor-general of what remained as occupied Poland. As the chief regional administrator, he obtained the cooperation of **Hermann Göring** in economic matters, but the SS, under **Odilo Globocnik**, implemented the murder of Jews. The area became a depot for non-Aryan races providing endless slave labor and a site for mass extermination of European Jews.

The *Generalgouvernement* seemed to offer room for German population growth, but first the Polish nationals and the several million Jews who lived in the area had to be cleared. In a speech on December 16, 1941, Frank said,

> We cannot shoot these 3.5 million Jews, we cannot poison them, but we will take measures that will somehow lead to successful destruction; and this in connection with large-scale procedures which are to be discussed in the Reich, the Government-General must become as free of Jews as the Reich. . . . We must annihilate the Jews wherever we find them and wherever it is at all possible, in order to maintain the whole structure of the Reich.

Frank oversaw the segregation of Jews into ghettos, especially the enormous Warsaw ghetto, and into the Bełżec, Treblinka, Majdanek, and Sobibór extermination camps. Frank was responsible for the exploitation and murder of hundreds of thousands of Polish civilians, including their use of forced labor. Frank administered the destruction of Poland as a national entity with the murder of the country's leaders, educated elite, and clergy, and the extermination of nearly all Poland's Jews.

In 1942, he lost his positions of authority outside the *Generalgouvernement* after annoying Hitler with a series of speeches in Berlin, Vienna, Heidelberg, and Munich that openly criticized SS policies and racial issues. He was also involved in a power struggle with **Friedrich-Wilhelm Krüger**, the head of the SS and the police in the *Generalgouvernement*. Krüger himself was ultimately replaced by **Wilhelm Koppe**. Hitler removed Frank from his NDSAP roles but would not permit him to resign from his rank of governor-general, which Frank retained until he was forced to take flight from the advancing Soviet army.

Fleeing the Allies at the end of the war, Frank was arrested by American troops on May 3, 1945, at Tegernsee, Bavaria. Initially beaten, he twice attempted suicide. He stood trial at Nuremberg before the International Military Tribunal, and as an aid to his defense, he willingly turned over the 43 volumes of his diaries. The charges against him were numerous: he held a position of leadership in the Nazi Party and in the German government; he promoted the seizure of power by the Nazis through his maneuvering in the field of law; as governor-general of Poland, he committed war crimes and crimes against humanity; he advocated and administered a program of exterminating Jews; and he imposed upon the population of the *Generalgouvernement* a reign of terror, oppression, impoverishment, and starvation.

Frank was found guilty on counts three and four (war crimes and crimes against humanity) and was sentenced to death. He was hanged at Nuremberg on October 16, 1946.

FRANZ, KURT (1914–1998)

Kurt Franz was an SS officer known to be a cruel and sadistic commander of the Treblinka extermination camp. He was a major perpetrator of genocide during the Holocaust and one of the many concentration camp officers who were initially part of the *Aktion T-4* euthanasia program.

Kurt Hubert Franz was born on January 17, 1914, into a Catholic family in Düsseldorf. His father, a merchant, died early, and his mother remarried a man with a strong nationalistic outlook. From 1920 to 1928, Franz attended school and then trained as a cook, without completing his final examination. He joined several right-wing nationalist groups and served in the voluntary labor corps.

Franz joined the Nazi Party in 1932. He enlisted in the German army in 1935 and served in the kitchen of an artillery regiment. Discharged in October 1937, he joined the *SS-Totenkopfverbände* (Death's Head unit), training at Weimar. He then started as a cook and guard at nearby Buchenwald concentration camp, where he rose to the rank of *SS-Unterscharführer*.

In late 1939, Franz worked in **Adolf Hitler**'s chancellery. In the later part of 1941, he was assigned to cook at the *Aktion T-4* euthanasia headquarters. On April 20, 1942, he was promoted to *SS-Oberscharführer*, and later that spring, he was posted to Lublin in the *Generalgouvernement*. Sent to the Bełżec extermination camp, where he stayed until the end of August 1942, Franz worked as a cook, at the same time training the Ukrainian guards there.

In September 1942, Franz was transferred to Treblinka extermination camp, where, on the orders of **Christian Wirth**, he became deputy commandant. Franz's initial duties at Treblinka were overseeing work commandos, receiving transports, and moving Jews from the undressing rooms to the gas chambers. He became the main supervisor in day-to-day contact with prisoners at Treblinka and turned out to be the most dreaded guard there because of his brutality.

Franz made his rounds of the camp together with his St. Bernard dog, Barry, who was trained to follow Franz's command. Because of the dog's size, the target area when biting prisoners was invariably their genitalia or buttocks. When Franz was not there to give such orders to the dog, the dog permitted prisoners to pet and even tease him, without harming anyone.

In early 1943, after a selection for the gas chambers, Franz found three babies left by their mothers. It was observed that he lifted one of the children off the ground, kicked him in the air, and watched as his head split against the wall. Franz frequently enjoyed kicking and killing babies from the arriving transports. He especially enjoyed shooting with his pistol or hunting rifle at prisoners or those newly arriving. An expert at flogging prisoners, Franz never hit fewer than 25 or 50 lashes, which he carried out slowly and with great satisfaction.

Franz reviewed the prisoner roll call and took part in meting out the punishments. Once, when 7 prisoners had attempted to escape, Franz had them all shot; he then ordered a roll call and announced that any future attempted escapes would be dealt with by shooting 10 prisoners for every successful escapee.

Franz was also responsible for teaching "the Treblinka song" to those Jews in the *Sonderkommando*—those who were made to work in the crematoria instead of being immediately executed. They were tasked to memorize the entire song by nighttime on their first day at the camp and were ordered to sing the song as new transports were unloading and prisoners were going through the process of undressing.

From August 1943 to November 1943, Franz oversaw the end of *Aktion Reinhard*. During September and October 1943, the Jews did the physical work of dismantling Treblinka; and after this was done, some 30 to 50 were sent to dismantle Sobibór. The rest were shot and cremated on Franz's orders.

In late autumn 1943, Franz was transferred to Trieste as part of a major redeployment on the orders of the primary manager of the three *Aktion Reinhard* death camps (Bełżec, Sobibór, and Treblinka), **Odilo Globocnik**. Shortly after September 8, 1943, Franz, together with Christian Wirth and others, reached Trieste. Under Globocnik, they transformed an old rice mill on the fringe of Trieste into a prison center complete with a crematorium. It was known as Risiera di San Sabba. At San Sabba, thousands of Italian Jews, resistance members, and political dissidents were tortured and then murdered.

Franz was imprisoned by U.S. forces at the end of the war but escaped. Initially, he found work as a laborer until 1949, prior to reverting to his former occupation as a cook. He then worked in Düsseldorf for 10 years, until, on December 2, 1959, he was arrested and imprisoned after a search of his house found a photo album of Treblinka entitled "Beautiful Years."

In 1965, Franz was tried for the crimes he committed at Treblinka. He denied all the charges brought against him. He was found guilty of participating in the murder of at least 300,000 people as well as 35 specific counts of murder and attempted murder and was given a life sentence on September 3, 1965. Released from prison in 1993, he died on July 4, 1998, aged 84, in a senior citizen's home in Wuppertal.

FREISLER, ROLAND (1893–1945)

Roland Freisler was a preeminent lawyer and judge who served as president of the People's Court (*Volksgerichtshof*) in Nazi Germany from August 20, 1942, until his death on February 3, 1945, in Berlin. In this capacity, Freisler headed the show trials used by the Nazis to deal with opponents of the National Socialist regime and political dissent. Acting as judge, jury, and sometimes even as prosecutor, he handed down the death penalty or life imprisonment in 90 percent of all cases that came before him. While he presided over the First Senate of the People's Court, he was responsible for as many death sentences as all other sessions of the court put together for the entire time it existed.

Freisler contributed to the introduction into German law of racial categories and differential treatment based on race. In addition, he was responsible for the first laws allowing for the execution of juveniles in Germany. He was more extreme in his adherence to principles of racial purity than **Adolf Hitler**, arguing for a ban on any sort of mixed-blood intercourse or relationships, no matter how little "foreign blood" might be involved. He represented the Reich Ministry of Justice at the Wannsee Conference in January 1942, when the plans of the Final Solution were outlined.

Freisler was born on October 30, 1893, in Celle, Lower Saxony, and was baptized a Protestant on December 13, 1893. In 1914, he was at law school at the University of Jena when the outbreak of war interrupted his studies. He served as an officer cadet in 1914, and by 1915, he was a lieutenant. He won the Iron Cross First and Second Class for heroism in action. Wounded on the Eastern Front, in October 1915, he was captured by Russian forces. As a prisoner of war, he learned Russian and is reputed to have developed an interest in Marxism following the Russian Revolution. After the war, he returned to Germany with the reputation of being a convinced communist, something he always later denied. His subsequent career as a political official in Germany, however, was overshadowed by rumors about his possible communist past.

In 1919, he resumed his law studies and became a doctor of law in 1922. From 1924, he worked as a solicitor in Kassel. He was also elected a city councilor as a member of the *Völkisch-Sozialer Block*, an extreme nationalist splinter party.

Freisler joined the National Socialist German Workers' Party in July 1925 as part of the movement's left wing and served as defense counsel for party members who were regularly facing prosecutions for acts of political violence. As the Nazis transitioned from a fringe political beer-hall and street-fighting movement into a more formal political entity, Freisler was elected for the party to the Prussian Landtag and later became a member of the Reichstag.

In February 1933, after the Nazi takeover of Germany, Freisler was appointed director of the Prussian Ministry of Justice. He served there from 1933 to 1934 and then in the Reich Ministry of Justice from 1934 to 1942. Known to be interested in the procedures of Andrei Vyshinsky, the chief prosecutor of the Soviet purge trials, Freisler watched Vyshinsky's performances when he had been engaged in Soviet show trials in Moscow in 1938.

In October 1939, Freisler introduced the concept of "precocious juvenile criminal" in the Juvenile Felons Decree. This provided the legal basis for imposing the death penalty and penitentiary terms on juveniles for the first time in German legal history. From the period 1933 to 1945, the Reich's courts sentenced at least 72 German juveniles to death.

Despite Freisler's mastery of legal texts, mental agility, dramatic courtroom verbal dexterity and verbal force, and zealous conversion to National Socialist ideology, Adolf Hitler never appointed him to a government post beyond the legal system. This might have been attributable to the fact of his being politically compromised through family association with his brother Oswald Freisler, who was also a lawyer. Oswald, who had a habit of wearing his Nazi Party membership badge in court, had appeared as the defense counsel in court against the regime's authority several times in its program of increasingly politically driven trials with which it sought to enforce its control of German society. Propaganda minister **Joseph Goebbels** reproved Oswald Freisler and reported his actions to Hitler, who in response ordered Oswald's expulsion from the party. Oswald Freisler committed suicide in 1939.

On January 20, 1942, Freisler, representing the Reich justice minister **Franz Schlegelberger**, attended the Wannsee Conference of senior governmental officials to provide expert legal advice in planning the destruction of European Jewry. Then on August 20, 1942, Hitler named Freisler as president of the People's Court (*Volksgerichtshof*). The court had jurisdiction over a broad array of "political offenses," viewed by Freisler as destruction of the defensive capability of the Nazi state. The accused brought before him were accordingly punished severely, and death penalty was meted out in most cases.

Freisler became infamous for the aggressive way he presided during trials, aiming at total humiliation of the defendants. He became notorious for insulting and abusing defendants in a highly personalized fashion from the bench, often shouting at the steady stream of defendants passing before him on their way to their deaths—particularly in cases of resistance to the authority of Nazi Germany. His speech would become shrill, although in his rages he ensured that he controlled his voice for dramatic purposes, using a mastery of the art of courtroom performance. This practice earned him the nickname "Raving Roland."

The People's Court almost always agreed with the prosecution. In 90 percent of all cases, the court's verdict was the death penalty or a sentence of life in prison. The number of death sentences rose sharply under Freisler's tenure, and being brought before it was equivalent to a death sentence. Under Freisler's management, the *Volksgerichtshof* sent more than 5,000 Germans to their death without a fair trial.

Some *Volksgerichtshof* hearings under Freisler moved at an astonishing pace. In February 1943, he presided over the trial of three Munich University students who belonged to the dissident White Rose group. On February 22, 1943, 21-year-old Sophie Scholl; her 22-year-old brother, Hans Scholl; and 24-year-old Christof Probst were arrested for distributing antiwar leaflets at the university four days earlier. Brought before Freisler, they were tried and found guilty in less than an hour, without evidence being presented or arguments made by either side. The three were guillotined just six hours after their arrest.

Another of Friesler's victims was a Catholic priest, Joseph Müller, who told a political joke. The joke itself did not bring about Müller's conviction. His work with youth raised Nazi ire, as his teachings contradicted Nazi dogma. Throughout the trial, Freisler ranted and raved, even helping witnesses find appropriate words of scorn. He screamed accusations of collusion, hostility, and intentional undermining of the German people's will to carry on the war. Müller was sentenced to death and guillotined on September 11, 1944. His family received a bill for the cost of the execution.

Freisler's most notorious case came in the wake of the failed July 20, 1944, coup attempt against the Nazi regime. The trials began in the People's Court on August 7, 1944, with Freisler presiding. The first eight men accused were Erwin von Witzleben, Erich Hoepner, Paul von Hase, Peter Yorck von Wartenburg, Helmuth Stieff, Robert Bernardis, Friedrich Klausing, and Albrecht von Hagen. All were condemned to death by hanging, and the sentences were carried out at Berlin's Plötzensee prison within two hours of the verdicts being passed.

The way that Freisler humiliated the July 20 coup conspirators in his courtroom—bellowing at them nonstop and denying them the right to wear belts or suspenders so that their trousers fell—prompted even members of Hitler's entourage to recommend that his authority be curtailed. The accused were unable to consult their lawyers, who were not seated near them. None of them could address the court at length, and Freisler interrupted any attempts to do so.

On February 3, 1945, during a Saturday session of the People's Court, American Eighth Air Force bombers attacked Berlin. Government and Nazi Party buildings were hit, including the Reich Chancellery, the Gestapo headquarters, the Party Chancellery, and the People's Court.

According to one report, Freisler adjourned court and ordered that the day's prisoners be taken to a shelter, but he paused to gather files. No one is quite sure how he died. Some witnesses claim that he was crushed to death by falling masonry, while others claim that he bled to death outside of the bombed courthouse. His body was found crushed beneath a fallen masonry column, clutching the files he had retrieved. Among those files was that of Fabian von Schlabrendorff, a July 20 bomb-plot member who was on trial that day and was facing execution. Freisler's death saved Schlabrendorff, who, after the war, became a judge of the Constitutional Court of the Federal Republic of Germany.

Freisler is interred in the plot of his wife's family at the Waldfriedhof Dahlem cemetery in Berlin. His name is not shown on the gravestone.

FRICK, WILHELM (1877–1946)

Wilhelm Frick, a prominent German Nazi politician who served as Reich minister of the interior in **Adolf Hitler**'s cabinet from 1933 to 1943, was responsible for Nazifying Germany during the initial years of the dictatorship by putting in place legislation that implemented Nazi racial policy and removed Jewish citizens from public life, abolished political parties, and sent political dissidents to concentration camps. From August 1943, Frick was also the protector of Bohemia and Moravia.

He was born on March 12, 1877, in Alsenz, Rheinland-Pfalz, the youngest of four children of teacher Wilhelm Frick and his wife Henriette. Frick completed high school in Kaiserslautern in 1896 and studied law between 1896 and 1900 at Göttingen, Munich, Berlin, and Heidelberg, where he received his doctorate in 1901. From 1900, he served as an administrator, and in 1903, he passed the examination for admission to the Bavarian civil service. In 1904, he was appointed as a public prosecutor in the Munich Police Department. In 1910, Frick married Elizabetha Emile Nagel, with whom he had two sons and a daughter. Their marriage ended in an ugly divorce in 1934. He was rejected as unfit for service during World War I.

In 1919, Frick took over the leadership of the Political Police in Munich. Using the powers of his new office to support radical right-wing groups, Frick offered

Wilhelm Frick served as Reich minister of the interior between 1933 and 1943. Particularly in the early years of the Third Reich he laid the foundations for Hitler's dictatorship and oversaw the persecution of political opponents and Jews. In this image, Frick is greeting officers in newly annexed Austria in 1938. (Library of Congress)

members of *Freikorps*, who committed political killings, the opportunity to escape. In February 1923, Frick became head of the Munich Criminal Police. In close contact with Adolf Hitler, he became Hitler's liaison man at Munich Police Headquarters, and on November 8 to 9, 1923, while still director of the Munich Criminal Police, Frick took part in the 1923 Munich Beer Hall Putsch, Hitler's failed effort to seize power. Frick was arrested along with others; tried for treason in 1924, he was sentenced to 15 months' imprisonment and dismissed from his police post. He avoided prison, however, when the far-right National Socialist Freedom Party picked him as a representative to the Reichstag. He was duly elected in May 1924, where he continued to serve from that point onward as leader of the National Socialist group in the assembly.

On January 23, 1930, Frick was appointed as minister of the interior in Thuringia with responsibility for education, and in this capacity, he founded a chair for racial research at the University of Jena. Frick also used his power as the first National Socialist minister in a provincial government to dismiss communist and Social Democratic officials and to rid the Thuringian police force of officials who supported the Weimar Republic, replacing them with Nazis. He proscribed several newspapers, banned the antiwar film *All Quiet on the Western Front*, and forbade the playing of jazz music. Rampant antisemitic propaganda flourished. Frick organized special German freedom prayers to be said in Thuringian schools, which lauded the *Volk*, national honor, and military might while at the same time decried "traitors."

Using his influence as interior minister, Frick granted Hitler German citizenship, applying a law that extended citizenship to anyone appointed to a German official position by naming Hitler as a councilor for the state of Braunschweig. Frick was removed from office by a Social Democratic motion of no confidence in the Thuringian Landtag Parliament on April 1, 1931, but he remained in the Reichstag as a member of the NDSAP.

After Hitler came to power on January 30, 1933, he appointed Frick as minister of the interior, a key position he held until August 1943. In this role, he had direct responsibility for many measures taken against Jews, communists, Social Democrats, and other opponents of the regime. He also had control over drafting and implementing the laws that gradually eliminated Jews from the German economy and public life, culminating in the Nuremberg Laws on Race, which reduced Jews to second-class status. Frick was one of only three Nazis in the original Hitler cabinet; Hitler was chancellor, and **Hermann Göring** was minister without portfolio. Initially Frick had no authority over the police, as law enforcement had been previously a state and local matter.

Frick's power grew owing to his involvement in the Reichstag Fire Decree and the Enabling Act of 1933. Already in July 1933, he had implemented the Law for the Prevention of Hereditarily Diseased Offspring including forced sterilizations, which later culminated in the killings of the *Aktion T-4* euthanasia program supported by his ministry. He was responsible for drafting many of the *Gleichschaltung* (coordination) regulations that consolidated the Nazi regime. Under the Law for the Reconstruction of the Reich, which centralized authority throughout Germany, the state governors became responsible to his office. In 1935, Frick was granted sole power to appoint the mayors of all municipalities with populations greater than 100,000, except for Berlin and Hamburg, where Hitler reserved the right to appoint the mayors.

It was Frick who framed the extraordinary law that declared all Hitler's actions during the Blood Purge of the SA in June 1934 to be legal. Frick was responsible for many of the prewar antisemitic laws, such as the Law for the Restoration of the Professional Civil Service and the Nuremberg Laws of September 1935. Frick took a leading part in Germany's rearmament and drafted laws introducing universal military conscription, both in violation of the Versailles Treaty, and extending the Wehrmacht military-service law to Austria after the 1938 *Anschluss*, as well as to the regions of Czechoslovakia annexed under the Munich Agreement. When the various countries to be incorporated into the Reich were invaded, Frick was placed at the head of the central departments responsible for these incorporations.

From the mid-to-late 1930s, Frick lost favor within the Nazi Party after a power struggle involving attempts to resolve a lack of coordination within the Reich government. For example, in 1933, he tried to restrict the widespread use of protective custody *(Schutzhaft)* orders used to send people to concentration camps, only to be overridden by **Heinrich Himmler**. Although nominally Himmler's superior, Frick failed to impose any legal limitations on the power of the Gestapo and the SS; nor did he seriously interfere with their encroachment on his area of jurisdiction. His power was greatly reduced in 1936, when Hitler named Himmler chief of all German police forces. This effectively united the police with the SS and made it independent of Frick's control, since Himmler was responsible only to Hitler. A long-running power struggle between the two culminated in Frick being replaced by Himmler as interior minister in 1943.

On August 24, 1943, Frick succeeded Himmler when he was appointed *Reichsprotektor* of Bohemia and Moravia, a position he held until the end of the war, although real authority was concentrated in the hands of his subordinate Karl-Hermann Frank. In this role, Frick oversaw and approved the pillaging of the Protectorate, the execution of hostages, and other punishments that took place up until the end of the war. In Prague, Frick used ruthless methods to counter dissent. Frick was captured in May 1945 and tried before the International Military Tribunal at Nuremberg. For his role in formulating the Enabling Act as minister of the interior and the later Nuremberg Laws, he was convicted of planning, initiating, and waging wars of aggression; war crimes; and crimes against humanity. He was also found guilty of crimes against humanity committed in concentration camps in the Protectorate of Bohemia and Moravia. He was sentenced to death and was hanged at Nuremberg on October 16, 1946.

G

GEBHARDT, KARL (1897–1948)

Karl Gebhardt was a German physician who, as the consulting surgeon of the Waffen-SS, ran the Hohenlychen Sanatorium and directed a series of cruel and unethical surgical experiments on concentration camp prisoners at Ravensbrück and Auschwitz.

Karl Franz Gebhardt was born on November 23, 1897, in Haag, Upper Bavaria. He served in the Bavarian infantry in World War I, was wounded in action, and was awarded the Iron Cross First Class; he was also a prisoner of war of the British for a brief period. Gebhardt received his medical degree in 1922 from the University of Munich. In 1923, he joined the *Freikorps Oberland* and took part in the Beer Hall Putsch. In 1924, he interned at the University of Munich's surgical clinic, and upon completing his internship, residency, and postresidency work by 1932, he joined the Nazi Party in 1933.

In 1935, Gebhardt became an associate professor of medicine in Berlin and a member of the SS. He was named superintendent of the Hohenlychen Sanatorium in 1935, transforming it from a tuberculosis clinic to an orthopedic medicine facility. There he established the first sports-medicine clinic in Germany. It also treated amputees and patients with disabilities.

Gebhardt became director of the Medical Department at the Academy for Exercise and Physical Training in 1936 and was the chief physician for the 1936 Berlin Olympics. By this stage, he had built a distinguished career and had published widely in the field of sports medicine. Not coincidentally, he was also interested in aspects of physical therapy.

In 1937, Gebhardt became chair of orthopedic surgery at the University of Berlin. Highly regarded in Germany and beyond, in 1938, he was named personal physician to **Heinrich Himmler** (a friend from his youth), which further cemented his reputation in Germany. He was also appointed president of the German Red Cross.

In 1940, after the onset of war, Gebhardt advertised for an assistant doctor who would take medical care of women prisoners at Ravensbrück concentration camp, and as a result, he appointed Dr. **Herta Oberheuser**.

Also in 1940, Gebhardt served a tour of duty with SS Second Division. On May 27, 1942, Himmler sent Gebhardt to Prague to attend upon **Reinhard Heydrich**, who had been gravely wounded in an assassination attempt. Despite a fever, Heydrich's recovery appeared to progress well. Theodor Morell, Hitler's personal physician, was also sent to Prague and suggested the use of sulfonamide, a new antibacterial drug. Gebhardt disdained the use of sulfonamide, which he considered worthless, thinking Heydrich would make a full recovery without antibiotic use. Heydrich died of sepsis, however, on June 4, 1942.

Gebhardt was accused of failing to treat Heydrich appropriately. To demonstrate his innocence, he commenced a series of bizarre and cruel medical experiments on concentration camp prisoners, chiefly at Ravensbrück and Auschwitz. On July 27, 1942, working with Oberheuser, he brought 75 women prisoners, mostly Polish intelligentsia, for experimentation. There he supervised experiments that saw prisoners' legs or arms broken, usually without anesthetic, to gauge the body's ability to heal itself. Amputations were also carried out, and infections were either introduced into the wounds or allowed to fester to test various drugs to ward off sepsis and gangrene. Nearly all these internees died. Those who survived became lame and hopped because of the experiments; as a result, they were known as the "rabbits."

The Ravensbrück experiments were slanted in Gebhardt's favor; women in the sulfonamide-treated experimental group received little or no nursing care, while those in the untreated control group received better care. Not surprisingly, those in the control group were more likely to survive the experiments. One particularly bizarre experiment involved amputating camp prisoners' limbs and attempting to transplant them onto German soldiers wounded on the Russian front.

Gebhardt treated **Albert Speer** in early 1944 for fatigue and a swollen knee, nearly killing him until he was replaced by another doctor. Gebhardt had permission from Himmler for his vivisection of women at both Ravensbrück and Auschwitz.

After the war, Gebhardt was arrested by Allied authorities and stood in the dock during the Doctors' Trial at Nuremberg along with 22 other doctors, from December 9, 1946, to August 20, 1947. Accused of crimes against humanity and war crimes, he was found guilty and sentenced to death on August 20, 1947. He was hanged on June 2, 1948, in Landsberg Prison.

Gebhardt's assistant, Fritz Fischer, who worked in the hospital at Ravensbrück as a surgical assistant to Gebhardt, was also tried and convicted at Nuremberg. Initially condemned to life imprisonment, Fisher's sentence was reduced to 15 years in 1951. Released in March 1954, he regained his medical license and was employed by the chemical company Boehringer Ingelheim, until his retirement. He died in 2003 at the age of 90.

Herta Oberheuser, another of Gebhardt's assistants at Ravensbrück, was sentenced to 20 years in prison but was released in April 1952 and became a family doctor in Stocksee, Germany. In 1956, a Ravensbrück survivor recognized her, and her medical license was revoked in 1958. She died on January 24, 1978, at the age of 66.

GLOBKE, HANS (1897–1973)

Hans Globke was a Nazi lawyer who helped draft antisemitic laws stripping Jews of their rights. He worked with **Adolf Eichmann** in the SS Department of Jewish Affairs. After the war, he rose to become one of the most powerful figures in the

West German government. Serving as national security adviser to Chancellor Konrad Adenauer, he was the main liaison with the CIA and NATO.

Hans Globke was born on September 10, 1898, in Düsseldorf, into a Roman Catholic family. His father, Josef Globke, was a draper; his mother was named Sophie. When he finished his secondary education at the elite Catholic *Kaiser-Karl-Gymnasium Aachen* in 1916, he was drafted into the army. After World War I, he studied law and political science at the universities of Bonn and Cologne, graduating from the University of Giessen in 1922. Globke finished his assessment examination in 1924, briefly serving as a judge in the police court at Aachen. He became deputy police chief of Aachen in 1925 and a government assessor in 1926. In December 1929, he entered the Prussian civil service and quickly rose through the ranks. During this period, he was a member of the conservative Catholic Center (*Zentrum*) Party.

In November 1932, two months before **Adolf Hitler** became chancellor, Globke wrote a set of rules to make it tougher in Prussia for Germans of Jewish ancestry to change their last names to anything less recognizably Jewish, and he followed this up with guidelines for its implementation the following month. Globke stayed in the civil service after Adolf Hitler came to power.

In 1933, he helped draw up the Enabling Act, the emergency law that gave Hitler total power. Two years later, Globke helped to draft the first two Nuremberg Laws, designed to isolate Jews from the rest of society in the Third Reich by stripping them of their political and civil rights. In 1936, he coauthored with **Wilhelm Stuckart** the highly influential commentary on the 1935 Nuremberg Laws.

Although he thus participated at a high level in the administration of Nazi Germany, his request to join the Nazi Party was turned down because of his former *Zentrum* links. He remained a favored person within the regime, however. Later, Globke created the laws that forced all Jews to take on the names Israel or Sarah and that gave all property belonging to concentration camp victims to the German government. During the war, he helped **Heinrich Himmler** enforce these laws all over occupied Europe.

When the war ended in 1945, American authorities arrested Globke. He was not tried; it was felt he had only enabled the Nazis but was never a Nazi himself. Later, he was a witness during the Nuremberg Trials.

Globke held several administrative posts in West Germany beginning in 1946, and none of the Western Allies protested his nominations. In September 1949, he joined the newly created Chancellery of the Federal Republic, becoming state secretary there in 1953. He acted as the highest adviser to Chancellor Konrad Adenauer and influenced staff recruitment. He was also a key player in establishing the West German security services.

Globke's activities during the Nazi period were criticized by the Social Democratic opposition in Parliament in 1951, 1953, and again in 1955 to 1956, and for that reason, he tried to keep a low profile. Adenauer, on the other hand, had him promoted and even decorated with a high West German order.

Globke's actions during the Nazi period became a major issue in the debate over his guilt. His supporters claimed that Globke had strong links to the anti-Hitler bomb plot of July 20, 1944, and that his legal explanations of the race laws could be viewed as a softened approach to Nazi racial legislation. His opponents accused him of being a leading figure in the persecution of Jews.

In 1960, the East German government, which had access to most of the relevant Nazi files, began a campaign to discredit Globke, even comparing him to Adolf Eichmann. This resulted in his trial in absentia in July 1963, in which the court sentenced him to life imprisonment for war crimes, crimes against humanity, and murder. The final judgment was not accepted by the West German authorities, who at the same time conducted a separate investigation into the case, although without it ever coming to trial.

The debate about Globke's culpability was as much about personal guilt as it was about the reintegration of former Nazi officials into the West German government. Globke resigned his position in October 1963, when Adenauer also resigned, and died on February 2, 1973.

GLOBOCNIK, ODILO (1904–1945)

Odilo Globocnik was a prominent Austrian Nazi official and the primary architect of the Holocaust in German-occupied Poland.

Odilo Lothar Ludwig Globocnik was born on April 21, 1904, in Trieste, then part of the Austro-Hungarian Empire, to an Austrian Slovene family. His father Franz, a Habsburg cavalry lieutenant, did not have enough funds to buy an officer's marriage permit, so he left the service and was given a job in the postal service. His mother was Hungarian, and both grandmothers had German heritage. In 1914, the family left Trieste for Cseklész (modern-day Bernolákovo, Slovakia), and his father was recalled to active duty.

As a teenager, Globocnik joined the pro-Austrian militia fighting the Slovene volunteers and later the Yugoslav army during the Carinthian War, from 1918 to 1919. In 1920, he worked as an underground propagandist for the Austrian cause during the Carinthian plebiscite, later enrolling in a school for mechanical engineering, from which he graduated with honors. During this time, he took on odd jobs, such as carrying suitcases at the train station, to financially support his family.

In 1922, Globocnik became involved in a Nazi-style paramilitary group. Being a building tradesman in Klagenfurt, he joined the Austrian Nazi Party in 1931 and the SS on September 1, 1934. As the Nazi Party was illegal in Austria, he was arrested four times between 1933 and 1935, spending some 11 months in jail. In 1936, he was appointed provincial party leader in Kärnten (Carinthia), and prior to Germany's annexation of Austria in 1938, he formed Nazi cells in various Austrian provinces. He played a pivotal role in the annexation, receiving personal instructions from **Adolf Hitler** at the Reich Chancellery in Berlin.

Hitler rewarded Globocnik by appointing him as gauleiter of Vienna on May 24, 1938. From this base, Globocnik and those in his circle, who distrusted the Catholic Church, launched a crusade against it; they confiscated property, closed Catholic organizations, and sent many priests to the concentration camp at Dachau. Anger at the treatment of the Church in Austria grew quickly, and October 1938 saw the first act of overt mass resistance to the new regime when a rally numbering thousands left Mass in Vienna chanting, "Christ is our Führer," prior to being dispersed by police.

Hermann Göring relieved Globocnik of his post at the end of January 1939, owing to financial irregularities, including foreign-currency speculation, theft of Jewish valuables purloined by the state, and mismanagement of party funds. With his removal as gauleiter of Vienna, Globocnik's career seemed over.

He then enlisted in the Waffen-SS and saw action in the invasion of Poland in September 1939, where he distinguished himself in combat. On November 9, 1939, *SS-Reichsführer* **Heinrich Himmler**, who had always admired Globocnik's loyalty, appointed him SS chief of the Lublin District in the General Government of Poland. Further to Globocnik's responsibilities for Lublin's SS and police matters, in July 1941, Himmler appointed him as his "Plenipotentiary for the Construction of SS and Police bases in the former Soviet areas." His base commanders were Georg Michalsen, Kurt Classen, **Hermann Höfle**, and **Richard Thomalla**. **Hermann Dolp** was also prominent in the construction of these bases at Minsk and Mogilev. Globocnik and these five SS officers would play a leading part in *Aktion Reinhard* one year later.

With the start of the Final Solution during the summer of 1941, Globocnik stated that after the "resettlement" of the Jews in the *Generalgouvernement*, the Polish population from Lublin should be resettled to the East as part of the larger program to move the Slavic nations behind the Ural Mountains and prepare this region for German colonization. This was an important element of what became known as *Generalplan Ost*. This action would be organized first in the Lublin district; German colonists, mainly from Bessarabia and Bukovina, would replace Poles. The Zamość region was chosen by Himmler and Globocnik as a laboratory for the whole of *Generalplan Ost*.

Some 110 villages in the Zamość region were resettled between 1942 and 1943, often accompanied by mass executions. Many villages were destroyed in the course of this action. Approximately 50,000 Poles were deported to the transit camps in Zwierzyniec and Zamość. From these, they were sent to Auschwitz, Majdanek, and labor camps in Germany. Thousands escaped to the forests, and the economy of the Lublin district totally collapsed.

Globocnik's role in Lublin and his key role in supervising the *Aktion Reinhard* death camps in addition to *Generalplan Ost* created conflict between him and Ernst Zörner, the civil governor of the Lublin district. The Polish underground started to resist Globocnik's resettlement plan; Zörner pressured the SS authorities to stop the resettlement of Poles, arguing that because of large-scale resistance, industrial sabotage, and mass escapes of Polish peasants from the villages, the plan was not working. Governor **Hans Frank** reported his concerns to Berlin, and Himmler issued an order to stop the resettlement action. As *Aktion Reinhard* had to be completed, Globocnik was left alone.

At a meeting with Himmler on October 13, 1941, Globocnik proposed exterminating the Jews in assembly-line fashion in a concentration camp utilizing gas chambers. The next day, Himmler held a five-hour meeting with **Reinhard**

Heydrich to discuss "executions," following which several extermination-camp gassing sites were developed or proposed. Days later, Himmler forbade all further Jewish emigration from Reich territory in view of the forthcoming Final Solution of the Jewish Question.

Globocnik implemented the Final Solution between 1941 and 1945. He supervised the final liquidation of the ghettos and, carrying out Himmler's orders, oversaw the construction and management of three *Aktion Reinhard* death camps—Bełżec (1941), Sobibór (1942), and Treblinka (1942)—where Jews from all over Europe were murdered. Not only did *Aktion Reinhard* kill at least 1.7 million Jews, but it also provided stolen assets, valuables, and removable property amounting to 178 million Reichsmarks.

Appointed by Himmler as head of the SS firm OSTI (*Ostindustrie GmbH*), Globocnik created a small army of Jewish slave laborers. Of these, 45,000 were forced into labor camps like Trawniki and Poniatowa to perform all sorts of manual labor under the most horrific conditions. Globocnik was also responsible for a network of work camps in the Lublin district, including another extermination site, Majdanek.

Following the completion of *Aktion Reinhard* and the cessation of the *Generalplan Ost*, in September 1943, Globocnik was ordered to Trieste to serve as the local SS leader and police commissioner in the portion of Italy still controlled by German forces. There he led the persecution of partisans and Jews in Istria (northern Italy and the northern Adriatic coast).

In October 1944, Globocnik married Lore Peterschinegg, head of the Carinthian *Bund deutscher Mädel* (League of German Girls).

At the end of the war, Globocnik fled into the Alpine highlands but was apprehended by British forces on May 31, 1945, near Paternion, Austria. After a brief interrogation, he committed suicide by poison at 11.30 a.m. the same day, by biting into a hidden cyanide capsule. Overall, it is estimated that Globocnik was directly responsible for the deaths of as many as 1.5 million Jews.

GLÜCKS, RICHARD (1889–1945)

Richard Glücks was a high-ranking Nazi official in the SS. From November 1939 until the end of World War II, he oversaw the Inspectorate of Concentration Camps (*Amt D: Konzentrationslagerwesen*) under the SS Main Economic and Administrative Office (*SS-Wirtschafts- und Verwaltungshauptamt*, or WVHA).

The son of a fire-insurance agent, Glücks was born on April 22, 1889, in Odenkirchen, in the Rhineland. After completing his secondary education in Düsseldorf, he worked in his father's business, leaving to become a volunteer in the German army artillery in 1909. In 1913, he visited the United Kingdom before moving to Argentina as a trader, but when World War I broke out, he returned to Germany on a Norwegian ship to rejoin the army in January 1915. He was given command of an artillery unit. Glücks was awarded the Iron Cross First and Second Class, and after the war, he served in the Westphalian *Freikorps*, from 1919 to 1920. In March 1920, Glücks became a liaison officer between the German forces and the

Military Inter-Allied Commission of Control, the organization that regulated the restrictions regarding military rearmament laid down by the Treaty of Versailles. Glücks stayed in that role until 1924, when he joined the staff of the Sixth Prussian Division.

On March 1, 1930, Glücks joined the NSDAP, and on November 16, 1932, he moved into the SS. He rose through the ranks to command his own SS unit, and on April 1, 1936, he became chief of staff to **Theodor Eicke**, who was then inspector of concentration camps. Eicke moved on to become field commander of the Death's Head SS division in 1939, and on November 15, 1939, **Heinrich Himmler** promoted him to be the new inspector of concentration camps. Glücks reported to Himmler, but as Glücks had never served inside a concentration camp, he gave his camp commanders more autonomy in operating their respective commands. Glücks looked at the use of forced labor in the concentration camps, urged commandants to lower the death rate as it went counter to his department's economic objectives, and ordered that inmates be made to work continuously.

On February 21, 1940, Glücks recommended to Himmler and **Reinhard Heydrich** that Auschwitz, a former Austrian cavalry barracks in Poland, was a suitable site for a new concentration camp. On March 1, 1941, he accompanied Himmler and senior directors of the I. G. Farben industrial conglomerate on a visit to Auschwitz, where they decided to expand the camp to accommodate up to 30,000 prisoners, establish an additional camp at Birkenau capable of housing 100,000 POWs, and construct a factory; this facility and its camp prisoners would then be placed together with the camp prisoners for the use of I. G. Farben. By May 1940, under Glücks's orders, **Rudolf Hoess**, the first commandant of Auschwitz, commenced construction of the Auschwitz complex.

Days after the Wannsee Conference in January 1942, Glücks started to implement the Final Solution. Himmler ordered Glücks to prepare his camps to take 100,000 Jewish men and 50,000 women being deported from the Reich to augment the Soviet prisoners as forced laborers. In July 1942, he met with Himmler to plan medical experiments on camp inmates. From his visits to Auschwitz, Glücks knew of the mass murders and atrocities happening there, and Hoess routinely reported to Glücks on the status of the extermination activities.

In 1942, the entire concentration camp system moved under the authority of **Oswald Pohl** to the WVHA, with the inspectorate now reporting to that department. Glücks continued to manage the camp administration until the end of the war. In January 1945, he was decorated for his contributions to the Reich in managing the 15 largest camps and the 500 satellite camps, which employed upward of 40,000 members of the SS. Glücks, together with Pohl, managed the entire Nazi camp system. All written and oral extermination orders were transmitted by Heinrich Himmler through Pohl and Glücks, to be passed on to the various concentration camp commanders. Not only did Glücks exercise full control over the medical services at Auschwitz and other camps, as he was responsible for the SS doctors who made the selections for extermination, but also he decided, together with Himmler and Pohl, how many Jewish deportees should be liquidated and how many spared for hard labor.

The WVHA offices in Berlin were destroyed by Allied bombing on April 16, 1945. With the advance of the Red Army forces, Glücks and his wife, Alice, fled to Flensburg, where they were captured by the British. There has been ongoing discussion regarding his fate, but the consensus is that he committed suicide on May 10, 1945, by swallowing a cyanide capsule.

GOEBBELS, JOSEPH (1897–1945)

Joseph Goebbels was a leading Nazi politician who became the Nazi Party's minister for propaganda and public enlightenment. Serving from 1933 until 1945, Goebbels ran **Adolf Hitler**'s propaganda efforts. His ministry used modern media—including film, radio, and the press—to create a cult around Hitler and spread the Nazi message abroad. Goebbels organized the notorious Nuremberg Party Rallies that began in 1929 and was also the impetus behind the *Kristallnacht* pogrom of November 9 to 10, 1938, during which Jewish businesses and synagogues were destroyed and thousands of Jews were sent to concentration camps. One of Hitler's closest and most devoted followers, Goebbels was known for his deep, virulent antisemitism. Goebbels remained dedicated to Hitler even after the war turned against Germany. Following Hitler's suicide, Goebbels served as chancellor of Germany for a single day before he and his wife, Magda, poisoned their six children and took their own lives.

Joseph Goebbels was a master propagandist and orator who served as Nazi Germany's first and only minister for Propaganda and Public Enlightenment across the duration of the regime between 1933 and 1945. One of Adolf Hitler's closest and most devoted followers, he was known for his deep, virulent antisemitism. Following Hitler's suicide, Goebbels served as chancellor of Germany for a single day; then he and his wife, Magda, poisoned their six children and took their own lives. (Library of Congress)

Paul Joseph Goebbels was born on October 29, 1897, in Rheydt, in the German Rhineland, into a strict middle-class Catholic family. He was the son of Fritz Goebbels, a bookkeeper in a factory, and his wife Maria. As he was a bright student, his parents hoped that he would study for the priesthood. In 1914, Goebbels was unable to join the German army because he was less than five feet tall and had a bad limp from a congenital foot deformity and a bone operation as a child. Instead, he served with a Patriotic Help Unit in his hometown. Goebbels completed his education at a Christian gymnasium, completing his university entrance examination in 1916. Goebbels would say later that his limp resulted from a wound suffered while fighting in the war.

After the war, instead of joining the clergy, Goebbels studied German literature and attended several universities, including Bonn, Freiburg, Würzburg, and Munich. During his college years, he fell away from his Catholic faith. In 1921, he earned his doctorate from Heidelberg University. His doctoral supervisor, Max Freiherr von Waldberg, was Jewish; in April 1933, he would be forced to resign from Heidelberg University owing to his non-Aryan status under the Third Reich's Civil Service Law.

After completing his doctorate, Goebbels embarked on a 10-year literary career writing novels, plays, and poems. His first novel, *Michael: Ein Deutsches Schiksal* (*Michael: A German Destiny*), based on his experiences at university, was not published until 1929, when the Nazi Party's publisher accepted it. Goebbels developed the theory that his works remained unpublished because the publishing companies were owned by Jews. By this stage a rabid antisemite, in 1922, he joined the emerging National Socialist German Workers' Party and was given the initial task of organizing the party's youth. When he tried to find steady work after university, he was rejected as a reporter by the newspaper *Berliner Tageblatt*. In 1924, he gave up trying to work in journalism and entered politics.

Goebbels's sharp intelligence, his gift of oratory, his flair for theatrical effects, his reckless pragmatism, and his revolutionary dogma flourished in service to the party. Over the following few years, Goebbels was an active Nazi and met Hitler upon his release from jail in 1925. In prison, Hitler made plans to restructure the party and appointed Goebbels in 1929 to manage the NSDAP in the Rhineland, where he was also to act as secretary to prominent Nazi Gregor Strasser.

In October 1926, Goebbels was promoted to district commissioner (*Gaulieter*) for Berlin. He reorganized the Berlin branch of the party and built its weekly newspaper, *Der Angriff*, into a strong political weapon promoting German nationalism and opposing the ruling Weimar government. Goebbels attacked Berlin's Jewish police chief, Bernhard Weiss, launching a heavy propaganda campaign against him. When he was informed by a friend that Weiss was a loyal German with an exemplary military record, Goebbels commented that he had nothing against Weiss and that the attacks were run to put the Nazis constantly in the national spotlight.

In 1928, Goebbels, **Hermann Göring**, and 10 other Nazis were elected to the Reichstag. Goebbels became the party's head of propaganda. Over the next years, he ran the NSDAP electoral strategy. When Adolf Hitler became chancellor in January 1933, he appointed Goebbels as minister for public enlightenment and propaganda, which was the vehicle for Goebbels to show his true propaganda skills.

On May 1, 1933, Goebbels organized a massive parade on what was designated the Day of National Labor, an event that marked the end of the German trade-union movement. On May 10, 1933, he then supervised the burning of 20,000 books written by Jewish or anti-Nazi authors. As minister for public enlightenment and propaganda, Goebbels began to control all cultural aspects of German life—including art, music, literature, and mass media—which resulted in a mass flight of Jewish artists and authors. Before long, the contents of all of Germany's newspapers, books, novels, plays, and films were subjected to the ministry's control. His large budget enabled Goebbels to bribe artists to cooperate with Nazi Party policies and threaten with violence those who did not. It was Goebbels's strategy that by controlling art, literature, and other forms of German culture, he could bring about a spiritual mobilization of the German people.

Goebbels used publicity and marketing ideas in the political realm, bringing out eye-catching slogans and psychology into political advertising. His propaganda posters were designed to include bright-red ink and a large typeface for attention-grabbing headlines, and his innumerable rallies generated immense support for the regime—as well as instilled fear among the Jewish population.

Goebbels controlled what was seen in the cinemas. *Hitlerjunge Quex*, made in 1933, told the story of a German boy brought up in a communist family who broke away from his background, joined the Hitler Youth, and was murdered by communists for doing so. *The Eternal Jew* was a film denigrating the Jews, comparing them to rats spreading disease. Goebbels ordered that many comedies should be made to give Germany a "lighter" look so that the cinemas were not just full of serious films with a political message.

Goebbels adapted modern media for propaganda purposes with masterly skill. To make sure that every German could hear Hitler speak, he organized the sale of cheap radios called the People's Receivers, which cost only 76 Reichsmarks. There was also a smaller version costing just 35 Reichsmarks. If Hitler was to give speeches, Goebbels reasoned, every German should be able to hear him. Loudspeakers were put up in streets so that people could not avoid the Führer's words, and cafés and bars were ordered to broadcast Hitler's public speeches.

Goebbels himself detailed his own role in the Nazi rise to power in two books: *Der Kampf um Berlin* (*The Struggle for Berlin*), published in 1932, and *Vom Kaiserhof zur Reichskanzlei* (*From Kaiserhof to the Reich Chancellery*), in 1934. His unpublished diary covering the years 1942 to 1943 was discovered among his papers after his death and published in 1948.

On February 18, 1943, Goebbels delivered a "total war" speech at the Sports Palace in Berlin, urging Germans to devote themselves entirely to the German war effort and warning that a German defeat would mean the destruction of Western civilization at the hands of Jews and communists. Goebbels was a supporter of sending Jews to concentration camps and ghettos to the East, and he pushed for Jews in his jurisdiction, Berlin, to be sent first. On July 25, 1944, Hitler designated Goebbels as the Reich plenipotentiary for total war.

A womanizer, Goebbels's reprehensible private life endangered his status in the party. In 1931, in a Protestant ceremony, Goebbels married Magda Quandt, with whom he would later have six children. Notwithstanding the marriage, he had several affairs, the behavior that angered Hitler and undermined Goebbels's standing.

After World War II started in 1939, Goebbels attempted to influence Hitler's war strategy, but while Hitler acknowledged Goebbels's work as propaganda minister, he disregarded his military advice and excluded him from assisting in the war effort. Despite this slight, Goebbels continued to strongly support the party, even after war turned against Germany. Goebbels remained the party's main propaganda voice until the war's end.

By 1945, the Nazi war machine had been destroyed on the Eastern Front, and the Reich was doomed. In the final days of the war, Goebbels moved his wife, Magda, and their six children into Hitler's bunker in Berlin. Hitler's final act as German leader, before he killed himself, was to appoint Goebbels to the office of Reich chancellor. On May 1, 1945, with the soldiers of the Red Army surrounding Berlin, Goebbels helped his wife to poison their children and then shot her before committing suicide.

GOETH, AMON (1908–1946)

Amon Goeth was an Austrian Nazi officer who was commandant of the Kraków-Płaszów concentration camp in German-occupied Poland for most of the camp's existence during World War II. Decades after his execution in 1946 for war crimes, Goeth became infamous as an icon of Nazi evil after his depiction in Stephen Spielberg's film *Schindler's List* (1993), the story of Oskar Schindler, the industrialist who shielded over 1,000 Jews during the Holocaust.

Amon Leopold Goeth was born on December 11, 1908, in Vienna, Austria, to a wealthy book-publishing family. In 1926, he joined an Austrian Nazi youth group while studying agriculture in Vienna. He was a member of the antisemitic paramilitary *Heimwehr* (Home Guard) from 1927 to 1930, abandoning them to join the Austrian branch of the Nazi Party and the SS in September 1930. From 1928 until 1939, he was employed by a military and technical book publisher in Vienna.

On June 19, 1933, the Austrian Nazi Party was declared illegal. Operating in exile from Munich, Goeth couriered radios and weapons on behalf of the party into Austria. Arrested by the authorities, he was released in December 1933 for lack of evidence. He was arrested again after Austrian chancellor Engelbert Dollfuss was assassinated in July 1934 in a failed Nazi coup.

While living in Munich, Goeth suspended his SS and Nazi Party activities until 1937, instead helping his parents to develop their publishing business. In 1938, he married Anny Geiger; their child Paul was born in 1939 but died within a few months. They had another son, Werner, in 1940 and a daughter, Ingeborg, in 1941. Even though the family maintained a permanent home in Vienna throughout World War II, Goeth later separated from his wife and started a relationship with a beautician, Ruth Irene Kalder, with whom he had a daughter, Monika.

On March 5, 1940, he was drafted into the Wehrmacht, with the rank of *Unterfeldwebel*. Later the same year, he transferred into the SS and was promoted to *SS-Obersturmführer*.

After serving at Teschen (Cieszyn) and Kattowitz (Katowice), Goeth was transferred to **Odilo Globocnick**'s staff in Lublin in June 1942 to participate in Jewish deportations. Little is known of the six-month period he served during *Aktion Reinhard*, although transcripts of his later trial indicate that he was responsible for rounding up and transporting Jews to be murdered. Goeth also played a leading role in the destruction of a number of Jewish ghettos, including Rzeszów in 1942, from where the Jews were deported to the death camp at Bełżec.

After conflict with *SS-Sturmbannführer* **Hermann Höfle**, Globocnik's chief of staff for *Aktion Reinhard*, Goeth was instructed in early 1943 to build a new camp at Płaszów employing forced labor, which he would command after it had been built. Goeth served at Kraków-Płaszów from February 11, 1943, until September 13, 1944.

The site chosen for this *Arbeitslager* (labor camp) was the Jewish cemetery on the outskirts of Lublin. Huts were constructed in desecration of the freshly dug graves, gravestones were crushed to form an access road, and, within one month, the new camp was ready. On March 13, 1943, the Kraków ghetto was liquidated, and several thousands of people not deemed fit for work were sent to extermination camps to be murdered. During the liquidation of the ghetto, Goeth personally shot some 50 children, while hundreds of people were murdered on the streets. Survivors were sent to the camp at Płaszów.

Goeth created a regime of terror in which torture and murder were the order of the day. His behavior was, to some extent, conditioned by excessive alcohol consumption and lack of sleep, but there was more to it than that. His two dogs were trained to attack Jews, and almost daily, he killed prisoners as his cruelty took on an increasingly ominous character. Over time, it seemed, he became more ruthless and unpredictable.

Oskar Schindler's enamelware factory, staffed with Jewish slave labor, was moved adjacent to Płaszów after the liquidation of the ghetto. He skillfully worked on Goeth to ensure that his workers survived the brutal regime the commandant had created. In time, Goeth permitted Schindler to move his workers to quarters outside the camp, where their odds for survival improved.

On September 3, 1943, in addition to his duties at Płaszów, Goeth took charge of the liquidation of the ghetto at Tarnów, which had been home to 25,000 Jews at the start of World War II. During the liquidation, Goeth confiscated for himself Jewish property, furniture, furs, clothing, jewelry, tobacco, and alcohol, which were later found by the Gestapo in storage at Brunnlitz (Brněnec). Ten thousand Tarnów Jews were deported to Płaszów, and 4,000 were killed. The 8,000 Jews who remained were loaded onto a train for Auschwitz, but less than half survived the journey; most of them were deemed unsuitable for forced labor and were murdered immediately on their arrival at Auschwitz.

Goeth also supervised the closure of the forced-labor camp in Szebnie near Jaslo. The liquidation began on September 21, 1943, with the killing of 700 Jewish prisoners, who were driven in trucks to a forest in Tarnowiec, where they were shot at Goeth's command. Under the leadership of *SS-Sturmbahnführer* Wilhelm Haase, Goeth also prepared plans for the liquidation of ghettos in Bochnia and Przemyśl.

By April 1944, Goeth had been promoted to *SS-Hauptsturmführer* and was appointed a reserve officer of the Waffen-SS. In early 1944, the status of the Kraków-Płaszów labor camp changed to a permanent concentration camp under the direct authority of the *SS-Wirtschafts- und Verwaltungshauptamt* (SS Main Economic and

Administrative Office, or WVHA). Concentration camps were more closely monitored by the SS than labor camps, so conditions improved slightly when the designation was changed.

On September 13, 1944, Goeth was arrested in Kraków by the SS and charged with theft of Jewish property (which belonged to the state, according to Nazi legislation); failure to provide adequate food for the prisoners under his charge; violation of concentration camp regulations regarding the treatment and punishment of prisoners; and allowing unauthorized access to camp personnel records by prisoners and noncommissioned officers for the purpose of large-scale fraud. He was also interrogated by the *Sicherheitspolizei* (Security Police, or SiPo) for passing on unauthorized information to a civilian named Grunberg about the liquidation of the Kraków ghetto. Grunberg, a German sympathetic to the Jews, passed the information on to Oskar Schindler, who in turn warned the ghetto leaders.

Moreover, Goeth could not explain where the 80,000 Reichsmarks that were found in his villa came from. He was dismissed from his position, but due to the war situation and Germany's looming defeat, the charges against him were dropped in early 1945. SS doctors then diagnosed him as suffering from mental illness, and he was committed to a sanitorium in Bad Tölz, where he was arrested by the U.S. military in May 1945.

The Americans agreed to a request by Polish authorities to extradite Goeth to Poland, where he was tried before the Supreme National Tribunal on charges of committing mass murder during the liquidations of the ghettos in Kraków and Tarnów and of the camps at Płaszów and Szebnie. He was found guilty of personally ordering the imprisonment, torture, and extermination of individuals and groups of people. He was also convicted of homicide, the first such conviction at a war crimes trial, for "personally killing, maiming and torturing a substantial, albeit unidentified number of people."

Amon Goeth was sentenced to death in Kraków on September 5, 1946. He was hanged in the former camp at Płaszów on September 13, 1946.

GÖRING, HERMANN (1893–1946)

Hermann Göring was a German political and military leader as well as one of the most powerful figures in the Nazi Party. A World War I fighter-pilot ace, he received the *Pour le Mérite*. In World War II, he became an air force marshal and head of the Luftwaffe. **Adolf Hitler** appointed Göring as his second in charge and successor. Göring played a pivotal role in German foreign policy regarding Austria and Czechoslovakia, in implementing the Holocaust against Europe's Jews, and in plundering the art and valuables of occupied Europe.

Hermann Wilhelm Göring was born on January 12, 1893, in Rosenheim, Bavaria, to a former cavalry officer and judge, Heinrich Ernst Göring. His father, who had been the first governor-general of German South West Africa, had five children from a prior marriage; Hermann was the fourth of five other children by Heinrich's second wife, Franziska Tiefenbrunn. When Göring was born, his father was

As commander in chief of the Luftwaffe, Hermann Göring was one of the most powerful figures in the Nazi Party. He played a pivotal role in crafting German foreign policy regarding Austria and Czechoslovakia, in implementing the Holocaust against Europe's Jews, and in plundering the art and valuables of occupied Europe. Tried and sentenced to death at Nuremberg, he committed suicide by swallowing a cyanide pill just two hours prior to his planned execution. (Library of Congress)

German consul general in Haiti; his mother returned to Bavaria only to give birth and then left her six-week-old baby for three years. She only saw her son again when the family returned to Germany in 1896.

Hermann Göring's godfather, Dr. Hermann Epenstein, was a wealthy half-Jewish physician, army doctor, and businessman. Franziska Göring was Epenstein's mistress, and in 1894, Epenstein restored a ruined castle, Mauterndorf, in Salzburg, Austria. Hermann Göring considered this as the castle of his youth. In 1897, Epenstein bought the large Burg Veldenstein castle north of Nuremberg, and the Göring family moved there.

Göring was interested in a career as a soldier from a very early age. He became a mountaineer and scaled Mont Blanc as well as German and Austrian mountains. At 16, he entered officers' training school at Gross Lichterfelde, Berlin, graduating with distinction. In 1912, he was commissioned in the Prince Wilhelm Regiment (112th Infantry) of the Prussian army.

When World War I broke out in August 1914, Göring served around Mülhausen, a garrison town close to the French frontier. In 1915, he was hospitalized with rheumatism, a result of damp trench warfare. While recovering, his friend Bruno Loerzer urged him to transfer to the air corps of the German army. Göring's initial request was rejected, but by 1916, he was accepted and sent for pilot training. Seriously wounded in aerial combat, he took nearly a year to recover and was awarded the Iron Cross First Class. On July 7, 1918, he was named commander of the famed Flying Circus, the squadron of Baron Manfred von Richthofen. Credited with 22 aerial victories in World War I, Göring was awarded the coveted *Pour le Mérite* medal.

In the last days of the World War I, Göring was ordered to retreat with his squadron but refused. Like many others, he believed the stab-in-the-back legend, which held that the German army had not lost the war but was betrayed by German Marxists, Jews, and Republicans in the civilian leadership.

After the war, Göring remained in aviation and briefly worked at Fokker. Most of 1919 was spent in Denmark and Sweden flying in civil aviation. Göring left Stockholm in 1921 to study political science at Munich University, becoming a close associate of Adolf Hitler. On February 3, 1922, he married a baroness, Carin von Kantzow.

Göring joined the Nazi Party in 1922. His aristocratic background and his prestige as a war hero made him a prize recruit. In December 1922, Hitler gave Göring charge of the SA, which Göring built dramatically in strength. Nazism offered him the promise of action, adventure, comradeship, and an outlet for his lust for power. He participated in Hitler's failed Beer Hall Putsch on November 8 to 9, 1923, was seriously wounded, and became addicted to morphine for pain relief. He fled Germany after the putsch but returned after a pardon in 1927, when he rejoined the NSDAP. In 1928, he was elected to the Reichstag and was its president from 1932. He knew many key players in industry, banking, and the military, and he played a key role in the Nazi ascent to power.

Carin Göring's health had been weakened by tuberculosis, and the day after she attended her mother's funeral in Stockholm, she suffered a heart attack. She died of heart failure on October 17, 1931. Göring later built his Karinhall estate to honor his late wife.

After Hitler became chancellor in January 1933, Göring gained further power and influence. His many roles included minister without portfolio, minister of the interior for the state of Prussia, and minister of the air force (Luftwaffe). In rebuilding the Luftwaffe, he became a key player in all major policy decisions affecting its composition and training.

On February 27, 1933, just one month after Hitler had been sworn in as chancellor, an arson attack on the Reichstag building in Berlin occurred. One of the first to arrive on the scene, Göring exploited the fire (which many suspected that he had engineered) in order to implement a series of emergency decrees that destroyed the last remnants of civil rights in Germany, imprisoned communists and Social Democrats, and banned the left-wing press.

On April 26, 1933, Göring established the Gestapo (*Geheime Staatspolizei*), which was intended to crush all resistance to Nazism. On April 20, 1934, Göring handed over control of the Gestapo to **Heinrich Himmler**.

On June 30, 1934, Himmler and Göring affected the SS purge of leaders of the paramilitary SA, including Ernst Röhm, who had become a threat to Hitler's power. Göring personally went over the lists of detainees and determined who should be shot. At least 85 people were killed between June 30 and July 2, in a period that became known as the Night of the Long Knives.

On April 10, 1935, Göring married actress Emmy Sonneman, and at the ceremony, no fewer than 200 Luftwaffe fighter planes flew over the couple as an honor guard.

In 1936, Göring was appointed to oversee the Four-Year Plan, giving him power over the German economy. On December 17, 1936, in a secret meeting, Göring told leading German industrialists that the war for which Germany was preparing was on the horizon.

The creation of the state-owned Hermann Göring Works in 1937, a gigantic industrial complex employing 700,000 workers and a capital of 400 million Reichsmarks, enabled Göring to make a fortune. So also did the confiscation of Jewish properties. Some he acquired for himself for a nominal price, while he collected bribes for allowing others to steal Jewish property. He took kickbacks from industrialists for favorable decisions as Four-Year Plan director and money for supplying arms to Spanish Republicans in the Spanish Civil War—even though Germany was supporting Franco and the Nationalists.

Göring used his position to indulge in ostentatious luxury and bought grand estates, hunting lodges, and a large art collection. He also owned a personal train complete with separate sleeping coaches for him and his wife and a car that was set up as a cinema. He remained genuinely popular with the German masses, who regarded him as manly, honest, and more accessible than the Führer.

As head of the Four-Year Plan, Göring pressured for Austria to be incorporated into the Reich. On February 12, 1938, he met with Austrian chancellor Kurt von Schuschnigg, threatening Austria with invasion if it would not concur to peaceful unification. Schuschnigg's subsequent resignation on March 11, 1938, and the German invasion of Austria the next day were arguably down to Göring's machinations more than Hitler's and should be seen as his victory.

In July 1938, Göring once more involved himself in foreign affairs, suggesting to the British government that he make an official visit to discuss Germany's intentions for Czechoslovakia. At the Nuremberg Party Rally in September 1938, Göring and other speakers denounced the Czechs as an inferior race that must be conquered. Again, Göring's intrigues paid off. British prime minister Neville Chamberlain undertook three summit meetings with Hitler, leading to the Munich Agreement on September 29, 1938. This not only gave the Czech Sudetenland to Germany but opened the way to the German occupation of the remainder of Bohemia and Moravia in March 1939—once more owing to Göring's diplomatic maneuverings.

Following the *Kristallnacht* pogrom of November 9 to 10, 1938, Göring fined the German Jewish community 1 billion Reichsmarks and ordered the elimination of Jews from the German economy, the Aryanization of their property and businesses, and their exclusion from schools, resorts, parks, forests, and the like. On November 12, 1938, he warned of a "final reckoning with the Jews" should Germany come into conflict with a foreign power.

At the start of World War II, Göring had built the Luftwaffe into a formidable force. His planes performed superbly in the Blitzkrieg campaigns against Poland, the Low Countries, Norway, and France.

Then from July 10, 1940 to October 31, 1940, the Luftwaffe waged large-scale attacks against the United Kingdom in the Battle of Britain, as Göring was convinced that by Operation Eagle he could secure the surrender of the British through air power alone. Göring made a fatal tactical error when he switched to massive night bombings against London on September 7, 1940, which saved the Royal Air

Force sector-control stations from destruction and gave the British fighter defenses time to recover. The Luftwaffe lost planes and experienced bomber crews that it was unable to replace, and Hitler was forced to abandon Operation Sea Lion, the planned invasion of England.

On November 5, 1940, Göring issued an order to loot the art treasures at the Louvre museum in Paris, many of which were to be distributed to German museums and private Nazi collections, with a large portion of the art reserved for himself. On May 23, 1941, Göring ordered the plunder and destruction of Soviet industrial centers, justifying this on the basis that the conquered Soviet population would be no more than laborers for Germany.

On June 29, 1941, Hitler named Göring as his successor and heir, with a promotion to the rank of *Reichsmarschall* (a rank above field marshal created just for him), placing him above all other military leaders in Germany.

On June 22, 1941, Adolf Hitler launched Operation Barbarossa, a massive invasion of the Soviet Union, an offensive initially opposed by Göring, who favored a Mediterranean strategy instead. In training, doctrine, and fighting ability, the German forces invading Russia represented arguably the 20th century's finest combat army, but the ultimate failure of Barbarossa to achieve its objectives was the crucial turning point in World War II. Nazi Germany was henceforth forced to fight a two-front war against a coalition possessing vastly superior resources.

Systematic killing of men, women, and children began in June 1941 after the onset of Operation Barbarossa. On July 31, 1941, Göring commissioned **Reinhard Heydrich** to prepare and submit a plan for a "final solution to the Jewish question" (*Endlösung der Judenfrage*) in territories under German control and to coordinate the participation of all government organizations involved. Accordingly, the Wannsee Conference was held on January 20, 1942, in Berlin, with Heydrich emphasizing that once mass deportation was complete, the SS would take charge of the exterminations. The minutes of the conference estimated the Jewish population of the Soviet Union to be 5 million, with another 3 million in Ukraine.

Göring's opposition to Operation Barbarossa had political ramifications, with blame cast in his direction for suggesting that the Luftwaffe, with only a limited transport capacity, could supply the Sixth Army at Stalingrad. By mid-1943, enemy fighters were accompanying bomber squadrons deeper and deeper into German territory. Public opinion turned against Göring, as Allied air raids on Germany became increasingly effective and the Luftwaffe seemed unable to defend Germany itself. Progressively marginalized, Göring spent more time at his estate of Karinhall, where he indulged his interests in hunting and stealing art collections.

As the Soviets approached Berlin, Hitler's efforts to defend Germany became futile. His birthday, celebrated at the *Führerbunker* in Berlin on April 20, 1945, was a leave-taking for many top Nazis, Göring included. Göring had already evacuated Karinhall, loading all his plundered treasures onto 24 heavy trucks and several train cars. He arrived at his estate at Obersalzberg on April 22, 1945, to learn that Hitler, in a diatribe against his generals, had that day admitted publicly that the war was lost and that he intended to remain in Berlin to the end and commit suicide.

On April 23, 1945, Göring learned that Hitler considered him to be in a better position than the Führer to negotiate a peace settlement. After consulting a number of senior government officials, Göring sent a telegram to Hitler stating that in accordance with Hitler's decree of June 29, 1941, Göring would take power over Germany if Hitler could not respond by midnight. The head of the Party Chancellery, **Martin Bormann**, portrayed this as a treasonous attempt by Göring to wrest power from Hitler, who demanded Göring's immediate resignation; without it, he would be executed for high treason. Hitler removed Göring from all offices and ordered that he and his staff be placed under house arrest at Obersalzberg. Bormann made an announcement over the radio that Göring had resigned for health reasons. On April 30, 1945, Hitler committed suicide.

On May 9, 1945, accompanied by his wife and daughter, Göring surrendered to elements of the U.S. Ninth Infantry Division. On May 21, 1945, he was transferred to the secret American camp Ashcan, where other senior Nazis were imprisoned. Tried at the International Military Tribunal at Nuremberg, Göring was unrepentant. Found guilty and sentenced to death, on October 15, 1946, only two hours before his planned execution, Hermann Göring, aged 53, committed suicide by swallowing cyanide.

GREISER, ARTHUR (1897–1946)

Arthur Greiser was a Nazi politician, *SS-Obergruppenführer*, and *Reichsstatthalter* of the German-occupied territory of Wartheland.

Arthur Karl Greiser was born January 22, 1897, in Schroda (Środa Wielkopolska), Prussia, to a local bailiff. In 1903, he began to study at the *Königlich-Humanistische Gymnasium* (Royal Humanities College) in Hohensalza, Posen (Poznań). Owing to Posen's geographical location close to Prussian Poland, Greiser learned to speak Polish fluently as a child.

In 1914, Greiser quit school without earning a diploma. He joined the navy in August 1914, and in 1917, he became a naval aviator. He earned the Iron Cross First and Second Class as well as other military decorations. Shot down and wounded later in the war, on September 30, 1919, he was classified as 50 percent war disabled and discharged from naval service.

After the war, he returned home to Posen, now Poznań and part of Poland. From 1919 to May 1921, he served in the *Freikorps Grenzschutz Ost* and fought in the Baltic States. He joined the Nazi Party and SA on December 1, 1929, and then the SS on September 29, 1931. In 1935, Greiser became the Senate president of the Free City of Danzig (Gdańsk).

On September 8, 1939, after Germany invaded Poland, Greiser was named as head of the military government in Poland. On October 21 and 26, 1939, he was appointed district leader (gauleiter) and administrator of *Reichsgau Posen* (renamed Wartheland on January 29, 1940). Greiser would hold these positions until the end of the war.

Reichsgau Posen was potentially very rich. It had been a major agricultural area providing food to Germany before 1914 and possessed an excellent rail and road network as well as a comparatively healthy and well-educated workforce. The capital, Litzmanstadt (Łódź), had developed a sophisticated industrial base during the 19th century.

A fervent racist who eagerly practiced an "ethnic cleansing" program to rid the Warthegau of Poles, Greiser removed Polish civilians from various regions and resettled them with ethnic Germans, 350,000 of whom were refugees from Eastern European states occupied by the Soviet Union. Some of the people removed were murdered systematically, while others were deported further east. Greiser approved the creation of SS detachments that operated as mobile killing squads murdering Jews, mental patients, and other groups deemed "subhuman" in accordance with Nazi philosophy. **Wilhelm Koppe**, a subordinate to Greiser, was put in charge of the Final Solution in the Wartheland, and between late 1941 and April 1942, Koppe was responsible for killing 150,000 Jews using gas vans.

Greiser was fully aware of the Holocaust. Early in 1940, he was on record challenging **Hermann Göring** over efforts to delay the expulsion of Łódź Jews to the *Generalgouvernement*. On September 18, 1941, **Heinrich Himmler** informed Greiser that he intended to transfer 60,000 Czech and German Jews to the Łódź ghetto up to the spring of 1942, when they would be "resettled." The first transport arrived a few weeks later, and Greiser sought and received permission from Himmler to kill 100,000 Jews in his area.

Greiser then instructed Koppe to manage the overcrowding. Koppe and **Herbert Lange** managed the problem by experimenting with gas vans at a country estate at Chełmno, creating the first killing unit, which murdered around 150,000 Jews between late 1941 and April 1942. On October 6, 1943, Greiser held a national assembly of senior SS officers in Posen, at which Himmler bluntly spoke of the mass executions of civilians. Greiser's mass murder actions were coordinated by Herbert Mehlhorn.

On January 20, 1945, Greiser ordered a general evacuation of Posen (having received a telegram from **Martin Bormann** relaying **Adolf Hitler**'s order to leave the city). Greiser left Posen the same evening and reported to Himmler's personal train in Frankfurt am Oder. There, Greiser found that Bormann had tricked him. Hitler had announced that Posen must be held at all costs, and Greiser was now viewed as a deserter and coward, particularly by **Joseph Goebbels**, who, in his diary on March 2, 1945, labeled Greiser "a real disgrace to the Party." Posen fell under Russian control on January 28, 1945, and Greiser surrendered to the Americans in Austria near the end of the war.

Greiser was later tried by the Polish Supreme National Tribunal. His defense against war crimes charges was that he was following orders, but he was nonetheless found guilty of several charges including mass murder, torture, and the systematic destruction of Polish culture and identity. On July 21, 1946, aged 49, Arthur Greiser was executed by hanging at Fort Winiary in Poznań in what would become the last public execution in Polish history.

GRESE, IRMA (1923–1945)

Irma Grese, sometimes called the "Beautiful Beast," was an SS officer during World War II who served as a guard in the concentration camps at Ravensbrück, Auschwitz, and Bergen-Belsen.

Irma Ida Ilse Grese was born in Wrechen, Germany, on October 7, 1923. She was the third of five children of Berta and Alfred Grese, a farming family. In 1936, Grese's mother committed suicide after learning that Alfred Grese had engaged in an extramarital affair.

Grese, a poor student, was bullied by her classmates, dropped out of the school in 1938 aged 14, and joined the *Bund deutscher Mädel* (League of German Girls, or BdM). She was then employed in several casual jobs, including two years at an SS sanatorium.

By the time Grese was 18 years old, she was accepted to work at the women's concentration camp Ravensbrück, where she served as an *Aufseherin* (female guard), bringing to the position both her passion for the Nazi cause and her brutality.

In March 1943, Grese moved to the harsher camp environment at Auschwitz-Birkenau. By the middle of 1944, she was a senior guard. She was an active participant in prisoner selections for the gas chambers and was especially feared by inmates; survivors later gave evidence about her tortures and the "pure unabashed evil" ways in which she terrified prisoners.

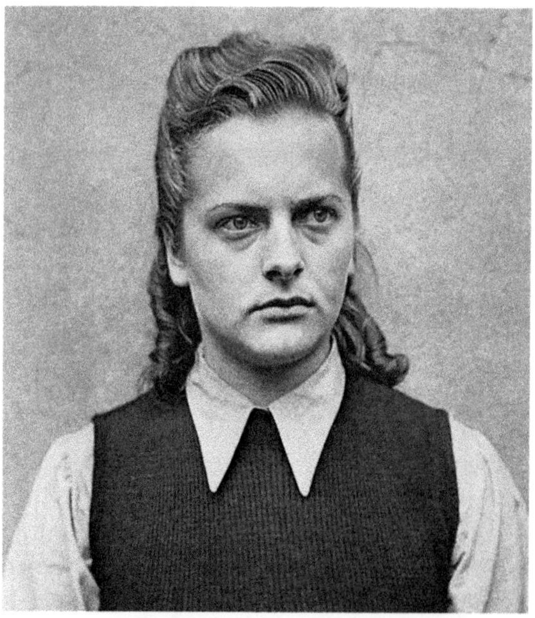

Irma Grese was a guard at Ravensbrück, Auschwitz, and Bergen-Belsen concentration camps and was infamous among prisoners for her many acts of sadistic cruelty and bloodshed. Arrested at the end of the war and placed on trial for crimes against humanity, she was one of three female guards (along with Juana Bormann and Elisabeth Volkenrath) found guilty and sentenced to death. She was hanged on December 13, 1945, at just 22 years of age. (Corbis via Getty Images)

Grese gained infamy as a nymphomaniac and a sadist, who had sexual relationships with chosen prisoners and many of the male SS guards. The prisoners described acts of cruelty and bloodshed, such as beating the prisoners bare-handed and making them hold heavy stones over their head for long stretches. The prisoners also were cowed by indiscriminate shootings. When Grese was especially angry, she was known to use trained and allegedly half-starved dogs to attack prisoners, who were also fearful of her because she was responsible for selecting prisoners for the gas chambers. Survivors reported that Grese wore heavy boots and carried a whip and a pistol, testifying that she enjoyed using both physical and psychological methods to torture inmates. Other accounts claimed that she beat some women inmates to death and flogged others using a plaited whip. Grese became a symbol of terror and the most feared guard in the camp.

One surviving prisoner, Olga Lengyel, wrote that Grese had a fondness for selecting not just the sick and the weak but any woman who had retained her beauty. She later recalled that Grese had numerous lovers among the SS in the camp, including **Josef Mengele**, and that her scrupulous personal grooming, tailored clothing, and overuse of perfume were all part of a deliberate act of hostility against the ragged women who were her prisoners.

On April 17, 1945, Grese transported prisoners from Ravensbrück to Bergen-Belsen. When British troops arrived there soon thereafter, Grese was standing at the camp entrance, along with the commandant, **Josef Kramer**, offering help. They were immediately arrested, along with other SS personnel who had not already fled. A few months later, Grese was put on trial as a war criminal.

Irma Grese was one of the 45 defendants accused of war crimes at the Belsen Trials, conducted by the British military in Lüneburg, Germany, which ran from September 17 to November 17, 1945. The charges of war crimes were derived from the Geneva Convention of 1929 concerning the management of prisoners, and the accusations against Grese addressed her abuse and murder of those imprisoned at the camps.

During the Belsen trials, the press branded Grese as the "Beautiful Beast" alongside Kramer, who was nicknamed the "Beast of Belsen." Even though a total of 16 women guards were charged with similar ghastly accusations, Grese was one of only 3 female guards sentenced to death, along with **Juana Bormann** and **Elisabeth Volkenrath**. Found guilty, she was hanged on December 13, 1945, aged just 22.

GÜRTNER, FRANZ (1881–1941)

Franz Gürtner was a German jurist and leading member of the conservative German National People's Party (DNVP). An old-school bureaucrat, Gürtner was sympathetic to right-wing radicals, such as **Adolf Hitler**. On June 2, 1932, he was appointed German minister of justice and continued in that role in Hitler's cabinet after January 1933 until his death on January 29, 1941. Gürtner provided official sanction and legal grounds for a series of criminal actions under the Hitler administration.

He was born in Regensburg, southeast Germany, on August 26, 1881. The son of a locomotive engineer, he studied law at the University of Munich and then served as an officer in France and Palestine during World War I. He was awarded an Iron Cross for bravery.

After the war, Gürtner resumed a successful legal career and was appointed Bavarian minister of justice on November 8, 1922, a position he held until 1932. A member of the conservative German Nationalist Party, Gürtner also developed strong nationalist beliefs and, like many in Weimar Germany, was infuriated by the terms of the Treaty of Versailles and the 1923 Franco-Belgian occupation of the Ruhr. As he was sympathetic toward right-wing radicals such as Hitler, it was understood that Gürtner used his influence to help Hitler when he was put on trial after the failed Beer Hall Putsch in 1923. Tried for treason, Hitler received a five-year jail term, which was spent in some comfort at Landsberg Prison. He had only served nine months before Gürtner used his judicial authority to obtain his early release. Gürtner also persuaded the Bavarian government to legalize the banned Nazi Party and allow Hitler to speak again in public.

In June 1932, Gürtner was appointed minister of justice in the cabinet of Franz von Papen. He was retained by Hitler as minister of justice and was given responsibility for coordinating jurisprudence in the Third Reich.

Though a non-Nazi conservative, Gürtner was authoritarian by inclination. He fully supported the Reichstag Fire Decree, which effectively wiped out civil liberties in Germany. Indeed, on the day before the Reichstag fire, he proposed a bill that was almost as heavy handed and would have instituted severe restrictions on civil liberties under the pretense of keeping the communists from launching a general strike. In office, Gürtner merged the association of the German judges with the new National Socialist Lawyers' Association and provided a veil of constitutional legality for the Nazi state.

In 1933, Gürtner came into conflict with one of his subordinates, **Roland Freisler**, over issues relating to *Rassenschande* (racial shame)—sexual relationships between Aryans and non-Aryans—which Freisler wanted immediately criminalized. Gürtner, in a meeting, pointed out many practical difficulties with Freisler's proposal. This did not, however, stop the passing of the Nuremberg Laws in 1935, criminalizing such relations.

In the weeks following the Nazi Party purge known as the Night of the Long Knives from June 30 to July 2, 1934, Gürtner demonstrated his loyalty to the Nazi regime by writing a law that added a legal veneer to the purge. Signed into law by both Hitler and Minister of the Interior **Wilhelm Frick**, the Law Regarding Measures of State Self-Defense retrospectively legalized the murders committed during the purge. Gürtner even quashed some initial efforts by local prosecutors to take legal action against those who carried out the murders.

As Reich minister of justice with extensive powers, Gürtner opened the first session of the People's Court on July 14, 1934. After nominating all the judges and public prosecutors, Hitler invariably rubber-stamped Gürtner's nominations and swore the judges in personally. In return, Gürtner signed Nazi laws and mediated between the Nazi regime and conservative jurists to gain their cooperation.

Yet Gürtner also tried to protect the independence of the judiciary and at least a facade of legal norms. The ill-treatment of prisoners in concentration camps under the jurisdiction of local SA leaders provoked a sharp protest from the Ministry of Justice. Gürtner observed that prisoners were being beaten to the point of unconsciousness with whips and blunt instruments, commenting that such treatment revealed a level of brutality and cruelty that was totally alien to German sentiment and feeling. Gürtner also complained about confessions obtained by the Gestapo under torture. In both protests, he found himself at odds with Hitler. By the end of 1935, it was already apparent that neither Gürtner nor Frick would be able to impose limitations on the power of the Gestapo or control the SS camps, where thousands of detainees were being held without judicial review.

In 1936, Gürtner, acting upon Hitler's direction, ordered that the *Fallbeil*, a variation on the guillotine, replace the hand ax as the official method for all civil executions throughout Germany. He then joined the Nazi Party in 1937 and found himself providing official sanction and legal grounds for a series of criminal actions, beginning with the institution of *Ständegerichte* (drumhead courts-martial). During the war, this court tried Poles and Jews in the occupied eastern territories and issued decrees that opened the way for implementing the Final Solution.

Upon the outbreak of war, the Ministry of Justice found that its power was swiftly eroded by internal security forces, which did not adhere to formal judicial processes. The Gestapo and SD became judge, jury, and executioner in many issues, and few in the ministry were brave enough to query their work. In 1939 the SS won the right to order the summary execution of any person deemed subversive or disloyal; all compromise with the state judicial system was abandoned.

A district judge and member of the Confessing Church, Lothar Kreyssig, wrote in 1940 to Gürtner protesting that the T-4 euthanasia program was illegal, since no law or formal decree from Hitler had authorized it. Gürtner promptly dismissed Kreyssig from his post, telling him, "If you cannot recognise the will of the Führer as a source of law, then you cannot remain a judge."

Gürtner then provided legal backing and support to any act carried out on behalf of Hitler—normally explaining that such action was required to defend the Fatherland. On this basis, Hitler expected Gürtner to legally justify any actions taken by Nazi organizations as well. The usual legal explanation invariably oriented around a "defense of the Fatherland" argument.

Franz Gürtner was still minister of justice when he died in Berlin on January 29, 1941. His death completed **Heinrich Himmler**'s supremacy of the legal and justice system, as Gürtner's replacement at the justice ministry, State Secretary **Franz Schlegelberger**, never had Gürtner's authority; nor was he in any position to challenge the might of the SS.

H

HAGEN, HERBERT (1913–1999)

Herbert Martin Hagen was an *SS-Sturmbannführer* with specific responsibilities regarding the Jewish question.

Born on September 20, 1913, in Neumünster, Schleswig-Holstein, he joined the SS in October 1933 in Kiel, where, from May 1934, he was mentored by Franz Six, head of the press office of the *Sicherheitsdienst* (Security Service, or SD) at the headquarters of *SS-Reichsführer* **Heinrich Himmler**. In September 1934, the SD main office moved from Munich to Berlin, with Hagen employed in Central Division I.3 (Press and Museum). From the summer of 1936 onward, he lectured at the German Academy of Politics. At the age of 24, he became one of the youngest service chiefs of the Reich security apparatus.

In 1937, he headed Division II/112 (Jews) at SD headquarters, and in this capacity, he and his subordinate **Adolf Eichmann** traveled to the British Mandate of Palestine to assess the possibility of Germany's Jews voluntarily emigrating there. Feival Polkes, an agent of the Haganah, had earlier met with Eichmann in Berlin in February 1937, and it was at his invitation that Hagen and Eichmann went to Palestine. They left Berlin on September 4, 1937, and disembarked at Haifa with forged press credentials on October 3, traveling on to Cairo. Once there, meetings took place on October 10 and 11, 1937, but they were unable to strike a deal. Polkes had hoped that he could negotiate for more Jews to be allowed to leave under the terms of the Haavara (transfer) Agreement of August 25, 1933, but Hagen refused any relaxation, claiming that a strong Jewish presence in Palestine might lead to the establishment of an independent Jewish state. Eichmann and Hagen attempted to return to Palestine a few days later but were denied entry after the British authorities refused them the required visas.

Upon returning to Germany, Hagen moved into the press office of the SD, from where he traveled throughout the country spreading the gospel of Nazi antisemitism. With the *Anschluss* between Germany and Austria, Hagen and Eichmann journeyed to Vienna to work in the establishment of SD there.

When World War II broke out, the SD, the Gestapo, and the Criminal Investigation Department were brought together under the auspices of the *Reichsicherheitshauptamt* (Reich Security Main Office, or RSHA) on September 27, 1939. Hagen moved into the RSHA-Amt VI (Foreign Intelligence Service) although he was still involved with RSHA-Amt VI H2 (Jewish Questions and Antisemitism), as he had been earlier.

With the German occupation of France in 1940, Hagen moved to Paris, and on August 1, 1940, he was appointed the head of 1 of the 11 French departments of the SD, basing himself in Bordeaux. From here, Hagen instituted measures to deport Jews to their death. He once more worked with Eichmann, who was by now head of RSHA-Amt IV B4 (Jews and Clearances). On October 24, 1941, in an internment camp at Souges, northwestern France, Hagen was directly responsible for the execution by hanging of 50 hostages, having drawn up a death list specifically for this purpose. Then, in December 1941, Hagen set up a concentration camp for the Jews of the Mérignac region on the southern Atlantic coast.

On May 5, 1942, Hagen was appointed to the position of political assistant of **Carl Oberg**, who commanded the SS and police forces in France. He was deputized by Oberg to oversee anti-Jewish matters, while at the same time remaining active in other security activities under the leadership of *SS-Obersturmburführer* Helmut Knochen. Hagen then organized raids in Paris to deport Jews. A fluent speaker of French, he communicated the exact meaning of German demands to members of the Vichy regime, and in this way, Hagen took a leading role in working to suppress the resistance movement and at the same time organizing the transfer of workers and deportation of Jews from France.

On July 2, 1942, Hagen took part in a meeting that included the secretary-general of the French police, **René Bousquet**, who agreed to seize and hand over to the Germans for deportation 40,000 foreign Jews living in France. Hagen made an agreement with Vichy prime minister **Pierre Laval** that the latter, if asked what was happening to the Jews, would answer that Jews transferred from unoccupied France to the occupied zone were being transported to the *Generalgouvernement* in Poland. By August 1943, Hagen was demanding from Bousquet that Jews be denied French nationality as a means of easing their deportation.

In September 1944, Hagen was transferred to Carinthia in southern Austria and given command of an *Einsatzkommando* (special action squad) for engaging in antipartisan activities on the Yugoslav border.

He remained here until the end of the war, when he was arrested by British forces on May 13, 1945, and imprisoned in Carinthia's capital, Klagenfurt. Shunted from place to place (including Italy and British prisons in Lower Saxony and Hamburg), he was handed by the British to the French occupation forces in November 1946. The investigation over the following year established Hagen's responsibility for the deportation of Jews as a member of the SD in France. It was not until March 18, 1955, however, that Hagen was finally convicted for having been instrumental in the deportation of the Jews from France and condemned to lifelong forced labor by a military court in Paris.

However, under the terms of a treaty signed at Paris between the Federal Republic of Germany and the three Western powers (France, Britain, and the United States) on October 23, 1954, the remaining restrictions on German law regarding the prosecution of National Socialist crimes were abolished. This led to some categories of war criminals, such as Hagen, effectively receiving amnesties from any further prosecution because they could not be tried and punished for the same crime twice. Secure in the knowledge that he would be safe provided he did not leave Germany or go to France, Hagen settled down to a life in the corporate world.

In July 1978, the German State Prosecutor's Office brought an action against Hagen and two other leading former Nazis, **Kurt Lischka** and Ernst Heinrichsohn, in Cologne. Over the next 15 months, the court learned that Hagen not only knew about the Nazi program to exterminate the Jews but was, in fact, a central figure in its implementation and was heavily involved in the deportation of Jews from France for a lengthy period. It was concluded that during his period in command, some 70 transports with 70,790 Jews were sent to the concentration camps in the East, of which at least 35,000 were killed in the gas chambers. On February 11, 1980, the Cologne Regional Court announced its verdict, and he was sentenced to 12 years imprisonment, to be served at the Hamm prison, in the Ruhr.

Released after only serving four years of his sentence, Hagen retired to private life. In 1997, he lived in a senior citizens' home near Warstein, in the state of North Rhine-Westphalia, and he died on August 7, 1999, in nearby Rüthen.

HARSTER, WILHELM (1904–1991)

Wilhelm Harster was an *SS-Gruppenführer* and Holocaust perpetrator. He served as chief of security and police forces in the German-occupied Netherlands from 1940 to 1944 and in Italy from 1944 to 1945.

Harster was born on July 21, 1904, at Kelheim, Bavaria. His father was a lawyer and police officer. Harster attended grammar school in Munich, and in 1920, aged 16, he became a member of the *Freikorps Bund Oberland*. Harster joined the Reichswehr (the Germany army under the Weimar Republic) and remained a reservist after his training.

He took his law degree from the University of Munich in 1927, and in 1929, he joined the Stuttgart police force. Soon, he moved on to the political police.

On May 1, 1933, only three months after **Adolf Hitler**'s accession to office, Harster joined the NSDAP. In November 1933, he became a member of the SS, and in October 1935, the SD, eventually rising to *Gruppenführer*.

From March 31, 1938, to June 1, 1940, Harster led the State Police Regional Office in Innsbruck. As a Gestapo chief, he participated in the planning and executing the *Kristallnacht* pogrom there in November 1938.

In June 1940, after the onset of war the previous September, Harster was recalled to active duty and served from July 1940 in a machine-gun company. On July 19, 1940, only weeks after the German invasion of the Netherlands on May 10, 1940, he was posted there as commander of the SD, where he served until August 1944.

In 1941, Harster gave permission for "sharpened interrogation" (a euphemism for torture) of communist prisoners. This permission came after discussions with his Gestapo counterpart at the RSHA in Berlin, *SS-Gruppenführer* **Heinrich Müller**. It was initially not allowed for other prisoners, but in 1942, the sharpened interrogation process was extended. It was said that the screams of those being tortured could be heard coming from Harster's office.

In early May 1943, in a letter to the German commanders of concentration camps in the Netherlands, Harster reported on talks he had with the RSHA in Berlin and spoke of recent instructions from Hanns-Albin Rauter, the highest SS and police leader in the occupied Netherlands, reporting directly to *SS-Reichsführer* **Heinrich Himmler** and the Nazi governor of the Netherlands, **Arthur Seyss-Inquart**. A clear statement regarding the extermination of the Dutch Jews, it was titled *Endlösung der Judenfrage in Niederlanden* ("Final Solution of the Jewish Question in the Netherlands"). As head of the SD in the Netherlands, Harster managed the mustering and transportation of the Dutch Jews and was ultimately implicated in the deaths of 104,000 Jews in the Holocaust.

After his role in the occupation of the Netherlands, Harster was redeployed as commander of the SD under General **Karl Wolff** in German-occupied parts of Italy from August 29, 1943. Here, he had contact with *SS-Sturmbannführer* **Christian Wirth**, inspector of the *Aktion Reinhard* death camps and former commandant of Bełżec.

Harster was captured by British forces on May 10, 1945, and between then and 1947, he was a prisoner of war. At the insistence of the Dutch, in 1947, Harster was extradited to the Netherlands to stand trial for war crimes committed while he headed the SD in Holland. He was imprisoned there until 1949. In 1949, Harster was convicted and given a 12-year prison term for his role in the persecution, deportation, and murder of the Dutch Jews and for negligence in failing to supervise the staff at the Amersfoort concentration camp.

He was released in 1953, having spent a total of eight years in prison. He returned to West Germany and took up a civil service position in Bavaria. By 1963, however, he was compelled to leave that job when his past deeds in the Netherlands came under more scrutiny, although he was permitted to keep his pension.

In 1967, German judicial authorities filed a new trial against Harster, in which he was charged with being coresponsible for the murder of thousands of Dutch Jews at Sobibór and Auschwitz. Convicted, he was given a 15-year jail sentence, with credit for time served. He was released in 1969.

Harster's release caused an uproar in some circles, and the Dutch Auschwitz Committee formally petitioned the West German chancellor not to pardon Harster; the pardon, however, went forward in 1969. Harster died in Bavaria on December 25, 1991, aged 87.

HEIM, ARIBERT (1914–1992)

Aribert Heim was an Austrian SS doctor, also known as "Dr. Death." During World War II, he served at the Mauthausen-Gusen concentration camp, torturing and killing inmates by various methods, such as directly injecting toxic compounds into the hearts of his victims.

Aribert Ferdinand Heim was born on June 28, 1914, in Bad Radkersburg, Austria, into a middle-class family, and his father was a police officer. Heim was handsome, intelligent, and athletic and played professional ice hockey. He studied medicine in Graz and earned his doctorate in Vienna, graduating in 1940 aged 36.

Heim joined the Austrian Nazi Party in 1935, and after the *Anschluss* with Germany, he joined the SS. He volunteered for the Waffen-SS in the spring of 1940, rising to the rank of *SS-Hauptsturmführer*.

In October 1941, Heim was sent to Mauthausen-Gusen concentration camp, near Linz, as a camp doctor, where he was known to inmates as "Dr. Death." Between October and December 1941, he was stationed at Ebensee camp near Linz, where he carried out experiments on inmates. He was known for performing often-fatal operations and experiments, including injecting various solutions (gasoline, water, phenol, and poison) into Jewish prisoners' hearts to see which induced a quicker death. He also operated on prisoners without anesthesia and removed organs from healthy inmates, leaving them to die on the operating table.

A former camp inmate gave evidence that an 18-year-old Jewish man came to the clinic with a foot inflammation. The 18-year-old was asked by Heim why he was so fit and replied that he had been a football player and swimmer. Instead of treating the prisoner's foot, Heim placed him under anesthesia, cut him open, took out his kidneys, and castrated him. The young man was then decapitated. As the head apparently had perfect teeth, Heim boiled the flesh off the skull for use as a paperweight. Other survivors referred to Heim removing tattooed flesh from prisoners and using the skin to make seat coverings, which he gave to the commandant of the camp. Heim, who also served as a doctor at Buchenwald and Sachsenhausen, became notorious for collecting skulls.

In February 1942, Heim began serving under *SS-Obergruppenführer* Karl Maria Demelhuber in the Sixth SS Mountain Division Nord in Northern Finland, where he was an SS doctor in hospitals in the city of Oulu.

Heim was captured by U.S. soldiers on March 15, 1945, and sent to a prisoner-of-war camp. He was released and avoided immediate prosecution due to the omission of his time at Mauthausen from his American-held file in Germany. Following his release, Heim married, set up practice as a civilian doctor working as a gynecologist in Baden-Baden and Bad Nauheim, and fathered two sons.

One late afternoon in 1962, Heim telephoned his home and was told that police were waiting there for him. Based on his previous experiences, he presumed that an international warrant for his arrest was to be served. He went immediately into hiding. Much later, Heim's son Rüdiger revealed that Heim drove across France and Spain to Morocco, Libya, and finally to Egypt. Over time, Heim acquired a reputation as the most wanted Nazi still at large. There were sightings reported of him in Latin America, Europe, and Africa.

Heim lived for many years in Cairo, Egypt, aided by family members and lawyers in Germany, who channeled money to him. Eventually he converted to Islam at the Al-Azhar mosque and lived under the alias Tarek Hussein Farid. He was never made to answer for his crimes in life. He died in Egypt of intestinal cancer on August 10, 1992, aged 78, and was buried in a pauper's grave in Cairo.

HEISSMEYER, AUGUST (1897–1979)

August Heissmeyer, a general in the Waffen-SS, was head of the Inspectorate of Concentration Camps and director of the elite training schools of SS youth. As such, he played a huge role both in developing the infrastructure for the Holocaust and in conditioning German youth for the role they would play in bringing it about.

Heissmeyer was born on January 11, 1897, in Gellersen, Lower Saxony. Upon finishing school, he joined the German army and served with distinction as a junior officer during World War I, in which he was decorated with the Iron Cross First Class. After the war, he went back to school but found it difficult to settle back to a civilian routine. Like many frustrated veterans unable to succeed economically, he was drawn to right-wing politics, and in 1923, he first encountered the National Socialist Party. He became an early convert to the Nazi cause when he joined the party in 1925.

At the start of 1926, Heissmeyer became a member of the SA, where he was an active and successful senior leader. This was followed by membership of the SS in January 1930. In 1932, he obtained a position at the *SS-Amt*, the central command office of the SS created in 1931. In 1933, this was renamed the *SS-Oberführerbereichen* and was given responsibility for all SS units across the country. This then became the SS Main Office (*SS-Hauptamt*, or SS-HA) on January 30, 1935, with Heissmeyer in command.

Heissmeyer was promoted to *SS-Obergruppenführer* on November 9, 1936. Accompanying this promotion was a move to another SS institution, the National Political Institutes of Education (*Nationalpolitische Erziehungsanstalten*, or NPEA). These bodies—secondary boarding schools commonly abbreviated by the name *Napola* (an abbreviation for *Nationalpolitische Lehranstalt*, or National Political Institution of Teaching)—had as their mission the "education of national socialists, efficient in body and soul for service to the people and the state."

Being elite schools, they were separate from the regular education system and regulated by a highly selective intake that accepted only the "worthiest" Aryan candidates. Those admitted were meant to become Germany's future leaders and had to operate in a highly competitive, strictly militaristic environment featuring a politically charged curriculum based on physical strength, ideological indoctrination, and racialized programs. By the time war broke out in September 1939, the *Napolas* were essentially preparatory schools for entry into the Wehrmacht and Waffen-SS. Two of Heissmeyer's own sons attended *Napolas* administered by their father.

Heissmeyer went further once war broke out. In 1939, he was appointed *SS-Oberabschnittsleiter "Ost"* (senior section leader east), and in 1940, he was further promoted as higher SS and police leader (*Höherer SS und Polizeiführer*, or SS-HSSPF) for the Spree area, with command of police forces in the region covering Berlin-Brandenburg. Considering that he had a responsibility for the *Napola* students' military training, he set up his own section, the *Dienststelle SS-Obergruppenführer Heissmeyer*, to enhance the wartime chances of the young men in his care.

In 1940, Heissmeyer took over the Inspectorate of Concentration Camps from the outgoing inspector, **Theodor Eicke**, who had assumed command of a frontline SS division when the war broke out. Through his command of the *SS-Totenkopfverbände*, Heissmeyer effectively ran the concentration camp network across Germany and occupied Europe. He remained in charge until May 1942, a crucial time in the Holocaust during which the mass murder of Jews began in earnest. He left the position when a new inspector of concentration camps, *SS-Gruppenführer* **Richard Glücks**, was appointed.

On November 14, 1944, as the Reich began to collapse, Heissmeyer was promoted to *SS-Oberstgruppenführer* (general of the Waffen-SS)—the highest military rank available in the SS. Many SS men were given Waffen-SS commissions at this time so that if they were captured in combat, they would be treated according to the rules of war and not shot out of hand. Heissmeyer's was far from being a paper commission, however; in April 1945, he was given command of a combat unit, *Kampfgruppe Heissmeyer*, and ordered to defend the Spandau airfield outside Berlin with a scratch division comprised of *Volkssturm* (home guard detachments established on the direct order of **Adolf Hitler**, comprising males aged between 16 and 60 years) and boys from the Hitler Youth.

With the final collapse of Germany, Heissmeyer and his wife, **Gertrud Scholtz-Klink** (leader of the National Socialist Women's League, or *NS-Frauenschaft*), fled Berlin. Captured in the summer of 1945 and imprisoned in a Soviet prisoner-of-war camp near Magdeburg, they managed to escape soon after. In October 1945, a haven was provided for them by Princess Pauline of Württemberg, who, as director of the German Red Cross for the Rhineland, Hesse, Nassau, and Westphalia, had known Scholtz-Klink during the war. Princess Pauline arranged for the couple to live quietly in the village of Bebenhausen, where they spent the next three years under the alias of Heinrich and Maria Stuckebrock.

On February 29, 1948, Heissmeyer was captured by French authorities near Tübingen. Held for trial the following month, he served 18 months in prison before being released in 1949. In 1950, his case was reopened, and he was forced to appear before a denazification court. His sentence was reevaluated, and he was sentenced to three years' imprisonment. After his release, he went to live in Schwäbisch Hall, Württemburg, where he became a director of the local Coca-Cola bottling plant. He died on January 16, 1979, five days after his 82nd birthday.

August Heissmeyer is not to be confused with his nephew, **Kurt Heissmeyer**, who was also an SS officer. A physician involved in medical experimentation on concentration camp inmates, he rose to prominence owing personal connections—in particular, through his uncle August and a friend, the SS general **Oswald Pohl**. In 1959, after living for many years as a successful medical practitioner in East Germany, Kurt Heissmeyer was identified and put on trial. In 1966, he was convicted and sentenced to life imprisonment. He died on August 29, 1967, aged 61.

HEISSMEYER, KURT (1905–1967)

Kurt Heissmeyer was an SS physician involved in medical experimentation on concentration camp inmates, including children.

He was born on December 26, 1905, in Lamspringe, Lower Saxony. His father was a physician, and his mother was a pastor's daughter; together, his parents ran an authoritarian family home. His uncle was *SS-Obergruppenführer* **August Heissmeyer**; his aunt, married to August Heissmeyer, was **Gertrud Schloss-Klink**, the head of the Nazi Women's League (*NS-Frauenschaft*). At university in Marburg, Heissmeyer joined the antisemitic *Arminia* fraternity.

Heissmeyer was licensed to practice medicine in 1933 and began specialist training in Freiburg before moving to the famous Davos-Clavadel clinic in Switzerland. Heissmeyer then became a resident at the Auguste-Victoria Hospital in Berlin. In 1937, he joined the Nazi Party. Building on his new party links, he became senior physician at Hohenlychen, a prestigious SS convalescent health spa at Uckermark, 70 miles north of Berlin, in 1938. Later he was elevated to assistant director. In this role, Heissmeyer fraternized with politicians and SS leaders from Berlin, including members of the administration of nearby Ravensbrück concentration camp.

Heissmeyer advanced his career by undertaking original research and publishing his scientific findings. In 1943, he wrote a paper entitled "Principles of Present and Future Problems of TB Sanatoriums." His thesis, which, unknown to him, had first been proposed and disproved by Austrian researchers A. and H. Kutschera-Aichbergen, was that the injection of live tuberculosis bacilli into subjects would act as a vaccine. He also claimed that Jews, as *Untermenschen* (subhumans), have less resistance to tuberculosis than racially superior patients and that, due to their inherent weakness, Jewish subjects would be more useful for his research.

In spring 1944, a meeting was held at Hohenlychen between Heissmeyer and others, including **Leonardo Conti**, **Karl Gebhardt**, and Ernst Grawitz. Conti was the chief physician of the SS, Gebhardt was the medical director of Hohenlychen, and Grawitz was the state secretary for health in the Ministry of the Interior and, as head of the SS health services, also responsible for medical experiments on prisoners. At the meeting, Heissmeyer proposed his experiment seeking a cure for tuberculosis, in which his subjects would be Jewish concentration camp prisoners. After the meeting, Gebhardt asked Conti if Heissmeyer could use prisoners from Ravensbrück. Conti and Grawitz both agreed, with the only other permission needed from *SS-Reichsführer* **Heinrich Himmler**. Through Heissmeyer's personal Nazi connections (his uncle, SS General August Heissmeyer, and his close acquaintance, SS General **Oswald Pohl**), Himmler's permission was obtained. The experiments were to take place, however, at the Neuengamme concentration camp near Hamburg rather than at Ravensbrück.

Heissmeyer initially experimented on adult prisoners. By November 1944, he had observed that the condition of all "his" inmates had worsened following subcutaneous tubercle inoculation. The medical records from only 32 adult experiments have been preserved, but it is believed that Heissmeyer experimented on over 100 individuals.

Undaunted, Heissmeyer was anxious to complete the second phase of his research. He ordered 20 children with the intention of immunizing them against tuberculosis. He wanted Jewish children, it was said, because they represented an inferior and weaker race. Thus, in 1944, Heissmeyer had 20 Jewish children, 10 boys and 10 girls all between the ages of 5 and 12, transferred from Auschwitz to Neuengamme. His theory was that injections of living tuberculosis bacteria would grant their recipients immunity to the disease.

As Heissmeyer began his experiments on the children, Allied forces were crossing the Rhine. With a worsening of the children's condition, he thought it would be valuable to see how the axillary glands of the children had reacted to the bacteria and ordered a Czech inmate surgeon to perform lymph-node dissections. Heissmeyer removed the children's lymph glands and then began injecting the bacteria into the children's lungs and bloodstreams.

The children grew weaker and were confined to their barracks. Heissmeyer did not know what to do with the 20 sick and dying Jewish children and sought Oswald Pohl's advice. In March 1945, while the U.S. Third Army advanced into Germany, Pohl and **Rudolph Hoess**, the Auschwitz commandant, visited Neuengamme. It was Hoess who decided the children's fate.

The Hamburg SS had taken over a bombed-out school, converted into a satellite camp of Neuengamme, at number 92/94 Bullenhuser Damm, two years earlier. The children were taken to this place. On April 20, 1945, when the British were less than three miles from the camp, the 20 children, along with the children's 2 French physicians and 2 Dutch caretakers, were murdered by being hanged on hooks in the basement at Bullenhuser Damm.

On April 21, 1945, Heissmeyer fled Hohenlychen in civilian clothing and returned to Thuringia, where he worked in his father's medical practice. He eventually settled in Magdeburg in postwar East Germany, where, for the next 18 years, he enjoyed a successful practice as the director of the only private TB clinic in East Germany. Heissmeyer's practice was so large that he was able to purchase homes for each of his three children, and he was recognized as one of Magdeburg's outstanding citizens.

Heissmeyer would have continued leading a prosperous life if, in 1959, the West German magazine *Stern* had not published an article deploring the omission of Nazi crimes from the curricula of German schoolchildren and referring specifically to the murders of the children at Bullenhuser Damm. A retired economist from Nuremberg began researching this murder and identified Heissmeyer's role. Four years later, after verification of his identity, Heissmeyer was arrested by the East German General Prosecutor's Office, charged with crimes against humanity, and imprisoned in Berlin. He initially denied the accusations but eventually led investigators to a box he had buried in the garden of his house in Hohenlychen, which contained documents and photographs relating to his experiments on children.

Heissmeyer's trial began on June 21, 1966. Found guilty, he was sentenced to life imprisonment. At his trial he stated, "I did not think that inmates of a camp had full value as human beings." When asked why he did not use guinea pigs, he responded, "For me there was no basic difference between human beings and guinea pigs." He then corrected himself: "Jews and guinea pigs." Heissmeyer was unrepentant to the very end. Fourteen months after being sentenced, on August 29, 1967, he died of a heart attack.

HERING, GOTTLIEB (1887–1945)

Gottlieb Hering was an SS commander who served in *Aktion T-4* before becoming the last commandant of Bełżec extermination camp during *Aktion Reinhard*. He was also responsible for liquidating the Jewish labor camp at Poniatowa.

Hering was born on June 2, 1887, in Warmbronn, near Leonberg, Baden-Württenberg. After leaving school, he worked as an agricultural laborer on local farms, before being conscripted into the German army in 1915. He fought with a machine-gun regiment on the Western Front and was awarded the Iron Cross First Class.

In December 1918, released from the army, Hering joined the police service and served at Göppingen, Württemberg. Later, Hering worked in the Stuttgart criminal investigation division (Kripo), where he met **Christian Wirth**. Hering rose to the level of *Kriminalinspector*. He retained his position after the ascent to office of the Nazis, and between December 1939 and December 1940, he served in a team of Kripo officers in occupied Poland, specifically Gdynia (renamed Gotenhafen by the Nazis), where ethnic Germans were being resettled on the Baltic coast.

From late 1940, Hering had a range of roles in the *Aktion T-4* program. As part of this, in 1941, he served at Bernberg in the registry office and then later in the registry at Hadamar euthanasia center. He then worked at Sonnenstein euthanasia center as an assistant supervisor and became the office manager at the Hartheim Castle euthanasia center.

After *Aktion T-4* was suspended, Hering was posted briefly to the SD in Prague. In July 1942, he transferred to Bełżec death camp, reporting to Christian Wirth. One month later, he was promoted to commandant of Bełżec when Wirth moved on to become chief inspector of *Aktion Reinhard*. Within the overall program, the task of Bełżec was to destroy the Jewish communities of Eastern Poland, specifically Warsaw, Lublin, Kraków, and Lvov. *SS-Reichsführer* **Heinrich Himmler** was so impressed by Hering's management that he promoted him to *SS-Hauptsturmführer*. Toward the end of the operation, the mass graves at Bełżec were opened and the corpses incinerated, while the gas chambers and other buildings were destroyed. The site was plowed over, trees were planted, and peaceful-looking farmhouses were constructed.

After Belźec ceased functioning in March 1943, Hering became commandant of the Jewish labor camp at Poniatowa. On November 3 to 4, 1943, German police killed the remaining Jews at Poniatowa during *Aktion Erntefest* (Operation Harvest Festival).

On October 14 to 15, 1943, prisoners at Sobibór rose in rebellion, killing several guards and making a mass escape. Within five days, *SS-Reichsführer* Heinrich Himmler ordered **Friedrich-Wilhelm Krüger** to carry out *Aktion Erntefest*, which included the liquidation of Sobibór. Krüger delegated this task to Jakob Sporrenberg, the newly appointed HSSPF for Lublin. Other elements of the *Aktion* were carried out simultaneously in three camps—Poniatowa, Trawniki, and Majdanek—to prevent rumors transferring from one camp to another.

In late October 1943, the Jews at Poniatowa were told to dig two deep trenches, 95 meters long, 2 meters wide, and 1.5 meters deep, as defenses against air attacks. On November 3, 1943, the camp was surrounded by a police unit, which had been directed to murder all the Jews. They were taken to the trenches and shot. Some resisted by not coming out of their barracks, so the barracks were set on fire; all of those remaining inside were burned alive. About 150 Jews were left to clean the area and cremate the corpses. Fifty Jews who hid during the massacre joined them. Two days later, these 200 Jews were shot because they refused to cremate the corpses. In their place, 120 Jews were brought in from other camps to carry out this work.

In September 1943, after the Italian armistice, the port city of Trieste was seized by Wehrmacht troops. Here, at Risiera di San Sabba, the Germans built the lone Italian concentration camp with a crematorium, which operated from April 4, 1944. About 5,000 South Slavs, Italian anti-fascists, and Jews died at San Sabba, while thousands more transited there before transfer to other concentration camps.

In 1944, after *Aktion Erntefest*, Hering went to Trieste, where he again replaced Christian Wirth—this time as chief of *Sonderkommando R1*, after Wirth was killed by partisans. In Trieste, he joined fellow SS men from *Aktion Reinhard*, including **Odilo Globocnik** and those under his command, many of whom had been known to Hering for a long time already.

On May 1, 1945, Yugoslav partisans conquered most of Trieste. The German garrison refused to surrender to anyone other than New Zealanders, as Yugoslavs were reputed to shoot German prisoners. The Second New Zealand Division, under General Bernard Freyberg, arrived in Trieste on May 2, 1945, and the German forces surrendered that evening. They were immediately turned over to the Yugoslav forces.

On October 9, 1945, Gottlieb Hering died in mysterious circumstances (possibly suicide) at St. Catherine's Hospital in Stetten im Remstal, near Kernen, Germany.

HEYDRICH, REINHARD (1904–1942)

Reinhard Heydrich was a high-ranking German Nazi official and one of the main architects of the Holocaust. An SS general, he headed the Reich Main Security Office, the SS and police agency most directly concerned with implementing the Nazi plan to murder the Jews of Europe.

Reinhard Tristan Eugen Heydrich was born in Halle, near Leipzig, Germany, on March 7, 1904, to a cultured Catholic musical family. His father, a Wagnerian opera singer, founded the Halle Conservatory of Music, and his mother was a skilled pianist. Heydrich was bullied at school because he had a high-pitched voice and was teased that he had Jewish blood (his grandmother had married for a second time after the birth of Heydrich's father, to a man with a Jewish-sounding name). There was strong discipline in the home, where Heydrich was beaten, but he grew up driven to excel at academics, music (violin), athletics (fencing), horsemanship, and sailing.

The German defeat in World War I brought social chaos, inflation, and economic ruin to most German families, including Heydrich's. Consequently, at the age of 16, he joined one of the many *Freikorps* groups that arose around the country—right-wing, antisemitic organizations of ex-soldiers involved in violently opposing communists on the streets. He desired to join the group in order to overcome the many persistent (though false) rumors regarding his Jewish ancestry. Heydrich believed that the German army was not defeated militarily in the war but was "stabbed in the back" and brought down by the German home front collapsing.

In March 1922, aged 18, Heydrich sought the free education, adventure, and prestige of a naval career, but this ended suddenly in 1931, when he became engaged to his future wife, Lina von Osten, and put aside another girlfriend who was from a prominent naval family. The girl's father made an official complaint, and after proceedings before a court of honor, Heydrich was immediately discharged from the service.

That same year, Heydrich joined the Nazi Party and became active in the SA in Hamburg. **Heinrich Himmler** noted Heydrich's managerial abilities and Aryan appearance and appointed him as the founding head of the *Sicherheitsdienst* (SD), the SS intelligence body tasked with locating and overcoming resistance to the Nazi Party through arrests, deportations, and murders. An *SS-Brigadeführer* by 1933, Heydrich built the SD into a powerful operation. Both **Adolf Hitler** and Himmler quickly became aware of the rumors of Heydrich's Jewish blood spread by Heydrich's enemies in the Nazi Party, and because of these rumors, Heydrich developed an immense hostility toward Jews.

In January 1933, following the Nazi seizure of power, Heydrich and Himmler administered the mass arrests of communists, trade unionists, Catholic politicians, and other opponents. An unused munitions factory at Dachau, near Munich, quickly became a concentration camp for political prisoners. By April 1934, Himmler took control of the new Secret State Police (*Geheime Staatspolizei*, or Gestapo), with Heydrich, his second in command, running the organization.

Two months later, in June 1934, Himmler and Heydrich, along with **Hermann Göring**, successfully plotted the downfall of powerful SA chief Ernst Röhm by spreading false rumors that Röhm and his 4 million SA storm troopers intended to seize control of the Reich and carry out a new revolution. In the purge, known as the Night of the Long Knives, the SA leadership was liquidated. Feared even within party ranks for his ruthlessness and known as the "Blond Beast," Heydrich thereafter helped create the Nazi police state.

Heydrich also prompted Soviet leader Joseph Stalin into conducting a purge of top Red Army generals in 1937, by supplying evidence to Soviet secret agents of a possible military coup. Within Germany, Heydrich took part in bringing down two powerful conservative German generals who had opposed Hitler's long-range war plans, announced in November 1937. War Minister Werner von Blomberg and the commander in chief of the army, Werner von Fritsch, were framed by unfounded character attacks; they were forced out, eliminating their influence. Following their dismissal, Hitler took over as army commander in chief.

Following the Nazi annexation of Austria in March 1938, the SS rounded up anti-Nazis and Jews. Heydrich established the Gestapo Office of Jewish Emigration, headed by Austrian native **Adolf Eichmann**; it became the sole office permitting Jews to leave Austria, and it took their assets in return for safe passage. Almost 100,000 Austrian Jews left, many of whom had handed over all their wealth to the SS. A similar office was set up in Berlin. Heydrich also helped organize the *Kristallnacht*, the pogrom targeting Jews throughout Germany and Austria on November 9 to 10, 1938.

Following the invasion of Poland on September 1, 1939, Heydrich took charge of the RSHA (Reich Main Security Office). On Heydrich's orders, Jews not shot outright were forced into overcrowded, walled-in ghettos in Warsaw, Kraków, and Łódź. By mid-1941, half a million Polish Jews had died from starvation and disease.

Heydrich established the *Einsatzgruppen*, killing squads charged with executing Jews and members of opposition groups, in German-controlled Poland and later the Soviet Union. After the Nazi invasion of the Soviet Union in June 1941, he sent four *Einsatzgruppen*, marked A, B, C, and D, into the Soviet Union with orders to politically "pacify" the occupied areas by search and execution measures. All communists taken into custody were shot, along with suspected partisans, saboteurs, and anyone considered to be a security threat. The *Einsatzgruppen* followed the German army deep into Soviet territories and the Ukraine, aided by volunteer units of ethnic Germans who lived in Poland as well as volunteers from Latvia, Lithuania, Estonia, and Ukraine.

On July 31, 1941, on Hitler's order, Hermann Göring ordered Heydrich to put together the administrative material and financial measures necessary to carry out "the desired final solution of the Jewish question." On January 20, 1942, Heydrich convened the Wannsee Conference in Berlin with 15 top Nazi bureaucrats to coordinate the Final Solution, under which the Nazis would eliminate all the Jews of Europe, an estimated 11 million people. To replace emigration, the conference's alternative proposal was "deportation to the East," a euphemistic solution approved by Hitler. This referred to mass deportations of Jews to ghettos in Poland and then on to the planned extermination complexes at Bełżec, Sobibór, and Treblinka. The plan forced the Jews to form Jewish Councils (*Judenräte*) who kept lists of names and assets, thereby partly organizing, administering, and financing the Final Solution themselves. By mid-1942, mass gassing of Jews using Zyklon B (hydrogen cyanide) began at Auschwitz in occupied Poland.

In September 1941, while still retaining his other duties, Hitler appointed Heydrich as deputy Reich protector of Bohemia and Moravia. His headquarters were in Prague. Shortly after, Heydrich created a ghetto for Jews at Theresienstadt. Although he offered incentives to Czech workers for food and privileges if they filled Nazi production quotas and displayed loyalty to the Reich, Heydrich's agents cracked down on the Czech resistance movement. Heydrich would travel between Germany and his headquarters in Prague in an open-top green Mercedes without an armed escort in order to underscore how far he had intimidated and pacified the Czechs.

On May 27, 1942, against the expressed wishes of the local population who feared reprisals, British-trained Czech commandos ambushed Heydrich's car, seriously wounding him. He died a few days later, on June 4, 1942. In retaliation, Hitler ordered the murder of thousands of Jews; he also wanted to kill 10,000 Czech political prisoners, but Himmler persuaded him that the Czechs were needed to supply Germany's industrial needs. Nonetheless, more than 13,000 Czechs were arrested, and 5,000 were murdered in reprisals. False information led the Nazis to believe that the assassins were hiding in Lidice, a village near Prague; they also found a radio resistance transmitter in Ležáky. The Germans took revenge on Lidice by killing all 199 men in the town, arresting the 195 women and sending them to Ravensbrück concentration camp, and taking the 95 children, 8 of whom were given to German families. Lidice was demolished on June 9, 1942, and the ruins bulldozed. In Ležáky, all adults were murdered; the children disappeared, except for two who were handed over to Nazi families, and the town was razed.

Heydrich's funeral in Berlin was remembered as the largest of its kind in Nazi Germany.

HIMMLER, HEINRICH (1900–1945)

Heinrich Himmler, a leading member of the NSDAP and a key official in the government of **Adolf Hitler**, was head of the entire Nazi police force, including SD and the Gestapo; minister of the interior, and commander of the Waffen-SS and the Home Army. As the Reich leader of the *Schutzstaffel* (SS), Himmler administered the death camps in the East and oversaw the mass murder of Jews and other peoples during the Holocaust.

Heinrich Luitpold Himmler was born in Munich, Germany, on October 7, 1900, to devout Catholic, middle-class parents: Joseph, a teacher, and Anna Maria. He was named after his godfather, Prince Heinrich of Bavaria, whom his father had taught. In 1913, Himmler's family moved to Landshut, about 40 miles northeast of Munich, where his father became assistant principal of the local high school. An intelligent and studious boy, Himmler struggled to overcome a sickly disposition. Awkward in social situations, he compensated by reading racist German writers who condemned what they identified as a strong Jewish influence in Germany. The young Himmler was interested in dueling and current events, and in 1915, he began training with the Landshut Cadet Corps.

Taking an emergency high school diploma, in 1917, he applied to the navy as a trainee officer but was rejected because he wore glasses. He then enlisted with the reserve battalion of the 11th Bavarian Regiment in December 1917. His father's connections ensured Himmler's acceptance for officer training, which he began on January 1, 1918. Himmler was still in training when the war ended with Germany's defeat in November 1918, denying him the opportunity to see combat or complete his officer training. Upon his discharge on December 18, 1918, he formalized his high school qualification and graduated in July 1919.

In April 1919, Himmler joined the *Freikorps Lauterbach* and came to Munich under Kurt Eisner to fight in street battles against the communists. His application to join the army was rejected. In October 1919, following a brief farm apprenticeship and an illness, Himmler studied agronomy from 1919 to 1922 at the Munich Technical High School. Here, he joined numerous clubs, including the German Society for Breeding Studies. He completed his diploma in 1922.

After Foreign Minister Walther Rathenau's murder on June 24, 1922, Himmler turned further toward the radical right. Disappointed by his inability to find a military career and unable to afford his doctoral studies, he took a low-paying job as a laboratory assistant and salesman in a fertilizer company, remaining until

September 1923. After a few months, he resigned to join Ernst Röhm's paramilitary Imperial War Reich Flag Society. Soon after this, he joined the National Socialist Party and took part in Hitler's failed Beer Hall Putsch on November 8 to 9, 1923. While Himmler was not charged for his role in the putsch because of insufficient evidence, he was able to find work as an agronomist and had to move back to his parents' home.

Arguably the second most powerful man in Germany after Hitler, Heinrich Himmler was head of the entire Nazi police force, including the SS, the SD, and the Gestapo. As head of the SS, Himmler administered the death camps in the East and oversaw the mass murder of Jews as well as countless other victims during the Holocaust. At the end of the war he was captured by British forces but never stood trial for his crimes; on May 23, 1945, he swallowed a hidden cyanide capsule and committed suicide. (Keystone/Getty Images)

These failures made him more irritable and aggressive; he alienated himself from friends and family, and during 1923 to 1924, he abandoned Catholicism. Occult Germanic mythology became his religion, instead, while politically the NSDAP appealed to him because its positions reflected his own views. While he was not swept up by Hitler's charisma, Himmler read his works and admired him greatly.

From mid-1924, Himmler worked as secretary and personal assistant to party secretary Gregor Strasser, whom Hitler appointed party propaganda head in 1926. Himmler traveled the whole of Bavaria, giving speeches and handing out writings. From late 1924, Strasser placed him in charge of the NSDAP's offices in Lower Bavaria; Himmler was responsible for bringing in new members when the party was refounded in February 1925. In 1926, Himmler was appointed as deputy gauleiter of Oberbayern and Swabia. From then until 1930, he was also acting propaganda leader of the NSDAP.

Himmler also made a reputation for himself in the party as a speaker and organizer. His speeches emphasized race consciousness, the need for German expansion and settlements, and long-standing opposition toward Germany's enemies: "Jewish" capital, Marxism (i.e., socialism, communism, and anarchism), liberal democracy, and the Slavic peoples. His background in agriculture placed Himmler comfortably in a party that stressed the myth of "blood and soil," and he was obsessed with notions of selective breeding and racial perfection. In 1927, Himmler was appointed deputy *Reichsführer* of the *Schutzstaffel* (SS), a post he held until his appointment as *SS-Reichsführer* on January 6, 1929.

On July 3, 1928, Himmler married Margarete Boden, who bore him a daughter, Gudrun, on August 8, 1929. They set up a poultry farm at Waldtrudering, near Munich, but Himmler was not a successful farmer. After Gudrun's birth, he left both his wife and the farm.

On January 6, 1929, Himmler was appointed to head Hitler's personal bodyguard, the black-shirted SS, at that time a small body of 280 men. The SS was subservient to the SA and had two major functions: to serve as bodyguards for Hitler and other Nazi leaders and to market subscriptions for the Nazi Party newspaper, the *Völkischer Beobachter*. From this foundation, Himmler developed the elite corps of the Nazi Party. By 1930, the SS had grown to 2,700 men, and Himmler had managed to make it into an organization independent from the SA. Himmler was elected to the Reichstag for the constituency of Weser-Ems.

In April 1931, Himmler used his SS troops to crush a revolt by the Berlin SA against Hitler's leadership. The suppression of the SA mutiny showed the SS to be an internal party police organization showing unconditional loyalty to Hitler through its motto "My honor is loyalty."

In 1931, Himmler commissioned his close associate, **Reinhard Heydrich**, to create the Security Service SD, which, in August 1934, became the main intelligence organization of the party. It kept watch on Hitler's internal opponents and gathered intelligence on other political parties as well as local and federal government officials. On January 25, 1932, Himmler was appointed the security chief of the NSDAP headquarters in Munich, the so-called Brown House.

By January 1933, when the Nazis seized power, the SS numbered more than 52,000 officers, and Himmler had taken charge of two key responsibilities for Germany: internal security and guardianship over racial purity. In March 1933, Himmler was appointed head of the Munich police and took over responsibility for the structure and management of the concentration camp at Dachau. On April 1, 1933, the Bavarian state government was dismissed, and Himmler became the political police commander; by January 1934, he extended his control of the police force in all German states except for Prussia and Schaumburg-Lippe. On April 20, 1934, because of growing tension between the Nazi leadership and the SA, **Hermann Göring** appointed Himmler as inspector of the Secret State Police (Gestapo). The joining of the Gestapo with Heydrich's SD resulted in Himmler administering tight control over the whole system, adding also to the size and influence of the SS.

Himmler and Heydrich were instrumental in convincing Hitler to purge the leadership of the SA. As a result, Himmler and the SS were the main participants in the June 1934 purge that became known as the Night of the Long Knives. Himmler was personally involved in the arrest and murder of SA leaders and Hitler's political opponents in Berlin. By July 1934, Himmler, as *SS-Reichsführer*, reported directly to Hitler, making him one of the most powerful men in Germany. With total control over the concentration camps, the SS had sole responsibility for their construction and management throughout Germany, while the Gestapo was able to act against supposed opponents of the regime without reference to the judicial system.

In February 1938, Himmler used the SD to force Werner von Fritsch and Werner von Blomberg to resign from their army leadership posts, elevating Hitler to complete control over Germany's military. In August 1938, against the opposition of the Wehrmacht, Hitler gave a military role to the SS, which later formed the Waffen-SS; although assigned to the Wehrmacht, these units remained under Himmler's control as *SS-Reichsführer*. This overrode the arms monopoly of the army and gave Himmler authority over an independent armed force.

Shortly after World War II broke out on September 3, 1939, the administration of the Gestapo, the Criminal Police, and the SD merged to create the *Reichsicherheitshauptamt* (RSHA), operating under the SS. Heydrich became head of the RSHA, reporting directly to Himmler. Then on October 7, 1939, Himmler was appointed *Reichskommissar* for the consolidation of German nationality, with responsibility for displacing and oppressing the local population in the occupied territories in accordance with Nazi racial ideology.

Upon the occupation of Poland, the SS assumed responsibility to purge the enemies of the German Reich in the occupied territories. The *Einsatzgruppen*, special squads under Heydrich's direct command, organized the expulsion, persecution, and murder of hundreds of thousands of Poles and Jews. Himmler described the massive eradication policy as a "heavy duty" for his subordinates.

In 1941, following Germany's invasion of the Soviet Union, Hitler transferred Himmler to police security in the areas occupied by the Wehrmacht, and with this, he became the main contributor to the Final Solution of the Jewish Question, the deportation and murder of the European Jews. People considered to be "subhuman" from all over Eastern Europe were next incarcerated into camps and ghettos to prevent organized resistance and to permit German population expansion into the occupied territories. Later, those Jews who were not summarily shot were herded into ghettos and then later sent to death camps, where they were gassed and burned in crematoria. Himmler himself often visited execution sites and the camps and was the person most active in turning Hitler's violent hatred toward Jews and other peoples into an extermination program. His brilliant organizational skills had awful consequences for the Jews. It was Himmler who ensured that the deportations took place and that the camps all ran on business lines so that they paid for themselves and made profits where possible.

In 1942, Himmler was given control to impose Nazi criminal law over all Russians, Poles, and Jews in the occupied territories as well as power to exploit the large number of prisoners of war as slave labor for the war economy. Himmler laid down and implemented the *Generalplan Ost*, which used force to expel and relocate millions of Poles, Czechs, Ukrainians, and White Ruthenians, deemed to be "sub-human," to Siberia—at the same time, moving ethnic Germans into newly conquered territories.

In January 1943, after the assassination of Heydrich the previous summer, **Ernst Kaltenbrunner** became head of the SD and the RSHA, replacing Himmler, who had been in charge of management before June 1942. Meanwhile, Himmler continued to increase his power and accumulate more offices. On August 25, 1943, Hitler appointed Himmler as minister of the interior, and on October 4, 1943, in a three-hour speech in Posen to top-ranking SS officers, he spoke openly about the "extermination" of the Jews.

In February 1944, at Himmler's insistence, Hitler dismissed Admiral Wilhelm Canaris as chief of Germany's military intelligence service, the *Abwehr*. The *Abwehr*'s functions were taken over by the RSHA, and areas previously the responsibility of the *Abwehr* were divided between Gestapo and the RSHA.

On July 20, 1944, an attempt was made on Hitler's life by a group of army officers. Himmler himself oversaw the arrest, prosecution, and execution of those responsible. This unsuccessful assassination brought Himmler further power and the entry into the Wehrmacht, as Hitler appointed him, on July 21, 1944, to be the successor of General Friedrich Fromm as a leading commander of the army. He also became commander in chief of Army Group Vistula.

On December 2, 1944, Himmler took over Army Group Oberrhein in order to build up a new defensive line, but by January and February 1945, it became obvious that he lacked the military skills necessary for a commander in chief. To avoid further responsibility, Himmler escaped to an SS hospital and was replaced in March 1945.

By the spring of 1945, Himmler's loyalty to Hitler was beginning to waver, as Germany was clearly losing the war. Having made desperate attempts to conceal and destroy evidence of his monstrous crimes, Himmler sought to arrange a German surrender to the Western Allies; hoping to avoid capture by the Red Army, he counted on the anticommunist sentiment of the West to negotiate an anti-Soviet alliance that would include Germany.

In April 28, 1945, when Hitler learned that Himmler, as his successor and possible mediator, had made unauthorized peace overtures to the Western Allies, Himmler was dismissed from all offices and party membership and Hitler prepared an arrest warrant against him. The notorious former SS leader was now unwelcomed in the new German government. He attempted to escape the ruined country through British lines under a false name. He was captured, however, and on May 23, 1945, while in British custody at Lüneburg, he committed suicide by swallowing a cyanide capsule.

HIPPLER, FRITZ (1909–2002)

Fritz Hippler was a German filmmaker who ran the film department in the Propaganda Ministry of the Third Reich, under **Joseph Goebbels**. He was born on August 17, 1909 and brought up in Berlin. The son of a minor official who died in France during World War I, he was only 10 years of age when the Treaty of Versailles was signed, but during his teenage years, he developed an intense hatred toward the Weimar Republic. In 1927, he joined the Nazi Party and became a member of the SA. When he was old enough, he became a law student at universities in Heidelberg and Berlin, and by 1934, he had earned his PhD at the University of Heidelberg.

In 1932, he became a Nazi Party district speaker and was promptly expelled from the University of Berlin for inciting violence. On April 19, 1933, however, the newly installed National Socialist education minister, Bernhard Rust, overthrew all existing disciplinary actions against students associated with the Nazi Party, enabling Hippler's return. He then became the district and high school group leader for Berlin-Brandenburg in the National Socialist German Students' League. On May 22, 1933, following Goebbels's lead on May 10, Hippler gave a speech to his fellow students that precipitated a march from the student house to Opera Square with a collection of banned books, which were then publicly burned.

In 1936, Hippler became an assistant to the artist, photographer, and film director Hans Weidemann. In this capacity, he worked on the production of newsreels and learned the techniques behind documentary filmmaking. His work was undertaken through the Reich Propaganda Ministry, and with it came a promotion in 1938 to the rank of *SS-Hauptsturmführer*. In January 1939, he took over Weidemann's position, meaning that he now worked directly for Goebbels. By August 1939, Hippler had been promoted to head the film department at the ministry. Among his tasks he determined which foreign films would be allowed on German screens and what parts of them would be cut.

He also produced and directed movies. In 1940, Hippler directed *Der Feldzug in Poland (The Campaign in Poland)*, a propaganda film demonstrating the superiority of German arms in the first phase of World War II from September 1939 onward.

His most famous—indeed, infamous—creative work was undoubtedly another feature-length film from 1940: *Der Ewige Jude (The Eternal Jew)*, arguably one of the most offensive antisemitic propaganda movies ever made. The film consists of documentary footage combined with materials filmed shortly after the Nazi occupation of Poland. Hippler shot footage in the Jewish ghettos of Łódź, Warsaw, Kraków, and Lublin, the only such footage, as it turned out, shot specifically for the film. The rest of the film consisted of stills and archival footage from other feature films—footage that the film presented as if it was an additional documentary film. The film itself covered four essential tropes: "degenerate" Jewish life as seen in the Polish ghettos; the nature of Jewish political, cultural, and social values; Jewish religious ceremonies, instruction, worship, and ritual slaughter; and **Adolf Hitler** as the savior of Germany from the Jews.

Even though the Nazis had not themselves yet decided on mass annihilation as the means to destroy Europe's Jews, the intention of the film was to prepare the German population for the coming Holocaust. However, the movie did not have the desired impact on the German public, owing to the fact that a major motion picture, *Jud Süss* (Veit Harlan, 1940), had already appeared to rapturous acclaim employing top box-office stars and building on captivating period drama. By contrast, *Der Ewige Jude* was a documentary based on limited original footage, still images, and archival film clips. Unlike *Jud Süss*, therefore, which was a great commercial success, *Der Ewige Jude* was a failure at the box office. As a propaganda film, it was shown more for training purposes to troops on the Eastern Front and SS members than it was in cinemas, although a few foreign-language voice-overs were made, and the film was exported to countries occupied by Germany.

Hippler, for his part, was honored by Adolf Hitler, and his career was made. In October 1942, he was appointed director in charge of Reich filmmaking, with responsibility for all control, supervision, and direction of German movies. He now became second only to Goebbels, and by 1943, he was promoted to *SS-Obersturmbannführer*.

Such a career trajectory, though impressive, generated resentment in some quarters—no less than from Goebbels himself. The *Reichsminister* had long kept a watching brief on Hippler, whom he saw as sometimes impertinent, often immature, disorganized, and too fond of alcohol. In this latter area, Goebbels had a point. Hippler indeed suffered from an addiction to alcohol, and it was for this that Goebbels finally dismissed him in June 1943. Hippler was stripped of his SS rank, and a trumped-up accusation was brought against him that he had denied having a Jewish great-grandmother. Hippler was sent to an infantry-replacement battalion and underwent mountain infantry training. Released from active duty, he was then given the task of shooting newsreel footage as cameraman until February 1945. At the end of the war, he was taken by the British as a prisoner of war.

In 1946, he was tried for directing *Der Ewige Jude* and sentenced to two years in prison. Staging a comeback after his release, he collaborated on documentary movies under another name. In a 1981 memoir, he claimed that Goebbels was the real creator of *Der Ewige Jude*, having directed large parts of it himself and giving Hippler the credit. Later, he stated that he regretted being listed as the director of the movie because it unfairly resulted in his treatment after the war. In his opinion, he had nothing to do with the killing of Jews and only shot some footage for a film that Goebbels himself then put together. Moreover, he claimed that at the time he had little knowledge of the Nazis' murderous policies toward the Jews and was not aware of the Holocaust as it was taking place. He said that if he could, he would "annul" everything about the film, which had caused him such personal difficulties in his subsequent life.

Fritz Hippler lived in Berchtesgaden, Bavaria, until his death on May 22, 2002, aged 92.

HIRT, AUGUST (1898–1945)

August Hirt was a physician with an interest in anatomy. During World War II, he carried out mustard-gas experiments on inmates at the Natzweiler-Struthof concentration camp and also arranged for the murder of 86 Auschwitz inmates so that their bodies could be used as part of his research on skeletons for his collection of "Judeo-Bolshevik" skulls as specimens at the Institute of Anatomy in Strasbourg.

Hirt was born on April 28, 1898, in Mannheim, Baden, to a Swiss businessman father. In 1914, aged 16 and still a high school student, he volunteered to fight for Germany in World War I. In October 1916, he suffered a bullet wound in his upper jaw; he was awarded an Iron Cross and returned home to Mannheim in 1917.

Hirt studied medicine at the University of Heidelberg, and in 1922, he took out his doctorate in medicine with a thesis investigating the nervous system of dinosaurs. He worked at the Anatomical Institute in Heidelberg, and in 1925, he started teaching at Heidelberg University. By 1930, he was a professor there.

Hirt had taken out German citizenship in 1921, giving him dual Swiss and German nationality. On April 1, 1933, he joined the SS; he joined the Nazi Party on May 1, 1937, and within two months, he had attained the rank of *SS-Hauptsturmführer*. From March 1, 1942, he was a staff member at the *Rasse- und Siedlungshauptamt der SS* (SS Race and Settlement Main Office, or RuSHA), the organization in charge of ensuring "racial and ideological purity" among members of the SS. In 1944, he attained the rank of *SS-Sturmbannführer*.

The *Ahnenerbe* was a Nazi initiative dedicated to researching the history, culture, and anthropology of the Aryan race. Its aim was to establish that Nordic peoples once ruled the earth. The *Institut für Wehrwissenschaftliche Zweckforschung* (Institute for Military Scientific Research), which performed wide-ranging human-subject medical research, became part of the *Ahnenerbe* during World War II. The institute was managed by Wolfram Sievers, who had founded the organization on the orders of *SS-Reichsführer* **Heinrich Himmler**. Himmler appointed Sievers as institute director with two divisions, one headed by Sigmund Rascher and the other by August Hirt.

Hirt was regard as an expert on the deadly mustard-gas toxin. Fearing that the Allies might use it against Germany, Himmler tasked Hirt to find an antidote. Prior to World War II, Hirt had carried out mustard gas experiments with rats, but with the onset of war, he sought to repeat these experiments on humans in the Natzweiler-Struthof concentration camp, near Strasbourg. Chosen inmates were subjected to mustard gas through a drip in the arm; within a few hours, they experienced burns over their bodies and suffered excruciating pain. Some inmates went blind; others died. The corpses were then dissected to remove and study the damaged organs.

In 1942, Hirt—now head of the department of anatomy at the Reich University in Strasbourg, working under the aegis of the *Ahnenerbe*—proposed to collect skulls of "Judeo-Bolsheviks" who embodied the "disgusting but characteristic subhuman" as part of his research on race. Himmler approved the proposal; he wanted the RuSHA to review all children of mixed marriages and their progeny for three or four generations. Descendants with "Jewish features" could be sterilized, if not murdered. To enable this, the SS needed a clearer understanding of Jewish "race traits."

Hirt thus sought to create a museum of "subhumans," in which the so-called Jewish traits would be exhibited. Himmler allowed Hirt to choose any prisoners from Auschwitz he needed. In August 1943, Wolfram Sievers, together with Hirt and anthropologists Bruno Beger and Hans Fleischhacker, selected 115 individuals at Auschwitz: 79 Jewish men, 30 Jewish women, 2 Poles, and 4 "Asians" whose nationality was not determined. These were the people who would be used to create a specimen collection of Jews. Of those selected, 89 people (60 men and 29 women) were sent to Natzweiler-Struthof on July 30, 1943. Three men died en route. The victims were fed to improve their appearance for the casts that would be made of their bodies. Divided into four groups, they were successively gassed in the small-scale gas chamber at Natzweiler-Struthof by **Josef Kramer** during August 1943. Their corpses were sent to Hirt at Reich University in Strasbourg, where their skeletons were prepared as an anthropological display.

Hirt stored the bodies in alcohol-filled tanks. In September 1944, the rapid approach of French troops led to the project being abandoned and to Himmler ordering the destruction of all traces of the collection. Part of Hirt's skull collection is said to have been moved to Mittersill Castle, in Salzburg, Austria, in the fall of 1944. On liberating Strasbourg, the Allies found corpses and the partial remains preserved in formalin of 86 bodies. The corpses were buried on October 23, 1945, before being transferred in 1951 to the Jewish cemetery of Strasbourg-Cronenbourg. The names of the victims were not known.

Hirt escaped from Strasbourg in September 1944 and hid in Tübingen, southern Germany. He was tried in absentia for war crimes at the Military War Crimes Trial at Metz on December 23, 1953. Unknown to the tribunal, however, Hirt had committed suicide on June 2, 1945, aged 47, at Schluchsee, Baden-Württemberg.

HIRTREITER, JOSEF (1909–1978)

Josef Hirtreiter was an SS officer who worked at Treblinka during the *Aktion Reinhard* phase of the Holocaust in Poland. In 1951, he was the first SS man brought to trial for war crimes committed at Treblinka.

Josef Hirtreiter was born on February 1, 1909, in Bruchsal, near Karlsruhe. After completing elementary school, he trained as a locksmith but failed the final examination. He then worked as an unskilled construction worker and bricklayer. On August 1, 1932, he became a member of the SA and the Nazi Party.

In October 1940, after the invasion of Poland, Hirtreiter was assigned to the Hadamar euthanasia center, an extermination facility of *Aktion T-4*. He worked in the kitchen and the office and was also involved in cremating corpses.

In summer 1942, he was called up to join the Wehrmacht; he was in the army for only a short time before being sent back to Hadamar. Shortly after his return, Hirtreiter was assigned to *Aktion Reinhard* and transferred to Berlin; from there, **Christian Wirth** sent him to the camp complex at Lublin in occupied Poland. On August 20, 1942, along with seven other T-4 veterans, Hirtreiter arrived at Treblinka. There, he acquired the rank of *SS-Scharführer*. He served at Treblinka II, in the receiving area, between October 1942 and October 1943. He became known by the nickname "Sepp," a diminutive of Josef. Because of his cruelty, he soon became the terror of Jewish prisoners and became notorious as a murderer of infants and small children.

In October 1943, Hirtreiter moved on to Sobibór to assist with the liquidation of the camp. Then, after the closure of Treblinka in October 1943, he was ordered to Italy, where he joined a police unit for antipartisan cleansing operations.

After the *Aktion Reinhard* camps were liquidated, most operatives were sent to Trieste in Italy, tasked with assisting with the suppression of partisan activities. **Franz Stangl**, Hirtreiter's camp commander, suggested that while he had been told he was being sent to Trieste to set up the Risiera di San Sabba killing center there, senior Nazi politicians realized that the staff and commanders of *Aktion Reinhard* could incriminate their superiors. Consequently, operatives were sent to dangerous areas where some of them, such as Wirth, were killed.

Hirtreiter was arrested by the Allies in July 1946 for having served at Hadamar and jailed in Darmstadt. He was released due to a lack of incriminating evidence that he was complicit in murdering mentally ill people.

He was then rearrested in 1951, after testimony from former Treblinka prisoner Szyja (Sawek or Jeszajahu) Warszawski, who survived, wounded, in a burial pit and slipped away under the cover of night. Hirtreiter was charged in March 1951 at Frankfurt am Main and convicted for killing children, many aged one or two, during the unloading of the transports. He was known to grab them by their feet and smash their heads against the walls of boxcars. He was also found guilty of beating two prisoners (because money had been found on them) until they were unconscious, hanging them by their feet, and finally killing them with a shot to the head.

Hirtreiter was sentenced to life imprisonment on March 3, 1951. He was the first of the Treblinka extermination camp SS officers tried over a decade later at Düsseldorf. Released from prison in 1977 due to illness, he died six months later, on November 27, 1978, in a home for the elderly in Frankfurt.

HITLER, ADOLF (1889–1945)

Adolf Hitler was a German politician who was the founder and head of the Nazi Party, chancellor of Germany from 1933 to 1945, and führer (leader) of the Nazi State from 1934 to 1945. In his efforts to implement a racial policy in which Germans and Aryans became the master race over Europe, he led his Third Reich into actions, which resulted in the deaths of 35 million people.

Adolf Hitler, the fourth of six children, was born on April 20, 1889, at Braunau-am-Inn, Austria, the son of Alois Hitler, a German customs clerk, and his third wife Klara, an indulgent, hardworking Austrian. He was a slow learner, did poorly in school, and was frequently beaten by his strict, authoritarian father. His mother tried to shield him, but he was only freed from his father's cruelty, at the age of 14, by his father's death. Hitler dropped out of high school when 16 years old. An aspiring artist, he went to Vienna in October 1907 but twice failed to be accepted into the Vienna Academy of Fine Arts. His mother died from cancer in 1908.

Bitter at his rejection by the academy, he spent five difficult years in Vienna, where he learned politics from the inflammatory speeches of the populist Christian Socialist mayor, Karl Lueger, and picked up Lueger's stereotyped, obsessive antisemitism with its concerns about "purity of blood." This shaped the hatred of Jews, Marxists, liberals, and the Hapsburg rulers that he retained throughout his life. He lived a hand-to-mouth existence, working occasional odd jobs and selling his sketches through taverns, where he also gave political speeches to customers. Although Austrian, Hitler became a German nationalist, and in 1913, he moved to Bavaria in the German Empire.

From wild racial theories in Vienna, Hitler took the concept of the "Eternal Jew" as the symbol and cause of all chaos, corruption, and decadence in culture, politics, and the economy. He viewed the press, prostitution, syphilis, capitalism, Marxism, democracy, and pacifism as means in which "the Jew" conspired to undermine the German nation and the purity of the creative Aryan race.

Adolf Hitler became the leader of the Nazi Party in 1921 and was chancellor of Germany between 1933 and 1945. He served as undisputed Führer ("leader") of the Nazi State from 1934 onward. As dictator, he initiated World War II by invading Poland in September 1939 and then, implementing an extreme policy of racial exclusivism, presided over a regime that perpetrated the Holocaust of Europe's Jews. Hitler thereby became one of the most notorious mass murderers in history. (Photos.com)

With the outbreak of World War I, Hitler enlisted in the 16th Bavarian Infantry Regiment of the German army, in which he served until 1919. He was assigned a role as a regimental messenger runner but also saw combat; during those years, he received four decorations for bravery, including the prestigious Iron Cross First Class. In Flanders in 1918, he was temporarily blinded in a gas attack; he spent several months recuperating and was promoted from private to corporal, receiving the Iron Cross Second Class. When the war ended, he was posted to an intelligence unit in the army and assigned to spy on certain radical political parties. One of these was the German Workers' Party. Hitler was finally mustered out of the German army in 1919.

The June 1919 Treaty of Versailles imposed on defeated Germany severe economic penalties, causing great hardship for the German people. On September 16, 1919, the thoroughly disenchanted Hitler joined the same German Workers' Party (DAP), which had originally been his surveillance target. The DAP was the creation of Dietrich Eckart, who spread doctrines of mysticism and antisemitism, and Hitler soon managed to convert the party into the National Socialist German Workers Party (NSDAP), of which he became the leader in 1921.

In 1920, Hitler's intelligence handler, Munich-based Colonel Karl Haushofer, adopted the swastika insignia, and Hitler himself designed the Nazi Party banner, using the swastika symbol and placing it in a white circle on a red background. In 1921, Haushofer founded the paramilitary storm troopers (*Sturmabteiling*, or SA), composed of German veterans of World War I and undercover military intelligence officers. These storm troopers helped Hitler to organize the failed coup, the infamous Beer Hall Putsch, against the Bavarian government in Munich.

The attempted coup took place on November 8 to 9, 1923, and proceeded with help from SA leader Ernst Röhm, **Hermann Göring**, and General Erich von

Ludendorff. Hitler and his coconspirators stormed the *Bürgerbräukeller*, a Munich beer hall, where members of the Bavarian state government were gathered. The coup was crushed by police and military units; Hitler was convicted of treason, sentenced to five years in jail, and imprisoned in Landsberg Prison. He only served nine months before a general amnesty was declared, but while there, he dictated to his deputy, Rudolf Hess, the first volume of his autobiography and political manifesto, *Mein Kampf* (*My Struggle*). In it, he openly displayed his antisemitism, as well as Germany's urgent need for *Lebensraum* (living space), or territorial expansion in the East. The book was not taken seriously, however, and its warning signs went unheeded.

Released in 1924, Hitler worked to build up the Nazi Party. He generated support by attacking the Treaty of Versailles, while promoting pan-Germanism, antisemitism, and anticommunism—all of which proceeded from propaganda that denounced international capitalism and communism as being part of the Jewish conspiracy.

After his failed putsch, Hitler resolved to overthrow the established Weimar Republic by working within the system, and his demagoguery, as well as general economic unrest, led to increasing Nazi representation at all levels of government via elections held during the 1920s. The Great Depression, which began in 1929, gave Hitler's goals a tremendous boost, as Germans turned to him for leadership in Germany's national economic crisis. Hitler was provided with a personal bodyguard unit named the *Schutzstaffel*, or SS, and the Nazis began to gain considerable support in Germany through their network of army and war veterans. By 1932, the Nazis had become the largest party in the Reichstag, although they never achieved a majority of votes or seats.

Hitler ruled the NSDAP through an autocratic style, asserting the leader principle (*Führerprinzip*), which relied on total obedience of all subordinates to their superiors. He viewed leadership as a pyramid, with himself—the infallible leader—at the peak, demanding total loyalty of all party members to himself. Party roles were filled through appointment by those of higher rank, who demanded unquestioning obedience to the will of the leader. Hitler's leadership style was to give contradictory orders to his subordinates and to foster distrust, competition, and infighting, which consolidated and maximized his own power.

The electorate responded to Hitler's promises of jobs, security, and a greater Germany. In 1932, Hitler ran for the presidency against 84-year-old Paul von Hindenburg. Hitler came second in both rounds of the election, gaining more than 36 percent of the vote in the final count, and these results set Hitler up as a strong force in German politics. Hindenburg reluctantly agreed to appoint him as chancellor on January 30, 1933, in a coalition government with strong support from right-wing German industrialists and bankers, who saw in Hitler their bulwark against communism.

Hitler used his position as chancellor to form a de facto legal dictatorship. When the Reichstag was set on fire on the night of February 27, 1933, Hitler projected this as a communist plot to overthrow the state in response to his appointment as chancellor. The resulting Decree for the Protection of the People and the State (also known as the Reichstag Fire Decree) suspended basic rights in the German Constitution, restricting the right to assembly, freedom of speech, and freedom of the press, among other rights; allowed detention without trial; and removed all restraints on police investigations.

Hitler also engineered the passage of the Enabling Act in 1933, which gave his cabinet full legislative powers for a period of four years and allowed for deviations from the constitution. The regime could arrest and incarcerate political opponents without specific charge, dissolve political organizations, and suppress publications. The central government was given authority to overrule state and local laws and to overthrow state and local governments. This law became a permanent feature of the Nazi police state. By the end of June 1933, all other political parties had effectively ceased to exist, and on July 14, 1933, the Nazi Party was declared the only legal political party in Germany.

Military opposition was also punished. The demands of the SA for more political and military power led to the infamous Night of the Long Knives, a major purge that took place from June 30 to July 2, 1934. Ernst Röhm and other SA leaders, along with certain of Hitler's political enemies, were rounded up and shot.

When Hindenburg died in August 1934, Hitler combined the offices of chancellor and president to become the "uncontested leader" (Führer) of the German nation. Unrestrained, he now whipped up passionate support for his regime through his speeches and elaborate propaganda at mass meetings, in which his audiences attained a degree of hysteria. Moreover, from 1933 until the outbreak of war in 1939, the regime instituted hundreds of laws and regulations to restrict and exclude Jews in German society. These laws were issued throughout all levels of government, making good on the Nazis' pledge to persecute Jews.

On April 1, 1933, Hitler commenced a national boycott of Jewish businesses. On April 7, 1933, this was followed by the Law for the Restoration of the Professional Civil Service, which banned Jews from state service. Laws limited the number of Jewish students permitted to attend schools and universities, restricted Jews working in medical and legal professions, and canceled the licenses of Jewish tax consultants. The German Student Union called for "Action against the Un-German Spirit," prompting students to burn more than 25,000 books and ushering in an era of censorship and incessant Nazi propaganda. By 1934, Jewish actors could no longer perform in films or theaters, and on September 15, 1935, the Nuremberg Laws defined a "Jew" as anyone with three or four grandparents who were Jewish, regardless of whether the person considered himself or herself Jewish or observed the religion. The Nuremberg Laws also set out the Law for the Protection of German Blood and German Honor, forbidding marriage (or even sexual relations) between non-Jewish and Jewish Germans, and the Reich Citizenship Law, which deprived "non-Aryans" of the benefits of German citizenship.

In 1936, Germany held the winter and Berlin summer Olympic Games, and Hitler softened his antisemitic speeches and actions in order to avoid world criticism and an adverse impact on tourism. Once the Olympics were over, however, the oppression of Jews resumed and intensified, with the Aryanization of Jewish businesses—a process involving the firing of Jewish workers and the seizure of

Jewish businesses by non-Jewish owners. Jews were isolated from German society; they were banned from public schools, universities, theaters, sports events, and Aryan localities. Jewish doctors were forbidden from treating Aryan patients. Jews had to carry identity cards, and from the fall of 1938, Jews had to have their passports stamped with a red letter *J*.

On the night of November 9 to 10, 1938, a spate of vicious anti-Jewish pogroms swept Germany, Austria, and parts of the Sudetenland. Nazis destroyed synagogues; vandalized Jewish homes, schools, and businesses; and murdered around 100 Jews in the *Kristallnacht*, the so-called Night of Broken Glass (a reference to the broken glass resulting from the destruction). It raised the Nazi persecution of Jews to a higher level of barbarity; at least 30,000 Jewish men were arrested in the wake of the pogrom and sent to concentration camps.

Hitler's racial eugenic program also targeted children with physical and developmental disabilities, a precursor to later euthanasia programs for adults. Hitler's regime also victimized homosexuals, arresting an estimated 100,000 men from 1933 to 1945. Some of these were imprisoned or sent to concentration camps, where they were forced to wear pink triangles to distinguish them as gay prisoners; the Nazis considered their homosexuality a crime and a disease.

In a series of military moves intended to overturn the hated provisions of the Versailles Treaty, Hitler reoccupied the Rhineland (1936), restoring it to Germany; established the Rome-Berlin Axis (1936) with Benito Mussolini's Fascist Italy; and annexed Austria to Germany (1938). At the Munich Conference of September 1938, Hitler convinced Britain and France (without Czechoslovak participation) to permit him to annex the Sudetenland of western Czechoslovakia, containing many ethnic Germans. Within six months of that agreement and much to the humiliation of the French and British leaders, Hitler decided to annex the rest of Czechoslovakia in March 1939. Then in August 1939, he surprised the Western world by signing a nonaggression pact with the Soviet Union, negotiated by his foreign minister **Joachim von Ribbentrop**. This ensured the stability of Germany's vulnerable eastern border and enabled Germany and the USSR to invade Poland in September 1939.

The invasion of Poland brought Germany into a state of war with Britain and France on September 3, 1939, in defense of their ally Poland. The German army's newly developed blitzkrieg tactics, however, saw Poland crushed within three weeks. By June 1940, France had been conquered, and British troops had been thrown out of Europe via the beaches of Dunkirk. Between July 10 and October 31, 1940, Germany then waged and lost the Battle of Britain, in which the German Luftwaffe attempted to weaken Britain prior to a land invasion by the German army. With Germany's defeat in the air, the invasion was postponed.

Hitler then looked to other parts; Greece and Yugoslavia were subdued, along with most of North Africa, but on June 22, 1941, in Operation Barbarossa, Hitler committed his single biggest mistake of the war when German forces invaded the Soviet Union. The initial operation comprised more than 4 million German troops, with additional forces from Germany's allies Romania, Italy, Slovakia, Hungary, Croatia, Spain, and Finland. Three Nazi armies invaded Russia: Army Group

North besieged Leningrad for 900 days, Army Group Center reached the outskirts of Moscow, and Army Group South occupied Ukraine. Early Soviet losses were massive; the Red Army was forced back deep into Russia. After a series of initial successes, however, the German armies were stopped with the outline of the city of Moscow in sight. Hitler did not permit his men to retreat for the winter, and when Soviet forces counterattacked, they inflicted the first German land defeat.

Enraged, Hitler fired most of his leading generals, was dismissive of the rest, and took over as commander in chief of the armed forces. For the next four years, Germany waged a losing war in the east against greater numbers of Soviet forces. In December 1941, Hitler aggravated his miscalculations by declaring war on the United States after the Japanese attack on Pearl Harbor.

In addition to waging a war of aggression, Hitler launched arguably the greatest crime against humanity ever committed: using the policy of a racially pure Aryan nation, Hitler turned his hatred of Jews into a national policy of mass extermination through the creation of numerous death camps. Jews were deported from occupied countries, used as slave labor, and then dispatched in gas chambers when unable to work further. In this manner, an estimated 6 million Jews perished in Hitler's Final Solution.

After catastrophic losses at Stalingrad in January 1943, German forces on the Eastern Front had to withdraw. As the course of the war turned against Hitler, so did certain cliques in the German military. By 1944, several attempts had been made on Hitler's life, including one by Colonel Claus von Stauffenberg, who exploded a bomb at Hitler's East Prussian headquarters on July 20, 1944. By now, the Third Reich's days were clearly numbered, but Hitler embarked on several desperate gambits to stave off defeat. In a spectacular but futile attempt to turn the tide of the war back to Germany's favor, he directed construction of numerous "superweapons," including jet fighters, pilotless bombs, and guided missiles. After surviving the July 1944 assassination attempt, he squandered Germany's final military reserves in the ill-fated Battle of the Bulge in France (December 16, 1944 to January 16, 1945) but failed to defeat the Western Allies.

In the final days of the war, British, U.S., and Soviet armies were advancing on Berlin. By April 1945, the avenging Soviets had all but surrounded Berlin, and Hitler was a virtual captive in his command bunker deep underground. On April 30, 1945, Hitler and his wife of a few hours, his long-term mistress, Eva Braun, committed suicide in the bunker rather than face capture. He and his followers brought about the most devastating war in history, the genocide of 6 million people, and the disgrace and humiliation of Germany.

HOESS, RUDOLF (1900–1947)

Rudolf Franz Ferdinand Hoess (also spelled Höss) was commandant of the Auschwitz concentration and death camp between 1940 and 1943. He was born on November 25, 1900, in Baden-Baden, Germany, the only son of three children born into a strict Roman Catholic family. His father was a former army officer who served in German East Africa (Tanganyika) and ran a successful tea and coffee business. Hoess was a lonely child with no playmates his own age until he entered elementary school. His father wanted him to train for the priesthood, but he turned against Catholicism in his early teens, after his priest told his father about something Hoess had spoken about during confession.

When World War I commenced, Hoess was keen to join the army and tried three times join the front line as a 14-year-old, but on each occasion, he was sent home because he was too young. After his father's death, Hoess lied about his age and enlisted in his father's and grandfather's old regiment when he was 15. He was posted to the Middle East Front, served in Turkey and Palestine, and at 17, he became the youngest noncommissioned officer in the army. Hoess was wounded three times and was awarded the Iron Cross and other military decorations.

After the war, Hoess returned to Germany and completed his secondary education. Like many young veterans at a loose end, he joined a *Freikorps* group and was completely comfortable in that right-wing militaristic environment. In early 1922, he was first introduced to **Adolf Hitler**. Conservative, racist, and extremely nationalistic, Hoess joined the Nazi Party in 1922 and renounced his affiliation with the Catholic Church.

Fighting in the streets against communists and "traitors," Hoess and members of the *Freikorps* (including **Martin Bormann**) were arrested in June 1923 after beating the local schoolmaster to death for handing over to France a "patriot" engaged in sabotage during the French occupation of the Ruhr. Hoess was sentenced to 10 years' jail and remained in prison until July 1928.

Hoess emerged from prison a hero to right-wing nationalists and married Hedwig Hensel in 1929. Between 1930 and 1943, they had five children: two sons and three daughters, who later lived with him at Auschwitz. Hoess responded to a call to action from **Heinrich Himmler**, and on April 1, 1934, he joined the SS. In December 1934, Hoess was appointed as a block leader at Dachau concentration camp, where he was mentored by **Theodor Eicke**. Hoess was a model guard and worked his way up the ranks. In August 1938, he was transferred to Sachsenhausen, and in 1939, after the invasion of Poland, he joined the Waffen-SS. Hoess performed his duties so well that when Himmler created a new camp in Upper Silesia in April 1940, he chose Hoess as its first commandant.

On May 1, 1940, Hoess was deployed to a prison camp consisting of old army barracks near the town of Auschwitz (Oświęçim). He had orders to devise a compound for 10,000 prisoners, and he resolved to develop a camp more efficient than either Dachau or Sachsenhausen. Some 700 prisoners—Soviet prisoners of war and Poles, including peasants and intellectuals—arrived in June 1940 and were told that they would not survive more than three months.

During the three and a half years in which Hoess commanded the camp, he developed the huge complex known as Auschwitz-Birkenau, consisting of three separate facilities on 8,000 hectares (20,000 acres), embracing a vast number of satellite subcamps.

In June 1941, Hoess met with Himmler in Berlin and learned that Hitler had given the order for the Final Solution of the Jewish Question. Hoess said later that Himmler had chosen Auschwitz as a killing site because of its isolation and easy rail access. Hoess was ordered to keep this information secret and was informed that **Adolf Eichmann** would be giving him all operational orders. Eichmann arrived at the camp four weeks later.

In October 1941, Hoess cleared a huge area around Auschwitz I, which remained the camp's administrative center, and built a second camp, Auschwitz II, called Birkenau, which became Auschwitz's killing center. Hoess was closely involved in selecting the best methods for killing large numbers of people. He set up experiments in which a truck's exhaust fumes were piped back into a sealed cabin to asphyxiate those trapped inside. Finding that trucks took too long to kill large numbers of people, he implemented gas chambers. Eventually, he used a disinfectant, Zyklon-B, which killed faster and more thoroughly than exhaust fumes.

During standard camp operations, two to three trains carrying 2,000 prisoners each would arrive daily, for periods of four to six weeks. The prisoners were unloaded at Birkenau; those fit for labor were marched to barracks either in Birkenau or one of the Auschwitz camps, while those unsuitable for work went immediately to the gas chambers. At first, small gassing bunkers were located deep in the woods in order to avoid detection. Later, four large gas chambers and crematoria were constructed at Birkenau in order to make the killing more efficient and to handle the increasing rate of extermination.

In May 1942, Hoess built a third camp, Auschwitz III, or Monowitz, to provide slave labor for German chemical firm I. G. Farben's synthetic-rubber works and later for other German industries. By 1943, Auschwitz was an enormous complex, at its height housing about 100,000 prisoners. It is estimated that 2.5 million people died there—mostly Jews, but also Roma, Soviet prisoners of war, and many other nationalities and ethnic groups.

Hoess lived at Auschwitz in a villa with his wife and children. He was a loving family man who returned to his home after completing a day's work at Auschwitz.

In December 1943, Hoess was rewarded for his efforts at Auschwitz with a promotion to deputy inspector of concentration camps under **Richard Glücks**. He was replaced as Auschwitz commandant by **Arthur Liebehenschel** on November 10, 1943, after which he traveled all over Germany inspecting and improving camp operations. As the German army retreated across Europe, he then began to arrange for the dismantling of some of the camps.

On May 8, 1944, Hoess returned to Auschwitz to supervise the destruction of the Jews of Hungary, in which 430,000 Hungarian Jews were transported to the camp and killed in 56 days between May and July. Even Hoess's expanded facility could not handle the huge number of corpses, and the camp staff had to dispose of tens of thousands of bodies by burning them in open pits.

When Germany surrendered in May 1945, Hoess knew that he was a wanted man and went into hiding. In March 1946, he was discovered and arrested. He was a witness at the trial of the major war criminals at Nuremberg and was then turned over to the Polish government, who had demanded his extradition. He was tried for murder and various war crimes and was found guilty. He never denied what he did, but like most Nazis on trial, he claimed simply to have been following orders.

Hoess was taken to Auschwitz, the scene of so many of his crimes, and hanged there on April 15, 1947.

HÖFLE, HERMANN (1911–1962)

Hermann Höfle (not to be confused with an SS general of the same name) was an Austrian-born *SS-Sturmbannführer*, who was **Odilo Globocnik**'s deputy in the *Aktion Reinhard* program, acting as his key deportation and extermination specialist.

Hermann Julius "Hans" Höfle was born on June 19, 1911, in Salzburg, Austria. He joined the Austrian Nazi Party in 1930, when it was an illegal movement, and became a member of the NSDAP on August 1, 1933. Höfle was imprisoned in Salzburg between late 1935 and January 1936 because of his political activity. A trained mechanic, he had at one time been a Salzburg taxi driver and owner of a taxi company.

In 1937, Höfle was head of the SS unit *Sturmbann 1/76*. The first action in which he took part was *Kristallnacht* on November 9 to 10, 1938. He aroused the interest of **Adolf Eichmann**, who recommended him to Globocnik. Completing training at officers' school in Dachau, Höfle worked in the Sudetenland briefly prior to the outbreak of World War II.

After Poland was invaded by Germany, Höfle served as an officer with the police auxiliary unit (*Selbstschutz*) in Nowy Sącz in the Kraków district. From November 1940, he was the head of the Jewish forced-labor camps working near Bełżec on a system of antitank trenches.

Höfle was also involved in the construction of SS and police bases in the occupied East as part of *Aktion Reinhard*. During 1941, he served in Mogilev, after which he returned to Lublin, where he worked under Globocnik and was drawn into planning *Aktion Reinhard*. On March 16, 1942, he met with several other planners of *Aktion Reinhard* and the German civil administration to organize deportations to Bełżec. It took no time for him to become second in command to Globocnik within the program and Globocnik's key deportation and extermination expert. In Lublin, Höfle instructed SS members, including those who transferred from *Aktion T-4*, in what their *Aktion Reinhard* duties should be. As chief of staff, he made all recruits sign a secrecy pledge regarding their service.

Höfle played a key role in deportation actions in Mielec, Lublin, Rzeszów, Warsaw, and Białystok, and he acted as Eichmann's escort whenever he visited Bełżec and Treblinka. Höfle coordinated the deportation of Jews from the General Government to extermination camps. He was also in charge of receiving transports to Bełżec from Germany and the former Czechoslovakia. All deportation orders were run from Höfle's office.

Around May 1942 in the General Government, Polish workers to be sent to the Reich were replaced with Jewish laborers. Deportation trains from the Reich and Slovakia were stopped in Lublin, and able-bodied Jews were selected for work in the General Government; the others were sent on to their deaths in Bełżec. Many Jews were thus temporarily spared death and used for forced labor in a policy implemented by Höfle himself.

Höfle oversaw the deportation of Jews from the Warsaw ghetto, known as *Grossaktion Warschau*, which started on July 22, 1942. Already there had been random killings in the days leading up to the operation, and many of those connected to the *Judenrat* (Jewish Council) were taken hostage. This was to intimidate the *Judenrat* leaders into accepting the forthcoming measures.

Early on the first day, Höfle, together with a company of SS and state officials, told Adam Czerniaków, the chairman of the Warsaw *Judenrat*, that all Jews with very few exceptions were to be sent to the East. Exemptions included German factory workers with valid work permits as well as *Judenrat* employees and their families. Deportees could carry with them 15 kilograms of baggage, food for three days, money, gold, and other valuables. The order required 6,000 Jews to arrive at the *Umschlagplatz* (collection point) daily by 4:00 p.m. in order to board the deportation trains. Every evening, Höfle required a report sent to his office in Lublin on the daily statistics of Jews deported to Treblinka. He was thus very aware of the horrendous conditions in the transports and the death of many Jews en route to the camps.

On January 11, 1943, Höfle sent a message from Lublin to the HSSPF in Kraków and to Eichmann in Berlin. This became known as the Höfle Telegram, documenting the total number of deportations of Jews to the *Aktion Reinhard* camps through December 31, 1942. It listed the number of deaths in the extermination camps during a 14-day period in 1942 and gave a figure for the whole year of 1942 as 1,274,166.

After Globocnik had left for Trieste in September 1943, Höfle remained in Lublin and was associated with *Aktion Erntefest* (Harvest Festival) in November 1943, when the inhabitants of the Jewish labor camps in the Lublin district were killed. Approximately 43,000 Jews were murdered during this operation, which was the single largest German massacre of Jews in the entire war. After leaving Lublin, Höfle served various missions in Brussels and the Netherlands, and finally rejoined Globocnik in Trieste.

Höfle was not immediately brought to justice. On May 31, 1945, British troops captured both him and Globocnik in Carinthia, southern Austria. Höfle remained in British custody between 1945 and 1947, and on October 30, 1947, he was released to continue his earlier occupation as a car mechanic in Salzburg. On July 9, 1948, after an extradition request by the Polish government, he fled to Italy, where he lived under a false name until 1951. Later, he returned to Austria before moving on to the Federal Republic of Germany. There he was employed briefly as an informant for U.S. Army Counterintelligence.

Höfle was finally arrested in January 1961 in Salzburg. From there, he was transferred to Vienna, where he hanged himself in his cell on August 21, 1962.

HOPPE, PAUL-WERNER (1910–1974)

Paul-Werner Hoppe was an *SS-Obersturmbannführer* and the commandant of Stutthof concentration camp from September 1942 until April 1945.

He was born on February 28, 1910, in Berlin. His father, an architect, died when Hoppe was two and a half years old, and the orphaned boy was sent to live with his mother's family in Braunschweig. In 1919, Hoppe returned to Berlin and lived with his uncle, also an architect, who adopted him. Hoppe completed high school with average marks.

He then became an apprentice gardener. In 1931, he returned to Berlin to study landscape design, where he joined the student group of the Nazi Party, ridiculing his uncle as a "democrat." Thereupon, his uncle threw him out and cut off his financial support. Hoppe had to abandon his studies but was able to resume them later with support from the Nazi student organization. In early 1933, he joined the NSDAP, and in October 1934, he applied to join the SS, seeking to become an officer. He completed his landscape design qualification but chose instead a career with the SS. In 1936, he married Charlotte Baranowski, the daughter of Hermann Baranowski, camp commandant of Sachsenhausen.

Hoppe graduated as an SS officer in late 1937. From 1938 to 1939, he was assigned to the Inspectorate of Concentration Camps under *SS-Obergruppenführer* **Theodor Eicke**. Hoppe was instrumental in helping Eicke form the *SS-Totenkopf* division in the fall of 1939, serving as Eicke's adjutant.

When war broke out in 1939, Eicke took Hoppe, then 29, to the front, where he was given command of an infantry company in April 1941. In 1942, Hoppe received a severe leg wound fighting the Red Army near Novgorod Oblast (northwestern Russia) and was badly hurt again in a car accident in France. These injuries ruined his effectiveness as a combat soldier.

After Hoppe convalesced, *SS-Gruppenführer* **Richard Glücks** recommended him for the position of commandant of Stutthof concentration camp near Danzig, to replace *SS-Obersturmbannführer* Max Pauly, who had held this office until August 31, 1942. A promotion to *SS-Sturmbannführer* and commandant of Stutthof were approved, and in September 1942, Hoppe took up his new position. Hoppe's training in the concentration camp system under Eicke would now pay off.

A few months after taking command at Stutthof, Hoppe was called to Berlin by Glücks, who informed him of **Adolf Hitler**'s order regarding the Final Solution. Large transports of Jews from Lithuania were arriving at Stutthof, and a few weeks later, Hoppe was again called to Berlin. Glücks told him he was to gas with Zyklon B any Jewish prisoners who were not fit to work. Hoppe returned to Stutthof to plan out the arrangements, and **Rudolf Hoess** visited the camp to offer his advice in the use of the gas. The gassing of prisoners began in September or October 1944 and lasted for several weeks.

As the Soviets advanced westward, it was decided by Albert Forster, gauleiter of Danzig, and SS Higher and Police Leader **Fritz Katzmann**, headquartered in Danzig, to evacuate Stutthof. The evacuation order was signed by Hoppe on January 25, 1945, and evacuations began immediately under the command of *SS-Hauptsturmführer* Teodor Meyer. The destination of the death march was a subcamp of Stutthof near Lauenburg in Pomerania, about 87 miles southwest of Stutthof.

After the mass evacuation, Hoppe became commandant of Wöbbelin concentration camp, a subcamp of Neuengamme near Ludwigslust. From mid-April 1945, Wöbbelin served as a reception center for evacuation transports from dissolved concentration camps about to be overrun by the Red Army, and it soon turned into a death camp. On April 15, 1945, more than 2,500 concentration camp inmates arrived from elsewhere after days of transport, often without adequate food and completely exhausted. The camp organization at Wöbbelin was not prepared for it. The SS did not primarily kill by force but left the prisoners to die by starvation, disease, and exhaustion. In the 10 weeks of its existence, more than 1,000 of the 5,000 prisoners who were sent there died.

In the early afternoon of May 2, 1945, Wöbbelin was occupied by soldiers of the 82nd U.S. Airborne Division and the 8th U.S. Infantry Division. On May 3, 1945, they found more than 500 bodies "stacked like cordwood" and buried between the barracks and in pits behind. Shocked by the conditions found, Divisional Commander James M. Gavin ordered that civilians from surrounding areas visit the camp.

Hoppe was captured by the British in April 1946 in Holstein. He was sent to Camp 165 in Watten, Scotland, from August 1947 until January 1948, when he was sent on to internment in Fallingbostel, in the British Zone of Occupation in West Germany. While awaiting extradition to Poland, Hoppe escaped and found his way to Switzerland, where he worked as a landscape gardener under a false identity for three years before returning to West Germany. He was arrested on April 17, 1953, in Witten, North Rhine-Westphalia.

He was tried and convicted as an accessory to murder in 1955. On June 4, 1957, the district court in Bochum resentenced Hoppe to nine years, and he was released in 1966. Paul-Werner Hoppe died aged 64 on July 15, 1974, in Bochum.

HÖPPNER, ROLF-HEINZ (1910–1998)

Rolf-Heinz Höppner was a German lawyer and *SS-Obersturmbannführer* in the Reich Security Main Office (RSHA), responsible for the deportation of Jews and Poles and the settlement of ethnic Germans in the German-occupied area of Poland known as the Wartheland. Owing to a series of memoranda from Höppner to his superior officer, **Adolf Eichmann**, commencing on July 16, 1941, the Nazi murder program moved to a new level, which brought about indiscriminate mass death by gassing.

Höppner was born on February 24, 1910, in Siegmar-Schönau, Saxony. He studied law at the University of Leipzig, passing both state examinations. As early as 1931, Hoeppner was a member of the National Socialist Party and the SS. Initially, he undertook voluntary press work with the *Sicherheitsdienst* (SD), and in early 1934, he was hired by the SD as a speaker. He was then involved in personnel and organizational issues, rising to become head of the Central Resettlement Office in Posen (Poznán), a position he held until June 1944.

As head of resettlement, Höppner was responsible for the "resettlement of foreign nationals," namely the deportation of Jews and Poles to the *Generalgouvernement* and the settlement of ethnic Germans in Wartheland. In that capacity, on July 16, 1941, Höppner, now one of the leading officers on the general staff of the police and the SS in the Warthegau, wrote a now-notorious memorandum to Adolf Eichmann, in which he summarized several meetings that had been held in the local governor's office in Posen to solve the Jewish question in the Reich. Höppner noted that some of the solutions suggested might perhaps sound bizarre but that nonetheless they would, in his view, perform well.

One proposal suggested that in place of ghettos like Łódź, all 300,000 Jews should be concentrated into a massive camp, built in barrack form, where the inmates would perform slave labor. This establishment could be supervised by a much smaller police presence, and able-bodied Jews could be pulled out as required and used for work. Höppner suggested that all Jewish women of child-bearing age should be sterilized so that "the Jewish problem is completely liquidated with this generation."

Apparently, Höppner was aware that such a huge prison system could not be built within a few months. He therefore added a further point that extended the application of Nazi policy: "The Jews are at risk this winter of starving. It should seriously be considered whether the most humane solution would be to liquidate the Jews unfit for work by any quick acting means. In any case, it would be more pleasant than letting them starve." This liquidation was directed at Jews who were "not fit to work" rather than "all Jews."

Five weeks after Höppner's memorandum, additional Nazi policies were introduced. The so-called euthanasia campaign, known as *Aktion T-4*, had to be interrupted, following the emergence of rumors and criticism from the Catholic Church in Germany regarding the murder of those with physical and psychological handicaps.

On September 3, 1941, Höppner sent a long memorandum to Eichmann expressing his concern that with the expansion of the German Reich, several racially undesirable groups would have to be deported and that this would have to be on a large scale. He proposed that vast areas of the Soviet Union could be used for this purpose after the war. There were 11 million Jews in Europe, but the overall population of Europeans incapable of Aryanization was many times larger than that. Höppner raised the question of whether such people should be assured of a "certain continuous life" or whether they should be completely eradicated. In this regard, he returned to the "fast-acting agent" to which he referred in his memorandum of July 16, 1941.

As it turned out, such a fast-acting agent already existed—namely, murder by carbon monoxide gas. This had already begun under **Herbert Lange** in 1939 in the Wartheland as part of *Aktion T-4* and was expanded considerably from the summer of 1941 onward. On December 8, 1941, members of the *SS-Sonderkommando Kulmhof* began the systematic gassing of tens of thousands of Jews at Chełmno. Just before this, on November 1, 1941, construction work began at Bełżec extermination camp, followed by two more camps at Sobibór and Treblinka. The fast-acting agent suggested by Höppner now took on a life of its own and saw the ultimate realization of the Holocaust.

On June 21, 1944, Höppner was promoted to *SS-Obersturmbannführer* and was called to the Reich Security Main Office in Berlin in July 1944 to head up the legal system in Office Group III A.

Höppner was arrested in July 1945 near Flensburg, Schleswig-Holstein. He appeared as a defense witness at the Nuremberg Trial, which examined the responsibility of the Reich Security Main Office for the murders of the *Einsatzgruppen*.

In 1947, Höppner was delivered to Poland for trial, and on March 15, 1949, he was sentenced to life imprisonment. He was released on December 12, 1956, as part of a general Polish amnesty and went to live in the Federal Republic of Germany, where he worked as a senior civil servant in the Housing Ministry. He died on October 23, 1998, in a nursing home in Bad Godesberg.

HUDAL, ALOIS (1855–1963)

Alois Hudal was an Austrian-born bishop in the Roman Catholic Church whose pro-Nazi sentiments were demonstrated not only by his 1937 book, *The Foundations of National Socialism*, that praised **Adolf Hitler** and his National Socialist policies but also by the far-reaching lengths he went to after World War II to help Nazi war criminals escape punishment for their wrongdoings and reach sanctuary in countries beyond the reach of Allied justice.

Alois Hudal was born on May 31, 1885, in Graz, Austria. The son of a shoemaker, he studied theology in Graz from 1904 to 1908 and was ordained a priest on July 19, 1908. After he received a doctorate in canon law in 1911 in Graz, he went to Rome from 1911 to 1913, where he obtained a second doctorate on the religious and moral ideas of the Book of Proverbs. He returned to Austria in 1914, having obtained a teaching position on the faculty of the University of Graz.

Hudal served as a military chaplain in World War I, and in 1917, he spoke against national chauvinism from the pulpit. Hudal set up connections with the Vatican, meeting Pope Pius XI in 1922. With his help, Hudal returned to Rome in 1923 as rector of a leading theological seminary in Rome for German-speaking seminarians, the *Collegio Teutonico di Santa Maria dell' Anima.* He led the seminary for the next 30 years. Viewed by the Vatican as the primary representative of the Austrian Church, in 1930, Hudal was appointed as a papal consultant.

Hudal, who held antisemitic views conflating Jews and communists, saw in Nazism a welcome ally against communism and liberalism. Once the Nazis took power in Germany in 1933, he adopted a more nationalistic and antisemitic line. His invectives against Jews, whom he accused of wanting to dominate the world, then became more frequent.

Hudal's 1937 book, *The Foundations of National Socialism*, embraced the Nazi Party and reflected his belief that a working relationship should be established between Catholicism and Nazism. It was in direct opposition with the foreign policy of Pope Pius XI, whose 1937 encyclical, *Mit brennender Sorge* (*With Burning Sorrow*), condemned Nazism. Publication of the book ended Hudal's influence among his fellow clerics and resulted in him being ostracized from the Vatican's inner circle, including Eugenio Pacelli, cardinal secretary of state and soon-to-be Pope Pius XII. Suffering this rebuff, Hudal then isolated himself in his college.

If his Vatican-centered cohort withdrew contact, however, his National Socialist supporters did not. Indeed, suggestions have been made that Hudal was a Nazi intelligence agent during World War II, operating via the German SS officer **Walter Rauff**.

With the onset of a likely German defeat in the war, certain Nazis considered their position and the punishments they could encounter in the event of an Allied victory. With this, Hudal and several others created what became known as ratlines, by which Nazi war criminals could escape Europe with forged papers, visas, passports, and letters of recommendation, many of which were written by Hudal himself. This would enable them to avoid being held accountable for their actions. Thus, many resettled in South America, especially Argentina.

Nazi war criminals who benefitted from Hudal's help included the commander of the Treblinka extermination camp, **Franz Stangl**; the "Angel of Death" from Auschwitz, **Josef Mengele**; **Adolf Eichmann**, who was central to enabling the realization of the Final Solution throughout Europe; **Gustav Wagner**, the commandant at Sobibór; **Alois Brunner**, organizer of deportations from France and Slovakia; Erich Priebke, organizer of the mass killing of civilians carried out in Rome on March 24, 1944; Eduard Roschmann, the "Butcher of Riga"; Walter Rauff, who was instrumental in introducing mass death by mobile gas chambers; and **Klaus Barbie**, the "Butcher of Lyon." Hudal's efforts also benefitted leaders of the notorious *Ustashe*, the collaborationist government installed by the Nazis in Croatia. These figures included Milivoj Ašner, **Ante Pavelić**, Dinko Šakić, and Vjekoslav Vrančić.

Similarly, Hudal's protection enabled some Nazis, such as the Austrian **Otto Wächter**, to live in Rome after the war with impunity. These activities caused a scandal when a Bavarian newspaper revealed them in 1947, and Hudal was finally forced to resign as rector of the *Collegio Teutonico di Santa Maria dell' Anima* in 1952. He spent his last years at Grottaferrata, having never regretted his actions.

Hudal's behavior in supporting the Nazi government and aiding the escape from justice of thousands of Nazi war criminals is beyond dispute. In his defense, he claimed that he was acting out of Christian mercy for the men of the Nazi regime.

The role, if any, Pope Pius XII and the Vatican may have played in those actions remains controversial. There are two sides to the argument. One position is that Pius XII and others in the Vatican sanctioned and funded Hudal's activities dedicated to the welfare of Nazi fugitives through the Vatican Relief Commission, which was unreservedly supported by the very highest levels of the Vatican and used the Vatican bank to provide for its financial needs. The other side asserts that this position is nonsense; Hudal himself, in his memoir published posthumously, stated that Pius XII knew nothing of the ratlines. The argument acknowledges that Hudal aided Nazi war criminals to escape justice and concedes that fleeing Nazis may have crept into the Church's programs to help refugees find a new start outside of Europe, but it unconditionally rejects the allegation that Pius XII or the Vatican supported or authorized, let alone financed, Hudal's efforts.

Hudal (known to some as the "Brown Bishop") believed right up to his death on May 13, 1963, that protecting some of the most barbaric Nazi war criminals was nothing more than what any good Christian should do.

J

JECKELN, FRIEDRICH (1895–1946)

Friedrich Jeckeln was a high-ranking Nazi official who served as an SS leader and police leader (HSSPF) in the occupied Soviet Union during World War II. Heavily involved in directing the activities of the *Einsatzgruppen*, he was responsible for planning, organizing, and overseeing the deaths of over 100,000 Jews, Slavs, Roma, and other "undesirables." As such, he was one of the major Nazi mass murderers.

Jeckeln was born in Homburg in the Black Forest on February 2, 1895. He studied engineering for a term at the polytechnic at Köthen, and then in 1914, just before the outbreak of World War I, he began his military service. He served through the whole war, initially as a gunner on the Western Front. In 1916, after a severe injury, he served in the nascent air corps, where he began pilot training. He was discharged on January 20, 1919, having reached the rank of lieutenant.

After the war, Jeckeln was a farm manager on an estate near Danzig owned by a Jew, Paul Hirsch. In 1918, aged 23, he married Hirsch's daughter, Charlotte. The couple had three children but separated in 1926. Jeckeln's antisemitism can be linked to the breakdown of the marriage and disagreements with his father-in-law. Jeckeln remarried a wealthy German woman in 1929 and had two more children, but he did not maintain his first wife or the children from his first marriage.

Like many Germans, Jeckeln was disillusioned with Germany's defeat in World War I, and he served in one of the many paramilitary *Freikorps* units until 1924. He joined the National Socialist Workers' Party (NSDAP) on October 1, 1929. On March 15, 1930, he joined the SS and rose quickly to the rank of *SS-Sturmbannführer*. By 1932, he was a member of the Reichstag representing the NSDAP for Braunschweig.

At the same time, he engaged in domestic terror against the party's opponents, carrying out bombings mainly against the communists. On July 4, 1933, in response to the death of an SS man, 11 communist militants were murdered, and Jeckeln used his position in the police to ensure that the murders, known as the Rieseberg Killings, were never properly investigated. From 1933 to 1936, Jeckeln was commander of the regional section of the NSDAP in Braunschweig and was appointed in 1933 an *SS-Gruppenführer*.

From 1933, the Jews of Braunschweig found their businesses boycotted and their families targeted on the street by SS men. Jeckeln later played a very prominent role in organizing the *Kristallnacht* pogrom of November 9 to 10, 1938 in Braunschweig.

In May and June 1940, Jeckeln fought on the Western Front commanding the *Totenkopfverbände* regiment of **Theodor Eicke** while participating in the French campaign. In July 1941, he was named HSSPF of occupied Ukraine. Between

August 10 and September 1, his troops massacred 23,600 Ukrainian and Hungarian Jews in Kamenez-Podolski. He was closely involved in the massacre of Jews at Babi Yar, outside of Kiev, where 33,771 people were massacred between September 29 and 30, 1941. Jeckeln was also responsible for other massacres in Rowno and Dnepropetrovsk.

On October 11, 1941, Jeckeln was appointed HSSPF in the Baltic and Belorussia, and he was transferred to Riga, Latvia. Here, he took charge in liquidating the ghetto to make room for the future deportations of the Jews of the Reich. On November 30 and December 8, 1941, he participated with his troops, supported by Latvian auxiliaries, in the massacre of 25,000 Jews, including 21,000 women and children, in the Rumbula Forest.

At Riga, Jeckeln invented the killing style known as "sardine packing." After forcing people from their homes, the Security Police organized them into columns of 500 to 1,000 people and drove them to the killing grounds, where pits had already been dug. The victims were stripped of their clothing and valuables and forced to run through a double cordon of guards. They were then either shot immediately at the edge of the pits or were ordered to lie facedown between the legs of those already shot and then killed. The latter method saved much-needed space. Anyone not killed outright was simply buried alive when the pit was covered up.

The Riga massacre showed that mass shooting was not a feasible means of resolving the Jewish problem. It was time consuming and psychologically burdensome for the killers. This led to a search for new ways of "evacuating" large numbers of people in a way that would not cause stress for the killers. The result would see the second phase of the Holocaust commence, with the construction of extermination camps and gas chambers.

At the beginning of 1942, Jeckeln and his staff participated in *Aktion Sumpffieber* (marsh fever), during which his troops eliminated thousands of Jews from various ghettos under the guise of fighting against the partisans. In February 1945, he was appointed commander in chief of the Breslau region.

Arrested at the end of the war, Jeckeln and other accomplices were brought before the Soviet military court in Riga. On February 3, 1946, he was sentenced to death and was hanged the same day in front of thousands of people near the Duna River.

K

KALTENBRUNNER, ERNST (1903–1946)

Ernst Kaltenbrunner was an Austrian-born senior SS general during World War II. Between January 1943 and May 1945, he was the chief of the Reich Main Security Office (*Reichssicherheitshauptamt*, or RSHA) and chief of the Security Police. In the latter role, he controlled the Gestapo, Criminal Police, and Security Service (SD). He was a leading figure in the Final Solution.

Ernst Kaltenbrunner was born on October 4, 1903, in Ried, Upper Austria, the son of lawyer Hugo Kaltenbrunner and his wife Therese. His middle-class family home was influenced by the idea of a "Greater Germany," as well as antichurch causes. Kaltenbrunner was educated at the state high school in Linz, where he became childhood friends with **Adolf Eichmann**. After finishing school, in 1921, he commenced studying chemistry at the Graz University of Technology. He joined the arms-carrying fraternity *Arminia*, and as a keen fraternity member and duelist, he became prominent in student politics. In 1923, Kaltenbrunner switched to the study of law, while at the same time working as a coal carrier. He became a spokesman for his *Arminia* fraternity and for nationalist students at the university and took part in anti-Marxist and anticlerical demonstrations.

Obtaining his doctorate in law from Graz University in 1926, he worked at a law firm in Salzburg for a year before opening his own law office in Linz. He became a legal consultant for the NSDAP in 1929, joining the party on October 18, 1930. He joined the SS on August 31, 1931. He became a legal consultant to the SS in 1932, at the same time as he began working at his father's law practice. By 1933, Kaltenbrunner was head of the National Socialist Lawyers' League in Linz. Kaltenbrunner himself was an intimidating figure. At six feet four inches tall, weighing 220 pounds, he had a powerful build, dark features, and deep scars (possibly from fencing or from a car accident) on both sides of his face.

In January 1934, Kaltenbrunner and other National Socialists were jailed by the Dollfuss government for conspiracy. While in prison, he led a hunger strike, forcing the government to release 490 Nazi Party members. In 1935, he was jailed again for high treason. This charge was dropped, but Kaltenbrunner was sentenced to six months' imprisonment for conspiracy and lost his license to practice law.

On January 14, 1934, Kaltenbrunner married Elisabeth Eder, also from Linz and a Nazi Party member, with whom he had three children. In addition to these children, in 1945, Kaltenbrunner had twins with his long-time mistress, Gisela Gräfin von Westarp.

He was released from prison in 1935 and appointed by his leaders in Germany to command the entire Austrian division of the SS. In 1937, at the instigation

Born in Austria, Ernst Kaltenbrunner was head of the Reich Security Main Office and chief of the Security Police in which he controlled the Gestapo, Criminal Police, and Security Service. During World War II he was a key figure in orchestrating and carrying out the Final Solution. In 1945 he was arrested and placed on trial at Nuremberg for war crimes and crimes against humanity; found guilty, he was sentenced to death and hanged on October 16, 1946. This image shows him testifying during the trial in 1946. (Keystone-France\Gamma-Rapho via Getty Images)

of **Heinrich Himmler**, he was promoted to *SS-Oberführer* and began working with **Arthur Seyss-Inquart** to implement the Austrian *Anschluss* (union) with Germany. After the *Anschluss*, which took place on March 12, 1938, Kaltenbrunner became state secretary for public security and a member of the Reichstag. During 1938 and 1939, Kaltenbrunner was also involved in the organization of the Austrian Gestapo, the establishment of the concentration camp Mauthausen, and the persecution of Austria's Jews.

On January 30, 1943, in the wake of the assassination of **Reinhard Heydrich**, Kaltenbrunner took over his principal functions as head of the RSHA, reporting directly to Himmler. At Kaltenbrunner's instigation, anyone arrested and placed into "protective custody" (*Schutzhaft*) was transferred to concentration camps. Using the RSHA intelligence network, the persecution and arrest of Jews, members of resistance organizations, and other opposition groups was ongoing.

The commandant of Auschwitz, **Rudolf Hoess**, specifically stated that "all the mass executions in the gas chambers took place under the direct orders, the supervision and the overall responsibility of the RSHA. I received orders directly from the RSHA to proceed with these mass executions." This placed responsibility directly at Kaltenbrunner's feet.

Heydrich had made the RSHA more politically powerful than the Wehrmacht, and Kaltenbrunner derived the benefit from Heydrich's assassination. In February 1944, he contrived to have Admiral William Canaris's *Abwehr* (German military intelligence) completely abolished and its remnants transformed into the RSHA's Military Branch, to be directed by Walter Schellenberg. With the unseating of Canaris, Kaltenbrunner established an intelligence service monopoly.

Kaltenbrunner's power increased markedly after the attempted assassination of **Adolf Hitler** on July 20, 1944, and he was responsible for actively seeking out and calling for the execution of all those accused of plotting against the Führer.

In December 1944, Kaltenbrunner, along with other SS generals, was granted the rank of general of the Waffen-SS so that if they were captured by the Allies, they could be considered as military officers rather than police officials.

On April 18, 1945, Himmler named Kaltenbrunner commander in chief of German forces remaining in Southern Europe. Kaltenbrunner organized his intelligence agencies as a stay-behind underground net, but in late April 1945, he shifted his headquarters from Berlin to Altaussee, where he had often vacationed. While there, he thwarted the efforts of local governor August Eigruber to destroy the irreplaceable collection of more than 6,500 paintings and statues stolen by the Nazis from museums and private owners across occupied Europe, with the intention of placing them in Hitler's planned *Führermuseum* in Linz. Eigruber was determined to prevent the collection from falling into the hands of "Bolsheviks and Jews" by destroying it with explosives. Kaltenbrunner countermanded the order and had the explosives removed, saving world treasures such as Michelangelo's *Madonna of Bruges*, stolen from the Church of Our Lady in Bruges; Jan van Eyck's *Ghent Altarpiece*, stolen from St. Bavo Cathedral in Ghent; and Vermeer's *The Astronomer* and *The Art of Painting*.

With the end of the war looming in 1945, Kaltenbrunner moved his headquarters again, giving orders that all prisoners were to be killed. He was arrested by the Americans in the Austrian mountains after attempting to pass as a doctor. In November 1945 at the International Military Tribunal in Nuremberg, Kaltenbrunner was charged with conspiracy to commit crimes against peace, war crimes, and crimes against humanity. He rejected all responsibility for the charges against him and stressed during cross-examination that all decrees and legal documents that bore his signature were "rubber-stamped" and filed by his subordinates.

Kaltenbrunner's close control over the RSHA meant that he was deemed to have direct knowledge of and command responsibility for mass murders by the *Einsatzgruppen*, deporting citizens of occupied countries for forced labor, establishing concentration camps and committing racial and political undesirables to them for slave labor and mass murder, screening of prisoner-of-war camps and executing racial and political undesirables, seizure and destruction of public and private property, persecution of Jews and Roma, and persecution of churches.

Kaltenbrunner claimed he was an intelligence leader, not a mass murderer. The tribunal concluded, instead, that he was an active authority and participant in many instances of war crimes and crimes against humanity. He was found guilty of war crimes and crimes against humanity, sentenced to death, and hanged in Nuremberg on October 16, 1946.

KATZMANN, FRITZ (1906–1957)

Fritz Katzmann was a Holocaust perpetrator responsible for mass murder in the cities of Katowice, Radom, Lvov (Lviv, Lemberg), Danzig (Gdansk), and other parts of Nazi-occupied Poland. On June 30, 1943, Katzmann submitted to **Friedrich-Wilhelm Krüger** a top-secret report, known as the Katzmann Report, summarizing *Aktion Reinhard* in Galicia up to that point of the year. The report was used as evidence at the Nuremberg Trials after World War II.

Friedrich ("Fritz") Katzmann was born on May 6, 1906, in Langendreer, Westphalia, into a coal miner's family. After elementary school, he became a carpenter but lost his job and was unemployed from 1928 to 1933. In December 1927, he joined the SA; in September 1928, the NSDAP; and in July 1930, the SS. On April 20, 1933, he was promoted to *SS-Sturmbannführer*.

From the beginning of April 1933 until early April 1934, Katzmann served in a municipal role in Duisburg. On January 30, 1934, he was promoted to *SS-Obersturmbannführer*, after which he served full-time in the SS. On August 17, 1934, he was appointed an *SS-Standartenführer*, having taken part in the Night of the Long Knives on June 30, 1934. From April 4, 1934, until March 21, 1938, Katzmann was stationed in Berlin.

Between mid-August 1936 and mid-August 1942, Katzmann was a member of the People's Court (*Volksgerichtshof*). On March 21, 1938, he commanded an SS unit in Breslau; later in the year, on November 9, 1938 (the day of *Kristallnacht*), he was promoted to *SS-Oberführer*.

From November 1939 to July 1941, Katzmann was higher SS and police leader (*Höherer SS- und Polizeiführer*, or HSSPF) in Radom, Poland, in charge of the ghettoization process of Radom's 32,000 Jews. Under his command, they were subjected to theft, terror, and murder.

On June 21, 1941, immediately in advance of the invasion of the Soviet Union, Katzmann was promoted to SS-*Brigadeführer*. Thereafter, until April 20, 1943, he was HSSPF for Galicia, based in Lvov. On September 26, 1941, he was further promoted to SS police major general.

In November 1941, Katzmann ordered 80,000 Jews confined to the Lvov ghetto. In the city outskirts, he also established the Janowska concentration camp. The number of those killed at Janowska has been a matter of dispute, ranging from the unlikely Soviet figure of up to 500,000 to a more realistic number of victims estimated at 35,000 to 40,000. It has been further approximated that up to 60,000 Jews were murdered overall on Katzmann's command by the end of 1941. In 1942, Katzmann organized further transports that took at least 80,000 Jews from Lvov to the death camp of Bełżec.

Katzmann was promoted *SS-Gruppenführer* and lieutenant general of police on January 30, 1943. During the first half of 1943, he organized the death of over 140,000 Jews in the district of Galicia.

On June 30, 1943, just over two years after arriving in Lvov, Katzmann submitted his report entitled "Solution of the Jewish Question in the District of Galicia," to the HSSPF of the General Government, Friedrich-Wilhelm Krüger. Katzmann described in detail his actions and the Jewish resistance that resulted from them. One of the report's conclusions was that by June 27, 1943, a total of 434,329 Jews had been expelled and that the district of Galicia was now free of Jews (*Judenrein*), except for those who were under Krüger's direct control.

With Galicia *Judenrein*, Katzmann's job was seen to be completed, and he was thus transferred elsewhere. From April 20, 1943, to May 8, 1945, he was SS commander of Military District XX (Vistula/Danzig/West Prussia), headquartered in Danzig. He oversaw the organization of gas chambers and crematoria at Stutthof concentration camp, where tens of thousands more Jews were murdered. On July 1, 1944, he was promoted to *SS-Obergruppenführer* in the Waffen-SS.

Katzmann experienced the end of the war on the island of Fehmarn, off the coast of Schleswig. He escaped immediate prosecution, living under a false identity in Württemberg as Bruno Albrecht. In March 1956, Bruno Albrecht was registered in Darmstadt, where his family lived, but a planned transfer to Argentina did not materialize, owing to Katzmann's ill health at that time. He died on September 19, 1957, in the Alice Hospital in Darmstadt.

KITTEL, BRUNO (1922–?)

Bruno Kittel was an SS officer involved with Jewish issues in France, Latvia, and Lithuania during World War II. He was notorious for having been responsible for administering the liquidation of the Vilna ghetto in September 1943, having already overseen the massacre of Jews in two small communities nearby, Kena and Bezdonys, on July 8 to 9, 1943. It has been estimated that some 240 Jews were killed in Kena, and 300 to 350 were killed in Bezdonys.

Born in Austria in 1922, Kittel trained as an actor in Berlin and Frankfurt. Prior to the outbreak of war, he was known as an actor, singer, and musician (his preferred instruments were saxophone and piano). He joined the SS, reached the rank of *SS-Oberscharführer*, and was sent to France and Riga to learn how to manage Jewish matters.

Deployed to Vilna in June 1943, where he played his saxophone on local radio, Kittel was the youngest of his colleagues there, and his reputation as a passionate and cruel antisemite preceded him. Zealous in hunting down Jews, his reputation extended throughout occupied Poland. At the end of June 1943, for example, he ordered 418 Jewish forced laborers murdered in retaliation for the flight of 6 Jews to the partisans.

A city of 200,000 people, 30 percent of whom were Jewish, Vilna was known as the "Jerusalem of the North," with 106 synagogues, despite a 60 percent Catholic presence. Approximately 265,000 Jews lived in Lithuania at the time of German occupation in 1941; by the end of World War II, 95 percent of them had been exterminated. No other Jewish population was so devastated in the Nazi-occupied areas of Eastern Europe.

A ghetto was established at Vilna by the Nazi military administration in September 1941. Owing to Nazi depredations, by the beginning of 1942, its population had been reduced to just 15,000, and in June 1943, **Heinrich Himmler** ordered the ghetto's final liquidation. The SS chief and commander of *Einsatzkommando* 3 in Vilna, Rolf Neugebauer (who was later transferred to Kovno/Kaunas, and, deeper into the war, Budapest), ordered Kittel to oversee the destruction of the ghetto, which he undertook on September 22 to 23, 1943. Most of the inhabitants were taken to the nearby Ponary Forest and were shot or sent to extermination camps in Poland or to work camps in Estonia, where almost all of them died. Of those remaining, most were women and children transported to extermination camps such as Auschwitz. About 2,000 men were sent to the Klooga concentration camp in Estonia, and up to 1,700 of the younger women were sent to the Kaiserwald concentration camp in Latvia.

Constantly smiling, Kittel was remembered as elegant, polite, and refined. He was young, and his manner was intended to be calming. When executing victims, it was said that he pleaded with them not to be nervous so that he could perform his murders calmly, quietly, and deliberately.

Following the liquidation of the Vilna ghetto, Kittel continued his deadly procession. On October 15, 1943, he visited the Kailis forced-labor camp near Vilna, which had received a number of Jewish prisoners from the ghetto. Selecting 30 inmates at random, he had them dispatched to the killing fields at Ponary on a whim. The camp itself was liquidated, and its remaining workers were executed at Ponary, on July 3, 1944, although this was long after Kittel had left the vicinity.

Kittel's remaining activities during the war are sketchy. It is known that on March 27, 1944, he was present in Kovno, where he was involved in what became known as the *Kinderaktion*, when the Germans came for the ghetto's remaining 1,700 children. Under Kittel's watching eye, the ghetto's 130 Jewish police were then taken at gunpoint to a nearby SS base known as the Ninth Fort, where they were tortured for information regarding the hiding places of other Jewish children as well as partisans. Kittel selected upward of 40 of these men and arranged for their summary execution.

With the advance of the Russians, Kittel took leave of all his SS activities and disappeared without trace. His trail ran cold, and he was thus never held responsible or prosecuted for his crimes during the war.

KLIMAITIS, ALGIRDAS (1923–1988)

Algirdas Klimaitis was a Lithuanian collaborator with the Nazis during World War II. The militia he commanded was notorious for its role in the Kovno (Kaunas) pogrom in June 1941 and was active during Operation Barbarossa.

Algirdas Jonas Klimaitis was born in 1923 in Lithuania. For some time, he traded in livestock but went bankrupt. Later, he began writing for newspapers and worked as a far-right-wing journalist. Prior to World War II, he edited the tabloid newspaper *Dešimt centų* (*Ten Cents*) and was a member of the *Voldemarininkai*, a right-wing nationalistic movement following Augustine Voldemar, who had negotiated for independence for Lithuania at Versailles. Klimaitis was a supporter of anticommunist and antisemitic ideals.

On Sunday, June 22, 1940, Nazi Germany attacked the Soviet Union. The next day, the Lithuanian Activist Front (*Lietuvos Aktyvistų Frontas*, or LAF) seized the radio station and announced the establishment of a provisional Lithuanian government. Two days later, on Wednesday, June 25, the German army entered Kovno, the country's second-largest city. Lithuanians rejoiced because they were rid of the Soviet presence that had been occupying their country, but the German military was indignant that the Lithuanians had given themselves the status of an independent country. General Wilhelm Schubert met with Lithuanian leaders and announced that any possibility of an independent Lithuania would never be achieved.

SS-Brigadeführer **Franz Walter Stahlecker** was commandant of *Einsatzgruppe A*, tasked to pacify occupied Lithuania. As the head of the SiPo and SD, Stahlecker sought local movements that would "self-cleanse" their communities of Jews and achieve this as rapidly as possible. It was important to establish as "unshakable and provable facts" that the liberated population took such measures against the Bolshevik and Jewish enemy on its own initiative without any German instructions.

From the Germans' viewpoint, this was necessary in Lithuania, for, in some places such as Kovno, Jews had armed themselves and taken an active part in sniping and arson. In addition, the Jews of Lithuania had cooperated closely with the Soviets.

Stahlecker sought dependable people who would provide cover for the SD's action. He identified a local Lithuanian military representative named Simkus and an army faction calling itself the Iron Wolf. Stahlecker spoke with Jonai Dainauskas, head of the Interim Lithuanian Security Police, to prepare pogroms, but Dainauskas refused. Stahlecker reported to *SS-Reichsführer* **Heinrich Himmler** that "It suddenly turned out that organizing a larger-scale Jewish pogrom is not quite easy." Instead, Stahlecker used two groups of partisans who had fought in Kovno against the Soviets. The first group was 600 men, mainly civilian workers under the leadership of Algirdas Klimaitis; the second was about 200 men following a physician, Dr. Zygonys. Stahlecker authorized Klimaitis and Zygonys to recruit an auxiliary police force.

On the night of June 25 to 26, Stahlecker instigated a pogrom led by Klimaitis's unit, making it appear that this was a spontaneous Lithuanian affair not initiated by the Germans. The Lithuanian auxiliaries set fire to synagogues and about 60 homes in the old Jewish quarter and began shooting Jews in the streets. On the first night, some 1,500 Jews were killed. On the second night, 2,300 more Jews were murdered. The chance for plunder provided a powerful motive; after the owners were killed, the auxiliaries looted homes and warehouses and ripped valuables from bodies. In addition to these 3,800 people, a further 1,200 people were killed in surrounding towns and villages by June 28.

In Kovno, film and photographs were used to establish, as far as possible, that these first "spontaneous" measures against Jews and communists were carried out by Lithuanians. Between June 24 and July 2, two *Einsatzkommandos* (9 and 7) arrived in Vilnius and organized snatch squads, which kidnapped Jews and either held them in Lukiskiai Prison or took them into the Ponary Forest and shot them.

Klimaitis was not operating under the authority of the Lithuanian Provisional Government. The acting prime minister of Lithuania, Juozas Brazaitis-Ambrazevičius, claimed in his memoirs that the Provisional Lithuanian Government sent Generals Stasys Pundzevičius and Mikė Rėkaitis to instruct Klimaitis not to create pogroms and not to serve under Stahlecker. When Klimaitis met the two generals, he attempted to justify the pogroms, and in response, the generals informed him that his behavior was blackening Lithuania's name and that Klimaitis was doing the Nazis' dirty work for them. Klimaitis justified his actions on the basis that Stahlecker was threatening to eliminate him if he did not follow orders. The generals advised Klimaitis to disappear, which he soon did.

Lithuanians who continued with pogroms against the Jews were commanded by the leader of the LAF, Aleksandras Bendinskas. Klimaitis did not participate in these later massacres.

On Saturday, June 28, 1940, the few remaining Lithuanian rebel groups operating in Kovno were disarmed and disbanded. Those deemed "reliable" were then selected and formed into five police companies. The next day, the Kaunas Military Command established the National Defense Forces Battalion. The Lithuanian Interim Government hoped it would be the beginning of the Lithuanian army, but instead the battalion began murdering Jews. Overall, across the duration of the Nazi occupation, the total number of Jews liquidated in Lithuania was 71,105.

After the war, Algirdas Klimaitis settled in Hamburg, Germany, where he lived quietly until discovered in the 1970s. The Hamburg Public Prosecutor's Office filed a lawsuit against him, but he died on August 28, 1988, without facing trial.

KLOPFER, GERHARD (1905–1987)

Gerhard Klopfer was a lawyer, senior official of the Nazi Party, and assistant to **Martin Bormann** in the Party Chancellery. One of the most influential and knowledgeable bureaucrats of the Nazi regime, he participated in the Wannsee Conference in January 1942, which discussed how to murder Jews in the most efficient and effective manner.

Gerhard Klopfer was born in the East Prussian town of Schreibersdorf on February 18, 1905, the son of a farmer who was also a provincial official. He attended the local high school prior to studying at the universities of Breslau and Jena, where his academic focus was on law and political science. He also served as a temporary volunteer in the Ulm Artillery Regiment in December 1923. His doctoral thesis from the University of Jena in 1927 was in employment relations, which led to his appointment as a judge. Through his university life, he met **Wilhelm Stuckart**, who later became secretary of state at the Reich Ministry of the Interior.

Klopfer joined the Nazi Party on April 10, 1933, and the SA on April 15, 1933. On November 1, 1933, he was appointed as a state prosecutor in Düsseldorf. Positions were available because the new Nazi regime had dismissed many civil servants, especially Jews. Klopfer was promoted in quick time, and on December 1, 1933, he was transferred to the Prussian State Ministry for Agriculture, Lands, and Forests.

On August 1, 1934, Klopfer was promoted to government counselor, and on December 8, he took up a role in the Gestapo. A loyal and reliable party member, on April 18, 1935, he became a staff member of the Representatives of the Führer, headed by Rudolf Hess and Martin Bormann, Hess's former deputy. Klopfer joined the SS on September 15, 1935, and remained a member until May 1945. In 1938, Klopfer personally took part in implementing the regulations of the Nuremberg Laws and was responsible for seizing Jewish businesses. When Hess flew to England on an unauthorized mission in 1941, Klopfer became Bormann's assistant and head of the state division of the Party Chancellery. In this role, he deputized for Bormann at the Wannsee Conference on January 20, 1942.

Klopfer was one of the most notable and knowledgeable bureaucrats of the Nazi regime. As head of Constitutional Law Section III of the chancellery and Martin Bormann's deputy, he managed issues relating to "race and national character," economic policies, cooperation with the Reich Security Main Office, and the basic politics of occupation. In November 1942, as state secretary, he restricted the rights of Jews living in mixed marriages.

Klopfer therefore had extensive power of patronage within the Nazi Party, and Bormann often left him to handle appointments to party positions. As Bormann's deputy, he was a signatory to the call to arms of Germany's youth and elderly, in the age range of 16 to 60 years (the so-called *Volkssturm*) in the final stage of the war. In 1944, he was promoted to *SS-Gruppenführer*.

As the Red Army closed in on Berlin in 1945, Klopfer fled from Berlin and went into hiding. It was not until March 1, 1946, that he was arrested by agents of the Counter Intelligence Corps (CIC) in Munich with false papers in the name of Otto Kunz. He was sent first to the Dachau Detention Center before being transferred to the Ludwigsburg and Nuremberg-Langwasser camps.

Klopfer was interrogated some 10 times by American prosecutors between March 1947 and January 1948, during which he sought to minimize his importance and maximize his ignorance. He was a witness during the Wilhelmstrasse trials of many of the former Nazi state secretaries at Nuremberg in 1948. Under questioning, Klopfer denied having anything to do with the destruction of the Jews, admitting only to hearing rumors about it. He stated that in 1935 he had been commanded against his will to organize the party and that his professional abilities had been the reason for his rapid promotion; all political responsibility was with his superior, Martin Bormann. When confronted with the minutes of the Wannsee Conference, Klopfer did not recall the wording as set out in the protocol and said that he had always assumed that the Jews were only to be "resettled."

Although he was marked for prosecution in a new U.S. military tribunal case, the plan to place him on trial was canceled on the grounds of insufficient evidence. The United States was facing new priorities owing to the Cold War, and Western unity became more important than the pursuit of criminal justice. Evidence prepared against Klopfer by U.S. authorities was handed over, along with additional documentation, to a German investigative commission. The implementing legislation of the Basic Law 131 allowed thousands of former Nazi officials to return to the state service, and the impunity laws adopted by the Bundestag in 1949 and 1954 reversed essential measures of the Allied denazification process.

Klopfer settled in Ulm, resuming his law practice there in 1956. The District Attorney's Office in Ulm, responding to pressure from the Central Office for the Prosecution of Nazi Crimes in Ludwigsburg, initiated inquiries into Klopfer's role in the Final Solution, but proceedings against him were dropped once and for all on January 29, 1962.

Klopfer was to live longer than any other participant in the Wannsee Conference, dying on January 28, 1987, at a home for the elderly outside the Baden-Württemberg city of Heilbronn.

KOCH, ILSE (1906–1967)

Ilse Koch was the wife of the commandant of the Nazi concentration camps at Buchenwald and Majdanek. In 1947, she became one of the first prominent Nazis to be tried twice by two different regimes for her behavior during the Third Reich: first by the U.S. military and then by the German government.

Margarete Ilse Köhler was born on September 22, 1906, in Dresden, the daughter of a factory foreman. At 15 years old, she studied accountancy, later working as a bookkeeping clerk. In 1932, she joined the Nazi Party. In 1934, she met Karl Otto Koch in 1934 through friends in the SA and SS and got engaged. She started work in 1936 as a guard and secretary at Sachsenhausen concentration camp near Berlin, which Karl Koch commanded. They were married later in 1936, and she changed her name to Ilse Koch. In 1937, her husband was made commandant of Buchenwald, and she went there with him.

At Buchenwald, it is claimed that Ilse Koch assisted a prison doctor to complete his thesis on criminality and tattooing by ordering selected prisoners to be murdered and skinned so as to retrieve the tattooed parts of their bodies. It was here that she acquired her reputation as a sadist, beating prisoners with her riding crop and forcing them to perform physically exhausting activities for her own amusement. Ilse Koch's abuses were evidenced at trial. She was a rabid antisemite, called Jews "swine," and had derision for anyone not fitting the Nazi ideal. She would order her dog to attack on command anyone she viewed as a threat to her person. If laundry was not done to her liking or if anyone spoke out of turn, the miscreant would be executed.

Evidence was given at trial that her hobby was collecting lampshades, book covers, and gloves made from the skin of specially murdered concentration camp inmates, as well as shrunken human skulls. An anecdote tells of a 19-year-old American soldier who, after the war, found several lampshades with beautifully painted butterflies and birds; then, he and his three buddies went out and vomited when they identified that the lampshades were made of human skin.

In 1940, Ilse Koch constructed an indoor sports arena costing over 250,000 Reichsmarks, most of which had been seized from the inmates. Her husband, suspected of enriching himself by skimming profits from the camp that should have gone to the SS, was relieved of command at the end of 1941. He was transferred to Lublin to establish the Majdanek concentration and extermination camp, but Ilse Koch remained at Buchenwald.

On August 24, 1943, Ilse and Karl Koch were arrested on the orders of the SS and police leader for Weimar, who was responsible for supervising Buchenwald. They were charged with making themselves privately wealthy by theft and embezzlement and with murdering prisoners to prevent them testifying. Ilse Koch was jailed until 1944, when she was cleared for lack of evidence; her husband was found guilty, sentenced to death in Munich by an SS court, and executed by firing squad at Buchenwald on April 5, 1945.

Ilse Koch went to live with her surviving family in the town of Ludwigsburg, where she was arrested by U.S. authorities on June 30, 1945, after having been identified by a former Buchenwald inmate as the fierce redheaded woman who was perverse and brutally cruel. The prisoners called her the "Witch of Buchenwald," which the press transformed into the "Bitch of Buchenwald."

In 1947, Koch was charged with aiding, abetting, and participating in the murders at Buchenwald. Among the physical evidence against her was a lampshade made of human tattooed skin, which outraged international public opinion. The trial began on April 11, 1947, and on August 19, 1947, she was sentenced to life imprisonment for "violation of the laws and customs of war." On June 8, 1948, after two years of her sentence, the interim military governor of the American Zone in Germany reduced her life sentence to four years imprisonment on the basis that "there was no convincing evidence that she had selected inmates for extermination . . . to secure tattooed skins, or that she possessed any articles made of human skin."

The Bavarian government gave notice that if Koch was released, new proceedings would be brought against her. She was freed in October 1949, and after bureaucratic wrangling between the U.S. government and the government of East Germany, she was handed over to West German authorities, who arrested her.

Public opinion was irate. In 1949, she was put on trial a second time, now before a West German court. On November 27, 1950, the trial commenced before the District Court at Augsburg. It lasted seven weeks, during which 250 witnesses were heard, including 50 for the defense. The 16 prosecution witnesses gave evidence that she had brutally abused prisoners in the camp, using the power that her husband had arbitrarily granted her to perpetrate sadistic and perverse acts on Buchenwald's inmates. The heart of the trial became the famous articles made of human skin.

At least four separate witnesses for the prosecution testified that they had seen Koch choose tattooed prisoners who were then killed or that Koch had seen or been involved in the process of making human-skin lampshades from tattooed skin. However, this charge was dropped by the prosecution when they could not prove that the lampshades or any other items were made from human skin.

On January 15, 1951, the court gave its verdict. It ruled that the previous trials in 1944 and 1947 were not a bar to proceedings (being tried twice for the same offence), as at the 1944 trial, Koch had only been charged with receiving, whereas in 1947 she had been accused of crimes against foreigners after September 1, 1939, and not with crimes against humanity, for which Germans and Austrians had been defendants both before and after that date. On January 15, 1951, she was sentenced to life imprisonment and permanent forfeiture of civil rights.

On September 1, 1967, Ilse Koch, then 60, hanged herself in her cell at Aichach women's prison.

KOPPE, WILHELM (1896–1975)

Wilhelm Koppe was a Waffen-SS general responsible for mass crimes against Poles and Jews in the General Government and elsewhere during the German occupation of Poland in World War II.

Karl Heinrich Wilhelm Koppe was born on June 15, 1896, in Hildesheim, Lower Saxony, to Robert Koppe, a bailiff, and his wife. He attended a private school in Stolzenau and the *Realgymnasium Harburg-Wilhelmsburg*, completing his high school education in 1914. In October 1914, he volunteered to serve in the Schleswig-Holstein Pioneer Battalion No. 9 and served on the Western Front in January 1915. In December 1916, he became a lieutenant of the reserve, and from January 1917 until December 1918, he served as battalion gas officer of the Pioneer Battalion No. 9. Wounded in Flanders, he was discharged at the end of the war.

In the interwar period, he was an independent merchant and owner of a wholesale business in food and tobacco products. Koppe joined the Nazi Party on January 9, 1930, serving from December 1930 to January 1932 as the press officer of the party's Harburg-Wilhelmsburg branch. He joined the SA in 1931 and the SS in 1932. Prior to World War II, he was a regional SS and SD commander, first in Münster and then in Danzig, Dresden, and Leipzig. From 1933 to 1945, he was an NSDAP member of the German Reichstag.

In October 1939, after the German invasion of Poland, Koppe became the SS and police leader in Reichsgau Wartheland, based in Posen (Poznań), under the command of **Arthur Greiser**. Koppe actively implemented Nazi racial ideals in his region, declaring in November 1939 that he would make Posen "free from Jews." He thereupon ordered many executions and deportations of Poles and Polish Jews. Later, Koppe took charge of the deportation of the Jews to the Łódź ghetto and the Chełmno extermination camp.

On November 12, 1939, Koppe announced to the *Generalgouvernement* the long-term goals of the deportations. These were to transform the conquered Polish territories into German settlements. To this end, so-called *Volksdeutsche* (ethnic Germans living outside of Germany proper) were to be resettled. He stated further that all Jews and Polish intellectuals were equivalent to dangerous criminals, so the cleansing and safeguarding of the area could only be achieved when all had been removed. That was also necessary to create jobs for Germans moving to the newly conquered territory.

Koppe also was active in the Nazi euthanasia program as the overall commander of *Sonderkommando Lange*. Toward the end of May 1940 and until June 1940, Koppe organized the mass murder, using gas vans, of some 1,558 Germans and around 500 Poles with disabilities in the East Prussian transit camp Soldau.

On January 1, 1942, on the orders of *SS-Reichsführer* **Heinrich Himmler**, with whom he had established a good working relationship, Koppe was promoted to SS general and placed in charge of the police. On September 11, 1943, he took over in Kraków from **Friedrich-Wilhelm Krüger** as state secretary and general procurator for the armament of the governor-general for the occupied Polish territories, reporting to **Hans Frank**. In this new role, he participated in the activities at Chełmno and in operations against the Polish resistance. Koppe organized the execution of more than 30,000 Polish patients suffering from tuberculosis and ordered that all men identified as resistance fighters should be executed and the rest of their families sent to concentration camps.

On July 1, 1944, Koppe was appointed as general of the Waffen-SS and the police. On July 7, 1944, he was the target of an unsuccessful assassination attempt by the Polish resistance; he survived, but five members of the resistance were killed.

As the Eastern Front approached Poland, Koppe ordered that all prisoners under his command be executed rather than rescued by the Soviets. In 1945, he was appointed as commander of the special staff of the Army Group Vistula, and from April 4, 1945, to May 8, 1945, he held the positions of senior SS and police leader in Munich.

In April 1945, shortly before Germany's collapse, Koppe issued himself personal-identity cards with changed name, date of birth, and birthplace. Under the alias of Lohmann, his wife's surname, he then went into hiding. He worked as a director of the Sarotti chocolate factory in Bonn, Germany, managing to remain undetected until 1960.

On December 30, 1960, due to an anonymous street advertisement in Bonn, Koppe was arrested and held in custody until he was released on bail of 30,000 deutsche marks on April 19, 1962. Meanwhile, in 1961, criminal proceedings were initiated against him by the *Landgericht Bonn*, for the mass murder of 145,000 people during the first phase of the Chełmno exterminations. **Adolf Eichmann**, on trial in Israel during 1961, did not help Koppe's position when he made statements against Koppe that further incriminated him. These, in turn, were sent to the prosecutor's office in Bonn.

Koppe's trial opened on October 9, 1964. It was postponed due to an illness which held up the proceedings, and on August 25, 1966, the Bonn court decided not to prosecute; instead, it released him on the grounds of "mental decay." The German government then rejected a Polish request for extradition. Koppe died on July 2, 1975, in Bad Godesberg, near Bonn, where he is buried.

KRAMER, JOSEF (1906–1945)

Josef Kramer was a German SS officer who served as the commandant of Auschwitz-Birkenau and Bergen-Belsen concentration camps. Called the "Beast of Belsen" by camp prisoners, he was directly responsible for the death of tens of thousands of Jews.

Kramer was born in Munich on November 10, 1906, an only child in a strict Roman Catholic family. In 1915, the family moved to Augsburg, and Kramer initially worked as a bookkeeper. After losing his job, he was mostly unemployed from 1925 until 1933.

In December 1931, he joined the NSDAP, followed by the SS a month later. In 1934, he became a concentration camp guard, initially working at Dachau before moving on to Sachsenhausen and later to Mauthausen. On October 16, 1937, he married Rosina, a schoolteacher, with whom he had three children.

In 1940, Kramer was assigned to assist **Rudolf Hoess**, the newly installed commandant at Auschwitz. He accompanied Hoess to inspect the Auschwitz location as a possible site for a new plant for synthetic coal oil and rubber, a vital industry given Germany's shortage of oil. *SS-Reichsführer* **Heinrich Himmler** was impressed by Kramer's attention to strict discipline.

Kramer served from May 1941 to August 1943 as commandant of the Natzweiler-Struthof concentration camp in Alsace-Lorraine, France. Here, he personally carried

Josef Kramer served as the commandant of Auschwitz-Birkenau concentration camp between May and November 1944, and Bergen-Belsen from December 1944 until the camp's liberation on April 15, 1945. Responsible for the death of thousands of people, he was known by camp inmates as the "Beast of Belsen." While there he instituted a regime of strict discipline and sadism, and lengthy roll calls, harsh labor, and insufficient food became common features of camp life. At the end of the war he was detained by the British army, convicted of war crimes, and hanged. (George Rodger/The LIFE Picture Collection/Getty Images)

out the gassing of 80 Jewish men and women, part of a group of 87 selected at Auschwitz to become anatomical specimens in a proposed Jewish skeleton collection to be housed at the Anatomy Institute at the Reich University of Strasbourg under the direction of **August Hirt**, an anatomist at the Strasburg Medical University.

At the beginning of May 1944, Kramer returned to Auschwitz with Hoess to assist in the mass murder of Hungarian Jewry. Between May 15 and July 9, 1944, approximately 430,000 Hungarian Jews were deported, for the most part to Auschwitz. Kramer was the commandant of the killing center at Auschwitz, known as Auschwitz II, between May and November 1944. After the war, several witnesses declared that they had seen Kramer regularly during the selections of people to be murdered in the gas chambers that took place immediately after the arrival of a transport.

In December 1944, Kramer was appointed as commandant of the camp at Bergen-Belsen. He brought to Belsen the strict discipline and sadism he had already demonstrated, and lengthy roll calls, harsh labor, and insufficient food became common features of camp life.

As Nazi Germany began to disintegrate in early 1945, more and more transports brought prisoners to the already overcrowded Belsen. Vast numbers began to die each day from typhus, and Kramer undertook virtually nothing to improve living conditions. The large stocks of medicines and medical instruments he had at his disposal were not made available to the prisoners, among whom were several doctors.

With a population of 15,257 inmates at the end of 1944, the number soared to 44,000 by March 1945. By April, order in the camp had vanished, while Allied bombings had disrupted water and food supplies. As the typhus epidemic raged, the camp's crematorium could no longer handle the increasing number of bodies. Corpses were simply left to rot, and with Allied armies penetrating Germany, prisoners from camps at risk of being overrun were transported to Belsen. During the week of April 13, 1945, more than 20,000 additional prisoners were transported to the camp, and numbers increased even more.

On April 15, 1945, British troops liberated Belsen. They found some 40,000 starving survivors along with around 35,000 unburied corpses scattered throughout the camp. To his own surprise, Kramer was arrested.

Josef Kramer was imprisoned at the Hameln jail, and on September 17, 1945, he was tried along with 44 other camp staff by a British military court at Lüneburg. The prosecution detailed the horrific conditions of Bergen-Belsen and presented evidence of Kramer's time spent at Auschwitz. Anita Lasker-Wallfisch, a cellist and surviving member of the Auschwitz Women's Orchestra, testified that Kramer took part in selections for the gas chamber. His defense argued that he was merely following orders in a time of war and had been following German laws, but this defense was not accepted by the court.

Kramer wrote during his defense that he was a fanatical Nazi and did only what he thought was right. He wrote that he was thankful that he and his family were not born Jews, since that would mean they would have had to die. He wrote that he did not see the inmates as people and never did what was forbidden by SS rules.

Josef Kramer was found guilty on November 17, 1945. He was hanged on December 13, 1945, aged 39, in Hameln.

KRÜGER, FRIEDRICH-WILHELM (1894–1945)

Friedrich-Wilhelm Krüger, a senior member of the SA and the SS, was notorious for his actions in Poland during World War II. From 1939 and 1943, he was the higher SS and police leader in the General Government in German-occupied Poland. In that role, he was responsible for crimes against humanity, including the establishment of concentration camps, forced labor, and mass murder. At the same time, he had a major responsibility for the Holocaust in Poland. His brother, Walter Rudolph Krüger, was also a Waffen-SS general.

Friedrich-Wilhelm Krüger was born on May 8, 1894, into a military family in Strassburg (Strasbourg), Elsass (Alsace), Germany, the son of Colonel Albert Krüger. His father was killed on August 6, 1914, while serving as a regimental commander in World War I. Krüger discontinued high school to undertake training as a cadet in military academies in Karlsruhe and Gross-Lichterfelde. On March 22, 1914, he joined the Prussian army as a lieutenant in an infantry regiment. He served this regiment as a platoon and company commander, was wounded in combat three times, and earned the Iron Cross First and Second Class.

After the war in 1919, Krüger became a staff officer with the 20th Infantry Division, leaving the army in May 1920 as a first lieutenant. At the same time, from August 1919 to March 1920, he served in the *Freikorps von Lützow*. He returned to civilian employment, working in the book trade until 1923. He married Elisabeth on September 16, 1922, and had five children: two from his wife and three foster children. From 1924 to 1928, he served as a director of a refuse company, after which he set up his own business as an independent merchant.

Krüger became a member of the NSDAP in November 1929 and joined the SS in August 1930. He was commissioned as an *SS-Sturmführer* on March 16, 1931. In April 1931, he became a member of the SA. Due to the influence of his friend **Kurt Daluege**, in 1932, Krüger was elected as SA group leader in the personal staff of the SA chief Ernst Röhm.

In 1933, he was elected to the Reichstag, serving as a member until the end of the war in 1945. He took charge of SA training and was promoted in June 1933 to *SA-Obergruppenführer*. After the Röhm Putsch of June to July 1934 (which he avoided), Krüger moved back to the SS.

From March 1936 to October 1939, Krüger ran the SS border units, and between May 1938 and October 1939, he was also inspector of *Allgemeine-SS* mounted units. With the outbreak of war, he was promoted to the position of higher SS and police leader *Ost* for the General Government based in Kraków, one of the highest posts in occupied Poland. In this position, he was responsible for, among other things, the running of counterinsurgency operations in the concentration camps, the establishment of forced-labor camps, the use of police and SS in the deportation of Jews from the Warsaw ghetto, the carrying out of Operation Harvest Festival (*Aktion Erntefest*), the fight against resisters in the General Government, and the ethnic cleansing of hundreds of thousands of Polish farmers from the area around Zamość. Krüger became a police general on August 8, 194, and commanded *Oberabschnitt "Ost"* (Senior District East) from mid-September 1939 to October 1943, as well as being deputy governor (*Reichskommisar*) for the General Government from April 1942 until his departure from Poland.

Krüger's actions throughout this time caused massive suffering for both Jews and Poles, as he was deeply implicated in carrying out Nazi racial policies. *SS-Reichsführer* **Heinrich Himmler** gave Krüger responsibility to complete the destruction of Polish Jewry. During the Warsaw Ghetto Uprising from April 19 to May 16, 1943, SS General **Jürgen Stroop** sent his daily reports on the suppression of the uprising and the ghetto's subsequent liquidation directly to Krüger. Poles involved with the resistance movement ordered Krüger's death, but on April 20, 1943, an assassination attempt in Kraków failed when two bombs missed hitting his car.

Political disagreements framed as competence disputes with Governor-General **Hans Frank** led to Krüger's dismissal on November 9, 1943, and his replacement by **Wilhelm Koppe**. After his dismissal, Krüger requested a combat assignment, which was granted. From November 1943 until April 1944, he served as a divisional commander with the Seventh SS Volunteer Mountain Division Prinz Eugen in Nazi-occupied Yugoslavia, which fought against partisans until December 1944. While ostensibly engaged in these actions, this unit became notorious for committing atrocities against the civilian population.

On May 20, 1944, Krüger was appointed a full general of the Waffen-SS. From May to August 1944, he led the Nord Division in Northern Finland. Then from August 1944 until February 1945, he was commanding general of the Fifth SS Mountain Corps, which, along with elements of other Waffen-SS units, helped to hold a vital bridgehead in the Vardar Corridor in Macedonia that helped 350,000 German soldiers escape from possible encirclement by the advancing Soviets.

In February 1945, after the Red Army in the Vistula-Oder operation had broken through the German Eastern Front, Krüger commanded the Fifth *SS-Freiwilligen-Gebirgs-Korps*, subordinated to the Ninth Army of the Vistula Army Group. During April and May 1945, he was commander of a combat unit of the *Ordnungspolizei* (Orpo) at Army Group South.

At the end of the war, in American captivity, Krüger took his own life in Gundertshausen, Upper Austria, on May 10, 1945.

L

LAMBERT, ERWIN (1909–1976)

Erwin Lambert was an SS corporal who supervised construction of the gas chambers for the *Aktion T-4* euthanasia program at Hartheim, Sonnenstein, Bernburg, and Hadamar and then at Sobibór and Treblinka extermination camps. The gas chamber he built killed more people than previous efforts in the extermination program.

Erwin Hermann Lambert was born on December 7, 1909, at Schildow, a small town near Berlin, to Hermann and Minna Lambert. His father was killed in 1915 in World War I, and his mother remarried; his stepfather owned a construction company in Schildow. Lambert belonged to the Evangelical Church, and after completing elementary school, he became an apprentice locksmith. After a year, he decided to become a mason's apprentice, qualifying in three years. He then studied a further three semesters at a Berlin construction school, working on practical jobs with various building companies. He was always employed—initially as a mason, then as a master mason, and afterward as a foreman for various Berlin construction companies.

Lambert joined the NSDAP in March 1933, and from 1938 to 1939, he worked for the party in Schildow. At that time, he was not yet a member of any of the party's paramilitary organizations. In late 1939, on the recommendation of the local office of the German Labor Front (*Deutsche Arbeitsfront*), *Aktion T-4* sought to recruit Lambert. In January 1940, he accepted the offer.

Lambert became a member of the Charitable Foundation for Sanatoria in Berlin, one of several front organizations. Dr. Carl Schneider, a psychiatrist who was a senior researcher for *Aktion T-4*, briefed Lambert about his tasks and the Reich's requirements of secrecy. Lambert's first assignment was the renovation of the villa at Tiergartenstrasse 4 (after which *Aktion T-4* was named). The central office then instructed him to install gas chambers and crematoria at clinics at Hartheim, Sonnenstein, Bernburg, and Hadamar.

The experience gained from *Aktion T-4* qualified Lambert as a specialist for murder plants wherever they were needed. In spring 1942, he was ordered to Treblinka and reported to **Richard Thomalla**, who oversaw the construction of Treblinka's first gas chambers. In August 1942, Lambert was photographed demolishing a glass factory chimney, the bricks from which were used in the construction of the larger gas chambers in Treblinka. Then under the instruction of **Christian Wirth**, Lambert built fixed gas chambers at Sobibór and Treblinka with the help of Ukrainian volunteers, using the slave labor of Jewish inmates.

On his first visit to Treblinka, Lambert built various barracks, the fences within the camp, and the ammunition bunker. During his second visit, he built the large new gas chamber. On a subsequent visit, he undertook repair and conversion work on existing buildings.

Lambert then went to Sobibór with Lorenz Hackenholt, who built and operated the gas chamber at the Bełżec extermination camp. Reporting to the commandant, **Franz Reichleitner**, he was given exact guidelines for construction of the gas chambers. The warehouse was already in operation as a gassing facility, but the old installation was not big enough and reconstruction was necessary.

Lambert directed construction in several nearby labor camps, such as Dohorucza and Poniatowa in Opole. He later stated that he was an uninvolved expert dedicated exclusively to his work and not interested in the conditions that surrounded it. In the spring of 1943, however, he again carried out conversions and repairs at Treblinka and the Hartheim T-4 center. Finally, Lambert took part in the relocation of the T-4 office from central Berlin to Gut Steineck near Schönfliess.

After *Aktion Reinhard* ended during 1943, Lambert spent several weeks over Christmas on home leave before being transferred to Trieste in early 1944 as a police sergeant. In January 1945, he was also required to install crematoria at the Italian concentration camp Risiera di San Sabba, in Trieste. More than 3,000 corpses were cremated here, while thousands more were transported elsewhere. In order to hide the evidence of their acts as the war was ending, the Nazis destroyed the crematorium.

On May 15, 1945, Lambert was captured by the British and delivered to the Americans, who brought him to a camp in Aalen, Württemberg. During his denazification hearing, Lambert was classified as a "follower" (*Mitläufer*). He settled in Stuttgart, where he became a self-employed tiler.

On March 28, 1962, Lambert was arrested and tried at the first Treblinka trial. He was convicted in the district court in Düsseldorf on September 3, 1965, for assisting in the murder of at least 300,000 people and was sentenced to four years' imprisonment. Having already served this time, he was freed. At the Sobibór trial in 1966, he denied involvement in the killing operations, claiming that he had only suspected the building would be used for killing. Lambert was acquitted.

Erwin Lambert died on October 15, 1976, in Stuttgart.

LANGE, HERBERT (1909–1945)

Herbert Lange was one of the main perpetrators of the Nazi murder of patients in Germany and occupied Poland during the *Aktion T-4* euthanasia program. At the end of 1939, he became the head of the so-called *Sonderkommando Lange*, and by the following summer, his unit had murdered more than 6,000 Polish and Jewish patients from hospitals and nursing homes in the area known to the Nazis as the Warthegau, in East and West Prussia, and in other annexed areas. As of December 1941, *Sonderkommando Lange* was using gas vans to kill tens of thousands of Jews and Roma classed as "unfit to work" in the extermination camp of Chełmno, of which Lange was the first commandant until April 1942. Later, he commanded *Sonderkommando Lange* in carrying out the extermination of Jews from the Łódź ghetto.

Herbert Lange was born in Menzlin, Western Pomerania, on September 29, 1909. He enrolled to study law at university but failed to graduate. He subsequently joined the Nazi Party on May 1, 1932. Three months later, he enlisted in the SA, led by Ernst Röhm, and in 1934, he joined the SS. By 1935, he had become a deputy police commissioner.

In 1939, Lange joined *Einsatzgruppe Naumann* (EG VI), which consisted of about 150 men. In the wake of the German army's invasion of Poland, he entered Poland with EG VI during the September campaign. On November 9, 1939, he was promoted to the rank of *SS-Untersturmführer*.

On September 12, 1939, as part of his duties, Lange was ordered to build a concentration camp at Posen (Poznán). This became known as KZ Fort VII and was part of the huge Prussian fortifications encircling the city. For a very short time, from October 10 to 16, Lange was the camp commandant. Once he had established the camp, however, he moved on.

From mid-October 1939, he headed up his own special unit, *Sonderkommando Lange*, and in early in 1940, this was tasked with the extermination of mentally ill people in the Nazi administrative area known as the Wartheland. By mid-1940, Lange and his men had been responsible for the murder of about 1,100 patients in Owińska, 2,750 patients at Kościan, 1,558 patients and 300 Poles at Działdowo, and hundreds of Poles at Fort VII, where the mobile gas chamber (*Einsatzwagen*) was invented. The unit, equipped with a gas van, shuttled between hospitals picking up patients and killing them with carbon monoxide.

Lange's effectiveness in organizing these murders was highly regarded by the SS hierarchy. He was promoted to *SS-Obersturmführer* on April 20, 1940, and his unit was permanently stationed at the Soldau concentration camp. Later, Lange was responsible for mass killing activity in the Konin region, but officially from the end of November 1940 to late 1941, he was head of the economic crimes department of the Criminal Police.

SS and police authorities established the Chełmno killing center for the single purpose of annihilating the Jewish population of the Wartheland, including the inhabitants of the Łódź ghetto. It was the first stationary facility where poison gas was used for mass murder of Jews, and Lange was tasked with the liquidation of 100,000 Jews from the region. In April 1942, Lange's unit was renamed *Sonderkommando Kulmhof* and introduced improvements to the extermination process. Lange constructed cremation pits to replace mass graves. He was succeeded by **Hans Bothmann**, who formed *Sonderkommando Bothmann* later in 1942. At a very minimum, 152,000 people were killed at the camp, with later estimates charging up to 180,000 victims.

Lange held the position of commander of the Chełmno extermination camp from December 7, 1941, until February 21, 1942. He was then transferred to the Reich Main Security Office (*Reichssicherheitshauptamt*, or RSHA). Here, he served under **Arthur Nebe** as a criminal investigator and went to the Balkans on an anti-partisan mission.

In March 1944, Lange returned to the already-inactive death camp at Chełmno as part of *Sonderkommando Bothmann* and resumed gassing operations for the final 10 transports of Jews.

In 1944, army officers led by Klaus von Stauffenberg attempted to assassinate Hitler, and Lange aided in catching the conspirators. His work in this endeavor was so highly regarded that he was promoted to *SS-Sturmbannführer*.

The circumstances of Lange's death are unclear, but it is believed that he was killed in action during the Battle of Berlin, probably around April 20, 1945.

LANGE, RUDOLF (1910–1945)

Rudolf Lange was a prominent Nazi police official and a key *Einsatzkommando* officer who was present at the Wannsee Conference in January 1942. Lange commanded the Nazi Party Intelligence Organization (*Sicherheitsdienst*, or SD) and the Nazi Security Police (SiPo) in Riga, Latvia. He was a mass killer who was largely accountable for the extermination of the Jewish population of Latvia. *Einsatzgruppe A*, which operated within his area of command, killed over 250,000 people in less than six months.

Lange was born on November 18, 1910, in Weisswasser, Saxony, the son of a railway construction supervisor. He finished high school in 1928 and studied law at the Friedrich Schiller University Jena. He received a doctorate in law in 1933 and joined the *Sturmabteilung* (SA) in November of that year, having been recruited by the Gestapo.

Feeling that this had been a bad career move, in 1936, Lange joined the *Schutzstaffel*, or SS. Within a year, he had absorbed the values of SS morality and ideology, leading him to resign his church membership by 1937. In May 1938, soon after the *Anschluss* of Austria with Germany, Lange was transferred to the Gestapo in Vienna to supervise and coordinate the fusion of the Austrian police system with that of Germany. He was then transferred to Stuttgart in June 1939, where he became a Gestapo administrator. By 1940, he was Berlin's deputy head of police.

In 1941, Lange was promoted to the rank of SS major, and on June 5, 1941, he reported to Pretzsch, Saxony, and the command staff of *Einsatzgruppe A*, headed by *SS-Brigadeführer* **Franz Walter Stahlecker**. Lange was placed in charge of *Einsatzkommando* 2, or EK2. He was one of the few people aware of the Führer Order (*Führerbefehl*) dealing with the so-called Jewish problem in Latvia. Sent to Riga, he became chief of the Riga Gestapo and Criminal Police in July 1941.

From the beginning of his involvement in Latvia, Lange gave orders to squads of Latvians, such as the *Arājs Kommando*, to carry out massacres in the smaller cities. Another local group receiving orders from Lange was the *Vagulāns Kommando*, responsible for the Jelgava massacres in July and August 1941. Lange personally supervised some of the executions and ordered that all SD officers should personally participate in the killings.

Between November 25 and November 29, 1941, Jews from the Reich itself were also sent to Riga. As construction of the Riga concentration camp had not begun, Jews coming off trains from Berlin, Frankfurt, Munich, Vienna, and Breslau were summarily shot without evaluating whether they were suitable for work. In addition, Lange planned and executed the murder of 24,000 Latvian Jews at the Rumbula Forest near Riga from November 30 to December 8, 1941.

By December 1941, Lange's EK2 had killed about 60,000 Jews from Latvia, as well as those from Germany and Austria. That month, he was named commander of the Security Police and Security Service in Latvia. As his department served as the focus of all SD operations in Latvia, Lange is widely recognized as one of the primary perpetrators of the Holocaust in Latvia. On January 20, 1942, representing **Friedrich Jeckeln**, Lange participated in the Wannsee Conference in Berlin to discuss the Final Solution. By now, he was the deputy head of all SS task forces in Latvia. Although he was the lowest-ranking SS officer present at Wannsee, his on-site experience in conducting the mass murder of deported Jews was considered as valuable for the conference; he had, after all, been responsible for the mass killings on the outskirts of Riga that murdered 35,000 people in two days, and he was able to report firsthand on killing procedures.

Lange also carried out further killing operations against Jews, political opponents, and partisans in Latvia using gas vans. Later in 1942, he was promoted to *SS-Obersturmbannführer* in Riga, where he remained until 1945. He assumed command of the SD and SiPo for the Reichsgau Wartheland, situated in Posen (Poznań), Poland.

In January 1945, Lange was promoted to *SS-Standartenführer*. Posen, which lay on the main route between Warsaw and Berlin, had to be cleared by the Red Army before the final assaults designed to capture Berlin and end the war could begin. Bitter fighting saw the outlying forts reduced and city blocks seized, as the Soviets succeeded in pushing the German defenders toward the city center. The manner of his death is unclear. One report states that he committed suicide on February 16, 1945; another states that he was killed in battle on February 23, 1945. He was posthumously awarded the German Cross in Gold for his actions in the Battle of Posen.

LAVAL, PIERRE (1883–1945)

Pierre Jean-Marie Laval was a French politician who served twice as prime minister of France during the Third Republic. During Germany's occupation of France in World War II, Marshal Philippe Pétain and Pierre Laval, as leading members of the French government, surrendered vast resources to the Nazi war effort and facilitated the deportation of tens of thousands of Jews to their death in Nazi concentration camps.

Laval was born on June 28, 1883, in Châteldon, in the Auvergne. His parents, Baptiste and Claudine, ran a small inn, and his father operated the local mail coach. Laval left school at 12 years old to drive for his father, and after that, his education was sporadic. Through persistence and talent, however, he attended university and earned degrees in geology and law. Drafted into the military, his term of service was cut short for medical reasons.

Laval married in 1909 and practiced law in Paris. By May 1914, he had won a seat as a socialist in the Chamber of Deputies, representing Aubervilliers in north east Paris from 1914 to 1919. He voted against the Treaty of Versailles, as, in his view, it imposed too harsh a penalty on Germany and provided no reliable mechanism of enforcement. This did not endear him to retribution-minded French voters, and with a right-wing upswing, he lost his seat. He used his subsequent period out of Parliament to focus on ensuring his income, earning money sufficient to enable him to move back into politics. In 1924, he was reelected and again represented Aubervilliers until 1927. He then served as a senator for the Seine from 1927 to 1936 and as senator for Puy-de-Dâme from 1936 to 1944. He also served as Aubervilliers' mayor from 1923 to 1944.

On January 22, 1936, Laval resigned as prime minister after the Hoare-Laval Pact scandal, an attempt by Britain and France to end war in Abyssinia by giving Italian dictator Benito Mussolini two-thirds of the country. Many of Laval's backers felt that the pact humiliated France, and he lost enormous support as a result. On May 5, 1936, Italy conquered Addis Ababa.

In September 1939, France and Britain declared war on Germany because of its invasion of Poland. On May 10, 1940, after several months of a "phony war" in which very little fighting occurred in the West, Germany attacked France and rapidly broke through French lines.

The French government fled Paris, establishing itself in Vichy. The victorious Nazis then divided France into two parts: occupied France, which the Nazis governed, and Vichy France, which remained nominally independent though under ultimate German authority. Although officially government for the whole of France, the Vichy regime effectively controlled only the south of the country.

Laval was brought back into mainstream French politics in support of Marshal Pétain. On July 10, 1940, Laval used his influence in the National Assembly to give Pétain full powers, and the next day, Laval again became prime minister. In this capacity, he cooperated with German policy demands, including antisemitic measures and the export of forced French labor to serve the German war effort.

Laval quickly began removing the rights of French Jews and organizing the roundup and deportation of those not born in France. In October 1940, Pétain and Laval met with **Adolf Hitler** at the small French town of Montoire, agreeing on a policy of collaboration, but on December 13, 1940, Pétain dismissed Laval to placate other members of his government. Laval was placed under arrest, but he was released on December 15, 1940.

On August 25, 1941, as Laval was seeing off French volunteers going to fight in Russia alongside Germany, he was shot four times by a student and seriously wounded. He was discharged from hospital on September 30, 1941, but it took him a considerable period before he regained full health.

On March 27, 1942, just three weeks before Laval's return to power, the first convoy of Jewish deportees to Auschwitz was sent from Drancy and Compiègne. **Theodor Dannecker**, head of the Gestapo in Paris, then anticipated the deportation of all adult Jews living in occupied and unoccupied France. Doing so, however, would require the cooperation of police forces in the occupied zone, as well as collaboration from the Vichy government.

On April 14, 1942, Pétain named Laval chief of government with special powers in Vichy France, and on April 18, he once more became prime minister, with additional roles as information minister, interior minister, and foreign minister.

At the start of July 1942, Laval stated his intention to deliver to Germany foreign Jews living in unoccupied France, in exchange for a collective exemption of French-born Jews from both zones. When asked to reconsider his decision to include in the convoys children under 16 years (initially not asked for by the Germans), Laval refused and replied that not one of those children may stay in France. Of the 11,000 children under the age of 16 who were deported, most of them at Laval's personal insistence, none returned.

Laval claimed after the war to have delivered the foreign Jews to avoid the deportation of French-born Jews, but he never asked for nor obtained the slightest written assurance from the Germans on that issue. Thousands of French Jews were deported later, and in 1942 alone, more than 43,000 Jews, both foreign and French born, were deported, most of them arrested by French police. The year 1943 saw 11,000 Jews deported, with another 17,000 in 1944. It has been estimated that 80 percent were arrested by the French police and that 97 percent of all those deported perished in gas chambers or were exterminated through slave labor in Nazi concentration camps.

When the Allied forces landed in North Africa in November 1942, Germany occupied the Vichy zone, reducing the Pétainiste state to little more than a puppet regime. Laval and Pétain now believed it was of paramount importance to prove that France retained its sovereignty, leading them to do much of the Germans' dirty work for them. If Jews had to be rounded up, they considered that it would be better that the French police seize them rather than the Germans.

In January 1943, Laval oversaw the creation of the French Militia (*Milice*), a police force under the leadership of Joseph Darnand but with Laval officially the president. In six months, the *Milice* recruited more than 35,000 men and played the key role in the hunt for Jews and members of the resistance, who were either tortured and executed summarily or deported to concentration camps. That same year, Laval handed over prewar premiers Léon Blum, Paul Reynaud, and Edouard Daladier to the Nazis.

Laval encouraged French collaboration on an economic level as well. He negotiated the transfer of French skilled laborers to work in German war industries, eventually compelling compliance by drafting French workers. This measure drove many such men into the countryside to join the resistance. In addition, he organized the export of French material resources to Germany so that by 1943, more than 40 percent of French agricultural and industrial output was devoted to the Nazi war effort.

In July 1944, Laval appeared sincerely horrified by the assassination of his former friend and colleague of government Georges Mandel, liquidated by the *Milice*. There was a certain irony in this: Mandel, né Rothschild, was Jewish—and French born.

Laval served as prime minister until August 1944. His policy was to ensure that as much of France as possible escaped the destruction and loss of life he had seen in Poland. He did what he could to avoid giving the Germans any form of military help, but regardless of the motives underlying his efforts, many saw Laval, Pétain, and their supporters as collaborators.

After the success of D-Day in June 1944 and the liberation of Paris in August 1944, it was only a matter of time before the whole of France was liberated. The Vichy government relocated to Germany, where it fell apart as the Allied forces continued to advance.

Laval fled to Spain in May 1945. He was deported from there to Austria, where he was turned in to the French. Charged with plotting against the security of the state and collaborating with the enemy, his trial began at 1:30 p.m. on Thursday, October 4, 1945. A sentence of death was pronounced, with the execution set for the morning of October 15. Laval attempted suicide at Fresnes Prison on the day of his execution but failed, as the cyanide capsule hidden in his jacket had lost its potency. Later that day, October 15, 1945, aged 61, Laval was shot in the courtyard of Fresnes Prison.

LIEBEHENSCHEL, ARTHUR (1901–1948)

Arthur Liebehenschel was a German SS leader who commanded the Auschwitz and Majdanek extermination camps during World War II.

He was born on November 25, 1901, in Posen (Poznań). As a student, he read economics and public administration. In January 1919, Liebehenschel left Posen, and from April 1, 1919, to August 1919, he took part in *Freikorps Graf Dohna*, focusing on border-guard duties. He served in the German army from April 10, 1919, to October 1931 and was discharged with the rank of sergeant major.

On January 2, 1932, Liebehenschel joined the NSDAP, and on November 8, he became a member of the SS. From 1932 to August 1, 1934, Liebehenschel served as an assistant to the physicist Walter Gerlach, and then after August 4, 1934, he became a senior officer at the notorious Columbia House prison in Berlin. On leaving in 1936, Liebehenschel served at the Lichtenburg concentration camp, where he remained until August 1, 1937. From then until to May 1940, Liebenhenschel worked as chief of staff of the leader of the *SS-Totenkopfverbände*, **Theodor Eicke.**

From January 5, 1940, to June 1, 1940, Liebehenschel was the chief of staff in the Concentration Camp Inspectorate, transferring on June 1, 1940, to a roving commission visiting the camps in person. He held this position until March 3, 1942. On November 14, 1941, he sought details of all SS members involved in executions so they could receive the War Merit Cross II with Swords, but six days later, he sent out an addendum stating the award should be for "special tasks essential to the war." The term "executions" was not to be used.

When the WVHA was founded, Liebehenschel was assigned to the new *Amtsgruppe D* (Concentration Camps) as head of Office D I (Central Office), and he held that role from March 16, 1942, to November 10, 1943, working under **Oswald Pohl** and a representative of the Inspector of Concentration Camps, **Richard Glücks**. During that term, he regulated the concentration camps and their processes.

On August 8, 1942, he sent out orders to concentration camp commanders to avoid the courts becoming involved in ill-treatment of prisoners, as this could negatively influence the judiciary's view of camp conditions. In that notice,

Liebehenschel noted that at Auschwitz prisoners were ill treated by German criminal inmates supported by the SS, who could incite the actions of the criminals but, for doing so, were never to be punished. Liebehenschel issued orders of various kinds to camp commandants covering a variety of topics: the treatment of Soviet prisoners of war, the concealment of brothels and crematoria in camps, the immediate cessation of the transfer of ashes of Czechs and Jews to their family members, the implementation of the *Nacht und Nebel* (night and fog) decree, the use of gold from teeth, and the need to camouflage the incidence of deaths in the camps.

Liebehenschel had married Gertrud, with whom he had three children: a boy and two girls. The marriage failed, and Liebehenschel had started a relationship with Richard Glücks's secretary, Anneliese. Liebehenschel had been divorced by his wife in early December 1943 and had left his family because of the affair. Annaliese had been in a sexual relationship with a Jewish man in 1935 and had been held in protective custody in Düsseldorf for three weeks for contravening the race laws (*Rassenschande*). Oswald Pohl wanted Liebehenschel to end the relationship with Annaliese, but as Annaliese was expecting a child in 1944, *SS-Reichsführer* **Heinrich Himmler** approved Liebehenschel's petition for marriage over Pohl's opposition.

Initially, Liebehenschel was transferred out of Berlin because of the divorce and the affair, and on November 11, 1943, he was appointed commandant of Auschwitz. Liebehenschel was put in overall charge of the camp complex as well as Auschwitz I (main camp), with Friedrich Hartjenstein heading Auschwitz II (Birkenau) and Heinrich Schwarz, Auschwitz III (Monowitz). Liebehenschel did not last long as commandant of Auschwitz, however, and was dismissed on May 8, 1944. His lengthy dispute with Pohl about his divorce and rebellion against Pohl when Himmler stepped in on the question of remarriage were probably the only reasons for the dismissal.

Liebehenschel was appointed to head the camp at Lublin-Majdanek on May 19, 1944, succeeding Martin Gottfried Weiss. The camp had been evacuated because of the Soviet advance into German-occupied Poland, but Liebehenschel's remit was wider than just the camp itself; as commandant, he was also assigned to take charge of labor camps at Warsaw, Radom, Budzyń, and Bliżyn. Leibehenschel served there until August 1944.

In August 25, 1944, he was relocated to Trieste, Italy, to work for **Odilo Globocnik** as head the SS Manpower Office there. Almost all the team members in Globocnik's command came from the *Aktion Reinhard* camps, and his zone of operations, created on October 1, 1943, covered the Italian provinces of Udine, Gorizia, Trieste, Pula, and the Slovene regions of Ljubljana, Susak, and Bakar.

After the war, Arthur Liebehenschel was arrested by the U.S Army and extradited to Poland on November 27, 1946. After being convicted of crimes against humanity by the Supreme National Tribunal at the Auschwitz Trial in Kraków, he was sentenced to death on December 22, 1946. He was executed by hanging on January 24, 1948. Others executed at the same time included Hans Aumeier, Maximilian Grabner, Carl Möckel, and **Maria Mandl**.

LISCHKA, KURT (1909–1989)

Kurt Werner Lischka was Gestapo chief and commandant of the security police in Paris during the German occupation of France in World War II.

Kurt Werner Lischka was born on August 16, 1909, in Breslau (Wrocław) to the family of a bank official. He passed his baccalaureate in 1927 and then studied law and political science in Berlin. After obtaining his degree, he worked in district courts and in the Provincial Court of Appeal in Breslau. He joined the SS on June 1, 1933, eventually reaching the ranks of *SS-Sturmbannführer* in 1938 and *SS-Obersturmbannführer* on April 20, 1942.

On September 1, 1935, Lischka joined the Gestapo, initially as a reference person for religious affairs. A hard worker with a reputation for zeal, self-control, and audacity, in 1938, he became a doctor of law. At 29 years old, he was promoted to head the *Referat IVB* office of the Gestapo in charge of religious denominations, Jews (the Jewish question), Freemasons, emigrants, and pacifists. He organized and carried out the first mass arrests of German Jews on June 16, 1938, transferring between 2,000 and 3,000 men to Buchenwald and Sachsenhausen, 10 percent of whom died during the first two months. On October 28, 1938, Lischka organized the deportation of over 20,000 Jews to the Polish border, precipitating the events that would in due course lead to the November pogrom of November 9 to 10, 1938. On that night, Lischka took part in the arrest of some 30,000 German Jews in what became infamous as *Kristallnacht*, the Night of Broken Glass.

By the end of 1938, Lischka was appointed head of the Reich Center for Jewish Emigration in Berlin, which robbed Jews of their property before their emigration.

In January 1940, Lischka became head of the Gestapo in Cologne, and in November 1940, he was transferred to France. Here, he became deputy to Helmut Knochen, senior commander of the SiPo-SD in the Occupied Zone. His skills as an organizer were used to structure a small SiPo-SD commando that had just been set up in Paris. In January 1943, Lischka became responsible, with **Theodor Dannecker**, for organizing the Vel' d'Hiv roundup of thousands of Paris Jews, who were deported, via Drancy, to their deaths at Auschwitz-Birkenau. Lischka was instrumental in planning and supervising the deportation and subsequent murder of tens of thousands of French Jews, together with others the Third Reich considered to be "undesirable."

In September 1943, Lischka, suspected of corruption, was recalled to Berlin. Criminal proceedings against him commenced, but charges were dismissed on June 27, 1944. In November 1943, he was given a key role in the central administration of the Nazi police service and assigned to the IV D1 unit of the Reich Security Main Office in the Protectorate of Bohemia and Moravia with responsibility for reprisals. In this capacity, he was the right-hand man of **Heinrich Müller**, the Gestapo chief. Lischka was a member of the Special Commission of 20 July 1944, the investigative team tasked with identifying and punishing the plotters involved with the failed assassination attempt and coup against **Adolf Hitler** on that date.

In April 1945, Lischka was evacuated to Schleswig-Holstein, and his services ended on May 3, 1945. At the end of the war, he lived and worked under a false identity as a farmworker, but on December 10, 1945, he was arrested by British soldiers and imprisoned in British and then French internment camps.

Due to his activity in occupied Czechoslovakia, where he was implicated in the killing of Czech resistance members, Lischka was extradited to Prague in 1947 for war crimes. He was released on August 22, 1950, and he settled in Cologne, West Germany.

On September 18, 1950, Lischka was sentenced to life imprisonment in absentia by a French military court for his wartime role in the Final Solution in occupied France. However, due to the 1955 closed transition agreement, Lischka, like many other war criminals, was protected against extradition, so he did not stand trial in France. For many years, French courts sought a retrial in for his activities in France, but in vain.

Lischka thus spent more than 25 years as a free man, working under his own name in the Federal Republic of Germany. One of his positions was as a judge in the Federal Republic, his life sentence in France notwithstanding.

Impatient with years of legal delays, French Nazi hunter Serge Klarsfeld and his German-born wife, Beate, attempted to kidnap Lischka in 1974 and take him back to France by force. Although the kidnapping attempt was foiled, it gained widespread publicity for the case against Lischka. The following year, facing heavy political pressure, Bonn finally ratified an accord with France that cleared the way for a new trial. Due in part to Klarsfeld's success at gathering incriminating documents, the trial went unusually swiftly. In 1980, Lischka was sentenced to 10 years' imprisonment, but in 1985, he was released early on health grounds. He and his wife then lived in a retirement home in Brühl, where he died on May 16, 1989.

M

MACKERT, ALICE (1916–2012)

"Alice La Blonde" was the nickname given to Alice Mackert, who served as the secretary-general of the Gestapo in Nice, France, during the German occupation of the area.

She was born in Switzerland in 1916. Moving to France in 1937, she took in sewing in Alençon. She arrived in Nice in 1943 as support staff to the Gestapo following the German invasion of Vichy France after the withdrawal of the Italian occupying forces from the region. She became the mistress of Alfred Schultz, her boss and one of the local Gestapo leaders. Schultz had been a former professor of French and served in Nice as an interpreter on behalf of the German police. Allegedly, Mackert was also the mistress of **Alois Brunner** during the last few weeks he was in Nice.

The Hermitage Hotel, housing the Gestapo in Nice, was built in 1905 for European tourists who came south for the summer. It served as a hotel from 1905 until 1939, except during World War I, when it acted as a military hospital.

After the fall of France on June 22, 1940, Nice was in the unoccupied zone, and despite the anti-Jewish legislation introduced by the Vichy regime, it became a haven for Jewish refugees who fled to the south hoping to stay out of the Nazis' reach. The Italian Armistice Commission partially requisitioned the hotel.

On June 2, 1941, the law required that all Jews must be registered. As early as June 25, 1941, the prefect of Alpes-Maritimes asked the mayors to provide him with "a preliminary list of all Jews or Jews deemed to be Jewish in your commune: these lists should be secretly established, in order to allow a first check on subsequent declarations." The prefect estimated that there were 15,000 Jews in the department.

On September 8, 1943, Italy surrendered, and the Germans moved into Nice. Two days later, Alois Brunner, a top aide to **Adolf Eichmann**, took possession of the Hermitage Hotel, where he set up his headquarters. He immediately started organizing some of the war's most violent raids against the Jews. Teams of SS officers routinely patrolled the city, snatching anyone off the street who "looked" Jewish. A bounty of 3,500 francs was paid to those who denounced a male Jew, and from November 1943, this was increased by "performance bonuses." From September 10, 1943, up to the time Brunner left Nice, a total of about 80 days, no fewer than 2,142 Jews were rounded up. At the Hotel Hermitage, they were registered and then sent to the death camps via the nearby train station.

Alice La Blonde flourished in this environment, and the basements of the hotel functioned as torture rooms. She was reputed to be a sadistic and brutal torturer who used a sharp whip. Described as being "elegantly depraved" by the paper *La Liberté*, she was feared by all, even her leaders.

She was responsible for attempting to trap and denounce Bishop Paul Rémond. The Germans wanted to move against Rémond but were held back by their concern that Rémond was very popular; accordingly, they created a trap. Alice showed up at Rémond's residence with two Jewish-looking children and begged Rémond to "hide them as you have hidden so many others." The bishop had been briefed about Alice as a known Gestapo agent ever since she had entered the local boys' vocational school looking for Jewish boys to arrest. She was reputed to be "a piece of work" and was easily recognizable by her dyed blond hair (as one observer recalled, "too blonde to be believed"). The bishop continued to repeat that he had no facilities at the residence to take in children. Alice became increasingly agitated and started to plead loudly that the children needed help, but Rémond continued to deny her help and showed her politely to the door.

At the end of the war, Alice La Blonde was arrested. On May 6, 1946, at the request of the director general for services and research, the investigating judge signed the decision to divest the Nice Court of Mackert and granted her a closed hearing. She was well defended by an excellent legal team. Despite the evidence of 32 witnesses, no testimony ultimately was considered to have proven her guilt, despite compelling evidence pointing to her antisemitism and support of the Gestapo's actions in arresting and deporting Jews.

At dawn on June 1, 1946, Mackert left the New Prison at Nice for transport to Marseille. On December 3, 1946, the *Nouvelliste Valaisan* reported that the military court trial of Alice La Blonde had commenced, referring to Alice as the Nice Gestapo's torturer. Before the military court of the ninth region, she denied being the mistress of an *Abwehr* officer named Baina, who had executed six members of the resistance. However, her cruelty in insisting on sending the Jewish wife and children of a non-Jewish soldier serving for France was upsetting to the judge.

On December 6, 1948, the *Jewish Telegraph* reported that the French woman Alice Mackert, who had aided the Gestapo and who was responsible for the death of about 5,000 Jews, had been sentenced to hard labor for life. Notwithstanding that she was suspected of double dealing and that her persona was a symbol of Gestapo horrors and collaboration, inexplicably Alice Mackert was surreptitiously spirited out to the United States after the success of her appeal on points of law. She was traced to Ohio, where she died at the advanced age of 98 in 2012.

MAGNUSSEN, KARIN (1908–1997)

Karin Magnussen was a German biologist, teacher, and researcher at the Kaiser Wilhelm Institute of Anthropology, Human Heredity, and Eugenics during the Third Reich, propagating National Socialist racial doctrine. At the Kaiser Wilhelm Institute, she was known for her studies of heterochromia iridis (different-colored eyes) using iris specimens supplied by **Josef Mengele** from Auschwitz concentration camp victims.

She was born on February 9, 1908, in Bremen, Germany, into the middle-class home of landscape painter and ceramist Walter Magnussen. She completed her schooling in Bremen and then studied biology, geology, chemistry, and physics at the University of Göttingen.

Magnussen joined the National Socialist German Students' League (NSDStB) while she was still an undergraduate. By 1931, aged 23, she was a member of the NSDAP. The same year, she became a leader of the League of German Girls (BdM) and a member of the National Socialist Teachers League. As a BdM leader, she gave lectures on racial and demographic politics in Bremen. She graduated in 1932, having passed examinations in botany, zoology, and geology. In July 1932, her doctoral thesis, "Studies on the Physiology of the Butterfly Wing," was accepted, after which she studied at the Zoological Institute of the University of Göttingen. In 1935, she commenced work in the Nazi Racial Policy Office in Hanover, and in 1936, she completed writing *Race and Population Policy Tools*, which was published in 1939.

In 1936, Magnussen topped state examinations for high school teaching positions, and from 1936 to 1941, she was employed in Hanover as a secondary-school teacher. In the autumn of 1941, having received a scholarship, she suspended her teaching position and transferred to the Kaiser Wilhelm Institute for Anthropology, Human Genetics, and Eugenics (KWI-A) in Dahlem, Berlin. Her value to the KWI-A was in her party connections and her credentials as a biologist.

It was originally intended that at the KWI-A, Magnussen would assist human geneticist Hans Nachtsheim, but he refused a request from the director, **Eugen Fischer**, to hire her because she was "a fanatical Nazi and antisemite." Magnussen worked instead under another famous geneticist, Otmar Freiherr von Verschuer, and remained one of his assistants even after he became director of the KWI-A in 1942, upon Fischer's retirement. At the KWI-A, Magnussen met Dr. Josef Mengele, who worked there temporarily.

From July 1943, a research-funding organization, the *Deutsche Forschungsgemeinschaft* (DFG), promoted Magnussen's study to "explore the heritage conditionality for the development of eye color as a basis for racial and ethnicity studies." In the third published edition of *Race and Population Policy Tools* in 1943, Magnussen wrote that the war then in progress "is not just about the preservation of the German people, but is about which races and peoples should live in the future on European soil . . . Judaism has significant influence in all of the enemy states." Magnussen warned of "the many dangers" that confronted Germany, ranging from Africans, Roma, and especially Jews, whom she viewed as a treacherous 1 percent of the German population.

Magnussen's interest in eye coloring continued. First, she bred rabbits with exactly the same hereditary characteristics—that is, heterochromia—as in humans. In the summer of 1944, she used them to test "the effect of several hormones and pharmacologically active substances on the pigmentation in the eyes of various color breams," as the DFG reported.

From a colleague, she learned that more twins and family members with heterochromic irises would be found in a Sinti community in Mechau, northern

Germany. Members of various families were taken in the spring of 1943 to the KWI-A. They were photographed before being sent to Auschwitz, where Mengele had worked since late May 1943 as camp physician. A report by an inmate physician indicated that six twins and a family with eight members were selected from the Roma ("Gypsy") camp and killed so that their eyes could be "harvested" for Magnussen's and von Verschuer's research.

Magnussen's experiments on rabbits were replicated by Mengele on Sinti human subjects. An eyewitness at Auschwitz reported that several SS doctors carried out experiments on newborn babies to change the color of their eyes.

At the Kaiser Wilhelm Institute, Magnussen examined the eyes of murdered prisoners sent to her by Mengele. She received sufficient number of eyes for her research to assure that the research agenda of the KWI-A would be supported. Magnussen used the scientific method to conclude that eye color is not only genetically but also hormonally determined.

Mengele pledged to Magnussen to give her an uninterrupted supply of victims' eyes for further research and evaluation, and as a result, the second half of 1944 saw Magnussen receive several deliveries of eyes taken from Auschwitz victims. A Hungarian prisoner pathologist working as a slave laborer for Mengele in Auschwitz, Miklós Nyiszli, noted after the autopsy of Sinti twins that they died not because of illness but because of a chloroform injection to the heart. Nyiszli had to prepare their eyes and send them to the KWI-A.

At least until the spring of 1945, Magnussen was known to be working in Berlin. After World War II, she moved to Bremen again and continued her research, which was published in 1949 as *On the Relationship between Histological Distribution of Pigment, Iris Color and Pigmentation of the Eyeball of the Human Eye*. At least in the Soviet Zone of Occupation, Magnussen's publications appeared on the list of prohibited literature.

In September 1946, the Berlin office of the U.S. Counsel for War Crimes and its chief research analyst, Manfred Wolfson, recommended that both von Verschuer and Magnussen be arrested. British and American officials decided to permit the resumption of German medical science and to forego the prosecution of other crimes. The Kaiser Wilhelm Institutes were too heavily implicated with the Nazi programs of racism, death, and pseudoscience, and the KWI was renamed as the Max Plank Institute. A commission was set up to investigate charges against von Verschuer. Led by a judge, four members of the commission looked not only at specific guilt but also at the scientific value of Verschuer's work. They determined that his link to Auschwitz crimes was established, and he was judged to be a "racist fanatic." Verschuer's career at the KWI-A now ended, he counterattacked that the denunciations derived from "communist agents."

Wolfson recommended that Magnussen be arrested and interrogated. Those adjudicating at the Nuremberg Doctors' Trial decided that publicizing German medical atrocities could undermine public confidence in clinical science. In order to avoid the appearance that the entire German medical community could no longer be trusted, the tribunal presented medical researchers as having been "perverted" by the manipulative control of the SS and as poisoned by Nazism. It stated that the human experiments were so ill conceived as not to be worthy of the status of science. The tribunal held further that any additional investigation of hospitals and universities was undesirable, because, if undertaken on a large scale, it might result in the removal of large numbers of highly qualified medical personnel at a time when their services were most needed.

On September 19, 1949, the Dahlem Commission, a tribunal of von Verschuer's peers, reversed the prior findings of the Nuremberg Doctors' Tribunal and cleared von Verschuer. It also played down the significance of the Mengele link by stressing that Mengele was only a camp doctor who would have followed SS regulations against spreading information about Auschwitz as an extermination camp. Thus, they ruled that the ties of the German medical community—especially those at the Kaiser Wilhelm Institutes—were not in any way linked with the death camps and the SS and that medical personnel, such as Mengele, who were directly involved with the death camps were identified as the most responsible for the atrocities of National Socialism.

Karin Magnussen wanted to continue to study the eyes of Roma but was advised to refrain from every attempt to publish her material on this subject for the time being, as there were still Auschwitz Roma victims who could implicate her. Efforts to explore her culpability continued throughout the rest of her life, but she was able to live to almost 90 without any public acknowledgment of her involvement with Auschwitz.

In 1949, scientific-journal editor Alfred Kuhn refused to provide Magnussen a vehicle for her research data on eyes. In rejecting her work, Kuhn stated that "we have discovered that you also worked with human material on Gypsy eyes from the Auschwitz camp in KWI for Anthropology. It is inconceivable to me how it is possible to have a relationship of any kind with a person connected with this institution."

Both Otmar von Verschuer and Karin Magnussen carried out research on human material supplied by Josef Mengele from Auschwitz. Verschuer apparently preferred not to ask for any details about the circumstances under which Mengele had obtained his material. Magnussen, on the other hand, effectively egged Mengele on. Publicly, at least, she never demonstrated any contrition for the part she played in the atrocities that took place at Auschwitz.

With the end of World War II, Karin Magnussen taught biology at a Bremen grammar school for girls. A popular teacher, she ran interesting classes in which students were able to study live and dead rabbits.

Until 1964, Magnussen published essays in scientific journals. She retired in August 1970, but even in old age, she justified Nazi racial ideology. In 1980, in a conversation with geneticist Benno Müller-Hill, she noted that the Nuremberg Laws did not go far enough. She also denied until the end that Mengele had killed children so that she could continue her research.

In 1990, Magnussen moved into a nursing home. A family member recalled that as Magnussen's home was being broken up to assist with the move, several jars with eyes from Auschwitz were found, which were then disposed of. Karin Magnussen died in Bremen on February 19, 1997, at the age of 89. Otmar Frieherr von

Verschuer remained a respected scientist in Germany and became dean of the University of Münster, as well as an honorary member of numerous scientific societies.

MANDL, MARIA (1912–1948)

Maria Mandl (also spelled Mandel) was an Austrian SS guard, notorious as a top-ranking official at the Auschwitz-Birkenau extermination camp.

She was born on January 10, 1912, in Münzkirchen, Upper Austria, the third daughter of Franz Mandl, a shoemaker, and his wife Mandlanna. She completed elementary school and then did a year at a commercial school. She spent 18 months abroad with her sister, who was a cook in Switzerland, before becoming a housemaid in Innsbruck. Afterward she worked for the Austrian post office, but following the *Anschluss* in March 1938, all government employees were dismissed if they had not pledged their loyalty to the NSDAP. Later the same year, Mandl joined the SS, at a time when the SS were looking for single women aged between 21 and 45.

Mandl moved to Munich in September 1938, where, through her uncle who was a police inspector, she became a guard at the SS camp in Lichtenberg, the first women's concentration camp, on October 15, 1938. She worked here until May 14, 1939. A survivor of Lichtenberg, Linda Haag, recalled only one guard, Mandl, whom she described as standing out from all other guards because of her brutality and violence. She would flog any woman who broke camp rules, tying the naked woman to a wooden post and beating her until she could no longer lift her arms.

From May 15, 1939, to October 6, 1942, Mandl worked as a guard at Ravensbrück, where as a superintendent she assisted Dr. **Herta Oberheuser** with her search for human experiments. Due to her prior experience, Mandl rose quickly through the ranks. Newly recruited camp guards would begin their training (which could last anywhere between one and six months depending on the recruit's background), at Ravensbrück, where they were taught how to punish prisoners and how to maintain work speed for those engaged in slave labor.

On January 4, 1941, Mandl became a member of the NSDAP prior to joining the German Women's League. She was transferred to Auschwitz on October 7, 1942, where she worked until November 30, 1944. She immediately became senior officer of the women's camp at Birkenau, taking over from Johanna Langefeld, who was dismissed for being too "soft" on Polish prisoners. Mandl was feared and called the "Beast" because of her brutality. A sadistic murderer, she especially liked to select women and children for the gas chambers.

From 1942 onward, Mandl served as the camp leader at Birkenau. Every single female in Auschwitz, prisoner or guard, answered to her, and she answered directly to the commandant, **Rudolf Hoess**. Mandl's responsibilities in Auschwitz were to oversee the roll call (which could last up to five hours), selections for killing, and medical experiments conducted by Dr. **Josef Mengele**.

As a music lover, she developed the women's orchestra in Birkenau in the spring of 1943. The musicians were treated better than the other inmates; their barracks were clean, and they got better food than other prisoners. The conductor of the women's orchestra was Alma Rosé, the niece of Gustav Mahler, and the orchestra also included two professional musicians, cellist Anita Lasker-Wallfisch and vocalist/pianist Fania Fénelon, each of whom wrote memoirs of their time in the orchestra. Wallfisch, for example, recollected being told to play Schumann's *Träumerei* for Mengele, while Fénelon's account, *Playing for Time*, was made into a film of the same name. Mandl's establishment of the orchestra enhanced her status, both with Mengele, who attended many performances, and with **Heinrich Himmler**. Fénelon wrote that the orchestra members were scheduled to be shot to death on the same day as their liberation by British troops.

Mandl often had a Jewish prisoner serve as her "personal pet," carrying out tedious tasks until she was tired of that person—upon which she would have the "pet" executed. When it was time for the prisoners to line up, she would wait for one to look at her, and then she would have that person executed.

Mandl admired **Dorothea Binz**'s teaching of "malicious pleasure" and was known to have kicked to death a Jewish woman for curling her hair. Any prisoner who dared to look at her risked being sent to the gas chambers. While Mandl was at Auschwitz, she appointed the infamous female guards **Irma Grese** and Therese Brandl, her private secretary.

With the advance of the Soviet army, Mandl moved camps, and from November 1944 to May 1945, she was a guard at a camp known as Mühldorf. In May 1945, she fled Mühldorf before the advance of the Americans into the mountains of southern Bavaria to her birthplace, Münzkirchen. Her father, who had broken off contact with her when she became a camp guard, would not provide her with refuge. On October 8, 1945, while residing with her sister in Luck, she was arrested by soldiers of the U.S. Army and imprisoned with others in the war crimes prison in Dachau.

On April 4, 1946, the Polish Department of War Crimes sought Maria Mandl's extradition, and on November 11, 1946, she was delivered into Polish custody and imprisoned in Montelupich prison. On March 5, 1947, her trial began in Kraków; it concluded on December 22, 1947. For her part in the selections for the gas chambers and medical experiments and for her torture of countless prisoners, Maria Mandl was condemned to death as a war criminal by Poland's Supreme People's Court. She was executed on January 24, 1948, at the age of 36.

MENGELE, JOSEF (1911–1979)

Josef Mengele was an SS physician stationed at Auschwitz during World War II. A member of the team of doctors responsible for the selection of victims to be killed in the gas chambers and for performing deadly human experiments on prisoners, he was nicknamed the "Angel of Death."

Mengele was born in Günzburg, near Ulm, Bavaria, on March 16, 1911, the oldest of three sons of Walburga and Karl Mengele, a prosperous manufacturer of agricultural implements. As a boy, he was cultured, bright, well liked, and a good scholar. He graduated from Gunzburg High School in 1930 and was accepted into Munich University. With no political interests until this time, he joined the Nazi Party at university to boost his career as a scientist. Mengele joined the *Stalhelm*

Nicknamed the "Angel of Death," Josef Mengele was an SS physician stationed at Auschwitz during World War II. Obsessed with the study of human genetics, he was renowned for performing deadly human experiments without anesthetic and overseeing "selections" of arriving prisoners. He was known to conduct experiments on children and was especially fascinated with twins. This image is of Mengele, in 1960, in Paraguay, one of the locations to which he fled after the war. (Bettmann/Getty Images)

(Steel Helmet) militia in 1931; in 1934, the SA incorporated the Stalhelm into its ranks, making Mengele by default a Brownshirt. Soon after this, Mengele developed a problem with his kidneys that saw him leave the *Stalhelm* but enabled him to concentrate on his studies. In 1935, he earned a PhD in physical anthropology, with a dissertation that dealt with racial differences in the structure of the lower jaw—allegedly enabling researchers to tell the difference between Jews and non-Jews.

In 1936, Mengele passed the state medical examination, after which he went to Leipzig to work at a clinic. In January 1937, he was invited to join the Institute for Hereditary Biology and Racial Hygiene in Frankfurt, where he became the assistant of Dr. Otmar von Verschuer, a leading scientific figure widely known for his research with twins.

Also in 1937, Mengele rejoined the Nazi Party, and in May 1938, he became a member of the SS. On July 28, 1939, he married Irene Schönbein, whom he had met while studying in Leipzig. Upon the outbreak of war in September 1939, Mengele was unable to enlist immediately because of his kidney problem, but in 1940, he was accepted into the Waffen-SS.

In 1941, Lieutenant Mengele was awarded the Iron Cross Second Class in the fighting in Ukraine. In January 1942, he was pronounced unfit for duty, promoted to the rank of captain, awarded the Iron Cross First Class, and posted to the Race and Resettlement Office in Berlin.

On May 24, 1943, Mengele's next assignment saw him appointed as medical officer of Auschwitz-Birkenau's *Zigeunerfamilienlager* (Gypsy Family Camp), where his work was funded by a grant from his mentor, Otmar von Verschuer. Here, he studied human genetics. In August 1944, the camp was liquidated, and all its inmates gassed, after which Mengele became chief medical officer of the main infirmary camp at Birkenau. He was not, however, the chief medical officer of the Auschwitz complex overall; his superior was the SS garrison physician, **Eduard Wirths**.

SS doctors carried out a selection process on new arrivals to Auschwitz. The doctors "selected" (chose) those who were "fit" for work, while the others (children under 14, the elderly, sick, and women with children) were sent to the line of those picked for immediate death. Some of the SS officers had to get drunk before a selection, but Mengele was reported to enjoy the process and even showed up at selections to which he was not assigned. He was the only doctor as Auschwitz to wear his medals; his uniform was always tailored, and he wore white gloves. He exploited his good looks to trick women into believing whatever he said. He had an unpredictable personality, and everyone, including other SS officers, feared him.

Mengele believed that twins held the mysteries behind how Aryan genetic features, such as blond hair and blue eyes, were passed on. Accordingly, some 1,500 sets of twins were brought to him through the selection process. Once selected, these twins kept their own hair and clothes, were tattooed, were measured in height and weight, and had a brief history taken. In the morning, twins reported for roll call and ate a small breakfast, and Mengele would talk with some of them, give them a candy, or even occasionally play a game.

Life for the twins was bearable until they were taken for experiments. Each day, twins had to give blood—from fingers, limbs, and, for smaller children, from the neck. About 10 cubic centimeters of blood was drawn daily in a painful and frightening process. Sometimes so much blood was drawn that one twin would faint; huge blood transfusions were made from one twin to another. Mengele attempted to change eye color by injecting chemicals or giving drops that caused pain, infections, or temporary or permanent blindness. He injected lethal germs, carried out sex-change operations, and removed organs and limbs, all without anesthesia. He attempted to create Siamese twins by sewing their backs together and trying to connect blood vessels and organs; however, after a few days, gangrene would set in, and the twins inevitably died. Other experiments included isolation endurance, spinal taps without anesthesia, castrations, amputations, the removal of sexual organs, and incestuous impregnations. Some samples of the bodies were sent to von Verschuer for further study. Of the 1,500 pairs of twins chosen by Mengele at Auschwitz, only 200 survived.

Mengele also had an interest in people with physical abnormalities, such as dwarves, midgets, and hunchbacks, and on these, too, he carried out pseudoscientific experiments.

The SS abandoned Auschwitz on January 27, 1945, and Mengele was transferred to Gross Rosen camp in Lower Silesia, working as the camp doctor. After Gross Rosen was evacuated at the end of February 1945, Mengele worked in other camps for a short time, and on May 2, 1945, he joined a Wehrmacht medical unit led by Hans Otto Kahler, his former colleague at the Institute of Hereditary Biology and Racial Hygiene in Bohemia. The unit fled west to avoid capture by the Soviets, and members were taken as prisoners of war by the Americans. Unaware that Mengele's name already stood on a list of wanted war criminals, however, U.S. officials quickly released him.

From July 1945 until May 1949, Mengele operated under false papers naming him as Fritz Hollmann and worked as a farmhand in a small village near Rosenheim, Bavaria, staying in contact with his wife Irene and an old friend, Hans Sedlmeier. Sedlmeier arranged Mengele's escape to Argentina via Innsbruck, possibly assisted by the ODESSA network.

In 1954, five years after Mengele escaped to Buenos Aires, his wife Irene divorced him. On July 25, 1958, in Nueva Helvecia, Uruguay, Mengele married Martha Mengele, widow of his deceased brother, Karl. His crimes having been well documented at the International Military Tribunal and other postwar courts, West German authorities issued a warrant for his arrest in 1959. As José Mengele, he received citizenship in Paraguay in 1959. In 1960, a request was issued for his extradition to West Germany. Alarmed by the capture of **Adolf Eichmann** in Buenos Aires, Mengele moved several times throughout South America, and in 1961, he apparently moved to Brazil, where he lived with Hungarian refugees Geza and Gitta Stammer, working as manager of their farm about 200 kilometers outside São Paulo. In the seclusion of his Brazilian hideaway, Mengele was safe.

In 1974, when his relationship with the Stammer family was coming to an end, other Nazis in hiding, including Hans Ulrich Rudel, discussed relocating Mengele to Bolivia, where he could spend time with **Klaus Barbie**. Mengele rejected this proposal, preferring to stay in São Paulo for the last years of his life. In 1977, his only son, Rolf, who had never known his father, visited him in São Paulo and found him to be an unrepentant Nazi who claimed that he "had never personally harmed anyone in his whole life."

Mengele's health had been deteriorating for years, and he died on February 2, 1979, at a vacation resort in Bertioga, Brazil. He was swimming in the Atlantic Ocean when he suffered a massive stroke and drowned. He was buried in Embu das Artes, under the name Wolfgang Gerhard, whose identity he had used since 1976. These remains were exhumed on June 6, 1985, and a team of forensic experts determined that Mengele had taken Gerhard's identity, died in 1979 of a stroke while swimming, and was buried under Gerhard's name. Dental records later confirmed the forensic conclusion.

Mengele had evaded capture for 34 years. After the exhumation, the São Paulo Institute for Forensic Medicine stored his remains and attempted to repatriate them to the remaining Mengele family members, but the family rejected them and turned over his diaries to investigators. The bones have been stored at the São Paulo Institute for Forensic Medicine ever since.

MIETE, AUGUST (1908–1978)

August Miete was an SS officer who worked in the *Aktion T-4* program at the Grafeneck and Hadamar euthanasia centers and then at Treblinka extermination camp.

August Wilhelm Miete was born on November 1, 1908, in Westerkappeln, North Rhine-Westphalia, the son of a miller and farmer. He finished school before his father died in 1921. Miete and his brother then took over running the family farm and mill. As an adult, he married and became a family man with three children and remained at the mill and farm until May 1940.

Around this time he expressed interest in becoming one of Germany's settlers in the conquered East and inquired officially about how this could be achieved. Joining the Nazi Party at once to help realize this, he was drafted into the agricultural service, where he became caretaker of a big property that included a clinic for the insane. After eight days, he was ordered to the Grafeneck euthanasia center, where he remained until the fall of 1940.

Miete then moved on to another euthanasia center at Hadamar, which was still under construction. Becoming involved in the murder process there, he supervised workers who removed and then burned corpses from the gas chambers. He remained at Hadamar until the summer of 1942. At the end of June, he was ordered to Berlin; from there, he was posted to *Aktion Reinhard* in Lublin and then sent to Treblinka, where he served until November 1943.

He was generally acknowledged to be one of the cruelest of the SS men at Treblinka. The prisoners there nicknamed him the "Angel of Death." He was assigned by the commandant, *SS-Sturmbannführer* **Christian Wirth**, to the train station where new prisoners arrived as well as the undressing yard at Camp I, where he supervised selections for the forced-labor *Sonderkommando*. He walked among the Jewish prisoners, looking for those fit to work or those who should be dispatched to their death immediately.

An infirmary (*Lazaret*) had been established at Treblinka, to which these prisoners were taken. All children were also taken, regardless of their state of health. In addition to his other duties, Miete was given charge of the *Lazaret*, and he carried out most of the killings. He would have each victim stand near a pit in which a fire was always going, take out his gun, and shoot point-blank.

Miete did not act alone in this murderous work. His major accomplice was a junior officer, *SS-Unterscharführer* Willi Mentz, born in 1904 and known by the prisoners as "Frankenstein." Mentz, a sawmill worker and milkman before becoming a policeman, joined the NSDAP in 1932. His trajectory was like that of Miete: Grafeneck, Hadamar, and then Treblinka, where he worked at the *Lazaret*. Mentz wore a white doctor's coat at the *Lazaret*, and while serving there, he shot thousands of Jews. In December 1943, Mentz was sent for a period to Sobibór. From there, Mentz served in Italy during *Aktion R*, killing Jews and partisans.

August Miete, his commander at Treblinka, made it a point for his officers to search each prisoner. Beatings were commonplace and intensified if Miete found items of value. Miete also sought out victims from other parts of the camp to be brought to the *Lazaret* and shot, and he colluded with other officers, such as **Kurt Franz**, to find weak, injured, or sick Jews who could be "processed" at the *Lazaret*. Their fate was foreordained.

With the closure of Treblinka in November 1943, after the end of *Aktion Reinhard*, Miete was sent to Trieste and, after a brief time there, to Udine, which was under direct German administration after Italy's surrender to the Allies in September 1943. In the fall of 1944, Miete moved from Udine to upper Italy, attached to a demolition unit.

With the end of the war, Miete was captured by the Americans but was soon released. He returned to the family farm and mill, where he worked until 1950, and then he worked as the managing director of the Savings and Loan Association in Lotte, not far from his original home. He was arrested again on May 27, 1960, and held in pretrial detention at Düsseldorf-Derendorf. On September 3, 1965, he was found guilty at the First Treblinka Trial of participating in the mass murder of at least 300,000 people, as well as of the murder of at least 9 named victims. Miete was sentenced to life imprisonment, but there is uncertainty as to his fate after then. He is believed to have died in prison on July 25, 1978.

Willi Mentz was arrested and charged with complicity in the mass murder of 700,000 Jews during the First Treblinka Trial in 1965. He was sentenced to life imprisonment. On March 31, 1978, he was released from prison due to poor health, and he died on June 25, 1978, in Niedermeien.

MÜLLER, HEINRICH (1900–?)

Heinrich Müller served as a German police official in both the Weimar Republic and Nazi Germany. As head of the Gestapo, together with his deputy **Adolf Eichmann**, he directed the investigation, collection, and deportation to ghettos, concentration camps, and death camps of Jews and various other groups deemed socially, racially, and politically undesirable.

Müller was born on April 28, 1900, in Munich, to working-class Catholic parents. In 1918, during World War I, he served as a spotter pilot and was decorated several times for bravery. In 1919, he joined the Bavarian police force. After seeing the revolutionary Red Army shoot their hostages in Munich in April 1919 during the Bavarian Soviet Republic, Müller acquired a hatred of communism and engaged in suppressing communist uprisings in Germany's turbulent postwar environment. During the Weimar Republic, Müller was appointed head of the Munich Political Police Department, where he met many members of the Nazi Party, including **Heinrich Himmler** and **Reinhard Heydrich**. He was not himself yet a Nazi, supporting instead the more dominant Bavarian People's Party.

On March 9, 1933, during the Nazi takeover of the state of Bavaria that deposed the government of Minister President Heinrich Held, Müller recommended that his superiors use force against the Nazis. Notwithstanding, Müller's hatred of communism, his professionalism and skill as a policeman, and his firm authority over his subordinates were all qualities that endeared him to Heydrich, even if Müller himself had been reluctant to join the movement. Müller finally joined the Nazi Party in 1939, not because of any ideological convictions but because doing so enhanced his career prospects. That same year, he became chief of the Gestapo, and as "Gestapo Müller," he implemented Hitler's policies against Jews and other groups deemed a threat to the state. Eichmann, who headed the Gestapo's Office of Resettlement and then its Office of Jewish Affairs, was Müller's immediate subordinate.

Müller was a key participant at the Wannsee Conference on January 20, 1942, at which Heydrich, head of the Reich Security Main Office (RSHA) and Müller's superior, announced that **Hermann Göring** had directed the evolution and implementation of the Final Solution. Under Müller's management, the Gestapo was instrumental in the deportation process of Europe's Jews, and Gestapo officials served as vital intelligence links, reporting *Einsatzgruppen* actions on the Eastern Front to **Adolf Hitler**.

Müller was also involved in a variety of other criminal and counterespionage matters occurring within the Third Reich. In 1938, he was active in falsifying proceedings against Werner von Blomberg, who had been minister of war since 1935, and Werner von Fritsch, commander in chief of the Wehrmacht, forcing both men from office. In 1939, Müller assisted in fabricating a "Polish" assault on the Gleiwitz radio station, which was used to justify Germany's attack upon Poland on September 1, 1939, and thereby initiated World War II. In May 1942, Müller also headed up the criminal investigation of Heydrich's assassination, successfully tracking down his killers.

In March 1944, Müller signed the Bullet Order, which authorized the shooting of escaped prisoners of war. Müller's quick and harsh interrogation of the members of the July 1944 bomb plot to kill Hitler earned him the Knight's Cross and the War Service Cross with Swords, conferred in October 1944. Müller was also heavily involved in security and counterintelligence operations that funneled misinformation to the Soviet Union throughout the war. Müller's Gestapo team caught and turned Soviet agents, which was among the greatest Soviet intelligence setbacks of the war.

Müller was highly regarded for the ruthless efficiency with which he carried out his duties, and although he was late joining the Nazi Party, he remained among the last to leave Hitler's bunker at the end of the war. He was last seen there on the evening of May 1, 1945, the day after Hitler's suicide. For a long time, it was thought that he had escaped to Syria, but to this day, his fate remains a mystery despite speculation and investigation by West German police, the Central Intelligence Agency, and British intelligence agencies.

N

NEBE, ARTHUR (1894–1945?)

Arthur Nebe became the head of the Nazi *Kriminalpolizei* (Criminal Police, or Kripo) and took command of *Einsatzgruppe B* from June to November of 1941 in the Soviet Union. He had a key role in the security and police apparatus of Nazi Germany and was a major Holocaust perpetrator.

He was born in Berlin in 1894, the son of a Berlin elementary school teacher. Nebe volunteered for service during World War I, served with distinction, and was wounded twice by gas. In 1920, Nebe joined the Berlin city police as a detective, was promoted in 1924 to police commissioner, and authored a criminology textbook.

Nebe joined the NSDAP and the SS in 1931, and then the SA. In April 1933, he became chief of the State Police and was tasked with reorganizing the criminal police in the Reich. In September 1939, he was promoted to *SS-Gruppenführer* and given command of *Amt V* of the RHSA (responsible for the criminal police), reporting directly to **Reinhard Heydrich**.

In 1939, Nebe loaned **Christian Wirth**, one of his police commissioners, to the *Aktion T-4* campaign, the program of involuntary euthanasia of those with disabilities. In 1939, as SS head of the Kripo, he discussed actions against the Sinti and Roma, and later, he recommended sending Berlin's Roma population to the East along with the Jews. In October 1939, **Adolf Eichmann**, acting on Nebe's orders, put Roma on the transports with Jews to Nisko.

Across the period June to November 1941 Nebe commanded of *Einsatzgruppe B*, the extermination unit based in Minsk, and during this time, he was credited with 46,000 murders. In Nebe's report of July 23, 1941, he argued that it was impractical to shoot Jews to rid the Reich of the Jewish problem because there were so many to be killed and not enough men to kill them. By August 1941, he realized that his *Einsatzgruppe* members found it a problem to kill the Jewish women and children included in the killing quota.

In August 1941, at **Heinrich Himmler**'s request, Nebe organized a mass shooting of 100 people in Minsk. Himmler attended the shooting, vomiting after what he saw. Himmler told Heydrich that he was concerned for the mental health of the SS men and tasked Nebe to find new methods of mass murder that were less distressing for those doing the killing. Nebe experimented by murdering Soviet mental patients with explosives near Minsk. After that, under his command, gas vans were created from converted trucks, and these were trialed on a small group of 32 people with disabilities, killing them by motor-vehicle exhaust at Mogilev in September 1941.

At the end of November 1941, Nebe returned to Berlin to resume his command of the Kripo. By now, he was convinced that Germany would lose the war. In 1942, Nebe contacted the German resistance and warned Hans Oster and Hans von Dohnańyi about their impending arrest by the Gestapo. Despite this, on June 28, 1944, an unrepentant Nebe wrote a letter recommending the use of Roma for human experiments, such as the drinking of seawater.

Arthur Nebe's life and death after the attempted assassination of **Adolf Hitler** in the bomb plot of June 20, 1944, remains unclear. Exculpatory stories have been spun that over time, he developed serious doubts about the Nazi regime. One account even asserts that as early as 1941 to 1942, when Nebe was assigned to *Einsatzgruppe B*, he saved thousands of Russian civilians from execution by falsifying figures and claiming credit for slaughters that were never actually carried out. This notwithstanding, there is little doubt that *Einsatzgruppe B* was responsible for the 46,000 deaths between June and November 1941, when the unit was under Nebe's command.

Nebe disappeared three days after the July 1944 bomb plot. His fate and whereabouts were then shrouded in mystery. One account states that he was betrayed by a rejected mistress, sentenced to death by the People's Court (*Volksgerichtshof*), and hanged on March 2, 1945. He was, however, also rumored to have disappeared into Latin America after 1945. According to historian Robert Wistrich, Nebe pursued business activities in Hamburg until his death on April 4, 1960, without being brought to account for his wartime crimes. Sightings of Nebe were allegedly made in Turin, Italy, in September 1956 and in Ireland in the winter of 1960.

O

OBERG, CARL (1897–1965)

Carl Oberg was the head of the SS and police in occupied France from 1942 to 1945. In this capacity, he deported over 40,000 Jews from France and earned the title of the "Butcher of Paris."

Carl Albrecht Oberg was born in Hamburg on January 27, 1897, the son of a professor of medicine. When aged 17, he enlisted in the German army in August 1914, fighting as a lieutenant on the Western Front by September 1916 during his military service. He was decorated with an Iron Cross for bravery.

In 1920, Oberg took part in the Kapp Putsch in Berlin, which attempted to overthrow the Weimar Republic in response to the Republic's attempt to demobilize two *Freikorps* brigades. In January 1921, Oberg was business manager in Flensburg of the Escherich Organization, an antisemitic paramilitary group. He served as liaison between various German army units, the government, and local patriotic leagues and militias in Schleswig. In 1926, he returned to Hamburg as the representative of a wholesale paper merchant, and in 1928, he took a job with a wholesale tropical-fruit firm, which failed because of the world economic crisis. Oberg remained unemployed until the end of 1930, when he bought a tobacco kiosk in Hamburg with the help of a small family loan.

Upon meeting **Reinhard Heydrich** in May 1933, Oberg asked him for a job and in consequence joined the *Sicherheitsdienst* (Security Service, or SD). He was promoted to SS captain in March 1934, major in July 1934, and colonel in 1935. Acting as Heydrich's right-hand man in the SD, he was respected for his bureaucratic efficiency and discipline, until differences between the two men led Oberg to return to the SS in Mecklenburg, where he commanded an SS regiment and later headed the SS Brigade IVA in Hanover until December 1938.

Oberg was appointed police president at Zwickau in Saxony in January 1939. With the war situation and the intensification of anti-Jewish measures, he became SS and police leader in Radom in September 1941, where he murdered Jews and rounded up Poles to work as slave laborers. Oberg was promoted to *SS-Gruppenführer* in April 1942. On May 7, 1942, he was sent to Paris as **Heinrich Himmler**'s personal representative in order to take command of the SS and SD in occupied France.

In France, Oberg was responsible for managing anti-Jewish policy and destroying the French Resistance. In 1942, already known as the "Butcher of Paris," Oberg was responsible for organizing the roundup of Jews, resulting in their temporary incarceration in the Paris *Velodrome d'Hiver* (Winter Velodrome).

On Heydrich's orders, Oberg and others were responsible for the deportation of over 40,000 Jews from France to extermination camps in the East, with the assistance of the Vichy French police headed by **René Bousquet**.

By early 1943, Oberg hesitated to follow some of the orders he received from Himmler and **Adolf Hitler**. Himmler ordered Oberg to make 100,000 arrests and use explosives to demolish the crime district in Marseille. Instead, Oberg worked with the French police and oversaw 6,000 arrests, 20,000 people displaced, and a partial destruction of the harbor area. In 1944, he blocked an attempt to establish an *Einsatzkommando* of the Waffen-SS in France.

After the Allied invasion of Normandy in June 1944 and the liberation of Paris by August of that year, Oberg and his men retreated to Germany in December 1944, where he was appointed commander in chief of the Weichsel (Vistula) Army, formed on January 24, 1945, under Himmler's direct orders.

Oberg was arrested by the U.S. military in June 1945. Convicted of war crimes, he was sentenced to death by a British court before receiving another death sentence from the French in October 1954. However, in 1958, the death sentence was commuted to life imprisonment by French president René Coty, and it was later reduced to 20 years' hard labor. Oberg was released on November 28, 1962, and was pardoned by President Charles de Gaulle in 1965. He died on June 3, 1965, in Germany.

OBERHEUSER, HERTA (1911–1978)

Herta Oberheuser was a Nazi physician who conducted cruel and sadistic medical experimentation on concentration camp inmates at Auschwitz and Ravensbrück concentration camps between 1940 and 1943.

She was born on May 11, 1911, in Cologne. Her father was an engineer. Young and blond, for many, she would come to represent the Nazi ideal.

Growing up in Düsseldorf, she received her medical degree in Bonn in 1937, with specialty training in dermatology. She then worked in a specialized clinic for skin conditions in Düsseldorf until she obtained her license as a dermatologist in 1940. Earlier, she had joined the League of German Girls (BdM) in 1935, volunteering to serve as an unpaid medical assistant in the Düsseldorf branch. In 1937, she became a member of the NSDAP as an intern and later as a physician for the BdM. She quickly found a post at the municipal pediatric clinic (*Kinderstation*) in Düsseldorf. The Third Reich's physicians could boast of having the highest percentage of Nazi Party members of any profession—an astonishing 45 percent.

In 1940, she applied for a job advertised in a Nazi medical journal for the "medical care of female criminals" at the Ravensbrück concentration camp. It paid a significantly higher salary than the one she was earning in Düsseldorf. Oberheuser applied and was accepted. She later gave evidence that it was almost impossible for a woman to join a surgical department in Germany and that it was not until Ravensbrück that she got the chance.

Oberheuser began as a camp doctor assisting the head physician, **Karl Gebhardt**, who was chief SS surgeon and personal physician to *SS-Reichsführer* **Heinrich Himmler**. She also worked closely with Fritz Fischer, infamous for his experiments with sulfonamide on female prisoners.

At Ravensbrück, Oberheuser and other doctors would perform gruesome experiments. Oberheuser single-handedly gave children deadly injections of oil and the barbiturate Evipan, after which she removed their limbs and vital organs and studied her handiwork.

Oberheuser had unlimited power over life and death. At her later trial, evidence was presented that she had given a teenager a lethal injection because he had wet his bed. Another example was that a prisoner had complained about thirst, so Oberheuser cruelly gave him water into which she had put vinegar.

Karl Gebhardt had attended **Reinhard Heydrich** after he was the victim of an assassination action in Prague in May 1942. When Heydrich died subsequently due to fatal gangrene and putrefaction of his wounds, Gebhardt's medical skills were questioned. Some SS argued that Heydrich might have lived if Gebhardt had treated him with huge doses of sulfanilamide, alleging that this would have cleared the severe infection. Himmler then asked Gebhardt to prove by experiment if sulfanilamide was effective against gangrene and putrefaction in severely wounded German soldiers. If these experiments were successful, lives could be saved.

This led to the establishment of a branch of the Hohenlychen Sanatorium within the Ravensbrück concentration camp. Hoping to expand their knowledge of infections and ways to fight them, Gebhardt and Oberheuser intended to use the camp's inmates as subjects for their medical experiments. The results of the initial experiments were disappointing, because they failed to replicate actual combat injuries. Later experiments sought to correct this, and inmates were subjected to gunshot wounds infected with dirt and foreign material. They also endured severed muscles and broken bones, and their wounds were then injected with streptococcus, gas gangrene, and tetanus. Those prisoners who survived these experiments were often crippled for life. Further, Oberheuser deliberately caused injuries to her victims by shattering limbs with heavy hammers prior to cutting open body parts without anesthesia. To simulate the combat wounds of German soldiers, she rubbed foreign objects—such as wood, rusty nails, shards of glass, pebbles, dirt, or sawdust—into the cuts.

She also conducted experiments involving bone and muscle transplantation and oversaw the transfer of other inmates to Hohenlychen to conduct unnecessary amputations and transplants. The goal of these experiments was to provide "spare parts" for wounded German soldiers. Once a subject's usefulness had passed, Oberheuser hastened death with injections of gasoline. The time from the injection to death was between three and five minutes, with the victim being fully conscious until the last moment.

On July 27, 1942, 75 women (mostly Polish political prisoners) were ordered to the commandant's headquarters. Almost all of them were young; their ages ranged from 16 to 45, with most in their early 20s. The majority were members of the intelligentsia, either students or teachers. Once there, Oberheuser physically examined the women and evaluated their suitability for experimentation. Those chosen had their legs cut and bacteria strains placed in the wounds. The subsequent infections were then treated with new sulfanilamide drugs. All the experiments were conducted without the subjects' consent. Because these women became lame and hopped, they were known as the "rabbits." These women had been promised that their participation in the experiments, which was involuntary, would result in a commutation of their death sentences, but this promise was never kept. Several of the women were executed after the experiments had been terminated.

With the end of the war, Oberheuser was the only woman to stand trial at the Nuremberg Doctors' Trial. On August 20, 1947, she was found guilty for her part in conducting human experimentation at Ravensbrück and at Hohenlychen. Originally sentenced to 20 years' imprisonment, her sentence was later reduced to 10 years, and she was released in 1952 after serving only 5 years.

After her release in 1952, Oberheuser immediately returned to practice as a doctor, establishing a thriving family medical practice in Stocksee, a village in Schleswig-Holstein. In 1956, a survivor of Ravensbrück recognized her, and in 1958, her career completely ended and her license to practice medicine was withdrawn for good.

Herta Oberheuser died on January 24, 1978, in a retirement home near the city of Linz am Rhein, Rhineland-Palatinate, West Germany.

OHLENDORF, OTTO (1907–1951)

Otto Ohlendorf was an SS officer and head of one of the mobile killing squads (*Einsatzgruppen*) responsible for the deaths of some 90,000 innocent civilians, most of them Jews, between 1941 and 1942. He was head of the *Sicherheitsdienst* (SD) Interior, responsible for intelligence and security within Germany.

The son of a farmer, he was born on February 4, 1907, in Hoheneggelsen, Lower Saxony, and attended high school in Hildesheim, where he was educated in the humanities. Ohlendorf studied economics and law at universities in Leipzig and Göttingen, before obtaining a doctorate in jurisprudence from the University of Pavia, Italy. He completed his studies in law in July 1933.

In 1925, Ohlendorf joined the Nazi Party, becoming a member of the SS in 1926. In 1933, he became research director of the Institute of World Economy at the University of Kiel, where he focused on the study of Italian fascism and German National Socialism. In 1936, he became an economic adviser to the SD, where he provided information and reported on German public opinion for Nazi leaders.

In 1939 at the age of 32, the middle-class and university-educated Ohlendorf was headhunted by **Reinhard Heydrich** to lead RSHA Office III at the Berlin Headquarters, a position which he held until the end of the war. In June 1941, with the German invasion of the Soviet Union, Ohlendorf was given command of *Einsatzgruppe D*, a mobile killing unit operating in the Crimea and southern Ukraine and attached to the German Eleventh Army. Ohlendorf's men were responsible for mass killing of Jews in Kherson, Nikolaiev, and Podilia. At Simferopol, on December 13, 1941, Ohlendorf's unit murdered around 14,300 civilians, mainly Jews.

A conscientious and efficient officer, at his later trial, Ohlendorf gave evidence that he had ordered at least five men to fire on victims simultaneously so that no one would be personally responsible for any single killing. During his approximately one-year command of *Einsatzgruppe D*, as many as 90,000 people were murdered. Ohlendorf was very concerned about the emotional upset experienced by his troops from their face-to-face killing, especially of women and children.

In spring 1942, this concern for staff welfare resulted in an order from *SS-Reichsführer* **Heinrich Himmler** that, in the future, women and children were to be killed only in gas vans.

In June 1942, Ohlendorf left the front line and returned to his SS work in Germany, serving in the Reich Economic Secretariat. In 1943, he became deputy director general in the Reich Ministry of Economic Affairs. By the end of 1943, he had contemplated the possibilities of a German military defeat and began planning the reconstruction of the postwar German economy. In 1944, he was promoted to SS-*Gruppenführer*.

With the end of the war in 1945, he was taken prisoner by Allied authorities and placed on trial for war crimes. At the Nuremberg Trial of several key *Einsatzgruppen* officials, Ohlendorf was the lead defendant and testified to the killing methods employed. He described how naked victims were shot into antitank ditches and ravines. All their valuables were confiscated and handed over to the finance ministry. He sent out inspectors to ensure that the murders met the following conditions: first, the public was excluded from the area; second, military execution was carried out by firing squad; third, arrival of transports and carrying out of the liquidation was undertaken in a smooth manner to avoid unnecessary excitement, as otherwise the victims would have to be beaten to keep them in order; and fourth, property was supervised to prevent looting.

He showed no remorse for his murders and asserted that his unit's crimes were no more odious than the "push-button" killers who had unleashed the atomic bombs over Japan in 1945. Justifying his actions as military necessity, he claimed that the Jews were a permanent danger to German troops who could have attacked Germany one day and that their children were individuals who would grow up and would, as the children of parents who had been killed, be a danger no less than that of their parents.

Ohlendorf's trial ended in the early spring of 1948, and in April, he was sentenced to death. After spending some three years as a prisoner at the Landsberg Prison, he was hanged there on June 8, 1951. His testimony was useful in convicting several others besides himself.

P

PAPON, MAURICE (1910–2007)

Maurice Papon was a French civil servant during the 1930s who led the police in major prefectures and in Paris during the Nazi occupation. He was the only Frenchman convicted of complicity in crimes against humanity committed in France during World War II, in a trial that took place from 1997 to 1998.

Papoon was born into a middle-class family on September 3, 1910, in Gretz-Armainvilliers in the Seine-et-Marne department. Papon's father was a glassworker and local mayor. His family had republican, center-left views. Papon was educated in Paris, studying law and political science at the *Lycée Louis-le-Grand* and the *École des Sciences Politiques*. In 1929, he entered the *Faculté de Droit et de Lettres* in Paris.

While a student, Papon joined the socialist youth movement. In February 1931, he began working as a ministerial adviser on the staff of Jacques-Louis Dumesnil, Prime Minister **Pierre Laval**'s minister for air. In 1935, Papon joined the Ministry of the Interior, working under Maurice Sabatier, a specialist in Islamic law, where his tasks covered Moroccan and Tunisian affairs.

At the start of World War II, Papon served in Tripoli and Syria with the French infantry. He was demobilized in October 1940, with the outset of the German occupation.

Papon had the choice of joining Charles de Gaulle's Free French forces or remaining with the pro-Nazi collaborationist government of Marshal Philippe Pétain. He opted to remain in the unoccupied zone. He rejoined Sabatier at the Ministry of the Interior and was promoted to head the administration of that department in March 1941.

In May 1942, he was appointed general secretary of the Gironde prefecture, based in Bordeaux. The mayor of Bordeaux, Adrien Marquet, was an ex-socialist who endorsed Laval. In Bordeaux, Papon implemented policies on transport, fuel, German requisitions, and general relations with the occupiers. He was also responsible for the office known as Service of Jewish Questions. Administration of this small branch of about 12 people under Pierre Garat obliged him to apply Vichy laws against the Jews.

The Service of Jewish Questions had two essential functions. The first was applying regulations arising from the *Statut des Juifs*, major anti-Jewish legislation enacted by the Vichy government on October 3, 1940, and renewed in summer 1941. Papon's department also was responsible for Aryanizing Jewish property and goods, which involved the naming of an administrator to take over and dispose of Jewish assets. Central to these issues was the *fichier*, the card index held in Papon's office identifying the prefecture's Jews, compiled and brought up to date by the service. The *fichier* was used by the service to prepare operations for the arrest of Jews and their transfer to the transit camp at Drancy. Papon was involved in arrests and deportations of Jews from Bordeaux and signed off at all stages of Jewish roundups, signing documents ordering arrests by French police and gendarmes.

The record of Bordeaux during the occupation showed that 285 hostages were shot; 900 political deportees never returned from the camps to which they were sent; and 1,560 Jews, of whom 223 were children, were deported to their death in Auschwitz. These figures do not include resisters or forced-work casualties who also lost their lives.

Papon's prefecture was responsible for the nearby internment camp of Mérignac. Prisoners then were transferred to the Bordeaux rail station, from where they were sent to Drancy. Between July 18, 1942, and June 5, 1944, 11 convoys left Bordeaux, carrying men and women, small children, the elderly, and the sick. Almost all perished at Auschwitz.

By late 1943, around the time the war began to turn, the Germans considered Papon pro-American, and in mid-1944, he started providing information on German movements to the French Resistance. Two days before Bordeaux was liberated in 1944, Papon transformed himself into a supporter of de Gaulle and an anti-Vichyite.

When Allied armies liberated Bordeaux in August 1944, Papon was given a position in the new government. For working with the resistance, he was awarded the *Carte d'Ancien Combattant de la Résistance.*

From January 1947 to 1949, Papon served as prefect of Corsica, before a succession of positions saw him serving the French Republic in a number of areas: prefect of the Constantine region in Algeria (1949), secretary-general of the Protectorate of Morocco (1954), and prefect of Paris police (March 1956 to June 1966).

In 1968, Papon was elected to the National Assembly as a Gaullist representing the Cher region, and he was reelected in 1973 and 1978. In April 1978, President Valéry Giscard d'Estaing appointed him budget minister. Despite this successful career, on May 6, 1981, facts about his past actions under the Vichy regime surfaced when a French newspaper published documents signed by Papon demonstrating his responsibility in the deportation of Bordeaux Jews to Drancy between 1942 and 1944.

In 1983, Papon was accused of crimes against humanity, but the charges were deferred in 1988. Seven years later, however, he was indicted on "complicity in crimes against humanity." His trial began in October 1997, and in April 1998, he was found guilty of illegal arrest and incarceration of over 1,000 Jews between 1942 and 1944. He was sentenced to 10 years in prison, but during his appeal, he fled to Switzerland, where he was arrested, sent back to France, and imprisoned at Fresnes prison in Paris. In September 2002, a French court released him on the grounds of ill health. Maurice Papon died on February 17, 2007, in Pontault-Combault, France.

PAVELIĆ, ANTE (1889–1959)

Ante Pavelić was a Croatian ultranationalist dictator who founded and headed the fascist organization the *Ustashe* in 1929. From 1941 to 1945, he ran the Independent State of Croatia, a fascist puppet state carved out of parts of Yugoslavia by Nazi Germany and Fascist Italy. Pavelić and the *Ustashe* persecuted many racial minorities and political opponents in Croatia during the war, including Serbs, Jews, Roma, and anti-fascist Croats.

Ante Pavelić was born on July 14, 1889, in Bradina, Bosnia-Herzegovina, to Mile and Mary. His elementary school was a Muslim *makteb*, and then when his parents moved, he attended a Jesuit school in Travnik. Health problems interrupted his education in 1905 and again in 1908. Early in high school, he joined the Party of Rights (an anti-Serb movement). Pavelić completed his education in Zagreb, and in 1910, he began studying law at the University of Zagreb.

The founder and head of the fascist paramilitary *Ustashe* movement, Ante Pavelić was an ultra-nationalistic dictator of the puppet state of Croatia from 1941 to 1945. Styling himself as the *Poglavnik* ("leader"), his regime subjected Croatia to four years of terror, in which tens of thousands of Jews, Serbs, Muslims, Roma, and other minorities were expelled or executed in an attempt to create a purely Croatian state. *Ustashe* forces also established concentration camps in which large numbers of victims were exterminated. (ullstein bild/Getty Images)

Pavelić was called up to serve in the Austro-Hungarian navy, but the military medical commission at the Pula naval base questioned his fitness. Instead, he worked from August 1914 to March 1915 as a mason constructing the naval building in Sibenik. During that time, he lived with a Jewish family. At the end of March 1915, he was recalled to Pula, where the medical commission concluded that Pavelić was not capable of military service and released him. He became a trainee lawyer of Aleksandar Horvat, then president of the Party of Rights, and obtained his doctor of law in July 1915. As an employee and friend of Horvat, Pavelić frequently participated in important party meetings, from time to time assuming Horvat's duties. In 1918, Pavelić became an independent lawyer.

Elected to the *Skupstina* (Yugoslav Parliament) in 1920, Pavelić represented the Party of Rights. On August 12, 1922, in the church of St. Marka in Zagreb, he married Mary Lovrenčević. The daughter of renowned journalist Martino Lovrenčević, also a member of the Rights Party, she was Jewish on her mother's side. Together, they had three children.

After election to the assembly in Belgrade in 1927, Pavelić became a member of the Croatian Bloc. He was an eyewitness to the assassination of Stjepan Radić, founder of the Croatian People's Peasant Party (*Hrvatska pučka seljačka stranka*), who was shot in the assembly by Serb radical politician Puniša Račić on June 20, 1928.

In 1928, Pavelić founded an armed Croatian group and invited Croats openly to start an armed rebellion, which immediately caused the group to be declared illegal. In 1929, King Alexander suspended the constitution and initiated a government crackdown on nationalist activities, a move which saw Pavelić flee to Italy. In 1930, he formed the Croatian Liberation Movement, known as the *Ustashe*.

With covert Italian support, Pavelić launched a terror campaign against the Yugoslav state. In October 1934, *Ustashe* gunmen assassinated King Alexander and French foreign minister Louis Barthou at Marseille, for which a Yugoslav court sentenced Pavelić to death in absentia.

With the German invasion and defeat of Yugoslavia in April 1941, Pavelić and his supporters established the Independent State of Croatia with the backing of Italy, which occupied the country. Following the Italian surrender in 1943, Pavelić's *Ustashe* regime transferred its allegiance to Germany and remained a German client until the end of the war.

Pavelić, who proclaimed himself *Poglavnik* (leader), subjected Croatia to four years of abject terror. Bands of *Ustashe* militia roamed the countryside, expelling or executing scores of Jews, Serbs, Muslims, Roma, and other minorities to create a purely Croatian state. Copying the Nazis, the *Ustashe* also established concentration camps in which tens of thousands of victims were exterminated. Ultimately, the lawlessness and violence of Pavelić's regime alienated it from most Croatians and swelled the ranks of the Yugoslav partisans.

Under Pavelić's sponsorship, a Croatian Muslim division was formed in Bosnia and was visited by the mufti of Jerusalem, **Haj Amin al-Husseini**. Pavelić's regime incited the destruction of Orthodox Serb churches and the forcible conversions of Serbs to Catholicism.

The regime was generally recognized as the most murderous Nazi puppet state in all of occupied Europe. Indeed, German officers were themselves horrified by scenes of atrocities committed by the *Ustashe*, and they forced an end to the bloodshed, the arrest of one of the most notorious *Ustashe* leaders, and the disarming of a *Ustashe* detachment. **Joachim von Ribbentrop**'s chief envoy in the Balkans, **Edmund Veesenmayer**, reported to Berlin that Pavelić had only two wishes: first, to obtain German recognition of Croatia and, second, to thank Hitler in person and promise him his undying loyalty.

It is estimated that by early 1945 Pavelić's murderous policies had resulted in the deaths of some 30,000 Jews, 29,000 Roma, and anywhere between 300,000 and 600,000 Serbs. Moreover, such excesses also aroused grotesquely ironic protests from Pavelić's German overlords, who complained that *Ustashe* abuses were hindering the establishment of order necessary for the exploitation of Croatia's economic resources.

Pavelić never faced a war crimes tribunal. After Germany's defeat in May 1945, he escaped to Rome, where he was shielded in the Vatican until 1948. He then went to Argentina, where he served as an adviser to President Juan Perón. Pavelić was badly wounded in a 1957 assassination attempt by Yugoslavia's secret police, which compelled him to flee to fascist Spain. He died in Madrid on December 28, 1959.

PETRI, ERNA (1920–2000)

Erna Kürbs was born on May 30, 1920, to a farmer from Herressen in Thuringia. In July 1938, she married Horst Petri, an SS officer and protégé of Richard Walter Darré, chief of the Race and Resettlement Office. Horst Petri shared Darré's vision of the agricultural mission of the Nazi Party, which saw the soldier-farmer as the model for German expansion into the East. From the summer of 1942 onward, Horst Petri was posted to the Ukrainian city of Lvov (Lviv) during the German occupation, where he administered an estate called Grzenda. In uniform, Horst Petri participated in the murder and deportation of the local Jewish population. At home, he routinely mistreated the forced laborers at Grzenda.

As the wife of the SS manager of the Grzenda estate, Erna Petri also mistreated those working on the farm, and she delivered several female Ukrainian workers to a concentration camp. In 1943, she killed four Jewish men who escaped from a nearby camp onto the property.

One summer's day in 1943, Erna Petri, by then a mother of two children, noticed six Jewish boys aged 6 to 12 sitting alongside the road near the estate. Reasoning that they had probably escaped from a train heading for Sobibór, she saw that the children were at once terrified and hungry. She calmed them down and brought them food from her kitchen, but believing that all Jews roaming the countryside were to be captured and shot, she waited for her husband to return to the estate so that she could hand over the children to him. However, as he was late getting home, Erna Petri decided to shoot the six children herself.

While providing hospitality to her husband's SS colleagues, she had overheard them speaking about the mass shootings of Jews and that the most effective way to kill was a single shot to the back of the neck. She led the children to the same pit in the woods where other Jews had been shot and buried. With a World War I pistol that her father had given her, she executed the six children in the manner described by the SS men.

In 1962 in Erfurt, East Germany, Erna Kürbs Petri and Horst Petri were tried for the crimes they committed at Grzenda between 1942 and 1944, including mass extermination. The victims of the crime were listed as foreign laborers, German soldiers, Jews, and civilians whose nationalities were given as Soviet, German, and Polish. The Petris were described as a "management couple in charge of the SS-estate Grzenda."

Horst Petri was charged on a number of counts: mistreating numerous persons employed at the estate, in part causing incurable damage to their health; participating in chasing after and rounding up Jews who had fled from deportation transports and shooting Jews who were caught in the process; participating in the shooting of the Jewish population of a town adjacent to the estate; deporting Jewish forced laborers to concentration camps; participating in the shooting of 15

Ukrainian farmers who were reported to have delivered food supplies to the partisans; and shooting at a German soldier.

Erna Kürbs Petri was charged with participation in chasing after escaped Jews, shooting Jewish men and children who had been caught or who were discovered wandering, mistreating girls employed at the estate, and delivering Ukrainian female workers into a concentration camp. During the hearing into her conduct, she gave evidence that she had been hardened and desensitized through her contact with the SS men and that through such contact, she wanted to show them that she as a woman could comport herself like a man: "So I shot four Jews and six Jewish children. I wanted to prove myself to the men." She added that at the time in that region, it was known that Jewish persons and children were being shot, which she added also caused her to kill them.

The couple was found guilty by the East German court. Horst Petri was sentenced to death, and Erna Petri was given a sentence of 30 years in jail. She died in 2000 in a small hamlet in East Germany.

POHL, OSWALD (1892–1951)

Oswald Pohl was a senior SS officer who, as head of the *SS-Reichssicherheitshauptamt* (SS Main Economic and Administrative Office, or RSHA) and the chief administrator of the Nazi concentration camps, became one of the most powerful men in the SS and supervised its economic needs as well as the administration of the concentration camp system.

Oswald Ludwig Pohl was born on June 30, 1892, in Duisburg-Ruhrort, the fifth of eight children of the blacksmith Hermann Pohl and his wife Auguste. After graduating from school in 1912, he enlisted in the German Imperial Navy and served throughout World War I, rising to the position of paymaster. On October 1918, he married for the first time.

At war's end, Pohl attended courses at a trade school and began studying law and state theory at the *Christian Albrechts Universität* in Kiel. He dropped out in 1919, however, instead becoming active with the *Friekorps Brigaheae Löwenfeld*, working in Berlin and drawing on his naval training as paymaster. In 1920, he participated in the failed right-wing Kapp Putsch.

In 1924, Pohl was accepted into the Weimar Republic's new navy (*Reichsmarine*). He joined the SA in 1925, and on February 22, 1926, he joined the Nazi Party.

Pohl met **Heinrich Himmler** in 1933 and soon became his protégé. In 1934, Himmler appointed Pohl to head the administration of the *Allgemeine-SS*, the largest branch of the SS. He took financial charge of the SS Death's Head units, the Waffen-SS, and the SS Budget and Building Department, which oversaw the construction of concentration camps. By 1939, Pohl was administering the concentration camp system.

In this role, he identified the commercial possibility of forced labor. Shortly after the *Anschluss* with Austria in March 1938, Pohl and Himmler went to the town of Mauthausen and resolved that the SS-operated *Deutsche Erd- und Steinwerke GmbH* (German Earth and Stone Works Company, or DEST) would begin excavating granite using concentration camp prisoners as slave laborers.

On January 19, 1942 (ironically, one day before the Wannsee Conference that would determine the future operation of the Final Solution), Himmler consolidated all the offices for which Pohl was responsible into one, creating the RSHA. In 1942, as leader of the *SS-Wirtschafts- und Verwaltungshauptamt* (SS Economic and Administrative Department, or WVHA), Pohl was the third most powerful man in the SS, surpassed only by Himmler and **Reinhard Heydrich**. Pohl administered the entire Waffen-SS, operated over 20 concentration and labor camps, ran all SS and police building projects, and took charge of all SS business concerns.

On December 12, 1942, after divorcing his first wife, he married Eleonore von Brüning, widow of Ernst Rüdiger von Brüning, the son of one of the founders of the *Hoechster Farbwerke*, which became part of I. G. Farben in 1925.

Supervising the concentration and labor camps supplied Pohl with some 600,000 slave laborers. Pohl reorganized the camps in such a way as to exploit their victims' labor, using his slave workforce to meet the needs of the SS and renting them out to meet the labor needs of private industries.

Pohl also devised the idea of sending back to Germany all personal possessions of Jews who had been gassed—including hair, gold teeth, clothes, wedding rings, and other jewelry—and using them or turning them into cash. This operation was all part of the SS emphasis on being efficient and financially independent.

On March 12, 1943, Pohl was named chairman of the board of directors for Eastern Territories Industries, Inc. Despite intending to use concentration camp prisoners to work in the expanding SS industries, he was limited by the Nazi ideology of exploitation and racial extermination. He refused to allow any increases in rations to starving prisoners slaving in the quarries of Gross-Rosen concentration camp, when there were administrative complaints in favor of providing more food to the inmates. Rather, he believed that concentration camp prisoners should serve the greater interests of the Reich, which also meant completely "exhausting forced labor"—working them to death.

By 1944, 250,000 slave laborers were working in private armament industries; many industries opened factories inside or adjoining the camps. As needs grew, Pohl and the WVHA also seized the labor of surviving Jews in the ghettos and eastern camps.

Pohl and the WVHA also controlled all SS-owned industries, such as the German Excavating and Quarrying Company, the German Equipment Company, the German Experimental Establishment for Foodstuff and Nutrition, and the Society for Exploitation of Textiles and Leatherworks. Industries not owned by the SS were indirectly controlled by the WVHA, including mineral-water production and the furniture industry. Jewish-owned and foreign industries were also seized by the WVHA.

At the end of World War II, Pohl first hid in Upper Bavaria and then near Bremen. He was captured by British troops on May 27, 1946, and was sentenced to death by an American military court on May 27, 1946. Imprisoned rather than immediately executed, he repeatedly appealed his case. He rejoined the Catholic Church, and in 1950, he published a book, *Credo: My Way to God*. Oswald Pohl was hanged on June 7, 1951, at Landsberg Prison.

PRÜTZMANN, HANS-ADOLF (1901–1945)

Hans-Adolf Prützmann was a high-ranking SS official who, from June to November 1941, was higher SS and police leader (*Höherer SS- und Polizeiführer*, or HSSPF) in Latvia. He set up ghettos in Riga and ran operations carried out by *Einsatzgruppen* units. He also organized the Nazi *Werwolf* guerrillas at the end of World War II.

Hans-Adolf Prützmann was born on August 31, 1901, in Tolkemit (Tolkmicko), East Prussia. On completing his education, he studied agriculture in Göttingen before joining several *Freikorps* between 1918 and 1921, although he did not engage in any military action. In 1923, he discontinued his studies, and in 1924, he joined a new *Freikorps*, which fought along the border region of Upper Silesia.

Prützmann worked for seven years as a farmworker in Pomerania, Brandenburg, and East Prussia before enrolling in the SA in 1929. Radicalized by his involvement in the *Freikorps*, he left the SA in 1930 and joined the NSDAP and the SS that year. His career from that point had a rapid trajectory. From July 1932, he was a member of the Reichstag, a position he held until 1945. In November 1933, he was appointed *SS-Brigadeführer* and progressed to *SS-Gruppenführer* in February 1934. At the same time, he took on the leadership in Stuttgart of the SS upper section southwest.

Between March 1937 and May 1941, Prützmann was HSSPF northwest, based in Hamburg, and in April 1941, he was appointed police lieutenant general.

From June to November 1941, he held the post of HSSPF for Latvia. This gave him effective control of the whole country, which he shared with Hinrich Lohse, who had been appointed *Reichskommissar Ostland* on July 17, 1941, after Germany took charge of the Baltic States. As HSSPF Latvia, Prützmann oversaw the SD and was the person responsible for implementing the Final Solution there.

The Nazis were divided about how to handle the Jewish problem in Latvia. Lohse, who was backed by **Alfred Rosenberg**, wanted to imprison Jews in ghettos, pilfer all their wealth, and have them work as forced labor in support of Germany's war effort. Prützmann's superior, *SS-Reichsführer* **Heinrich Himmler**, wanted to murder the Jews of Latvia immediately. At the beginning of August 1941, when a subordinate asked Prützmann where the Baltic Jews were being evicted to, he reportedly replied that the deportation was not to a place but to the afterlife.

Annoyed at the slowness with which the SD was murdering Jews in Latvia, Himmler flew to Kovno (Kaunas) on July 29, 1941, to ramp up mass killings in the Baltic States. By November 1941, some 30,000 of Latvia's roughly 70,000 Jews had been killed. In mid-November 1941, Himmler replaced Prützmann with **Friedrich Jeckeln**, the HSSPF from Ukraine, while Prützmann was reassigned to replace Jeckeln. When Jeckeln took over as HSSPF Latvia, Prützmann reported that large numbers of Jews had already been killed. Responsible for forcing the Jews of Latvia into ghettos, Prützmann's actions allowed them to be murdered more readily by Jeckeln.

Prützmann held the position of HSSPF Ukraine and Russia-South from November 1941 until the summer of 1944. In July 1942, he decided to train the foresters in Zhytomyr to carry out tasks similar to the police units. Besides Jewish refugees, partisans in the forests also needed to be confronted, apprehended, and shot.

A unit of 272 SS men who worked for *Sonderkommando Russland* in Ukraine kept headquarters at Prützmann's offices in Kiev.

In his capacity as *SS-Gruppenführer*, Prützmann took part in a meeting of several others of similar rank on October 4, 1943, in Posen (Poznań), where Himmler spoke openly about the extermination of the Jews. To fight partisans, Prützmann also commanded *Kampfgruppe Prützmann* in Ukraine during early summer 1944; the unit that saw constant action in the forests. For his efforts, Prützmann received high decorations including the German Cross in Gold.

One of his last promotions came in September 1944, when Prützmann was appointed by Heinrich Himmler as general inspector of special defense (*Generalinspekteur für Spezialabwehr*) and was tasked with establishing a unit that would serve as a last-ditch guerrilla service, the *Werwolf* force. While stationed in Ukraine, Prützmann had studied the guerrilla tactics used by Soviet partisans, and at *Werwolf* headquarters, he sought to teach these tactics to the unit's members. *Werwolf* troops were intended to serve as military formations that would engage in clandestine operations behind enemy lines once Germany had been overrun and occupied. As things turned out, despite the mystery and allure the *Werwolf* detachments represented, they did not produce the anticipated results and were ineffective against the might of Allied combat troops in the last days of the war.

Shortly before the war ended, Prützmann was captured by the Allies. He committed suicide while in custody, on May 21, 1945.

Q

QUISLING, VIDKUN (1887–1945)

Vidkun Quisling was a Norwegian military officer and politician who collaborated with Nazi Germany and headed the government of Norway after the country was occupied during World War II.

Vidkun Abraham Lauritz Jonssøn Quisling was born in Fyresdal, Norway, on July 18, 1887, the son of Lutheran minister and genealogist Jon Lauritz Quisling and his wife Anna, the daughter of wealthy shippers. Both parents were from old and distinguished Telemark families.

Quisling entered the army in 1911 and graduated as Norway's best-ever war-academy cadet. He rose to the rank of major before serving as Norwegian military attaché in Petrograd from 1918 to 1919 and in Helsinki from 1919 to 1921. He carried out relief work in Russia under the famed Arctic explorer and humanitarian Fridtjof Nansen and later for the League of Nations. Quisling represented British interests at the Norwegian legation in Moscow from 1927 to 1929, as Britain and Soviet Russia had no diplomatic relationship. Between 1931 and 1933, he was the Norwegian minister of defense, gaining notoriety for putting down a strike by workers in the hydroelectric industry.

A capable army officer and government administrator, Quisling became controversial through his support of Germany's Nazi Party. He resigned from the government on May 17, 1933, to help form the fascist *Nasjonal Samling* (National Unity) Party, which stood for suppression of communism and unionism; the party, however, failed to gain a seat in the *Storting* (Parliament). After 1935, when the party changed from its religious base to a more pro-German and antisemitic policy, support from the Church waned. Over time, the party became more extremist, and party membership fell to about 2,000 members after the German invasion.

With the party's failure to win electoral support, in 1939, Quisling met with **Adolf Hitler** and put his case for a German occupation of Norway, which would place the *Nasjonal Samling* in power. During the German invasion of Norway in April 1940, as the king and government fled north, Quisling attempted a coup d'état to make him minister president, but this failed within five days, as the Germans refused to support him.

Germany set up a new government, with **Josef Terboven** as Reich commissioner reporting directly to Hitler. Quisling participated in the occupation government.

On February 1, 1942, Quisling attained greater political power, heading the Norwegian state administration jointly with Terboven and serving as Norway's minister president in a *Nasjonal Samling* government. Quisling's regime brought in a collaborationist program of Nazification and implemented the Final Solution, in which more than 1,000 Norwegian Jews were transported to German concentration camps. His policies, including converting churches and schools to National Socialism, were opposed by most Norwegians, and his policy to carve out an autonomous Norwegian fascist identity was impeded both by interference from Berlin and by Norwegian partisan resistance.

Germany took control over law and order in Norway. After the deportation of the Jews, Norwegian officers were also deported; in addition, there was an attempt to deport students from the University of Oslo. In 1944, Quisling forced compulsory military service on servants of the royal family.

On January 20, 1945, in his final trip to visit Hitler, Quisling promised Norwegian support to Germany if the Nazis agreed to a peace deal with Norway. The Nazis instead implemented a scorched-earth policy in northern Norway, including shooting Norwegian civilians who refused to evacuate the region. Upon being asked to sign the execution order of thousands of Norwegian "saboteurs," Quisling refused. He was convinced that the Nazi refusal to sign a peace agreement would seal his reputation as a traitor.

Following the liberation of Norway in May 1945, Quisling was imprisoned to await trial for war crimes. During the subsequent court proceedings, he claimed that he had acted for the greater good of Norway, but he was found guilty of charges including embezzlement, murder, and high treason and was sentenced to death. He was executed by firing squad at Akershus Fortress, Oslo, on October 24, 1945. His name, Quisling, has subsequently become synonymous with that of collaborator and traitor.

R

RADEMACHER, FRANZ (1906–1973)

Franz Rademacher was a German diplomat in charge of the so-called Jewish desk (*Judenreferat D III*) in the Ministry of Foreign Affairs between May 1940 and April 1943.

Born on February 20, 1906, in the town of Neustrelitz, Mecklenburg, he studied law in Rostock and Munich, receiving his license to practice in April 1932, prior to entering the civil service. In 1932, he joined the SA (*Sturmabteilung*), and in March 1933, he became a member of the Nazi Party. He joined the Foreign Office in 1937 and served several years overseas as a diplomat before being appointed head of D III in 1940. An avowed antisemite, he was recognized by those around him as a Jewish expert. Given this, he sought to elevate the role of the Foreign Office in Jewish affairs, particularly in finding a way to remove the Jews from German life.

He suggested that all Jews falling into the German sphere—which, given the conquest of Poland, had increased considerably—be expelled and deported to the French island of Madagascar, off the coast of Africa in the Indian Ocean. Throughout the spring and summer of 1940, he worked hard on developing his plan, along the way alienating himself from the Jewish expert at the SS, **Adolf Eichmann**, who was attempting to take control of the project himself. The question over who was ultimately to have ownership of the scheme became moot, however, when Germany failed to defeat Britain in 1940 and thereby had to abandon the plan, owing to Britain's continued dominance of the sea lanes.

In October 1941, Rademacher became directly involved for the first time in the mass murder of Jews. At the request of the local foreign ministry representative in Belgrade who had asked for the city's Jews to be deported, he was sent to Serbia to help occupation authorities there find a local solution to the Jewish question. Rademacher, who normally operated from Berlin, traveled to Belgrade to see firsthand whether the problem could be resolved. An agreement was reached without any further ado to shoot 1,300 Jews in situ. Upon his return to Berlin, Rademacher then filed a travel-expense claim, describing the reason for his trip as the "liquidation of Jews in Belgrade."

From this beginning, Rademacher became involved more deeply in the developing Holocaust. He employed the Foreign Office as the vehicle for organizing the deportation of Jews from France, Belgium, and the Netherlands to the extermination camps, by demanding that governments allied to Germany surrender their Jewish citizens. In this way, Rademacher's office was able to reduce any minimizing external complications that could otherwise have held the deportations back. Within Germany, he liaised closely with the SS to smooth the path leading to the deportations. As a leading bureaucrat in foreign affairs, Rademacher exercised great skill in carrying out the requirements of his office and brought external policy and race policy together in a relationship that was literally murderous.

In the spring of 1943, Rademacher became caught up in internal departmental politics. His immediate superior, Martin Luther, involved Rademacher in a plot to supplant **Joachim von Ribbentrop** as foreign minister. Luther was arrested and sent to Sachsenhausen concentration camp. Rademacher was dismissed from the Foreign Office and forced to join the navy as an officer for the remainder of the war, where he served in an intelligence unit. The Foreign Office was reorganized, Rademacher's division was closed, and all foreign matters relating to Jews were transferred to the responsibility of Eberhard von Thadden, a lawyer who was head of the office's Inland II unit.

With the end of the war, Rademacher was arrested by British military police in November 1945. Although released, he subsequently became one of the few Nazi diplomats to be investigated. In February 1952, he was brought to trial in Germany for the murders he had overseen in Serbia and was convicted by a German state court in Nuremberg-Furth. Appealing the case in 1953, he jumped bail while proceedings were taking place and fled to Syria with the aid of Nazi sympathizers in September of that year. The court convicted him in absentia and sentenced him to three years and five months' imprisonment.

His whereabouts were known while in the Middle East, and in 1962, he became the subject of a failed assassination attempt at the hands of Israeli spy Eli Cohen. To some degree, this was the beginning of Rademacher's end. In 1963, he was arrested on charges of spying; released in 1965 owing to ill health, he returned voluntarily to Germany, penniless, in 1966. He was arrested at Nuremberg airport on November 30, 1966, faced a new trial, and was again convicted of war crimes. On this occasion, he was sentenced to five and a half years' imprisonment, with the court ruling that he could be released owing to what it considered to be time served. A German high court overruled this judgment in 1971 and ordered another new trial. Rademacher appealed this action, but before proceedings could begin, he died on March 17, 1973.

RASCH, OTTO (1891–1948)

Otto Rasch was a high-ranking SS officer in the German-occupied eastern territories of the Soviet Union, who commanded *Einsatzgruppe C* until October 1941, focusing on northern and central Ukraine.

Emil Otto Rasch was born on December 7, 1891, in Friedrichsruh, Schleswig-Holstein. During World War I, he fought as a naval lieutenant. After the war, he studied philosophy, law, and political science in Leipzig and received doctorates in law and political economy; he was known as "Dr. Dr. Rasch," to accord with German academic tradition. In 1931, he became a lawyer, practicing in Dresden.

Rasch enrolled in the NSDAP in September 1931 and the SS in 1933. After **Adolf Hitler** took power in January 1933, Rasch became mayor of Radeberg, a small town just north of Dresden. This was followed by a term as mayor of Wittenberg from 1934 to 1936, where he was investigated for corruption; allegedly, he renovated his villa at the expense of his constituents, which ruined any hopes for a political future with the NSDAP.

In 1936, Rasch was employed full-time by the *Sicherheitsdienst* (SD), and on October 1, 1937, he assumed command of the State Police in Frankfurt am Main. After the *Anschluss* with Austria in March 1938, Rasch, now based in Linz, became director of security for Upper Austria. In June 1938, he joined the RSHA, and in March 1939, he was appointed chief of the Security Police (SiPo) and SD in Prague. In November 1939, as SiPo and SD inspector, Rasch was transferred to Königsberg, East Prussia.

Rasch took an active part in the Gleiwitz incident of August 31, 1939—a covert Nazi attack on a German radio station, which was used as a pretext for the invasion of Poland. With the subsequent outbreak of war in September 1939, Rasch took part in the Polish campaign.

In February 1940, with the agreement of head of the SD **Reinhard Heydrich**, Rasch created the Soldau transit camp, where more than 600 people were liquidated. From June to October 1941, Rasch was commandant of *Einsatzgruppe C*, which operated in Ukraine, following up the rear of the advancing German Army South.

In August 1941, Rasch met with his subordinates to discuss how best to implement a Hitler order dealing with the mass extermination of whole groups in the occupied eastern territories. Rasch's view was that his commanders would have to be tougher than they had been up to now, would have to shoot more Jews, and would have to participate personally in the killings. The only exceptions that could be made related to those deemed "indispensable" as workers. All others would have to be killed.

In a report to Berlin on October 20, 1941, Rasch took credit for the massacre of nearly 50,000 people. Among these was the massacre of Babi Yar, where 33,771 Jews were massacred in two days across September 29 to 30, 1941.

Rasch was discharged from his position in October 1941, and **Max Thomas**, a physician, took over the leadership of *Einsatzgruppe C*. At the beginning of 1942, as a reward for his service, Rasch returned to Germany, where he became the director of the Continental Oil company until 1945.

At Nuremberg, Rasch was indicted with other *Einsatzgruppen* officials before a U.S. military court; the trial lasted from June 3, 1947, to August 10, 1948. Erwin Schulz, who had asked to be relieved of duty as commandant of *Einsatzgruppe C*, testified that Rasch distinguished himself by extreme ruthlessness and had ordered all *Einsatzgruppen* personnel, including the commanding officers, to participate personally in the mass shootings so that all members would share in their culpability.

The charges against Rasch were dropped on February 5, 1948, because he had Parkinson's disease and associated dementia and was considered unfit to stand trial. On November 1, 1948, he died in Wehrstedt, Saxony, at the age of 56.

RAUFF, WALTER (1906–1984)

Walter Rauff was an SS commander who served from January 1938 as an aide of **Reinhard Heydrich**, first in the SS and later in the Reich Security Main Office (RSHA). Rauff was among those with responsibility for nearly 100,000 deaths during World War II, in the implementation of the Nazis' genocide by mobile gas chamber; his victims included communists, Jews, Roma, and the disabled.

Walter Rauff was born on June 19, 1906. In 1924, at the age of 18, he joined the German navy as a cadet. After serving as a midshipman in South America and Spain, he was promoted to lieutenant in 1936 and given command of a minesweeper. In 1937, he was sanctioned for conduct unbecoming an officer (adultery) and resigned. His good friend and former fellow naval officer, **Reinhard Heydrich**, then deputy commander of the SS under **Heinrich Himmler**, gave Rauff the job of putting the SS and its security service, the *Sicherheitsdienst* (SD), onto a war footing.

After the conquest of Norway in 1940, Rauff headed the SD there for three months. That year, he was reinstated in the navy and commanded a fleet of minesweepers in the English Channel. He was promoted to lieutenant commander in April 1941, but shortly afterward, Heydrich summoned him back to SS headquarters. When Heydrich was appointed *Reichsprotektor* of Bohemia and Moravia, Rauff accompanied him to Prague as his technical assistant.

In 1941 to 1942, Rauff was appointed head of the SS Technical Department, responsible for the development and use of mobile gas vans used to murder people deemed enemies of the German state. Rauff's main rationale for using gas vans was that the shooting of noncombatant men, women, and children was a considerable burden for those doing the killing and that this burden removed by using the gas vans. Rauff delegated the task of keeping the gas vans operating in the Soviet Union and other Nazi-occupied areas to an SS chemist, August Becker, who kept Rauff fully informed on the gas-van killing operations.

Tens of thousands of people, most of them Jews, were murdered in this way. It was, however, too slow and cumbersome for the Nazis, who went on to develop fixed gas chambers using Zyklon B as the killing agent. Rauff returned to Berlin in June 1942, after Heydrich's assassination by the Czech resistance.

A month after German Field Marshal Erwin Rommel's defeat of the British at Tobruk in June 1942, the SS set up a special extermination unit to follow in the wake of Rommel's Afrika Korps. The unit, commanded by Rauff, carried out "executive measures on the civilian population," the Nazi euphemism for mass murder of Jews and partisans. From July 1942 to May 1943, Rauff commanded an *Einsatzkommando* in North Africa.

Rauff's hope to exterminate Jews in the Middle East was brought to an abrupt halt by the British Eighth Army's defeat of Rommel at El Alamein in October 1942. Rommel withdrew the remnants of his army to Tunisia, where it remained until May 1943, enabling Rauff's SS to commence the persecution of local Jews. More than 2,500 Jews in Nazi-occupied Tunisia died in a network of SS slave-labor camps before the Germans withdrew. Rauff's men also stole jewels, silver, gold, and Jewish religious artifacts. Forty-three kilograms of gold were taken from the Jewish community on the island of Djerba alone.

In July 1943, after a brief stay in Berlin, Rauff was made commander of an *Einsatzkommando* in Corsica, and from September 1943 until the end of the war, he was the SS commandant in Milan, where he took charge of all Gestapo and SD operations throughout northwest Italy. In both Tunisia and northern Italy, Rauff earned a reputation for utter ruthlessness, as he was responsible for the indiscriminate execution of both Jews and local partisans.

Rauff remained in Italy until the end of the war. As SS commandant, he took part in the secret negotiations that led to the surrender of the Nazis in northern Italy. Arrested by the Allies on April 30, 1945, he escaped from an American internment camp in Rimini and hid in a number of Italian convents, apparently under the protection of Bishop **Alois Hudal**.

His route after leaving Italy remains controversial and unclear. Allegedly, in 1947, he was recruited for Syrian intelligence but fled to Lebanon after a coup in Syria in 1949. After Lebanon, Rauff returned to Italy and gained a transit pass for Ecuador, where he and his family settled. Before sailing for Ecuador in December 1949, Rauff allegedly worked for a while for Israeli intelligence in Egypt, although this has been denied by Rauff's family.

Rauff settled in Quito, Ecuador. In 1953, he was reportedly in Buenos Aires, heading an anticommunist group. In 1958, he moved to Chile, obtained permanent residency status there a year later, and became a cattle and fish merchant. His son, also named Walter, joined the Chilean naval academy and was the protégé of Chief of Staff General Carlos Prats, a supporter of socialist President Salvador Allende.

From 1958 to 1963, Rauff was covertly employed by the Federal Intelligence Service of West Germany as a South American spy. His contact, Wilhelm Beissner, knew Rauff from the time when both were employed in the RSHA. In 1960, Rauff traveled to Germany in order to claim his pension for the time served in the German navy; he had no trouble with the German authorities.

When Hans Strack, the German ambassador to Chile, was ordered by Germany to request Rauff's extradition, Strack, a supporter of exiled war criminals, delayed forwarding the application for 14 months—enough time for Chile to refuse the extradition request on the grounds that the country's statute of limitations on murder cases had expired. In December 1962, Rauff was arrested but was freed by a Chilean Supreme Court decision five months later. Salvador Allende's election as Chilean president in 1970 made no change to Rauff's status. Allende argued that he could not reverse the Supreme Court's 1963 decision.

Under Augusto Pinochet's military dictatorship, Rauff may have served as an adviser in Chilean secret police, the *Dirección de Inteligencia Nacional* (National Intelligence Directorate, or *DINA*). Pinochet's regime resisted all calls for Rauff's extradition to stand trial in West Germany or Israel.

The last request to extradite Rauff to West Germany was presented by renowned Nazi hunter Beate Klarsfeld in 1983; it was rejected. The Pinochet regime alleged that Rauff had been a peaceful Chilean citizen for over 20 years and that the Supreme Court's 1963 decision had closed the case. In January 1984, the director general of Israel's Ministry of Foreign Affairs, David Kimche, officially requested

Rauff's outright expulsion in a meeting with Chilean foreign minister Jaime del Valle, but the request was turned down. A month later, West Germany repeated its extradition request. Chile said that the case would be reopened only if it were presented with evidence of new crimes. The court's position was that extraditing Rauff would not serve any public interest in Chile, since he had lived in the country for many years and his behavior was always beyond reproach.

Walter Rauff died of lung cancer in May 1984.

REICHLEITNER, FRANZ (1906–1944)

Franz Reichleitner was an Austrian member in the SS who participated in *Aktion Reinhard* during the Holocaust.

Franz Karl Reichleitner was born on December 2, 1906, in Ried im Traunkreis, Austria-Hungary. He worked for the Criminal Police and held the rank of *Kriminalsekretär*. He joined the NSDAP in 1936 and the SS in 1937, rising to *SS-Hauptsturmführer*.

After the *Anschluss* in March 1938, Reichleitner worked as a member of the Gestapo in Linz, still with the rank of *Kriminalsekretär.* It was here that he first met **Franz Stangl**, who was to be the future commandant of the extermination camps at Sobibór and Treblinka.

In spring 1940, Reichleitner served with *Aktion T-4* in the killing center at Hartheim Castle, near Linz. In November 1940, Franz Stangl was also transferred to Hartheim, where the two shared a room. After the appointment of **Christian Wirth** as inspector of all euthanasia institutions, Stangl was his successor as office manager in Hartheim, and Reichleitner became Stangl's deputy. At Hartheim, in addition to the activities of the special registry office, the office manager was responsible for control of the death book, the processing of correspondence, and similar matters. These were also local police matters, so Stangl and Reichleitner worked closely together.

Further cementing their personal relationship, Reichleitner married a young woman from Steyr, Anna Baumgartner, who was a friend of Stangl's wife, Theresa. On September 1, 1942, Reichleitner, then aged 36, was appointed to the position of commandant at Sobibór, replacing Stangl, who, in turn, had been transferred to Treblinka.

Reichleitner preferred to operate out of public gaze, and his command of Sobibór was recognized as stricter than that of Stangl. He relied on his subordinates, who were highly intimidated by his authority and his unpredictability, based, it was said, on the fact that he was a heavy drinker. As a result, Sobibór was highly disciplined and meticulously managed. Under Reichleitner's command, all functions went smoothly, and transports arriving on any given day were liquidated efficiently. Reichleitner always turned himself out with great style and wore gloves, but he had no direct contact with the Jews who arrived on the transports. *SS-Reichsführer* **Heinrich Himmler** visited Sobibór on February 12, 1943. Impressed with Reichleitner's efficiency, he promoted the commandant to the rank of *SS-Hauptsturmführer*.

On October 14, 1943, a major revolt took place at Sobibór. Over 300 of the 600 prisoners escaped, with some loss of life among the SS guard detachment.

Reichleitner was on leave the day of the revolt, but upon his return and proceeding from Himmler's direct order, he oversaw that those prisoners remaining in the camp were shot. Within a few days, Sobibór was ordered closed, and in succeeding weeks, there was a concerted effort to remove all traces of the camp's existence, including what had taken place there.

Reichleitner's future was already somewhat mapped out, however. On September 13, 1943 the overall head of *Aktion Reinhard*, **Odilo Globocnik**, had been appointed to coerce the area around Trieste and exterminate the local Jewish community. With the closure of Sobibór, Reichleitner, like so many of the other perpetrators of *Aktion Reinhard*, was transferred to Trieste, Italy, on antipartisan duties. While serving in this capacity, Franz Reichleitner was killed by partisans on January 3, 1944, in the Fiume district.

RIBBENTROP, JOACHIM VON (1893–1946)

Joachim von Ribbentrop was a German diplomat and politician who served as Nazi foreign minister between 1938 and 1945. A friend of **Adolf Hitler**, Ribbentrop was instrumental in negotiating the Nazi-Soviet Nonaggression Pact that freed Germany to invade Poland in September 1939. He managed the diplomatic moves that persuaded Germany's Axis partners to expel their Jews for deportation to German killing centers as well as to abandon their Jewish citizens living in Germany.

Ulrich Friedrich Willy Joachim von Ribbentrop was born in Wesel, in the Rhineland, on April 30, 1893, to Richard Ulrich Joachim Ribbentrop, a career army officer, and his wife Johanne. He attended school in Germany and Switzerland and spent time in France and Britain as a child.

In 1910, he began working as clerk with a German importing firm based in London, before moving to Canada, where he worked for the Molsons Bank in Montreal. He then worked for an engineering company on the reconstruction of the Quebec Bridge and with the National Transcontinental Railway on the Canadian Pacific Railroad. He followed this with employment as a journalist in New York and Boston but returned to Germany to recover from tuberculosis. He then went back to Canada, where he set up a small business importing German wines. Shortly before the outbreak of World War I, he returned to Germany; joining the German army, he served on the Eastern Front, receiving the Iron Cross Second Class. After being seriously wounded in 1917, he was assigned to the German military mission in Turkey.

After the war, Ribbentrop worked as a wine and champagne salesman for the French firm Pommerey in the Rhineland until his marriage in 1920 to the daughter of a wealthy wine producer. This made him financially independent. Initially, his name was Joachim Ribbentrop, but in 1925, he persuaded a distant ennobled relative to adopt him so that he could inherit the noble "von," adding this to his last name.

On May 1, 1932, Ribbentrop joined the NSDAP. He moved quickly up the party hierarchy and became one of Adolf Hitler's closest confidants. In January 1933, he participated in the secret discussions between Franz von Papen, Hitler, and

President Paul von Hindenburg in Berlin, resulting in the dismissal of Kurt von Schleicher as minister of defense and the nomination of Hitler to take up the post of chancellor on January 30, 1933. After Hitler took power, Ribbentrop became a commissioner and special envoy for the Foreign Affairs Ministry. In 1934, he became the German special commissioner for disarmament to the government of the United States. It was Ribbentrop's responsibility to ensure that the world believed that Germany sincerely wanted an arms-limitation treaty while at the same time ensuring that no such treaty ever emerged.

In August 1934, Ribbentrop founded an agency, Ribbentrop Services (*Dienstelle Ribbentrop*). Funded by money from the NSDAP, it was located directly across the road from the Ministry of Foreign Affairs on Berlin's Wilhelmstrasse. The agency was staffed by journalists, diplomats, members of the NSDAP and the Hitler Youth, dissatisfied businessmen, former reporters, and ambitious Nazi Party members. Ribbentrop Services engaged in collecting information on foreign affairs, functioning as an alternative foreign ministry independent of, and often contrary to, the official Foreign Office. The *Dienststelle* also competed with other Nazi Party units working in the foreign policy arena, including the foreign operation section of the Nazi Party (NSDAP/AO) led by Ernst Bohle, and the Nazi Party Office of Foreign Affairs, (APA) led by **Alfred Rosenberg**. When Ribbentrop was appointed as minister of foreign affairs in February 1938, the *Dienststelle* itself lost its importance and about one-third of its staff followed Ribbentrop to the Foreign Office.

In August 1936, Ribbentrop was appointed as the German ambassador to Britain. His main task was to persuade the British government not to get involved in German territorial disputes and to work together with Germany against the communist government of the Soviet Union. Ribbentrop presented his credentials to King George VI on February 5, 1937, outraging Britain when he gave the king the Hitler salute. He also upset the British government by posting SS guards outside the German Embassy in London and by flying swastika flags on official cars. On February 4, 1938, Ribbentrop replaced Constantin von Neurath as Germany's foreign minister.

Ribbentrop was not popular with the older members of the Nazi Party; nearly all disliked him. **Joseph Goebbels** and **Hermann Göring** considered him to be a snob and a social climber who married into money and bought his title. His diplomatic effort as German ambassador to Britain indicated that he was also inept. Despite efforts made by State Secretary Ernst von Weizsäcker and British prime minister Neville Chamberlain to exclude Ribbentrop from the negotiations at Munich, he participated and tried to pressure Hitler to foment a war with Czechoslovakia. The resultant diplomatic round, however, saw the Sudetenland given to Germany without violence. Even though Germany was able to annex Austria and Czechoslovakia successfully through diplomacy, Ribbentrop regarded them as his failures, because he was not able to provide Germany an opportunity to deploy its military.

As Germany's foreign minister, Ribbentrop worked closely with Adolf Hitler in his negotiations with the British and French governments. He participated in the signing of the Pact of Steel with Benito Mussolini on May 22, 1939. On August 23, 1939, the Nazi-Soviet Nonaggression Pact (also called the

Ribbentrop-Molotov Pact) was signed in Moscow, defining each dictator's future sphere of influence in Eastern Europe. The pact partitioned Poland and gave Germany the right to annex the Baltic States, buying time for the Nazis and the Soviets to consolidate their power bases. A week later, Hitler invaded Poland.

On September 27, 1940, Germany, through Ribbentrop, formed the Tripartite Pact with Japan and Italy, providing for mutual assistance against the United States. This lulled the Soviet Union into a false sense of security that it would not be attacked by the three allies.

With the outbreak of war, Ribbentrop remained foreign minister only through Hitler's backing. Even this support faded, however, after Foreign Office personnel were implicated in the July 20, 1944, bomb plot to assassinate Hitler.

After the unconditional surrender of Germany, the pursuit of high officials serving Hitler began immediately. Ribbentrop escaped capture for a full month, but the Allies arrested him in Hamburg on June 15, 1945. He was transferred to Nuremberg, where, before the International Military Tribunal, he was accused of war crimes as one of the leading representatives of Nazi Germany. Ribbentrop and the Foreign Office were fully involved in a wide variety of breaches of the laws and usages of war, and Ribbentrop himself supported and encouraged the Nazi program against the Jews. His assent resulted in the transportation of Jews from foreign countries to concentration and death camps, even though he denied knowledge of Germany's racial policies resulting in extermination. The tribunal found him guilty on all four counts (conspiracy, crimes against peace, war crimes, and crimes against humanity) and sentenced him to death. Joachim von Ribbentrop was hanged on October 16, 1946.

ROSCHMANN, EDUARD (1908–1977)

Eduard Roschmann, subsequently known as Federico Wegener, was a member of the SS and commandant of the Riga ghetto during 1943.

He was born on November 25, 1908, in Graz, Austria, the son of a brewery manager. He studied law in Graz for six semesters but left without finishing his degree and started a business as a wine dealer, later working in his father's brewery.

In 1927, Roschmann joined the Austrian Fatherland Front (*Vaterländische Front*, or VF), which was part of the paramilitary home guard (*Heimatschutz*) movement. In 1938, after the union of Austria with Germany, Roschmann, aged 20, was admitted to the NSDAP and the SS.

In January 1941, he began working at the Reich Security Main Office (*Reichssicherheitshauptamt*, or RSHA) in Berlin. As the main Nazi security agency, the RSHA was tasked with combating the enemies of the Third Reich both within and outside Germany. Roschmann served with the Gestapo and came into close contact with the commander of the SiPo and the SD in Latvia, **Rudolf Lange**.

After the capture of the Latvian capital Riga by the Wehrmacht on July 1, 1941, Roschmann was sent to Latvia as a member of a task force of the Security Police and the SD. On July 21, 1941, a decision was made to set up a ghetto to assist in the control and supervision of Riga's Jews, and by October 25, 1941, all 30,000

Jews were collected there. The higher SS and police leader (*Höherer SS- und Polizeiführer*, or HSSPF) in Latvia was **Hans-Adolf Prützmann**. His successor in that office was **Friedrich Jeckeln**.

In March 1942, the German agencies in charge of the Riga ghetto and an improvised concentration camp about four kilometers away, Jungfernhof, killed 3,740 German, Austrian, and Czech Jews who had been transported to Latvia. These inmates were the elderly, the sick, and children. The victims were told that they would be moved to a better camp called Dünamünde sited outside of Riga, but there was no such camp; the Jews were transported to a forest area north of Riga and shot.

Roschmann was appointed as commandant of the Riga ghetto, a position he held from January to November 1943. In addition to local murders, Roschmann also deported thousands of Jews to their death at Auschwitz-Birkenau. While commandant, Roschmann was nicknamed the "Butcher of Riga."

With the advance of the Red Army in October 1944, the SS fled by sea to Danzig, taking several thousands of prisoners with them. Many did not survive the trip. Roschmann then headed south toward the Austrian border and traded his SS attire for a Wehrmacht uniform. He was hidden in the homes of friends near Graz until mid-1945. Detained later as a prisoner of war and released in 1947, he visited his wife in Graz, was recognized by a former camp inmate, and was arrested by British military police, but he managed to escape during his transfer to the military prison camp at Dachau.

Roschmann then traveled to Italy via Austria, and in 1948, with the aid of Bishop **Alois Hudal**, he obtained a new passport in the name of Federico Wegener. He managed to flee from Genoa to Argentina, where he established a timber import-export company.

In 1955, he married his secretary, Irmtraud Schubert, even though he was still legally married, and in 1958, he moved to Germany, where he continued his business interests. An arrest warrant for bigamy was issued through the Regional Court of Graz, but Roschmann returned to Argentina before the warrant could be executed. Due to the illicit marriage with his secretary, his wife left Roschmann and married someone else in West Germany in 1958. In 1960, an international arrest warrant was issued against Roschmann for suspected war crimes. He took out an Argentinean passport in 1968.

In summer 1972, a British writer, Frederick Forsyth, sought the help of Nazi hunter Simon Wiesenthal in writing a story about a fugitive Nazi war criminal. Wiesenthal agreed on one condition: that the fictional criminal was Eduard Roschmann, the Butcher of Riga. Wiesenthal wanted to give Roschmann visibility and, in this way, seek his capture. Forsyth accepted and included an invented scene to make Roschmann unpopular among the Nazi fugitives. The ensuing book, *The Odessa File*, was a great success.

In October 1976, an extradition request was handed over by the German Embassy in Buenos Aires; it was rejected, and a further request was repeated in May 1977. On July 5, 1977, a spokesman for Argentina's president Jorge Rafael Videla announced that the request for extradition would be considered. Roschmann left straight away for Paraguay.

On July 25, 1977, Roschmann was hospitalized for cardiovascular problems. He suffered a heart attack and died on August 10, 1977. On August 19, 1977, Interpol confirmed the identity of the Butcher of Riga, who died in a hospital in Asunción, Paraguay. Roschmann was buried in a pauper's grave.

ROSENBERG, ALFRED (1893–1946)

Alfred Rosenberg was a leading Nazi racial theorist and influential ideologue of National Socialism. He held several important state posts under the Nazis and was one of Nazism's most significant intellectuals.

Alfred Ernst Rosenberg was born on January 12, 1893, in Reval, Russia (Tallinn, Estonia), to an Estonian mother and Baltic German father from Latvia. He studied architecture in Riga, and with the approach of German forces in World War I, he went to Moscow, where he studied engineering. In 1915, he married Hilda Leesmann, an Estonian, in Moscow, and received his doctorate in 1917. A czarist supporter during the Russian Revolution of 1917, he fled to Paris after the communist victory and followed this up by a further move to Munich in 1918. Rosenberg was an antisemite, influenced by Houston Stewart Chamberlain's ideas on racial theory.

Rosenberg equated Jews with Bolshevism and communist revolution ("Judeo-Bolshevism") and was heavily involved in the postwar ultranationalist scene in Munich. He joined the German Workers' Party (the forerunner to the Nazi Party) in January 1919 and began writing for its flagship newspaper, the *Völkischer Beobachter*, becoming the paper's senior editor in 1923. Rosenberg became a German citizen in 1920 and gradually assumed the position of chief party ideologue. His antisemitic writings spread the notorious antisemitic forgery, *The Protocols of the Elders of Zion*, and he denounced the Weimar Republic as an anomaly resulting from defeat and controlled by "Jewish traitors."

In 1923, Rosenberg divorced his first wife, Hilda. On November 9, 1923, he participated in the failed Munich Beer Hall Putsch, which resulted in **Adolf Hitler**'s arrest for treason. Rosenberg then became Hitler's personal choice to serve as interim party leader while the Führer himself was in prison, a role he played until Hitler's release.

He married his second wife, Hedwig Kramer, in 1925; the marriage lasted until his death. The couple had two children: a son, who died in infancy, and a daughter, Irene, who was born in 1930.

Upon Hitler's release, Rosenberg returned to journalism. From 1929, Rosenberg headed the new National Socialist Society for Culture and Learning, and in 1930, he was elected to the Reichstag as a Nazi deputy from Hesse-Darmstadt. The year 1930 saw the publication of his major work, *The Myth of the Twentieth Century*, which became the most popular party work after Hitler's *Mein Kampf*. The *Myth* was a pompous pseudoscientific study, which claimed that the Germans represented a pure Nordic race destined to rule Europe. It argued that the Aryan and Jewish "races" were in conflict, and it attacked "international Jewry," Freemasons, Christianity, and the Jesuits, among others.

Alfred Rosenberg, nicknamed "Hitler's Philosopher," was considered to be the leading ideologue in Nazi Germany. His major work, *The Myth of the Twentieth Century*, was published in 1930, and it became the most popular party work after Hitler's *Mein Kampf*. Appointed by Hitler to serve as minister for the Occupied Eastern Territories, Rosenberg then assumed a key role in the development of the Nazis' "Final Solution of the Jewish Question." Tried at the International Military Tribunal in Nuremberg, he was sentenced to death and executed on the morning of October 16, 1946. (United States Holocaust Memorial Museum, courtesy of William Gallagher)

After Hitler attained office in January 1933, Rosenberg headed the foreign policy office. In 1934, he was made Hitler's deputy for supervising the spiritual and ideological training of the Nazi Party. His visit to Britain that year was intended to show that the Nazis would not be a threat, but as a propaganda trip, it was a failure. When Rosenberg laid a wreath bearing a swastika at the Tomb of the Unknown Soldier, a British war veteran threw it into the Thames.

Rosenberg reshaped Nazi racial policy throughout the years, but it always included Aryan supremacy, extreme German nationalism, and rabid antisemitism. Rosenberg also viewed homosexuality, particularly lesbianism, as a hindrance to the expansion of the Nordic population. He argued for a new "religion of the blood" based on the supposed innate promptings of the Nordic soul to defend its noble character against racial and cultural degeneration.

In 1938, Hitler approved Rosenberg's proposal for a new, fully Nazified university system that would provide a base for future party and state elites in racist ideology. In January 1940, Rosenberg founded the *Hohe Schule* (High School). Within this school was the Institute for Research into the Jewish Question, intended to legitimize Nazi antisemitic policies by proving the existence of a "Jewish conspiracy," based on books and archives stolen from Jewish organizations at home and abroad. The libraries of the *Hohe Schule* were filled with looted Jewish art. Rosenberg formed a Nazi task force that looted European art treasures by the trainload, confiscating art, furniture, rugs, and even appliances from Jewish homes. Founded in October 1940, the Rosenberg Task Force (*Einsatzstab Reichsleiter Rosenberg*, or ERR) was the most successful Nazi body involved in art plunder. By the end of war, it had shipped almost 1.5 million railcar loads of artwork and artifacts from German-controlled Europe to the Reich.

In early 1941, Rosenberg edged into Hitler's inner circle in preparation for the German attack on the Soviet Union. His early life in Russia, together with his anti-Bolshevism, made him the Nazi authority on the Soviet Union. On July 17, 1941, following the invasion of the USSR, Hitler appointed Rosenberg as head of the Reich Ministry for the Occupied Eastern Territories, in charge of all Soviet lands falling to Germany stretching from the old Polish border to the Ural Mountains.

Rosenberg's all-consuming ambition for power was undermined by his frequent fights with competitors, his ineptitude in constructing alliances, and his reputation as a poor administrator. In late 1941, as the Wehrmacht stalled before Moscow, Rosenberg's influence lessened, but his office still comprised the Baltic States and parts of Byelorussia (Belarus) and Ukraine. In occupied regions not under military rule, Rosenberg's ministry installed Reich commissioners together with an intricate civilian rule down to the level of rural districts.

Rosenberg received daily reports on the effect of German policies aimed at "pacifying" the local population in the occupied territories. A strong believer in Judeo-Bolshevism, Rosenberg had no difficulties in targeting members of Soviet elites and Jews for destruction. The areas under his charge were the first to see the Final Solution of the Jewish Question carried out through the systematic murder of Jewish men, women, and children. By the end of 1941, more than half a million Jews had been annihilated; Estonia, part of his ministry, was the first German-occupied region declared to be "free of Jews." From November 1941, trains with Jews deported from the Reich arrived in the East. SS and police, together with Rosenberg's officials, made sure that the deportees were either killed immediately on arrival or exploited in forced-labor projects that few were expected to survive.

Despite its persistent power struggles with the SS and other German agencies, Rosenberg's Ministry for the Occupied Eastern Territories took a key role in the development of the Final Solution. It was the only government agency to send two representatives (Alfred Meyer and Georg Leibbrandt) to the Wannsee Conference convened by **Reinhard Heydrich** on January 20, 1942, in Berlin.

Disappointed by his lack of power and influence, Rosenberg wrote to Hitler in October 1944 and attempted to resign his position. Hitler ignored his letter.

Allied troops captured Rosenberg at the end of the war in the Murwick hospital. Tried at the International Military Tribunal in Nuremberg as one of the principal Nazi leaders, he claimed to be ignorant of the Holocaust, notwithstanding that his deputy, Meyer, and his employee Leibbrandt were both present at Wannsee. Rosenberg was found guilty on all four counts of the indictment for conspiracy to commit aggressive war, crimes against peace, war crimes, and crimes against humanity. He was sentenced to death and executed with other condemned codefendants at Nuremberg on the morning of October 16, 1946. His body was cremated, and his ashes scattered in the Isar River.

ROTHAUG, OSWALD (1897–1967)

Oswald Rothaug was a Nazi jurist. In June 1933, he was named a prosecutor at Nuremberg, and in April 1937, he became the regional court director in Schweinfurt and the director of Nuremberg's Special Court (*Sondergericht*). In 1938, he became a member of the Nazi Party and worked closely with the SD (*Sicherheitdienst*). In 1942, he sentenced a 25-year-old Polish slave laborer to death, explaining that the inferiority of the defendant was obvious given that he was part of Polish subhumanity. Rothaug sought after and presided over the trial of Leo Katzenberger in March 1942, ordering his execution in May 1943 for so-called racial defilement. Following the trial, Rothaug was brought to Berlin as a member of the People's Court (*Volksgerichthof*).

Oswald Rothaug was born on May 17, 1897, in Mittelsinn, Bavaria. The son of a primary school teacher, his education was interrupted from 1916 to 1918 while he was in the German army. He passed his final law examination in 1922 and the state examination for the higher administration of justice in 1925.

In December 1925, he began his career as a jurist, first as an assistant to an attorney in Ansbach and later as assistant judge at various courts. In 1927, he became a public prosecutor in charge of criminal cases, rising to senior public prosecutor in Nuremberg in June 1933. Between April 1937 and May 1943, he was director of the Nazi Special Courts in Nuremberg, except for a period in August and September of 1939, when he was serving in the Wehrmacht.

In 1938, Rothaug formally joined the NSDAP. The start of his membership was dated to May 1937, the date of his application, and although he alleged he was not a member, he worked close with the SD as an "honorary collaborator" on legal matters.

He was an up-and-coming judge when, in 1942, the case of 68-year-old Lehman Israel "Leo" Katzenberger came before him. Katzenberger was a shoe wholesale merchant and head of the Jewish community in Nuremberg. He was accused of the crime of "racial pollution" because of his alleged sexual intercourse with a younger Aryan woman named Irene Seiler, the daughter of a close non-Jewish friend. In fact, the investigation showed that they had a relationship, but it was one of debtor and creditor: Katzenberger had loaned Seiler some money, and she was renting an apartment and shopfront from him.

Both Katzenberger and Seiler denied the charge, and the original police report indicated that there was no evidence of a sexual relationship. In response, Rothaug had Katzenberger's case transferred from a more traditional criminal court to a *Sondergericht* established by the Nazi regime to try racial and political enemies of the state. Rothaug, a proud member of the Nazi Lawyer's League, was excited about drawing this assignment. So clear was he in his bias that he sent tickets to the Nazi hierarchy to attend the trial.

Katzenberger never had a chance. During the proceedings, Rothaug tried with all his power to encourage the witnesses to make incriminating statements against the two defendants, who were barely heard by the court, as their statements were passed over or disregarded. During the course of the trial, Rothaug took the opportunity to give the audience a National Socialist lecture on the subject of the Jewish question. The witnesses found it extremely difficult to give testimony because of the way in which the trial was conducted, since Rothaug constantly anticipated the evaluation of the facts and expressed his own views on racial matters instead.

The punishment for racial pollution was not death, but an eyewitness appeared who gave evidence that Katzenberger had been seen leaving Seiler's house after dark. This opened the door to a different wartime law offence involving the death penalty: committing a crime during blackout hours.

In delivering his findings, Rothaug stated that Katzenberger's visits to Seiler under the protection of the blackout served at least the purpose of keeping relations going, arguing that it did not matter whether sexual relations took place during these visits or whether the two only conversed; in his view, the very nature of the two interrelating on any level was sufficient to prove Katzenberger's race treason. He sentenced Katzenberger to the guillotine, and the sentence was carried out on June 2, 1942. Irene Seiler, who testified that no sexual relationship existed between herself and Katzenberger, was convicted of perjury and sentenced to two years' jail with hard labor.

From May 1943 to April 1945, Rothaug was public prosecutor at the People's Court in Berlin. Here he handled national cases of high treason and, from January 1944, cases concerning the undermining of public morale in the Third Reich.

At the end of the war, Rothaug was arrested by the Allies and taken before the International Military Tribunal sitting at Nuremberg in the Judges Trial in 1947. In the tribunal's view, it was not concerned with the legal incontestability under German law of cases like Katzenberger's. The tribunal found that the evidence established beyond a reasonable doubt that Katzenberger was condemned and executed because he was a Jew and that others before Rothaug met the same fate because they were Poles. Their execution was in conformity with Nazi policies of persecution, torture, and extermination. In this context, Rothaug was a knowing and willing instrument in the Nazi program of persecution and extermination.

During their findings, the tribunal also stated that Rothaug's manner and methods made his court an instrument of terror and won the fear and hatred of the population. The tribunal stated that, from the evidence of his closest associates as well as his victims, Oswald Rothaug represented the personification of both Nazi intrigue and cruelty. The court held that under any civilized judicial system Rothaug, a sadistic and evil man, could have been impeached and removed from office or convicted of malfeasance in office because of the scheming malevolence with which he administered injustice.

Oswald Rothaug was found guilty of crimes against humanity but was found not guilty of war crimes through the abuse of the judicial and penal process and membership in a criminal organization. On December 14, 1947, he was sentenced to life imprisonment for crimes against humanity. His sentence was later reduced to 20 years, and he was released on parole on December 22, 1956. He died in Cologne a free man in 1967.

ROTHENBERGER, CURT (1896–1959)

Curt Rothenberger was a German jurist and leading figure in the Nazi Party. Upon the Nazi seizure of power, Rothenberger, **Hans Frank**, and **Roland Freisler** formed an unofficial group that changed the legal process by installing loyal party men into leading judicial positions.

Curt Ferdinand Rothenberger was born on June 30, 1896, in Cuxhaven, Lower Saxony; his father was a customs agent in Hamburg. From 1905, Rothenberger attended the *Wilhelm-Gymnasium*, a school well attended by Jewish boys.

Completing his secondary schooling in August 1914, he was too young to volunteer for World War I, but in April 1915, he received his call-up papers in Kiel. He served until 1918 as a field gunner on the Western Front, rising to the rank of lieutenant.

While still a student, Rothenberger became close friends with a Jewish boy, Kurt Enoch. Serving together in the war, they remained in touch until Rothenburger's sympathies for the Nazis rendered their connection imprudent. Enoch later emigrated from Germany.

After the war, Rothenberger returned to Hamburg and enrolled in a specially designed course for war veterans at the University of Hamburg. In 1919, he volunteered to join *Freikorps Bahrenfeld*. He passed his first state examination in March 1920, served a shortened legal clerkship, obtained his doctoral thesis, and passed the second state law examination. In June 1922, Rothenberger was appointed an auxiliary district court judge in Hamburg. He became an investigating judge in 1927, and in 1928, he was promoted to the Government Council in the State Justice Administration. In mid-1929, he moved into health administration, working as a senior government counsel.

At the end of 1931, Rothenberger was Hamburg candidate for a position as assistant judge in Leipzig, but he was not appointed due to his young age; at just 35 years, he was considered too young for such a senior position. His career aspirations now overcame any morals or ethics. While he had been mentored by at least two Jewish professors, he now tied his career to the Nazi Party's success. For tactical reasons, he did not join the party but was a backroom adviser assisting the Nazis.

On March 8, 1933, Rothenberger was elected as justice senator. Once in place, he fired two Jewish prosecutors even before the Law for the Restoration of the Professional Civil Service—the Aryan Law of April 7, 1933—was passed. Rothenberger was not publicly aligned to the NSDAP, so the radical changes he made to the judiciary were not immediately evident. However, by the time he was done, he had sacked 31 Jewish judges and prosecutors. In the purge of Hamburg's judicial system, some 30 percent of Hamburg's lawyers lost their offices.

Rothenberger became president of the Hanseatic Higher Regional Court on April 1, 1935, and from May 16, 1935, he also served as president of the Hamburg Higher Administrative Court.

Rothenberger initiated a monitoring system in all courts. He held weekly pre-case discussions, in which each judge presented the most important cases coming up in the forthcoming week. Rothenberger stated how each case should proceed and at the same time criticized "unacceptable" judgments from the previous week. Over time, he decided almost every case personally. On some occasions, he intervened in the cases of other judges, directing an outcome. He always blocked any charges against men of the SA or SS.

With the onset of World War II, justice was even more controlled. After Reich Minister of Justice **Franz Gürtner** died in January 1941, **Franz Schlegelberger** was acting justice minister. Rothenberger now identified a new career for himself in Berlin. In April 1942, he wrote to **Adolf Hitler** with a series of reform proposals, leading to Hitler approving changes to the judicial system based on these submissions. On August 20, 1942, Hitler dismissed Schlegelberger and on the same day replaced him with **Otto Georg Thierack**, with Rothenberger appointed as state secretary in charge of judicial reform.

One of Rothenberger's first acts was to make a deal with *SS-Brigadeführer* **Bruno Streckenbach**, whereby prisoners deemed as "antisocial" were to be removed from jails and given to the SS to be worked to death in concentration camps. *SS-Reichsführer* **Heinrich Himmler** decreed that Jews and Roma would join recidivists and those with sentences of 80 years or over in this "antisocial" category.

Rothenberger soon returned to his original reform plans and sought to give the Nazi Party a closer role in the training of judges. He argued that justice at the highest level should remain with a proper, trained judiciary, an idea interpreted by the head of the Party Chancellery, **Martin Bormann**, as not going far enough. Others saw Rothenberger's ideas as unwarranted attacks on the judiciary.

From December 1942, Thierack tried to get rid of his unpopular secretary of state, as his reforms were causing friction at a time when the war was beginning to turn against the Nazis and stability was necessary. Bormann eventually dismissed Rothenberger in late 1943 on the unusual charge of plagiarism. He returned, disappointed, to Hamburg. There he was appointed by Gauleiter Karl Kaufmann as Hamburg's commissioner for total warfare. In September 1944, Rothenberger commenced practice as a public notary.

In May 1945, Rothenberger was arrested by the Allies and interned in Neumünster, near Hamburg. He became one of the defendants at the Judges' Trial, which commenced at Nuremberg on January 4, 1947, and on December 4, 1947, he was sentenced to seven years in prison. The tribunal found that Rothenberger had furthered the program of racial persecution and contributed significantly to the degradation of the Ministry of Justice and the courts in their submission to the will of Hitler, the Nazi Party, and the police. Rothenberger was found guilty for participating in the perversion and bending of the legal system.

In August 1950, he was released early from Landsberg Prison and settled in Schleswig-Holstein, before returning to Hamburg in 1954. His request for a review of his pension was rejected by the City of Hamburg. In 1959, a report was published on Rothenberger's activities during the Nazi era. Shamed, Rothenberger committed suicide on September 1, 1959, in Hamburg.

S

SANDBERGER, MARTIN (1911–2010)

Martin Sandberger was a senior SS official and a Holocaust perpetrator. He oversaw *Sonderkommando 1a* of *Einsatzgruppe A* and was commander of the SiPo and SD in Estonia. Sandberger organized the murder of Jews in the Baltic States and the deportation of Italian Jews to Auschwitz.

Sandberger was born on August 17, 1911, in Charlottenburg, Berlin, the son of a manager working for I. G. Farben. After finishing high school with honors, he studied law at the Universities of Munich, Cologne, Freiburg, and Tübingen. In 1931, he joined the Nazi Party and the SA. During 1932 to 1933, he was a Nazi student leader in Tübingen, in an environment in which two of his student colleagues went on to command *Sonderkommando 1b* and *Sonderkommando 4a* respectively.

By 1935, Sandberger had obtained his doctorate in law. In 1936, he joined the SS in a unit headed by **Gustav Adolf Scheel**, and by 1938, he was an *SS-Sturmbannführer* and had made contact with **Hans Frank**, the incumbent president of the academy of German law and later governor-general of Poland.

Following the German invasion and occupation of Poland in September 1939, *SS-Reichsführer* **Heinrich Himmler** began implementing a program designed to drive out the native Polish population in certain areas and replace them with ethnic Germans (*Volksdeutsche*) from outside the Reich. On October 13, 1939, Himmler appointed Sandberger to take charge of the Northeast Central Immigration Office, tasked with the "racial evaluation" of the arriving immigrants.

Sandberger was also responsible for German resettlement policies elsewhere. In mid-January 1940, 160 Jews from Schneidemühl (Pila) in western Prussia were deported to Lublin so that Baltic Germans could settle there. In May 1940, Sandberger was transferred to Alsace in France, along with his mentor **Gustav Adolf Scheel**, who had selected Sandberger as his aide.

In April 1941, Himmler ordered Sandberger to coordinate the removal of Slovenes from northeastern Slovenia, and in June 1941, he was appointed commander of *Sonderkommando 1a* of *Einsatzgruppe A*. During the first two weeks following the German invasion of the Soviet Union on June 22, 1941, Sandberger traveled into the occupied territories with **Franz Walter Stahlecker**, the commander of *Einsatzgruppe A*, to learn of events firsthand.

Sandberger said that as early as the spring of 1941 and two weeks prior to Operation Barbarossa, he was informed about **Adolf Hitler**'s order to kill all Jews in the Soviet Union. He received this information, he said, from a speech by an RSHA official, **Bruno Streckenbach**, while attending Gestapo headquarters in Berlin.

Each of the four *Einsatzgruppen* followed the various armies of invasion, which had their own theaters of operation. For *Einsatzgruppe A*, the operation of *Einsatzkommando 1a* stretched from the Baltic States and Belarus to Leningrad. Sandberger commanded 105 men from various departments of the RSHA, including 18 men from the Gestapo, 11 from Kripo, and 8 from the SD. Estonia was *Sonderkommando 1a*'s main area of operation. Prior to World War II, out of a population of 1 million living in Estonia, 4,500 were Jews.

During Operation Barbarossa, Sandberger's men, along with *Einsatzkommando 2*, entered Riga and incited local collaborators to destroy synagogues and liquidate Jews. After the alleged butchering of a German soldier by a Jew, 100 Jews were executed by way of reprisal, and such practices were continued in Estonia. On August 28, 1941, Sandberger and his unit moved into the capital, Tallinn. Many Estonians treated Germany as a liberator who would end the Soviet occupation. Due to the close cooperation of the Estonian police, a large German occupation force was unnecessary.

Antisemitism among the Estonian population never rose to the level where pogroms could erupt spontaneously. Many Jews had already fled Estonia prior to the German occupation (only about 1,000 remained), and immediately after the invasion, Estonian militias began arresting Jews. Sandberger took things a step further and ordered the arrest of all men and women fit for labor in Tallinn as well as Riga so that they could be employed as peat diggers. Sandberger also issued orders to wear the Star of David, along with an array of anti-Jewish measures of a kind prevailing for Jews in Germany.

On October 12, 1941, steps were taken to exterminate the entire Jewish population of Estonia. Sandberger became commander of the Security Police and SD on December 3, 1941. During the winter, at Sandberger's command, Estonian Jews who had been deployed as forced labor were also murdered. In a report of July 1, 1942, Sandberger reported the death of 921 Jews, meaning he had successfully completed his mission and that Estonia was "free of Jews."

In September 1943, Sandberger was transferred to Verona, Italy, as head of the Gestapo. During his time in Italy, the deportation of Jews in Rome was carried out in October 1943, with a total of 1,015 Jews deported to Auschwitz. Only 10 survived.

Sandberger returned to Berlin in early January 1944 and spent the rest of the war as head of the foreign agency branch of the SD in the RSHA, reporting to Walter Schellenberg. As Schellenberg's assistant, he acted as liaison with Heinrich Himmler.

In 1945, Sandberger was promoted to *SS-Standartenführer*, but after the collapse of the Third Reich, he went into hiding in an alpine cabin in Austria. On May 25, 1945, he surrendered voluntarily to American officers in Kitzbühl, in the Tirol.

Due to his extensive knowledge of the German intelligence services, the Allies showed great interest in Sandberger. He tried to delay or avoid prosecution by disclosing what he knew under interrogation and to play down his responsibility for the crimes committed. Until internal reports of the *Einsatzgruppen* were discovered, Sandberger was able to convince British investigators that his activities in Tallinn had involved no criminal actions on his part. He could not ultimately escape prosecution, however. He was indicted, along with 23 others, during the *Einstazgruppen* Trial, which took place in Nuremberg between September 1947 and April 1948.

Hiding behind Hitler's directives, Sandberger stated that the order to exterminate Jews was legitimate as Hitler was the supreme authority and his orders had to be obeyed. The tribunal, on the other hand, found that Sandberger willingly obeyed these commands, and he was found guilty on all counts. On April 10, 1948, Judge Michael Musmanno sentenced Martin Sandberger to death by hanging. Despite political pressures, General Lucius D. Clay confirmed Sandberger's death sentence in 1949, but in 1951, the sentence was commuted to life imprisonment. During the period of his trial, the Cold War had begun, and in many cases, pleas by West German politicians and clergymen not to execute their fellow countrymen were accepted.

Sandberger's father also used his connections with the West German president, Theodor Heuss, who in turn contacted the U.S. ambassador, James B. Conant, with the request for a pardon. Numerous pleas for leniency were made by influential individuals, including Minister of Justice Wolfgang Haussmann and Bishop Martin Haug. The vice president of the West German Parliament, Carlo Schmid, expressed concern about Sandberger's conditions in Landsberg Prison and spoke out in favor of a commutation. These and other well-connected people lobbied for Sandberger's release.

By late 1957, there were only four war criminals still held in prison in West Germany. One of them was Sandberger, who was released from Landsberg on January 9, 1958.

In the years that followed, Martin Sandberger was the highest-ranking member of the SS known to be alive. He lived in the open, under his own name, in a Stuttgart retirement home, until he died on March 30, 2010, at the age of 98.

SCHEEL, GUSTAV ADOLF (1907–1979)

Gustav Scheel was a leader of both the National Socialist German Students' League and the German Student Union. He became an *Einsatzgruppe* commander in occupied Alsace, and in 1940, he organized the deportation of the Jews of Karlsruhe (Baden-Württemberg). From November 1941 to May 1945, Scheel was a gauleiter and *Reichsstatthalter* (local governor) in Salzburg.

Gustav Adolphus Scheel was born on November 22, 1907, in Rosenberg, North Baden, into the family of a Protestant pastor. He was educated in Freiburg, Tauberbischofsheim, and Mannheim. While still a schoolboy at the end of World War I, he joined in with various German patriotic youth groups.

During the summer semester of 1928, Scheel began training at Tübingen University for the Protestant ministry, studying law, politics, economics, and theology. At the same time, he deepened his ties to right-wing student circles and, in the winter of 1928 to 1929, to the *Verein Deutscher Studenten* (VDSt), a support group for German student fraternities. Within a year, he was the group's chairman.

In 1929, Scheel joined the National Socialist German Students' League (*Nationalsozialistischer Deutscher Studentenbund*, or NSDStB). On October 1, 1930, he joined the SA, followed by the Nazi Party on December 1, 1930. Scheel first began studying medicine at Tübingen University before returning to Heidelberg, where he continued his studies. At the University of Heidelberg, he was a Nazi spokesman, and as NSDStB college group leader (*Hochschulgruppenführer*), he led Nazi student rallies against a Jewish professor of mathematics and pacifist, Emil Julius Gumbel. Their agitation led to Gumbel's removal in 1932.

In 1933, as chairman of the Heidelberg General Students' Board and a member of the vice chancellor's leadership staff, Scheel played a key role in influencing the university's appointments and personnel policy. He fought to exclude "students of Jewish lineage" from the "benefits of social institutions at the university." Following this line, in May 1933, Scheel was one of the main speakers at Heidelberg involved in the public burning of books proscribed by the Nazi regime.

In 1934, Scheel passed his state examination and graduated as a medical doctor. Later that same year in September, he became a member of the SS and began work full-time with the SD. Between 1935 and 1939, he ran the SD in Stuttgart. With his student activist background, he attracted to the SD many young Nazi academics who later went on to commit mass murder in the name of the Third Reich. Among them were **Walter Stahlecker**, **Martin Sandberger**, Erwin Weinmann, Albert Rapp, Erich Ehrlinger, and Eugen Steimle, all of whom went into various divisions of the RSHA to become leaders of murder squads with the *Einsatzgruppen*. In 1936, Scheel was appointed by Reich Education Minister Bernhard Rust as leader (*Reichsstudentenführer*) of the German Students' Union.

In 1940, after the Battle of France, Scheel became the SiPo commandant in Alsace. In October 1940, he organized the deportation of thousands of the Jews of Karlsruhe (about 40 miles from Mannheim) to Gurs, France.

Scheel's career continued to flourish. On May 1, 1941, he rose to the rank of *SS-Brigadeführer* and police major general for the Alpenland district in Austria. He was installed as gauleiter and *Reichsstatthalter* in Salzburg in November 1941. Upon learning of the existence of resistance groups in Salzburg, he organized a widespread wave of arrests, and as a result, several railway workers were put to death.

In 1944, Scheel took over from Walter Schultze as *Reichsdozentenführer* (Reich leader of university teachers). Schultze, who had served in this capacity since 1935, was also involved in the *Aktion T-4* campaign and was responsible for the death of nearly 400 Germans with disabilities. Scheel was also appointed a member of the executive board of the Reich Research Council (*Reichsforschungsrat*, or RFR). In August 1944, he was elevated to the rank of *SS-Obergruppenführer*, while simultaneously holding numerous other offices.

With the onset of a possible defeat for Nazi Germany in 1944 to 1945, Scheel was given responsibility for organizing the *Volkssturm* (home guard) in Salzburg. When **Adolf Hitler** drew up his last will on April 29, 1945, he nominated Scheel to take over the portfolio of Reich minister for science, national education, and culture in the next cabinet.

At the end of the war, Scheel aided the grand mufti of Jerusalem, **Haj Amin al-Husseini**, to escape arrest by the Allies by providing him with a guide to take him across the border and to safety in Switzerland.

Ten days after Salzburg was occupied by the Americans on May 4, 1945, Scheel was arrested and interned. He spent a considerable period in custody but was finally released in time for Christmas on December 24, 1947. Soon after, however, he was again arrested and transferred to Heidelberg to face a denazification hearing. In 1948, he was sentenced to five years in a labor camp as a *Hauptschuldiger*, or major offender. He was again released on December 24, this time in 1948. After his release, Scheel first worked as on the docks at Hamburg before resuming his medical practice in the summer of 1949.

After an appeal proceeding in 1952, Scheel belonged to the neo-Nazi Naumann Circle, along with other former Nazi leaders, such as **Werner Best** and Werner Naumann. It was alleged that this group was attempting to infiltrate West German political parties, and as result, Scheel was arrested in January 1953 by British police, who suspected him of building up a secret organization. Handed across to German authorities, he faced a trial, which was suspended on December 3, 1954, for lack of evidence of wrongdoing.

From February 1954 to April 8, 1977, Scheel was the owner of a medical practice in Hamburg. He died there on March 25, 1979, aged 71.

SCHLEGELBERGER, FRANZ (1876–1970)

Louis Rudolph Franz Schlegelberger was state secretary in the German Reich Ministry of Justice and served as justice minister during the Third Reich. He was the highest-ranking defendant at the Judges' Trial in Nuremberg.

Schlegelberger was born on October 23, 1876, into a pious Protestant family from Königsberg, where he attended *gymnasium* and sat his school-leaving examination in 1894. He began studying law in Königsberg in 1894, continuing his legal studies in Berlin from 1895 to 1896. In 1897, he passed the state legal examination. At the University of Königsberg (by some accounts, the University of Leipzig), he graduated as a doctor of law on December 1, 1899.

On December 9, 1901, Schlegelberger passed his state law examination. Two weeks later, he became an assessor at the Königsberg local court, and on March 17, 1902, he was made an assistant judge at the Königsberg State Court. On September 16, 1904, he became a judge at the State Court in Lyck (now Ełk, Poland). In early May 1908, he went to the Berlin State Court and in the same year was appointed assistant judge at the Berlin Court of Appeals (*Kammergericht*). In 1914, he was appointed to the *Kammergericht* Council (*Kammergerichtsrat*) in Berlin, where he stayed until 1918.

On April 1, 1918, Schlegelberger became an associate at the Reich Justice Office, receiving appointment later in the year to the Secret Government Court and Executive Council. In 1927, he took on the post as ministerial director in the German Ministry of Justice. From 1922, Schlegelberger also taught in the Faculty of Law at the University of Berlin as an honorary professor.

On October 10, 1931, Schlegelberger was appointed state secretary at the Ministry of Justice under **Franz Gürtner** and kept this job until Gürtner's death in 1941.

After the Nazi Party came to power in 1933, Schlegelberger objected to a decree retroactively imposing the death penalty on those blamed for the Reichstag Fire, on the basis that decree was a violation of the ancient legal maxim *nulla poena sine lege* ("no punishment without law"). On January 30, 1938, following **Adolf Hitler's** orders regarding judges in the Third Reich, Schlegelberger joined the Nazi Party.

In March 1940, Schlegelberger proposed that lawyers be expelled from their profession if they did not fully and without reservation support the National Socialist state. As minister of justice, he reiterated that call in a conference of German jurists and lawyers in April 1941. The first item on the conference agenda was the Nazi regime's T-4 euthanasia program; Schlegelberger announced the Führer's policies so that judges and public prosecutors understood that they may not use legal means to oppose the policy against the will of the Führer.

After Franz Gürtner's death in 1941, Schlegelberger became provisional Reich minister of justice for the years 1941 and 1942, while still holding his post as state secretary. **Otto Thierack** was appointed after Schlegelberger's acting position expired. During Schlegelberger's period in office, the number of judicial death sentences rose sharply. He drafted the Poland Penal Law Provision (*Polenstrafrechtsverordnung*), under which Poles were executed for tearing down German wall posters and proclamations.

Schlegelberger's work assisted the institutionalization of torture in the Third Reich. After defendants accused of political crimes started to show signs of torture, Schlegelberger's justice ministry legalized such acts, to such an extent that the Reich Ministry of Justice even established a standard club to be used in beatings so that torture would at least be regularized.

In 1941, a police captain named Klinzmann was convicted of torture for beating an arson confession out of a Jewish farm laborer. When the German Supreme Court refused to hear Klinzmann's appeal, Schlegelberger created a new procedure called "cancelation," giving the Reich a means to end every trial independently of judicial decisions. Klinzmann was set free.

On October 24, 1941, Schlegelberger wrote to the chief of the Reich Chancellery, Hans Lammers, informing him that acting under the Führer Order of October 24, 1941, Schlegelberger had handed over to the Gestapo for execution a Jew named Markus Luftglass, sentenced by the Special Court (*Sondergericht*) in Katowice to two and a half years in prison for the crime of hoarding eggs. That was clearly a violation of the legal maxim "no punishment without law."

In November 1941, Schlegelberger was among those whom **Reinhard Heydrich** invited to attend the Wannsee Conference. As things turned out, his subordinate, **Roland Freisler**, attended as Schlegelberger's deputy. After the conference, Schlegelberger supported efforts to apply a more restrictive definition of the persons subjected to the Final Solution. In a letter dated April 5, 1942, to Lammers, he suggested that "mixed people" should be given a choice between "evacuation to the East" or sterilization, writing that "The measures for the final solution of the

Jewish question should extend only to full Jews and descendants of mixed marriages of the first degree, but should not apply to descendants of mixed marriages of the second degree. . . . There is no national interest in dissolving the marriage between such half-Jews and a full-blooded German."

Schlegelberger wrote several books on the law and at the time of his retirement was called the "Last of the German Jurists." Some of those texts commenting upon German law were still of use and available for purchase in 2018. Upon his retirement as justice minister on August 24, 1942, Adolf Hitler thanked Schlegelberger with a huge financial endowment and permitted him to purchase an estate with the money, something outside the rules then in force; clearly, Hitler held Schlegelberger in high esteem.

After the war, Schlegelberger was one of the main accused indicted in the Nuremberg Judges' Trial of in 1947. He was sentenced to life imprisonment for conspiracy to perpetrate war crimes and crimes against humanity. The judgment stated, in part,

> Schlegelberger supported the pretension of Hitler in his assumption of power to deal with life and death in disregard of even the pretense of judicial process. By his exhortations and directives, Schlegelberger contributed to the destruction of judicial independence. It was his signature on the decree of 7 February 1942 which imposed upon the Ministry of Justice and the courts the burden of the prosecution, trial, and disposal of the victims of Hitler's Night and Fog. For this he must be charged with primary responsibility.

In 1950, the 74-year-old Schlegelberger was released from prison on health grounds by the American high commissioner for Germany. He then lived in Flensburg until his death at the age of 93, on December 14, 1970.

Schlegelberger was perceived as a reluctant supporter of Hitler's rule and given a lenient sentence. From the available records, it appears that Schlegelberger's acutest regrets dealt with what he experienced rather than what he helped inflict on others. Given his record, he was the model for the character of Ernst Janning, the penitent German jurist portrayed by Burt Lancaster in the multi-award-winning motion picture *Judgment at Nuremberg* (Stanley Kramer, 1961), a depiction of the Judges' Trial at Nuremberg.

SCHOLTZ-KLINK, GERTRUD (1902–1999)

Gertrud Scholtz-Klink was a Nazi Party member and leader of the National Socialist Women's League (*NS-Frauenschaft*) during the period of the Third Reich.

She was born Gertrud Emma Treusch on February 9, 1902, into an antisemitic Christian family in Adelsheim, Baden, where her father was the district surveyor. Her father died when she was eight, leaving her mother to raise her and her two brothers. Leaving school in 1918, she worked as a nurse in Berlin during the last days of World War I. At the age of 18, she married an elementary school teacher, Eugen Klink, with whom she had six children, one of whom died in infancy. In the early 1920s, they joined the National Socialist German Workers' Party (NSDAP), and Eugen Klink became a Nazi district officer. In 1930, he died of a heart attack at a Nazi rally.

During their time together, Gertrud Klink saw her role as one of helping her husband in his party activities—looking after the organization of party kitchens during events, sewing, or organizing day care for the children of the party's female members. In 1929, she became leader of the NSDAP women's section in Baden.

In 1932, she married a country doctor, Günther Scholtz, taking the surname Scholtz-Klink. They divorced in 1938, because he did not share her passion for Nazi politics.

When the Nazis came to power in 1933, **Adolf Hitler** appointed Scholtz-Klink as *Reichsführerin* (Women's Leader) and head of the National Socialist Women's League (*NS-Frauenschaft*). She then established one of the largest women's organizations in history, which was fundamentally concerned with issues relating to the family, particularly motherhood. A woman's role in Nazi Germany was to be considered sacrosanct; it was a woman's selfless duty to give birth to as many children as possible, to take care of her body to ensure maximum fertility, and to make a good German home for her husband and sons. Presenting a male child to the Führer was the greatest form of contribution a German woman could make to her Fatherland.

In July 1936, Scholtz-Klink was promoted as head of the Women's Bureau in the German Labor Front (*Deutsche Arbeitsfront*), responsible for persuading women to work to the advantage of the Nazi government. In 1938, she argued that "the German woman must work and work, physically and mentally she must renounce luxury and pleasure." Scholtz-Klink had the same impact over German women in the Nazi Party that Hitler had over Germany as a whole, and in this sense, she served Nazi needs perfectly.

Just as the SS under **Heinrich Himmler** oversaw the separation of Jews from mainstream German life, so Scholtz-Klink directed the disconnection between women and the daily life of Nazi-dominated male society. She spoke often against women participating in government or public life, saying that "Anyone who has seen the Communist and Social Democratic women scream on the street and in the parliament, will realize that such an activity is not something which is done by a true woman." Elsewhere, she alerted her members that they had to "deny the Liberal-Jew-Bolshevik theory of 'women's equality,'" as any acceptance of it "dishonors them."

Under the close supervision of **Heinrich Himmler**, Scholtz-Klink supervised the running of six-week training programs for young women known as "Nazi bride schools." The course of instruction ensured that women learned how to become good wives in service to the Nazi state. An important part of the course saw to it that women acquired detailed knowledge of race and genetics, and instruction was also given on how young women could become perfect partners for SS soldiers.

The *NS-Frauenschaft* was thus the breeding ground for the master race. The private sphere of women became inextricably bound up with masculinist Nazi ideology. The Nazi state sought strict control over female reproduction, as women's bodies provided the means for engineering racial purity. This was the front line of Nazi racial thinking transformed into action, in which, as she said in another of her speeches, "the mission of woman is to minister in the home and in her profession to the needs of life from the first to last moment of man's existence."

Many years later, American scholar Claudia Koonz interviewed Scholtz-Klink about the situation in Nazi Germany regarding the Jews. As this fitted into the male sphere, however, Scholtz-Klink denied any involvement. She knew that Jewish women were denied access to *Frauenschaft* activities, but she did not go out of her way to help any Jews seeking assistance because, she said, she "did not know any." At the same time, she considered the treatment of Jews to be legal and therefore beyond the realm of judgment—particularly by women. This, Koonz suggested, was a case of "spectator guilt," in which Scholtz-Klink and her enormous organizational machine saw to it that millions of German women could not intervene in any moral capacity against the barbarities of the Third Reich.

Scholtz-Klink led the *NS-Frauenschaft* from February 1934 to 1945. She divorced Günther Scholtz in 1938, and in 1940, she married her third husband, *SS-Obergruppenführer* **August Heissmeyer**. They combined their families. She had six children (one died in infancy); Heissmeyer had five from a previous marriage. Later, they had another child together. In 1944, the Nazi Party advertised Scholtz-Klink and her 11 children as a "fertility model" for the Third Reich. What it did not add was that Scholtz-Klink and Heissmeyer made frequent trips to visit prisoners in women's concentration camps, such as at Moringen, Lichtenburg, and Ravensbrück, in line with Heissmeyer's role as inspector of concentration camps.

After World War II, Scholtz-Klink and Heissmeyer fled Berlin. Captured in the summer of 1945 and imprisoned in a Soviet prisoner-of-war camp near Magdeburg, they managed to escape soon after. In October 1945, a haven was provided for them by Princess Pauline of Württemberg, who, as director of the German Red Cross for the Rhineland, Hesse, Nassau, and Westphalia, had known Scholtz-Klink during the war. Princess Pauline and her nurse were both later indicted by a U.S. military government court for "having concealed two prominent Nazis." Princess Pauline arranged for the couple to live quietly in the village of Bebenhausen, where Scholtz-Klink spent the next three years under the alias of Maria Stuckebrock. On February 28, 1948, however, she was identified and arrested. A French military court sentenced her to 18 months in prison on the charge of forging documents, and in May 1950, a reevaluation of her sentence penalized her with an additional 30 months.

After her release from prison in 1953, Scholtz-Klink settled back in Bebenhausen. In her 1978 book, *Die Frau im Dritten Reich* (*The Woman in the Third Reich*), she confirmed her ongoing support for Nazism, beliefs she held through to her death, at the age of 97, on March 24, 1999.

SCHÖNGARTH, KARL EBERHARD (1903–1946)

Karl Georg Eberhard Schöngarth was born on April 22, 1903, in Leipzig, Saxony. His father was a builder. After graduating from high school in 1920, he served in the *Freikorps*. In 1922, he joined the Nazi Party and earned his living as a bank employee. He served in the army in 1924 and then began studying law. His doctor of law was awarded in June 1929, and he worked as a university professor at

Leibnitz University in Hanover. From June 1932, Schöngarth was a legal assessor in Magdeburg, Erfurt, and Torgau.

On March 1, 1933, he joined the SS, and in May, he rejoined the NSDAP, before joining the Gestapo in 1935. From November 1935 to 1936, he was assigned to the press section in the Berlin Gestapo, and during the first half of 1936, he also acted as a political lawyer. From May 1936 to 1937, Schöngarth oversaw the Gestapo office in Arnsberg. During 1937 to 1938, he ran the Gestapo offices in Bielefeld, Westphalia, Dortmund, and Münster.

In 1939, he became the chief government counsel to the SS and then, from October 1939 to March 1941, an inspector for the *Sicherheitspolizei* (Security Police, or SiPo) and the *Sicherheitsdienst* (Security Service, or SD) in Dresden. From January 30, 1941 (the day he was promoted to the rank of *SS-Oberführer*), to January 14, 1943, he commanded the SiPo and SD in the *Generalgouvernement* in Poland. A fanatical enemy of the Jews, Schöngarth believed their "extermination" necessary and wanted to toughen his SiPo-SD commanders with the necessary "steel hardness" to be able to carry out their murderous actions. During the execution of Jews in Lvov (Lviv), for example, he informed officers under his command that any SS officer failing to carry out an order of execution would himself be shot and that he would support any officer who shot his comrade for this failure.

Schöngarth was characterized by an outstandingly fast intellectual grasp, strong willpower, and an impressive appearance, which commanded respect and obedience. His experience and prominent position within the security services of the *Generalgouvernement*, together with his ideologically safe political approach, led to his chief of the RSHA, **Reinhard Heydrich**, inviting Schöngarth to attend the Wannsee Conference on January 20, 1942, where he participated in the discussion of the Final Solution to the Jewish Question (*Endlösing der Judenfrage*).

Schöngarth was promoted to *SS-Brigadeführer* and police major general on January 30, 1943, and in July, he was transferred to the Fourth SS Police Division in Greece, where he served until early July 1944.

From early July 1944 until the end of the war, Schöngarth was the senior commander of the SiPo and SD in The Hague, Holland. After his immediate chief, Hanns-Albin Rauter, was wounded in 1945 in an ambush by Dutch resistance fighters, Schöngarth ordered the execution of 260 Dutch hostages in retribution. With the unsuccessful attempt on Rauter's life, Schöngarth served in his place as higher SS and police leader in The Hague during March and April 1945.

In 1945, Schöngarth was captured by the British. Tried for war crimes, he was found guilty on February 11, 1946, and was sentenced to death by hanging. Schöngarth was executed on May 15 or 16, 1946, at Hameln Prison.

SEYSS-INQUART, ARTHUR (1892–1946)

Arthur Seyss-Inquart was a prominent Austrian SS official and Reich commissioner in the Netherlands, largely responsible for the persecution of Dutch Jews.

He was born on July 22, 1892, in Stonařov, Moravia (Austria-Hungary), the youngest of six children of the ethnic-Czech school principal Emil Zajtich and his

German-speaking wife, Auguste Hyrenbach. The family moved to Vienna in 1907, where they changed the Czech Slavic name of Zajtich to the German Seyss-Inquart.

Seyss-Inquart studied law at the University of Vienna before enlisting in the Austro-Hungarian army in August 1914. During World War I, he saw action in Russia, Romania, and Italy and was badly wounded. He was awarded war medals for bravery, and in 1917, while on convalescent leave, he completed his final examinations for his degree.

In 1911, Seyss-Inquart met Gertrud Maschka; they married in 1916 and had three children. After the war, he became a lawyer in Vienna, where he developed right-wing views, and in 1921, he set up his own successful legal practice. He was a strong advocate of union with Germany (*Anschluss*) during the 1930s. Seyss-Inquart joined the cabinet of Chancellor Engelbert Dollfuss in 1933, and after Dollfuss's murder in 1934, he became a state councilor under Kurt Schuschnigg. In February 1938, to appease **Adolf Hitler**'s threats, Schuschnigg appointed Seyss-Inquart as his minister of the interior. Initially, Seyss-Inquart was not a member of the Austrian National Socialist Party, but by 1938, sympathetic to the party's views, he became a respectable advocate for the Austrian Nazis.

On March 11, 1938, Schuschnigg was threatened with a German invasion aimed at preventing a plebiscite on the *Anschluss* issue; on the same day, Schuschnigg resigned as Austrian chancellor, and Seyss-Inquart was appointed in his place by Austrian president Wilhelm Miklas. Also on this day, Seyss-Inquart joined the National Socialist Party. The next day, German troops crossed the border at Seyss-Inquart's invitation; shortly afterward, Hitler announced the union of Austria with Germany, basing his action on Seyss-Inquart's revocation of the post–World War I Treaty of St. Germain.

Seyss-Inquart drafted the legislation reducing Austria to a province of Germany and signed it into law on March 13. With Hitler's approval, he remained the Reich representative in the former Austria and received the honorary SS rank of *Gruppenführer*. In May 1939, he was made minister without portfolio in Hitler's cabinet.

Following the German invasion of Poland on September 1, 1939, Seyss-Inquart became administrative chief for southern Poland and then became a deputy to Governor-General **Hans Frank**. Seyss-Inquart was involved in the forcible transfer of Polish Jews into ghettos, in the seizure of strategic supplies, and in the "extraordinary pacification" of the resistance movement. Displeased with the atrocities committed by SS forces and unable to exert any influence over policies, he asked for a new appointment.

In May 1940, he duly became Reich commissioner of the newly occupied Netherlands, reporting to Hitler. Seeking to create a climate conducive to a program of Nazification, he found that Dutch Nazis, under local fascist leader Anton Adriaan Mussert, were not generally supported by the Dutch population. He therefore saw that had no alternative but to work in a moderate environment, among traditional elites.

An avowed antisemite, within a few months of his arrival in the Netherlands, Seyss-Inquart took measures to remove Jews from the government, the press, and leading positions in industry. There were two concentration camps in the

Netherlands: Herzogenbusch, near Vught, and Kamp Amersfoort, near Amersfoort. In addition, there was a preexisting transit camp for Jews at Westerbork. Under Seyss-Inquart's administration, around 140,000 Dutch Jews were registered, and a ghetto was established in Amsterdam. The first movement of Dutch Jews to Buchenwald started in February 1941. Later, many were sent directly to Auschwitz-Birkenau. By the end of the war, it is estimated that 110,000 Dutch Jews had been murdered.

In late 1941, political parties other than Mussert's were banned, and many former government officials were imprisoned. Seyss-Inquart's regime now engaged in a variety of activities. It oversaw the recruitment of Dutch workers to be relocated in the Reich, was wholly responsible for the deportation of scores of thousands of Dutch Jews to the extermination camps, and worked to ensure German exploitation of the Dutch economy.

When Hitler committed suicide in April 1945, Seyss-Inquart was appointed as foreign minister (replacing **Joachim von Ribbentrop**) in the new German government of Admiral Karl Dönitz. He was captured shortly before the end of hostilities, and the Dönitz government lasted mere days. He was charged with war crimes and tried at Nuremberg. Specifically, the charges against him cited his heavy-handed repression of Dutch resisters, the placement of thousands of Jews in the Amsterdam ghetto, and the deportation of some 110,000 Jews to death camps in the East, where all but 5,000 perished—leading to an overall loss of 75 percent of Dutch and foreign Jews between 1940 and 1945. Seyss-Inquart was found guilty and was hanged on October 16, 1946.

SIX, FRANZ (1909–1975)

Franz Six was an *SS-Brigadeführer* who, after a career as a senior university academic in history and political science, became a Nazi official and leader of an *Einsatzgruppe* destined to operate in what would become occupied Britain.

Franz Alfred Six was born in Mannheim, Baden-Württemberg, on August 12, 1909. The son of a furniture dealer, he finished high school in 1930 and enrolled at the University of Heidelberg, where he studied sociology, journalism, and political science. He became an activist in the Heidelberg National Socialist German Students' League (*Nationalsozialistischer Deutscher Studentenbund*, or NSDStB). His doctoral studies were supervised by Professor Arnold Bergstraesser, who, owing to his Jewish ancestry, was dismissed from his university post under the Nazis and forced to flee to the United States.

Six earned his doctorate in 1934 and, in 1936, his habilitation, enabling him access to a university teaching career at the University of Königsberg. In 1937, Six became a professor of journalism there; in 1939, he took the chair of foreign political sciences at the University of Berlin, and the following year he became dean of the university's Faculty of International Studies and head of the German Foreign Studies Institute.

A committed Nazi, Six built for himself a second career within the Nazi hierarchy. He joined the NSDAP in 1930 and the SA in 1932, where he served the party as a student organizer. In 1935, he joined the SS and became a member of the SD working as head of its press office in Berlin. The head of the SD, **Reinhard Heydrich**, noticed Six as a rising star and, in 1937, appointed him as head of Amt VII of the Reich Security Main Office—that is, the de facto head of the domestic security service involved with ideological and propaganda warfare. He would hold this position until 1943.

From this position, Six made a major contribution relative to Jewish and racial policy as well as antisemitic persecution by the SD. His role in this regard was largely suppressed after the war, with his subordinate, **Adolf Eichmann**, much more visible.

Six, together with the head of the Gestapo, **Heinrich Müller**, was given responsibility for organizing preparations for police activities prior to the attack on Poland in September 1939. As a key member of the SD, he was thoroughly apprised of the plans of **Adolf Hitler** and **Heinrich Himmler**, as well as Heydrich, to liquidate the Polish elites and leadership cohorts.

On September 17, 1940, Six was appointed by Hitler to eliminate anti-Nazi elements in Britain following a successful Wehrmacht invasion. In such an event, a list (*Sonderfahndungsliste G. B.*, or Special Search List Great Britain) of up to 2,800 of those to be wiped out had earlier been compiled by another senior SD officer, Walter Schellenberg. Not only were prominent British individuals to be captured; potentially subversive organizations were to be destroyed, the free media was to be shut down, much of the male population was to be enslaved, and *Einsatzkommandos* were to be sent out across Britain—to London, Manchester, Birmingham, Bristol, Liverpool, and either Edinburgh or Glasgow—to wipe out resisters and all Jews.

With the German defeat in the Battle of Britain, plans for *Einsatzgruppe England* were abandoned, and on June 20, 1941, immediately before Operation Barbarossa, Six was redeployed to *Einsatzgruppe B* under overall command of **Arthur Nebe**, directing *Vorkommando Moscow* (SK 7c), the *Einsatzkommando* tasked with weakening enemy resistance and destroying Jews. In dispatches to Berlin in July and August 1941, Six took responsibility for killing 144 people. He reported on the unit's involvement in shooting operations in the Smolensk area, including the shooting of 38 "intellectual Jews, who tried to provoke dissatisfaction and unrest in the newly erected Smolensk ghetto." As a reward for his "exceptional service," Himmler promoted Six to *SS-Oberführer* on November 9, 1941.

Six next became lead of the Cultural Policy Department in the Foreign Office in September 1942. Here, he worked closely on propaganda with the Press Department, in particular on matters justifying the persecution of the Jews. Six wrote extensively, and his pamphlets sold rapidly. He argued continually that the Jewish question had to be dealt with as a matter of urgency and "brought to a solution" internationally. Again, he was rewarded for his work, and on January 31, 1945, he was promoted *SS-Brigadeführer*.

Toward the end of war, Six went into hiding, first near Salzburg and then as farmhand Georg Becker in Hesse. He was arrested by the Americans in January 1946.

At the 1948, *Einsatzgruppen* trial, he was tried as a war criminal, although the tribunal could not link him directly to the mass murders for which he was charged. He was sentenced to 20 years in prison; this was later commuted to 10 years, and Six was released in October 1952 by the U.S. high commissioner for Germany, John J. McCloy.

In 1957, after his release from Landsberg Prison, Franz Six became head of advertising with the Porsche Motor Company. He maintained his writing as before and retained his title of professor before retiring on a full pension to Friedrichshafen in southern Germany.

Six was called as a defense witness during the trial of Adolf Eichmann in Jerusalem in 1961; he testified but did not travel to Israel, for fear that he would have been arrested as a war criminal. Between 1963 and 1968, the Berlin prosecutor investigated Six for his involvement in the Final Solution, but no action was taken, as his attorneys claimed successfully that his poor health rendered him unfit to stand trial.

At the end of his life, Franz Six retired to a luxury house in Caldaro (Kaltern) in the Bolzano district of the South Tyrol. He died in his sleep on July 9, 1975.

SPEER, ALBERT (1905–1981)

Adolf Hitler's chief architect, Albert Speer, served as Reich minister for armaments and war production for most of World War II. He used his organizational skills and the labor of millions of concentration camp prisoners, forced laborers, and prisoners of war to keep the military armed and fighting.

Berthold Konrad Hermann Albert Speer was born on March 19, 1905, the second of three sons of an upper-middle-class family in Mannheim. He became an architect, as his father and grandfather had before him. In 1918, the family moved permanently to their summer home, Villa Speer, on Schloss-Wolfsbrunnenweg, Heidelberg, where Speer took up skiing and mountaineering. Because his parents' income was limited by the 1923 hyperinflation crisis, Speer began architectural studies at the University of Karlsruhe; when the crisis abated, he transferred to study at the Technical University of Munich. In 1925, he transferred again, to study under Heinrich Tessenow at the Technical University of Berlin. Passing his exams in 1927, Speer became Tessenow's assistant, teaching some classes while continuing his graduate studies.

Speer, apolitical as a young man, attended a Berlin Nazi rally in December 1930 at the urging of some of his students, and he joined the Nazi Party on March 1, 1931. He found in Adolf Hitler not only an inspiring speaker but also the answer to his concern about communism and his belief that Germany needed to return to its past glory.

In 1931, Speer gave up his position as Tessenow's assistant and moved back to Mannheim, where he managed his father's properties. In July 1932, Nazi Party official Karl Hanke proposed to **Joseph Goebbels** that he use Speer to renovate the party's Berlin headquarters. After completing this assignment and providing acceptable plans for the Nuremberg Party rally of 1933, Speer was in constant contact with Hitler, who appointed him the Nazi Party's chief architect in early 1934. His projects included building the huge Nuremberg stadium designed to hold over 300,000 people and the German pavilion for the 1937 International Exposition in Paris. Soon, Speer was the inspector general of the Reich.

World War II prevented the realization of many of Speer's architectural plans, including the rebuilding of Berlin. However, when Fritz Todt, Hitler's minister for armaments and war production, died in an airplane accident on February 8, 1942, Speer's proven efficiency and business skills made him ideal to take over as minister.

The German economy was not up to wartime production; Speer's first task was to bring it up to that level. No fewer than five Supreme Authorities had jurisdiction over armament production, while the Ministry of Economic Affairs declared in November 1941 that conditions did not permit any increase in armament production. Moreover, few women worked in factories, which were running only one shift. Speer centralized power over the war economy in himself. Since so much of the German economy was based on military production, he found himself effectively in charge of the entire economy.

Speer's results were impressive. By 1943, he had markedly increased tank and airplane production and had dramatically reduced the time required to bring a German submarine from planning to launch, despite Germany being the subject of massive Allied bombing.

In order to optimize the use of German and slave labor, Speer wanted Karl Hanke appointed as a labor leader. Instead, Hitler, under **Martin Bormann**'s influence, appointed Fritz Sauckel. Rather than increasing female participation and better organizing German labor, as Speer favored, Sauckel imported more slave labor from the occupied nations as workers for Speer's armament factories. On December 10, 1943, Speer visited the underground *Mittelwerk V-2* rocket factory that used concentration camp labor. He claimed, after the war, that he had been shocked by the conditions there.

By 1943, even as the Allies had gained air superiority over Germany, tank production more than doubled, production of planes increased by 80 percent, and production time for submarines was reduced from one year to two months. Output would continue to increase until the second half of 1944.

Because of Allied raids on aircraft factories, Hitler authorized the creation of a governmental task force composed of the Reich Aviation Ministry, Armaments Ministry, and SS personnel, the aim of which was to ensure the preservation and growth of fighter-aircraft production. This continued to improve until late 1944, with Allied bombing destroying just 9 percent of German fighter aircraft production, which more than doubled from 1943 to 1944.

In January 1944, Speer fell ill for three months with complications from an inflamed knee, resulting in his detachment from day-to-day operations. With Hitler's support, he was able to fight off the efforts of others—including Bormann, **Hermann Göring**, and **Heinrich Himmler**—to take over some of his areas of responsibility.

Speer's task force increased the exploitation of slave labor, especially in aviation manufacturing. The SS provided 64,000 prisoners for 20 separate projects at the peak of construction activities. A high mortality rate was associated with the underground construction projects, with the workforce involving 80,000 to 90,000 inmates from the subcamps of Mittelbau-Dora, Mauthausen-Gusen, Buchenwald, and other camps. On August 1, 1944, Speer reformed the task force into the *Rüstungsstab* (armament staff) and then operated with the same model of operation for all top-priority armament programs.

Speer's formation of the *Rüstungsstab* now consolidated key arms-manufacturing projects for the three branches of the military under the authority of his ministry. The task force managed the development and production activities of the *Volksjäger* (people's fighter), as part of the Emergency Fighter Program.

After Hitler's death, Speer worked in the short-lived government of Karl Dönitz, Hitler's successor, until arrested by the British. As he attained his success in greatly increasing Germany's weaponry using forced labor (including millions of Jewish concentration camp prisoners and prisoners of war) in factories around the Reich, in horrid conditions that resulted in death for many of the workers, he was charged with planning and/or participating in a war of aggression, conspiring to plan a war of aggression, war crimes, and crimes against humanity. He was convicted on the last two charges. He stood trial as one of the defendants at the International Military Tribunal at Nuremberg.

During the trial, Speer was the only defendant who acknowledged responsibility for the crimes of the Reich and for his role in them. He contended that he knew nothing of the extermination of the Jews and that he plotted to kill Hitler in 1945—contentions that were and continue to be seriously doubted—but his was a unique response to the charges of the tribunal. Speer was sentenced to and served 20 years in Spandau Prison, from which he was released on October 1, 1966. He then authored three books, including *Inside the Third Reich* and *Spandau: The Secret Diaries*. Speer died in London on September 1, 1981.

STAHLECKER, FRANZ WALTER (1900–1942)

Franz Walter Stahlecker was commander of the SS security forces for the *Reichskommissariat Ostland* from 1941 to 1942, commanding *Einsatzgruppe A*, the most murderous of the four *Einsatzgruppen* active in German-occupied Eastern Europe.

Stahlecker was born on October 10, 1900, in Sternenfels, Baden-Württemberg. He was the second son of a wealthy Protestant pastor, Paul Stahlecker, and his wife Anna. His strict German nationalist family moved in 1905 to the university town of Tübingen, where Stahlecker's father became headmaster of the girls' secondary school there. On completing high school, Stahlecker served in the German military during World War I.

In 1919, after demobilization, he joined the antidemocratic, right-wing, and armed Tübingen student battalion, where he fought against the political left. He also participated in militant nationalist and antisemitic organizations, such as the German *Volkschutz* and *Trutzbund*, which gravitated toward the recently established National Socialist Party. In 1921, Stahlecker became a member of the NSDAP.

Stahlecker studied at the University of Tübingen, completing his law degree in 1924 and receiving his doctorate in law in 1927. There, he befriended **Martin Sandberger**, Erich Ehrlinger, and Eugen Steimle, who later became his accomplices in mass murder.

In 1927, Stahlecker joined the Württemberg state service, and by the fall of 1930, he took charge of an employment office as an administrator. In 1932, he married Luise-Gabriele von Gültlingen, who came from old Swabian imperial nobility.

In 1932, Stahlecker rejoined the Nazi Party and was appointed head of the Württemberg Gestapo in 1934. On August 20, 1938, he became head of the Central Agency for Jewish Emigration in Vienna, whose overall head was **Adolf Eichmann**. After this, he became the higher SS and police leader of the Protectorate of Bohemia and Moravia, reporting to Karl Hermann Frank.

In mid-October 1939, Eichmann and Stahlecker decided to begin implementation of the Nisko Plan, which called for the expulsion and resettlement of Poland's Jews into the inaccessible corner of the territory of the *Generalgouvernement* bordering the cities of Lublin and Nisko. The plan was devised in September 1939, after the invasion of Poland, and was implemented between October 1939 and April 1940. It was the brainchild of **Adolf Hitler**, with help from **Alfred Rosenberg** and **Heinrich Himmler** and with added participation from Eichmann, **Heinrich Müller**, **Hans Frank**, and **Arthur Seyss-Inquart**. **Odilo Globocnik**, the SS and police leader of the new Lublin District, was put in charge of the reservation. In total, about 95,000 Jews were deported to the Lublin Reservation. The main camp of the entire complex was set up in Bełżec, and in March 1942, it became the first Nazi extermination camp of *Aktion Reinhard*.

A clash with **Reinhard Heydrich** caused Stahlecker to move to the Foreign Office, and in 1940, he was sent to Norway to serve as higher SS and police leader there. Stahlecker was highly ambitious and had strong organizational and intellectual skills. When Germany invaded the Soviet Union in 1941, he became an *SS-Brigadeführer*, a major general in the police, and was appointed to command *Einsatzgruppe A*. The mission of *Einsatzgruppe A* was to hunt down and annihilate Jews, Roma, communists, and other "undesirables," by following Army Group North as it overran the Baltic States and areas of Russia west of Leningrad.

Stahlecker founded the infamous extermination group called the *Arājs Kommando*. After the entry of *Einsatzgruppe A* into Riga, contact between Stahlecker and a local Latvian nationalist leader, Viktors Arājs, was established on July 1, 1941. Stahlecker instructed Arājs to set up a commando group, which came to be composed of far-right-wing students and former officers. All the members were volunteers and free to leave at any time. On July 2, 1941, Stahlecker told Arājs that his commando had to unleash a spontaneous-looking pogrom.

The *Arājs Kommando* thus collaborated in Nazi atrocities, including the killing of Jews, Roma, and mental patients, as well as civilian massacres along Latvia's eastern border with the Soviet Union. It murdered the Jews of the Riga ghetto, and in the Rumbula massacre of November 30 and December 8, 1941, it murdered up to 26,000 Jews deported from Germany. Some of the *Arājs Kommando*'s men also served as guards at the Salaspils concentration camp. Contemporary Nazi newsreels prominently featured the *Arājs Kommando* in order to project the image that anti-Jewish activity in the Baltic States was local and not directed by Nazis. The unit numbered about 30 to 500 men during the period that it participated in the killing of the Latvian Jewish population and was disbanded in the final phases of the war.

By the winter of 1941, Stahlecker reported to Berlin that *Einsatzgruppe A* had murdered some 249,420 Jews and other Soviet citizens. In November 1941, he was made higher SS and police leader of the Ostland, comprising Estonia, Latvia, Lithuania, and Belarus. In December 1941, he established Nazi concentration camp Jungfernhof, which operated near Riga.

Stahlecker was killed on March 23, 1942, in a clash with Soviet partisans near Krasnogvardeysk, Russia.

STANGL, FRANZ (1908–1971)

Franz Paul Stangl was an Austrian-born police officer who worked in the *Aktion T-4* euthanasia program and was commandant of Sobibór and Treblinka extermination camps.

He was born in Altmunster, Austria, on March 26, 1908. His father, a night watchman who ruled his family with iron discipline, died in 1916. As a young man, Stangl played and taught the zither to support his family. He completed his public schooling in 1923 and then was apprenticed as weaver, qualifying as a master weaver in 1927. He moved to Innsbruck in 1930, applied to join the Austrian federal police, was accepted in early 1931, and trained for two years at the federal police academy in Linz, where he described his trainers as "sadists."

Stangl became a member of the Austrian Nazi Party in 1931, membership of which was forbidden to Austrian police at that time. In 1935, he was made a detective in the town of Wels. After the *Anschluss* between Austria and Germany on March 12, 1938, Stangl was assigned to the *Schutzpolizei* (later called the Gestapo) in Linz, where he was posted to the Jewish Bureau. In May 1938, he joined the SS, reaching the rank of captain.

In 1940, Stangl was transferred back to Upper Silesia, where he became deputy to **Christian Wirth**, head of the entire Nazi euthanasia program. He became a superintendent of the T-4 euthanasia program at the Euthanasia Institute at Schloss Hartheim, where mentally and physically handicapped people were sent to be murdered.

Hartheim operated as a training center for the industrial murder of human beings. Stangl and many others who would later murder Jews during the *Aktion Reinhard* campaign received their technical and psychological training there. Staff from *Aktion T-4* were deployed to work in the gas chamber and crematoria complexes in the death camps, where they implemented the Final Solution. After leaving Hartheim in 1942, Stangl was transferred to Poland and worked under the SS leader **Odilo Globocnik**. In Poland, Stangl was commandant of the death camp at Sobibór between March and September 1942.

Stangl was then transferred to manage Treblinka, the largest of the three *Aktion Reinhard* camps in occupied Poland, which he commanded from September 1942 through the camp's closure in August 1943. He proved to be a highly efficient and dedicated organizer of mass murder, receiving an official commendation as the "best camp commander" in Poland. Always dressed in white riding clothes and carrying a whip, Stangl's reputation was built on his skills as an administrator. He was not a sadist but took pride and pleasure in running the death camp like clockwork; he regarded his victims as "cargo to be dispatched." Stangl was responsible for the murder of most of Treblinka's approximately 900,000 Jewish victims.

Franz Stangl was commandant of the death camp at Sobibór between March and September 1942, and the related death camp at Treblinka, which he commanded from September 1942 until the camp's closure in August 1943. Escaping immediate justice after the war, he was eventually tracked down and extradited to West Germany in 1967, where he was tried and found guilty of complicity in the mass murder of 900,000 Jews at Treblinka. On June 28, 1971, he suffered a heart attack and died in prison in Düsseldorf. (ullstein bild via Getty Images)

In August 1943, along with Globocnik, Stangl was transferred to Trieste, where he helped organize the campaign against Yugoslav partisans and local Jews. Due to illness, he returned to Vienna in early 1945.

At the end of the war in 1945, Stangl was captured by the Americans and briefly imprisoned as a member of the SS who had been involved in antipartisan activities in Yugoslavia and Italy. His earlier service in Poland was not known at this time. In late 1947, Stangl was handed over to the Austrians in connection with his involvement in the euthanasia program at Schloss Hartheim, and he was transferred to an open, civilian prison in Linz. On May 30, 1948, Stangl walked out of the prison with his Austrian colleague from Sobibór, SS Sergeant **Gustav Wagner**. Austrian Roman Catholic Bishop **Alois Hudal**, a Nazi sympathizer, helped Stangl and Wagner escape through a ratline and reach Syria using a Red Cross passport.

Arriving in Damascus, Stangl was joined by his wife and family. He worked there for three years as a mechanical engineer in a textile mill. In 1951, the Stangl family emigrated to Brazil, and in 1959, after working in a variety of jobs, Stangl became an engineer at a Volkswagen factory in São Bernardo do Campo, still using his own name.

Although Stangl's responsibility for the mass murder of men, women, and children was known to the Austrian authorities, it took until 1961 for his name to appear on the official Austrian list of wanted criminals and a warrant to be issued for his arrest. As he never used an assumed name, it is not clear why it took so long to apprehend him. It then took another six years, through February 28, 1967, before Stangl was tracked down by Nazi hunter Simon Wiesenthal and arrested by Brazilian federal police.

After extradition to West Germany, he was tried for coresponsibility in the mass murder of 900,000 Jews at Treblinka. Stangl admitted to these killings but argued, "My conscience is clear. I was simply doing my duty." He was sentenced to life imprisonment on October 22, 1970. In prison, British journalist Gitta Sereny questioned Stangl across 70 hours of interviews, attempting to understand him in the role as a mass murderer. He again claimed that his conscience was clear, and in his last interview with Sereny, he stated that he "never intentionally hurt anyone . . . But I was there [and] in reality I share the guilt."

On June 28, 1971, the day after Sereny completed the last of her interviews, Stangl suffered a heart attack and died in Dusseldorf Prison.

STRAUCH, EDUARD (1906–1955)

Eduard Strauch was an *SS-Obersturmbannführer*, commander of *Einsatzkommando* 2, and chief of two Nazi organizations, the SiPo and the SD, first in Belarus and then in Belgium. In October 1944, he was transferred to the Waffen-SS.

Strauch was born on August 17, 1906, in Essen. His father was a factory foreman. After World War I, his parents lost money because of hyperinflation, and, as schoolboys, Strauch and his brother worked to augment the family's income. Strauch was radicalized and joined the right-wing Young German Order, to which he belonged until the end of 1927.

After he began studying theology at the universities of Erlangen (Erlangen-Nuremberg) and Münster, he changed direction and instead studied law. He graduated with a degree in jurisprudence.

On August 1, 1931, Strauch joined the Nazi Party and the SA. On December 1, 1931, he became a member of the SS, and in 1934, he began working for the SD. He remained there until the outbreak of war in September 1939.

With the start of Operation Barbarossa in June 1941, Strauch assumed command of *Einsatzkommando* 2, which was part of *Einsatzgruppe A*, whose assigned territory was the Baltic region and northern Russia. From November 4, 1941, *Einsatzgruppe A* was under the command of **Franz Walter Stahlecker**. The higher SS and police leader (*Höherer SS-und Polizeiführer*, or HSSPF) covering the same territory was **Friedrich Jeckeln**. On November 27, 1941, the Jews of the Riga ghetto were informed they would be deported farther east. Three days later, on November 30, Strauch and 20 men under his command, together with Latvian SS units led by Victors Arājs, took part in the murder of some 15,000 Jews in the Rumbula forest near the city. On December 8, 1941, another 10,000 went to their deaths. After disrobing and handing over their valuables, the Jews were murdered by both Latvian and German *Sonderkommandos*. As a reward for this service, Strauch was promoted to commander of the SiPo and the SD and transferred to Belarus.

In the spring of 1942, many children in the Minsk ghetto were caught in the streets and thrown into gas vans. On March 2, 1942, alone, the Germans killed 200 to 300 children in a kindergarten, along with medical staff and educators. By the end of July 1942, Strauch organized a major massacre at Minsk, and the first victims were those unable to work. Soon, mass pogroms were organized. In the entire period dating from the German occupation of Minsk by the end of August 1941 (before Strauch's arrival) right up to July 28, 1942, 71,000 Jews from the Minsk ghetto were killed. On October 21 to 23, 1943, another 22,000 from other parts of Europe were brought in to be killed. All in all, of the 100,000 Jews in the Minsk ghetto, only 2 to 3 percent survived.

Strauch was also in charge of the Maly Trostenets camp; in this small village, 12 kilometers southeast of Minsk, between 60,000 and 65,000 people, mostly Jewish, were exterminated between May 1942 and June 1944. In the forest area Blagovshchina, near Maly Trostenets, Strauch had nearly 16,000 Jews from the "Old Reich" and the occupied German territories shot or asphyxiated in gas vans.

The small Belarusian city of Slutsk had been occupied on June 26, 1941, and Jews had formed a majority before the war. Soon after the occupation, a ghetto was established. After that, thousands were murdered in October 1941 by the Gestapo and Lithuanian militias. On February 5, 1943, Strauch assembled several dozen SS officers and men, as well as the regular security police, and together with a company of Latvian military volunteers, they took part in the extermination of the ghetto's Jews. The number of Jewish victims murdered during the existence of the ghetto was about 18,000; overall, it is estimated that a total of 30,000 civilians were killed in and around Slutsk during the war.

In July 1943, the Nazi general commissioner for White Russia, Wilhelm Kube, reported on his discussion with Strauch and referred to him as the particularly adept leader of the SD who had just affected the murder of tens of thousands of Jews in the past 10 weeks.

Despite such reports, Strauch had personal issues within the SS. He was sometimes exposed to criticism because of his alcoholism, and his activities were, it was said, "predominantly instinctual," especially "under the deterrent effect of alcohol." *SS-Obergruppenführer* **Erich von dem Bach-Zelewski**, who was HSSPF in the Minsk area, described Strauch as "the worst human I ever met in my life." A possible promotion of Strauch to *Standartenführer* was denied owing to negative evaluations like Bach-Zelewski's.

On April 5, 1944, Strauch was appointed SiPo and SD commander for Belgium and northern France. Stationed in Brussels, he was tasked with eliminating the Belgian resistance movement. By the time of his arrival, the Belgian Jews had already been deported. In October, Strauch was transferred into the Waffen-SS.

At the *Einsatzgruppen* trial in Nuremberg, Strauch was found guilty of crimes against humanity and was sentenced to death. Unlike his codefendants

Otto Ohlendorf and **Paul Blobel**, Strauch was not hanged, however, but extradited to Belgium. In Liège, he was charged with shooting prisoners of war, and in 1949, he was again sentenced to death. The sentence was never carried out, owing to the defendant's mental illness. Strauch died in a sanatorium in Uccle, Belgium, in custody, on September 15, 1955.

STRECKENBACH, BRUNO (1907–1977)

Bruno Streckenbach was an *SS-Gruppenführer*. In Kraków, during May 1940, he led mass arrests and the death of the members of the Polish intelligentsia, and from 1941, he was responsible for the murder of thousands of Jews as an SS *Einsatzgruppen* leader.

Bruno Heinrich Streckenbach was born on February 7, 1902, in Hamburg, the son of a customs official. He served in the final year of World War I, and in 1919, aged 17, he joined a local *Freikorps*. In 1920, he started working in business, and in 1930, he joined the NSDAP, becoming a member of the SS in September 1931.

In December 1933, Streckenbach was appointed head of the Hamburg Gestapo until, in 1938, *SS-Reichsführer* **Heinrich Himmler** promoted him to Security Police inspector in the 10th Military District. There, he was also the head of the Munich Gestapo. He developed a reputation for exceptional brutality. In Munich, there was a high death rate among prisoners; on Streckenbach's orders, their bodies were immediately cremated, without any forensic examination.

When Germany invaded Poland on September 1, 1939, **Reinhard Heydrich**, the head of the *Sicherheitsdienst*, created five *Einsatzgruppen* to follow in the wake of the German military. They were later reinforced by members of the *Ordnungspolizei* (Orpo) and Waffen-SS men coming from the *Totenkopfverbände* ("Death's Head Units") employed in the concentration camps. Streckenbach commanded *Einsatzgruppe I* from August 1939 to November 1939, serving in the Neutitschen, Bielsko, and Rzeszów areas, where he was responsible for the murders of thousands of Jews. After November 1939, personnel from this *Einsatzgruppe* were assigned to SS and SD units in Kraków.

On October 31, 1939, Streckenbach informed **Hans Frank**, governor-general of Poland, about Himmler's intention to deport all Jews who lived in the regions of Poland that were now part of the Reich and to replace them with 1 million Poles "of good origin" who could be considered racially acceptable for Germanization.

In November 1939, Streckenbach was appointed commander of the Security Police and the SD for the *Generalgouvernement*. Under a decree dated November 28, 1939, the Nazi-appointed Jewish Council (*Judenrat*) was placed under the control of the civilian authorities, and at a meeting in Kraków two days later, Streckenbach—together with Hans Frank, **Friedrich-Wilhelm Krüger**, **Otto von Wächter**, and others—informed the meeting that the Security Police were "very interested" in the Jewish question and that "sooner or later all questions pertaining to Jewish matters would have to be referred to the Security Police," regardless of whatever else happened. It was later agreed that the civilian authorities would cooperate with Streckenbach's forces.

Streckenbach was also involved in *Generalplan Ost*, the Nazi plan for the expulsion of more than 50 million non-Germanized Slavs of Eastern Europe beyond the Ural Mountains and into Siberia. In their place, up to 10 million Germans would be settled in an expanded living space, or *lebensraum*. As part of this, Streckenbach oversaw the expulsion and relocation of approximately 88,000 Poles from the former western Polish provinces into the *Generalgouvernement*.

As a senior SS officer, Bruno Streckenbach was involved in *Generalplan Ost*, the Nazi plan for the expulsion of the Slavs of Eastern Europe. They, in turn, would be replaced by millions of Germans who would be settled in response to the Nazi demands for *lebensraum* ("living space"). In May 1940 he led mass arrests of members of the Polish intelligentsia in Kraków and was later responsible for the murder of thousands of Jews as a leader of *SS Einsatzgruppe I*. Streckenbach escaped punishment after the war, and lived freely until October 28, 1977, when he died in Hamburg at 75 years of age. (Fetzer/ullstein bild via Getty Images)

The Reich's military planning committee planned the *A-B Aktion* (*Ausserordentliche Befriedungsaktion*, or Extraordinary Pacification Operation) during February and March 1940, and Hans Frank ordered its commencement for May 16, 1940. This was directed against the Polish intelligentsia. Streckenbach oversaw the arrest and murder of 3,500 Polish intellectuals, who were mostly murdered in the forest near Palmiry, not far from Warsaw.

In June 1940, SD chief **Reinhard Heydrich** ordered Streckenbach's transfer from Kraków. He was sent to Berlin as the head of *Amt I*, the staff department of the Reich Main Security Office.

Just prior to the German invasion of the Soviet Union, in May 1941, Streckenbach received top-secret orders to proceed to the police barracks at Pretzsch on the Elbe. He replaced **Werner Best** in training future *Einsatzgruppen* commanders and was required to give a three-week training course for handpicked members of the SD, Gestapo, Waffen-SS, and Orpo, who were to be instructed for *Einsatzgruppen* service. Veterans of earlier German atrocities in Poland now became members of one of four newly constituted *Einsatzgruppen* destined for Soviet Russia as part of Operation Barbarossa.

Streckenbach detailed the mission of the *Einsatzgruppen*: They were to seize and destroy all political and racial enemy groups, such as Bolsheviks, Roma

("Gypsies"), partisans, and Jews. In addition, they were to report on and evaluate material seized during the campaign and to gather information from agents among the Soviet population. Streckenbach ordered that all enemies of the Reich were to be deported to concentration camps and executed. Jews were especially singled out for *Sonderbehandlung* (special treatment), meaning extermination. A follow-up meeting took place on June 17, 1941, in Heydrich's office in Berlin, and on July 2, the *Einzsatzgruppen* and their constituent *Einsatzkommando* groups received their written instructions.

On November 9, 1941, Streckenbach was promoted to *SS-Gruppenführer* and police general and was placed in charge of security forces operating behind the front lines of Army Group North. With Reinhard Heydrich's death on June 4, 1942, Streckenbach had assumed that he would be promoted to the post of head of the Security Police and SD; instead, **Ernst Kaltenbrunner** took the position.

That September, Streckenbach requested transfer to a frontline unit, and accordingly, he took command of 8th SS Cavalry Division Florian Geyer, with the rank of *SS-Obersturmführer*. By April 1943, Streckenbach was in command of the division's antitank battalion. In the autumn of 1943, he replaced Hermann Fegelein as a divisional commander and was promoted to *SS-Oberführer* on January 30, 1944. From April 1944 to May 8, 1945, Streckenbach had command of the 19th Waffen Grenadier Division of the SS (2nd Latvian), and in November 1944, he became an *SS-Gruppenführer*. He was heavily decorated for his military service.

In May 1945, Streckenbach was taken prisoner in the Soviet Union, and in 1952, he was sentenced to serve 25 years in prison. He was released on October 10, 1955, as part of the post-Stalin thaw, which resulted in the release of Germans from Soviet prisoner-of-war camps and gulags.

West German attempts in 1972 to bring him to justice failed. He faced trial in 1973, but the case was dismissed due to his ill health; heart disease did not guarantee that he would survive until the end of the trial. In addition, the court counted his imprisonment in Soviet captivity as time served.

Bruno Streckenbach escaped punishment for his crimes against humanity and lived free and unconstrained until October 28, 1977, when he died in Hamburg, aged 75.

STREICHER, JULIUS (1885–1946)

Julius Streicher was a rabidly antisemitic German politician and prominent member of the Nazi Party prior to World War II. He founded and published the anti-Jewish newspaper *Der Stürmer*, which became a central element of the Nazi propaganda machine.

He was born on February 12, 1885, in Fleinhausen, Bavaria, one of nine children of elementary teacher Friedrich Streicher and his wife Anna. He followed his father and also became an elementary teacher, and in 1909, he moved on to the administration of a secondary school in Nuremberg. In 1913, Streicher married Kunigunde Roth, a baker's daughter, who died in 1943, after 30 years of marriage. They had two children. Streicher joined the German army in 1914, and during World War I, he won the Iron Cross First and Second Class for bravery. By the time of the Armistice in November 1918, he had attained the rank of lieutenant.

With the end of the war, Streicher was demobilized and returned to Nuremberg. He resumed teaching, but by 1919, he became involved in right-wing politics. In 1920, in response to the failed communist revolution of 1918, Streicher founded the Nuremberg chapter of the German Socialist Party, which, far from being socialist, was a strongly antisemitic, anti-Catholic, and intensely nationalistic entity, which considered that Jews had conspired with Bolshevik traitors in trying to subject Germany to communist rule.

Streicher sought to move the German Socialists toward greater levels of antisemitism, which aroused so much opposition that he left the group and in 1921 joined the German Workers' Party. In 1921, he heard **Adolf Hitler** speak, identified him as a mentor, and in 1922 joined the Nazi Party. He merged his personal following with Hitler's, almost doubling the party membership and making him one of Adolf Hitler's earliest political associates.

In May 1923, Streicher founded and began publishing *Der Stürmer* (*The Stormer*), an antisemitic newspaper that served as a useful tool for Nazi propaganda and that reinforced the party's racial policies. A weekly, it produced violent, obscene, and pornographic stories and cartoons about "Jewish perfidy." *Der Stürmer* often published caricatures of Jews depicting them as ugly characters with exaggerated facial features and misshapen bodies. It ran accusations of blood libel, such as that Jews killed children, sacrificed them, and drank their blood. It also included sexually explicit, anti-Catholic, anticommunist, and antimonarchist propaganda. Streicher described Jews as sex offenders who violated the innocent and carried out bizarre sex crimes. He also frequently reported attempts of Jewish child molestation.

Der Stürmer never lacked details about sex, names, and crimes to keep readers aroused and entertained. The accusations were for the most part wildly inaccurate and were rarely investigated. Through the adaptation and amalgamation of almost every existing antisemitic stereotype, myth, and tradition, *Der Stürmer*'s virulent attacks were aimed at the dehumanization and demonization of Jews. The paper was not an official publication of the Nazi Party; as it was published privately by Streicher, it did not display the swastika in its logo. It provided Streicher with a lucrative income and made him a multimillionaire.

Streicher participated in Hitler's failed Beer Hall Putsch on November 8 to 9, 1923, marching with Hitler in the front row of the demonstrators and braving the bullets of the Munich police. His loyalty earned him Hitler's lifelong trust and protection, and Streicher became one of Hitler's few intimates. Streicher was elected in 1924 to the Bavarian legislature (*Landtag*), a position he held until 1932, which gave him a modicum of parliamentary immunity that helped him resist efforts to silence his racist message.

Streicher's early campaigns against Jews made extreme claims that came just short of violating a law that might get the paper shut down. *Der Stürmer* alleged that the Jews had caused the unemployment and inflation Germany suffered during the 1920s. When the Nazi Party was legalized again in 1925, after having been suppressed owing to the putsch, Hitler appointed Streicher as gauleiter of the Bavarian region of Franconia, including Nuremberg.

Streicher was fired from his teaching position in 1923 for his involvement in the putsch, enabling him to focus on his newspaper. He managed to substantially increase its readership while engaging in illicit right-wing political activities.

After Hitler came to power in January 1933, Nazi control of the German state apparatus gave the gauleiters enormous power, which Streicher wielded happily in Nuremberg. In 1933, he organized the April 1 one-day boycott of Jewish businesses, which was used as a model for other antisemitic commercial measures. In 1935, he helped create the political environment leading to the creation of the Nuremberg Laws on race. In the meantime, his newspaper and other publishing ventures reached the pinnacle of success. Hitler declared that *Der Stürmer* was his favorite newspaper and saw to it that each weekly issue was posted for public reading in every town and village in special glassed-in display cases known as *Stürmerkasten*. The newspaper reached a peak circulation of 600,000 in 1935.

Streicher's excesses, however, brought condemnation even from other Nazis. His outrageous personal behavior included unconcealed adultery, several furious verbal attacks on other gauleiters, and striding through the streets of Nuremberg cracking a bullwhip. He was viewed by many Nazi leaders as a loose cannon—narcissistic, volatile, and greedy. He was accused of keeping Jewish property seized after *Kristallnacht* in November 1938. His political downfall came in 1939, after an incident in which he tried publicly to humiliate **Hermann Göring**. The Supreme Nazi Party Court pronounced Streicher "unfit for leadership" and stripped him of his party posts, effectively banishing him from the inner echelons of the Nazi Party. He was forbidden to issue any public statements, and by 1940, he had been stripped of his rank and other offices. Streicher was permitted to continue publishing *Der Stürmer*, however, which he did until early 1945.

When Germany surrendered to the Allies in May 1945, Streicher said he was suicidal; instead, he married his former secretary, Adele Tappe. On May 23, 1945, Allied troops captured Streicher in Waidring, Austria; although he first attempted to hide his true name, he soon admitted his identity.

Streicher was taken into custody, charged with crimes against humanity, and tried by the International Military Tribunal at Nuremberg. His publishing and speaking activities were a major part of the evidence presented against him. The prosecutors argued that Streicher's role in provoking Germans to kill Jews made him an accessory to murder, as much to blame as those who carried out the killing. Evidence was given that Streicher continued to publish his provocative articles and speeches when he knew that Jews were being slaughtered.

Streicher was convicted of crimes against humanity and sentenced to death on October 1, 1946. He was hanged, along with the other condemned, at Nuremberg, on October 16, 1946.

STRIPPEL, ARNOLD (1911–1994)

Arnold Strippel was an *SS-Obersturmführer* and member of the *SS-Totenkopfverbände* who operated the Nazi concentration camps. While assigned to the camp at Neuengamme in 1945, he was given the task of murdering the child victims of a tuberculosis medical experiment conducted by the SS doctor **Kurt Heissmeyer**.

Arnold Strippel was born on June 2, 1911, in Unshausen, north Hesse. Between the ages of 6 and 14, he attended elementary school in Unshausen. He completed three years training in his uncle's construction company and then worked there as a carpenter. Later, he worked on his parents' farm. In May 1940, at age 28, Strippel married; a son was born from the marriage.

In the spring of 1934, Strippel applied to work with the SS. He began his service in October 1934 as a security guard in the Sachsenburg concentration camp. From 1937, Strippel was employed at Buchenwald; there, he soon became a *SS-Rapportführer* (rapport leader), overseeing morning and evening roll call, camp discipline, and training for junior SS personnel. An *SS-Rapportführer* was usually a midlevel noncommissioned officer (often an *Oberscharführer* or *Hauptscharführer*) specific to the *Totenkopfverbände*.

From March to October 1941, Strippel worked as an *SS-Scharführer* at the Natzweiler concentration camp in France and, from October 1941, as an *SS-Untersturmführer* at Majdanek in Poland.

After a brief time working in the main camp at Ravensbrück, in June 1943, he was set to the Ravensbrück subcamp of Karlshagen II, a scientific experimental site where the V2 rocket would later be produced. From October 1943, Strippel was stationed at KZ Herzogenbusch, in the Netherlands.

From May 1944, *SS-Obersturmführer* Strippel was deployed at Neuengamme concentration camp, and from December 1944 to early May 1945, he managed all of Neuengamme's subcamps in the Hamburg region.

Strippel was known to be cruel and impulsive. During six tours of duty in various concentration camps, he became adept at torture. His favorite methods included simple beatings with his fists and feet or with various whips and clubs. He frequently indulged in tree hanging, where prisoners were suspended by their arms, which were bound behind them.

Karl Heissmayer, a physician who had close personal Nazi connections (his uncle was SS General **August Heissmeyer**, and his close acquaintance was SS General **Oswald Pohl**), was given permission to conduct human experiments to test body responses to tuberculosis injections. While he had initially asked for the trials to be held at Ravensbrück, the experiments eventually took place at Strippel's Neuengamme.

In 1944, Heissmeyer initially experimented on adult prisoners, but by November 1944, he found that the experiments had not delivered the results for which he had hoped. He then ordered 20 Jewish children, 10 boys and 10 girls, all between the ages of five and twelve, transferred from Auschwitz to test his thesis. Heissmeyer began his experiments just as Allied forces were crossing the Rhine.

As the children grew weaker, Heissmeyer sought advice as to what should be done. On April 20, 1945, when the British were less than three miles from the camp, **Rudolf Hoess**, commandant of Auschwitz, determined that the children should be eliminated by poison. Strippel agreed. Lacking poison, as directed by Berlin, he improvised.

Two years earlier, the Hamburg SS had taken over Bullenhuser Damm, a bombed-out school, and converted it into a satellite camp of Neuengamme. Strippel delegated *SS-Unterscharführer* (and *Rapportführer*) Wilhelm Dreiman to attach four ropes to ceiling pipes at Bullenhuser Damm. The children's French physicians, Gabriel Florence and René Quenouille, and their Dutch caretakers, Anton Hölzel and Dirk Deutekom, were hanged. So were six Russian prisoners from Neuengamme. Another guard, Johann Frahm, told the 20 children to get undressed; they were going to be vaccinated against typhus. Instead, each of the children received an injection of morphine, and most fell asleep. The six who remained awake were given a second injection.

Frahm lifted the weakest child, Georges Kohn, and brought him into an adjacent room, where two nooses hung from hooks on the wall. Frahm placed the boy into one of the nooses, but he was so frail that the noose would not tighten. Frahm placed the child in a bear hug and pulled down, causing the noose to close. Two at a time, the children were brought into the boiler room and hanged in the same manner. Strippel and other officers supervised the murders; following this, 18 more Russian prisoners were hanged.

Strippel then took the initiative for disposing of the bodies. The next night, he returned to Bullenhuser Damm, in the same truck that had originally transported the children. The corpses were loaded and returned to Neuengamme, where they were cremated under the direction of *SS-Unterscharführer* Wilhelm Brake. The war in Europe ended 17 days later.

Most of those involved in the murders, including Johann Frahm, were captured soon after the war ended. Once tried, all were executed by hanging in October 1946. Others escaped capture and punishment. One, Hans Petersen, fled to Denmark, where he served a short prison sentence in 1946 for his membership in the SS and died in Sonderburg in December 1967. Another, Hans Klein, was not pursued; he became an instructor of forensic medicine at the University of Heidelberg.

After the massacre at Bullenhuser Damm, Arnold Strippel also went into hiding, working as a farmhand in Hesse. In 1948, he presented himself at the American internment camp in Darmstadt and was dismissed after receiving proper documentation. In mid-December 1948, however, he was recognized in Frankfurt by a former Buchenwald torture victim. Police were summoned, and Strippel was arrested.

The first trial against Strippel began on May 31, 1949, in Frankfurt. He was charged with murdering 21 Jewish prisoners at Buchenwald and of torturing others. On June 1, 1949, he was sentenced to 21 life terms plus an additional 10 years. Strippel began his detention in Butzbach prison, where he was given a privileged post in the prison hospital.

In 1969, lawyers arranged for the arrest order against Strippel to be rescinded, and he left Butzbach on April 21, 1969. In October 1969, a new trial, lasting five months, began. The court upheld that while Strippel had participated in the murders of 21 Jews in Buchenwald, he had not actually fired any fatal shots. He was sentenced to time served in Butzbach and received 121,500 deutsche marks in compensation. Strippel moved to Frankfurt-Kalbach, where he worked as an accountant, purchased a home, and lived quietly until 1975, when he was accused of complicity in the murder of 41 inmates at Majdanek. Found guilty, he was ordered not to leave Germany.

On December 12, 1983, the Hamburg public prosecutor filed charges against Strippel for the murders of the children at Bullenhuser Damm and 22 Neuengamme inmates. After three years of additional legal wrangling, Strippel was deemed unfit to stand trial. He disappeared from public view and died on May 1, 1994, in Frankfurt-Kalbach.

STROOP, JÜRGEN (1895–1952)

Jürgen Stroop was an SS general during World War II. He was in command of Nazi troops during the Warsaw Ghetto Uprising of 1943 and wrote the Stroop Report, a book-length account of the operation.

He was born Josef Stroop on September 26, 1895, in Detmold, in the state of Lippe, Germany. His father, Konrad Stroop, was Lippe's chief of police; his mother, Katherine Stroop, was a devoutly religious woman who allegedly subjected her son to childhood physical abuse. After an elementary education, he was apprenticed with the land registry in Detmold. During World War I, he served in several infantry regiments on the Western Front. Wounded in action in October 1914, he returned after eight months' leave and fought in Russian Poland, Lithuania, Belarus, Austrian Galicia, and Romania. He was awarded the Iron Cross Second Class on December 2, 1915.

After demobilization, Stroop returned to the land registry. He joined the National Socialist Party and SS in 1932, and, in 1933, he was appointed leader of the state auxiliary police. Later he worked for the SS in Münster and Hamburg.

In September 1938, Stroop was promoted to the rank of colonel, initially serving in the Sudetenland. After Germany's invasion of Poland in September 1939, he commanded the SS section in Gnesen (Gniezno). He was then transferred to nearby Posen (Poznań) to head the so-called self-defense group of local ethnic Germans.

In May 1941, Stroop changed his name from Josef to Jürgen in honor of his dead infant son. From July 7 to September 15, 1941, he served with the SS on the Eastern Front and received further military awards.

On September 16, 1942, he was promoted to SS general and posted as an inspector of the SiPo and SD of the higher SS as well as police leader for Russia.

In this position, he worked to help secure a key logistical route for German forces on the Eastern Front. From October 1942, Stroop commanded an SS garrison at Kherson, before becoming the SS and police leader (SSPF) for Lvov (Lviv) in February 1943.

Stroop is notorious for his role in the suppression of the Warsaw Ghetto Uprising. *SS-Reichsführer* **Heinrich Himmler** sent him to Warsaw on April 17, 1943, to crush the revolt. Stroop was put in charge of 2 Waffen-SS battalions, 100 infantry troops, units of local police, and local Security Police. It was the function of the latter to accompany SS units in groups of six or eight, as guides and experts in ghetto matters.

Stroop ordered the entire ghetto to be systematically burned down and blown up, building by building. Except for a few Jewish fighters who made it to the Aryan side of Warsaw via the sewers, nearly all of the survivors—including men, women, and children—were either killed on the spot or deported to extermination camps.

Stroop expressed bewilderment that the ghetto's Jewish combatants, whom he viewed as "subhumans," had fought so tenaciously against his men. After the uprising was suppressed, he ordered that Warsaw's Great Synagogue be blown up and destroyed, as a symbol of Nazi victory and the total subjugation of the Jews. He then formally assumed the position of SS and police leader of Warsaw, and on June 18, 1943, he was presented with the Iron Cross First Class for the Warsaw ghetto "action."

Stroop created a detailed 75-page report with 69 pictures, along with communiqués relevant to the suppression of the uprising. The report covered the period April 24, 1943, to May 24, 1943. Bound in black leather and entitled *The Jewish Quarter of Warsaw Is No More!* the report was intended as a souvenir album for Heinrich Himmler and Stroop's immediate superior, **Friedrich Jeckeln**.

Stroop was subsequently placed in charge of the SS and police in Greece on September 8, 1943. The local civilian administration found his methods and behavior unacceptable and withdrew cooperation, forbidding the local Order Police from having anything to do with him. This made his position untenable, and he was consequently removed. On November 9, 1943, he was appointed commander of the SS in Wiesbaden, serving there until the end of the war.

Stroop was involved in the purge of anti-Nazi Germans that followed the failure of the July 20, 1944, bomb plot against the life of **Adolf Hitler**. For his involvement, Stroop claimed to have offered Field Marshal Günther von Kluge a choice between suicide and a show trial before notorious judge of the People's Court, **Roland Freisler**. Kluge demanded his day in court, and Stroop personally shot Kluge in the head. Himmler announced that the field marshal had committed suicide.

Between October 1944 and March 1945, nine men of the U.S. Army Air Corps were summarily executed after being shot down and captured in Stroop's district.

On May 10, 1945, carrying forged discharge papers, Stroop surrendered to the American forces in the village of Rottau, Bavaria. It was two months before he admitted to his actual identity on July 2, 1945. He was then prosecuted during the Dachau Trials. He pretended no knowledge of the killings of the American servicemen, even though as senior commander of the SS and police, he would have given the orders for their execution. After an eight-week trial, Stroop was convicted on March 21, 1947, for shooting the American POWs and sentenced to death by hanging. In November 1947, however, before the sentence was carried out, he was extradited to Poland.

Stroop's trial in Poland began on July 18, 1951, at the Warsaw Criminal District Court. It lasted for just three days. He was convicted on July 23, 1951, and on the evening on March 6, 1952, he was hanged at Mokotów Prison for crimes against humanity.

STUCKART, WILHELM (1902–1953)

Wilhelm Stuckart was a Nazi Party lawyer who cowrote the Nuremberg race laws in 1935 and a follow-up commentary in 1936. His notoriety also emanated from his attendance at the Wannsee Conference in January 1942, which was called to settle procedural, jurisdictional, and legal questions regarding the mass murder of Europe's Jews.

Stuckart was born on November 16, 1902, in Wiesbaden. The son of a railway employee, he had a Christian upbringing. In 1919, he joined the far-right *Freikorps* to resist Allied occupation in the Rhineland, centering on the French in the Ruhr Valley. He began his studies of law and political economy in 1922 at the University of Munich. He joined the Nazi Party in December 1922 and remained a member until the party was banned after the failed Beer Hall Putsch of 1923. To support his parents, Stuckart had to defer his studies temporarily, only completing his degree in 1928.

Passing the bar examination in 1930, Stuckart served as a district court judge. There he renewed his association with the Nazi Party and provided party comrades with legal counseling. As judges were prohibited from being politically active, Stuckart's mother joined the party on his behalf.

From 1932 to 1933, Stuckart was a member of the SA, working as the movement's lawyer in Stettin. On the recommendation of **Heinrich Himmler**, he joined the SS on December 16, 1933; eventually, by 1944, he had reached the rank of *SS-Obergruppenführer*.

Stuckart's quick rise in the German state administration was unusual for a person of modest background and would have been impossible without his long dedication to the National Socialist cause. Having been a party member since December 1922—that is, before the Beer Hall Putsch—he held the coveted Gold Party Badge (*Goldenes Parteiabzeichen*), a special award given to all Nazi Party members with low registration numbers and unbroken Party membership).

On April 4, 1933, he became mayor and state commissioner in Stettin; he was also elected to the Prussian Council of State. On May 15, 1933, he was appointed ministerial director of the Prussian Ministry of Education and the Arts, and on June 30, 1933, he was made a state secretary.

In 1934, Stuckart was intimately involved in the dubious acquisition, by the Prussian State under its prime minister **Hermann Göring**, of the Guelph Treasure of Brunswick. A unique collection of early medieval, religious, precious metalwork and one of the most important church treasuries to have survived from medieval Germany, the treasure was at that time in the hands of several German-Jewish art dealers from Frankfurt. Disagreements with his superior led Stuckart to leave the ministry and move to Darmstadt, where he worked for a few weeks as president of the superior district court.

On March 7, 1935, he began serving in the Reich Ministry of Interior, with responsibility for constitutional law, citizenship, and racial laws. In this role, on September 13, 1935, he, together with Bernhard Lösener and Franz Albrecht Medicus, was given the task of cowriting the antisemitic Law for the Protection of German Blood and German Honor and the Reich Citizenship Law. Together, these are better known as the Nuremberg Laws, which enacted the legal basis of Nazi racial policy, removing Jewish participation in Aryan society. The laws deprived Jews of citizenship, prohibited Jewish households from having German maids under the age of 45, prohibited any non-Jewish German from marrying a Jew, and outlawed sexual relations between Jews and Germans. Drafted in two days, the laws were imposed by the Reichstag on September 15, 1935.

In 1936, Stuckart, as the chairman of the Reich Committee for the Protection of German Blood, coauthored, with **Hans Globke**, the Nazi government's official Commentary on German Racial Legislation in elaboration of the Reich Citizenship and Blood Protection Laws. The commentary explains the basis of these laws on the concept of *Volksgemeinschaft* (people's community), to which every German was bound by common blood. The individual was not a member of society (a concept viewed by the Nazi legal theorists as Marxist) but a born member of the German *Volk*, through which he or she acquired rights. The interests of the *Volk* were to always override those of the individual. People born outside of the *Volk* were seen to possess no rights and, in fact, to represent a danger to the purity of the people's community. As such, antimiscegenation legislation was justified, even necessary.

On August 18, 1939, Stuckart signed a confidential decree regarding the Reporting Obligations of Deformed Newborns, which became the basis for the Nazi regime's euthanasia of children.

In October 1939, Stuckart was given the task of investigating the comprehensive rationalization of the state administrative structure by decentralization and simplification. He proposed that the state and party should effectively be combined in an overarching concept of the Reich and cooperate at the highest levels of power so that ground-level friction between the institutions could be solved by referencing upward. The transformation of the state administration from a technical apparatus for the application of norms to a means of political leadership was the central idea in Stuckart's model. The ideal Nazi civil servant was not to be a passive lawyer of the bygone "liberal constitutional state" but a "pioneer of culture, colonizer and political and economic creator." The administrative structure of the *Reichsgaue* (district), where the party and state authorities were combined and the gauleiter, or district head, fielded almost dictatorial powers over his domain, reflected Stuckart's theorization.

In 1940, he participated in the preparatory measures designed to deprive Jews of their German citizenship, and by 1941, he had worked out a proposal that Jews inside the German Reich should wear distinguishing marks.

At the Wannsee Conference on January 20, 1942, which discussed the imposition of the Final Solution of the Jewish Question (*Endlösung der Judenfrage*), Stuckart represented **Wilhelm Frick**, then interior minister. According to the conference minutes, Stuckart objected to the SS ignoring the Nuremberg Laws in fulfilling the Final Solution and pointed out the bureaucratic problems of such a radical course of action, insisting that mandatory sterilization for persons of "mixed blood" (*Mischlinge*) instead of evacuation (extermination) would preserve the spirit of the Nuremberg Laws.

However, **Reinhard Heydrich**, chairing the meeting, informed Stuckart that the decision to exterminate the Jews had been made by **Adolf Hitler** and that according to the *Führerprinzip*, Hitler's word was above all written law. Stuckart and several others at the conference recognized that Hitler had not given (or must give) this order in writing.

Heydrich called a follow-up conference on March 6, 1942, which further discussed the problems of "mixed blood" individuals and mixed-marriage couples. At this meeting, Stuckart argued that only first-degree *Mischlinge* (persons with two Jewish grandparents) should be sterilized by force, after which they should be allowed to remain in Germany and undergo a "natural extinction." He was also concerned about causing distress to German spouses and children of interracial couples.

In May 1945, Stuckart served briefly as interior minister in Karl Dönitz's Flensburg government, the three-week-long government of Nazi Germany following Hitler's suicide on April 30. With the end of the war, he was arrested and tried by the Allies in the Ministries Trial for his role in formulating and carrying out anti-Jewish laws. The court characterized him as an ardent Jew-hater who pursued his antisemitic campaign from the safety of his ministerial office. Former colleague Bernhard Lösener testified that Stuckart had been aware of the murder of the Jews even before the Wannsee Conference. The defense argued that his support for the forced sterilization of *Mischlinge* was in order to prevent or delay even more drastic measures. Unable to resolve the question, the court sentenced him in April 1949 to 3 years and 10 months imprisonment, which, because of his preceding detention, was counted as having been served.

In 1951, he was tried in a denazification court and classified as a "fellow traveler" (*Mitläufer*) of the Nazis. For this, he was fined 500 deutsche marks in 1952.

Stuckart was killed on November 15, 1953, near Hanover, West Germany, in a car accident one day before his 51st birthday. Ever since, there has been speculation that the accident was set up by persons hunting down Nazi war criminals still at liberty.

SZÁLASI, FERENC (1897–1946)

Ferenc Szálasi was the leader of the infamous pro-Nazi Arrow Cross Party and headed the Hungarian government for the final six months of Hungary's

Ferenc Szálasi was the leader of Hungary's pro-Nazi Arrow Cross Party (or *Nyilas*) during World War II, and head of the government from October 1944 until the country was occupied by Soviet forces. Prior to and during the short six months of Szálasi's regime, over 500,000 Jews died from maltreatment or were murdered. Szálasi fled Hungary but was captured, tried in a Hungarian court in Budapest, and hanged on March 12, 1946. (UtCon Collection/Alamy Stock Photo)

involvement in World War II, after Germany occupied Hungary and removed Miklós Horthy. During his brief rule, Szálasi's men murdered between 10,000 and 15,000 Jews.

Szálasi was born on January 6, 1897, in Kassa, Hungary (now Košice, Slovakia), into a strict family. His father, also named Ferenc Szálasi, was a soldier, and his mother, Erzsébet, was very religious. Szálasi completed his military training in the Theresian Military Academy of Wiener Neustadt and was promoted to lieutenant in 1915. Serving in the Austro-Hungarian army during World War I, he was on the front line for 36 months. He was promoted to captain in 1924, appointed to the general staff in 1925, and was a major by 1933.

The Treaty of Trianon in 1920 severely decreased the size of Hungary's territory and population. With his own ideological program for the country's restoration, in 1930, Szálasi joined the right-wing Hungarian Life League, a "race-protecting" organization, and published his Plan for the Construction of the Hungarian State.

Szálasi resigned from the military in 1934. In 1935, he founded the fascist Party of National Will and, in 1937, the Hungarian National Socialist Party. Both parties focused on patriotism, anticommunism, and antisemitism, and both were banned for being too extreme. Szálasi was jailed for treason.

In 1939, Szálasi founded the Arrow Cross Party (*Nyilas*), which won 25 percent of the votes in the Hungarian Parliament that year; it was banned by Hungarian Regent Admiral Miklós Horthy when World War II broke out. *Nyilas* diverged from Nazism in its goal of creating Greater Hungary rather than a Nazi-dominated Europe and in its policy of Jewish emigration rather than extermination. With time, this would change.

The Hungarian army suffered huge losses at Stalingrad in 1942 and 1943, and Horthy and Prime Minister Miklós Kállay identified that Germany could be defeated. At this time, most of the Jews of the rest of Europe had been murdered by *Einsatzgruppen* and deportations to death camps. As the Hungarian government had consistently rejected Nazi demands for implementation of the Final Solution, only the large Hungarian Jewish community remained almost intact. With Horthy's tacit approval, Kállay began looking into the possibility of negotiating a separate armistice with the Western Allies.

To forestall this, Germany occupied Hungary on March 19, 1944. Horthy remained as regent; Kállay was dismissed, and Germany appointed General Döme Sztójay as prime minister. Sztójay, who had earlier been Hungarian minister to Berlin, was fervently pro-German and pledged Hungary to continue the war and collaborate with the Germans in deporting the Hungarian Jews.

In April 1944, Jews living outside Budapest (roughly 500,000) were concentrated in regional areas, from which they were rounded up by Hungarian paramilitary police and dispatched to hastily improvised ghettos located in towns. In some of these, Jews had to live outdoors without shelter or sanitary facilities; food and water was totally inadequate, and medical care nonexistent. They were forbidden to leave these ghettos and were watched over by police. None of these places existed for more than a few weeks, and many were closed within days.

In mid-May 1944, the Hungarians, together with the German SD under **Adolf Eichmann**'s control, began methodically to deport the Jews. The Hungarian paramilitary police rounded them up and forced them onto deportation trains. Within two months, nearly 440,000 Jews had been deported in 145 trains, mostly to Auschwitz. By the end of July 1944, the only major Jewish community left in Hungary was that in Budapest.

Because of the deteriorating military situation and threats of war crimes trials from Allied leaders, Horthy halted the deportations on July 7, 1944. In August, he dismissed the Sztójay government and resumed efforts to negotiate for an armistice with the Soviet Union, whose army was now close to invading. By the middle of October 1944, Horthy was finalizing negotiations with the Soviets when the Germans orchestrated a coup d'état that saw Horthy arrested. The antisemitic Szálasi was appointed prime minister.

Under Szálasi's regime, deportations of Jews resumed; attention was now directed to the previously untouched community in Budapest. Arrow Cross gangs produced a rule of random terror; the Jews were transferred to "yellow star" houses, making them defenseless to Arrow Cross gang members. Jews were marched to the banks of the Danube and shot into the river, while many others died from the brutal conditions of forced labor to which the Arrow Cross subjected them.

In November 1944, a ghetto was established for about 70,000 of Budapest's Jews. Assisting Eichmann, Szálasi ordered that about 25,000 Jewish men and 10,000 Jewish women be marched out of the city to build anti-Soviet fortifications. In addition, also beginning in November 1944, Szálasi ordered that a further 80,000 Jews be mobilized and marched toward the Austrian border on additional building projects. Many who were too weak to continue marching in the bitter cold were shot along the way.

In January 1945, with the Soviets already in Pest, Hungary signed an armistice. Buda was liberated on February 13, 1945, and Soviet troops pushed the last

German units and their Arrow Cross collaborators out of western Hungary by early April 1945.

Of the approximately 825,000 Jews living in Hungary in 1941, about 63,000 died or were killed before the German occupation of March 1944. Prior to and during the short six months of Szálasi's government, over 500,000 Jews died from maltreatment or were murdered. Some 255,000 Jews, less than one-third of those who had lived within enlarged Hungary in March 1944, survived the Holocaust.

Ferenc Szálasi fled Hungary but was captured and returned by American troops in May 1945. He was tried in a Hungarian court in Budapest, found guilty of war crimes and high treason, and was hanged on March 12, 1946.

T

TERBOVEN, JOSEF (1898–1945)

Josef Antonius Heinrich Terboven was the Nazi-imposed commissioner for Norway during the German occupation of that country during World War II.

Of Dutch descent, Terboven was born on May 23, 1898, in Essen, Germany. In World War I, serving in the German field artillery and the newly created air force, Terboven was awarded the Iron Cross and rose to the rank of lieutenant.

On February 13, 1919, Terboven started studying law and political science at the University of Munich before moving to Freiburg, where he became involved in extremist politics. Without completing his studies, he dropped out of university. In 1923, he joined the NSDAP, but after he and others took part in the Beer Hall Putsch in Munich on November 8 to 9, 1923, the party was outlawed.

Terboven then worked as a bank clerk in Essen between February 1, 1923, and June 30, 1925, when he was laid off. On August 4, 1925, he rejoined the NSDAP and worked full-time for the Nazi Party as a member of the SA, helping set up the party in Essen. From 1927 until December 15, 1930, Terboven edited a National Socialist newspaper in Essen, but he was imprisoned for three months in 1929 for publication of a proscribed newspaper. He stood unsuccessfully for election in May 1928 but was appointed gauleiter (Nazi district chief) in Essen in 1928.

On June 29, 1934, Terboven married Ilse Stahl, the former secretary and mistress of **Joseph Goebbels**. **Adolf Hitler** was the guest of honor at the wedding; the next morning, Hitler flew south to direct the massacre of the SA leadership (the Röhm Putsch, or Night of the Long Knives), the plans for which had been drawn up during the wedding celebrations.

Terboven was made senior president of the Rhein province in 1935 and gained a reputation as a petty and ruthless despot.

On April 24, 1940, prior to the completion of Germany's military invasion of Norway on June 7, Terboven was made *Reichskommissar* with supervisory authority over the civilian administration. He moved into the crown prince's residence at Skaugum in September 1940 and made the Norwegian Parliament's buildings his headquarters.

On September 17, 1941, Terboven decreed that SS and German police tribunals would be given authority over Norwegian citizens breaking the laws of the occupation authorities, and he introduced harsher and more repressive measures to combat sabotage and resistance. He arrested Norwegian teachers who had defied certain actions taken by the German High Command and used them to build fortifications. Terboven also established concentration camps in Norway, such as Falstad, near Levanger, and Bredtvet, in Oslo, in late 1941.

Day-to-day matters were initially administered by an acting Norwegian state cabinet, but the members of the governing commission were Terboven appointees working under his control. All proposed legislation had to be submitted to Terboven for approval. On February 1, 1942, a "national government" headed by Norwegian collaborator **Vidkun Quisling** was established, and Quisling was given the title of minister president. Effectively, however, he was given no real power. In September 1942, Quisling was informed that the final relationship between Germany and Norway could only be settled after the war.

Terboven's relations with the SS and police were good, and he gave them freedom to implement their policies and activities. Despite the small size of Norway's Jewish population (approximately 1,800 in total), Terboven and his administration persecuted them relentlessly. By 1944, some 770 had been deported, of which only 24 returned after the war. Other Jews numbering over 930 fled to sanctuary in Sweden. The main deportation action occurred on the night of November 25 to 26, 1942, when German police acting under Gestapo orders arrested Jewish women, children, and sick people, who were transported to Oslo Harbor and placed on the ship *Donau*, alongside of Jewish men from the Berg detention camp. These 532 Jews disembarked at Stettin and transferred to Auschwitz, arriving on December 1, 1942. On February 25, 1943, another 158 Jews interned at Bredtvet were deported aboard the *Gotenland*. A further 45 Jews left Oslo on the *Monte Rosa* on November 26, 1942. All were sent to Auschwitz. Earlier, in 1941 to 1942, 11 more Jews had been deported to concentration camps.

General Nikolaus von Falkenhorst, who commanded German military forces in Norway (sometimes as many as 400,000 men), attempted to reach an understanding with the Norwegian people; his troops were under his orders to treat Norwegians with courtesy. By contrast, Terboven commanded a force of 6,000, of which 800 were part of the secret police. From 1941, he focused on crushing the irregular military resistance against the Germans, declaring martial law in Trondheim in 1942, and ordering the destruction of the village of Telavåg in reprisal for a partisan attack on Nazi officers. The devastation that followed has been compared to similar events at Lidice in Czechoslovakia and Oradour-sur-Glane in France.

Terboven became renowned for ordering retaliatory measures in a variety of other actions, leading him to develop a fearsome reputation throughout Norway.

On May 22, 1943, Terboven arrested Norwegian Protestant bishops who came to put to him their concerns about his harsh conduct. In November 1943, he ordered the arrest of students at the University of Oslo; the men were transferred to a special camp in Germany, and the women were dismissed from the University, required to return home under house arrest and report regularly to the police. Terboven was disliked not only by Norwegians but also by many Germans. Joseph Goebbels's diary notes his annoyance at Terboven's "bullying tactics," as they turned the population against Germans. Notwithstanding, Terboven remained in ultimate charge of Norway until the end of the war in 1945. On December 18, 1944, von Falkenhorst was dismissed from his command for opposing certain of Terboven's policies.

In October 1944, as Soviet troops advanced into northern Norway, Terboven implemented a scorched-earth policy that resulted in widespread destruction, and 50,000 people forcibly evacuated and relocated.

As the tide of war turned against Germany, Terboven's personal aspiration was to organize a fortress Norway (*Festung Norwegen*) for the Nazi regime's last stand. When Hitler's successor, Admiral Karl Dönitz, ordered the political and military leaders of Norway to cooperate with Allied General Headquarters, Terboven demurred. As a result, on May 7, 1945, Dönitz dismissed Terboven from his post as *Reichskommissar*. A day later, with the announcement of Germany's surrender, Terboven committed suicide.

TESCH, BRUNO (1890–1946)

Bruno Emil Tesch (not to be confused with anti-Nazi resister Bruno Guido Camillo Tesch) was a German chemist and businessman who supplied Zyklon B gas to the Nazis used for murdering masses of Jews in death camps during World War II.

Tesch was born on August 14, 1890, in Berlin. He studied mathematics and physics for one semester in 1910 at the University of Göttingen, before completing his degree in chemistry at the University of Berlin in 1914. He then worked at the Kaiser Wilhelm Institute (KWI).

During World War I, Dr. Fritz Haber of KWI weaponized chlorine and other poisonous gases that were used during the Second Battle of Ypres. In 1919, Degesch (the *Deutsche Gesellschaft für Schädlingsbekämpfung mbH*) was established to explore the military use of hydrogen cyanide. Once developed, this was marketed as the pesticide Zyklon (cyclone), although it was banned after the war. In 1922, Degussa (*Deutsche Gold- und Silber-Scheideanstalt*, or German Gold and Silver Refinery) became sole owners of Degesch.

That year, chemists Walter Heerdt, Bruno Tesch, and Gerhard Peters, with the support of I. G. Farben (a German chemical and pharmaceutical conglomerate), researched the use of hydrogen cyanide as a fumigation agent. They invented and patented a process in which hydrogen cyanide could be manufactured and used in a solid form. Heerdt was named inventor of Zyklon B in the patent application, which was awarded to Dagesch, now a subsidiary of I. G. Farben, on December 27, 1926. The new product was labeled as Zyklon B to distinguish it from the earlier version. Heerdt was the only one of the inventors to receive patent rights. He set up the *Heerdt-Lingler GmbH* (Heli) of Frankfurt, to which Degesch gave the exclusive rights to distribute the insecticide Zyklon B west of the Elbe River.

Gerhard Peters joined Degesch and became its managing director during World War II. The company was designated by the German government to set the safety rules and standards for the use of Zyklon B, and it was given the authority to authorize shipments from the manufacturer to the customer after strict criteria were met.

In 1924, Tesch and Paul Stabenow, the sales representative for a Czech chemical company, cofounded Tesch & Stabenow (Testa), a pest-control company, in

Hamburg. Testa did not manufacture Zyklon B or any other chemicals. It was primarily a pest-control company specializing in the fumigation of commercial properties, such as warehouses and freighters in the Port of Hamburg.

In 1925, Testa received from Dagesch the exclusive rights to distribute Zyklon B east of the Elbe River. Stabenow left Testa in 1927, after which Tesch held a 45 percent share of the firm and Degesch held 55 percent, on the basis that Tesch would resume sole ownership in 1942. Karl Weinbacher, a German manager, worked at Degesch until 1924 and then at Testa, where he became manager in 1927 after Stabenow left. From 1928, Testa established itself as the largest distributor of Zyklon B.

In 1930, Degussa relinquished 42.5 percent ownership of Degesch to I. G. Farben and 15 percent to *Th. Goldschmidt AG* of Essen, in exchange for the right to market pesticide products of those two major companies through Degesch. Degussa retained managerial control of Degesch.

While Degesch owned the rights to the brand name Zyklon and the patent on the packaging system, the chemical formula was owned by Degussa. *Schlempe GmbH*, which was 52 percent owned by Degussa, owned the rights to a process to extract hydrogen cyanide from waste products of sugar-beet processing. This process was performed under license by two companies, *Dessauer Werke* and *Kaliwerke Kolin*, which also combined the resulting hydrogen cyanide with stabilizer from I. G. Farben and a cautionary agent from *Schering AG* to form the final product, which was packaged using equipment, labels, and canisters provided by Degesch.

The finished goods were sent to Degesch, who forwarded the product to two companies acting as distributors: Heli of Frankfurt and Testa of Hamburg. Their territory was split along the Elbe, with Heli handling clients to the west and south and Testa handling those to the east. Degesch owned 51 percent of the shares of Heli, and until 1942, it owned 55 percent of Testa. The company did not actually produce Zyklon B or other gases widely used for disinfection.

Testa oversaw shipping of the product and equipment to the SS and Wehrmacht, instructing the personnel about use on lice, the main carriers of typhus. When asked for advice on mass extermination of Jews by the Nazi state, Bruno Tesch suggested treating them like vermin by spraying prussic acid, the active ingredient in Zyklon B, into a sealed space. According to court testimony of his company's various employees, Tesch proceeded to share the know-how in a hands-on manner. By 1943, Karl Weinbacher, the company manager who received a percentage of the sales proceeds of Zyklon B, often acted as CEO with full authority on all business activities whenever Tesch was absent.

With the end of World War II, Weinbacher, Tesch, and Joachim Hans Drosihn, the firm's first gassing technician, were arrested on September 3, 1945. They were tried by a British military tribunal in Hamburg from March 1 to 8, 1946, also called the Testa Trial or the Zyklon B Trial.

Tesch, Weinbacher, and Drosihn were charged with having knowingly supplied the Zyklon B used in German concentration camps for the purpose of mass murder. Evidence was provided that 79,069 kilograms of Zyklon B were required in 1942 alone, 9,132 of which was slated specifically to kill humans at Sachsenhausen,

Neuengamme, and Auschwitz. In 1943, the demand rose to 12,174 kilograms, and by early 1944, nearly two tons arrived at Auschwitz monthly.

Tesch and Weinbacher were charged for knowingly selling poison gas to the SS, between January 1, 1941, and March 31, 1945, that would be used in violation of Article 46 of The Hague Convention of 1907. One witness for the prosecution was *SS-Rottenführer* **Pery Broad**, who had worked at Auschwitz.

Tesch and Weinbacher were convicted, condemned to death, and hanged on May 16, 1946, in Hameln Prison. Drosihn was acquitted, because he had no knowledge of corporate policy.

Dr. Gerhard Peters, director of Degesch, implicated himself during the I. G. Farben trial, saying that *SS-Obersturmführer* Kurt Gerstein, who was deeply involved in the gassing process, had told him that the German army needed Zyklon B without the additives whose smell warned people of its poisonous nature. In 1949, Peters was charged with murder, convicted, and sentenced to five years' imprisonment. In 1952, his conviction was confirmed on appeal and his sentence increased to six years. He was acquitted in a further appeal in 1953. He died on May 2, 1974. Walter Heerdt was reappointed as CEO of Degesch after the war and held this position until his death on February 2, 1957.

TEUDT, WILHELM (1860–1942)

On February 2, 1934, the Nazis in Germany, pursuing their ideal of a completely Jew-free society, began unveiling a new, Aryan version of the Bible. The first offering in this project was a rewritten Book of Psalms that eliminated all references to Jews, reworking the psalms in order to purge them of their "Jewish taint."

The updated version appeared in a hymnbook written by an eccentric author named Wilhelm Teudt. Born in 1860, Teudt, who studied theology and worked as a pastor from 1885 to 1908, was an amateur archaeologist who spent much of his time searching for an ancient Germanic civilization. In 1921, he joined the German National People's Party, and in 1933, at the age of 73, he moved on to the National Socialists, which, on January 30 that year, had come into office under **Adolf Hitler**.

Teudt's version had 75 psalms rather than the original 150. As an example of his efforts, his version of the 87th Psalm read as follows:

> The Lord loveth the height of Germany more than all the dwellings abroad.
>
> The Lord loveth the yew tree of the Odenwald and the oak of the Baltic.
>
> I will make mention of the vulgar Euphrates and the Ganges, where our forefathers ruled.
>
> Behold the lands of the Goths, the Longobards, and Andalusians: it shall be said our brothers were born and died there;
>
> But on Osning the Lord shall count those sprung from blood of the sons of Mannus: Ingo, Istu, and Ermin.

Osning is part of the Teutoberger Forest. Ingo, Istu, and Ermin were ancient Germanic gods.

The original states,

> His foundation is in the holy mountains.
>
> The Lord loveth the gates of Zion more than all the dwellings of Jacob.
>
> Glorious things are spoken of thee, O city of God. Selah.
>
> I will make mention of Rahab and Babylon to them that know me: behold Philistia, and Tyre, with Ethiopia; this man was born there.
>
> And of Zion it shall be said, This and that man was born in her: and the highest himself shall establish her.
>
> The Lord shall count, when he writeth up the people, that this man was born there. Selah.
>
> As well the singers as the players on instruments shall be there: all my springs are in thee.

Teudt maintained in his book's foreword that Jesus was of pure Aryan blood and that "His whole spirituality" was "foreign to Jews." He could not delete the whole of the Old Testament from Christian scripture, but he stated that many features of it were obnoxious and had to be pruned.

American readers knew of Teudt's removal of all references to Jews as he worked through the Old Testament. They read about it in the pages of their newspapers and discussed the issue in their churches. Of course, as with most things the Nazis began, Teudt's initiative did not stop there. Hitler's ultimate intention was gradually to "Nazify" the Church, beginning with the scriptural underpinnings upon which it rested. In 1939, he authorized the creation of what today would be called a think tank to rewrite the Bible completely; its charge was to remove all references to Jews and Judeo-Christian notions of compassion. Those appointed to work on this thoroughly Nazi version of the Bible had the brief of "cleansing" church texts "of all non-Aryan influences."

In addition to his work redrafting the psalms, Teudt's beliefs in German *völkisch* culture led him to develop theories that, even among his peers, were considered outlandish. Believing in an ancient, highly developed Germanic civilization, Teudt developed an interest in the 1920s in what he called "Germanic archaeology" through an investigation of Germanic pagan sacred sites. He held that he possessed a paranormal ability to pick up the vibrations of his Germanic ancestors, which provided him with the capacity to visualize ancient sites as he was excavating them.

His work studying ancient Saxon shrines attracted the interest of senior Nazis, who were obsessed with locating the spiritual elements of Aryanism. Developing an ever-deeper fascination with Saxon culture as the seedbed of all that Germanic culture would become, he viewed the conversion of the Germanic tribes to Christianity before the turn of the first millennium as the greatest catastrophe ever faced by Aryan civilization.

After Teudt joined the Nazi Party, Adolf Hitler appointed him to a professorial position. He founded or became a member of a number of esoteric research organizations, and his work garnered prizes and honors from the Nazis.

Wilhelm Teudt died on January 5, 1942, in Detmold, Lippe.

THIERACK, OTTO (1889–1946)

Otto Thierack was a Nazi jurist and politician who was the Reich minister of justice under **Adolf Hitler** between August 20, 1942, and April 30, 1945.

After Theirack assumed office on August 20, 1942, one of his first steps as justice minister was to direct the president of the People's Court that in criminal proceedings against the Jews, the decisive factor must always be their Jewishness rather than their culpability. Thierack not only made penal prosecution of all unpopular persons and groups harsher; he waived any pretense of legality and simply began handing "antisocial" prisoners (usually Jews, Poles, Russians, and Roma) over to the SS. Thierack came to an understanding with **Heinrich Himmler** that certain categories of prisoners were to be, to use their words, "annihilated through work." As Reich minister, Thierack ensured the reduction of clemency proceedings for those sentenced to death.

Otto Georg Thierack was born in Wurzen, Saxony, on April 19, 1889. His father was a merchant. In 1910, he commenced the study of law at the University of Marburg and received his doctorate in 1914 from the University of Leipzig. In World War I, he served as a volunteer in the German army, reaching the rank of lieutenant. He suffered a facial injury and was decorated with the Iron Cross Second Class.

After the war, he resumed his law studies, graduating in 1920 with his assessor (junior lawyer) examination. He then entered the judicial service of Saxony, and in 1921, he was appointed as a public prosecutor at the district court in Leipzig. In 1926, he became a prosecutor at the Supreme Court of Dresden.

In 1932, Thierack joined the Nazi Party and became the leader of the National Socialist Jurists' Organization (the *Rechtswahrerbund*), which led to his career as a leading Nazi judge. In 1933, after the Nazi assumption of power in Germany, he became the Saxon minister of justice. In 1935, he was appointed vice president of the Reich Court in Leipzig. At the same time, he represented the minister of justice in coordinating the integration of Nazi jurisdiction in the Reich.

On May 1, 1936, Thierack was appointed president of the People's Court (*Volksgerichtshof*), where he concentrated on tightening its jurisdiction. This court prosecuted people accused of crimes against the Third Reich in closed sessions and without the right of appeal. He held the position of president of the People's Court, interrupted by two periods in the German army in World War II, until 1942, when he was succeeded as president by **Roland Freisler**.

On April 23 to 24, 1941, Thierack was a participant in the meeting of judicial officers about the "destruction of life unworthy of life," in the context of *Aktion T-4* medical murders.

On September 9, 1942, now as justice minister, Thierack gave directions to the president of the People's Court that "in criminal proceedings against the Jews, the decisive factor is their Jewishness, rather than their culpability." The following month, he introduced monthly legal briefs that presented model rulings—decisions, with names left out—upon which German jurisprudence was to be based. He also introduced *Vorschauen* (previews) and *Nachschauen* (reviews), which required Presidents of the Higher State Courts to discuss with the Public

Prosecutor's Office and the state court president how a case was to be judged before the court's decision; the state court president then had to pass this on to the responsible criminal courts. This was to be done at least once every two weeks.

One year later, the Third Reich changed the laws again, this time removing Jews from the jurisdiction of the court altogether and leaving their fate in the hands of the police or the SS. This legalized the sending of "asocials" as well as certain foreign prisoners or forced laborers—Jews, Poles, Gypsies, Russians, and Ukrainians—directly to the SS and on to concentration camps in the East, where they would be "exterminated through work."

After Hitler's intervention, Thierack ordered that death sentences were to be enforced immediately. In the opinions of the trial court, the prosecutors, the attorney general, and other bodies, petitions for mercy were in principle no longer necessary.

In December 1942, at Thierack's instigation, the execution shed at Plötzensee Prison in Berlin was outfitted with eight iron hooks so that several people could be put to death at once by hanging (there had already been a guillotine there for some time). When a number of mass executions began on September 7, 1943, it also happened that some prisoners were hanged "by mistake." Thierack simply covered up these mistakes and demanded that the hangings continue. He was recognized to be ruthless in the furthering of his career, power hungry, and ambitious. His support staff described him as hardworking and resilient but also high handed and autocratic.

At the end of the war, Thierack was arrested by the Allies and imprisoned at the prisoner-of-war camp at Eselheide in 1945. He committed suicide in jail on November 22, 1946, before he could be put on trial at Nuremberg.

THOMALLA, RICHARD (1903–1945)

Richard Thomalla was an SS officer who headed the SS Central Building Administration at the Lublin reservation in occupied Poland. He was responsible for the construction of Bełżec, Sobibór, and Treblinka, all three of the *Aktion Reinhard* death camps.

Thomalla was born on October 23, 1903, in Sabine-bei-Annahof, Upper Silesia. A builder by trade, he was bilingual in German and Polish. He enlisted in the SS on July 1, 1932, and joined the Nazi Party a month later. His SS service took in Wohlau (Wołów) and Breslau (Wrocław) in Lower Silesia.

On September 6, 1940, Thomalla was transferred to the General Government, where he was a member of the *SS-Hilfspolizei* (auxiliary police) in Częstochowa and Radom. On August 22, 1940, he was transferred by **Friedrich-Wilhelm Krüger**, based in Kraków, to serve under *SS-Brigadeführer* **Odilo Globocnik**, in charge of police at Lublin. From August to October 1940, Thomalla was a section leader of the SS Border Defense Construction Service (SS-*Grenzschutz Baudienst*) in Bełżec, which stood on the line between the General Government and Soviet-occupied Galicia. Thomalla was tasked initially to build a construction depot in Zamość, about 40 kilometers north of Bełżec, for the Waffen-SS and police.

After Operation Barbarossa on June 22, 1941, Thomalla was also in charge of constructing SS bases (*SS-Stutzpunkte*) in Zwiahel (*Novohrád-Volýns'kyj*) and Kiev, in Ukraine. On November 1, 1941, construction began of the first *Aktion Reinhard* death camp, Bełżec, and Globocnik recalled Thomalla to Lublin in late 1941 (by some accounts, early 1942) to take over supervision of the project. Bełżec was completed in March 1942. At first, Polish workers were used, but these were later replaced by Jews from surrounding ghettos.

Thomalla then oversaw the construction of the other *Aktion Reinhard* camps at Sobibór and Treblinka and was the senior SS officer at each site until the respective camps became operational.

Thomalla proceeded to design and supervise the construction of Sobibór in March 1942, employing local inhabitants from the nearby towns and villages as construction workers. Special groups called *Sonderkommandos*, comprised of up to 80 Jews, were also taken from nearby ghettos to assist as slave labor. Thomalla served as commander of the Sobibór *Sonderkommando* during the construction phase, supervised by a Ukrainian guard unit trained at the concentration camp Trawniki. Upon the completion of Sobibór, the Jews of the *Sonderkommando* were killed. Thomalla's work over, he was replaced by a permanent commandant, **Franz Stangl**, in April 1942.

In late April to early May 1942, an SS team arrived in the Treblinka area and chose the site on which to build another of the *Aktion Reinhard* camps. The architecture was almost identical to that at Sobibór with some modifications, and building started around late May and early June 1942. Thomalla managed the construction, which was undertaken by the German construction firms Schönbronn of Leipzig and Schmidt-Münstermann of Warsaw. Thomalla remained at Treblinka for several weeks during construction, before **Irmfried Eberl** arrived as commandant.

In 1943, Thomalla ran the Waffen-SS construction offices in Riga and Mogilev. Then during 1943 to 1944, he took part in the SS subjugation *Aktion* in the Zamość district of Poland. He was last seen in Zamość in June 1944, a few weeks before the entry of the Red Army the following month.

Just before the end of the war, Thomalla was arrested by Soviet forces and imprisoned near the Czech city of Jičín (Titschein), northeast of Prague. He was killed there on May 12, 1945, apparently at the hands of Soviet security forces.

THOMAS, MAX (1891–1945)

Max Thomas was a German psychiatrist who served as an *SS-Gruppenführer* and police lieutenant general. He commanded *Einsatzgruppe C* in the occupied Soviet Union and later worked as the higher SS and police leader (*Höherer SS- und Polizeiführer*, or HSSPF) in the Black Sea area.

Max Thomas was born on August 4, 1891, in Düsseldorf. At the beginning of World War I, he volunteered for service in the German army, became an officer, and was awarded the Iron Cross First and Second Class. After the war, he studied law and medicine until 1922, going on to earn a doctorate in medicine before commencing practice as a specialist in psychiatry.

After the Nazi seizure of power in January 1933, Thomas joined the NSDAP on May 1, 1933, and in July, he became an officer in the SS. He then became councilor of the city of Fritzlar, Hesse, and took control of the management of a branch office of the SD. In 1939, as an *SS-Oberführer*, Thomas was appointed SiPo commander in a region of the Rhineland.

In 1940, Thomas moved to head Section IVB in charge of police intelligence within the RSHA—a subdepartment of which was IVB4, dealing with Jewish questions under the leadership of *SS-Obersturmbannführer* **Adolf Eichmann**.

On June 14, 1940, **Reinhard Heydrich**, head of the SD, dispatched Thomas to Paris to liaise with the military governor, General Otto von Stulpnagel, who loathed Thomas over the fact that he had sent 250 SD undercover operatives to Paris over his head. As military police, these men should have come under military control, not SD direction.

On July 27, 1940, Thomas was summoned back to RSHA headquarters in Berlin, where Heydrich had called together the heads of all the SD departments. They then traveled to Brussels to organize SD activities in Belgium. Thomas was given the twin tasks of establishing the SD in Brussels and serving as the higher representative of the SS for that city and Paris. Thus from June 1940 to the fall of 1941, he served as commander of the Security Police and the SD in Belgium and northern France.

In October 1940, a Special Command *SS-Reichsführer* **Heinrich Himmler** was set up under Thomas, who then transferred his headquarters to Paris. Otto von Stulpnagel, together with the senior SD and SiPo officer in Paris, Helmut Knochen, managed to have Thomas removed on the charge that he preferred Paris nightlife to setting up intelligence networks for the SS. Himmler was reported to have not been impressed with Thomas's attitude.

In October 1941, Thomas was promoted to *SS-Brigadeführer* and was transferred by Himmler to Kiev, Ukraine, where he succeeded *SS-Brigadeführer* **Otto Rasch** as the leader of *Einsatzgruppe C*, deployed near Army Group South in northern and central Ukraine. Nazi estimates recorded that *Einsatzgruppe C* had killed 26,000 people by the end of 1941, and with its alteration into a stationary unit in March 1942, Thomas, based in Kiev, took command of the liquidation of the Ukrainian Jewish ghettos. At least 300,000 Jews were killed in the *Aktion* that followed.

On November 9, 1942, Thomas was promoted to *SS-Gruppenführer*. He disagreed with *SS-Standartenführer* **Paul Blobel**, the leader of *Aktion 1005*, about the method of eradicating the mass graves as traces of the *Einsatzgruppen*.

Thomas, who was an active commander, had by now suffered a number of injuries while in the USSR, and he was discharged from leadership of *Einsatzgruppe C* on health grounds during the summer of 1943. In August 1943, he was appointed as HSSPF of the Black Sea operational area, but in December 1943, he was in a plane crash, and after a long period of hospitalization, he was assigned to a reserve unit in April 1944. Until November 1944, he had a desk assignment in the SS Personnel Office in Berlin.

Thomas disappeared at the end of the war but was located working as Dr. Karl Brandenburg in the town of Kleinostheim, Bavaria. On December 6, 1945, he attempted suicide and died at the Würzburg Luitpold Hospital. Because of this, he did not get to appear in the *Einsatzgruppen* trial at Nuremberg that took place between September 29, 1947, and April 10, 1948, and thus never stood trial for his crimes.

TISO, JOZEF (1887–1947)

Jozef Tiso was a Roman Catholic priest and Nazi collaborator who governed the satellite Slovak Republic from 1939 to 1945.

He was born on October 13, 1887, at Vel'ká Bytča, Slovakia (then Austria-Hungary). During his schooling, Tiso spoke Hungarian and studied several languages, including Hebrew and German. He was ordained a Roman Catholic priest in 1910 and worked to combat local poverty and alcoholism in his community. In 1915, he became director of the Theological Seminary of Nitra, while also teaching at a local high school.

After the breakup of the Austro-Hungarian Empire and the creation of Czechoslovakia, Tiso became a Slovak nationalist and career politician, with a political philosophy that was avidly pro-Slovak and antisemitic. In 1918, he helped found the Slovak People's Party (SPP), and in 1924, he became the dean and parish priest of the town of Bánovce nad Bebravou, a post he held until 1939. In 1924, the SPP became the largest political party in Slovakia, and Tiso represented it in the Czechoslovak Parliament in 1925. Between 1927 and 1928, he served as Czechoslovak minister of health.

Until 1938, Tiso's political career did not evince any overt demonstration of antisemitism, even as the SPP began to model itself on the Nazi Party and antisemitism became more acceptable. He was even accused by some right-wing radicals of being "soft" when it came to Jews.

With the death of SPP leader Andrej Hlinka in August 1938, Tiso took over as head of the party. It was in the interests of Germany to destroy the Czechoslovak state by assisting Slovakia to become independent, and in March 1939, with the encouragement of senior German diplomat **Edmund Veesenmayer**, Tiso sought to negotiate a treaty with Germany that would see the creation of an independent Slovakia. The Czechoslovak government deposed Tiso for promoting the breakup of the county, but he received **Adolf Hitler**'s support during a visit to Berlin on March 13, 1939; the following day, he proclaimed Slovak independence. The Germans occupied what remained of Czechoslovakia on March 15, 1939, and one day later, Tiso placed the new Slovak state under Germany's protection—primarily, it was clear, to avoid its annexation by Hungary.

Tiso was prime minister from March 14, 1939, until October 26, 1939, when he became president of an autonomous Slovakia, although he was forced to share power with the fascist paramilitary Hlinka Guard (*Hlinkova garda*). His government willingly collaborated with the Germans, allowing some tens of thousands of Slovakian Jews to be deported to German concentration camps. By expropriating Jewish property, Tiso showed support for Germany's policies as well as improved Slovakia's economic position.

In 1940, Germany first approached Slovakia with a demand to begin deporting Jews. Deportations started in March 1942, and at first, Tiso resisted pressure from the Vatican and Jewish groups to end them. They were stopped, however, despite German opposition, in October 1942, once Tiso learned that Germany not only used the Jews as forced laborers but had also begun systematically murdering them in camps. Public protests arose, as well as pressure from the Holy See, and Slovakia thus became the first state in the Nazi sphere to stop deportations of Jews. By that stage, though, some 58,000 Jews (75 percent of Slovak Jewry) had already been deported, mostly to Auschwitz, where only a minority survived.

On August 29, 1944, the Slovak Antifascist Uprising (supported by Edvard Beneš's Czechoslovak government in exile) was launched to oust Tiso and his government. Elements of the Slovak army began to desert, and German troops were sent to put down the uprising and occupy Slovakia.

With the troops came security police charged with rounding up Slovakia's remaining Jews. Despite losing domestic support, Tiso remained in office, but his presidency was relegated to a mostly titular role as Slovakia lost whatever de facto independence it had. Tiso now gave heartier support to the deportations, since he saw Jews as the leaders of the revolt. The deportation process was accelerated. Between October 1944 and the end of the war, 13,500 more Slovak Jews were deported, and 5,000 Jews were imprisoned. Some were murdered in Slovakia itself, in particular at Kremnička and Nemecká. By the end of the Holocaust, the Jewish population in Slovakia had collapsed to 24,000, from a population of 136,737 in 1930.

Tiso's government fell to the Red Army and Czech partisans in April 1945, when the Soviet Army conquered the last parts of western Slovakia. Tiso fled to Austria but was apprehended by U.S. authorities and extradited to Czechoslovakia, where he was tried and convicted of treason and war crimes. He was executed by hanging in Bratislava on April 18, 1947.

TURNER, HARALD (1891–1947)

Harald Turner was an SS commander in the German military administration of Serbia during World War II.

He was born on October 8, 1891, in Leun, Hesse, into a family where his father, William W. Turner, was a lieutenant in the German army. Turner Sr. was born in London in 1861 but later joined the Prussian army and served with District Command in Worms. His great-grandfather was probably a German-born cavalry officer who fought against Napoleon in Spain and at the Battle of Belle Alliance on June 18, 1815, in the aftermath of Waterloo.

From 1901, Harald Turner was a cadet at *Schloss Orienstadt*, sited at Diez on the Lahn. He attended a Prussian officer school from April 1906 to January 31, 1908, and entered the Prussian army on March 19, 1908, serving in the Lorraine Infantry Regiment No. 131. Shortly after, he attended Potsdam War School from October 1908 to July 1909, and on August 19, 1909, he became a lieutenant of the Second Company of his regiment.

In 1916, Turner married his fiancée, Adelheid "Heidi" Bechtel; their daughter, Irmingard, was born in 1917, and a son, Harald, was born in 1918. Turner served as a police officer in occupied Vilna (Vilnius) from December 1915 to July 1916 and reached the rank of captain on July 15, 1918. From December 13, 1918, to May 11, 1919, he acted as adjutant to the commander of the Wesel fortress.

Turner became a member of the *Freikorps Wesel* in Münster between June 1919 and March 1920 and was leader of the Beckum Rescue Service from October 1, 1919, to March 1, 1920. He commanded the staff quarters until April 1, 1920. That same month, he was taken into the Provisional National Army and served at Wesel in various administrative capacities from April 1, 1920, to May 1, 1922. Turner served at the Kreuznach Office between August 1, 1923, and April 1, 1924, and for the Trier Government Council from February 1926 onward. From April 1927 to February 1930, he studied law (obtaining his doctorate) prior to joining the SS on April 13, 1932. In January 1933, he became a leader of the *SS-Sturmbann II/5*.

Turner served as a higher-service government official in the supply office at Trier from February 12, 1933. Then he moved into a new role as the president of the government in Koblenz, where he remained from May 3, 1933, until January 17, 1936. He then became director and head of the personnel and salary department in the Prussian Ministry of Finance from February 1, 1936, a position he retained until May 1945.

On February 1, 1937, Turner became a major in the army reserve and a member of the Prussian State Council, where he served from 1938 until May 1945. He was promoted to *SS-Brigadeführer* on January 30, 1939. In June 1940, after seeing action in the Western campaign as head of the German military administration, he was sent to Paris as a key military administrator, serving there until February 1941.

Turner was appointed chief of staff of the German Military Administration in Serbia in April 1941, was promoted to lieutenant general in September 1941, and remained as chief of staff until 1943. On September 27, 1941, he became an SS group leader; his deputy was Georg Kiessel. In mid-August 1941, Turner suggested that all Jews be deported down the Danube to Romania or the *Generalgouvernement*, and although this was rejected, Turner pursued the matter further. **Adolf Eichmann**, operating through **Franz Rademacher**, eventually sent a reply saying that Jews could not be taken to Russia or the *Generalgouvernement*, since those places could not even take the Jews from Germany. Eichmann's proposed solution was that Turner work on killing them by shooting.

Soon after Turner received this response, massacres of Jews and Roma began. In an order dated October 26, 1941, Turner wrote that Jews and Roma represented a threat to public order and security, the more so as the Jewish intelligentsia had caused this war and had to be destroyed. On October 2, 1941, Yugoslav resisters killed 21 soldiers from a German communications unit in Topola. The military commander, Franz Böhme, then ordered Turner to kill 100 prisoners for every dead German, and Turner thereupon chose 2,100 Jews and communists from the concentration camps at Šabac and Belgrade.

Böhme and Turner were also responsible for the massacres in Kraljevo and Kragujevac the same month, when thousands of Jews were shot.

In March 1942, a gas van was delivered to Belgrade at the request either of Turner or Emanuel Schäfer, the chief of security forces in Belgrade. On April 11, 1942, Turner reported to **Karl Wolff**, of Himmler's personal staff, about the killings carried out with the aid of a "delousing car" (i.e., a gas van), stating that he would be using this van to kill Jews. Within two months, the SS had killed some 8,000 Jewish women and children from the Sajmište concentration camp in this van. On August 29, 1942, Turner bragged in a lecture given to the military commander of Southeast Europe that "Serbia is the only country where the Jewish question and the Gypsy question has been resolved."

In a 1942 letter to Wolff, Turner described the murderous nature of SS activities in the occupied territory, indirectly indicating that he intended to use vehicles most likely equipped with gas to murder Jews.

In early 1944, Turner was appointed deputy chief of the SS Race and Settlement Headquarters in Berlin. On February 18, 1944, he was confirmed in his position as an SS lieutenant general, with effect from January 30, 1944. However, in August 1944, at the SS school for junior military officers in Bad Tolz, he suggested that the SS should replace the NSDAP in command of the Reich. Because of this criticism of the NSDAP, he was relieved of his post and sent to fight at the front.

In 1945, Turner was imprisoned in a British prisoner-of-war camp. He was handed over to the government of Yugoslavia in 1945. He was tried in Belgrade for atrocities, massacres, and deportations. He was sentenced to death and shot in Belgrade on March 9, 1947.

U

ÜBELHÖR, FRIEDRICH (1893–1950?)

Friedrich Übelhör was a German politician, a Nazi Party official, and the Kalisz regional governor who ordered the construction of the Łódź ghetto on December 10, 1939.

He was born on September 25, 1893, in Rothenburg ob der Tauber, Bavaria. His father was a professor at the University of Würzburg. Übelhör graduated from high school in Würzburg in 1913 and joined an artillery regiment in 1914. He then served in World War I for four years, fought on the Western Front, served Army High Command, and received various war awards. He ended the war as a first lieutenant.

After the war, Übelhör served in the *Freikorps* of Paul von Lettow-Vorbeck and took part in the suppression of the Spartakus Uprising in Hamburg on July 19, 1919. He studied law and political science in Freiburg and Würzburg for five semesters but dropped out and did not complete his degree. He joined the Nazi Party in 1922, but the party was banned after **Adolf Hitler**'s failed coup attempt during November 8 to 9, 1923.

In 1924, Übelhör moved to Naumburg, and on April 4, 1925, he married Asta Popperoth, the daughter of the former higher regional court vice president Ludwig Popperoth. On June 30, 1925, he rejoined the NSDAP and became politically involved in the *Ortsgruppe Naumburg*, reorganizing the regional party structure. In 1931, he became Nazi Party county leader in Naumburg and was elected to the Reichstag on March 5, 1933. On January 25, 1934, *SS-Oberstumführer* Übelhör replaced Karl Roloff as mayor.

Poland was invaded in September 1939, and Łódź was occupied by the Germans on September 8, 1939. The inclusion of Łódź into the Reich brought with it new anti-Jewish legislation. On October 26, 1939, Übelhör was appointed as the provisional governor of Kalisch, in occupied Poland, with the rank of *SS-Obersturmbannführer*. On November 9, 1939, Łódź fell under the authority of Gauleiter **Arthur Greiser**, who sought the rapid and total Germanization of the areas under his command.

It took little time for the Jews of Łódź to be subjected to rigorous legal orders and bans. On November 14, 1939, Übelhör announced additional restrictive measures: Jews were to wear a distinguishing Jewish yellow patch on their clothing, and a curfew was introduced for Jews between the hours of 5:00 p.m. and 8:00 a.m. Übelhör's order to mark the Jews of Łódź was the first of its kind enacted in the Third Reich and had no previous basis in Nazi legislation. Unlike Übelhör's, **Reinhard Heydrich**'s later decree relating to the identification of Jews, published on October 1, 1941, did not apply to children under the age of six, and violations were not punished by death but with a fine or arrest. Übelhör's decree thus went beyond that of Heydrich, his superior.

The Jewish community had their businesses taken away. They were imprisoned in their own apartments, and, prevented from supporting themselves, they were left without any means to survive. Many Jews were shot, and many others froze to death. According to Nazi estimates, more than 71,000 Jews either left or were deported from Łódź during the first few months of the occupation.

On December 10, 1939, Übelhör produced a report on the feasibility of establishing a ghetto in Łódź. Estimating that there were some 320,000 Jews in the greater Łódź region, he reported that he would be able to collect them all into an enclosed ghetto. His report set out the boundaries of the ghetto and noted that preparation and execution of the plan would be carried out largely by German officers from different policing agencies. The ghetto would be enclosed in barbed wire and its borders guarded. A Jewish administration would be set up. Food and fuel for the ghetto was to be paid for by an exchange of materials, such as textiles, in order to obtain from the Jews "all their hoarded and hidden items of value." Übelhör thereupon ordered the construction of the ghetto; he was instrumental in the destruction of the Jewish population.

In early October 1941, Übelhör protested Heydrich's intention to deport 60,000 German Jews into the already overcrowded ghetto. In response, Heydrich threatened to draw "appropriate conclusions" if Übelhör did not take these Jews. By way of negotiations with **Adolf Eichmann**, it was agreed that only 20,000 Jews and 5,000 Roma would be sent to Łódź, with tens of thousands sent to other ghettos. In November 1941, to overcome Übelhör's concerns about ghetto arson started by Roma, Himmler advised Übelhör to shoot 10 Roma for every fire that broke out within the ghetto. Those who did not perish in the Łódź ghetto were killed by gas vans in January 1942 in Chełmno.

Übelhör was dismissed from his post as governor of Łódź in December 1942, after being accused of embezzlement by **Arthur Greiser**. The charges were ultimately unproven, but the suspicion damaged Übelhör's reputation and halted his advancement in the SS.

In October 1943, Übelhör fell into further disfavor when large quantities of textiles intended to produce winter clothing for soldiers fighting on the Eastern Front were found to have been sold at inflated prices. He was dismissed from office as president of the government of Merseburg on February 1, 1944; he would only return in January 1944, in the lesser role of governor of the Merseburg district.

Übelhör disappeared in the latter days of World War II and remained unaccounted for. He was declared legally dead in 1950.

V

VEESENMAYER, EDMUND (1904–1977)

Edmund Veesenmayer was a German diplomat and senior SS officer who facilitated the Holocaust in Hungary, Slovakia, and Croatia. A subordinate of **Ernst Kaltenbrunner** and **Joachim von Ribbentrop** and collaborator with **Adolf Eichmann**, he was responsible for a massive proportion of those murdered after the Holocaust hit Hungary in 1944.

He was born on November 12, 1904, in Bad Kissingen, Bavaria, the son of schoolteacher Franz Veesenmayer. From 1923 to 1926, he studied political science and obtained his doctorate from the University of Munich in 1928. Veesenmayer then lectured at the Munich Technical College and the Berlin School of Economics for four years.

Veesenmayer joined the Nazi Party in 1932 and the SS in 1934, making many friends and becoming an influential member of the party. By 1934, he had obtained a position in **Adolf Hitler**'s economic affairs office in Berlin. In the wake of the failed Nazi putsch in Austria in July 1934, Veesenmayer's first external role was to make clandestine arrangements for one of Hitler's long-held ambitions, the *Anschluss* with Germany. He was tasked with aligning the various factions of the outlawed Austrian Nazi Party with the party in Berlin, forcing the resignation of Chancellor Kurt Schuschnigg, and setting up key economic ties between Austria and Germany. For his efforts, on March 13, 1938, Veesenmayer was promoted by *SS-Reichsführer* **Heinrich Himmler** to *SS-Obersturmbannführer*. His next role was to tear Czechoslovakia asunder by assisting the Slovakian People's Party, led by **Jozef Tiso**, enter a treaty with Germany in March 1939, confirming Slovakia's subservience.

In early 1941, Veesenmayer was transferred to the German diplomatic staff in Zagreb, Croatia, to serve in the Balkans and support the creation of an independent Croatian state. There, he encouraged the deportation and murder of Croatian and Serbian Jews.

On March 19, 1944, Veesenmayer moved on to the German Embassy in Budapest. He worked very hard at furthering the Final Solution in conjunction with Eichmann and provided diplomatic cover for Eichmann's *Einsatzgruppen*.

Although Veesenmayer formally reported to Ribbentrop at the Foreign Office, he kept Ernst Kaltenbrunner at the RSHA fully apprised of the progress of securing the cooperation of the Hungarian authorities with German police in implementing the liquidation of Hungarian Jewry. Veesenmayer had to set aside his plans for greater Hungarian autonomy in conjunction with Regent Miklós Horthy and to submit to the harsh demands of the SS to expedite the deportation of Hungary's Jews.

A senior SS officer and diplomat, Edmund Veesenmayer was a leading facilitator of the Holocaust in Hungary, Slovakia, and Croatia. He organized the transfer by train of Jews from rural areas of Hungary to Auschwitz, resulting in the murder of well over 300,000 people. As such, Veesenmayer was directly responsible for the death of a huge proportion of Hungarian Jewry. In 1949 he was found guilty of war crimes and given a 20-year sentence, which was commuted to 10 years. After his release from prison, he lived in Darmstadt, where he died from heart failure on December 24, 1977, at the age of 73. (Chronos Media GmbH/ullstein bild via Getty Images)

Kaltenbrunner left Hungary on March 26, 1944, after securing the appointment of three Hungarians that augured no good for Jewry. Two men who had been active in the Arrow Cross (*Nyilas*) movement, László Baky and László Endre, were to run a Jewish Commissariat in the Ministry of the Interior, while another Arrow Cross man, Lieutenant Colonel László Ferenczy, was to convey orders to the Hungarian gendarmerie from Eichmann's SS.

On April 7, 1944, the first orders were issued for rounding up Jews in the least Hungarian areas. Roundups took place on April 15 to 16, 1944, at Ungvár (Uzhhorod) and Munkács (Mukachevo) in Ruthenia and at Nagykanisza near the Croatian border. On April 15, 1944, Veesenmayer expected only 5,000 Jews to be produced for deportation every three or four days, but two days later, expectations were raised to a total of 50,000 Jews to be exported for labor in the Reich during both April and May 1944.

In a telegram dated June 13, 1944, Veesenmayer reported to the Foreign Office that a total of 289,357 Jews in 92 trains of 45 cars had been transported from the Carpathian Mountains and Transylvania. On June 15, 1944, Veesenmayer cabled

Ribbentrop that some 340,000 Jews had so far been delivered to the Reich. He also announced that after final settlement of the Jewish question, the number of deported Hungarian Jews was expected to be around 900,000.

The Hungarian government under Döme Sztójay still expected to keep a labor force of 100,000 to 150,000 Jews in Hungary, but Baky, Endre, and Ferenczy, taking their orders from Eichmann, kept the Jews in such dreadful accommodations that they became an impossible burden to the civil administration—the classic method invented by Heydrich and expertly copied by Eichmann.

In 1949, in the Ministries Trial, Veesenmayer was found guilty of war crimes (crimes against humanity, slavery, and membership in a criminal organization) and was given a 20-year prison sentence. In 1951, the sentence was reduced to 10 years. He was released on December 16, 1951, due to the intercession of U.S. High Commissioner in Germany John J. McCloy. After his release, Veesenmayer worked in Iran between 1952 and 1955 as a representative for Toepfer, a manufacturer of agricultural machinery. He later lived in Darmstadt, where he died from heart failure on December 24, 1977, aged 73.

VOLKENRATH, ELISABETH (1919–1945)

Elisabeth Volkenrath was a German guard who trained at Ravensbrück concentration camp and, in 1943, became a supervisor (*Aufseherin*) at Auschwitz during World War II.

She was born Elisabeth Mühlau on September 5, 1919, in Schönau an der Katzbach, Silesia. Her father was a forest worker, and she had five siblings. After completing elementary school, Mühlau worked from 1933 to May 1938 as a nanny and kitchen hand. She became a hairdresser by trade, and in 1939, she was called up to work in a munitions factory. In October 1941, she joined the SS and began serving in concentration camps. Initially, she trained at Ravensbrück concentration camp, a major training center for women SS guards, under **Dorothea Binz**.

In August 1941, Mühlau was selected to work in Auschwitz-Birkenau, where she met her husband-to-be, Heinz Volkenrath. He, in turn, had worked at Auschwitz since 1941, as an *SS-Blockführer*. In March 1942, Mühlau volunteered for service at the Auschwitz main camp (*Stammlager*), where she served as a guard in the tailor shop. From there, she was transferred to the Auschwitz women's camp in August 1942, where she soon contracted typhus and was admitted to hospital. Upon release, she took over the parcel post in Birkenau from the end of December 1942, overseeing about 25 to 30 inmates. In this role, she supervised the incoming parcels, ensuring that they were searched by the Red Cross or inmate members prior to distribution to the corresponding inmates.

On August 15, 1942, she and Heinz Volkenrath became engaged, and in 1943, they were married. It was during this year that while serving as a senior concentration camp guard, Elisabeth Volkenrath took part in selections and the physical abuse of prisoners. In addition to her role of controlling the distribution of parcels to prisoners, she was also responsible for bread distribution in the warehouse. Elisabeth Volkenrath carried out these functions in the camp until September 1944.

After September 1944, she was transferred back to the main camp at Auschwitz, where she became an SS leader in the women's camp. In November 1944, she was promoted to be superintendent of the women's camp at Auschwitz. In this supervisory role, she oversaw three hangings, while ordering an increasing number of executions.

Promoted to senior concentration camp supervisor in November 1944, Volkenrath remained at Auschwitz until the final evacuation of the camp complex on January 18, 1945, when she was moved to Bergen-Belsen. She arrived at Belsen on February 5, 1945, only to fall ill. She resumed work some six weeks later, on March 22, 1945.

On April 15, 1945, Bergen-Belsen was liberated by British troops, who found more than 10,000 dead and about 60,000 survivors. Two days later, on April 17, 1945, Volkenrath was arrested. Along with the other guards, she was forced to take part in the mass burials of the corpses of the murdered inmates. Once the burials were completed, she was imprisoned with the other guards in the nearby town of Celle. Volkenrath stood trial with fellow guards **Irma Grese** and **Juana Bormann** in the Bergen-Belsen Trial, a British military tribunal for war crimes, which held hearings at Lüneburg, Germany.

During pretrial interviews and subsequent testimony, Volkenrath admitted to her supervisory positions in the camps but denied selecting prisoners for the gas chambers or beating prisoners. She did, however, admit to slapping the faces of women regularly in order to maintain discipline. Survivors of the camps, on the other hand, described her as the most hated woman in the camp.

On November 17, 1945, Volkenrath was found guilty of war crimes at both Auschwitz-Birkenau and Bergen-Belsen. She was convicted of committing numerous murders and making selections of prisoners for the gas chamber. She was sentenced to death, and on the morning of December 13, 1945, aged 26, she was executed at Hameln Prison.

W

WÄCHTER, OTTO VON (1901–1949)

Otto von Wächter was an Austrian lawyer, a Nazi politician, and a high-ranking member of the SS.

Baron Otto Gustav von Wächter was born on July 8, 1901, in northern Bohemia, the only son of General Josef von Wächter, a former Austrian army minister, and his wife Martha. His father served in the Austro-Hungarian army in World War I and received an award that gave him the title *Freiherr* (baron).

Between 1908 and 1913, Wächter lived in Trieste, Italy, where he attended primary school. During World War I, the family lived in Budějovice (Budweis), southern Bohemia, then a German-speaking district. Wächter graduated high school in 1919.

Skilled in swimming, climbing, and skiing, Wächter twice won Austrian rowing championships between 1919 and 1922. He completed his legal studies at the University of Vienna and received his doctorate in law in 1924.

From 1919 to 1922, Wächter was a member of an Austrian *Freikorps*. On April 1, 1923, aged 21, he took out membership in the then-banned Austrian Nazi Party. In October 1923, he also joined the German Nazi Party, but by 1925, he had dropped out due to internal party conflicts; he rejoined in October 1930. From 1931, Wächter served as a district office leader (*Gauamtsleiter*) in Vienna and chief trainer of the party in Austria. He enrolled in the SS on January 1, 1932.

Wächter was a leader of the failed Austrian putsch of July 25, 1934, which led to the murder of Chancellor Engelbert Dollfuss. He then fled to Germany, which cost him his Austrian citizenship in 1935, but he obtained German citizenship soon after. In 1937, Wächter started working in the relief organization of exiled Austrian Nazis in Berlin.

Following the *Anschluss* of March 1938, Wächter served under the Nazi governor of Austria, **Arthur Seyss-Inquart**, from May 24, 1938, to April 30, 1939. He headed the Wächter Commission, which was responsible for the dismissal and/or compulsory retirement of all Austrian officials who did not conform with the Nazi regime, as well as all Jewish officials in Austria.

Following the conquest of Poland in September 1939, the Nazis established the General Government in the central region of the country, which was administered by **Hans Frank**. Shortly after, **Adolf Hitler** appointed Wächter as governor of Kraków. On November 6, 1939, the local Gestapo chief, *SS-Obersturmbannführer* Bruno Müller, called a meeting of all staff and faculty of the Jagiellonian University to lecture them about German plans for Polish education. The entire faculty attended, and all were subsequently deported to Sachsenhausen concentration camp in what was called the *Sonderaktion Krakau* (Special Action Kraków). This was part of the Nazi plan to eliminate the Polish intellectual elite in the centers that were to become culturally German.

Wächter was also head of the Commission for Refugee Issues in Kraków. In this role, he ordered that by December 1, 1939, all Jews over 12 years old in the district of Kraków must put a distinguishing mark on their homes or would suffer severe punishment if they failed to do so. Further, also in December, he prohibited Jewish children from attending school in all public, private, and "Jewish schools." At the same time, he discussed with Hans Frank and **Friedrich-Wilhelm Krüger** what measures could be taken to compel Poles to do forced labor.

In December 1940, a decree for the expulsion of the city's 68,000 Jews appeared under Wächter's signature, as did a further decree issued on March 3, 1941, ordering the remaining 15,000 Jews to move into the newly created Kraków ghetto. At a government meeting on October 20, 1941, Wächter would say that a "radical solution to the Jewish issue is inevitable."

As governor of Kraków, Wächter was under the direct supervision of Hans Frank. Frustrated with the limitations of his role, Wächter was about to resign when he received a new posting in Galicia. The post of governor of Kraków was taken over by Richard Wendler, brother-in-law of *SS-Reichsführer* **Heinrich Himmler**.

After Operation Barbarossa on June 22, 1941, the eastern part of the former Austrian province of Galicia was attached to the General Government as the District of Galicia. On January 21, 1942, Wächter was appointed by Hitler as governor, based in the city of Lvov (Lviv).

Wächter showed himself to be an advocate of Frank's harsh attitude toward the Final Solution of the Jewish Question. In August 15, 1942, he obeyed an order to liquidate the ghetto and personally oversaw the transportation of 4,000 Jews to extermination camps.

In late 1942, Wächter visited the operational area known as *Reichskommissariat Ukraine*. There, he drew the conclusion that the best way to effectuate the Final Solution was through gassing.

While governor of Galicia, Wächter established a new Waffen-SS division under German supervision of people recruited from the local Ukrainian population. Its task was to fight against Soviet communists (which, by definition, included Jews as carriers of "Judeo-Bolshevik" ideas). After the disastrous German defeat at Stalingrad at the start of 1943, Wächter submitted the proposal to Himmler on March 1, 1943; by April 28, 1943, the SS Division Galicia was commissioned.

The loss of Galicia on July 26, 1944, to the advancing Red Army saw Wächter petition Himmler for transfer to the Waffen-SS. Himmler gave Wächter a new commission as head of "the Military Administration to the Plenipotentiary General of the German Wehrmacht in Italy," headed by *SS-Obergruppenführer* **Karl Wolff**. Wächter relocated to Gardone on the Lake Garda. In August 1944, Himmler gave Wächter the added responsibility of lieutenant general of the police. In the final stages of the war, he still headed the Eastern Affairs unit in the Reich Security Main Office.

Wächter remained with the First Division of the Ukrainian National Army until May 10, 1945, when he left to avoid being captured by the Soviets. He then successfully faked his death in Rome by drowning. He adopted a false identity as Alfredo Reinhardt and fled to Rome, where he hid for four years under the protection of Bishop **Alois Hudal**. In the spring of 1949, he crossed into South Tyrol in Italy, and in June, he began looking at options for moving to Brazil. On July 3, 1949, however, he contracted severe jaundice and died on July 14, 1949.

The dual German administration in the General Government meant that Wächter's role in Kraków was possibly not as extensive as that of others in occupied Poland. Moreover, notwithstanding his key role, little documentation exists about him in the Austrian State Archives or in Berlin Document Center. Famed Nazi hunter Simon Wiesenthal, who tried to hunt down Wächter after the war, considered him "the most hated among all Nazi fugitives," even though he managed to compile only a single folder on Wächter from his own exhaustive research. That folder is today part of the Simon Wiesenthal Archive, in Vienna.

WAGNER, GUSTAV (1911–1980)

Gustav Wagner, an Austrian staff sergeant in the SS and a deputy commander of the Sobibór extermination camp in German-occupied Poland, was known as the "Beast" and the "Wolf," because of his brutality to camp prisoners.

Born on July 18, 1911, in Vienna, Gustav Franz Wagner joined the Austrian Nazi Party in 1931. In 1934, he was arrested for painting swastikas and putting up Nazi posters, which was prohibited. To help him escape further arrest, the Nazi Party smuggled him over the border into Germany, where he worked with a local SA detachment, returning after the *Anschluss* with Austria in 1938.

From May 1940, he served in the *Aktion T-4* institution of Schloss Hartheim near Linz under the command of **Franz Stangl**, implementing the Nazi program of killing or sterilizing people with physical and mental disabilities. Because of Wagner's experiences at Hartheim, in March 1942, he was transferred to Sobibór in Poland, where he again worked with Stangl. After the camp was completed, Wagner was appointed deputy commandant and was responsible for the selection of prisoners.

Sobibór was a murder complex, where over a period of 15 months, 250,000 men, women, and children stepped off the train in the morning and were gassed by lunchtime. Their corpses were burned before dawn the next day. By then, their luggage had been sorted and packed for shipment to Germany. The victims were gassed by carbon monoxide.

Wagner's role was crucial. His initial job was to construct the factory—to build the structures and the wire fences (which were later electrified), make the antiescape trenches, place the minefields, build the gas chambers, and manage laying a small rail siding so that the trains could pull off the main line and discharge their cargoes.

He had responsibility for the daily interactions with prisoners and supervision of Sobibór's daily routine. During his visit to Sobibór on February 12, 1943, **Heinrich Himmler** promoted him to *SS-Oberscharführer*.

Wagner was remembered as one of the most brutal SS officers at the camp. Survivors have described him as a cold-blooded sadist. He regularly thrashed camp

Gustav Wagner was the deputy commander of the Sobibór extermination camp. He was remembered by prisoners as one of the most brutal of SS officers, with his violence earning him the nicknames "The Beast" and "The Wolf." He also spent time at the death camp of Treblinka, having learned much of his trade as a guard under the tutelage of Franz Stangl. Austrian Roman Catholic bishop Alois Hudal, a Nazi sympathizer at the Vatican, helped Wagner and Stangl escape Europe at the end of the war through a "ratline" and reach Syria using a Red Cross passport. Wagner was found dead with a knife in his chest on October 3, 1980, in São Paulo, Brazil. (Keystone Pictures USA/ZUMAPRESS.com)

inmates and killed Jews at whim without restraint. He rarely shot his victims but tortured them, using an ax, shovel, whip, or even his bare hands. He did not require any reason for doing so. Even other German SS guards in the camp were afraid of him.

In the spring of 1943, after two Jews escaped from Sobibór, Wagner took charge of securing the camp, and with a squad of Wehrmacht soldiers, he laid minefields around the perimeter to deter further escapes. This was ineffective. When a fully fledged revolt took place at Sobibór on October 14, 1943, Wagner was in Lublin, and the prisoners believed that his absence would improve their chances of success. After this, Wagner was ordered to assist in closing the camp. He was transferred to Treblinka and eventually to northern Italy, to the concentration camp of San Sabba. He then also fought in Yugoslavia against the partisans.

In 1945, after this last assignment, Wagner escaped the Allied advance. He was sentenced to death in absentia at Nuremberg. In late 1947, Wagner and Stangl were both held by the Austrians in connection with their involvement in the *Aktion T-4* program at Hartheim, but on May 30, 1948, they both escaped and disappeared. With the help of former colleagues, they crossed the border to South Tyrol and asked the Catholic agencies there to contact Rome.

Austrian Roman Catholic Bishop **Alois Hudal**, a Nazi sympathizer in the Vatican, helped Wagner and Stangl both escape through a ratline and to reach Syria using a Red Cross passport. On August 25, 1948, Wagner and Stangl both applied for a Red Cross travel document to migrate to Argentina, filling in the forms truthfully and using their real names. They gave their nationality as Austrian, saying that they had lost their nationality for political reasons, which made them stateless and entitled to assistance.

After three years in Syria, they both fled to Brazil, again with Bishop Hudal's help. Wagner was admitted as a permanent resident in 1950 and assumed the name of Günther Mendel.

After the Sobibór trial in West Germany in 1966, the West German searchers knew that Wagner was staying near his former boss, Stangl. It took until February 28, 1967, before Stangl was tracked down by Nazi hunter Simon Weisenthal, arrested, and extradited to West Germany. Weisenthal learned from evidence in Stangl's trial in Düsseldorf that Wagner had been hiding in Brazil since 1950 and asked the Brazilian police to locate Wagner, but they failed to do so.

Wiesenthal, together with a Brazilian journalist, eventually tracked down Wagner by posting in the paper a photograph of Germans in Brazil celebrating Hitler's 90th birthday and identifying one of the persons as Gustav Franz Wagner. It was not Wagner; but Wagner turned himself in to the Brazilian police because he feared that he would, like **Adolf Eichmann**, be kidnapped by the Mossad and sentenced to death in Israel or even be killed immediately by Israeli agents. He sought to hide his role in the death camps, but on May 31, 1978, when a Sobibór ex-prisoner, Stanislaw Szmajzner, saw the story on television about Wagner's arrest, he traveled to São Paulo and identified Wagner. There was now no doubt about Wagner's identity, and the Brazilian Ministry of Justice took him into custody.

On July 5, 1978, the Brazilian Supreme Court received the official request from West Germany for Wagner's extradition. After a series of court hearings involving the West German and Brazilian governments—and requests filed from Austria, Israel, and Poland that Wagner be extradited—the Brazilian attorney general rejected all attempts to bring Wagner to justice in Europe. As a result, he was never brought to trial, ostensibly due to the way the countries requested his extradition. The Brazilian Supreme Court's strict interpretation of the law also played a role.

Wagner died on October 3, 1980, aged 69, after he was found with a knife in his chest in São Paulo. His attorney stated that Wagner had committed suicide.

WIRTH, CHRISTIAN (1885–1944)

Christian Wirth, a German SS and police officer, was a perpetrator of the *Aktion T-4* program and a leading architect of *Aktion Reinhard*, the Nazi campaign to annihilate the Jews of Poland. Notorious for his sadism and brutality both to Jewish victims and his own SS staff at Nazi extermination camps, Wirth, nicknamed "Christian the Cruel" and "Wild Christian," implemented mass killings of Jews in three of the six Nazi death camps situated in Poland.

Born on November 24, 1885, in Oberbalzheim in Baden-Württemberg, Wirth was the son of a master cooper. After attending elementary and advanced training school, he became a carpenter. From 1905 to 1910, he was a member of the Württemberg Grenadier Regiment 123. He served as a policeman in Heilbronn in 1910, but he soon moved to Stuttgart, where he became a detective. During World War I, he volunteered to serve as a noncommissioned officer on the Western Front, where he was wounded. After the war, in June 1919, he returned to Stuttgart and was promoted quickly to police detective sergeant in charge of other detectives investigating homicides. His reputation for brutality was already well known, and his success rate for getting confessions from suspects was impressive.

Across 1922 to 1923 and then again from January 1, 1931, Wirth was a member of the NSDAP. In 1932, he was promoted to the position of criminal police inspector, taking a political role in the national police officers' association at Württemberg. In June 1933, he joined the SA, and on December 7, 1937, he became a member of the SD. In April 1939, he transferred to the SS. By the time war broke out in September 1939, Wirth had reached the rank of *Kriminalkommissar* in the Stuttgart Criminal Police (Kripo), a department of the Gestapo under **Arthur Nebe**.

Along with several other police officers, Wirth participated in the *Aktion T-4* euthanasia program, carried out and supervised by the Reich Chancellery and targeting Germans with mental and physical disabilities. Initially, the victims were killed by lethal injections, but later, gas vans and gas chambers were used.

In October 1939, Wirth was sent as administrator to a euthanasia unit in Brandenburg. He personally led the first gassing experiments there using carbon monoxide in a confined space. The experiment was attended by **Philipp Bouhler** and **Viktor Brack** of the Reich Chancellery. Bouhler introduced the idea to disguise future gas chambers as shower rooms so that victims would not become suspicious before the gassing started. Eventually, all gas chambers in the extermination camps would be camouflaged in this way.

Wirth was promoted to *SS-Obersturmfűhrer*, and from February 1940 until May 1940, he was stationed at the Grafeneck psychiatric killing center. Here he met *SS-Obersturmführer* Josef "Sepp" Kaspar Oberhauser, who later became his adjutant at Bełżec death camp. At Grafeneck was also situated *SS-Untersturmführer* **Kurt Franz**, named as commander of the camp at Sobibór in April 1942 and who was later himself transferred to take charge at Treblinka.

Wirth then worked briefly in the euthanasia facilities at Hadamar and Hartheim Castle. **Franz Stangl**, a future commandant at both Sobibór and Treblinka, met Wirth at Hartheim. In mid-1940, Wirth was appointed as head of the euthanasia program and inspector of all euthanasia centers in Germany and Austria. The euthanasia program was officially discontinued on August 24, 1941, as it gradually met with increasing opposition from the Catholic Church and relatives of the victims.

Many of those carrying out *Aktion T-4*, including Wirth, were able to put their experience gained with the gassings in the euthanasia facilities to perfect use in *Aktion Reinhard*. Three *Aktion Reinhard* death camps—Bełżec, Sobibór, and Treblinka—were built in German-occupied Poland, with the aim of gassing all Jews from the area known as the General Government.

By mid-March 1942, with Wirth as its first commandant and staffed by men he had met during *Aktion T-4*, Bełżec's killing capacity was operational. Bełżec was the first extermination camp where fixed gas chambers used carbon monoxide to kill the victims.

At Bełżec, Wirth earned a reputation for brutal efficiency and complete dedication to duty. He could also be hard on the German SS guards. He believed that they were lazy and ordered them to undertake route marches around the camp, which he personally led. Even the guards were taken aback by his brutality.

Wirth decided that the Jewish prisoners themselves were to do as much of the work as possible in the extermination process. He personally selected *Sonderkommando* workers from the first few trains that arrived at the camp and introduced a hierarchy into the *Sonderkommando*, appointing *oberkapos* and *kapos*—Jews who had the authority to supervise other Jews.

As Bełżec's commandant, Wirth sought to find the best ways to make the killing center run as efficiently as possible, seeking to ascertain the best ways to kill and dispose of the bodies of as many Jews as quickly as possible. Drawing on his *Aktion T-4* experience, he recognized the importance of deceiving the victims about the real purpose of the camp. He often made a welcoming speech to new arrivals, assuring them that they had come to a transit camp and that they had nothing to fear. He also recognized the importance of speed in this operation, moving the victims quickly from arrival to execution. He ordered that they be forced to run from one place to the next, always being beaten or whipped if they did not do so fast enough, so that they were terrified and disoriented.

Wirth's approach to the extermination process at Bełżec served as a model for the extermination camps Sobibór and Treblinka. In June 1942, Wirth moved from Bełżec and went to Berlin. **Gottlieb Hering**, whom Wirth had known for 20 years, took over at Bełżec in August 1942, as the second (and last) commandant. On August 1, 1942, Wirth reappeared, appointed as inspector of all three *Aktion Reinhard* camps. In this role, he directed all three commandants and was directly subordinate to **Odilo Globocnik**.

Wirth's first task was to reorganize Treblinka, which had become somewhat disordered over time. He took on the task with enthusiasm, ensuring that the gas chambers were enlarged and capable of dealing with more substantial numbers expected to arrive. Once he had finished at Treblinka, he moved on to Sobibór and did the same there. In December 1942, Wirth was given charge of the slave labor camps in the Lublin area.

In the summer of 1943, Wirth was promoted to *SS-Sturmbannführer*. After *Aktion Reinhard* was discontinued in the fall of 1943, Wirth and other officers were transferred to the region around Trieste in northern Italy. In addition to fighting partisans, Wirth's role was now to establish a death camp in San Sabba, which included a small gas chamber, to kill the Jews of Trieste. Globocnik was appointed local higher SS and police leader, and Globocnik, Wirth, and their colleagues were responsible for hunting down and arresting partisans and Jews.

In November 1943, Wirth temporarily returned to the Lublin district to take charge of *Aktion Erntefest* (Harvest Festival). As the *Aktion Reinhard* camps began to be closed, Wirth ensured that the Jewish laborers in Nazi camps, including Trawniki and Madjanek, were killed; some 42,000 Jews were murdered as a result.

Wirth lost his own life on May 26, 1944, aged 58, when he was killed by Yugoslav partisans in a street fight while traveling in an open-topped car on an official trip to Fiume. He was buried with full military honors.

WIRTHS, EDUARD (1909–1945)

Eduard Wirths was the chief SS doctor at Auschwitz from September 1942 to January 1945. He was significantly immersed in Nazi ideology in three crucial spheres: the claim of revitalizing the German race and *Volk*, the biomedical path to that revitalization through purification of genes and race, and the focus on Jews as a threat to this renewal and to the immediate and long-term health of the Germanic race. He was responsible for medical experimentation carried out at Auschwitz, including that by **Josef Mengele**.

Wirths was born at Geroldshausen, near Würzburg, on September 4, 1909, into a liberal Catholic family. His father served as a medical orderly in World War I. Eduard and his younger brother Helmut both became doctors. As a child, Eduard was meticulous, obedient, conscientious, and reliable; these traits continued into his adult life. The Wirths family was not known to be antisemitic or to be politically radical.

Wirths became a zealous Nazi while studying medicine at Würzburg University between 1930 and 1935. He joined the Nazi Party and the SA in 1933, applied to join the SS in 1934, and joined the Waffen-SS in 1939. With the onset of war, Wirths saw service in Norway and on the Eastern Front but was ruled medically unfit for combat in the spring of 1942 after he had a heart attack. He undertook special training for department leaders at Dachau concentration camp and served as chief SS psychiatrist at Neuengamme concentration camp during July 1942. In September 1942, now promoted to *SS-Hauptsturmführer*, he was appointed chief camp physician at Auschwitz, tasked with stopping the typhus epidemics that had afflicted SS personnel at the site.

Wirths improved conditions on the medical blocks, and he was well regarded by most prison doctors and inmates with whom he had contact. He was protective of prisoner doctors and other prisoners doing medical work. In August 1944, Wirth recommended Dr. Josef Mengele for promotion, referring to Mengele's "open, honest, . . . [and] absolutely dependable" character and "magnificent" intellectual and physical talents. Referring to Mengele's scientific experiments on prisoners, he also wrote of his "valuable contribution to anthropological science by making use of the scientific materials available to him."

Wirths was involved in ordering medical experimentation, particularly in gynecological and typhus-related tests, while his own primary research concerned precancerous growths of the cervix. He also had an interest in the sterilization of women through the removal of their ovaries by surgery or radiation. It is generally acknowledged that he never directly participated in such experiments himself; instead, he delegated them to subordinates. The victims of these experiments were Jewish women who had been imprisoned in Block 10 of the main camp in Auschwitz.

Wirths entrusted the responsibility for performing colposcopy procedures in Auschwitz to an inmate doctor, a German Jewish gynecologist named Maximillian Samuels, who was an expert in detecting precancerous growths in the cervix. Samuels was ordered to perform colposcopies on the female inmates in Block 10, remove parts of their cervix, study precancerous conditions of the cervix, and summarize his findings. In the fall of 1943, Samuels completed his research and submitted to Wirths his report, "Carcinoma: The Female Scourge of This World Is Curable." As soon as Samuels's task was finished, he was shot. Wirths sent the photographs and specimens for study to Dr. Hans Hinselmann, the physician who reportedly invented colposcopy, in Berlin. A colposcopy is today considered the gold standard for detecting cervical cancer in women with abnormal Pap smears, and the procedure has saved an untold number of women's lives.

While Wirths was busy in Auschwitz, his younger brother, Helmut Wirths, worked with Hinselmann at the *Frauenklinik Altona* ("Women's Clinic" in the northern city of Altona).

Like Hinselmann, Wirths's research focused on colposcopic examinations, and Wirths was trained in the procedure by Hinselmann.

Prior to the spring of 1943, selections of prisoners for gassing or work had been conducted by the camp commander and his subordinates. Wirths assumed medical control of prisoner selections at Auschwitz-Birkenau and insisted upon taking his own personal turn in performing selections.

Wirths was promoted to *SS-Sturmbannführer* in September 1944. Following the evacuation of Auschwitz in January 1945, he was transferred, along with many other former Auschwitz personnel, to the Mittelbau-Dora concentration camp in Thuringia. He held the position of chief camp physician until the camp's evacuation in April 1945.

Wirths was captured by the Allies at the end of the war and held in custody by British forces. He attempted suicide by hanging after a British officer made him recognize his responsibility in the death of some 4 million people. Eduard Wirths died on September 20, 1945, from injuries sustained during his suicide attempt.

WISLICENY, DIETER (1911–1948)

Dieter Wisliceny was an SS officer who was a key enforcer in the final phase of the Holocaust, rounding up Jews into ghettos and sending them to extermination camps. He served in Greece, Hungary, and Slovakia; introduced the yellow star, which distinguished Jews from non-Jews in occupied countries; and was involved in the deportation of Slovakian Jews in 1942, the Greek Jews from Salonika in 1943 to 1944, and the Hungarian Jews in 1944. Wisliceny's evidence at the Nuremberg trials was later important in the 1961 trial of **Adolf Eichmann** in Israel.

He was born on January 13, 1911, in Regulowken (now Możdżany), East Prussia, the son of a landowner. Wisliceny began studying theology before working briefly as a clerk in a construction firm. He was unemployed when he became a member of the NSDAP in 1931, and in 1934, he connected with both the SS and the SD. On joining the SD in July 1934, he befriended Adolf Eichmann, who had also just joined. At one stage, Wisliceny was Eichmann's superior in the SS. Both men served together from 1934 to 1937 in Berlin, maintaining friendly relations from 1937 until 1940, when Eichmann was sent to Vienna and Wisliceny was assigned to Danzig.

In 1940, Eichmann requested that Wisliceny work for him at the Reich Main Security Office (*Reichssicherheitshauptamt*, or RSHA) in Bratislava as an adviser on the Jewish question in Slovakia, but his role also covered Jews in Hungary and Greece. Wisliceny worked with Eichmann until September 1944.

Wisliceny acquired a reputation in Slovakia for accepting bribes. During the summer of 1942, he was bribed by the Bratislava-based Jewish Relief Committee to delay the deportation of Slovakian Jews. He also negotiated the ill-fated Europa Plan, initiated by Rabbi Michael Dov Weissmandel, to save the remnants of European Jewry for some $2 to $3 million, to be paid for by Jewish organizations abroad. Wisliceny accepted an initial bribe of $50,000 but did not halt the deportations.

As a specialist on "Jewish matters," Wisliceny met with Eichmann and other regional specialists at least annually, usually in November. While each representative reported on conditions in his territory, the number of persons affected by evacuation and extermination activities was kept secret. Those attending learned, however, the outcome of the Final Solution from the specialists reporting on each country.

From early 1943 to 1944, Wisliceny was assigned to Salonika, where, together with **Alois Brunner**, he introduced the definition of a Jew in accordance with the Nuremberg Laws. He ordered Jews to wear a yellow Star of David, required Jewish doctors and lawyers to affix such stars in their offices, and made Jewish tenants put stars on their apartment doors. Three ghettos were established, one of which, the Baron Hirsch quarter, was enclosed. These directives enabled the efficient roundup and deportation of Greece's Jews to Auschwitz. Wisliceny's mission to Salonika resulted in the ultimate destruction of Greek Jewry.

Wisliceny and his associates established themselves in villas formerly owned by Jews in the Hodos Velissariou district, and on March 15, 1943, 40 train cars carrying Jews left for Auschwitz. The next transport to leave went to Treblinka, arriving there on March 26, 1943. Between March 15 and August 11, 1943, more than 45,000 Jews from Salonika and other places in the German Occupation Zone of Greece were deported to Auschwitz.

Wisliceny's last assignment, in March 1944, saw him join Eichmann's Special Operations unit in Budapest, to arrange the deportation of Hungary's Jewish population to Auschwitz. The Hungarian and German governments had agreed that the German army would not enter Budapest. No mention was made of the Security Police, and a unit called Special Action Commando Eichmann (*Einsatzkommando Eichmann*), numbering about 800 members, was secretly organized from the Security Police and Waffen-SS. This began the extermination of the Hungarian Jews. Eichmann's men moved into Hungary on March 19, 1944, with all operations directed by Eichmann personally. Between April and October 1944, over 400,000 Hungarian Jews were deported to Auschwitz.

Wisliceny also served as liaison in the failed Blood for Goods negotiations, in which Eichmann offered to save the lives of 1 million Jews in exchange for goods supplied by the Allies, including 10,000 trucks. While detailed preparations were made for the deportation of all Hungarian Jews, a Hungarian Jewish emissary, Dr. Rudolf Kasztner, gave Wisliceny a large bribe to arrange a meeting with Eichmann to discuss the Jewish situation. Around April 8 or 10, 1944, a meeting was held in Eichmann's office between Kasztner, Joel Brand (another Jewish representative), and Eichmann. The negotiations failed, and the planned deportations continued. At this time, Budapest remained outside the scope of the deportations.

Recognizing that an agreement could eventually be achieved, Eichmann decided to send some 9,000 Hungarian Jews to Vienna. In August 1944, a further 3,000 were sent to Bergen-Belsen, from where, in December 1944, they were sent to Switzerland.

In November and December 1944, about 30,000 Jews were evacuated from Budapest to Austria under terrible conditions. The group was forced to walk about 180 kilometers to the Austrian border in rain and snow and without food. Many died. This was reported by the Hungarians to Eichmann, and Eichmann ended Wisliceny's participation in the Hungarian actions.

Wisliceny was arrested on May 12, 1945, near Altaussee, Austria. At Nuremberg, he was a witness for the prosecution and provided vivid details about the implementation of the Final Solution. In his evidence, Wisliceny claimed that in late April or early May 1942, Eichmann had shown him a secret order dated April 1942 signed by **Heinrich Himmler** that, on **Adolf Hitler**'s specific authority, designated Heydrich to immediately begin the "final disposition of the Jewish question." The order stated that the führer was to be kept informed as to the execution of this order. Wisliceny also said that at his last meeting with Eichmann in February 1945, at which time they were discussing their fates upon losing the war, Eichmann had told him, "I laugh when I jump into the grave because of the feeling that I have killed 5,000,000 Jews. That gives me great satisfaction and gratification." Wisliceny's evidence was produced in the 1961 Eichmann Trial in Jerusalem, Israel.

After the trial at Nuremberg concluded, Wisliceny was extradited to Bratislava, Czechoslovakia, where he was charged with complicity in mass murder. Convicted on February 27, 1948, he was sentenced to death by hanging. He escaped from prison on March 3, 1948, but was denounced by an innkeeper about 20 kilometers away. On May 4, 1948, he was hanged in Bratislava.

WOLFF, KARL (1900–1984)

Karl Wolff held the rank of *SS-Obergruppenführer* in the Waffen-SS. He became chief of staff to **Heinrich Himmler** and SS liaison officer to **Adolf Hitler** until 1943. He was the supreme head of the German police forces in Italy in 1945.

Karl Friedrich Otto Wolff was born on May 13, 1900, in Darmstadt, Hesse, the son of a wealthy district court judge. Completing his education at the Catholic school in Darmstadt in 1917, Wolff joined the German army, undertook four months' training, and volunteered on September 5, 1917, to serve with the Hessian Infantry Regiment on the Western Front. Wolff chose the army as his career, and as a lieutenant, he was one of the youngest officers ever appointed, having obtained his rank in 1918 at the age of 17. He was awarded the Iron Cross First and Second Class. After the war, Wolff was forced to leave the army due to the terms imposed on Germany by the Treaty of Versailles, and in December 1918, he joined a Hessian *Freikorps*, where he stayed until May 1920.

Wolff then started a two-year apprenticeship at the Bethmann bank in Frankfurt. In July 1922, he became engaged to Frieda von Röhmheld, whom he married in 1923. The couple moved to Munich, where Wolff worked for *Deutsche Bank* until hyperinflation led to his being laid off in June 1924. He then joined a public relations firm, and on July 1, 1925, he started his own public relations company in Munich, which he ran until 1933.

The appeal of a more powerful Germany drew Wolff to join the SS in July 1931 and the NSDAP in October the same year. Wolff rose through SS ranks, becoming an *SS-Sturmführer* in February 1932. After the Nazis came to power in 1933, he served briefly as an SS military liaison officer to the German army, and on June 15, 1933, he was selected by *SS-Reichsführer* Heinrich Himmler as his adjutant. In 1936, Wolff became Himmler's chief of staff. By early 1937, *SS-Gruppenführer* Wolff was the third in command of the entire SS.

As chief of staff, Wolff controlled access to Himmler, became head of the SS Chancellery, and supervised various SS organizations. His trajectory was rapid; by 1939, he was the liaison between Himmler and Hitler's general staff, as well as Himmler's "eyes and ears" at Hitler's headquarters. Around this time, he befriended **Odilo Globocnik**.

On September 8, 1939, Wolff ordered the Gestapo office in Frankfurt (Oder) to immediately arrest all male Jews of Polish nationality and their family members and to confiscate their wealth. As the war developed, he took part in meetings regarding the elimination of the Jews. He was aware of *Generalplan Ost* and the gas chambers. In August 1941, at **Arthur Nebe**'s invitation as commander of *Einsatzgruppe B*, Himmler and Wolff attended the shooting of Jews at Minsk. Repelled by the incident, Himmler resolved to implement alternate methods of killing, and by the spring of 1942, on his orders, Auschwitz had been greatly expanded to include new gas chambers where victims were killed by the pesticide Zyklon B.

Wolff's involvement in planning the transport and murder of the Jews of Warsaw in July and August 1942 was evidenced in the 1961 trial of **Adolf Eichmann**, which verified that up to 300,000 Jews were deported to die in the gas chambers of Treblinka. Wolff could not refute that he personally ordered several trains to start the deportations. He dealt constantly with Reich Railway Director Albert Ganzenmüller, and in a letter of August 13, 1942, referring to transports of Jews to Treblinka, Wolff thanked Ganzenmüller for his assistance and noted with pleasure that a train with 5,000 members "of the chosen people" had been running daily for 14 days. Under these conditions, the deportations could continue at an accelerated pace.

Wolff lost authority and power as differences arose between him and Himmler, especially after **Reinhard Heydrich** was assassinated in the summer of 1942. His influence was now threatened by other SS leaders, particularly Heydrich's successor at the RHSA, **Ernst Kaltenbrunner**, and Walter Schellenberg of the foreign intelligence service. In April 1943, Himmler sacked him as chief of staff and announced that he would personally take over Wolff's duties as liaison officer to Hitler.

Later in 1943, Wolff made something of a comeback when Hitler personally granted him a general's rank in the Waffen-SS. In September 1943, Wolff was transferred to Italy as higher SS and police leader (*Höherer SS- und Polizeiführer*, or HSSPF), and the German military governor of northern Italy. In that position, Wolff split duties with the head of the SD there, **Wilhelm Harster**, for security, prisons, and the supervision of concentration and forced-labor camps, as well as the deportation of forced laborers and the war against the partisans.

The Nazis entered Rome on September 10, 1943, and obtained registration lists of its Jewish community. On September 26, 1943, the community was ordered to hand over 50 kilograms of gold as a ransom and given 36 hours to do so or face the immediate deportation of 200 of their members. The gold payment merely postponed their fate. On October 16, 1943, the Germans entered the ancient ghetto to round up Jews for deportation. Most had gone into hiding. About 4,000 found sanctuary in various Roman Catholic institutions, including the Vatican. On October 18, 1943, however, 1,035 Jews were deported from Rome, and eventually a total of 2,091 Roman Jews were deported, approximately half of them to Auschwitz. By the end of World War II, only 102 of the deportees were still alive.

On December 9, 1944, Wolff was awarded the German Cross in Gold for using Italian units, with German troops in support, to destroy partisans and for the "maintenance of war production in the Italian territory."

By 1945, Wolff was acting military commander of Italy, and in March 1945, he used intermediaries to contact the U.S. Office of Strategic Services in Switzerland, under Allen W. Dulles, and negotiate the surrender of all German forces in Italy. In exchange, in a secret agreement, Wolff was promised that the Allies would not prosecute him for actions during his command in Italy.

Taken into American custody, Wolff escaped trial as an SS general and leading Nazi by providing evidence against his fellow Nazis at Nuremberg in 1946. In 1947, he retired to private life.

In 1949, the West German government arrested Wolff for war crimes. He was tried in Munich for the Minsk shootings, his part in the deportation and murder of at least 300,000 Jews from Warsaw to Treblinka and Sobibór, and the death of about 100 partisans and Jews on the Russian front. He was sentenced to four years in prison.

On June 9, 1958, **Otto Bradfisch**, the head of *Einsatzkommando 8*, was questioned by the Munich state prosecutor about the shooting of Jews and communists in Minsk in mid-August 1941. In his defense, Bradfisch claimed that the executions were legal, as proven by the presence of Himmler and Wolff at the shootings.

In 1961, evidence presented at the trial of Adolf Eichmann in Israel revealed that Wolff had organized the deportation of Italian Jews to the death camps in 1944, and Wolff was again arrested in 1964. Wolff stood trial in Munich. Charged as an accessory to the murder of more than 300,000 Jews while he was adjutant to Himmler between 1942 and 1943, Wolff was tried as a *Schreibtischtäter*, literally a "desk perpetrator," someone not physically present at the crime but culpable for reasons of administrative responsibility. The court concluded that Wolff served as Himmler's "eyes and ears" in deportations and was thus guilty of complicity in the killings. He was sentenced to 15 years in prison but only served half of this term. He was released in 1970 on medical grounds.

Karl Wolff died aged 84 on July 17, 1984, in a hospital in Rosenheim.

Primary Source Documents

The documents that follow, selected from tens of thousands of possibilities, represent a snapshot of some of the expressions of perpetration during the Holocaust. The exact time line of the Holocaust remains contested, and as a result, the documents included here have been introduced from across the entire period of the Third Reich, as the many examples shown in this book demonstrate. Indeed, the first documents predate the Nazi period itself, but they are crucial to any understanding of what was to come after 1933.

Many of the documents in this short collection have been taken from the voluminous record of the trials conducted at Nuremberg shortly after World War II. They reveal nothing less than the extremes of human nature, exposing both the savagery of the perpetrators and the suffering of the victims. An attempt has been made in this section to provide a varied range of sources that will give readers an idea of the types of documents available that illustrate Holocaust perpetration, whether from leaders, enablers, or collaborators.

1. Program of the National Socialist German Workers' Party, 1920

The Program of the National Socialist German Workers' Party, also referred to as the "25 Point Program," was initially the Party platform of German Workers' Party. When it was announced on February 24, 1920, however, Adolf Hitler took the opportunity to proclaim the new name of the Party he would henceforth shape. As the Party's official program, the intention was that it would remain unchanged until all its goals had been realized.

1. We demand the union of all Germans in a Greater Germany on the basis of the right of national self-determination.
2. We demand equality of rights for the German people in its dealings with other nations, and the revocation of the peace treaties of Versailles and Saint-Germain.
3. We demand land and territory (colonies) to feed our people and to settle our surplus population.
4. Only members of the nation may be citizens of the State. Only those of German blood, whatever their creed, may be members of the nation. Accordingly, no Jew may be a member of the nation.
5. Non-citizens may live in Germany only as guests and must be subject to laws for aliens.
6. The right to vote on the State's government and legislation shall be enjoyed by the citizens of the State alone. We demand therefore that all official appointments, of whatever kind, whether in the Reich, in the states or in the smaller localities, shall be held by none but citizens.

7. We demand that the State shall make it its primary duty to provide a livelihood for its citizens. If it should prove impossible to feed the entire population, foreign nationals (non-citizens) must be deported from the Reich.
8. All non-German immigration must be prevented. We demand that all non-Germans who entered Germany after 2 August 1914 shall be required to leave the Reich forthwith.
9. All citizens shall have equal rights and duties.
10. It must be the duty of every citizen to perform physical or mental work. The activities of the individual must not clash with the general interest, but must proceed within the framework of the community and be for the general good.

We demand therefore:

11. The abolition of incomes unearned by work.

The breaking of slavery of interest

12. In view of the enormous sacrifices of life and property demanded of a nation by any war, personal enrichment from war must be regarded as a crime against the nation. We demand therefore the ruthless confiscation of all war profits.
13. We demand the nationalization of all businesses which have been formed into corporations (trusts).
14. We demand profit-sharing in large industrial enterprises.
15. We demand the extensive development of insurance for old age.
16. We demand the creation and maintenance of a healthy middle class, the immediate communalizing of big department stores, and their lease at a cheap rate to small traders, and that the utmost consideration shall be shown to all small traders in placing of State and municipal orders.
17. We demand a land reform suitable to our national requirements, the passing of a law for the expropriation of land for communal purposes without compensation; the abolition of ground rent, and the prohibition of all speculation in land.
18. We demand the ruthless prosecution of those whose activities are injurious to the common interest. Common criminals, usurers, profiteers, etc., must be punished with death, whatever their creed or race.
19. We demand that Roman Law, which serves a materialistic world order, be replaced by a German common law.
20. The State must consider a thorough reconstruction of our national system of education (with the aim of opening up to every able and hard-working German the possibility of higher education and of thus obtaining advancement). The curricula of all educational establishments must be brought into line with the requirements of practical life. The aim of the school must be to give the pupil, beginning with the first sign of intelligence, a grasp of the notion of the State (through the study of civic affairs). We demand the education of gifted children of poor parents, whatever their class or occupation, at the expense of the State.
21. The State must ensure that the nation's health standards are raised by protecting mothers and infants, by prohibiting child labor, by promoting

physical strength through legislation providing for compulsory gymnastics and sports, and by the extensive support of clubs engaged in the physical training of youth.

22. We demand the abolition of the mercenary army and the formation of a people's army.
23. We demand legal warfare on deliberate political mendacity and its dissemination in the press. To facilitate the creation of a German national press we demand:
    a. That all editors of, and contributors to newspapers appearing in the German language must be members of the nation;
    b. That no non-German newspapers may appear without the express permission of the State. They must not be printed in the German language;
    c. That non-Germans shall be prohibited by law from participating financially in or influencing German newspapers, and that the penalty for contravening such a law shall be the suppression of any such newspaper, and the immediate deportation of the non-Germans involved.

    The publishing of papers which are not conducive to the national welfare must be forbidden. We demand the legal prosecution of all those tendencies in art and literature which corrupt our national life, and the suppression of cultural events which violate this demand.
24. We demand freedom for all religious denominations in the State, provided they do not threaten its existence nor offend the moral feelings of the German race.

    The Party, as such, stands for positive Christianity, but does not commit itself to any particular denomination. It combats the Jewish-materialist spirit within and without us, and is convinced that our nation can achieve permanent health only from within on the basis of the principle: *The common interest before self-interest.*
25. To put the whole of this program into effect, we demand the creation of a strong central state power for the Reich; the unconditional authority of the political central Parliament over the entire Reich and its organizations; and the formation of Corporations based on estate and occupation for the purpose of carrying out the general legislation passed by the Reich in the various German states.

The leaders of the Party promise to work ruthlessly—if need be to sacrifice their very lives—to translate this program into action.

Source: Jeremy Noakes and Geoffrey Pridham, eds. *Documents on Nazism, 1919–1945*. London: Jonathan Cape, 1974, pp. 37–40.

Commentary

The 25 points comprising the National Socialist German Workers' Party Program were composed by Adolf Hitler and Anton Drexler and were formally unveiled on February 24, 1920.

In the second volume of his book, *Mein Kampf*, Adolf Hitler explained the purpose of the program as being to give "a rough picture of the movement's aims," which formed "a political creed" intended to recruit new members and reinforce membership of those already in the party. Hitler made it clear that his thoughts would be translated into a plan of action. Although he declared that the program was designed to be "of limited duration" and that party leaders had no intention of establishing any new principles, subsequent events would demonstrate that the program was set in place to stay.

The first principle was to set the tone for all the others. A nationalistic statement, it left no room for doubt as to the Nazis' desire to expand Germany's current borders and define who could be classed as a German. Given that, point two demanded an overthrow of the post–World War I peace treaties of Versailles and St. Germain, something from which Hitler never retreated and which was to characterize his entire foreign policy down to 1939.

The program demanded control over all areas of public discourse. These included administration, law, economy, education, and government. With regard to national self-identification, perhaps of greatest importance were the points relating to race. Here, Hitler spelled out his objectives regarding Germany's Jews, leaving no possibility for them to be included in the national community (*Volksgemeinschaft*) in a future National Socialist state.

Overall, the 25-point program of the NSDAP showed Hitler's determination to establish a Germany built on racial purity that would be governed by a strong central authority unhampered by parliamentary procedures, rather than one that was divided over differing values or as a result of diverse national backgrounds or religious beliefs.

2. Adolf Hitler: Extracts From *Mein Kampf*, 1923

Adolf Hitler was incarcerated in Landsberg prison in 1923 following his failed attempt to overthrow the Weimar government. It was during his surprisingly short prison term that Hitler dictated Mein Kampf (My Struggle)*. Both an autobiography and an elaboration of his worldview, it serves as a disturbing harbinger of what was to come and provides some insight into the early thinking of the man most responsible for the Holocaust. Published in 1925, it became required reading during the Third Reich.*

Today it is difficult, if not impossible to say, for me to say when the word "Jew" first gave me ground for special thoughts. At home I do not remember having heard the word during my father's lifetime. I believe that the old gentleman would have regarded any special emphasis on this term as cultural backwardness. In the course of his life he had arrived at more or less cosmopolitan views which, despite his pronounced national sentiments, not only remained intact, but also affected me to some extent.

Likewise at school I found no occasion which could have led me to change this inherited picture. . . .

Not until my fourteenth or fifteenth year did I begin to come across the word "Jew," with any frequency, partly in connection with political discussions. This filled me with a mild distaste, and I could not rid myself of an unpleasant feeling that always came over me whenever religious quarrels occurred in my presence.

At that time I did not think anything else of the question.

There were few Jews in Linz. In the course of the centuries their outward appearance had become Europeanized and had taken on a human look; in fact, I even took them for Germans. The absurdity of this idea did not dawn on me because I saw no distinguishing feature but the strange religion. The fact that they had, as I believed, been persecuted on this account sometimes almost turned my distaste at unfavourable remarks about them into horror. . . . Then I came to Vienna. . . .

My views with regard to antisemitism thus succumbed to the passage of time, and this was my greatest transformation of all.

It cost me the greatest inner soul struggles and only after months of battle between my reason and my sentiments did my reason begin to emerge victorious. Two years later, my sentiment had followed my reason, and from then on became its most loyal guardian and sentinel.

At the time of this bitter struggle between spiritual education and cold reason, the visual instruction of the Vienna streets had performed invaluable services. There came a time when I no longer, as in the first days, wandered blindly through the mighty city; now with open eyes I saw not only the buildings but also the people.

Once, as I was strolling through the Inner City, I suddenly encountered an apparition in a black caftan and black hair locks. Is this a Jew? was my first thought.

For, to be sure, they had not looked like this in Linz. I observed the man furtively and cautiously, but the longer I stared at this foreign face, scrutinizing feature for feature, the more my first question assumed a new form: Is this a German?

As always in such cases, I now began to try to relieve my doubts by books. . . .

I could no longer very well doubt that the objects of my study were not Germans of a special religion, but a people in themselves; for since I had begun to concern myself with this question and to take cognizance of the Jews, Vienna appeared to me in a different light than before. Wherever I went, I began to see Jews, and the more I saw, the more sharply they became distinguished from the rest of humanity. . . .

The cleanliness of this people, moral and otherwise, I must say, is a point in itself. By their very exterior you could tell that these were no lovers of water, and, to your distress, you often knew it with your eyes closed. Later I often grew sick to my stomach from the smell of these caftan-wearers. Added to this, there was their unclean dress and generally unheroic appearance.

All this could scarcely be called very attractive; but it became positively repulsive when, in addition to their physical uncleanliness, you discovered the moral stains on this "chosen people."

In a short time I was made more thoughtful than ever by my slowly rising insight into the type of activity carried on by the Jews in certain fields.

Was there any form of filth or profligacy, particularly in cultural life, without at least one Jew involved in it?

If you cut even cautiously into such an abscess, you found, like a maggot in a rotting body, often dazzled by the sudden light—a kike!

What had to be reckoned heavily against the Jews in my eyes was when I became acquainted with their activity in the press, art, literature and the theatre. All the unctuous reassurances helped little or nothing. It sufficed to look at a billboard, to study the names of the men behind the horrible trash they advertised, to make you hard for a long time to come. This was pestilence, spiritual pestilence, worse than the Black Death of olden times, and the people was being infected with it! . . .

And now I began to examine my beloved "world press" from this point of view.

And the deeper I probed, the more the object of my former admiration shrivelled. The style became more and more unbearable; I could not help rejecting the content as inwardly shallow and banal; the objectivity of exposition now seemed to me more akin to lies than honest truth; and the writers were—Jews.

The relation of the Jews to prostitution and, even more, to the white-slave traffic, could be studied in Vienna as perhaps in no other city of Western Europe, with the possible exception of the southern French ports. If you walked at night through the streets and alleys of Leopoldstadt, at every step you witnessed proceedings which remained concealed from the majority of the German people until the War gave the soldiers on the eastern front occasion to see similar things, or, better expressed, forced them to see them.

When for the first time I recognized the Jew as the cold-hearted, shameless and calculating director of this revolting vice traffic in the scum of the big city, a cold shudder ran down my back.

But then a flame flared up within me. I no longer avoided discussion of the Jewish question; no, now I sought it. And when I learned to look for the Jew in all branches of cultural and artistic life and its various manifestations, I suddenly encountered him in a place where I would least have expected to find him.

When I recognized the Jew as the leader of the Social Democracy, the scales dropped from my eyes. A long soul struggle had reached its conclusion. . . .

Only now did I become thoroughly acquainted with the seducer of our people. . . .

The Jewish doctrine of Marxism rejects the aristocratic principle of Nature and replaces the eternal privilege of power and strength by the mass of numbers and their dead weight. Thus it denies the value of personality in man, contests the significance of nationality and race, and thereby withdraws from humanity the premiss of its existence and its culture. As a foundation of the universe, this doctrine would bring about the end of any order intellectually conceivable to man. And as, in this greatest of all recognizable organisms, the result of an application of such a law could only be chaos, on earth it could only be destruction for the inhabitants of this planet.

If, with the help of his Marxist creed, the Jew is victorious over the other peoples of the world, his crown will be the funeral wreath of humanity and this planet will, as it did thousands of years ago, move through the ether devoid of men.

Eternal Nature inexorably avenges the infringement of her commands.

Hence today I believe that I am acting in accordance with the will of the Almighty Creator: *by defending myself against the Jew, I am fighting for the work of the Lord.* . . .

His unfailing instinct in such things scents the original soul in everyone, and his hostility is assured to anyone who is not spirit of his spirit. Since the Jew is not the attacked but the attacker not only anyone who attacks passes as his enemy, but also anyone who resists him. But the means with which he seeks to break such reckless but upright souls is not honest warfare, but lies and slander.

Here he stops at nothing, and in his vileness he becomes so gigantic that no one need be surprised if among our people the personification of the devil as the symbol of all evil assumes the living shape of the Jew.

The ignorance of the broad masses about the inner nature of the Jew, the lack of instinct and narrow-mindedness of our upper classes, make the people an easy victim for this campaign of lies. . . .

They begin to tremble before the terrible enemy and thus have become his final victim.

The Jew's domination in the state seems so assured that now not only can he call himself a Jew again, but he ruthlessly admits his ultimate national and political designs. A section of his race openly owns itself to be a foreign people, yet even they lie. For while the Zionists try to make the rest of the world believe that the national consciousness of the Jew finds its satisfaction in the creation of a Palestinian state, the Jews again slyly dupe the dumb Goyim. It doesn't even enter their heads to build up a Jewish state in Palestine for the purpose of living there; all they want is a central organization for their international world swindle, endowed with its own sovereign rights and removed from the intervention of other states; a haven for convicted criminals and a university for budding crooks.

It is a sign of their rising confidence and sense of security that at a time when one section is still playing the German, Frenchman or Englishman, the other with open effrontery comes out as the Jewish race.

How close they see approaching victory can be seen by the hideous aspect which their relations with the members of other peoples takes on.

With Satanic joy in his face, the black-haired Jewish youth lurks in wait for the unsuspecting girl whom he defiles with his blood, thus stealing her from her people. With every means he tries to destroy the racial foundations of the people he has set out to subjugate. Just as he himself systematically ruins women and girls, he does not shrink back from pulling down the blood barriers for others, even on a large scale. It was and it is Jews who bring the negroes into the Rhineland, always with the same secret thought and clear aim of ruining the hated white race by the necessarily resulting bastardization, throwing it down from its cultural and political height, and himself rising to be its master.

For a racially pure people which is conscious of its blood can never be enslaved by the Jew. In this world he will forever be master over bastards and bastards alone.

And so he tries systematically to lower the racial level by a continuous poisoning of individuals.

And in politics he begins to replace the idea of democracy by the dictatorship of the proletariat.

In the organized mass of Marxism he has found the weapon which lets him dispense with democracy and in its stead allows him to subjugate and govern the peoples with a dictatorial and brutal fist.

He works systematically for revolutionization in a two-fold sense: economic and political.

Around peoples who offer too violent a resistance to attack from within he weaves a net of enemies, thanks to his international influence, incites them to war, and finally, if necessary, plants a flag of revolution on the very battlefields.

In economics he undermines the states until the social enterprises which have become unprofitable are taken from the state and subjected to his financial control.

In the political field he refuses the state the means for its self-preservation, destroys the foundations of all national self-maintenance and defense, destroys faith in the leadership, scoffs at its history and past, and drags everything that is truly great into the gutter.

Culturally, he contaminates art, literature, the theatre, makes a mockery of natural feeling, overthrows all concepts of beauty and sublimity, of the noble and the good, and instead drags men down into the sphere of his own base nature.

Religion is ridiculed, ethics and morality represented as outmoded, until the last props of a nation in its struggle for existence in this world have fallen.

Now begins the great revolution. In gaining political power the Jew casts off the few cloaks that he still wears. The democratic people's Jew becomes the blood-Jew and tyrant over peoples. In a few years he tries to exterminate the national intelligentsia and by robbing the peoples of their natural intellectual leadership makes them ripe for the slave's lot of permanent subjugation.

The most frightful example of this kind is offered by Russia, where he killed or starved about thirty million people with positively fanatical savagery, in part amid inhuman tortures, in order to give a gang of Jewish journalists and stock exchange bandits domination over a great people.

The end is not only the end of the freedom of the peoples oppressed by the Jew, but also the end of this parasite upon the nations. After the death of his victim, the vampire sooner or later dies too.

Source: Adolf Hitler. *Mein Kampf*. Translated by Ralph Manheim. Houghton Mifflin Harcourt. London: Hutchinson, 1974, *passim*.

Commentary

Mein Kampf (*My Struggle*) is a work in which Adolf Hitler set out his philosophy and his vision for Germany. It was published in two volumes, the first on July 19, 1925, and the second on December 11, 1926. By the end of 1933, more than 1.5 million copies had been sold. From 1934, the book was figuring in school primers, and in 1936, the Ministry of the Interior recommended that registrars present a copy to every bridal couple. The first complete text in English translation did not become available until 1938.

The book consisted of autobiographical recollections intermingled with reflections on political and social principles. Right from the start, Hitler noted the significance of his birthplace, Braunau-am-Inn, on the boundary between Germany and Austria. With this, he highlighted the necessity for the two countries to be joined together as one nation.

He then explained how his time in Vienna converted him to antisemitism, as he witnessed what seemed to him to be Jewish control of Social Democratic parties, the press, and immorality. Germany's defeat in World War I reinforced his beliefs in the notion of national betrayal by Jews, who sapped the will of the government and the middle classes to continue the war.

The extracts here show how the Jews, as a racial enemy, can simply never become Germans. Much of *Mein Kampf*, indeed, focused on Hitler's views on the centrality of race thinking as the answer to all national questions. Thus, he argued, a superior race that allowed itself to interbreed would decay, and the preservation of the purity of the German race was the prime responsibility of all Germans and of the state. Racial theory must be the foundation of a new political order.

3. Decree for the Protection of the People and the State, February 28, 1933

On February 28, 1933—one day after a fire had destroyed the Reichstag—Adolf Hitler, on the pretext that communist revolution was imminent, persuaded President Paul von Hindenburg to sign a decree that would suspend all the basic civil and individual liberties guaranteed under the constitution. As an emergency decree, it gave the government wide powers to ensure that threats to German society were removed. Significantly, it made no specific references to definite adversaries; while directing itself in this instance toward communism, it contained the menacing portent of later restrictions which might be applied toward other "enemies." Its terms enabled the new regime to begin to entrench itself in office, paving the way for the Nazi dictatorship and dismantling Germany's Weimar Republic.

On the basis of Article 48, Section 2, of the German Constitution, the following is decreed as a defensive measure against Communist acts of violence that endanger the state:

§ 1

Articles 114, 115, 117, 118, 123, 124, and 153 of the Constitution of the German Reich are suspended until further notice. Thus, restrictions on personal liberty, on the right of free expression of opinion, including freedom of the press, on the right of assembly and the right of association, and violations of the privacy of postal, telegraphic, and telephonic communications, and warrants for house searches, orders for confiscations as well as restrictions on property are permissible beyond the legal limits otherwise prescribed.

§ 2

If any state fails to take the necessary measures to restore public safety and order, the Reich government may temporarily take over the powers of the highest state authority.

§ 3

State and local authorities must obey the orders decreed by the Reich government on the basis of § 2.

§ 4

Whoever provokes, appeals for, or incites the disobedience of the orders given out by the supreme state authorities or the authorities subject to them for the execution of this decree, or the orders given by the Reich government according to § 2, can be punished—insofar as the deed is not covered by other decrees with more severe punishments—with imprisonment of not less than one month, or with a fine from 150 to 15,000 reichsmarks.

Whoever endangers human life by violating § 1 is to be punished by sentence to a penitentiary, under mitigating circumstances with imprisonment of not less than six months and, when the violation causes the death of a person, with death, under mitigating circumstances with a penitentiary sentence of not less than two years. In addition, the sentence may include the confiscation of property.

Whoever provokes or incites an act contrary to the public welfare is to be punished with a penitentiary sentence, under mitigating circumstances, with imprisonment of not less than three months.

§ 5

The crimes which under the Criminal Code are punishable with life in a penitentiary are to be punished with death: i.e., in Sections 81 (high treason), 229 (poisoning), 306 (arson), 311 (explosion), 312 (flooding), 315, paragraph 2 (damage to railways), 324 (general public endangerment through poison).

Insofar as a more severe punishment has not been previously provided for, the following are punishable with death or with life imprisonment or with imprisonment not to exceed 15 years:

1. Anyone who undertakes to kill the Reich President or a member or a commissioner of the Reich government or of a state government, or provokes such a killing, or agrees to commit it, or accepts such an offer, or conspires with another for such a murder;
2. Anyone who under Section 115, paragraph 2, of the Criminal Code (serious rioting) or of Section 125, paragraph 2, of the Criminal Code (serious disturbance of the peace) commits these acts with arms or cooperates consciously and intentionally with an armed person;
3. Anyone who commits a kidnapping under Section 239 of the Criminal Code with the intention of making use of the kidnapped person as a hostage in the political struggle.

§ 6

This decree enters into force on the day of its promulgation.

Source: Office of the U.S. Chief Counsel for the Prosecution of Axis Criminality. *Nazi Conspiracy and Aggression*. Vol. 3. Document 1390-PS. Washington, DC: U.S. Government Printing Office, 1946, pp. 968–70.

Commentary

The first step on the road to the Holocaust can be said to have taken place on the night of February 27, 1933, when the Reichstag building in Berlin was set on fire. The day after, on the pretext that it had been set by communists and that a left-wing revolution was imminent, the newly appointed chancellor, Adolf Hitler, persuaded President Paul von Hindenburg to sign a Decree for the Protection of the People and the State. Employing the decree as the legal basis for the imprisonment of anyone considered to be an opponent of the Nazis, the government detained hundreds of people in the first few days, and tens of thousands more in succeeding weeks.

The Reichstag Fire Decree, so called, was also used to suppress anti-Nazi publications. As the decree was not accompanied by any written guidelines regarding implementation, wide latitude was given to local authorities when carrying out its requirements. The decree would remain in force for the duration of the Nazi era and was an important element in establishing the one-party state of the Nazis. Together with an Enabling Act of March 24, 1933, it formed the legal basis for Hitler's dictatorship. Under its terms, the first concentration camps were established; within days, it became apparent that Jews (as political enemies) were also being targeted by the regime.

4. Article in *Der Stürmer* on the Hebrew Bible, January 1935

Published by the rabid antisemite Julius Streicher, Der Stürmer *was newspaper replete with antisemitic rants and crude, sometimes pornographic renderings of stereotypical Jewish males ravishing innocent Aryan girls and women. Its purpose was undeniable: to arouse in its readers a visceral anti-Jewish response that would eventually—and inevitably—spill over into violence. A leitmotif of the paper was the blood libel, the charge from the Middle Ages that Jews killed Christian children to make use of their blood for the preparation of matzah, the unleavened bread eaten during the Passover festival. This short extract from 1935 reflects the attitude often expressed in* Der Stürmer *regarding the Hebrew Bible.*

THE CHOSEN PEOPLE OF THE CRIMINALS

The history book of the Jews which is usually called the "Holy Scriptures" impresses us as a horrible criminal romance . . .

This "holy" book abounds in murder, incest, fraud, theft, and indecency.

Source: Office of the U.S. Chief of Counsel for the Prosecution of Axis Criminality. *Nazi Conspiracy and Aggression*. Red Series, vol. 5. Document 2697-PS. Washington, DC: U.S. Government Printing Office, 1946, p. 372.

Commentary

Undermining the authority and divinity of the Hebrew Bible related directly to the Nazi view of the Jews as inheritors of a tradition that threatened the Aryan race. The Bible was viewed by the Nazis as the founding document of the Jews' attempt to dominate the world. Therefore, disparaging the Hebrew Bible was a means of destroying Jewish claims to an overarching morality for all humanity and, as such, provided the Nazis with a way to elevate the building of their alternative: a racial civilization built on hierarchy and dominance.

This short extract from *Der Stürmer* further undercuts the scriptural basis of the Bible through its reference to it as a "history book," thereby removing it from any sort of divine authority and replacing it as a work created by humans (or, rather, subhumans). This made tangible a notion of "the Jewish enemy" so that readers could see that the Bible is in fact not divine but decadent. This is underscored through the addition of quotation marks when describing the Bible as a "holy" book.

Moreover, Streicher was happy to denigrate the first five books of the Christian Old Testament. Anyone who agrees with him that the Hebrew Bible "abounds in murder, incest, fraud, theft, and indecency" becomes complicit in the denigration; by implication, all people holding to their Christian beliefs must ipso facto stand against Nazism.

5. The Nuremberg Laws, 1935

The Nuremberg Laws were two constitutional laws issued by a special session of the Reichstag on September 15, 1935, at the annual Nazi Party Rally in Nuremberg. Both were designed to further exclude Jews from public life. The first, the Reich Citizenship Law, stated that only Germans or those related by blood could be citizens of Germany, thus excluding Jews from citizenship and in so doing further defining Aryans, Jews, and Mischlinge *(that is, persons of "mixed race"). The second, the Law for the Protection of German Blood and Honor, prohibited Jews from marriage with other Germans, extramarital affairs, the employment of German female domestic servants under the age of 45 in Jewish households, and the raising of the German flag by Jews. Any previous exclusions in effect for Jewish veterans of World War I were nullified. Ultimately, these laws paved the way for further exclusion of Jews and the expansion of additional antisemitic measures.*

I. THE REICH CITIZENSHIP LAW OF SEPTEMBER 15, 1935

The Reichstag has unanimously adopted the following law, which is herewith promulgated.

§ 1.

(1) A subject of the State is a person who belongs to the protective union of the German Reich, and who therefore has particular obligations towards the Reich.

(2) The status of subject is acquired in accordance with the provisions of the Reich and State Law of Citizenship.

§ 2.

(1) A citizen of the Reich is only that subject who is of German or kindred blood and who, through his conduct, shows that he is both willing and able to faithfully serve the German people and Reich.

(2) The right to citizenship is acquired by the granting of Reich citizenship papers.
(3) Only the citizen of the Reich enjoys full political rights in accordance with the provision of the law.

§ 3.
The Reich Minister of the Interior in conjunction with the Deputy of the Führer will issue the necessary legal and administrative decrees for implementing and supplementing this law.

II. FIRST REGULATION TO THE REICH CITIZENSHIP LAW OF NOVEMBER 14, 1935

On the basis of § 3, Reich Citizenship Law, of September 15, 1935 (RGBl [Reich Law Gazette] I, p. 1146) the following is ordered:

§ 1.
(1) Until further regulations regarding citizenship papers are issued, all subjects of German or kindred blood who possessed the right to vote in Reichstag elections at the time the Citizenship Law came into effect shall, for the time being, possess the rights of Reich citizens. The same shall be true of those to whom the Reich Minister of the Interior, in conjunction with the Deputy of the Führer, has given preliminary citizenship.
(2) The Reich Minister of the Interior, in conjunction with the Deputy of the Führer, can withdraw preliminary citizenship.

§ 2.
(1) The regulations in § I are also valid for Reich subjects of mixed Jewish blood.
(2) An individual of mixed Jewish blood is one who is descended from one or two grandparents who were fully Jewish by race, insofar as he or she does not count as a Jew according to § 5, Paragraph 2. One grandparent shall be considered as full-blooded if he or she belonged to the Jewish religious community.

§ 3.
Only the Reich citizen, as bearer of full political rights, exercises the right to vote in political affairs or can hold public office. The Reich Minister of the Interior, or any agency empowered by him, can make exceptions during the transition period, with regard to occupying public offices. The affairs of religious organizations will not be affected.

§ 4.
(1) A Jew cannot be a citizen of the Reich. He has no right to vote in political affairs, he cannot occupy a public office.
(2) Jewish civil servants will retire as of 31 December 1935. If these civil servants served at the front in the World War, either for Germany or her allies, they will receive in full, until they reach the age limit, full pension to which they were entitled according to the last salary they received; they will, however, not

advance in seniority. After reaching the age limit, their pensions will be calculated anew, according to the last salary they received, on the basis of which their pension was calculated.

(3) The affairs of religious organizations will not be affected.

(4) The employment status of teachers in Jewish public schools remains unchanged until new regulations for the Jewish school systems are issued.

§ 5.

(1) A Jew is anyone who descended from at least three grandparents who were fully Jewish by race. § 2, par. 2, second sentence will apply.

(2) A Jew is also anyone who descended from two fully Jewish grandparents, if:

(a) he belonged to the Jewish religious community at the time this law was issued or joined the community later;

(b) he was married to a Jewish person at the time the law was issued or married one subsequently;

(c) he is the offspring from a marriage with a Jew, in the sense of Section 1, which was contracted after the Law for the Protection of German Blood and German Honor became effective (RGBl. [Reich Law Gazette] I, page 1146 of September 15, 1935);

(d) he is the offspring of an extramarital relationship with a Jew, according to Section 1, and will be born out of wedlock after July 31, 1936.

§ 6.

(1) In case Reich laws or orders by the NSDAP and its organizations make demands for racial pureness that exceed § 5, they will not be affected.

(2) Any other demands for pureness of blood that exceed § 5 can only be made with permission from the Reich Minister of the Interior and the Deputy of the Führer. If any such demands have been made, they will be void as of January 1, 1936, if they have not been requested from the Reich Minister of the Interior in agreement with the Deputy of the Führer. These requests must be made to the Reich Minister of the Interior.

§ 7.

The Führer and Reich Chancellor can grant exemptions from the regulations laid down in the law.

Source: Office of the U.S. Chief Counsel for the Prosecution of Axis Criminality. *Nazi Conspiracy and Aggression*. Vol. 4. Documents 1416-PS and 1417-PS. Washington, DC: U.S. Government Printing Office, 1946, pp. 7–10.

Commentary

The collective term "Nuremberg Laws" was the name given to two antisemitic laws presented on September 15, 1935, at a special meeting convened at the annual Nuremberg Party Rally. The first of these was the Law for the Protection of German Blood and German Honor, forbidding intermarriage and extramarital sexual relations between Jews and "citizens of German blood." It also prohibited the employment of German females under 45 in Jewish households. The second was the Reich Citizenship Law, which announced that only those people of "German or kindred blood," exhibiting appropriate conduct, were eligible to be Reich citizens. The remainder were identified as state subjects, without citizenship rights but with obligations toward the Reich. Further, whatever previous exclusions were in effect for Jewish veterans of World War I were now nullified. A later decree was necessary to clarify or define who was Jewish for the purpose of these laws.

Many non-Jewish Germans henceforth became uncomfortable with their Jewish neighbors and gradually stopped socializing with them or shopping in Jewish-owned stores, many of which were forced to close due to a lack of customers. As Jews were no longer permitted to work in government service or government-regulated professions such as medicine and teaching, many middle-class business owners and professionals were required to take unskilled and basic employment. Soon after this, additional regulations were introduced that dismissed Jewish children from the state education system, forcing them into Jewish-only schools.

Some German Jews reacted to the Nuremberg Laws with a sense of relief; they thought that the worst was now over and that at least they finally knew where they stood and could get on with their lives, even if they had diminished rights. The Nuremberg Laws were, however, a further step in the removal of Jews from their participation in German life.

6. Article in *Der Stürmer* on Ritual Murder, April 1937

Der Stürmer, *the Nazi Party newspaper published by Julius Streicher, was one of the primary means by which the Party disseminated its propaganda. In addition to antisemitic stereotypes, including hooked noses, obsession with money, and the carnal danger Jewish men represented for Aryan girls and women, Streicher kept alive the "Blood Libel" myth stemming from the Middle Ages – the accusation that Jews used the blood of non-Jewish boys and girls to make unleavened bread (matzah) that is eaten during Passover. The picture that Streicher paints in this article from 1937 is a classic rendering of the accusation, including references to the "Talmud Jew" and supposed prayers from verses of the Hebrew Bible.*

RITUAL MURDER

The murder of the 10 years old Gertrud Lenhoff in Quirschied (Saarpfalz) . . . The Jews are our MISFORTUNE! . . .

Also the numerous confessions made by the Jews show that the execution of ritual murders is a law to the Talmud Jew. The former Chief Rabbi (and later monk) Teofiti declares that the ritual murders take place especially on the Jewish Purim (in memory of the Persian murders) and Passover (in memory of the murder of Christ).

The instructions are as follows:

The blood of the victims is to be tapped by force. On Passover, it is to be used in wine and matzos; thus, a small part of the blood is to be poured into the dough of the matzos and into the wine. The mixing is done by the Jewish head of the family.

The procedure is as follows: the family head empties a few drops of the fresh and powdered blood into the glass, wets the fingers of the left hand with it and sprays (blesses) with it everything on the table. The head of the family then says: "Dam Izzardia chynim heroff dever isyn porech harbe hossen maschus pohorus" (Exod. VII, 12) ("Thus we ask God to send the ten plagues to all enemies of the Jewish faith.") Then they eat, and at the end the head of the family exclaims: "Sfach, chaba, moscho kol hagoym!" ("May all Gentiles perish—as the child whose blood is contained in the bread and wine!")

The fresh (or dried and powdered) blood of the slaughtered is further used by young married Jewish couples, by pregnant Jewesses, for circumcision and so on. Ritual murder is recognized by all Talmud Jews. The Jew believes he absolves himself thus of his sins.

Source: Office of the U.S. Chief of Counsel for the Prosecution of Axis Criminality. *Nazi Conspiracy and Aggression*. Red Series, vol. 5. Document 2699-PS. Washington, DC: U.S. Government Printing Office, 1946, pp. 372–73.

Commentary

The accusation that Jews engaged in ritual murder of Christians for religiously prescribed reasons seems to have first emerged in England during the 12th century. The core of the accusation was that Jews murdered Christian children at Easter in emulation of the crucifixion of Jesus; over many centuries, widely spread folktales throughout Europe added that Jews also used the blood of these murdered children for their Passover rituals, most often through mixing the blood into matzah dough so that the Jews would literally devour the Christian life force throughout the Passover festival. The libel of a Jewish quest for Christian blood—often focusing on infants or small children and at other times on virgin girls—became a central charge motivating peasant reprisals in the form of pogroms and other acts of persecution. Given the proximity of Easter and Passover, March and April became months in which anti-Jewish violence often peaked in European countries. As Christians observed the death and resurrection of Jesus (as the Church taught, at the hands of the Jews), stories that Jews were still engaging in horrific practices against the innocents stirred up the most intense antagonism toward them.

In the modern era, blood libels took on an added dimension, with racial antisemites building on the blood libel tradition in Europe in order to harass, kill, and uproot a Jewish presence in lands developing modern forms of national identity and expression. In this extract from *Der Stürmer*, Julius Streicher presents the classic blood libel accusation, including references to the "Talmud Jew" and fabricated prayers from verses of the Hebrew Bible, which, he writes, are recited by Jews during the Passover service in the home, known as a seder. It was a further reinforcement for readers of the beastliness of the Jews and of the Jewish religious tradition.

7. Adolf Eichmann: Report Issued on His Activities in Vienna, August 22, 1938

Addressed to the Central Security Office by Adolf Eichmann, this document details his attempts to streamline the process of emigration for both "rich and poor Jews" in the

Central Office for Jewish Emigration, as a result of which the Central Office "prepares 200 Jews for emigration daily by supplying them with passports and supervising their departure."

On 22 August 1938, the Central Office for Jewish Emigration in Vienna was established by orders of the Reich Commissioner for reunification of Austria with the Reich. . . .

There were more and more instances in Vienna where Jews, eager to emigrate, had to stand in line for days and weeks to arrange the necessary paperwork for their emigration. Over that time there were many failures because of lack of organization and unqualified officials. This damaged our interest in forcing the Jews to emigrate from Austria. . . .

One of the problems with the emigration of Jews from Vienna is created by the activity of lawyers. Because of the complicated system, obtaining the necessary paperwork for a passport can take up to two or three months. For example, a certificate confirming that one does not have a criminal record may take 6–8 weeks to obtain. Rich Jews therefore employ Aryan lawyers to get the papers.

These lawyers manage to obtain favorable treatment by the authorities. They or their workers will come to an office with 20–30 applications and take up a great deal of the clerks' time, while poor Jews are standing in the street in a line that hardly moves for days. This has caused only problems. First, it has enabled the rich Jews to leave the country without problem, while the poor Jews stayed behind—this is contrary to our interest. Furthermore, it is already being said abroad that obtaining a passport in Vienna costs RM 1,000. The lawyers take enormous sums for each passport, and the rich Jews pay willingly.

Since obtaining a passport by the Central Office for Emigration takes only up to 8 days (We get the certificate from the police within 48 hours), lawyers have already approached some of the government and party offices. They have lost good business since the creation of the Central Office. Furthermore, the Central Office has not arranged for separate hours for these lawyers—a fact which increases their bitterness.

The aim of the Central Office for Emigration is to force the poor Jews to emigrate and to make the rich ones leave only if a number of poor Jews, proportionate to the rich Jews' capital, go as well.

Prior to the creation of the Central Office, papers and passports were provided without differentiation. The first Jew to come received documents, regardless of his emigration prospects. The result was that the papers would often expire while the Jews still had no possibility to emigrate. (The police document and the certificate of tax payment is good for only 4 weeks). These Jews had to go through the same process several times until they could emigrate. This caused heavy work loads for the authorities.

The Central Office for Emigration supplies the paperwork and passports only to those Jews who can emigrate. Many Jews hold visas that are valid for a limited time only. To prevent these visas from expiring, they are given top priority. The Jewish political organizations are looking for emigration possibilities for Jews. The period when Jews emigrated in groups is over, one has to concentrate on individual emigration. The Central Office prepares 200 Jews for emigration daily by supplying them with passports and supervising their departure.

Source: Yad Vashem Archive 051/OSO B1/70, http://www.yadvashem.org/odot_pdf/Microsoft%20Word%20-%203297.pdf. Reproduced by permission of Yad Vashem Publications.

Commentary

One of the problems facing the Nazis in their attempts to force the Jews of Austria to emigrate centered on the fact that in order to do so, Jews would, for the most part, be required to visit several offices to secure a variety of permissions and the coveted document stamps that went with them. The process was unwieldy and frequently lengthy, as Jews would be required to wait for one before being able to proceed to the next.

Given this, a means was developed to streamline the emigration procedure by centralizing all the steps into one location; this became bureaucratized as the Central Office for Jewish Emigration, established by Adolf Eichmann in Vienna in the summer of 1938. Every organization associated with emigration, whether public or private, was required to have a representative at the office, which was, in turn, responsible to the *Sicherheitsdienst* (SD, or Security Service) in Berlin. One of the features of the office was that the emigration of poorer Jews was facilitated through the office taking money from wealthier Jews and rerouting it to those less well-off; in this way, all were able to leave regardless of status, while the Reich did not have to pay anything at all.

In this document, Eichmann provides a summary report of how the Central Office was established and how it operates. He states triumphantly that by focusing on individual rather than group emigration, his office can process some 200 departures per day, which should solve the problem of how to speed up the emigration of Jews. At the same time, ideally, it would make the Jews pay for the process themselves. The success of the Central Office in Vienna, indeed, could even have acted as a precedent for other, similar, offices in other parts of the Reich—an unstated hope embedded in the positive report presented here.

8. Reinhard Heydrich: Instructions, November 10, 1938

Issued by SS-Grüppenführer *Reinhard Heydrich during the* Kristallnacht *pogrom of November 9-10, 1938, this document contains the following explicit instructions: German citizens or property are not to be destroyed, Jewish businesses and apartments are not to be looted, foreign nationals (including Jews) are to be left alone, Jewish archives are to be seized, and as many Jews as possible should be imprisoned. Because of this event, Nazi statistics subsequently listed some 91 Jews killed in the attacks, with 30,000 arrested and incarcerated in concentration camps. Jewish homes, hospitals, and schools were ransacked, as the attackers destroyed such buildings while avoiding German-owned ones. Over 1,000 synagogues were burned and over 7,000 Jewish businesses damaged or destroyed.*

Following the attempt on the life of Secretary of the Legation vom Rath in Paris, demonstrations against the Jews are to be expected in all parts of the Reich in the course of the coming night, November 9/10, 1938. The instructions below are to be applied in dealing with these events:

1. The Chiefs of the State Police, or their deputies, must immediately upon receipt of this telegram contact, by telephone, the political leaders in their areas—Gauleiter or Kreisleiter—who have jurisdiction in their districts and arrange a joint meeting with the inspector or commander of the Order Police to discuss the arrangements for the demonstrations. At these discussions the political leaders will be informed that the German Police has received instructions, detailed below, from the Reichsführer SS and the Chief of the German Police, with which the political leadership is requested to coordinate its own measures:
   a) Only such measures are to be taken as do not endanger German lives or property (i.e., synagogues are to be burned down only where there is no danger of fire in neighboring buildings).
   b) Places of business and apartments belonging to Jews may be destroyed but not looted. The police is instructed to supervise the observance of this order and to arrest looters.
   c) In commercial streets particular care is to be taken that non-Jewish businesses are completely protected against damage.
   d) Foreign citizens—even if they are Jews—are not to be molested.
2. On the assumption that the guidelines detailed under para. 1 are observed, the demonstrations are not to be prevented by the Police, which is only to supervise the observance of the guidelines.
3. On receipt of this telegram Police will seize all archives to be found in all synagogues and offices of the Jewish communities so as to prevent their destruction during the demonstrations. This refers only to material of historical value, not to contemporary tax records, etc. The archives are to be handed over to the locally responsible officers of the SD.
4. The control of the measures of the Security Police concerning the demonstrations against the Jews is vested in the organs of the State Police, unless inspectors of the Security Police have given their own instructions. Officials of the Criminal Police, members of the SD, of the Reserves and the SS in general may be used to carry out the measures taken by the Security Police.
5. As soon as the course of events during the night permits the release of the officials required, as many Jews in all districts—especially the rich—as can be accommodated in existing prisons are to be arrested. For the time being only healthy male Jews, who are not too old, are to be detained. After the detentions have been carried out the appropriate concentration camps are to be contacted immediately for the prompt accommodation of the Jews in the camps. Special care is to be taken that the Jews arrested in accordance with these instructions are not ill-treated.

Source: Yitzhak Arad, Yisrael Gutman, and Abraham Margaliot, eds. *Documents on the Holocaust: Selected Sources on the Destruction of the Jews of Germany and Austria, Poland, and the Soviet Union.* Jerusalem: Yad Vashem, 1981, pp. 102–4. Reproduced by permission of Yad Vashem Publications.

Commentary

The *Kristallnacht*, or the Night of Broken Glass (a sarcastic Nazi term for the largest prewar pogrom against the Jews of Germany), took place on the night of November 9 to 10, 1938. Supposedly conducted in retaliation for the murder of the third secretary of the German Embassy in Paris, Ernst vom Rath, by 17-year-old Jewish émigré Hershel Grynszpan, the pogrom was orchestrated behind the scenes by Joseph Goebbels, with Hitler's apparent consent.

In this document, Reinhard Heydrich, the head of the *Sicherheitsdienst* (SD, or Security Service), issues orders to all state police and SD leaders regarding how they are to proceed during the unfolding events of the night. While the document counsels a number of ways in which the police should be wary of allowing the violence to spread, Heydrich does not balk when it comes to the Jews; hence, while measures are to be taken that do not endanger German lives or property, "synagogues are to be burned down" but "only where there is no danger of fire in neighboring buildings." The overall result, for the Jews, was catastrophic. Even SS reports on November 11 were damning. Among the Jewish properties either vandalized or totally destroyed were 815 shops, 29 department stores, 171 dwellings, and 267 synagogues.

Further, Heydrich's instructions to the police were that the anti-Jewish "demonstrations"—presumably demonstrations of popular wrath against the Jews for vom Rath's murder—should not be prevented. The police were only to serve in a supervisory capacity for the sake of maintaining good order.

Nazi figures gave 91 Jews officially listed as killed during the demonstrations, although this is unquestionably an underestimation. Certainly, more than 30,000 Jews were arrested on the night and in the days immediately following, with tens of thousands more subsequently. Many were imprisoned in the concentration camps at Dachau, Sachsenhausen, and Buchenwald, and perhaps up to 1,000 lost their lives in the weeks that followed. The events of the *Kristallnacht* are now understood to have been a harbinger for the Holocaust, which was to come within a few years.

9. Extracts from a Conference on the Jewish Question Chaired by Hermann Göring, November 12, 1938

In a three-and-a-half-hour conference led by Hermann Göring, head of the Four-Year Plan and Number Two man in the Third Reich, discussion was held in response to Hitler's request that "the Jewish question be now, once and for all, coordinated and solved one way or another." The intention was to further isolate the Jewish community economically, in an effort to hasten Jewish emigration. One of the principal concerns of the meeting was to ensure that German insurance companies would not pay members of the Jewish community for the extensive destruction done to their homes, businesses, and synagogues that had occurred during the Kristallnacht *of two days earlier. Another area of significant discussion was the "aryanizing" of Jewish stores, factories, and large industrial concerns, as well as the imposition of various restrictions to be imposed on Jews in public life.*

Gentlemen! Today's meeting is of a decisive nature. I have received a letter written on the Führer's orders by the Stabsleiter of the Führer's deputy Bormann, requesting that the Jewish question be now, once and for all, coordinated and solved one way or another. And yesterday once again did the Führer request by phone for me to take coordinated action in the matter.

Since the problem is mainly an economic one, it is from the economic angle that it shall have to be tackled. Naturally a number of legal measures shall have to be taken which fall into the sphere of the Minister for Justice and into that of the Minister of the Interior; and certain propaganda measures shall be taken care of by the Minister for Propaganda. The Minister for Finance and the Minister for Economic Affairs shall take care of problems falling in their respective resorts.

In the meeting, in which we first talked about this question and came to the decision to aryanize the German economy, to take the Jew out of it, and put him into our debit ledger, was one in which, to our shame, we only made pretty plans, which were executed very slowly. We then had a demonstration, right here in Berlin, we told the people that something decisive would be done, but again nothing happened. We have had this affair in Paris now, more demonstrations followed and this time something decisive must be done!

Because, gentlemen, I have had enough of these demonstrations! They don't harm the Jew but me, who is the last authority for coordinating the German economy.

If today, a Jewish shop is destroyed, if goods are thrown into the street, the insurance company will pay for the damages, which the Jew does not even have; and furthermore goods of the consumer goods belonging to the people, are destroyed. If in the future, demonstrations which are necessary, occur, then, I pray, that they be directed, so as not to hurt us.

Because it's insane to clean out and burn a Jewish warehouse then have a German insurance company make good the loss. And the goods which I need desperately, whole bales of clothing and what-not, are being burned; and I miss them everywhere.

I may as well burn the raw materials before they arrive. The people of course, do not understand that; therefore we must make laws which will show the people once and for all, that something is being done.

I should appreciate it very much if for once, our propaganda would make it clear that it is unfortunately not the Jew who has to suffer in all this, but the German insurance companies.

I am not going to tolerate a situation in which the insurance companies are the ones who suffer. Under the authority invested in me, I shall issue a decree, and I am, of course, requesting the support of the competent Government agencies, so that everything shall be processed through the right channels and the insurance companies will not be the ones who suffer.

It may be, though, that these insurance companies may have insurance in foreign countries. If that is the case, foreign bills of exchange would be available which I would not want to lose. That shall have to be checked. For that reason, I have asked Mr. Hilgard of the insurance company, to attend, since he is best qualified to tell us to what extent the insurance companies are protected against damage, by having taken out insurance with other companies. I would not want to miss this, under any circumstances.

I should not want to leave any doubt, gentlemen, as to the aim of today's meeting. We have not come together merely to talk again, but to make decisions, and I implore the competent agencies to take all measures for the elimination of the Jew from German economy and to submit them to me, as far as it is necessary.

The fundamental idea in this program of elimination of the Jew from German economy is first, the Jew being ejected from the Economy transfers his property to the State. He will be compensated. The compensation is to be listed in the debit ledger and shall bring a certain percentage of interest. The Jew shall have to live out of this interest. It is a foregone conclusion that this aryanizing, if it is to be done quickly, cannot be made in the Ministry for Economy in Berlin. That way, we would never finish.

On the other hand, it is very necessary to have safety precautions so that the lower echelons, Statthalter, and Gauleiter will not do things unreasonably. One must issue correction directives, immediately.

The aryanizing of all the larger establishments, naturally, is to be my lot—the Ministry for Economy will designate, which and how many there are—it must not be done by a Statthalter or his lower echelons, since these things reach into the export trade, and cause great problems, which the Statthalter can neither observe, nor solve from his place.

It is my lot, so that the damage will not be greater than the profit, which we are striving for.

It is obvious gentlemen that the Jewish stores are for the people, and not the stores. Therefore, we must begin here, according to the rules previously laid down.

The Minister for Economic Affairs shall announce which stores he'll want to close altogether. These stores are excluded from aryanizing at once. Their stocks are to be made available for sale in other stores; what cannot be sold, shall be processed through the "Winterhilfe" or taken care of otherwise. However, the sales values of these articles shall always be considered, since the State is not to suffer but should profit through this transformation. For the chain and department stores—I speak now only of that, what can be seen, certain categories have to be established, according to the importance of the various branches.

The trustee of the State will estimate the value of the property and decide what amount the Jew shall receive. Naturally, this amount is to be set as low as possible. The representative of the State shall then turn the establishment over to the "Aryan" proprietor, that is, the property shall be sold according to its real value.

There begins the difficulties. It is easily understood that strong attempts will be made to get all these stores to party-members and to let them have some kind of compensations. I have witnessed terrible things in the past; little chauffeurs of

Gauleiters have profited so much by these transactions that they have now about half a million. You, gentlemen, know it. Is that correct?

(Assent)

Of course, things like that are impossible. I shall not hesitate to act ruthlessly in any case where such a trick is played. If the individual involved is prominent, I shall see the Führer within two hours and report to him.

We shall have to insist upon it, that the Aryan taking over the establishment is of the branch and knows his job. Generally speaking he is the one who must pay for the store with his own money. In other words, an ordinary business transaction is to be sought—one merchant selling, the other one buying a business. If there are party members among the contenders, they are to be preferred, that is if they have the same qualifications: first shall come the one who had the most damage, and secondly, selection should be according to length of Party membership.

Of course, there may be exceptions. There are party-members who, as may be proven, lost their business concessions by action of the Schuschnigg or Prague Government, and so went bankrupt. Such a man has naturally first option on a store for sale, and he shall receive help if he does not have the means to help himself. The trustee of the State can justify this help, if he is more business like in the transfer. This party-member should have the chance to buy the store for as cheap a price as possible. In such a case the State will not receive the full price, but only the amount the Jew received. Such a buyer may even receive a loan besides, so that he will get off to a good start.

I wish to make it clear that such a proceeding shall only be legal if the party-member has once owned such a store. For example, a party-member was the owner of a stationery store, and Schuschnigg took away the concession to operate it so that the man lost the store and went bankrupt. Now, if a Jewish stationery store is being aryanized, this party-member should get the store on conditions which he'll be able to fulfill. Such a case shall be the only exception though, in all other cases the procedure shall be of a strictly businesslike nature whereby the party-member, like I said before, shall have the preference, if he has the same qualifications as any other candidate, who is not a member of the party.

When selling for the actual value we shall find only about 60 Aryans ready to take over 100 Jewish stores. I don't think that we have a German for every Jewish store. You must not forget that the Jew sees his main activity in the field of trade, and that he owns 90% of it. I doubt that we'd have a demand big enough. I even doubt that we'd have enough people, particularly now since everybody has found his field of work.

Therefore, I ask the Minister for Economy to go beyond what we think ought to be done for the sake of the principle, in liquidating the establishments. I ask him to go further, even though there won't be any candidates. That'll be perfectly alright.

The transfer of stores and establishments shall have to be executed by the lower echelons, not through Berlin but through the Gaue and through the Reichstatthalterschaft. Therein shall be the seat of the members of the Board of Trustees, even if it consists of a few people only. The Statthalter and his people cannot do this job; the trustees will have to tackle it. But the Statthalter shall be the authority which supervises, according to the regulations given him, the trustees, particularly in dealings such as the transfer to party-members.

Naturally, these establishments cannot disappear all at once but we'll have to start by Monday, in a manner that shall make it obvious that a change has begun to materialize. Besides that, certain stores could be closed which will make things here easier.

Another point! I have noticed that Aryans took over a Jewish store and were then so clever to keep the name of the Jewish store as "formerly," or kept it altogether. That must not be; I cannot permit it. Because it may happen—what has just happened—stores were looted because their signboards bore Jewish names—because they had once been Jewish, but had been "aryanized" a long time ago. Names of former Jewish firms shall have to disappear completely, and the German shall have to come forward with his or his firm's name. I ask you to carry this out quite definitely. That much then regarding aryanizing of stores and wholesale establishments, particularly in regard to signboards and of all that is obvious!

Of the consequences resulting from this for the Jew, I shall speak later, because this is connected with other things.

Now for the factories. As for the smaller and medium ones, two things shall have to be made clear.

1. Which factories do I not need at all—which are the ones where productions could be suspended? Could they not be put to another use? If not, the factories will be razed immediately.
2. In case the factory should be needed, it will be turned over to Aryans in the same manner as the stores. All these measures have to be taken quickly, since Aryan employees are concerned everywhere. I'd like to say right now that Aryan employees shall have to be given employment immediately after the Jewish factory is closed. Considering the amount of labor we need these days, it should be a trifle to keep these people, even in their own branches. As I have just said; if the factory is necessary, it will be aryanized. If there is no need for it, it being abandoned shall be part of the procedure of transforming establishments not essential, for our national welfare into one that is essential for it—a procedure that shall take place within the next few weeks. For it, I shall still need very much space and very many factories.

If such a factory is to be transformed or razed, the first thing to be done is check the equipment. The questions arising will be: Where can this equipment be used? Could it be used after the place is transformed? Where else might it be needed badly? Where could the machinery be set up again? It follows that aryanizing factories will be an even more difficult task than the aryanizing of stores.

Take now the larger factories which are run solely by a Jewish owner, without control by a Board of Directors; or take corporations where the Jews might be in the Supervisory Council or Board of Directors. There the solution is very simple: the factory can be compensated in the same manner as in the sale of stores and factories; that is, at a rate which we shall determine, and the trustee shall take over the Jew's interest as well as his shares, which he in turn may sell or transfer to the State, which will then dispose of them. So, if I have a big factory, which belonged to a Jew or a Jewish corporation, and the Jew leaves, perhaps with his sons who were employed there, the factory will still continue to operate. Maybe a director will have to be appointed because the Jew has run the factory himself. But otherwise, particularly if the maintenance of the establishment is very essential everything will run smoothly.

Everything is very simple. I now have his shares. I may give them to some Aryan or to another group or I may keep them. The State takes them over and offers them at the stock market, if they are acceptable there and if it so desires, or it makes use of them in some other way.

Now, I shall talk of the very big establishments, those in which the Jew is in the Board of Directors, in which he holds shares etc., and so is either the owner or one of the co-owners; in any case in which he is greatly interested. There too, things are comparatively simple; he delivers all of his shares which shall be bought at a price fixed by the trustee. So the Jew gets into the account book. The shares shall be handled like I've just explained. These cases cannot be taken care of by the Gaue and Reichsstatthalter, but only by us here on top; because we are the only ones to decide where these factories are to be transferred to, how they may be affiliated with other establishments or to what an extent the State shall keep them or hand them over to another establishment belonging to the State. All this can only be decided here. Of course, the Gauleiter and Statthalter will be glad to get hold of the shares, and they'll make great promises to beautify our capital cities, etc. I know it all! It won't go! We must agree on a clear action that shall be profitable to the Reich.

The same procedure shall be applied where the Jew has a share in, or owns property of German economy. I am not competent enough to tell off hand in what forms that might be the case, and to what an extent he'll have to lose it. Anyway, the Jew must be evicted pretty fast from German economy.

Now, the foreign Jews. There we'll have to make distinctions between the Jews who have always been foreigners—and who shall have to be treated according to the laws we arranged with their respective countries. But regarding those Jews who were Germans, have always lived in Germany and have acquired foreign citizenship during the last year, only because they wanted to play safe. I ask you not to give them any consideration. We'll finish with these. Or have you any misgivings? We shall try to induce them through slight, and then through stronger pressure, and through clever maneuvering—to let themselves be pushed out voluntarily. . . .

Goebbels: In almost all German cities synagogues are burned. New, various possibilities exist to utilize the space where the synagogues stood. Some cities want to build parks in their place, others want to put up new buildings.

Goering: How many synagogues were actually burned?

Heydrich: Altogether there are 101 synagogues destroyed by fire; 76 synagogues demolished; and 7,500 stores ruined in the Reich.

Goering: What do you mean "destroyed by fire"?

Heydrich: Partly, they are razed, and partly gutted.

Goebbels: I am of the opinion that this is our chance to dissolve the synagogues. All these not completely intact, shall be razed by the Jews. The Jews shall pay for it. There in Berlin, the Jews are ready to do that. The synagogues which burned in Berlin are being leveled by the Jews themselves. We shall build parking lots in their places or new buildings. That ought to be the criterion for the whole country, the Jews shall have to remove the damaged or burned synagogues, and shall have to provide us with ready free space. . . .

I deem it necessary to issue a decree forbidding the Jews to enter German theaters, movie houses, and circuses. I have already issued such a decree under the authority of the law of the chamber for culture. Considering the present situation of the theaters, I believe we can afford that. Our theaters are overcrowded, we have hardly any room. I am of the opinion that it is not possible to have Jews sitting next to Germans in movies and theaters. One might consider, later on, to let the Jews have one or two movie houses here in Berlin, where they may see Jewish movies. But in German theaters they have no business anymore.

Furthermore, I advocate that the Jews be eliminated from all positions in public life in which they may prove to be provocative. It is still possible today that a Jew shares a compartment in a sleeping car with a German. Therefore, we need a decree by the Reich Ministry for Communications stating that separate compartments for Jews shall be available; in cases where compartments are filled up, Jews cannot claim a seat. They shall be given a separate compartment only after all Germans have secured seats. They shall not mix with Germans, and if there is no more room, they shall have to stand in the corridor.

Goering: In that case, I think it would make more sense to give them separate compartments.

Goebbels: Not if the train is overcrowded!

Goering: Just a moment. There'll be only one Jewish coach. If that is filled up, the other Jews will have to stay at home.

Goebbels: Suppose, though, there won't be many Jews going on the express train to Munich, suppose there would be two Jews in the train and the other compartments would be overcrowded. These two Jews would then have a compartment all themselves. Therefore, Jews may claim a seat only after all Germans have secured a seat.

Goering: I'd give the Jews one coach or one compartment. And should a case like you mention arise and the train be overcrowded, believe me, we won't need a law. We'll kick him out and he'll have to sit all alone in the toilet all the way!

Goebbels: I don't agree. I don't believe in this. There ought to be a law. Furthermore, there ought to be a decree barring Jews from German beaches and resorts. . . .

Goering: Particularly here in the Admiralspalast very disgusting things have happened lately.

Goebbels: Also at the Wannsee beach. A law which definitely forbids the Jews to visit German resorts!

Goering: We could give them their own.

Goebbels: It would have to be considered whether we'd give them their own or whether we should turn a few German resorts over to them, but not the finest and best, so we cannot say the Jews go there for recreation.

It'll also have to be considered if it might not become necessary to forbid the Jews to enter the German forests. In the Grunewald, whole herds of them are running around. It is a constant provocation and we are having incidents all the time. The behavior of the Jews is so inciting and provocative that brawls are a daily routine.

Goering: We shall give the Jews a certain part of the forest, and the Alpers shall take care of it that various animals that look damned much like Jews, – the Elk has such a crooked nose, – get there also and become acclimated.

Goebbels: I think this behavior is provocative. Furthermore, Jews should not be allowed to sit around in German parks. I am thinking of the whispering campaign on the part of Jewish women in the public gardens at Fehrbelliner Platz. They go and sit with German mothers and their children and begin to gossip and incite.

Goebbels: I see in this a particularly grave danger. I think it is imperative to give the Jews certain public parks, not the best ones—and tell them: "You may sit on these benches" these benches shall be marked "For Jews only." Besides that they have no business in German parks. Furthermore, Jewish children are still allowed in German schools. That's impossible. It is out of the question that any boy should sit beside a Jewish boy in a German gymnasium and receive lessons in German history. Jews ought to be eliminated completely from German schools; they may take care of their own education in their own communities.

Source: Office of the U.S. Chief of Counsel for the Prosecution of Axis Criminality. *Nazi Conspiracy and Aggression.* Red Series, vol. 4. Document 1816-PS. Washington, DC: U.S. Government Printing Office, 1946, pp. 425–57.

Commentary

Immediately after the *Kristallnacht* pogrom of November 9 to 10, 1938, Hermann Göring convened a meeting, the intention of which was to discuss what should happen next. The most pressing matter related to the economy, which was not surprising, given that Göring was head of the Four-Year Plan and that Germany was suffering from an acute shortage of foreign exchange. The fear of a flight of Jewish capital, linked to the added concern that there would be massive insurance claims stemming from the pogrom, led to the decision to hasten the program of Aryanizing the economy—that is, transferring all Jewish assets to non-Jewish or state control.

The extracts here, taken from the record of meeting, not only contain Göring's lengthy address to those present but also a discussion that includes Göring, Reinhard Heydrich, and Joseph Goebbels. Of particular importance is that part of the dialogue that moves beyond economic matters and considers discriminatory measures that can be introduced to cut Jews out of German life altogether: from separate carriages for Jews on trains, to distinctive park benches, to forbidding Jews to use theaters, beaches, and resorts, and to stop them from even entering forests.

The wide-ranging considerations that took place at this meeting were a taste of worse to come for the Jews, as they reinforced Nazi thoughts on the best ways to make Jewish lives so intolerable that the Jews would want to leave on their own accord. At this stage, there was no discussion of driving the Jews out; rather, the focus was on splitting the Jews off from any form of participation in German daily life. Henceforth, separate and thoroughly unequal existences would characterize the Aryan and Jewish populations in Germany, and if any should wish to leave as a result, so much the better. Eventually, it was hoped, the Jews would see that remaining in Germany was a thoroughly unviable proposition.

10. Regulation for the Elimination of Jews from the Economic Life of Germany, November 12, 1938

This document, issued by Hermann Göring and consisting of four regulations, relates to the implementation of the Four-Year Plan of October 18, 1936. In it, Jews are forbidden to operate and advertise retail stores, mail-order houses or sales agencies, run such enterprises, or be employed in any executive capacity in commercial venues.

On the basis of the regulation for the implementation of the Four-Year Plan of October 18, 1936 (Reichsgesetzblatt, I, p. 887), the following is decreed:

§ 1

(1) From January 1, 1939, Jews (§ 5 of the First Regulation to the Reich Citizenship Law of November 14, 1935, Reichsgesetzblatt, I, p. 1333) are forbidden to operate retail stores, mail-order houses, or sales agencies, or to carry on a trade [craft] independently.

(2) They are further forbidden, from the same day on, to offer for sale goods or services, to advertise these, or to accept orders at markets of all sorts, fairs or exhibitions.

(3) Jewish trade enterprises (Third Regulation to the Reich Citizenship Law of June 14, 1938—Reichsgesetzblatt, I, p. 627) which violate this decree will be closed by police.

§ 2

(1) From January 1, 1939, a Jew can no longer be the head of an enterprise within the meaning of the Law of January 20, 1934, for the Regulation of National Work (Reichsgesetzblatt, I, p. 45).

(2) Where a Jew is employed in an executive position in a commercial enterprise he may be given notice to leave in six weeks. At the expiration of the term of the notice all claims of the employee based on his contract, especially those concerning pension and compensation rights, become invalid.

§ 3

(1) A Jew cannot be a member of a cooperative.

(2) The membership of Jews in cooperatives expires on December 31, 1938. No special notice is required.

§ 4

The Reich Minister of Economy, in coordination with the Ministers concerned, is empowered to publish regulations for the implementation of this decree. He may permit exceptions under the Law if these are required as the result of the transfer of a Jewish enterprise to non-Jewish ownership, for the liquidation of a Jewish enterprise or, in special cases, to ensure essential supplies.

Source: Yitzhak Arad, Yisrael Gutman, and Abraham Margaliot, eds. *Documents on the Holocaust: Selected Sources on the Destruction of the Jews of Germany and Austria, Poland, and the Soviet Union*. Jerusalem: Yad Vashem, 1981, pp. 115–6. Reproduced by permission of Yad Vashem Publications.

Commentary

Proceeding from Göring's conference of the same day (see Document 9, above), this document is a regulation dated November 12, 1938, issued in the immediate aftermath of *Kristallnacht*. It embodies some of the preferences for Aryanization articulated by Göring at his meeting, specifically, in this case, the exclusion of Jews from all forms of economic enterprise, such as retail or other commercial activities. In addition, Jews were forbidden from serving in executive roles in any business-related enterprises.

The impact of this regulation for many German Jews was both profound and catastrophic. While large numbers of Jews were engaged in the professions, many others were merchants or otherwise occupied in commercial activities. Throwing them out of their means of earning a livelihood was a further reinforcement for them—if one was needed—that they no longer had a future in Germany and should immediately try to find a way to leave. Moreover, that this regulation should be handed down while they were still trying to absorb the shocks of *Kristallnacht* was a double blow. The "crystals," indeed, were all too frequently shards of glass from shattered windows of Jewish stores and other commercial enterprises.

This regulation, therefore, was a major prewar antisemitic measure. Its intention was twofold: to grab Jewish wealth for the Nazi state and, by doing so, to render Jewish life in Germany that much less sustainable.

11. Circular on "The Jewish Question as a Factor in German Foreign Policy in the Year 1938," January 25, 1939

In the year 1938 Nazi Germany annexed Austria, was handed the Sudetenland, and initiated the Kristallnacht *pogrom. In addition, the Evian Conference was held, at which no country expressed willingness to take in additional Jewish refugees. This document provides an overview of German foreign policy in 1938 as it was impacted by the Reich's desire to force the emigration of Jews to countries outside the Reich. Much of it focuses on the disposition of Jewish property upon emigration. The question of a Jewish state in Palestine is also referenced and found to be unacceptable, while noting the rise of antisemitism wherever Jewish immigrants have relocated outside of the Reich.*

It is certainly no co-incidence that the fateful year 1938 has brought nearer the solution of the Jewish question simultaneously with the realization of the "idea of Greater Germany," since the Jewish policy was both the basis and consequence of the events of the year 1938. The advance made by Jewish influence and the destructive Jewish spirit in politics, economy and culture paralyzed the power and will of the German people to rise again more perhaps even than the power-policy opposition of the former enemy allied powers of the World War. The healing of this sickness among the people was therefore certainly one of the most important requirements for exerting the force which in the year 1938 resulted in the joining together of Greater Germany, in defiance of the world. . . .

The necessity for a radical solution of the Jewish question arose however also as a consequence of the foreign political development, which resulted in a further 200,000 Jews in Austria in addition to the 500,000 of the Jewish Faith living in the Old Reich. The influence of Jewry on Austrian economy which had grown to enormous proportions under the Schuschnigg Regime, made immediate measures necessary, with the aim of excluding Jewry from German economy and utilizing Jewish property in the interests of the community. The action carried out as reprisal for the murder of Legation Counsellor vom Rath accelerated this process to such an extent that Jewish shops—till then with the exception of foreign business—disappeared from the streets completely. The liquidation of the Jewish wholesale trade, manufacturing trade, and of houses and real estate in the hands of Jews, will gradually reach a point where in a conceivable time there will no longer be any talk of Jewish property in Germany. Nevertheless it must be emphasized that this is no seizure of Jewish property without compensation, as for instance the confiscation of Church Property during the French revolution. On the contrary the dispossessed Jew receives Reich Bonds for his goods, and the interest is credited to him.

The final goal of German Jewish Policy is the emigration of all the Jews living in Reich territory. It is foreseen that already the thorough measures in the economic sphere, which have prevented the Jew from earning and made him live on his dividends, will further the desire to emigrate. Looking back on the last 5 years since the assumption of power, it is, however, obvious that neither the Law for the Reestablishing of the Professional Character of the Civil Service nor the Nurnberg Jewish laws with their executive regulations, which prevented any tendency of Jewry being assimilated, contributed to any extent to the emigration of German Jews. On the contrary every period of domestic political tranquility has resulted in such a stream of Jewish immigrants returning, that the Gestapo has been obliged to put Jewish immigrants with German passports into a training camp for political supervision.

The Jew was excluded from politics and culture. But until 1938 his powerful economic position in Germany was unbroken, and thereby his obstinate resolve to hold out until "better times" came. Indicative of the tactics of this "delaying" resistance is the programme of a Jewish Party recently formed in Poland, to fight against all Polish measures aimed at Jewish emigration. As long as the Jew can earn money in Germany, then in the opinion of World Jewry the Jewish bastion in Germany need not be given up.

But the Jew has underestimated the consequences and the strength of the National Socialist purpose. The powerful Jewish positions in Vienna and Prague collapsed in 1938 at the same time as the system of states in Central Europe created at Versailles to keep Germany down. Italy stood at Germany's side, with her racial Laws in the fight against Jewry. An expert on the Jewish question, Prof. Goga took over the Government in Bukarest with a programme aimed against Jewry, without however being able to carry it out because of overwhelming international pressure from Paris and London. Jewry in Hungary and Poland was subjected to special laws. Everywhere the success of German foreign policy now begins to shake Jewish strongholds which have been established for hundreds of years from Munich and in far off States, like the tremours of an earthquake.

It is also understandable that World Jewry, "which has selected America as its Headquarters" regards as its own downfall the Munich Agreement, which in American opinion signifies the collapse of the democratic front in Europe. For the system of parliamentary democracy has always, as experience proves, helped the Jews to wealth and political power at the expense of the people in whose country they live. It is certainly the first time in history that Jewry must evacuate a secure position.

This resolution was first formed in 1938. It showed itself in the efforts of the western democracies particularly those of the United States of America, to put the now finally determined Jewish withdrawal from Germany, in other words Jewish emigration, under international control and protection. The American president Roosevelt "who it is well known is surrounded by a whole row of exponents of Jewry among his closest confidants" called a State Conference as early as the middle of 1938 to discuss the refugee questions, which was held in Evian without any particular results. Both of the questions, the answering of which is the first essential for organized Jewish emigration remained unanswered: firstly the question of how this emigration should be organized and financed and secondly the question: emigrate *to where*?

In answer to the first question, International Jewry in particular did not appear willing to contribute. On the contrary the Conference—and later the Committee formed by it in London under the direction of Rublee, an American—regarded its main task as that of forcing Germany by international pressure to release Jewish property to the greatest possible extent. In other words Germany was to pay for the emigration of her 700,000 Jews with German national property. It is at the same time to be doubted whether International Jewry ever seriously desired the mass emigration of their fellow Jews from Germany and other states at all, unless there was an equivalent of a Jewish State. The tactics hitherto employed in Jewish proposals, were in every case aimed less at mass emigration of Jews than at the transfer of Jewish property.

It goes without saying, that the transfer of even a fraction of Jewish property, would be impossible from the point of view of foreign exchange. The financing of a mass emigration of German Jews is therefore still obscure. Questions could be answered casually thus, that Germany for her part reckoned that International Jewry—particularly relatives of Jews who have emigrated—would support this emigration as vigorously as it made it possible for its destitute fellow Jews to immigrate to Germany, at a time when Germany was so weak that she could not stop the stream of Jews from the East. It should be emphasized, however, that according to police and taxation records, the greater proportion of Jews immigrated to Germany without means and made money in a few years or decades, while the German people lost their possessions as a result of the reparations imposed by the Treaty of Versailles or joined the ranks of the unemployed. Consequently Germany for her part had no sympathy for the compassion, with which an ostensibly humanitarian world accuses Germany of illegally appropriating property which was taken away from the German people by Jewish business methods.

The second question, to what country should an organized Jewish emigration be directed, could similarly not be answered by the Evian Conference, as each of the countries taking part having announced that they were fundamentally concerned with the refugee problem, declared that they were not in a position to take large numbers of Jewish emigrants into their territory. After over 100,000 Jews even in 1933/34 had succeeded either legally or illegally in escaping abroad and establishing themselves in someone else's country either with the help of their Jewish relatives living abroad or circles sympathetically disposed from a humanitarian point of view, almost every State in the World has in the meantime hermetically sealed its borders against these parasitical Jewish intruders. The problem of Jewish emigration is therefore for all practical purposes at a standstill. Many States have already become so cautious, that they demand a permit made out by German authorities from Jews travelling in the ordinary way with German passports, saying that there is nothing against them returning.

The emigration movement of only about 100,000 Jews has already sufficed to awaken the interest if not the understanding of many countries in the Jewish danger. We can estimate that here the Jewish question will extend to a problem of international politics when large numbers of Jews from Germany, Poland, Hungary and Rumania are put on the move as a result of increasing pressure from the people of the countries where they are living. Even for Germany the Jewish problem will not be solved when the last Jew has left German soil.

It is even today an important duty of German policy to control and when possible direct the flow of Jewish emigration to be sure there is no incentive to cooperate with other countries such as Poland, Hungary and Rumania, who themselves are striving for the emigration of the Jewish sections of their population, in an attempt to solve this problem. From experience with this procedure interests clash, although directed towards the same goal, and retard the realization of Germany's urgent claim for German Jews to be admitted into other particular countries.

It is true that the Rumanian Government sent an official appeal to the Reich Government in the name of human ethics and justice, to join with them in an international action to solve the Jewish question. On the other hand, Poland at the end of October last year issued a decree, the execution of which has made it practically impossible for 60,000 Jews of Polish Nationality residing in Germany to return to Poland. As is well known, the Reich Government had then to decide to deport to Poland 60,000 Jews of Polish Nationality who will be followed by their families, shortly before the Polish Decree came into force. The Hungarian Government, it is true, appreciates the German Jewish policy in so far as they themselves have in mind the "Aryanization" of Hungarian-Jewish businesses in Germany, that is, Jewish owners of firms will be replaced by Hungarians. In general, however, it is apparent that the States concerned are more egotistically interested in deporting their own Jewish elements than in any international solution. Germany will therefore take the initiative herself, in order next of all to find ways, means and destination for Jewish emigration from Germany.

Palestine—which has already become the slogan of world opinion, as the land for the emigrants—cannot be considered as the target for Jewish emigration, because it is incapable of absorbing a mass influx of Jews. Under the pressure of Arab resistance, the British Mandatory Government has restricted Jewish immigration into Palestine to the minimum. For the time being Jewish emigration to Palestine was helped to a great extent, as far as Germany was concerned, by the signing of an agreement with the representatives of Jewry in Palestine, which made it possible to transfer Jewish property in the form of additional exports (Haavara-Agreement). Apart from the fact that emigration was made possible by this method for a small number of wealthy Jews only, but not for the mass of Jews without means, [Pencil note: Are there such people?] there were fundamental considerations of foreign policy against this type of emigration: the transfer of Jewish property out of Germany, contributed to no small extent to the building of a Jewish State in Palestine. Germany must regard the forming of a Jewish State, as dangerous, which even in miniature would form just such an operational base as the Vatican for political Catholicism. The realization that World Jewry will always be the irreconcilable enemy of the Third Reich, forces the decision to prevent any strengthening of the Jewish position. A Jewish State however would bring an international increase in power to World Jewry. Alfred Rosenberg expressed this idea in his speech in Detmold on 15 January this year as follows:

"Jewry is striving today for a Jewish State in Palestine. Not to give Jews all over the world a homeland but for other reasons: World Jewry must have a miniature State, from which to send exterritorial ambassadors and representatives to all countries of the world and through these be able to further their lust for power. But more than anything else they want a Jewish centre, a Jewish State in which they can house the Jewish swindlers from all parts of the world, who are hunted by the Police of other countries, issue them new passports and then send them to other parts of the world. It is to be desired, that those people who are friendly disposed to Jews, above all the Western Democracies who have so much space in all parts of the world at their disposal, place an area outside Palestine for the Jews, *of course in order to establish a Jewish Reserve and not a Jewish State*."

That is the programme expressing the foreign policy attitude of Germany towards the Jewish question. Germany is very interested in maintaining the dispersal of Jewry. The calculation, that as a consequence boycott groups and anti-German centres would be formed all over the world, disregards the following fact which is already apparent, the influx of Jews in all parts of the world invokes the opposition of the native population and thereby forms the best propaganda for the German Jewish policy.

In North America, in South America, in France, in Holland, Scandinavia and Greece, everywhere, wherever the flood of Jewish immigrants reaches, there is today already a visible increase in anti-semitism. A task of the German foreign policy must be to further this wave of anti-semitism. This will be achieved less by German propaganda abroad, than by the propaganda which the Jew is forced to circulate in his defense. In the end, its effects will recoil on themselves. The reports from German authorities abroad, emphasize the correctness of this interpretation.

The press and official correspondents continually report antisemitic demonstrations by the population of North America. It is perhaps indicative of the domestic political development in USA, that the listening-audience of the "Radio Priest" Coughlin, who is well known to be Anti-Jewish, has grown to over 20 millions. The Embassy in Montevideo reported on 12 December last year "that the Jewish influx continues for months, week by week. It goes without saying, that anti-semitism is growing"—Salonica reported on 30 November 1938: "that forces are at work to stir up the hate against the Jews" and that at the same time Greek Freemasonry is endeavoring to stem the anti-semitic movement. In France, the Paris Town Council (Stadtversammlung) was in April of this year to discuss a proposal, by which the naturalization of Jews was in future to be refused. The meeting on the Jewish question ended with the speaker being beaten up—Lyon reported on 20 December last year: "The immigration of Jewish refugees has lately led to undesirable occurrences. The antipathy towards the new intruders based on business and competitive grounds, which is general throughout France, is unmistakable." This aversion has grown to such an extent meantime that a Jewish defense has already been organized against the anti-semitism in France (Report Paris dated 19 November last year).—The Embassy at The Hague reported on 30 December last year: "Under the pressure of countless immigrants from Germany, who make themselves objectionable particularly in Amsterdam antisemitism is growing very much in Holland. And if this continues, it can easily come to pass that Dutchmen will not only appreciate Germany's action against the Jews but will also find themselves wishing to do the same as we."—The embassy at Oslo reported on 8th April last year: "While only a few years ago, the streets of Oslo were hardly marred by Jews at all, lately a great change has come about here. On the streets, in restaurants and above all in the coffee houses, Jews sit around in hideous cluster. The Norwegians are being crowded out, more and more. The Norwegian Press, which formerly did not understand the Jewish question at all, suddenly realized what it meant to have the Children of Israel invade the country like a swarm of locusts. It will be a very salutary lesson, which is being meted out to the Norwegians."

These examples from reports from authorities abroad, can, if desired, be amplified. They confirm the correctness of the expectation, that criticism of the measures for excluding Jews from German Lebensraum which were misunderstood in many countries for lack of evidence would only be temporary and would swing in the other direction the moment the population saw with its own eyes and thus learned, what the Jewish danger was to them. The poorer and therefore the more burdensome the immigrant Jew is to the country absorbing him, the stronger this country will react and the more desirable is this effect in the interests of German propaganda. The object of this German action is to be the future international solution of the Jewish question, dictated not by false compassion for the "United Religious Jewish minority" but by the full consciousness of all peoples of the danger which it represents to the racial composition of the nations.

Source: Office of the U.S. Chief of Counsel for the Prosecution of Axis Criminality. *Nazi Conspiracy and Aggression*. Red Series, vol. 6. Document 3358-PS, Washington, DC: U.S. Government Printing Office, 1946, pp. 87–95.

Commentary

This document is a summary of progress made regarding Jewish matters in 1938, as understood by the German Foreign Ministry. Issued on January 25, 1939, it notes a direct relationship between "the solution of the Jewish question" and "the realization of the 'idea of Greater Germany.'" It is clear in its conclusion that one was contingent upon the other.

These developments came about because of the *Anschluss* between Germany and Austria back in March. The addition of up to 200,000 more Jews into the Reich at a time when those in Germany were even then not yet leaving in sufficient numbers led to an urgent need to rethink the management of the Jewish issue. For the Foreign Office, this translated into the international implications of Nazi antisemitic policy; thus, the statement discusses the Evian refugee conference, the position of the United States toward the reception of Germany's Jews, and the attitude of other European countries with large Jewish populations.

Important in this context is the position of Palestine. This is something of which the Foreign Office was particularly aware, and while reference is made to the August 1933 Haavara Agreement between Nazi Germany and the Jewish Agency, the conclusion is drawn that too many Jews in Palestine—an unviable proposition in view of the fact that "it is incapable of absorbing a mass influx of Jews"—would be a "dangerous" proposition because it could lead to the formation of a Jewish state.

Finally, the document concludes that the Western world's criticism of German measures is unfounded owing to the "danger" presented by Jews internationally, a danger "to the racial composition of the nations" of the world.

12. Adolf Hitler: Extract from a Speech to the Reichstag, January 30, 1939

In its entirely, this speech was primarily concerned with the economic, political, military, and diplomatic recovery of Germany in the aftermath of the Versailles Treaty of 1919 after World War I. Hitler's antisemitism was reflected throughout the speech, but three-quarters of the way into it he made an important and often-quoted prophecy that if there should be another war (which, in his view, would have been caused by "international

Jewish financiers"), it would not result in a Jewish victory but, rather, "the annihilation of the Jewish race in Europe."

I believe that this problem will be solved—the sooner the better—for Europe cannot rest again before the Jewish problem has been eliminated. . . .

Once more I will assume the part of a prophet:

If the international Jewish financiers within and without Europe, succeeded in plunging the nations once more into a world war, then the result will be not the Bolshevization of the world and thereby the victory of Jewry—but the annihilation of the Jewish race in Europe.

Source: Office of the U.S. Chief of Counsel for the Prosecution of Axis Criminality. *Nazi Conspiracy and Aggression*. Red Series, vol. 5. Document 2663-PS. Washington, DC: U.S. Government Printing Office, 1946, pp. 367.

Commentary

On January 30, 1939, the sixth anniversary of Adolf Hitler's ascent to the chancellorship of Germany, he delivered a speech to the Reichstag lasting over two hours. The majority of the speech was not devoted to the subject of the Jews; instead, it recounted the history of the Nazi Party and its many successes.

Perhaps the lines most remembered, however, relate to a few comments he made toward the end of the speech, where he spoke unambiguously about the likely annihilation of European Jewry. If, he said, "the international Jewish financiers within and without Europe, succeeded in plunging the nations once more into a world war, then the result will be not the Bolshevization of the world and thereby the victory of Jewry—but the annihilation of the Jewish race in Europe." While this was not the first time there had been exterminatory invective thrown at the Jews, it was unquestionably the clearest statement yet made by Hitler himself in a public setting. Nor was it a slip of the tongue. Hitler was pleased with the words he said here and repeated his threat about the "annihilation of the Jewish race in Europe" in a number of additional speeches in the years that followed.

Moreover, not only did he repeat the words in other contexts; he also referred often to the speech's very existence. During these wartime addresses, interestingly, he would often erroneously and deliberately give the date of his speech as September 1, 1939, the day on which Germany invaded Poland and World War II was precipitated. This way, he was able to demonstrate how the destiny for the Jews he foresaw was being fulfilled at his command.

13. Hans Frank: Speech to His Cabinet, Kraków, December 16, 1941

Hans Frank was the Governor-General of the Generalgouvernement, *that portion of German-occupied Poland not incorporated into the Reich. Its Jewish population, as Frank observes in this extract, comprised more than two and a half million Jews. This speech is particularly significant in that it represents one of the first occasions in which extermination—not just relocation or ghettoization—of the Jews is discussed in such straightforward language, making it clear that annihilation is now the policy of the Reich. An interesting reference is made by Frank to a forthcoming conference that will take place in Berlin to discuss the extermination process. That conference is the Wannsee Conference, which would be held on January 20, 1942, as confirmed by Frank's statements that Dr. Bühler would attend and Reinhard Heydrich would chair the conference (as subsequent events would bear out).*

As far as the Jews are concerned, I want to tell you quite frankly that they must be done away with in one way or another. The Führer said once: should united Jewry again succeed in provoking a world war, the blood of not only the nations, which have been forced into the war by them, will be shed, but the Jew will have found his end in Europe. I know that many of the measures carried out against the Jews in the Reich at present are being criticized. It is being tried intentionally, as is obvious from the reports on morale, to talk about cruelty, harshness, etc. Before I continue, I want to beg you to agree with me on the following formula: We will principally have pity on the German people only, and nobody else in the whole world. The others, too, had no pity on us. As an old National Socialist, I must say: This war would only be a partial success if the whole lot of Jewry should survive it, while we would have shed our best blood in order to save Europe. My attitude towards the Jews will, therefore, be based only on the expectation that they must disappear. They must be done away with. I have entered negotiations to have them deported to the East. A great discussion concerning that question will take place in Berlin in January to which I am going to delegate the State-Secretary Dr. Bühler. That discussion is to take place in the Reich Security Main Office with SS-Lt. General Heydrich. A great Jewish migration will begin in any case.

But what should be done with the Jews? Do you think they will be settled down in the "Ostland," in villages? This is what we were told in Berlin: Why all the bother? We can do nothing with them either in the "Ostland" nor in the "Reichkommissariat." So, liquidate them yourself.

Gentlemen, I must ask you to rid yourself of all feeling of pity. We must annihilate the Jews, wherever we find them and wherever it is possible, in order to maintain there the structure of the Reich as a whole. This will, naturally, be achieved by other methods, than those pointed out by Bureau Chief Dr. Hummel. Nor can the judges of the Special Courts be made responsible for it, because of the limitations of the framework of the legal procedure. Such outdated views cannot be applied to such gigantic and unique events. We must find at any rate a way which leads to the goal, and my thoughts are working in that direction.

The Jews represent for us also extraordinarily malignant gluttons. We have now approximately 2,500,000 of them in the General Government, perhaps with the Jewish mixtures and everything that goes with it, 3,500,000 Jews. We cannot shoot or poison those 3,500,000 Jews, but we shall nevertheless be able to take measures which will lead, somehow, to their annihilation, and this in connection with the gigantic measures to be determined in discussions in the Reich. The General Government must become free of Jews, the same as the Reich. Where and how this is to be achieved is a matter for the offices which we must appoint and create here. Their activities will be brought to your attention in due course.

Source: Office of the U.S. Chief of Counsel for the Prosecution of Axis Criminality. *Nazi Conspiracy and Aggression*. Red Series, vol. 4. Document 2233-D-PS. Washington, DC: U.S. Government Printing Office, 1946, pp. 891–92.

Commentary

The year 1941 saw the start of the annihilation of the Jews, the process that was to become the Holocaust. With the Nazi invasion of the Soviet Union on June 22, 1941, the mass killing began, and soon thereafter, experiments in how to perfect the murder process started.

For Hans Frank, however, the issue was not one to be found in the Soviet Union; the urgency was to dispose of the large and, despite the authorities' best efforts, growing Jewish population in the *Generalgouvernement*.

The core of Frank's position is to be found in his second paragraph. For Frank, there is no doubt that the Jews will not be "resettled," as was often stated in the coded language characterizing Nazi statements. Proceeding from the discretionary powers delegated from Berlin, Frank knew instinctively that it was within his remit to "liquidate" (his term) the Jews, as a result of which he instructs those assembled before him to "rid yourself of all feeling of pity," comfortable in the knowledge that they "must annihilate the Jews, wherever we find them and wherever it is possible." He realizes that the task will be a difficult one given the millions of people involved and that "We cannot shoot or poison" them all. Nonetheless, he asserts, measures can be taken "which will lead, somehow, to their annihilation."

This is a document extraordinary for its unguarded bluntness, particularly in the Third Reich, where euphemistic language was the norm and matters relating to the mass murder of the Jews were rarely discussed overtly. The date of the meeting is also worth noting; it comes within days of Germany's declaration of war against the United States and the failure of the German army to take Moscow. From this point on, total war would have to be waged, and this applied also to the war against the Jews.

14. The Wannsee Protocol, January 20, 1942

Often misunderstood as the meeting where the Holocaust was decided, this record of the conference held at a villa on Lake Wannsee, Berlin, in January 1942 is a summary of events already in place. Convened by SS-Obergruppenführer *and Chief of the Security Police Reinhard Heydrich, the minutes were taken by* SS-Obersturmbannführer *Adolf Eichmann. Basing itself upon a presumption of 11,000,000 Jews still alive in Europe, the core of the discussion was focused on "preparations for the final solution of the Jewish question." While considerations of mass murder were not specifically recorded, there is little doubt that this was the primary matter of discussion at this meeting to coordinate the implementation of a decision that had already been taken to destroy the Jewish population of Europe.*

I. The following persons took part in the discussion about the final solution of the Jewish question which took place in Berlin, am Grossen Wannsee No. 56/58 on

January 20, 1942. Gauleiter Dr. Meyer and Reichsamtsleiter Dr. Leibbrandt (Reich Ministry for the Occupied Eastern Territories); Secretary of State Dr. Stuckardt (Reich Ministry for the Interior); Secretary of State Neumann (Plenipotentiary for the Four Year Plan); Secretary of State Dr. Freisler (Reich Ministry of Justice); Secretary of State Dr. Bühler (Office of the Government General); Under Secretary of State Luther (Foreign Office); SS-Oberführer Klopfer (Party Chancellery); Ministerialdirektor Kritzinger (Reich Chancellery); SS-Gruppenführer Hofmann (Race and Settlement Main Office); SS-Gruppenführer Müller and SS-Obersturmbannführer Eichmann (Reich Main Security Office); SS-Oberführer Dr. Schöngarth (Chief of the Security Police and the SD in the Government General Security Police and SD); SS-Sturmbannführer Dr. Lange (Commander of the Security Police and the SD for the General district Latvia, as deputy of the Commander of the Security Police and the SD for the Reich Commissariat "Eastland").

Security Police and SD

II. At the beginning of the discussion SS-Obergruppenführer HEYDRICH gave information that the Reich Marshal had appointed him delegate for the preparations for the final solution of the Jewish problem in Europe and pointed out that this discussion had been called for the purpose of clarifying fundamental questions. The wish of the Reich Marshal to have a draft sent to him concerning organisatory, factual and material interests in relation to the final solution of the Jewish problem in Europe, makes necessary an initial common action of all Central Offices immediately concerned with these questions in order to bring their general activities into line.

He said that the Reich Führer-SS and the Chief of the German Police (Chief of the Security Police and the SD) was entrusted with the official handling of the final solution of the Jewish problem centrally without regard to geographic borders.

The Chief of the Security Police and the SD then gave a short report of the struggle which has been carried on against this enemy, the essential points being the following:

a) the expulsion of the Jews from every particular sphere of life of the German people,
b) the expulsion of the Jews from the Lebensraum of the German people.

In carrying out these efforts, an increased and planned acceleration of the emigration of Jews from the Reich territory was started, as the only possible present solution.

By order of the Reich Marshal a Reich Central Office for Jewish Emigration was set up in January 1939 and the Chief of the Security Police and SD was entrusted with the management. Its most important tasks were

a) to make all necessary arrangements for the preparation for an increased emigration of the Jews,

b) to direct the flow of immigration,
c) to hurry up the procedure of emigration in each individual case.

The aim of all this being that of clearing the German Lebensraum of Jews in a legal way.

All the Offices realized the drawbacks of such enforced accelerated emigration. For the time being they had, however, tolerated it on account of the lack of other possible solutions of the problem.

The work concerned with emigration was, later on, not only a German problem, but also a problem with which the authorities of the countries to which the flow of emigrants was being directed would have to deal. Financial difficulties, such as the demand for increasing sums of money to be presented at the time of the landing on the part of various foreign governments, lack of shipping space, increasing restriction of entry permits, or canceling of such, extraordinarily increased the difficulties of emigration. In spite of these difficulties 537,000 Jews were sent out of the country between the day of the seizure of power and the deadline 31 October 1941. Of these as from 30 January from Germany proper approx. 360,000 Jews themselves, or rather their Jewish political organizations, financed the emigration.

In order to avoid the possibility of the impoverished Jews staying behind, action was taken to make the wealthy Jews finance the evacuation of the needy Jews, this was arranged by imposing a suitable tax, i.e. an emigration tax which was used for the financial arrangements in connection with the emigration of poor Jews, and was worked according to a ladder system.

Apart from the necessary Reichmark-exchange, foreign currency had to be presented at the time of the landing. In order to save foreign exchange held by Germany, the Jewish financial establishments in foreign countries were—with the help of Jewish organizations in Germany—made responsible for arranging for an adequate amount of foreign currency. Up to 30 October 1941, the foreign Jews donated approx. $9,500,000.

In the meantime the Reichsführer-SS and Chief of the German Police had prohibited emigration of Jews for reasons of the dangers of an emigration during wartime and consideration of the possibilities in the East.

III. Another possible solution of the problem has now taken the place of emigration, i.e. the evacuation of the Jews to the East, provided the Führer agrees to this plan.

Such activities are, however, to be considered as provisional actions, but practical experience is already being collected which is of greatest importance in relation to the future final solution of the Jewish problem.

from 15 March 1938 from Austria (Ostmark) appr. 147,000
from 15 March 1939 from the Protectorate, Bohemia and Moravia appr. 30,000.

Approx. 11,000,000 Jews will be involved in this final solution of the European problem, they are distributed as follows among the countries:

A
Germany proper 131,800
Austria 43,700
Eastern territories 420,000
General Government 2,284,000
Bialystok 400,000
Protectorate Bohemia & Moravia 74,200
Estonia free of Jews
Latvia 3,500
Lithuania 34,000
Belgium 43,000
Denmark 5,600
France/occupied territory 165,000
Unoccupied territory 700,000
Greece 69,600
Netherlands 160,800
Norway 1,300

B
Bulgaria 48,000
England 330,000
Finland 2,300
Ireland 4,000
Italy including Sardinia 58,000
Albania 200
Croatia 40,000
Portugal 3,000
Rumania including Bessarabia 342,000
Sweden 8,000
Switzerland 18,000
Serbia 10,000
Slovakia 88,000
Spain 6,000
Turkey (European Turkey) 55,500
Hungary 742,800
USSR 5,000,000
Ukraine 2,994,684
White Russia with exception of Bialystok 446,484

Total over
11,000,000

The number of Jews given here for foreign countries includes, however, only those Jews who still adhere to the Jewish faith as the definition of the term "Jew" according to racial principles is still partially missing there. The handling of the problem in the individual countries will meet with difficulties due to the attitude and conception of the people there, especially in Hungary and Rumania. Thus, even today a Jew can buy documents in Hungary which will officially prove his foreign citizenship.

The influence of the Jews in all walks of life in the USSR is well known. Approximately 5 million Jews are living in the European Russia, and in Asiatic Russia scarcely 1/4 million. The breakdown of Jews residing in the European part of the USSR, according to trades, was approximately as follows:

in agriculture 9.1%
communal workers 14.8%
in trade 20.0%
employed by the state 23.4%
in private occupations such as medical profession, newspapers, theater, etc. 32.7%

Under proper guidance the Jews are now to be allocated for labor to the East in the course of the final solution. Able-bodied Jews will be taken in large labor columns to these districts for work on roads, separated according to sexes, in the course of which action a great part will undoubtedly be eliminated by natural causes.

The possible final remnant will, as it must undoubtedly consist of the toughest, have to be treated accordingly, as it is the product of natural selection, and would, if liberated, act as a bud cell of a Jewish reconstruction (see historical experience).

In the course of the practical execution of this final settlement of the problem, Europe will be cleaned up from the West to the East. Germany proper, including the protectorate Bohemia and Moravia, will have to be handled first because of reasons of housing and other sociopolitical necessities.

The evacuated Jews will first be sent, group by group, into so-called transit-ghettos from which they will be taken to the East.

SS-Obergruppenführer HEYDRICH went on to say that an important provision for the evacuation as such is the exact definition of the group of persons concerned in the matter.

It is intended not to evacuate Jews of more than 65 years of age but to send them to an old age-ghetto—Theresienstadt is being considered for this purpose.

Next to these age-groups—of the 280,000 Jews still in Germany proper and Austria on 31 October 1941, approximately 30% are over 65; Jews disabled on active duty and Jews with war decorations (Iron Cross I) will be accepted in the Jewish old-age-ghettos.

Through such expedient solution the numerous interventions will be eliminated with one blow.

The carrying out of each single evacuation project of a larger extent will start at a time to be determined chiefly by the military development. Regarding the handling of the final solution in the European territories occupied and influenced by us it was suggested that the competent officials of the Foreign Office working on these questions confer with the competent "Referenten" from the Security Police and the SD.

In Slovakia and Croatia the difficulties arising from this question have been considerably reduced, as the most essential problems in this field have already been brought near to a solution. In Rumania the Government in the meantime has also appointed a commissioner for Jewish questions. In order to settle the question in Hungary it is imperative that an adviser in Jewish questions be pressed upon the Hungarian government without too much delay.

As regards the taking of preparatory steps to settle the question in Italy SS Obergruppenführer HEYDRICH considers it opportune to contact the chief of the police with a view to these problems.

In the occupied and unoccupied parts of France the registration of the Jews for evacuation can in all probability be expected to take place without great difficulties.

Assistant Under-Secretary of State LUTHER in this connection calls attention to the fact that in some countries, such as the Scandinavian states, difficulties will arise if these problems are dealt with thoroughly and that it will be therefore advisable to defer action in these countries. Besides, considering the small numbers of Jews to be evacuated from these countries this deferment means not essential limitation.

On the other hand, the Foreign Office anticipates no great difficulties as far as the South-East and the West of Europe are concerned.

SS-Gruppenführer HOFMANN intends to send an official from the Main Race and Settlement Office to Hungary for general orientation at the time when the first active steps to bring up the question in this country will be taken by the Chief of the Security Police and the SD. It was determined officially to detail this official, who is not supposed to work actively, temporarily from the Main Race and Settlement Office as assistant to the police attaché.

IV. The implementation of the final solution-problem is supposed to a certain extent to be based on the Nuremberg Laws, in which connection also the solution of the problems presented by the mixed-marriages and the persons of mixed blood is seen to be conditional to an absolutely final clarification of the question.

The chief of the Security Police and the SD first discussed, with reference to a letter from the Chief of the Reich Chancellery, the following points theoretically:

1) Treatment of Persons of Mixed Blood of the First Degree.

Persons of mixed blood of the first degree will, as regards the final solution of the Jewish question, be treated as Jews.

From this treatment the following persons will be exempt:

a) Persons of mixed blood of the first degree married to persons of German blood if their marriage has resulted in children (persons of mixed blood of the second degree). Such persons of mixed blood of the second degree are to be treated essentially as Germans.
b) Persons of mixed blood of the first degree to whom up till now in any sphere of life whatsoever exemption licenses have been issued by the highest Party or State authorities. Each individual case must be examined,

in which process it will still be possible that a decision unfavorable to the persons of mixed blood can be passed.

In any such case only personal essential merit of the person of mixed blood must be deemed a ground justifying the granting of an exemption. (Net merits of the parent or of the partner of German blood.)

Any person of mixed blood of the first degree to whom exemption from the evacuation is granted will be sterilized—in order to eliminate the possibility of offspring and to secure a final solution of the problem presented by the persons of mixed blood. The sterilization will take place on a voluntary basis. But it will be conditional to a permission to stay in the Reich.

Following the sterilizations the "person of mixed blood" will be liberated from all restrictive regulations which have so far been imposed upon him.

2) Treatment of Persons of Mixed Blood of the Second Degree.
Persons of mixed blood of the second degree will fundamentally be treated as persons of German blood, with exception of the following cases in which persons of mixed blood of the second degree will be treated as Jews:

a) The person of mixed blood of the second degree is the result of a marriage where both parents are persons of mixed blood.
b) The general appearance of the person of mixed blood of the second degree is racially particularly objectionable so that he already outwardly must be included among the Jews.
c) The person of mixed blood of the second degree has a particularly bad police and political record sufficient to reveal that he feels and behaves like a Jew.

But also in these cases exceptions are not to be made if the person of mixed blood of the second degree is married to a person of German blood.

3) Marriages between Full Jews and Persons of German Blood.
Here it must be decided from one individual case to another whether the Jewish partner is to be evacuated, or whether in consideration of the effects produced by such measure upon the German relatives of the mixed marriage he is to be committed to a ghetto for aged Jews.

4) Marriages between Persons of Mixed Blood of the First Degree and Persons of German Blood.

a) Without Children.

If no children have resulted from the marriage, the parents of mixed blood of the first degree will be evacuated or committed to a ghetto for old Jews. (The same treatment as in the case of marriages between full Jews and persons of German blood, Point 3).

b) With Children.

If the marriage has resulted in children (persons of mixed blood of the second degree) these children will be evacuated or committed to a ghetto together with the parents of mixed blood of the first degree, if they are to be treated as Jews. If the children are to be treated as Germans (regular cases) they will be exempt from evacuation and in that case the same applies to the parent of mixed blood of the first degree.

5) Marriages between Persons of Mixed Blood of the First Degree and Persons of Mixed Blood of the First Degree or Jews.

In the case of these marriages (including the children) all members of the family will be treated as Jews, therefore evacuated or committed to a ghetto for old Jews.

6) Marriages between Persons of Mixed Blood of the First Degree and Persons of Mixed Blood of the Second Degree.

Both partners will be evacuated, regardless of whether or not they have children, or committed to a ghetto for old Jews, since as a rule these children will racially reveal the admixture of Jewish blood more strongly than persons of mixed blood of the second degree.

SS-Gruppenführer HOFMANN advocates the opinion that sterilization must be applied on a large scale; in particular as the person of mixed blood placed before the alternative as whether to be evacuated or to be sterilized, would rather submit to the sterilization.

Under Secretary of State Dr. STUCKART maintains that the possible solutions enumerated above for a clarification of the problems presented by mixed marriages and by persons of mixed blood when translated into practice in this form would involve endless administrative work. In the second place, as the biological facts cannot be disregarded in any case, it was suggested by Dr. STUCKART to proceed to forced sterilization.

Further, for the purpose of simplifying the problem of mixed marriages it would be required to consider how it would be possible to attain the object that the legislator can declare: "This marriage has been dissolved."

Regarding the question of the effects produced by the evacuation of the Jews on the economic life, Under Secretary of State NEUMANN declared that the Jews assigned to work in plants of importance for the war could not be evacuated as long as no replacement was available.

SS-Obergruppenführer HEYDRICH pointed out that besides, according to the directives approved by him governing the carrying out of the evacuation program in operation at that time, these Jews would not be evacuated.

Under Secretary of State Dr. BÜHLER stated that it would be welcomed by the Government General if the implementation of the final solution of this question could start in the Government General, because the transportation problem there was of no predominant importance and the progress of this action would not be hampered by considerations connected with the supply of labor. The Jews had to be removed as quickly as possible from the territory of the Government General because especially there the Jews represented an immense danger as a carrier of epidemics, and on the other hand were permanently contributing to the disorganization of the economic system of the country through black market operations.

Moreover, out of the two and a half million Jews to be affected, the majority of cases was unfit for work.

Under Secretary of State BÜHLER further stated that the solution of the Jewish question in the Government General as far as the issuing of orders was concerned was dependent upon the chief of the Security Police and the SD, his work being supported by the administrative authorities of the Government General. He had this one request only, namely that the Jewish question in this territory be solved as quickly as possible.

Towards the end of the conference the various types of possible solutions were discussed; in the course of this discussion Gauleiter Dr. MEYER as well as Under Secretary of State Dr. BÜHLER advocated the view that certain preparatory measures incidental to the carrying out of the final solution ought to be initiated immediately in the very territories under discussion, in which process, however, alarming the population must be avoided.

With the request to the persons present from the Chief of the Security Police and the SD that they lend him appropriate assistance in the carrying out of the tasks involved in the solution, the conference was adjourned.

Source: *Trials of War Criminals before the Nuremberg Military Tribunals under Control Council Law No. 10*. Vol. 13. Document NG-2586. Office of the United States U.S. Chief Counsel for the Prosecution of Axis Criminality. Washington, DC: U.S. Government Printing Office, 1946, pp. 210–17.

Commentary

The conference on January 20, 1942, at a luxury villa on Berlin's Lake Wannsee, was convened to discuss the best way to coordinate the process of annihilation of the Jews beyond the work already being accomplished in the occupied Soviet Union by the *Einsatzgruppen*. The fundamental objective of the conference was thus to systematize and coordinate the Final Solution.

Those invited included a range of state secretaries whose bureaucratic departments would later become fully involved in the murders of Europe's Jews. Thus, this conference marked the official coordination of those efforts. Eight of the 15 participants had PhDs; many were lawyers by training. All were familiar with the work of mass killing already taking place in the areas under Nazi control.

Organized by the head of the SD, Reinhard Heydrich, the items for discussion included the use of mobile gas-killing vans and large-scale, stationary gas chambers. Other topics included estimating the size of Europe's Jewish population, organizing a systematic sweep of Europe to eliminate all Jewish remnants, and establishing criteria for dealing with mixed marriages and Jews of so-called "mixed-blood" (*Mischlinge*). The decision to annihilate 11 million European Jews, including those in Britain and all of the still-neutral countries, had already been made. Contrary to popular wisdom, the conference was not called to discuss whether or not to implement the Final Solution, but to discuss the various and best ways of achieving a *Judenrein* ("Jew-free") Europe.

The entire meeting lasted 90 minutes, with Adolf Eichmann serving as conference secretary. A stenographer carefully composed a complete record of the discussions, after which Heydrich gave Eichmann strict instructions about how to draw up the protocols based on the stenographic record. The result was a short summary document in which the purposes of the meeting were outlined, together with conclusions as to next steps. Thirty copies of these minutes were sent out, with instructions that all were to be destroyed later. One, however, remained; in 1947, Martin Luther's copy was located, enabling the story of the conference at Wannsee to be reconstructed.

15. Otto Ohlendorf: Extracts from Testimony Regarding the *Einsatzgruppen*, June 1941–June 1942

Einsatzgruppen *were mobile killing units that followed the German armies into Russia, tasked with the job of killing Jews and communists. There were four such units (A through D), each with approximately 750 men. The commander of* Einsatzgruppe D *was Otto Ohlendorf. It was in that capacity that he was responsible for the murder of 90,000 Jews during a single year, from June 1941 to June 1942, as a result of which he was tried in the* "Einsatgruppen *Trial" held in Nuremberg from September 1947 through February 1948. Ohlendorf was the lead defendant.*

The following extracts are from Ohlendorf's trial testimony. One of the areas of examination in this document is the close role that the Wehrmacht, the professional German military, played in support of the Einsatzgruppen, *something the Wehrmacht long denied. Ohlendorf provides a detailed description of how the Jews were executed, including the use and construction of gas vans used to kill women and children. He is being cross-examined by Colonel John Harlan Amen, a United States Army Intelligence officer and Nuremberg Prison Chief Interrogator.*

COLONEL JOHN HARLAN AMEN (Associate Trial Counsel for the United States): May it please the Tribunal, I wish to call as a witness for the Prosecution, Mr. Otto Ohlendorf.

COL. AMEN: When did you become a member of the SA?
OHLENDORF: In the year 1925.
COL. AMEN: When, if ever, did you join the SD?
OHLENDORF: In 1936.
COL. AMEN: What was your last position in the SD?
OHLENDORF: Chief of Amt III in the RSHA.
COL. AMEN: Did you tell us for what period of time you continued to serve as Chief of Amt III?
OHLENDORF: I was part-time Chief of Amt III from 1939 to 1945.
COL. AMEN: Turning now to the designation "Mobile Units" with the Army shown in the lower right hand corner of the chart, please explain to the Tribunal the significance of the terms "Einsatzgruppe" and "Einsatzkommando."
OHLENDORF: The concept "Einsatzgruppe" was established after an agreement between the Chiefs of the RSHA, OKW, and OKH, on the separate use of Sipo units in the operational areas. The concept "Einsatzgruppe" first appeared during the Polish campaign.

COL. AMEN: To the best of your knowledge and recollection, please explain to the Tribunal the entire substance of this written agreement.

OHLENDORF: I said, this was the relationship between the Army and the Einsatzgruppen and the Einsatzkommandos. The agreement specified that the army groups or armies would be responsible for the movement and the supply of Einsatzgruppen, but that instructions for their activities would come from the Chief of the Sipo and SD.

COL. AMEN: Let us understand. Is it correct that an Einsatz group was to be attached to each army group or army?

OHLENDORF: Every army group was to have an Einsatzgruppe attached to it. The army group in its turn would then attach the Einsatzkommandos to the armies of the army group.

COL. AMEN: And was the army command to determine the area within which the Einsatz group was to operate?

OHLENDORF: The operational area of the Einsatzgruppe was already determined by the fact that it was attached to a specific army group and therefore moved with it, whereas the operational areas of the Einsatzkommandos were then fixed by the army group or army.

COL. AMEN: Did the agreement also provide that the army command was to direct the time during which they were to operate?

OHLENDORF: That was included under the heading "movement."

COL. AMEN: And also to direct any additional tasks they were to perform?

OHLENDORF: Yes. Even though the Chiefs of the Sipo and SD had the right to issue instructions to them on their work, there existed a general agreement that the army was also entitled to issue orders to the Einsatzgruppen, if the operational situation made it necessary.

COL. AMEN: What position did you occupy with respect to this agreement?

OHLENDORF: From June 1941 to the death of Heydrich in June 1942, I led Einsatzgruppe D, and was the representative of the Chief of the Sipo and the SD with the 11th Army.

COL. AMEN: And when was Heydrich's death?

OHLENDORF: Heydrich was wounded at the end of May 1942, and died on 4 June 1942.

COL. AMEN: How much advance notice, if any, did you have of the campaign against Soviet Russia?

OHLENDORF: About 4 weeks.

COL. AMEN: How many Einsatz groups were there, and who were their respective leaders?

OHLENDORF: There were four Einsatzgruppen, Group A, B, C, and D. Chief of Einsatzgruppe A was Stahlecker; Chief of Einsatzgruppe B was Nebe; Chief of Einsatzgruppe C, Dr. Rasche, and later, Dr. Thomas; Chief of Einsatzgruppe Dl, I myself, and later Bierkamp.

COL. AMEN: To which army was Group D attached?

OHLENDORF: Group D was not attached to any army group, but was attached directly to the 11th Army.

COL. AMEN: Where did Group D operate?

OHLENDORF: Group D operated in the Southern Ukraine.

COL. AMEN: When did Group D commence its move into Soviet Russia?

OHLENDORF: Group D left Duegen on 21 June and reached Pietra Namsk in Romania in 3 days. There the first Einsatzkommandos were already being demanded by the Army, and they immediately set off for the destinations named by the Army. The entire Einsatzgruppe was put into operation at the beginning of July.

COL. AMEN: You are referring to the 11th Army?

OHLENDORF: Yes.

COL. AMEN: In what respects, if any, were the official duties of the Einsatz groups concerned with Jews and Communist commissars?

OHLENDORF: On the question of Jews and Communists, the Einsatzgruppen and the commanders of the Einsatzkommandos were orally instructed before their mission.

COL. AMEN: What were their instructions with respect to the Jews and the Communist functionaries?

OHLENDORF: The instructions were that in the Russian operational areas of the Einsatzgruppen the Jews, as well as the Soviet political commissars, were to be liquidated.

COL. AMEN: And when you say "liquidated" do you mean "killed"?

OHLENDORF: Yes, I mean "killed."

COL. AMEN: Prior to the opening of the Soviet campaign, did you attend a conference at Pretz?

OHLENDORF: Yes, it was a conference at which the Einsatzgruppen and the Einsatzkommandos were informed of their tasks and were given the necessary orders.

COL. AMEN: Who was present at that conference?

OHLENDORF: The chiefs of the Einsatzgruppen and the commanders of the Einsatzkommandos and Streckenbach of the RSHA who transmitted the orders of Heydrich and Himmler.

COL. AMEN: What were those orders?

OHLENDORF: Those were the general orders on the normal work of the Sipo and the SD, and in addition the liquidation order which I have already mentioned.

COL. AMEN: And that conference took place on approximately what date?

OHLENDORF: About 3 or 4 days before the mission.

COL. AMEN: So that before you commenced to march into Soviet Russia, you received orders at this conference to exterminate the Jews and Communist functionaries in addition to the regular professional work of the Security Police and SD; is that correct?

OHLENDORF: Yes.

COL. AMEN: Did you, personally, have any conversation with Himmler respecting any communication from Himmler to the chiefs of army groups and armies concerning this mission?

OHLENDORF: Yes. Himmler told me that before the beginning of the Russian campaign Hitler had spoken of this mission to a conference of the army groups and the army chiefs—no, not the army chiefs but the commanding generals—and had instructed the commanding generals to provide the necessary support.

COL. AMEN: So that you can testify that the chiefs of the army groups and the armies had been similarly informed of these orders for the liquidation of the Jews and Soviet functionaries?

OHLENDORF: I don't think it is quite correct to put it in that form. They had no orders for liquidation; the order for the liquidation was given to Himmler to carry out, but since this liquidation took place in the operational area of the army group or the armies, they had to be ordered to provide support. Moreover, without such instructions to the army, the activities of the Einsatzgruppen would not have been possible.

COL. AMEN: Did you have any other conversation with Himmler concerning this order?

OHLENDORF: Yes, in the late summer of 1941 Himmler was in Nikolaiev. He assembled the leaders and men of the Einsatzkommandos, repeated to them the liquidation order, and pointed out that the leaders and men who were taking part in the liquidation bore no personal responsibility for the execution of this order. The responsibility was his, alone, and the Führer's.

COL. AMEN: And you yourself heard that said?

OHLENDORF: Yes.

COL. AMEN: Do you know whether this mission of the Einsatz group was known to the army group commanders?

OHLENDORF: This order and the execution of these orders were known to the commanding general of the army.

COL. AMEN: How do you know that?

OHLENDORF: Through conferences with the army and through instructions which were given by the army on the execution of the order.

COL. AMEN: Was the mission of the Einsatz groups and the agreement between OKW, OKH, and RSHA known to the other leaders in the RSHA?

OHLENDORF: At least some of them knew of it, since some of the leaders were also active in the Einsatzgruppen and Einsatzkommandos in the course of time. Furthermore, the leaders who were dealing with the organization and the legal aspect of the Einsatzgruppen also knew of it.

COL. AMEN: Most of the leaders came from the RSHA, did they not?

OHLENDORF: Which leaders?

COL. AMEN: Of the Einsatz groups.

OHLENDORF: No, one can't say that. The leaders in the Einsatzgruppen and Einsatzkommandos came from all over the Reich.

COL. AMEN: Who was the commanding officer of the 11th Army?

OHLENDORF: At first, Ritter von Schober; later, Von Manstein.

COL. AMEN: Will you tell the Tribunal in what way or ways the commanding officer of the 11th Army directed or supervised Einsatz Group D in carrying out its liquidation activities?

OHLENDORF: An order from the 11th Army was sent to Nikolaiev stating that liquidations were to take place only at a distance of not less than 200 kilometers from the headquarters of the commanding general.

COL. AMEN: Do you recall any other occasion?

OHLENDORF: In Simferopol the army command requested the Einsatzkommandos in its area to hasten the liquidations, because famine was threatening and there was a great housing shortage.

COL. AMEN: Do you know how many persons were liquidated by Einsatz Group D under your direction?

OHLENDORF: In the year between June 1941 to June 1942 the Einsatzkommandos reported 90,000 people liquidated.

COL. AMEN: Did that include men, women, and children?

OHLENDORF: Yes.

COL. AMEN: On what do you base those figures?

OHLENDORF: On reports sent by the Einsatzkommandos to the Einsatzgruppen.

COL. AMEN: Were those reports submitted to you?

OHLENDORF: Yes.

COL. AMEN: And you saw them and read them?

OHLENDORF: I beg your pardon?

COL. AMEN: And you saw and read those reports, personally?

OHLENDORF: Yes.

COL. AMEN: And it is on those reports that you base the figures you have given the Tribunal?

OHLENDORF: Yes.

COL. AMEN: Do you know how those figures compare with the number of persons liquidated by other Einsatz groups?

OHLENDORF: The figures which I saw of other Einsatzgruppen are considerably larger.

COL. AMEN: That was due to what factor?

OHLENDORF: I believe that to a large extent the figures submitted by the other Einsatzgruppen were exaggerated.

COL. AMEN: Did you see reports of liquidations from the other Einsatz groups from time to time?

OHLENDORF: Yes.

COL. AMEN: And those reports showed liquidations exceeding those of Group D; is that correct?

OHLENDORF: Yes.

COL. AMEN: Did you personally supervise mass executions of these individuals?

OHLENDORF: I was present at two mass executions for purposes of inspection.

COL. AMEN: Will you explain to the Tribunal in detail how an individual mass execution was carried out?

OHLENDORF: A local Einsatzkommando attempted to collect all the Jews in its area by registering them. This registration was performed by the Jews themselves.

COL. AMEN: On what pretext, if any, were they rounded up?

OHLENDORF: On the pretext that they were to be resettled.

COL. AMEN: Will you continue?

OHLENDORF: After the registration the Jews were collected at one place; and from there they were later transported to the place of execution, which was, as a rule an antitank ditch or a natural excavation. The executions were carried out in a military manner, by firing squads under command.

COL. AMEN: In what way were they transported to the place of execution?

OHLENDORF: They were transported to the place of execution in trucks, always only as many as could be executed immediately. In this way it was attempted to keep the span of time from the moment in which the victims knew what was about to happen to them until the time of their actual execution as short as possible.

COL. AMEN: Was that your idea?

OHLENDORF: Yes.

COL. AMEN: And after they were shot what was done with the bodies?

OHLENDORF: The bodies were buried in the antitank ditch or excavation.

COL. AMEN: What determination, if any, was made as to whether the persons were actually dead?

OHLENDORF: The unit leaders or the firing-squad commanders had orders to see to this and, if need be, finish them off themselves.

COL. AMEN: And who would do that?

OHLENDORF: Either the unit leader himself or somebody designated by him.

COL. AMEN: In what positions were the victims shot?

OHLENDORF: Standing or kneeling.

COL. AMEN: What was done with the personal property and clothing of the persons executed?

OHLENDORF: All valuables were confiscated at the time of the registration or the rounding up and handed over to the Finance Ministry, either through the RSHA or directly. At first the clothing was given to the population, but in the winter of 1941–42 it was collected and disposed of by the NSV.

COL. AMEN: All their personal property was registered at the time?

OHLENDORF: No, not all of it, only valuables were registered.

COL. AMEN: What happened to the garments which the victims were wearing when they went to the place of execution?

OHLENDORF: They were obliged to take off their outer garments immediately before the execution.

COL. AMEN: All of them?

OHLENDORF: The outer garments, yes.

COL. AMEN: How about the rest of the garments they were wearing?

OHLENDORF: The other garments remained on the bodies.

COL. AMEN: Was that true of not only your group but of the other Einsatz groups?

OHLENDORF: That was the order in my Einsatzgruppe. I don't know how it was done in other Einsatzgruppen.

COL. AMEN: In what way did they handle it?

OHLENDORF: Some of the unit leaders did not carry out the liquidation in the military manner, but killed the victims singly by shooting them in the back of the neck.

COL. AMEN: And you objected to that procedure?

OHLENDORF: I was against that procedure, yes.

COL. AMEN: For what reason?

OHLENDORF: Because both for the victims and for those who carried out the executions, it was, psychologically, an immense burden to bear.

COL.AMEN: Now, what was done with the property collected by the Einsatzkommandos from these victims?

OHLENDORF: All valuables were sent to Berlin, to the RSHA or to the Reich Ministry of Finance. The articles which could be used in the operational area, were disposed of there.

COL. AMEN: For example, what happened to gold and silver taken from the victims?

OHLENDORF: That was, as I have just said, turned over to Berlin, to the Reich Ministry of Finance.

COL. AMEN: How do you know that?

OHLENDORF: I can remember that it was actually handled in that way from Simferopol.

COL. AMEN: How about watches, for example, taken from the victims?

OHLENDORF: At the request of the Army, watches were made available to the forces at the front.

COL. AMEN: Were all victims, including the men, women, and children, executed in the same manner?

OHLENDORF: Until the spring of 1942, yes. Then an order came from Himmler that in the future women and children were to be killed only in gas vans.

COL. AMEN: How had the women and children been killed previously?

OHLENDORF: In the same way as the men—by shooting.

COL. AMEN: What, if anything, was done about burying the victims after they had been executed?

OHLENDORF: The Kommandos filled the graves to efface the signs of the execution, and then labor units of the population leveled them.

COL. AMEN: Referring to the gas vans which you said you received in the spring of 1942, what order did you receive with respect to the use of these vans?

OHLENDORF: These gas vans were in future to be used for the killing of women and children.

COL. AMEN: Will you explain to the Tribunal the construction of these vans and their appearance?

OHLENDORF: The actual purpose of these vans could not be seen from the outside. They looked like closed trucks, and were so constructed that at the start of the motor, gas was conducted into the van causing death in 10 to 15 minutes.

COL. AMEN: Explain in detail just how one of these vans was used for an execution.

OHLENDORF: The vans were loaded with the victims and driven to the place of burial, which was usually the same as that used for the mass executions. The time needed for transportation was sufficient to insure the death of the victims.

COL. AMEN: How were the victims induced to enter the vans?

OHLENDORF: They were told that they were to be transported to another locality.

COL. AMEN: How was the gas turned on?

OHLENDORF: I am not familiar with the technical details.

COL. AMEN: How long did it take to kill the victims ordinarily?

OHLENDORF: About 10 to 15 minutes; the victims were not conscious of what was happening to them.

COL. AMEN: How many persons could be killed simultaneously in one such van?

OHLENDORF: About 15 to 25 persons. The vans varied in size.

COL. AMEN: Did you receive reports from those persons operating these vans from time to time?

OHLENDORF: I didn't understand the question.

COL. AMEN: Did you receive reports from those who were working on the vans?

OHLENDORF: I received the report that the Einsatzkommandos did not willingly use the vans.

COL. AMEN: Why not?

OHLENDORF: Because the burial of the victims was a great ordeal for the members of the Einsatzkommandos.

COL. AMEN: Now, will you tell the Tribunal who furnished these vans to the Einsatz groups?

OHLENDORF: The gas vans did not belong to the motor pool of the Einsatzgruppen but were assigned to the Einsatzgruppe as a special unit, headed by the man who had constructed the vans. The vans were assigned to the Einsatzgruppen by the RSHA.

COL. AMEN: Were the vans supplied to all of the different Einsatz groups?

OHLENDORF: I am not certain of that. I know only in the case of Einsatzgruppe D, and indirectly that Einsatzgruppe C also made use of these vans.

COL. AMEN: [W]ill you explain to the Tribunal why you believe that the type of execution ordered by you, namely, military, was preferable to the shooting-in-the-neck procedure adopted by the other Einsatz groups?

OHLENDORF: On the one hand, the aim was that the individual leaders and men should be able to carry out the executions in a military manner acting on orders and should not have to make a decision of their own; it was, to all intents and purposes, an order which they were to carry out. On the other hand, it was known to me that through the emotional excitement of the executions ill-treatment could not be avoided, since the victims discovered too soon that they were to be executed and could not therefore endure prolonged nervous strain. And it seemed intolerable to me that individual leaders and men should in consequence be forced to kill a large number of people on their own decision.

COL. AMEN: In what manner did you determine which were the Jews to be executed?

OHLENDORF: That was not part of my task; but the identification of the Jews was carried out by the Jews themselves, since the registration was handled by a Jewish Council of Elders.

COL. AMEN: Did the amount of Jewish blood have anything to do with it?
OHLENDORF: I can't remember the details, but I believe that half-Jews were also considered as Jews.

Source: *Trial of the Major War Criminals before the International Military Tribunal, Nuremberg*. Blue Series, vol. 4. Office of the United States. U.S. Chief Counsel for the Prosecution of Axis Criminality. Washington, DC: U.S. Government Printing Office, 1946, pp. 311–34.

Commentary

The Nuremberg trial testimony of Otto Ohlendorf, *SS-Gruppenführer* and commanding officer of *Einsatzgruppe D*, was a terrifying statement of how the mobile killing squads operated in the occupied Soviet Union. Colonel John Amen, the U.S. prosecutor, permitted Ohlendorf full rein to explain how the *Einstazgruppen* operated, and the matter-of-factness with which he presented his testimony makes for disturbing reading, even today.

While disclosing the intricacies of the murder process through shooting—the "Holocaust by bullets," to use the term coined by Holocaust scholar Fr. Patrick Desbois—Ohlendorf also disclosed details of how the gas vans operated in occupied Poland. While these details had been known in certain circles during the war, public disclosures of the kind made here were shocking for the public to hear.

Moreover, Ohlendorf described the disbursement of victims' property; the psychological impact of the murders on those doing the killing; and, importantly in the context of perpetration, the relationship between the *Einsatzgruppen* and the Wehrmacht, which, for several decades after the war, claimed an air of noncomplicity regarding the Holocaust.

All in all, this document, reproduced at length in this collection, is a key statement of how the early phase of the Holocaust was carried out in Poland and the Soviet Union. It is a demonstration of how the Nazis were able to engage in inhuman activities in pursuit of an antihuman ideology, and the way that Ohlendorf did so is both morally repugnant and very, very disturbing.

16. Heinrich Himmler: Order for the Completion of the Final Solution, July 19, 1942

By this single order, Reichsführer-SS Heinrich Himmler directed that the "resettlement of the entire Jewish population of the Government-General" be carried out and completed by December 31, 1942. Accordingly, all Jews in this densely populated region were to be gathered in "collection camps in Warsaw, Cracow, Czestochowa, Radom, and Lublin."

I herewith order that the resettlement of the entire Jewish population of the Government-General be carried out and completed by December 31, 1942.

From December 31, 1942, no persons of Jewish origin may remain within the Government-General, unless they are in collection camps in Warsaw, Cracow, Czestochowa, Radom, and Lublin. All other work on which Jewish labor is employed must be finished by that date, or, in the event that this is not possible, it must be transferred to one of the collection camps.

These measures are required with a view to the necessary ethnic division of races and peoples for the New Order in Europe, and also in the interests of the security and cleanliness of the German Reich and its sphere of interest. Every breach of this regulation spells a danger to quiet and order in the entire German sphere of interest, a point of application for the resistance movement and a source of moral and physical pestilence.

For all these reasons a total cleansing is necessary and therefore to be carried out. Cases in which the date set can not be observed will be reported to me in time, so that I can see to corrective action at an early date. All requests by other offices for changes or permits for exceptions to be made must be presented to me personally.

Source: Yitzhak Arad, Yisrael Gutman, and Abraham Margaliot, eds. *Documents on the Holocaust, Selected Sources on the Destruction of the Jews of Germany and Austria, Poland and the Soviet Union*. Jerusalem: Yad Vashem, 1981, pp. 275–76. Reproduced by permission of Yad Vashem Publications.

Commentary

The summer of 1942 saw an intensification of the killing processes of the Holocaust, during which *Aktion Reinhard*, named in honor of slain SD leader Reinhard Heydrich, swung into action. The operation was the code name given to the Nazi plan to murder the approximately 2 million Jews surviving in the *Generalgouvernement*.

The killing had started in the fall of 1941, but Heydrich's assassination in June 1942 led to a vengeance campaign and the development of murder processes at Bełżec, Sobibór, and Treblinka—the so-called Operation Reinhard camps.

Understanding the context in which this document appeared, therefore, is crucial. Himmler's order that the "resettlement of the entire Jewish population" was to be "carried out and completed" by the end of 1942 was a clear direction that the murder of 2 million Jews had six months to be achieved. By directing that the only Jews still permitted to be in the *Generalgouvernement* after December 31, 1942, could be those in "collection camps"—holding centers prior to deportation—Himmler was ordering that the ghettoization and slave-labor phases of Jewish existence had come to an end. Henceforth, "a total cleansing" would be carried out of the population in the *Generalgouvernement*, "with a view to the necessary ethnic division of races and peoples for the New Order in Europe." Into this could be read the extermination of a Jewish presence and the path made clear for the resettlement of Germans in the now-depopulated lands.

Acting upon this order, Nazi officials throughout the *Generalgouvernement*, led by Governor Hans Frank, breathed a sigh of relief. The *Generalgouvernement* would now be the major site of anti-Jewish activity, something that had been desired for the past two years.

This document, in short, was an order to take Holocaust killing up to the next and deadliest level.

17. Martin Luther: Joachim von Ribbentrop's Instructions on Speeding up Evacuation of Jews from Europe, September 24, 1942

In this document, Martin Luther, Foreign Office Undersecretary (Unterstaatssekretär), *conveys to State Secretary Ernst von Weizsäcker a decision made by Foreign Minister Joachim von Ribbentrop to expedite evacuation of Jews from various occupied countries in Europe. At this time, mass murders were occurring at extermination camps in Poland, including Auschwitz, where only two months earlier more than 4,000 children deported from Paris were exterminated. The reason given for the need to increase evacuations is that the Jews "stir up" others against the Nazi regime. In fact, the increased evacuations were part of the overall Nazi plan to deport as many Jews as possible to "the East," meaning to their deaths in the extermination camps.*

The Reich Foreign Minister has given me instructions today over the telephone to hurry as much as possible the evacuation of Jews from the various countries of Europe, because it is a known fact that the Jews stir up people against us everywhere and that they must be made responsible for attempts of murder and acts of sabotage. Upon a brief report concerning the present stage of evacuation of the Jews from Slovakia, Croatia, Rumania, and the occupied territories, the Reich Foreign Minister has given instructions now to start contacting the governments of Bulgaria, Hungary, and Denmark with the object of starting the evacuation of the Jews from these countries.

With regard to the settlement of the Jewish question in Italy, the Reich Foreign Minister has reserved for himself all steps to be taken. This question shall be discussed personally either between the Führer and the Duce or between the Reich Foreign Minister and Count Ciano.

Herewith to the State Secretary v. Weizsaecker with the request to take notice. All steps taken by us will be submitted to you at the time for your approval.

Source: *Trial of War Criminals before the Nuremberg Military Tribunals under Control Council No. 10*. Green Series, vol. 13. Document NG-1517. Office of the United States. U.S. Chief Counsel for the Prosecution of Axis Criminality. Washington, DC: U.S. Government Printing Office, 1946, pp. 255–56.

Commentary

Martin Luther, undersecretary at the Foreign Office, represented his minister, Joachim von Ribbentrop, at the Wannsee Conference in January 1942. In this document, issued nine months later, Luther conveys the content of a telephone conversation he had with Ribbentrop to the effect that deportations of Jews in the German-allied and German-occupied countries should be speeded up.

In this way, the Holocaust became a truly international affair. Luther, reporting to his immediate superior, Ernst von Weizsäcker, noted that Jews were already being "evacuated" (in the euphemistic code language of the Third Reich) from Slovakia, Croatia, and Romania—all allied countries—as well as from the German-occupied territories. Overtures were now to be made to other allied governments in Bulgaria and Hungary, as well as to the government of occupied Denmark "with the object of starting the evacuation of the Jews from those countries."

Given the more highly developed relationship between Germany and Italy, Luther noted, Ribbentrop would take charge of these negotiations personally; if they were not negotiated at the level of foreign minister with the Italian counterpart, Count Galeazzo Ciano, then Hitler and Mussolini would undertake to discuss developments themselves.

This document represents both a formalization and a broadening of the Holocaust as a truly Europe-wide Nazi project. In this case, the Foreign Office is exercising its jurisdiction over an area that was, in most other respects, a purely SS matter. It is with this in mind that we should read Martin Luther's involvement more clearly, as he was the conduit between the Wannsee Conference, at which the SS established its control over the Final Solution, and Ribbentrop.

18. Alice Mackert: Preliminary Interrogation, May 11, 1945

"Alice La Blonde" was the nickname given to Alice Mackert, who served as the secretary general of the Gestapo in Nice, France, during the German occupation. This document, reproduced here for the first time, is an excellent illustration of how far some collaborators went in their efforts to placate the Nazis—whether out of conviction or for ulterior motives. Born in Switzerland and an immigrant to France before the war, she arrived in Nice in 1943 as support staff to the Gestapo. As the document shows, she then had a very active life moving throughout Nazi-occupied Europe, engaging in denunciations of Jews, and mixing in high Nazi circles.

Herewith is Preliminary Interrogation Report of Alice MACKERT, mistress of OSTRICH, captured by Third Army in April 1945. Subject will be interrogated further at Camp 020 in the U.K.

Preliminary Interrogation of Alice MACKERT @ Antoinette LINSER

Alice MACKERT worked for SD Amt VI/S and was evidently highly esteemed and trusted by those with whom she worked. She was the former mistress of OSTRICH. She claims she is of Swiss nationality.

Before working for the SD MACKERT says that she was with the German army administration. She says that she worked for this service in Normandy from November 1940 until April 1942; from April to December 1942 at Lille and Sens; at Frankfort from December 1942 until April 1943; in Sens in April and then back to Frankfort where she stayed until July 1943. These statements are contrary to a report which says that MACKERT was in Alencon from 1939 until 1942 and that she was presumably engaged in espionage activities from 1940. The report also says that MACKERT became a naturalised German subject in 1942.

In July 1943 MACKERT went to work for Hauptsturmführer Dr. FISCHER @ SCHNEIDER, SD Referat 3b at 60 Avenue Foch, Paris. She says that she wrote reports on Brittany and the Basque country. While working for FISCHER, MACKERT did a penetration job for Standartenführer Dr. ADAM. Posing as ADAM's mistress, she was introduced to a group of German officers who frequented the Hotel

St. James in Paris and who were extremely well-informed as to German military plans.

In July 1943 MACKERT was sent to Nice with Dr. FISCHER who was to be Hauptsturmführer RETZECK's deputy at Cannes. MACKERT says that RETZECK was formerly a military instructor with the GFP at Rennes and she also states that the GFP was absorbed by the SD.

With RETZECK in Nice were the following: Hauptscharführer Dr. FILLMAN who had been in Paris; Hauptscharführer LAUSER who had been in Paris with FISCHER and who acted as a courier in Nice; Hauptscharführer SCHULZ (cover name); Sturmscharführer NAGEL; Oberscharführer NEBEL; Oberscharführer WOHLFAHRT; Untersturmführer MERBREIER @ GAUTHIER who had been at Boulevard Flandrin in Paris, later at Vichy and had also worked for Amt VI in Corsica. MERBREIER acted as liaison officer between the Italian consul and Amt VI and between Amt VI and Group MAX. According to MACKERT, Group MAX was an Italian intelligence network which was turned around and worked for Amt VI. Its chief was a Colonel BARANCO, an Italian, who, MACKERT says, is now in hiding in Italy. She says that he had all his teeth pulled out to change his appearance.

The head of Amt VI at Nice was Untersturmführer MOSER who was formerly with Amt VI at Montpellier. MOSER sent reports to RETZECK who forwarded them to 11 Boulevard Flandrin in Paris. MACKERT says that MOSER sent agents to Italy but not to Spain. He was still in Nice when MACKERT left in March 1944. With MOSER in Nice were: Sturmbannführer GOHL; WOEBEKING, deputy to MOSER; and a female secretary DREIBHOLZ who was from Coblenz. Also in Amt VI at Nice was Hauptscharführer SCHWINN, formerly a feldwebel in the Brandenburg Division and later with Jagdverband Sudwest and attached to SKORZENY. MACKERT says that she made out laisser-passer for SCHWINN's agents and also gave SCHWINN reports on the usefulness of his agents. She also says that at one time SCHWINN organised a group which he sent to penetrate the maquis. She saw SCHWINN for the last time in Berlin on 5 February 1945.

Also in Nice when MACKERT was there were MUELLER and KRAUSE (both cover names) with Amt IVb. The head of the Kripo in Nice was Oberscharführer NIVERA.

With the Abwehr at Nice was Rittmeister BUCHOLZ. MACKERT says the Abwehr called on the SD for aid in making arrests.

The Amt VI representative at Marseille, according to MACKERT, was SENNER. With him was a man named MARTIN who took care of SENNER's agents who were sent to Spain and Italy. MACKERT made out laisser-passer for SENNER's agents among whom were the SCHIFFMANN family, working in Spain, and the AGNELY family.

MACKERT says that RETZECK was transferred to Belgrade in March 1944 after some kind of trouble in Nice. She says that she thinks he may have been sent into Albania to fight the maquis. She last heard of him in connection with a proceeding against him in Paris in May 1944 in which she was supposed to be a witness against him. She says that KNAPP replaced RETZECK at Nice.

While at Nice MACKERT says that they had occasion to use a Fliegendes Kommando which was attached to Drancy prison in Paris. This kommando, which was the only one of its kind in France, was called upon by various Sipo and SD offices throughout France to deal with Jewish questions. MACKERT says that when there were Jewish problems in Nice the Fliegendes Kommando would arrive. If they needed a train for deportees or any other supplies, they were furnished by MACKERT's office.

In March 1944 MACKERT was transferred to Kaunas, Lithuania where she stayed until April when she went to Riga where she stayed until July 1944. In Riga she worked with Referat IVN under the Befehlshaber Ostland Oberst der Polizei Dr FUCHS who had previously been in the Balkans and later in Lithuania. While at Riga MACKERT acted as an interpreter, worked with agents and dealt with foreign workers, sentencing them to labour camps. MACKERT says that there was also a Fliegendes Kommando at Riga which worked with the guards of the ghetto dealing with Jewish questions.

In August 1944 MACKERT went to Berlin to the Berkaer Strasse where Hauptsturmführer MUELLER sent her to Obersturmbannführer BERNHARD who wanted her to act as interpreter for HITLER and HIMMLER. MACKERT did want to stay in Berlin and succeeded in being attached to SKORZENY. She was sent to Paris in August 1944 where she was with Sonderkommando HAGEDORN. She left with the kommando for Fischingen and Badenweiler. In October 1944 she acted as a courier between Badenweiler and BESEKOW in the Berkaer Strasse.

In November 1944 MACKERT accompanied a group of Amt VI/S agents to the Gasteinhuette at Schwarz, a pension requisitioned by SKORZENY for ski instruction for his agents. With MACKERT were the following: AMICO, BIANCHI, Daniel and Jacques MARISSAL, SORDI, BOURVEAU, Claude and Gerald AGNELY, GUY, Michel HARISPE, Edouard LOCQUET, PIERRE and RICARDO. MACKERT says that she saw the name of SKORZENY's wife, Amy, on the registry of the pension. The proprietor of the Gasteinhuette was a certain HACK and the ski instructors were Oberscharführer GROSS, a Swiss from Pontresil, and Unterscharführer AUER from Kitzbuhl. The men who took part in the kidnapping of MUSSOLINI had been sent to the Gasteinhuette for ski instruction.

MACKERT stayed at Schwarz until January 1945 when she returned to Berlin where she worked with Hauptsturmführer BESEKOW and Hauptsturmführer RADL, deputy and righthand man of SKORZENY. She went to Friedenthal at the end of January where she was working with BESEKOW taking care of French agents and reporting to Berlin on their usefulness. While at Friedenthal MACKERT saw RADL, BESEKOW, HAGEDORN, SCHMIEL, BRAUMFELD, DOBREWITCH, MAYER, ULLBRICH, secretary in SKORZENY's office, and Anna-Marie KRUGER, secretary to BESEKOW and SKORZENY.

The 12 February MACKERT left with Hauptsturmführer DOBREWITCH for San Remo. DOBREWITCH was with the Sipo at Verona. MACKERT passed through Verona, Milan and Genoa on her way to San Remo. At Milan she saw Sturmbannführer GOHL, the head of Amt VI at Milan and chief of all kommandos for Italy. She had previously seen him at Nice where he had been with Untersturmführer MOSER. GOHL did not wish to let MACKERT proceed to San Remo because orders had been received that all women were to be forbidden to go south of the Po. However, MACKERT had SKORZENY's orders and she was allowed to proceed.

At Verona MACKERT says that Hauptsturmführer Heinz TUNNAT was head of the Amt VMS kommando. He was chief for Southern Italy and employed only Italian agents.

In Genoa she says that the Amt VI office was in a Casa delli Estudianti.

At San Remo MACKERT worked with Obersturmführer NEISSER to whom she had brought a large sum of money from Berlin. She made out laisser-passer for SENNER's agents all of whom were to be sent to France except two who were destined for the Italian maquis. NEISSER and SENNER lived in the Villa Alice and about ten agents lived in the Villa Verdi. MACKERT says that Amt VI was entirely detached from the main office of the Sipo and SD.

While at San Remo MACKERT saw Rosita CASIER @ Yvonne or Rosita de VILLIERS who was a former mistress of BESEKOW. She had been suspected of playing a double game and had been sent to the Gasteinhuette at Schwarz and then had gone on to San Remo. She was supposed to return to Berlin but refused to go. As far as MACKERT knows she was still at San Remo when MACKERT left there.

MACKERT left San Remo 5 March 1945 and went to Wiesbaden. From there she went to Mayence where she was arrested.

Source: Central Intelligence Agency, FOIA Electronic Reading Room, Nazi War Crimes Disclosure Act Collection, https://www.cia.gov/library/readingroom/docs/NEBEL,%20LUDWIG%20%20%20VOL.%202_0116.pdf.

Commentary

Alice Mackert, known to many of her victims as "Alice La Blonde," served as the secretary-general of the Gestapo in Nice, France, during the German occupation of the area. As this document shows, however, the extent of her collaboration with the Nazis extended to much more than simple administration activities.

The document, which is a report of her initial interrogation after her capture by Allied forces at the end of World War II, refers to another of her aliases (Antoinette Linser). She gives an account of her life in France and elsewhere during the war, along the way exposing a curriculum vitae covering a broad expanse of territory—in France, Germany, Italy, and Latvia, to name just a few of the places in which she operated. At one point, she even went to Berlin, where there was an attempt to have her seconded to the staff of Adolf Hitler.

It is apparent that Mackert was deeply involved with the Gestapo, as is also shown by the vast number of contacts and acquaintances referred to in the interrogation report. Many of these would have been known to the Allied prosecutors; others, however, might have been less familiar, which would have underscored the value of Mackert's testimony. That said, she was certainly an important catch in her own right, particularly with regard to her activities as a Gestapo agent involved in anti-Jewish operations in Nice and in Riga.

Although the document does not refer to it, Alice La Blonde was known in Nice as a sadistic and brutal torturer who used a sharp whip on victims and was treated with caution even by other officials. Strong evidence pointed to her as an antisemite who employed every opportunity for self-aggrandizement and the opportunity to exercise her biases.

This document has been included in this collection as a representative sample of how some non-Germans saw their role during both the Holocaust and the Nazi occupation. While there was a vast range of motivations and justifications for collaborationist actions in support of the Gestapo's actions in arresting and deporting Jews, this one example shows that the Holocaust was not simply a Nazi or German project. It had many supporters and facilitators who undertook a wide variety of tasks.

19. Julius Streicher: Article in *Der Stürmer* Regarding Hitler's Promise to Free the World of Jews, January 28, 1943

Der Stürmer, *the Nazi Party tabloid published by Julius Streicher, was one of the primary means by which the Party disseminated its antisemitic propaganda. This extract from late January 1943 reflects Streicher's obsession with the complete destruction of the Jews, as he looks back to Hitler's speech to the Reichstag on January 30, 1939 in which he stated that the Jews would be annihilated in the event of another world war. He then characterizes what was happening to the Jews in January 1943—the extermination of two-thirds of all Jews in Europe was well on its way by then—as a fulfillment of Hitler's promise.*

When, with the outbreak of the Second World War, world Jewry again began to manifest themselves as warmongers, Adolf Hitler announced to the world, from the platform of the German Reichstag, that the World War conjured up by world Jewry would result in the self-destruction of Jewry. This prophecy was the first big warning. It was met with derision by the Jews, as were also the subsequent warnings. But now, in the fourth year of this war, world Jewry is beginning, in its retrospective reflections, to understand that the destiny of Jewry is finding its fulfillment at the hands of German National Socialism. That which the Führer of the German people announced to the world as a prophecy, at the beginning of this second World War, is now being fulfilled with unrelenting inevitability. World Jewry, which wanted to make big international business out of the blood of the warring nations, is rushing with gigantic steps towards its extirpation!

When Adolf Hitler stepped before the German people 20 years ago to submit to them the National Socialist demands which pointed into the future, he also made the promise which was to have the greatest effects in its results—that of freeing the world from its Jewish tormentor. How wonderful it is to know that this great man and leader is making action to follow this promise also! It will be the greatest ever to take place amongst mankind. As yet we are too close to the events of the present time to be able to applaud in pious devotion the action that has been commenced. But the day will come when the whole of humanity will enjoy an international peace such as it has longed for for thousands of years.

Source: *Nazi Conspiracy and Aggression*. Office of the U.S. Chief of Counsel for the Prosecution of Axis Criminality. (Washington, DC: U.S. Government Printing Office, 1946), Red Series, vol. Supplement A., pp. 1210–11, Document M-136.

Commentary

Julius Streicher was, arguably, second only to Adolf Hitler as the most notorious antisemite in history. His acknowledgment of the Holocaust in this document is worth noting. Referring to Hitler's Reichstag speech of January 30, 1939, in which the Führer made his infamous prophecy regarding the next war and the certain annihilation of Europe's Jews (see Document 12), Streicher alerts his readers to the fact that the prophecy is now being carried out.

Streicher's language is worth noting. Without providing details, he declares that "World Jewry" is now "rushing with gigantic steps towards its extirpation." Even though "we are too close to the events of the present time to be able to applaud in pious devotion," the actions that are currently being undertaken—probably Streicher, who by this stage was largely sidelined from the Nazi inner circle, did not himself know the closely guarded details—nevertheless "the day will come when the whole of humanity will enjoy the peace" thereby created. This peace, he writes, is one which has been "longed for thousands of years."

The propaganda value of an article such as this, appearing as it did in January 1943, was substantial. The Final Solution was then in its most intense phase, and although ordinary Germans (as well as Streicher) had little to no idea as to the minutiae of the killing process, the signs of Jewish disappearances were apparent everywhere. In this sense, Streicher's triumphalist statement, though light on details, was a recognition that the Jews were in the process of bearing the full force of the Führer's fury.

20. Jürgen Stroop: "The Warsaw Ghetto Is No More," May 16, 1943

SS General Jürgen Stroop's role in suppressing the Warsaw Ghetto Uprising on 1943, and his book-length account of that operation, made him one of the better-known Nazi officers during and after the Holocaust. Resistance against the Nazis began in January 1943 when, for the first time, Germans who entered the Warsaw Ghetto were met with small arms fire. They were forced to withdraw, but on April 19, 1943 they returned in force, this time under Stroop's command. Although outmanned and outgunned, the Jewish fighters were able to repel Stroop's forces. It was not until May 16, 1943, that the uprising was completely ended—an extraordinary feat of resistance.

The creation of special areas to be inhabited by Jews, and the restriction of the Jews with regard to residence and trading is nothing new in the history of the East. Such measures were first taken far back in the Middle Ages; they could be observed as recently as during the last few centuries. These restrictions were imposed with the intention of protecting the aryan population against the Jews.

Identical considerations led us as early as February, 1940 to conceive the project of creating a Jewish residential district in Warsaw. The initial intention was to establish as the Ghetto that part of the City of Warsaw which has the Vistula as its Eastern frontier. The particular situation on prevailing in Warsaw seemed at first to frustrate this plan. It was moreover opposed by several authorities particularly by the City Administration. They pointed in particular that disturbances in industry and trade would ensue if a Ghetto were founded in Warsaw, and that it would be impossible to provide the Jews with food if they were assembled in a closed area.

At a conference held in March 1940, it was decided to postpone the plan of creating a Ghetto for the time being, owing to the above objections. At the same time a plan was considered to declare the District of Lublin the collecting area for all Jews within the Government General, especially for the evacuated or fugitive Jews arriving from the Reich. But as early as April 1940, the Higher SS and Police Leader, East, Cracow, issued a declaration that there was no intention of assembling the Jews within the Lublin District. In the meantime, the Jews had increasingly taken to crossing the frontiers without permission and illegally. This noted especially at the limits of the Districts of Lowicz and Skierniewice. Conditions in the town of Lowicz became dangerous from the point of view of hygiene as well as from that of the Security Police, owing to these illegal migrations of Jews. The District President of Lowicz therefore, began to install Ghettos in his district in order to avoid these dangers.

The experiences in the district of Lowicz, after Ghettos had been installed, showed that this method is the only one suitable for dispelling the dangers which emanate repeatedly from the Jews.

The necessity of erecting a Ghetto in the City of Warsaw as well became more and more urgent in the summer of 1940, since more and more troops were being assembled in the district of Warsaw after termination of the French campaign. At that time the Department for Hygiene urged the speedy erection of a Ghetto in the interest of preserving the health of the German Forces and of the native population as well. The original plan of establishing the Ghetto in the suburb of Praga as intended in February 1940, would have taken at least 4 to 5 months, since almost 600,000 persons had to be moved. But since experience showed that greater outbreaks of epidemics might be expected in the winter months and since for this reason the District Medical Officer urged that the resettling action ought to be completed by 15 November 1940 at the latest, the plan of establishing a suburban ghetto in Praga was dropped; and instead, the area which hitherto had been used as a quarantine area for epidemics was selected for use as a Jewish residential area. In October 1940, the Governor ordered the Commissioner of the District, President for the City of Warsaw, to complete the resettlement necessary for establishing the Ghetto within the City of Warsaw by 15 November 1940.

The Ghetto thus established in Warsaw was inhabited by about 400,000 Jews. It contained 27,000 apartments with an average of 21/2, rooms each. It was separated from the rest of the city by partition and other walls and by walling-up of thoroughfares, windows, doors, open spaces, etc.

It was administered by the Jewish Board of Elders, who received their instructions from the Commissioner for the Ghetto, who was immediately subordinated to the Governor. The Jews were granted self-administration in which the German supervising authorities intervened only where German interests were touched. In order to enable the Jewish Board of Elders to execute its orders, a Jewish Police force was set up, identified by special armbands and a special beret and armed with rubber truncheons. This Jewish Police force was charged with maintaining order and security within the Ghetto and was subordinated to the German and Polish Police.

II

It soon became clear, however, that not all dangers had been removed by this confining the Jews to one place. Security considerations required removing the Jews from the city of Warsaw altogether. The first large resettlement action took place in the period from 22 July to 3 October 1942. In this action 310,322 Jews were removed. In January 1943 a second resettlement action was carried out by which altogether 6,500 Jews were affected.

When the Reichsführer SS visited Warsaw in January 1943 he ordered the SS and Police Leader for the District of Warsaw to *transfer to Lublin the armament factories and other enterprises of military importance which were installed within the Ghetto including their personnel and machines.* The execution of this transfer order proved to be very difficult, since the managers as well as the Jews resisted in every possible way. The SS and Police Leader thereupon decided to enforce the transfer of the enterprises in a large-scale action which he intended to carry out in three days. The necessary preparations had been taken by my predecessor, who also had given the order to start the large-scale action. I myself arrived in Warsaw on 17 April 1943 and took over the command of the action on 19 April 1943, 0800 hours, the action itself having started the same day at 0600 hours.

Before the large-scale action began, the limits of the former Ghetto had been blocked by an external barricade in order to prevent the Jews from breaking out. This barricade was maintained from the start to the end of the action and was especially reinforced at night.

When we invaded the Ghetto for the first time, the Jews and the Polish bandits succeeded in repelling the participating units, including tanks and armored cars, by a well-prepared concentration of fire. When I ordered a second attack, about 0800 hours, I distributed the units, separated from each other by indicated lines, and charged them with combing out the whole of the Ghetto, each unit for a certain part. Although firing commenced again, we now succeeded in combing out the blocks according to plan. The enemy was forced to retire from the roofs and elevated bases to the basements, dug-outs, and sewers. In order to prevent their escaping into the sewers, the sewerage system was dammed up below the Ghetto and filled with water, but the Jews frustrated this plan to a great extent by blowing up the turning off valves. Late the first day we encountered rather heavy resistance, but it was quickly broken by a special raiding party. In the course of further operations we succeeded in expelling the Jews from their prepared resistance bases, sniper holes, and the like, and in occupying during the 20 and 21 April the greater part of the so-called remainder of the Ghetto to such a degree that the resistance continued within these blocks could no longer be called considerable.

The main Jewish battle group, mixed with Polish bandits, had already retired during the first and second day to the so-called Muranowski Square. There, it was reinforced by a considerable number of Polish bandits. Its plan was to hold the Ghetto by every means in order to prevent us from invading it. The Jewish and Polish standards were hoisted at the top of a concrete building as a challenge to us. These two standards, however, were captured on the second day of the action by a special raiding party. SS Untersturmführer Dehmke fell in this skirmish with the bandits; he was holding in his hand a hand-grenade which was hit by the enemy and exploded, injuring him fatally. After only a few days I realized that the original plan had no prospect of success, unless the armament factories and other enterprises of military importance distributed throughout the Ghetto were dissolved. It was therefore necessary to approach these firms and to give them appropriate time for being evacuated and immediately transferred. Thus one of these firms after the other was dealt with, and we very soon deprived the Jews and bandits of their chance to take refuge time and again in these enterprises, which were under the supervision of the Armed Forces. In order to decide how much time was necessary to evacuate these enterprises thorough inspections were necessary. The conditions discovered there are indescribable. I cannot imagine a greater chaos than in the Ghetto of Warsaw. The Jews had control of everything, from the chemical substances used in manufacturing explosives to clothing and equipment for the Armed Forces. The managers knew so little of their own shops that the Jews were in a position to produce inside these shops arms of every kind, especially hand grenades, Molotov cocktails, and the like.

Moreover, the Jews had succeeded in fortifying some of these factories as centers of resistance. Such a center of resistance in an Army accommodation office had to be attacked as early as the second day of the action by an Engineer's Unit equipped with flame throwers and by artillery. The Jews were so firmly established in this shop that it proved to be impossible to induce them to leave it voluntarily; I therefore resolved to destroy this shop the next day by fire.

The managers of these enterprises, which were generally also supervised by an officer of the Armed Forces, could in most cases make no specified statements on their stocks and the whereabouts of these stocks. The statements which they made on the number of Jews employed by them were in every case incorrect. Over and over again we discovered that these labyrinths of edifices belonging to the armament concerns as residential blocks, contained rich Jews who had succeeded in finding accommodations for themselves and their families under the name of "armament workers" and were leading marvelous lives there. Despite all our orders to the managers to make the Jews leave those enterprises, we found out in several cases that managers simply concealed the Jews by shutting them in, because they expected that the action would be finished within a few days and that they then would be able to continue working with the remaining Jews. According to the statements of arrested Jews, women also seem to have played a prominent part. The Jews are said to have endeavored to keep up good relations with officers and men of the armed forces. Carousing is said to have been frequent, during the course of which business deals are said to have been concluded between Jews and Germans.

The number of Jews forcibly taken out of the buildings and arrested was relatively small during the first few days. It transpired that the Jews had taken to hiding in the sewers and in specially erected dug-outs. Whereas we had assumed during the first days that there were only scattered dug-outs, we learned in the course of the large-scale action that the whole Ghetto was systematically equipped with cellars, dug-outs, and passages. In every case these passages and dug-outs were connected with the sewer system. Thus, the Jews were able to maintain undisturbed subterranean traffic. They also used this sewer network for escaping subterraneously into the Aryan part of the city of Warsaw. Continuously, we received reports of attempts of Jews to escape through the sewer holes. While pretending to build air-raid shelters they had been erecting dug-outs within the former Ghetto ever since the autumn of 1942. These were intended to conceal every Jew during the new evacuation action, which they had expected for quite a time, and to enable them to resist the invaders in a concerted action. Through posters, handbills, and whisper propaganda, the communistic resistance movement actually brought it about that the Jews entered the dug-outs as soon as the new large-scale operation started. How far their precautions went can be seen from the fact that many of the dug-outs had been skilfully equipped with furnishings sufficient for entire families, washing and bathing facilities, toilets, arms and munition supplies, and food supplies sufficient for several months. There were differently equipped dug-outs for rich and for poor Jews. To discover the individual dug-outs was difficult for the units, as they had been efficiently camouflaged. In many cases, it was possible only through betrayal on the part of the Jews.

When only a few days had passed, it became apparent that the Jews no longer had any intention to resettle voluntarily, but were determined to resist evacuation with all their force and by using all the weapons at their disposal. So-called battle groups had been formed, led by Polish-Bolshevists; they were armed and paid any price asked for available arms.

During the large-scale action we succeeded in catching some Jews who had already been evacuated and resettled in Lublin or Treblinka, but had broken out from there and returned to the Ghetto, equipped with arms and ammunition. Time and again Polish bandits found refuge in the Ghetto and remained there undisturbed, since we had no forces at our disposal to comb out this maze. Whereas it had been possible during the first days to catch considerable numbers of Jews, who are cowards by nature, it became more and more difficult during the second half of the action to capture the bandits and Jews. Over and over again new battle groups consisting of 20 to 30 or more Jewish fellows, 18 to 25 years of age, accompanied by a corresponding number of women kindled new resistance. These battle groups were under orders to put up armed resistance to the last and if necessary to escape arrest by committing suicide. One such battle group succeeded in mounting a truck by ascending from a sewer in the so-called Prosta, and in escaping with it (about 30 to 35 bandits). One bandit who had arrived with this truck exploded 2 hand grenades, which was the agreed signal for the bandits waiting in the sewer to climb out of it. The bandits and Jews—there were Polish bandits among these gangs armed with carbines, small arms, and in one case a light machine gun, mounted the truck and drove away in an unknown direction. The last member of this gang, who was on guard in the sewer and was detailed to close the lid of the sewer hole, was captured. It was he who gave the above information. The search for the truck was unfortunately without result.

During this armed resistance the women belonging to the battle groups were equipped the same as the men; some were members of the Chaluzim movement. Not infrequently, these women fired pistols with both hands. It happened time and again that these women had pistols or hand grenades (Polish "pineapple" hand grenades) concealed in their bloomers up to the last moment to use against the men of the Waffen-SS, Police, or Wehrmacht.

The resistance put up by the Jews and bandits could be broken only by relentlessly using all our force and energy by day and night. *On 23 April 1943 the Reichsführer SS issued through the higher SS and Policeführer East at Cracow his order to complete the combing out of the Warsaw Ghetto with the greatest severity and relentless tenacity*. I therefore decided to destroy the entire Jewish residential area by setting every block on fire, including the blocks of residential buildings near the armament works. One concern after the other was systematically evacuated and subsequently destroyed by fire. The Jews then emerged from their hiding places and dug-outs in almost every case. Not infrequently, the Jews stayed in the burning buildings until, because of the heat and the fear of being burned alive they preferred to jump down from the upper stories after having thrown mattresses and other upholstered articles into the street from the burning buildings. With their bones broken, they still tried to crawl across the street into blocks of buildings which had not yet been set on fire or were only partly in flames. Often Jews changed their hiding places during the night, by moving into the ruins of burnt-out buildings, taking refuge there until they were found by our patrols. Their stay in the sewers also ceased to be pleasant after the first week. Frequently from the street, we could hear loud voices coming through the sewer shafts. Then the men of the Waffen-SS, the Police or the Wehrmacht Engineers courageously climbed down the shafts to bring out the Jews and not infrequently they then stumbled over Jews already dead, or were shot at. It was always necessary to use smoke candles to drive out the Jews. Thus one day we opened 183 sewer entrance holes and at a fixed time lowered smoke candles into them, with the result that the bandits fled from what they believed to be gas to the center of the former Ghetto, where they could then be pulled out of the sewer holes there. A great number of Jews, who could not be counted, were exterminated by blowing up sewers and dug-outs.

The longer the resistance lasted, the tougher the men of the Waffen-SS, Police, and Wehrmacht became; they fulfilled their duty indefatigably in faithful comradeship and stood together as models and examples of soldiers. Their duty hours often lasted from early morning until late at night. At night, search patrols with rags wound round their feet remained at the heels of the Jews and gave them no respite. Not infrequently they caught and killed Jews who used the night hours for supplementing their stores from abandoned dug-outs and for contacting neighboring groups or exchanging news with them.

Considering that the greater part of the men of the Waffen-SS had only been trained for three to four weeks before being assigned to this action, high credit should be given for the pluck, courage, and devotion to duty which they showed. It must be stated that the Wehrmacht Engineers, too, executed the blowing up of dug-outs, sewers, and concrete buildings with indefatigability and great devotion to duty. Officers and men of the Police, a large part of whom had already been at the front, again excelled by their dashing spirit.

Only through the continuous and untiring work of all involved did we succeed in catching a total of 56,065 Jews whose extermination can be proved. To this should be added the number of Jews who lost their lives in explosions or fires but whose numbers could not be ascertained.

During the large-scale operation the Aryan population was informed by posters that it was strictly forbidden to enter the former Jewish Ghetto and that anybody caught within the former Ghetto without valid pass would be shot. At the same time these posters informed the Aryan population again that the death penalty would be imposed on anybody who intentionally gave refuge to a Jew, especially lodged, supported, or concealed a Jew outside the Jewish residential area.

Permission was granted to the Polish police to pay to any Polish policeman who arrested a Jew within the Aryan part of Warsaw one third of the cash in the Jew's possession. This measure has already produced results.

The Polish population for the most part approved the measures taken against the Jews. Shortly before the end of the large-scale operation, the Governor issued a special proclamation which he submitted to the undersigned for approval before publication, to the Polish population; in it he informed them of the reasons for destroying the former Jewish Ghetto by mentioning the assassinations carried out lately in the Warsaw area and the mass graves found in Catyn; at the same time they were asked to assist us in our fight against Communist agents and Jews (see enclosed poster).

The large-scale action was terminated on 16 May 1943 with the blowing up of the Warsaw synagogue at 2015 hours.

Now, there are no more factories in the former Ghetto. All the goods, raw materials, and machines there have been moved and stored somewhere else. All buildings etc., have been destroyed. The only exception is the so-called Dzielna Prison of the Security Police, which was exempted from destruction.

III

Although the large-scale operation has been completed, we have to reckon with the possibility that a few Jews are still living in the ruins of the former Ghetto; therefore, this area must be firmly shut off from the Aryan residential area and be guarded. Police Battalion III/23 has been charged with this duty. This Police Battalion has instructions to watch the former Ghetto, particularly to prevent anybody from entering the former Ghetto, and to shoot immediately anybody found inside the Ghetto without authority. The Commander of the Police Battalion will continue to receive further direct orders from the SS and Police Führer. In this way, it should be possible to keep the small remainder of Jews there, if any, under constant pressure and to exterminate them eventually. The remaining Jews and bandits must be deprived of any chance of survival by destroying all remaining buildings and refuges and cutting off the water supply.

It is proposed to change the Dzielna Prison into a concentration camp and to use the inmates to remove, collect and hand over for reuse the millions of bricks, the scrap-iron, and other materials.

IV

Of the total of 56,065 Jews caught, about 7,000 were exterminated within the former Ghetto in the course of the large-scale action, and 6,929 by transporting them to T.II, which means 14,000 Jews were exterminated altogether. Beyond the number of 56,065 Jews an estimated number of 5,000 to 6,000 were killed by explosions or in fires.

Source: Office of the U.S. Chief of Counsel for the Prosecution of Axis Criminality. *Nazi Conspiracy and Aggression*. Red Series, vol. 3. Document 1061-PS. Washington, DC: U.S. Government Printing Office, 1946, pp. 718–28.

Commentary

Through the summer of 1942, the Germans deported or executed more than 300,000 Jews from the Warsaw ghetto, leaving fewer than 60,000 there. In order to obstruct future German deportations, some of the younger ghetto inhabitants formed the Jewish Fighting Organization (*Żydowska Organizacja Bojowa*, or ŻOB), and when, on April 19, 1943, Waffen-SS, police, and Wehrmacht units moved into the ghetto to finish the liquidation, the ŻOB, reinforced by fighters attached to a separate group, the Jewish Military Union (ZZW), struck with pistol fire, homemade hand grenades, and Molotov cocktails. The battle, beginning on April 19, lasted until May 16.

SS General Jürgen Stroop was sent to Warsaw by *SS-Reichsführer* Heinrich Himmler to suppress the revolt. He was given command of 2 Waffen-SS battalions, 100 infantry troops, units of local police, and local Security Police. He ordered the entire ghetto to be systematically burned down and blown up, building by building. Except for a few who made it into the Aryan side of Warsaw via the sewers, nearly all the survivors—including men, women, and children—were either killed on the spot or deported to extermination camps. On May 16, Stroop reported, "The Jewish Quarter of Warsaw is no more! More than 56,000 Jewish bandits have been captured."

In victory, he a compiled a detailed 75-page book-length account with 69 pictures, along with memoranda and communiqués relevant to the suppression of the revolt and illustrated with pictures of the devastation. The report covered the period April 24, 1943, to May 24, 1943. Bound in black leather and entitled *The Jewish Quarter of Warsaw Is No More!* the report was intended as a souvenir album and was later presented to Heinrich Himmler and General Friedrich-Wilhelm Krüger, while Stroop kept one for himself.

21. Heinrich Himmler: Order for Liquidation of Ostland Ghettos, June 21, 1943

This order from Reichsführer-SS *Heinrich Himmler to the chief of the SS Economic and Administrative Main Office, Oswald Pohl, requires that all Jews in ghettos in the* Ostland *region (Lithuania, Latvia, Estonia, and Belarus) be moved to concentration camps. Himmler provides more specific instructions regarding where Jewish male laborers should be assigned and reminds Pohl that nothing done pursuant to this order is to result in the reduction of productivity for the Wehrmacht. He also makes it clear that any Jews not able to serve the Nazis' needs were to be "evacuated to the East," the standard euphemism for deportation to the death camps in Poland.*

1. I order that all the Jews still remaining in ghettos in the Ostland area have to be collected in concentration camps.
2. I prohibit any taking out of Jews from concentration camps for [outside] work projects beginning 1 August 1943.
3. There has to be erected a concentration camp in the vicinity of Riga, to which has to be transferred all the manufacturing of clothing and equipment in outlying works maintained by the Wehrmacht. All private firms have to be cut out. The workshops are to become plain concentration camp workshops. The chief of the SS Economic and Administrative Main Office is requested to take care, that this reorganization does not cause any reduction in the necessary production for the Wehrmacht.
4. The biggest possible part of the male Jews has to be brought to the concentration camp in the oil shale area for the mining of oil shale.
5. Members of the Jewish ghettos not required are to be evacuated to the East.
6. Fixed day for the reorganization of the concentration camps is 1 August 1943.

Source: Office of the U.S. Chief of Counsel for the Prosecution of Axis Criminality. *Trials of War Criminals before the Nuremberg Military Tribunals under Control Council No. 10.* Green Series, vol. 5. Document NO-2403. Washington, DC: U.S. Government Printing Office, 1946, p. 626.

Commentary

Just as in his order of July 19, 1942, expelling all Jews from the *Generalgouvernement* (see Document 16), in this document, *SS-Reichsführer* Heinrich Himmler expands the scope of the Holocaust to the region of the occupied Soviet Union referred to by the Nazis as the "Ostland" (eastern lands).

Here, he orders that any Jew still found in the region should be apprehended and taken into concentration camps, where he or she is to be incarcerated. No Jews are permitted to remain at large, Jewish slave labor is to be restricted, and Jews are no longer to be assigned as *aussenarbeit* (labor outside the camp). All work should be undertaken under controlled conditions inside the concentration camp, and where camps do not yet exist, as in Riga, they will have to be built. Ominous here is the statement that any ghetto residents "not required" will have to be "evacuated to the East."

Himmler's order should be read within the context of the war on the Eastern Front in the middle of 1943. The summer campaign known as Operation Citadel (the Battle of Kursk) was the final strategic offensive the Germans were able to launch on the Eastern Front, and because of the timing, it represented one of the last opportunities for the SS to destroy the Jews of the Soviet Union. While Citadel was being planned, Himmler decided that the rear areas would need to be secured; thus, all Jews would have to be placed into thoroughly controlled spaces, where their labor would be exploited, or if this was impractical, they would be deported and killed. Given the context, it should be noted that this phase of the Holocaust was not a random occurrence and could be connected directly to the war situation Germany was then facing.

22. Heinrich Himmler: Extracts from Speech to Senior SS Officers, October 4, 1943

In October 1943, Reichsführer-SS *Heinrich Himmler delivered a three-hour speech to SS officers. The extracts below include his comments on such matters as the situation in the fifth year of the war, Russian leadership, foreigners in the Reich, the evacuation of the Jews, the principle of selection, and the future. While each section provides insights, a common theme throughout is that the only people who matter are Germans. Himmler says that members of the SS must be honest, decent, and loyal, but only "to members of our own blood." Elsewhere, "it is a crime against our own blood to worry about" others. Himmler also speaks of "the extermination of the Jewish race" without resort to euphemisms. The speech ends with these words: "We want to be worthy of being permitted to be the first SS men of the Führer Adolf Hitler. . . . Now let us remember the Führer Adolf Hitler who will create the Germanic Reich and will lead us into the Germanic future."*

I have considered it necessary, now at the beginning of the fifth year of war, to call you, the high leader corps of the SS and Police together. Sober as we always were, truthful toward ourselves, we will discuss several matters in this troop leader meeting. Just as I was accustomed to do during long years of peace, I will give you my opinion of the situation, as I see it, about our tasks, about what we have done and achieved, as well as about what the future holds for us, as briefly as possible.

The Russian Leadership

The 1941 attack.—In 1941 the Führer attacked Russia. That was, as we can well see now, shortly—perhaps 3 to 6 months—before Stalin prepared to embark on his great penetration into central and western Europe. I can give a picture of this first year in a few words. The attacking forces cut their way through. The Russian Army was herded together in great pockets, ground down, taken prisoner. At that time we did not value the mass of humanity as we value it today, as raw material, as labor. What after all, thinking in terms of generations, is not to be regretted but is now deplorable by reason of the loss of labor, is that the prisoners died, in tens and hundreds of thousands, of exhaustion and hunger. . . .

One basic principle must be the absolute rule for the SS men—we must be honest, decent, loyal, and comradely to members of our own blood and, to nobody else. What happens to a Russian, or to a Czech, does not interest me in the slightest. What the nations can offer in the way of good blood of our type we will take, if necessary by kidnapping their children and raising them here with us. Whether nations live in prosperity or starve to death interests me only so far as we need them as slaves for our culture; otherwise, it is of no interest to me. Whether 10,000 Russian females fall down from exhaustion while digging an antitank ditch interests me only so far as the antitank ditch for Germany is finished. We shall never be rough and heartless when it is not necessary, that is clear. We Germans, who are the only people in the world who have a decent attitude toward animals, will also assume a decent attitude toward these human animals. But it is a crime against our own blood to worry about them and give them ideals, thus causing our sons and grandsons to have a more difficult time with them. When somebody comes to me and says: "I cannot dig the antitank ditch with women and children, it is inhuman, for it would kill them," then I have to say, "You are a murderer of your own blood because if the antitank ditch is not dug, German soldiers will die, and they are sons of German mothers. They are our own blood." That is what I want to instill into this SS—and what I believe have instilled into them—as one of the most sacred laws of the future. Our concern, our duty is our people and our blood. It is for them that we must provide and plan, work and fight, nothing else. We can be indifferent to everything else. I wish the SS to adopt this attitude to the problem of all foreign, non-Germanic peoples, especially Russians. All else is vain, fraud against our own nation, and an obstacle to the early winning of the war. . . .

Foreigners in the Reich

We must also realize that we have 6 to 7 million foreigners in Germany. Perhaps it is even 8 million now. We have prisoners in Germany. None of them are dangerous so long as we take severe measures at the merest trifles. It is a mere nothing today to shoot 10 Poles, compared with the fact that we might later have to shoot tens of thousands in their place and compared to the fact that the shooting of these tens of thousands would then be carried out even at the cost of German blood. Every little fire will immediately be stamped out and quenched, and extinguished—otherwise—as in the case of a real fire—a political and psychological surface fire may spring up among the people. . . .

The Evacuation of the Jews

I also want to talk to you, quite frankly, on a very grave matter. Among ourselves it should be mentioned quite frankly, and yet we will never speak of it publicly. Just as we did not hesitate on 30 June 1934 to do the duty we were bidden and stand comrades who had lapsed up against the wall and shoot them, so we have never spoken about it and will never speak of it. It was that tact which is a matter of course and which I am glad to say, is inherent in us, that made us never discuss it among ourselves, never speak of it. It appalled everyone, and yet everyone was certain that he would do it the next time if such orders are issued and if it is necessary.

I mean the evacuation of the Jews, the extermination of the Jewish race. It's one of those things it is easy to talk about, "The Jewish race is being exterminated," says one Party Member, "that's quite clear, it's in our program—elimination of the Jews and we're doing it, exterminating them." And then they come, 80 million worthy Germans, and each one has his decent Jew. Of course the others are vermin, but this one is an A-1 Jew. Not one of all those who talk this way has watched it, not one of them has gone through it. Most of *you* must know what it means when 100 corpses are lying side by side, or 500, or 1,000. To have stuck it out and at the same time—apart from exceptions caused by human weakness—to have remained decent fellows, that is what has made us hard. This is a page of glory in our history which has never been written and is never to be written, for we know how difficult we should have made it for ourselves, if with the bombing raids, the burdens and the deprivations of war we still had Jews today in every town as secret saboteurs, agitators, and troublemongers. We would now probably have reached the 1916–1917 stage when the Jews were still in the German national body.

We have taken from them what wealth they had. I have issued a strict order, which SS Lieutenant General Pohl has carried out, that this wealth should, as a matter of course, be handed over to the Reich without reserve. We have taken none of it for ourselves. Individual men who have lapsed will be punished in accordance with an order I issued at the beginning which gave this warning; whoever takes so much as a mark of it is a dead man. A number of SS men—there are not very many of them—have fallen short, and they will die without mercy. We had the moral right, we had the duty to our people, to destroy this people which wanted to destroy us. But we have not the right to enrich ourselves with so much as a fur, a watch, a mark, or a cigarette, or anything else. Because we have exterminated a germ, we do not want in the end to be infected by the germ and die of it. I will not see so much as a small area of sepsis appear here or gain a hold. Wherever it may form, we will cauterize it. Altogether however, we can say that we have fulfilled this most difficult duty for the love of our people. And our spirit, our soul, our character has not suffered injury from it.

The Principle of Selection

We are a product of the law of selection. We have made our choice from a cross-section of our people. This people came into being aeons ago, through generations, and centuries, by the throw of the dice of fate and of history. Alien peoples have swept over this people and left their heritage behind them. Alien blood streams have flowed into this people, but it has, nevertheless in spite of horrible hardships and terrible blows of fate, still had strength in the very essence of its blood to win through. Thus, this whole people is saturated with and held together by Nordic-Phalian-Germanic blood, so that after all one could and can still speak of a German people. From this people of such varied hereditary tendencies as it emerged from the collapse after the years of the battle of liberation, we have now consciously tried to select the Nordo-Germanic blood, for we could best expect this section of our blood to contain the creative, heroic, and life preserving qualities of our people. We have gone partly by outward appearances and for the rest have kept these outward appearances in review by making constantly new demands, and by repeated tests both physical and mental, both of the character and the soul. Again and again we have sifted out and cast aside what was worthless, what did not suit us. Just as long as we have strength to do, thus will this organization [Orden] remain healthy. The moment we forget the law which is the foundation of our race and the law of selection and austerity toward ourselves, we shall have the germ of death in us and will perish, just as every human organization, every blossom in this world, does some time perish. It must be our endeavor, our inner law, to make this blossoming and fructifying last for our people as long as possible, bringing as much prosperity as possible and—don't be alarmed—if possible for thousands of years. That is why, wherever we meet and whatever we do, we must be mindful of our principle—blood, selection, and austerity. The law of nature is just this—What is hard is good, what is vigorous is good; whatever wins through in the battle of life, physically, purposefully, and spiritually, that is what is good—always taking the long view. Of course sometime—and this has happened often in history—someone can get to the top by deceit and cheating. That makes no difference to nature, to the fate of the earth, or to the fate of the world. Really, that is nature. Fate removes the impostor after a time—time not reckoned in generations of man but in historical periods. It must be our endeavor never to deceive ourselves but always to remain genuine, that is what we must continually preach and instill into ourselves, and into every boy and each one of our subordinates. . . .

The Future

When the war is won—then, as I have already told you, our work will start. We do not know when the war will end. It may be sudden, or it may be long delayed. We shall see. But I say to you now, if an armistice and peace comes suddenly, let no one think that he can then sleep the sleep of the just. Get all your commanders, chiefs, and SS Führers attuned to this; only then, gentlemen, shall we be awake, for then, so many others will fall into this sleep. I am going so to rouse the whole SS, and keep it so wide awake that we can tackle reconstruction in Germany immediately. Then Germanic work will be begun immediately in the General SS, for then the harvest will be ripe to be taken into the granary. We shall then call up age groups there by law. We shall then immediately put all our Waffen-SS units into excellent form, both as regards equipment and training. We shall go on working in this first 6 months after the war, as though the big offensive were starting on the next day. It will make all the difference, if Germany has an operative reserve, an operative backing, at the peace or armistice negotiations, of 20, 25, or 30 SS divisions intact.

If the peace is a final one, we shall be able to tackle our great work of the future. We shall colonize. We shall indoctrinate our boys with the laws of the SS organization. I consider it to be absolutely necessary to the life of our peoples, that we should not only impart the meaning of ancestry, grandchildren, and future, but feel these to be a part of our being. Without there being any talk about it, without our needing to make use of rewards and similar material things, it must be a matter of course that we have children. It must be a matter of course that the most copious breeding should be from this racial superstratum of the Germanic people. In 20 to 30 years we must really be able to present the whole of Europe with its leading class. If the SS, together with the farmers—we *together with our friend Backe*, then run the colony in the East on a grand scale, without any restraint, without any question about any kind of tradition, but with nerve and revolutionary impetus, we shall in 20 years push the national boundary 500 kilometers eastward.

I requested of the Führer already today, that the SS—if we have fulfilled our task and our duty by the end of the war—should have the privilege of holding Germany's eastern-most frontier as a defense frontier. I believe this is the only privilege for which we have no competitors. I believe not one person will dispute our claim to this privilege. We shall be in a position there to train every young age group in the use of arms. We shall impose our laws on the East. We will charge ahead and push our way forward little by little to the Urals. I hope that our generation will successfully bring it about that every age group has fought in the East, and that every one of our divisions spends a winter in the East every second or third year. Then we shall never grow soft, then we shall never get SS members who only come to us because it is distinguished or because the black coat will naturally be very attractive in peacetime. Everyone will know that "if I join the SS, there is the possibility that I might be killed." He has contracted in writing that every second year he will not dance in Berlin, attend the carnival in Munich, but that he will be posted to the Eastern Frontier in an ice-cold winter. Then we will have a healthy elite for all time. Thus, we will create the necessary conditions for the whole Germanic people and the whole of Europe: controlled, ordered, and led by us, the Germanic people, to be able in generations to stand the test in her battles of destiny against Asia which will certainly break out again. We do not know when that will be.

Then, when the mass of humanity of one to one and one-half billions line up against us, the Germanic people numbering, I hope, 250 to 300 millions and the other European peoples making a total of 600 to 700 millions (and with an outpost area stretching as far as the Urals or a hundred miles beyond the Urals) must stand the test in its vital struggle against Asia. It would be an evil day if the Germanic people did not survive it. It would be the end of beauty and culture, of the creative power of this earth. That is the distant future. It is for that we are fighting, pledged to hand down the heritage of our ancestors.

We see into the distant future because we know what it will be. That is why we are doing our duty more fanatically than ever, more devoutly than ever, more bravely, more obediently, and more thoroughly than ever. We want to be worthy of being permitted to be the first SS men of the Führer Adolf Hitler in the long history of the Germanic people which stretches before us.

Now let us remember the Führer Adolf Hitler who will create the Germanic Reich and will lead us into the Germanic future.

Our Führer, Adolf Hitler, Sieg Heil, Sieg Heil, Sieg Heil.

Source: Office of the U.S. Chief of Counsel for the Prosecution of Axis Criminality. *Trials of War Criminals before the Nuremberg Military Tribunals under Control Council No. 10*. Green Series, vol. 13. Document 1919-PS. Washington, DC: U.S. Government Printing Office, 1946, pp. 318–27.

Commentary

It was not often that senior members of the SS discussed the extermination of the Jews in an open forum such as in this document. Here, *SS-Reichsführer* Heinrich Himmler is completely candid in his statements regarding a variety of important issues.

While much of the document is a reinforcement of SS ideals regarding race—he speaks a lot, for instance, about "blood" and the necessity of safeguarding German purity at the expense of "lesser races"—Himmler's comments on the Jews and the Final Solution then being undertaken by the SS must have fallen on the fertilest ground. One of these statements has since entered Holocaust historiography as the quintessential admission of SS guilt and concealment. Referring directly to "the extermination of the Jewish race," he states that "This is a page of glory in our history which has never been written and is never to be written." Interestingly, Himmler invokes the Nazi Party purge of June 1934 as a precedent for this silence.

As a motivation to his officers to maintain their enthusiasm for the cause (especially given that the war has begun to turn against Germany), Himmler speaks confidently about the time after "the war is won." At this moment, he states, the real work of the SS will begin. Such work will be the racial reorganizing of Germany and of Europe, a task that will be enhanced through Hitler granting the SS "the privilege of holding Germany's eastern-most frontier as a defense frontier." In this way, Himmler reaffirms the often-quoted goal of the SS to be the new Teutonic Knights, upholders of civilization against the barbaric hordes to the East. He concludes with the admonition to his officers to "remember the Führer Adolf Hitler who will create the Germanic Reich and will lead us into the Germanic future."

23. Adolf Hitler: "My Political Testament," April 29, 1945

On April 29, 1945, one day before Adolf Hitler and his newlywed wife, Eva Braun, committed suicide as Allied forces approached Berlin, the Führer signed two documents: his private will and testament, and what he called his Political Testament. The latter, which is reproduced here, expresses his view that it was international Jewry that wanted a world war despite his best efforts to avoid one. He expels Hermann Göring and Heinrich Himmler from the Nazi Party and appoints a new cabinet. It is notable but not surprising that in his final statement—the last words he would impart to the world—he refers to "the universal poisoner of all peoples, international Jewry."

More than thirty years have now passed since I in 1914 made my modest contribution as a volunteer in the first world-war that was forced upon the Reich.

In these three decades I have been actuated solely by love and loyalty to my people in all my thoughts, acts, and life. They gave me the strength to make the most difficult decisions which have ever confronted mortal man. I have spent my time, my working strength, and my health in these three decades.

It is untrue that I or anyone else in Germany wanted the war in 1939. It was desired and instigated exclusively by those international statesmen who were either of Jewish descent or worked for Jewish interests. I have made too many offers for the control and limitation of armaments, which posterity will not for all time be able to disregard for the responsibility for the outbreak of this war to be laid on me. I have further never wished that after the first fatal world war a second against England, or even against America, should break out. Centuries will pass away, but out of the ruins of our towns and monuments the hatred against those finally responsible whom we have to thank for everything, International Jewry and its helpers, will grow.

Three days before the outbreak of the German-Polish war I again proposed to the British ambassador in Berlin a solution to the German-Polish problem—similar to that in the case of the Saar district, under international control. This offer also cannot be denied. It was only rejected because the leading circles in English politics wanted the war, partly on account of the business hoped for and partly under influence of propaganda organized by international Jewry.

I also made it quite plain that, if the nations of Europe are again to be regarded as mere shares to be bought and sold by these international conspirators in money and finance, then that race, Jewry, which is the real criminal of this murderous struggle, will be saddled with the responsibility. I further left no one in doubt that this time not only would millions of children of Europe's Aryan peoples die of hunger, not only would millions of grown men suffer death, and not only hundreds of thousands of women and children be burnt and bombed to death in the towns, without the real criminal having to atone for this guilt, even if by more humane means.

After six years of war, which in spite of all set-backs, will go down one day in history as the most glorious and valiant demonstration of a nation's life purpose, I cannot forsake the city which is the capital of this Reich. As the forces are too small to make any further stand against the enemy attack at this place and our resistance is gradually being weakened by men who are as deluded as they are lacking in initiative, I should like, by remaining in this town, to share my fate with those, the millions of others, who have also taken upon themselves to do so. Moreover I do not wish to fall into the hands of an enemy who requires a new spectacle organized by the Jews for the amusement of their hysterical masses.

I have decided therefore to remain in Berlin and there of my own free will to choose death at the moment when I believe the position of the Führer and Chancellor itself can no longer be held.

I die with a happy heart, aware of the immeasurable deeds and achievements of our soldiers at the front, our women at home, the achievements of our farmers and workers and the work, unique in history, of our youth who bear my name.

That from the bottom of my heart I express my thanks to you all, is just as self-evident as my wish that you should, because of that, on no account give up the struggle, but rather continue it against the enemies of the Fatherland, no matter where, true to the creed of a great Clausewitz. From the sacrifice of our soldiers and from my own unity with them unto death, will in any case spring up in the history of Germany, the seed of a radiant renaissance of the National-Socialist movement and thus of the realization of a true community of nations.

Many of the most courageous men and women have decided to unite their lives with mine until the very last. I have begged and finally ordered them not to do this, but to take part in the further battle of the Nation. I beg the heads of the Armies, the Navy and the Air Force to strengthen by all possible means the spirit of resistance of our soldiers in the National-Socialist sense, with special reference to the fact that also I myself, as founder and creator of this movement, have preferred death to cowardly abdication or even capitulation.

May it, at some future time, become part of the code of honour of the German officer—as is already the case in our Navy—that the surrender of a district or of a town is impossible, and that above all the leaders here must march ahead as shining examples, faithfully fulfilling their duty unto death.

Second Part of the Political Testament

Before my death I expel the former Reichsmarschall Hermann Goering from the party and deprive him of all rights which he may enjoy by virtue of the decree of June 29th, 1941, and also by virtue of my statement in the Reichstag on September 1st, 1939, I appoint in his place Grossadmiral Doenitz, President of the Reich and supreme Commander of the Armed Forces.

Before my death I expel the former Reichsführer-SS and Minister of the Interior, Heinrich Himmler, from the party and from all offices of State. In his stead I appoint Gauleiter Karl Hanke as Reichsführer-SS and Chief of the German Police, and Gauleiter Paul Giesler as Reich Minister of the Interior.

Goering and Himmler, quite apart from their disloyalty to my person, have done immeasurable harm to the country and the whole nation by secret negotiations with the enemy, which they conducted without my knowledge and against my wishes, and by illegally attempting to seize power in the State for themselves.

In order to give the German people a government composed of honourable men,—a government which will fulfill its pledge to continue the war by every means—I appoint the following members of the new Cabinet as leaders of the nation:

President of the Reich: Doenitz.
Chancellor of the Reich: Dr. Goebbels.
Party Minister: Bormann.
Foreign Minister: Seyss-Inquart.
Minister of the Interior: Gauleiter Giesler.
Minister for War: Doenitz.
C-in-C of the Army: Schoerner.
C-in-C of the Navy: Doenitz.
C-in-C of the Air Force: Greim.
Reichsführer-SS and Chief of the German Police: Gauleiter Hanke.
Economics: Funk.
Agriculture Backe.
Justice: Thierack.
Education and Public Worship: Dr. Scheel.

Propaganda: Dr. Naumann.
Finance: Schwerin-Grossigk.
Labour: Dr. Hupfauer.
Munitions: Saur
Leader of the German Labour Front and Member of the Reich Cabinet: Reich Minister Dr. Ley.

Although a number of these men, such as Martin Bormann, Dr. Goebbels etc., together with their wives, have joined me of their own free will and did not wish to leave the capital of the Reich under any circumstances, but were willing to perish with me here, I must nevertheless ask them to obey my request, and in this case set the interests of the nation above their own feelings. By their work and loyalty as comrades they will be just as close to me after death, as I hope that my spirit will linger among them and always go with them. Let them be hard, but never unjust, above all let them never allow fear to influence their actions, and set the honour of the nation above everything in the world. Finally, let them be conscious of the fact that our task, that of continuing the building of a National Socialist State, represents the work of the coming centuries, which places every single person under an obligation always to serve the common interest and to subordinate his own advantage to this end. I demand of all Germans, all National Socialists, men, women and all the men of the Armed Forces, that they be faithful and obedient unto death to the new government and its President.

Above all I charge the leaders of the nation and those under them to scrupulous observance of the laws of race and to merciless opposition to the universal poisoner of all peoples, international Jewry.

Given in Berlin, this 29th day of April 1945. 4:00 a.m.
Adolf Hitler

Source: Office of the U.S. Chief of Counsel for the Prosecution of Axis Criminality. *Nazi Conspiracy and Aggression*. Red Series, vol. 6. Document 3569-PS. Washington, DC: U.S. Government Printing Office, 1946, pp. 260–63.

Commentary

At around 4:00 a.m. on April 29, 1945, with Germany's defeat imminent, Adolf Hitler composed his final political testament in his Berlin bunker. The document, divided into two parts, is reproduced here. Prior to dictating it to his secretary, Traudl Junge, he married his mistress of many years, Eva Braun, in a civil ceremony. After disposing of his assets in his personal will, he then expressed his final thoughts.

In the document, he begins by discussing his life story up to that time, mentioning the three decades following World War I and the way that he had built his party. He then offers up the claim that neither he nor anyone else in Germany "wanted the war in 1939"; it was, rather, "desired and instigated exclusively by those international statesmen who were either of Jewish descent or worked for

Jewish interests." Hitler shows himself to have been a man of peace throughout the days leading up to the outbreak of war, even going so far as to recount his offer of peace to the British ambassador in Berlin three days before the invasion of Poland.

While much of the content resembles many of his speeches from earlier times, perhaps its most important elements can be found in the political line of succession he lays out after his death—a death which, he states, he will undergo "with a happy heart." He strips Heinrich Himmler and Hermann Göring from all their offices of state and their party membership, and he names Admiral Karl Dönitz to be the next führer and supreme commander of the armed forces. He then appoints a new cabinet, featuring Joseph Goebbels and Martin Bormann in key positions.

He also takes the opportunity—one final time—not only to blame the Jews for the war but also to command the German people to "scrupulous observance of the laws of race and to merciless opposition to the universal poisoner of all peoples, international Jewry." Thus, right to the very end of the war and his life, Hitler expressed no contrition or remorse for the destruction he had unleashed on Germany and continued to the very end with his antisemitic invective.

On the afternoon of April 30, 1945, a day and a half after he signed his last will and testament, Adolf Hitler and Eva Braun committed suicide.

24. Rudolf Hoess: Regarding Extermination at Auschwitz, May 1940–December 1943

In May 1940, SS-Obersturmbannführer Rudolf Hoess received his first senior posting when appointed to be the commandant of a new camp, which he would establish, at Auschwitz. His initial orders were to build a transit camp capable of accommodating ten thousand prisoners, but he later became responsible for carrying out the Nazi "Final Solution of the Jewish Question" at Auschwitz through the industrial mass murder of Jews sent from across Europe. In 1945 he was arrested by the Americans and transferred to Polish jurisdiction. The document produced here is an affidavit produced by Hoess and sworn at Nuremberg on April 5, 1946.

I, RUDOLF FRANZ FERDINAND HOESS, being first duly sworn, depose and say as follows:

1. I am forty-six years old, and have been a member of the NSDAP since 1922; a member of the SS since 1934; a member of the Waffen-SS since 1939. I was a member from 1 December 1934 of the SS Guard Unit, the so-called Deathshead Formation (Totenkopf Verband).
2. I have been constantly associated with the administration of concentration camps since 1934, serving at Dachau until 1938; then as Adjutant in Sachsenhausen from 1938 to May 1, 1940, when I was appointed Commandant of Auschwitz. I commanded Auschwitz until 1 December, 1943, and estimate that at least 2,500,000 victims were executed and exterminated there by gassing and burning, and at least another half million succumbed to starvation and disease, making a total dead of about 3,000,000. This figure

represents about 70% or 80% of all persons sent to Auschwitz as prisoners, the remainder having been selected and used for slave labor in the concentration camp industries. Included among the executed and burnt were approximately 20,000 Russian prisoners of war (previously screened out of Prisoner of War cages by the Gestapo) who were delivered at Auschwitz in Wehrmacht transports operated by regular Wehrmacht officers and men. The remainder of the total number of victims included about 100,000 German Jews, and great numbers of citizens, *mostly* Jewish) from Holland, France, Belgium, Poland, Hungary, Czechoslovakia, Greece, or other countries. We executed about 400,000 Hungarian Jews alone at Auschwitz in the summer of 1944.

3. WVHA (Main Economic and Administration Office), headed by Obergruppenfuehrer Oswald Pohl, was responsible for all administrative matters such as billeting, feeding and medical care, in the concentration camps. Prior to establishment of the RSHA, Secret State Police Office (Gestapo) and the Reich Office of Criminal Police were responsible for arrests, commitments to concentration camps, punishments and executions therein. After organization of the RSHA, all of these functions were carried on as before, but, pursuant to orders signed by Heydrich as Chief of the RSHA. While Kaltenbrunner was Chief of RSHA, orders for protective custody, commitments, punishment and, individual executions were signed by Kaltenbrunner or by Mueller, Chief of the Gestapo, as Kaltenbrunner's deputy.
4. Mass executions by gassing commenced during the summer 1941 and continued until Fall 1944. I personally supervised executions at Auschwitz until the first of December 1943 and know by reason of my continued duties in the Inspectorate of Concentration Camps WVHA that these mass executions continued as stated above. All mass executions by gassing took place under the direct order, supervision and responsibility of RSHA. I received all orders for carrying out these mass executions directly from RSHA.
5. On 1 December 1943 I became Chief of AMT I in AMT Group D of the WVHA and in that office was responsible for coordinating all matters arising between RSHA and concentration camps under the administration of WVHA. I held this position until the end of the war. Pohl, as Chief of WVHA, and Kaltenbrunner, as Chief of RSHA, often conferred personally and frequently communicated orally and in writing concerning concentration camps. On 5 October 1944, I brought a lengthy report regarding Mauthausen Concentration Camp to Kaltenbrunner at his office at RSHA, Berlin. Kaltenbrunner asked me to give him a short oral digest of this report and said he would reserve any decision until he had had an opportunity to study it in complete detail. This report dealt with the assignment to labor of several hundred prisoners who had been condemned to death—so-called "nameless prisoners."
6. The "final solution" of the Jewish question meant the complete extermination of all Jews in Europe. I was ordered to establish extermination facilities

at Auschwitz in June 1941. At that time there were already in the general government three other extermination camps; BELZEK, TREBLINKA and WOLZEK. These camps were under the Einsatzkommando of the Security Police and SD. I visited Treblinka to find out how they carried out their exterminations. The Camp Commandant at Treblinka told me that he had liquidated 80,000 in the course of one-half year. He was principally concerned with liquidating all the Jews from the Warsaw Ghetto. He used monoxide gas and I did not think that his methods were very efficient. So when I set up the extermination building at Auschwitz, I used Cyclon B, which was a crystallized Prussic Acid which we dropped into the death chamber from a small opening. It took from 3 to 15 minutes to kill the people in the death chamber depending upon climatic conditions. We knew when the people were dead because their screaming stopped. We usually waited about one-half hour before we opened the doors and removed the bodies. After the bodies were removed our special commandos took off the rings and extracted the gold from the teeth of the corpses.

7. Another improvement we made over Treblinka was that we built our gas chambers to accommodate 2,000 people at one time, whereas at Treblinka their 10 gas chambers only accommodated 200 people each. The way we selected our victims was as follows: we had two SS doctors on duty at Auschwitz to examine the incoming transports of prisoners. The prisoners would be marched by one of the doctors who would make spot decisions as they walked by. Those who were fit for work were sent into the Camp. Others were sent immediately to the extermination plants. Children of tender years were invariably exterminated since by reason of their youth they were unable to work. Still another improvement we made over Treblinka was that at Treblinka the victims almost always knew that they were to be exterminated and at Auschwitz we endeavored to fool the victims into thinking that they were to go through a delousing process. Of course, frequently they realized our true intentions and we sometimes had riots and difficulties due to that fact. Very frequently women would hide their children under the clothes but of course when we found them we would send the children in to be exterminated. We were required to carry out these exterminations in secrecy but of course the foul and nauseating stench from the continuous burning of bodies permeated the entire area and all of the people living in the surrounding communities knew that exterminations were going on at Auschwitz.
8. We received from time to time special prisoners from the local Gestapo office. The SS doctors killed such prisoners by injections of benzine. Doctors had orders to write ordinary death certificates and could put down any reason at all for the cause of death.
9. From time to time we conducted medical experiments on women inmates, including sterilization and experiments relating to cancer. Most of the people who died under these experiments had been already condemned to death by the Gestapo.

10. Rudolf Mildner was the chief of the Gestapo at Kattowicz *and as such was head of the political department at Auschwitz which conducted third degree methods of interrogation* from approximately March 1941 until September 1943. As such, he frequently sent prisoners to Auschwitz for incarceration or execution. He visited Auschwitz on several occasions. The Gestapo Court, the SS Standgericht, which tried persons accused of various crimes, such as escaping Prisoners of War, etc., frequently met within Auschwitz, and Mildner often attended the trial of such persons, who usually were executed in Auschwitz following their sentence. I showed Mildner throughout the extermination plant at Auschwitz and he was directly interested in it since he had to send the Jews from his territory for execution at Auschwitz.

I understand English as it is written above. The above statements are true; this declaration is made by me voluntarily and without compulsion; after reading over the statement, I have signed and executed the same at Nurnberg, Germany on the fifth day of April 1946.

Source: Office of the U.S. Chief of Counsel for the Prosecution of Axis Criminality. *Trial of the Major War Criminals before the International Military Tribunal, Nuremberg*. Blue Series, vol. 33. Document 3868-PS. Washington, DC: U.S. Government Printing Office, 1946, pp. 275–79.

Commentary

Rudolf Hoess was the longest serving commandant of Auschwitz. In this affidavit, he is completely candid, admitting his role in the Final Solution and estimating that approximately 3 million people, mostly Jews, were killed at Auschwitz during his three and a half years in command. He boasts of the improvements he made when constructing and running Auschwitz as compared to the way things were done at Treblinka. The objective and nonchalant manner of his statement here is startling, considering that he discusses, among other things, the selection process, the way the victims were kept unaware that they were headed for a gas chamber, and the fact that medical experiments were performed on prisoners who, as he explains, "had been already condemned to death by the Gestapo." Hoess was tried for murder by the Supreme National Tribunal in Poland. Sentenced to death on March 29, 1947, he was hanged on April 16 the same year.

25. Extracts from Judgment, Nuremberg Trial: "The Persecution of the Jews," September 30–October 1, 1946

The judgment handed down at the International Military Tribunal Trial of Major War Criminals, held in Nuremberg, Germany, includes a section on the persecution of the Jews. This document provides some of the essence of the judgment, beginning with the words: "The persecution of the Jews at the hands of the Nazi Government has been proved in the greatest detail before the Tribunal. It is a record of consistent and systematic inhumanity on the greatest scale." Referring to the murderous policies pursued during the war in the occupied territories, the judgment describes the selections made at the camps of who would go immediately to their death and who would die more slowly through slave labor. It also addresses the medical experiments conducted on the Jews, their deaths in the gas chambers, and the total number of Jews killed by the Nazis.

The persecution of the Jews at the hands of the Nazi Government has been proved in the greatest detail before the Tribunal. It is a record of consistent and systematic inhumanity on the greatest scale. Ohlendorf, Chief of Amt III in the RSHA from 1939 to 1943, and who was in command of one of the Einsatz groups in the campaign against the Soviet Union testified as to the methods employed in the extermination of the Jews. He said that he employed firing squads to shoot the victims in order to lessen the sense of individual guilt on the part of his men; and the 90,000 men, women, and children who were murdered in one year by his particular group were mostly Jews.

When the witness Bach Zelewski was asked how Ohlendorf could admit the murder of 90,000 people, he replied: "I am of the opinion that when, for years, for decades, the doctrine is preached that the Slav race is an inferior race, and Jews not even human, then such an outcome is inevitable."

The anti-Jewish policy was formulated in Point 4 of the Party Program which declared "Only a member of the race can be a citizen. A member of the race can only be one who is of German blood, without consideration of creed. Consequently, no Jew can be a member of the race." Other points of the program declared that Jews should be treated as foreigners, that they should not be permitted to hold public office, that they should be expelled from the Reich if it were impossible to nourish the entire population of the State, that they should be denied any further immigration into Germany, and that they should be prohibited from publishing German newspapers. The Nazi Party preached these doctrines throughout its history. *Der Stürmer* and other publications were allowed to disseminate hatred of the Jews, and in the speeches and public declarations of the Nazi leaders, the Jews were held up to public ridicule and contempt.

With the seizure of power, the persecution of the Jews was intensified. A series of discriminatory laws was passed, which limited the offices and professions permitted to Jews; and restrictions were placed on their family life and their rights of citizenship. By the autumn of 1938, the Nazi policy towards the Jews had reached the stage where it was directed towards the complete exclusion of Jews from German life. Pogroms were organized, which included the burning and demolishing of synagogues, the looting of Jewish businesses, and the arrest of prominent Jewish business men. A collective fine of 1 billion marks was imposed on the Jews, the seizure of Jewish assets was authorized, and the movement of Jews was restricted by regulations to certain specified districts and hours. The creation of ghettos was carried out on an extensive scale, and by an order of the Security Police Jews were compelled to wear a yellow star to be worn on the breast and back.

The Nazi persecution of Jews in Germany before the war, severe and repressive as it was, cannot compare, however, with the policy pursued during the war in the occupied territories. Originally the policy was similar to that which had been in force inside Germany. Jews were required to register, were forced to live in ghettos, to wear the yellow star, and were used as slave laborers. In the summer of 1941, however, plans were made for the "final solution" of the Jewish question in Europe. This "final solution" meant the extermination of the Jews, which early in 1939 Hitler had threatened would be one of the consequences of an outbreak of war, and a special section in the Gestapo under Adolf Eichmann, as head of Section B 4 of the Gestapo, was formed to carry out the policy.

The plan for exterminating the Jews was developed shortly after the attack on the Soviet Union. Einsatzgruppen of the Security Police and SD, formed for the purpose of breaking the resistance of the population of the areas lying behind the German armies in the East, were given the duty of exterminating the Jews in those areas. The effectiveness of the work of the Einsatzgruppen is shown by the fact that in February 1942 Heydrich was able to report that Estonia had already been cleared of Jews and that in Riga the number of Jews had been reduced from 29,500 to 2,500. Altogether the Einsatzgruppen operating in the occupied Baltic States killed over 135,000 Jews in three months.

Nor did these special units operate completely independently of the German Armed Forces. There is clear evidence that leaders of the Einsatzgruppen obtained the co-operation of Army commanders. . . .

Part of the "Final Solution" was the gathering of Jews from all German-occupied Europe in concentration camps. Their physical condition was the test of life or death. All who were fit to work were used as slave laborers in the concentration camps; all who were not fit to work were destroyed in gas chambers and their bodies burnt. Certain concentration camps such as Treblinka and Auschwitz were set aside for this main purpose. With regard to Auschwitz, the Tribunal heard the evidence of Höss, the commandant of the camp from 1 May 1940 to 1 December 1943. He estimated that in the camp of Auschwitz alone in that time 2,500,000 persons were exterminated, and that a further 500,000 died from disease and starvation. Höss described the screening for extermination by stating in evidence:

> "We had two SS doctors on duty at Auschwitz to examine the incoming transports of prisoners. The prisoners would be marched by one of the doctors who would make spot decisions as they walked by. Those who were fit for work were sent into the camp. Others were sent immediately to the extermination plants. Children of tender years were invariably exterminated since by reason of their youth they were unable to work. Still another improvement we made over Treblinka was that at Treblinka the victims almost always knew that they were to be exterminated and at Auschwitz we endeavored to fool the victims into thinking that they were to go through a delousing process. Of course, frequently they realized our true intentions and we sometimes had riots and difficulties due to that fact. Very frequently women would hide their children under their clothes, but of course—when we found them—we would send the children in to be exterminated."

He described the actual killing by stating:

> "It took from three to fifteen minutes to kill the people in the death chamber, depending upon climatic conditions. We knew when the people were dead because their screaming stopped. We usually waited about one half-hour before we opened the

doors and removed the bodies. After the bodies were removed our special commandos took off the rings and extracted the gold from the teeth of the corpses."

Beating, starvation, torture, and killing were general. The inmates were subjected to cruel experiments at Dachau in August 1942, victims were immersed in cold water until their body temperature was reduced to 28° Centigrade, when they died immediately. Other experiments included high altitude experiments in pressure chambers, experiments to determine how long human beings could survive in freezing water, experiments with poison bullets, experiments with contagious diseases, and experiments dealing with sterilization of men and women by X-rays and other methods.

Evidence was given of the treatment of the inmates before and after their extermination. There was testimony that the hair of women victims was cut off before they were killed, and shipped to Germany, there to be used in the manufacture of mattresses. The clothes, money, and valuables of the inmates were also salvaged and sent to the appropriate agencies for disposition. After the extermination the gold teeth and fillings were taken from the heads of the corpses and sent to the Reichsbank.

After cremation the ashes were used for fertilizer, and in some instances attempts were made to utilize the fat from the bodies of the victims in the commercial manufacture of soap. Special groups traveled through Europe to find Jews and subject them to the "final solution." German missions were sent to such satellite countries as Hungary and Bulgaria, to arrange for the shipment of Jews to extermination camps and it is known that by the end of 1944, 400,000 Jews from Hungary had been murdered at Auschwitz. Evidence has also been given of the evacuation of 110,000 Jews from part of Rumania for "liquidation." Adolf Eichmann, who had been put in charge of this program by Hitler, has estimated that the policy pursued resulted in the killing of 6 million Jews, of which 4 million were killed in the extermination institutions.

Source: Office of the U.S. Chief of Counsel for the Prosecution of Axis Criminality. *Trial of the Major War Criminals before the International Military Tribunal, Nuremberg*. Blue Series, vol. 1. Washington, DC: U.S. Government Printing Office, 1946, pp. 247–53.

Commentary

With the end of World War II, an international military tribunal (IMT), based in the German city of Nuremberg, sat to try 22 major Nazis. They were accused under any of four counts: crimes against peace, war crimes, crimes against humanity, and (the chief indictment) conspiring to commit any of the foregoing in a "Common Plan." The trials took place at Nuremberg's Palace of Justice from October 18, 1945, to October 1, 1946.

The major emphasis of the IMT was to bring to justice those who had upset the international order by waging aggressive war, not those who had exclusively committed crimes against humanity. For the IMT, the most criminal act was foisting aggressive war upon a world previously clearly committed to avoiding it. As a result, Nuremberg should be seen as more than simply a trial sitting in judgment on the Holocaust. When the tribunal (comprised of two judges each from Britain, France, the United States, and the Soviet Union) handed down its decisions, there were few surprises. Six of the accused were found guilty on all four counts and sentenced to hang; another six were found guilty of some counts and similarly sentenced. Others among the Nazis received long prison sentences ranging from 10 years to life, and three were acquitted.

Owing to the shocking revelations and film footage that came to light in evidence, however, there has been a perception in the popular awareness ever since that the trials were actually a judgment on the Holocaust, even though it was not on trial. The revelations that came through the trials served to confirm for people living in the Allied countries why the struggle against the Nazis had been too important to lose.

The extracts in this final document, therefore, are intended to serve as an illustration of how those meting out postwar justice viewed the heinous nature of the crimes over which they had just adjudicated. They provide a chilling and damning indictment of the perpetrators' actions across the wartime years of the Third Reich.

Chronology

This chronology seeks to outline the essential contours of some of the specific developments within the history of Nazi Germany, the Holocaust, and World War II. Given that the Holocaust played such a huge role in the affairs of nations and peoples, not all events, people, or places could be listed; doing so would, in one sense, make the chronology too unwieldy. Not only would this defeat the purpose of providing an accessible chronology; it would also lead to many of the events of the Holocaust becoming buried in the minutiae of other events.

1919	January 5: The German Workers' Party (DAP) is founded by Anton Drexler and Karl Harrer.
	June 28: Germany signs the Versailles Treaty, formally ending World War I.
	September 12: Adolf Hitler joins the DAP.
1920	February 24: The Nazi Party is established when the DAP is renamed, and it becomes the National Socialist German Workers' Party (NSDAP). Hitler presents a 25-point program, the Nazi Party Platform.
1922	October 24: Benito Mussolini and his Fascist Blackshirts March on Rome.
1923	November 9: Hitler leads an attempt to overthrow the government of Bavaria; he fails.
1924	February 24: Trial of Adolf Hitler for treason begins; he is found guilty and sentenced to five years in prison.
	April 1: Hitler commences his sentence at Landsberg Prison.
	December 19: Hitler is released from Landsberg, having served just eight months of his sentence.
1925	February 27: Hitler declares the Nazi Party (NSDAP) to be reestablished, with himself as leader (Führer).
	July 19: The first of two volumes of Hitler's *Mein Kampf* are published.
1930	January 23: Wilhelm Frick becomes the first NSDAP member to become a minister in a state government.
1933	January 30: Adolf Hitler is appointed chancellor of Germany by President Paul von Hindenburg.

	February 27–28: The Reichstag fire happens. Arrests of the Nazis' political opponents begin almost immediately.
	March 5: Reichstag elections occur. The Nazis gain 44 percent of the vote in manipulated elections.
	March 20: Dachau concentration camp is established.
	March 27: The Enabling Act is passed.
	April 1: Jewish businesses are boycotted across Germany.
	April 11: Nazis issue a decree defining who is a non-Aryan.
	April 21: Jewish ritual slaughter is banned.
	April 26: Hermann Göring establishes the Gestapo.
	May 10: Books written by Jews and "undesirables" are publicly burned.
	July 14: The Law for the Prevention of Offspring with Hereditary Defects is passed, forcing many Germans with "undesirable genes" to be sterilized.
	July 20: The Nazi government signs the Concordat with the Vatican.
	September 22: The Haavara Agreement is signed.
1934	January 26: Germany and Poland sign a nonaggression pact.
	June 30: *Sturmabteilung* (SA) leadership is purged, during what becomes known as the Night of the Long Knives.
	August 2: The German president, Paul von Hindenburg, dies. Hitler declares the office of president abolished and names himself Führer of Germany.
1935	September 15: The Nuremberg Laws are announced at the annual party rally.
	December 31: Jews holding civil service positions in Germany are dismissed.
1936	July 1: Hitler Youth membership becomes compulsory for all Aryan boys.
	August 1: The Summer Olympic Games begin in Berlin.
	October 25: The Rome-Berlin Axis is created.
1937	January 26: A new law is passed prohibiting Jews from working in any official capacity.
	March 21: Pope Pius XI issues the papal encyclical *Mit Brennender Sorge*.
	July 19: Buchenwald concentration camp is established.
1938	March 12: The *Anschluss* (union) of Austria with Germany is agreed. All German antisemitic decrees are applied immediately to Austria.

July 6–14: An international conference on refugees is held at Evian, France. No action follows to alleviate the situation of Jews.

August 1: The Nazi Office of Jewish Emigration is established to speed up the pace of Jewish emigration from Germany.

August 8: Mauthausen concentration camp is established in Austria.

August 11: Nazis destroy the Nuremberg synagogue.

August 17: The Nazis require Jewish women to add "Sarah" and men to add "Israel" to their names on all legal documents.

August 19: The Swiss government refuses entry to Austrian Jews seeking sanctuary.

September 27: German Jews are banned from practicing law.

September 29–30: The Munich Conference is held. Britain and France surrender the Sudetenland regions of Czechoslovakia to Germany by negotiation.

October 5: Passports belonging to German Jews are marked with the letter *J* to indicate their identity.

November 7: Ernst vom Rath, third secretary in the German Embassy in Paris, is shot and mortally wounded by Herschel Grynszpan. Vom Rath dies on November 9, precipitating *Kristallnacht*.

November 9–10: The *Kristallnacht* pogrom occurs in Germany and Austria. Nazi figures give 91 Jews killed and up to 10,000 arrested, with 267 synagogues destroyed; figures are likely much higher.

November 12: Retail businesses are forcibly transferred from Jewish owners.

November 16: Jewish children are forbidden from attending German schools.

December 2: Roma are required to be registered.

1939

January 1: Jews are banned from working with Germans under the Measure for the Elimination of Jews from the German Economy.

March 15: Germany invades Czechoslovakia.

March 28: Germany abrogates its nonaggression pact with Poland.

May 15: The first prisoners arrive at Ravensbrück.

June 17: The *SS St. Louis*, a ship carrying 936 Jewish passengers, returns to Europe after being denied entry into the United States and Cuba.

August 23: The Nazi-Soviet Nonaggression Pact is signed.

September 1: Germany invades Poland; a curfew is imposed on German Jews.

September 3: France and Britain declare war against Germany.

September 17: The Soviet Union invades Poland.

September 21: Reinhard Heydrich orders *Einsatzgruppen* commanders to establish ghettos in German-occupied Poland.

September 27: Warsaw surrenders. Jewish Councils are established in Poland. Adam Czerniakow becomes president of the Jewish Council in Warsaw.

October 8: A ghetto is established in Piotrkow Trybunalski, Poland.

November 9: Łódź is annexed by Germany.

November 23: Yellow stars are required to be worn by Polish Jews over the age of 10.

November 30: The Soviet Union invades Finland.

December 12: Labor camps are organized throughout Poland. Jews between the ages of 14 and 60 become forced laborers.

1940 February 8: Łódź ghetto is established.

March 12: The Treaty of Moscow is signed, bringing an end to the war between the Soviet Union and Finland.

April 1: Thousands of refugees are permitted into Shanghai, China.

April 9: Denmark and southern Norway are invaded and occupied by Germany. Heinrich Himmler issues a directive to establish a concentration camp at Auschwitz.

April 30: The Łódź ghetto is sealed off from the outside world.

May 7: Nearly 165,000 inhabitants are sealed in the Łódź ghetto.

May 10: France, the Netherlands, Belgium, and Luxembourg are invaded by Germany.

May 20: Auschwitz concentration camp established for Polish political prisoners.

June 4: Neuengamme concentration camp opens.

June 10: Italy declares war against Britain and France.

June 15: The Soviet Union occupies Latvia, Lithuania, and Estonia.

June 22: France surrenders to Germany. Marshal Philippe Pétain leads the pro-Nazi state established at Vichy.

June 27: Romania cedes the provinces of Bessarabia and Bukovina to the Soviet Union.

July 17: The first anti-Jewish measures are taken in Vichy France.

August 29: Hungary annexes Transylvania.

September 7: German forces begin aerial bombings of Britain.

September 27: The Tripartite Pact is signed by Germany, Italy, and Japan.

October 3: Vichy France passes its own version of the Nuremberg Laws.

October 7: Nazis invade Romania.

October 16: Germans officially establish the Warsaw ghetto.

November 4: Jewish civil servants in the Netherlands are dismissed.

November 16: The Warsaw ghetto, containing nearly 500,000 Jews, is sealed.

November 20–24: Hungary, Romania, and Slovakia join the Axis.

1941 January 2: The Iron Guard attempt a coup in Romania against government of Marshal Ion Antonescu.

January 21–26: The Romanian Iron Guard annihilates hundreds of Jews.

February 9: Dutch Nazis riot against Amsterdam Jews.

March 1: Construction of Birkenau begins.

April 6: Nazis invade Yugoslavia and Greece; Bulgaria annexes Thrace and Macedonia.

April 21: Natzweiler-Struthof concentration camp opens in France.

May 14: Thousands of Jews are rounded up in Paris at the Vel' d'Hiv.

June 22: Germany violates its nonaggression pact with the Soviet Union and invades (Operation Barbarossa); Hungary joins the Axis.

June 27: Białystok is occupied by Nazis. The Białystok ghetto is established.

July 2: Ukrainian nationalists murder thousands in Lvov (Lviv).

July 17: *Einsatzgruppen* are ordered to execute captured communists and Jews during the Soviet campaign.

July 20: The Minsk ghetto is established.

July 31: Adolf Eichmann is appointed to prepare the Final Solution.

September 1: The German euthanasia program is formally ended, following the deaths of some 100,000 people.

September 6: The Vilna ghetto is established.

September 19: Jews in Germany are ordered to wear yellow armbands bearing the Star of David. German troops occupy Kiev.

September 29: The *Einsatzgruppen* murders some 34,000 Jews at Babi Yar ravine, outside Kiev.

October 7: Birkenau is established as the primary mass-murder site of Auschwitz.

October 22–24: Romanian and German forces massacre an estimated 50,000 Jews in Odessa.

October 28: Approximately 9,000 Jews are killed outside of Kovno (Kaunas).

November 8: Plans are made for the creation of a ghetto in Lvov (Lviv).

November 24: Theresienstadt (Terezín) ghetto/concentration camp established.

December 7: The Night and Fog directive begins in Germany. Japan attacks Pearl Harbor, drawing the United States into World War II.

December 8: Chełmno extermination camp becomes fully operational; some 320,000 Jews will be murdered here.

December 11: Germany and Italy declare war on the United States.

1942

January 20: The Wannsee Conference takes place.

January 16: Deportations from Łódź begin.

February 23: Some 768 Jewish passengers, after being refused entry into Palestine, drown when the *SS Struma* sinks off of the Turkish coast.

March 1: Extermination by gas begins at Sobibór.

March 17: Killings begin at Bełżec extermination camp; it will see the murder of 600,000 Jews by the time it closes.

May 27: Reinhard Heydrich's car is ambushed; he is seriously wounded in the attack and dies shortly thereafter. In response, German soldiers destroy the Czech village of Lidice, murdering most of its inhabitants and sending the rest to concentration camps.

June 1: Jews in France, Holland, Belgium, Croatia, Slovakia, and Romania are ordered to wear yellow stars.

June 1: Treblinka extermination camp begins operation.

June 29–30: Following acts of armed resistance by Jewish partisans in the ghetto of Slonim, the Nazis set the ghetto on fire; they spend the next two weeks murdering between 7,000 and 10,000 Jews.

July 14: Mass deportation of Dutch and Belgian Jews to Auschwitz begins.

July 16: Over 4,000 children are taken from Paris and sent to Auschwitz; overall, some 12,887 Jews in Paris are sent through Drancy.

July 22: Mass deportation of Jews from the Warsaw ghetto to Treblinka begins.

July 23: Adam Czerniakow commits suicide in Warsaw.

July 28: The Jewish Combat Organization is formed in the Warsaw ghetto.

September 2–3: The Łachwa ghetto revolts, arguably the first ghetto revolt of the Holocaust.

October 15: The SS slaughters 25,000 Jews near Brest-Litovsk.

October 25: The deportation of Norwegian Jews begins.

October 22: The SS put down a revolt at Sachsenhausen by a group of Jews about to be sent to Auschwitz.

October 28: The first transport of Jews is sent from Theresienstadt (Terezín) to Auschwitz.

November 19: The Soviet army begins its counteroffensive at Stalingrad, causing the German army to begin its retreat.

December 24: The Jewish Combat Organization engages in armed operations against German troops in Kraków.

1943 January 18–21: Renewed deportations of Jews from the Warsaw ghetto begin following a visit from Himmler; Jewish resistance begins in the ghetto.

January 22: Deportations from the Warsaw ghetto end, following the deaths of 50 Nazi soldiers.

February 2: German forces surrender at Stalingrad.

February 16: Theodor Eicke, head of the Inspectorate of Concentration Camps, dies when his aircraft is shot down.

February 26: The first Roma arrive at Auschwitz.

February 27: The last Jews in Berlin are rounded up and deported through *Fabrikaktion* (Factory Action).

February 27–March 6: Non-Jewish wives and mothers undertake the Rosenstrasse protest in Berlin against the imprisonment of their Jewish husbands and children.

March 13–14: The Kraków ghetto is liquidated.

March 23: Nazi deportation of Greek Jews begins.

April 5: Approximately 4,000 Jews are massacred in the Ponary Forest, outside Vilna.

April 13: Mass graves are discovered in Katyn, Poland.

April 19: New deportations from the Warsaw ghetto start, and the Warsaw Ghetto Uprising begins.

May 8: Nazi forces capture the Jewish Combat Organization's command bunker at Miła 18.

May 16: SS General Jürgen Stroop reports that the "Jewish quarter of Warsaw is no more."

May 19: Nazis declare Berlin to be *Judenfrei* (cleansed of Jews).

June 2: Following resistance in Lvov (Lviv), 3,000 Jews are killed; another 7,000 are sent to the concentration camp at Janowska.

June 11: Himmler orders the liquidation of all ghettos in occupied Poland.

June 25–26: The Częstochowa ghetto revolts.

July 25: Mussolini's Fascist regime falls in Italy, and Mussolini is dismissed by King Victor Emmanuel III.

August 2: The Treblinka Uprising happens.

August 15–16: The uprising of the Białystok ghetto occurs.

August 23: Wilhelm Frick is named *Reichsprotektor* of Bohemia and Moravia.

September 3: The Allies invade southern Italy.

September 8: Italy surrenders to the Allies and declares war against Germany; German forces enter northern Italy in response.

October 1–2: German police begin deportations of Danish Jews; Danes respond with a rescue effort that saves the lives of 90 percent of the Jewish population.

October 14: The Sobibór Uprising occurs.

October 16: Nazis undertake a major raid and *razzia* (roundup) against the Jews of Rome, who are sent to Auschwitz

October 21: The Minsk ghetto is liquidated.

October 30: The Moscow Declaration is signed.

1944 January 22: U.S. president Franklin D. Roosevelt creates the War Refugee Board

March 19: Germany begins its occupation of Hungary; Adolf Eichmann is sent from Berlin to oversee the deportation of the Hungarian Jews.

May 15: The deportation of Jews from Hungary to Auschwitz begins; Jews from Ruthenia and Transylvania are deported.

May 16: Germans offer to free 1,00,000 Jews in exchange for 10,000 trucks.

June 23: The Swedish International Red Cross is allowed to visit Theresienstadt (Terezín).

June 30: The Kasztner Train departs from Budapest.

July 9: Raoul Wallenberg arrives in Hungary, where he distributes Swedish passports and sets up safe houses for Jews.

July 11: Deportations from Hungary are halted by order of Regent Miklós Horthy.

July 20: German officers fail to assassinate Hitler in the bomb plot.

July 24: Majdanek extermination camp is liberated by the Russians.

August 1–October 4: The Warsaw Revolt occurs.

August 2: Germany destroys the so-called Gypsy camp at Auschwitz, gassing some 3,000 in the process.

August 6: Łódź, the last Jewish ghetto in Poland, is liquidated; 60,000 Jews are sent to Auschwitz.

August 23: Romanian dictator Ion Antonescu is deposed and turned over to Soviet forces.

August 25: Paris is liberated.

October 7: The *Sonderkommando* revolt at Auschwitz; one of the gas chambers is destroyed, and 15 SS guards and 400 members of the *Sonderkommando* are killed.

November 8: Deportations resume in Budapest.

November 19: The Vatican and four other neutral powers in Budapest issue a collective protest to the Hungarian government calling for the suspension of Jewish deportations.

November 28: Himmler orders the gas chambers at Auschwitz destroyed.

December 24–29: Hungarian Arrow Cross fascists attack Jews in Budapest.

1945 January 17: Raoul Wallenberg is arrested by Soviet forces for espionage.

January 18: The evacuation of Auschwitz begins.

January 19: The Soviet Army liberates Łódź.

January 28: Soviet forces liberate Auschwitz.

April 9: The evacuation of Mauthausen begins.

April 11: American forces liberate Buchenwald.

April 12: U.S. president Franklin Delano Roosevelt dies and is succeeded by Harry S. Truman.

April 13: Soviets liberate Vienna.

April 15: British forces liberate Bergen-Belsen.

April 27: Soviet forces liberate Sachsenhausen.

April 28: Benito Mussolini is assassinated.

April 29: American forces liberate Dachau; Soviet forces liberate Ravensbrück.

April 30: Hitler commits suicide.

May 1: Joseph Goebbels kills his wife and children before shooting himself as Berlin is surrounded by the Soviet army.

May 2: Soviet forces capture Berlin.

May 3: Theresienstadt (Terezín) is surrendered to the International Committee of the Red Cross.

May 5: American forces liberate Mauthausen.

May 7: Germany surrenders to the Allies in Reims.

May 9: Wilhelm Keitel signs surrender documents in Berlin.

May 23: Heinrich Himmler commits suicide.

July 23: Marshal Philippe Pétain is tried for treason by France's High Court of Justice.

August 8: The London Charter Agreement is signed.

September 1: Japan surrenders to the Allies after the United States detonates atomic bombs at Hiroshima and Nagasaki, ending World War II.

October 15: Pierre Laval is hanged in France.

October 18: The International Military Tribunal of major war criminals begins at Nuremberg.

October 24: Vidkun Quisling is executed in Norway, after being found guilty of high treason.

1946 June 1: Ion Antonescu is executed in Bucharest following a guilty verdict at his May trial.

July 4: Forty-two Jews are killed in a pogrom in Kielce, Poland.

October 1: The International Military Tribunal ends.

October 15: Hermann Göring commits suicide in his cell at Nuremberg.

October 16: Death sentences are carried out at Nuremberg; those condemned are hanged.

Bibliography

The bibliography that follows is intended as a starting point for researchers and students of the Holocaust, with a specific focus on perpetration in all its forms. It does not pretend to be a complete listing of all works relating to those who carried out the Holocaust, nor could it be, within the scope of a listing of this size. New works are appearing literally every day, but at a bare minimum, the works in this listing could be considered as the core of any research project.

Where possible, we have added the names of those featured in this book alongside works where they feature. Unfortunately, there are still many stories remaining to be told or developed more, which is why not all the people featured in this volume have yet had studies done on their activities during the Holocaust.

Abbott, Peter, Nigel Thomas, and Martin Windrow. *Germany's Eastern Front Allies, 1941–45.* London: Osprey, 1982 (**Csatáry**).

Adele, Wendy, and Marie Sarti. *Women and Nazis: Perpetrators of Genocide and Other Crimes during Hitler's Regime, 1933–1945.* Palo Alto, CA: Academia Press, 2011 (**Binz**).

Adelson, Alan, and Robert Lapides (eds.). *Łódź Ghetto: A Community History Told in Diaries, Journals, and Documents.* New York: Viking, 1989 (**Biebow**; **Übelhör**).

Allen, Michael Thad. *The Business of Genocide: The SS, Slave Labor, and the Concentration Camps.* Chapel Hill, NC: University of North Carolina Press, 2002 (**Pohl**).

Aly, Götz. *"Final Solution": Nazi Population Policy and the Murder of the European Jews.* London: Arnold, 1999 (**Höppner**).

Angrick, Andrej. *Besatzungspolitik und Massenmord. Die Einsatzgruppe D in der südlichen Sowjetunion 1941–1943.* Hamburg: Hamburger Edition, 2003 (**Bierkamp**).

Angrick, Andrej, and Peter Klein. *The "Final Solution" in Riga: Exploitation and Annihilation.* New York and Oxford: Berghahn Books, 2009 (**Lange, R.**).

Annas, George J. *The Nazi Doctors and the Nuremberg Code: Human Rights in Human Experimentation.* Oxford: Oxford University Press, 1992 (**Magnussen**; **Oberheuser**).

Arad, Yitzhak. *Belzec, Sobibor, Treblinka: The Operation Reinhard Death Camps.* Bloomington, IN: Indiana University Press, 1987 (**Bauer**; **Eberl**; **Franz**; **Hering**; **Hirtreiter**; **Höfle**; **Lambert**; **Miete**; **Reichleitner**; **Thomalla**; **Wagner**; **Wirth**).

Arad, Yitzhak. *Ghetto in Flames: The Struggle and Destruction of the Jews in Vilna in the Holocaust.* Jerusalem: Yad Vashem, 1981 (**Kittel**).

Arendt, Hannah. *Eichmann in Jerusalem: A Report on the Banality of Evil.* New York: Penguin, 2006 (**Eichmann**; **Koppe**).

Askenasy, Hans. *Are We All Nazis?* Secaucus, NJ: Lyle Stuart, 1978.

Auschwitz-Birkenau State Museum. *KL Auschwitz Seen by the SS.* Oświęcim: Auschwitz-Birkenau State Museum, 1997 (**Broad**).

Bartov, Omer. *The Eastern Front, 1941–45: German Troops and the Barbarisation of Warfare.* Houndmills, UK: Palgrave Macmillan, 2001.

Bartrop, Paul R. *Surviving the Camps: Unity in Adversity during the Holocaust*. Lanham, MD: University Press of America, 2000 (**Eicke**).

Bauer, Yehuda. *Jews for Sale? Nazi-Jewish Negotiations, 1933–1945*. New Haven: Yale University Press, 1994 (**Becher**).

Baum, Steven K. *The Psychology of Genocide: Perpetrators, Bystanders and Rescuers*. Cambridge: Cambridge University Press, 2008.

Baumslag, Naomi. *Murderous Medicine: Nazi Doctors, Human Experimentation, and Typhus*. New York: Praeger, 2005 (**Magnussen**; **Wirths**).

Baxter, Ian. *Images of War: Himmler's Nazi Concentration Camp Guards*, Barnsley, UK: Pen and Sword, 2012 (**Bothe**).

Bennett, G. H. *The Nazi, the Painter and the Forgotten Story of the SS Road*. London: Reaktion Books, 2012 (**Jeckeln**).

Beorn, Waitman Wade. *Marching into Darkness: The Wehrmacht and the Holocaust in Belarus*. Cambridge, MA: Harvard University Press, 2014 (**Nebe**).

Birn, Ruth Bettina. *Die höheren SS- und Polizeiführer: Himmlers Vertreter im Reich und in den besetzten Gebieten*. Düsseldorf: Droste-Verlag, 1986 (**Katzmann**; **Scheel**).

Black, Monica, and Eric Kurlander (eds.). *Revisiting the "Nazi Occult": Histories, Realities, Legacies*. Rochester, NY: Camden House, 2015 (**Teudt**).

Black, Peter. *Ernst Kaltenbrunner: Ideological Soldier of the Third Reich*. Princeton, NJ: Princeton University Press, 1984 (**Kaltenbrunner**).

Blatt, Thomas Toivi. *From the Ashes of Sobibor: A Story of Survival*. Evanston, IL: Northwestern University Press, 1997 (**Bauer**).

Bloch, Michael. *Ribbentrop*. New York: Crown Publishers, 1992 (**Ribbentrop**).

Blood, Phillip W. *Hitler's Bandit Hunters: The SS and the Nazi Occupation of Europe*. Washington, DC: Potomac Books, 2006 (**Streckenbach**).

Borkin, Joseph. *The Crime and Punishment of I. G. Farben*. London: Andre Deutsch, 1979 (**Tesch**).

Bower, Tom. *Klaus Barbie: The Butcher of Lyons*. New York: Pantheon Books, 1984 (**Barbie**).

Braham, Randolph L. *The Politics of Genocide: The Holocaust in Hungary*. Vol. 1. New York: Columbia University Press, 1981 (**Becher; Szálasi**; **Veesenmayer**).

Bramsted, Ernst. *Goebbels and National Socialist Propaganda, 1925–1945*. East Lansing, MI: Michigan State University, 1965 (**Goebbels**).

Braun, Konstanze. *Dr. Otto Georg Thierack (1889–1946)*. Frankfurt am Main: Peter Lang, 2005 (**Thierack**).

Breitman, Richard. *The Architect of Genocide: Himmler and the Final Solution*. Hanover, NH: University of New England Press, 1991 (**Himmler**).

Breitman, Richard, Norman J. W. Goda, Timothy Naftali, and Robert Wolfe. *U.S. Intelligence and the Nazis*. New York: Cambridge University Press, 2005 (**Rauff**).

Broschell, Christopher. *Hitler's Money Machine: How Great Companies Stopped Worrying and Learned to Love the Reichsmark*. USA: CreateSpace, 2014 (**Boss**).

Browder, George C. *Foundations of the Nazi Police State: The Formation of the SIPO and the SD*. Lexington, KY: University of Kentucky Press, 1990 (**Schöngarth**).

Browder, George C. *Hitler's Enforcers: The Gestapo and the SS Security Service in the Nazi Revolution*. Oxford: Oxford University Press, 1996 (**Müller**).

Brown, Daniel Patrick. *The Beautiful Beast: The Life and Crimes of SS-Aufseherin Irma Grese*. Ventura, CA: Golden West Historical Publications, 1996 (**Grese**).

Brown, Daniel Patrick. *The Camp Women: The Female Auxiliaries Who Assisted the SS in Running the Nazi Concentration Camp System*. Atglen, PA: Schiffer Publishing, 2002 (**Binz**; **Bormann, J.**; **Mandl**; **Volkenrath**).

Browning, Christopher R. *Fateful Months: Essays on the Emergence of the Final Solution*. New York: Holmes and Meier, 1985 (**Turner**).

Browning, Christopher R. *The Final Solution and the German Foreign Office: A Study of Referat D III of Abteilung Deutschland, 1940–43*. New York: Holmes and Meier, 1978 (**Rademacher**; **Ribbentrop**).

Browning, Christopher R. *Nazi Policy, Jewish Workers, German Killers*. Cambridge: Cambridge University Press, 2000 (**Höfle**).

Browning, Christopher R. *Ordinary Men: Reserve Police Battalion 101 and the Final Solution in Poland*. New York: HarperCollins, 1992 (**Daluege**).

Browning, Christopher R. *The Origins of the Final Solution: The Evolution of Nazi Jewish Policy, September 1939–March 1942*. Lincoln, NE: University of Nebraska Press, 2004 (**Blobel**; **Rademacher**).

Browning, Christopher R. *The Path to Genocide: Essays on Launching the Final Solution*. Cambridge: Cambridge University Press, 1982 (**Turner**).

Bryant, Michael. *Eyewitness to Genocide: The Operation Reinhard Death Camp Trials, 1955–1966*. Knoxville, TN: University of Tennessee Press, 2016 (**Wirth**).

Buggeln, Mark. *Slave Labor in Nazi Concentration Camps*. Oxford: Oxford University Press, 2014 (**Pohl**).

Bullock, Alan. *Hitler: A Study in Tyranny*. London: Odhams, 1952 (**Hitler**).

Burrin, Philippe. *France under the Germans: Collaboration and Compromise*. New York: New Press, 1996 (**Laval**).

Buttar, Prit. *Between Giants: The Battle for the Baltics in World War II*. Oxford: Osprey, 2013 (**Arājs**; **Roschmann**).

Bytwerk, Randall L. *Julius Streicher: Nazi Editor of the Notorious Anti-Semitic Newspaper Der Stürmer*. New York: Cooper Square Press, 2001 (**Streicher**).

Calic, Edouard. *Reinhard Heydrich: The Chilling Story of the Man Who Masterminded the Nazi Death Camps*. New York: William Morrow, 1984 (**Heydrich**).

Campbell, Bruce. *The SA Generals and the Rise of Nazism*. Lexington, KY: University Press of Kentucky, 2004 (**Buch**).

Carruthers, Bob (ed.). *The Gestapo on Trial: Evidence from Nuremberg*. Barnsley, UK: Pen and Sword, 2014 (**Höppner**).

Cecil, Robert. *The Myth of the Master Race: Alfred Rosenberg and Nazi Ideology*. New York: Dodd, Mead, 1972 (**Rosenberg**).

Celinscak, Mark. *Distance from the Belsen Heap: Allied Forces and the Liberation of a Concentration Camp*. Toronto: University of Toronto Press, 2015 (**Kramer**).

Cervera, Suzanne. *Entre conformisme et scandale, le femmes du Comté de Nice au temps de la Libération*, https://www.departement06.fr/documents/A-votre-service/Culture/archives/recherches-regionales/dpt06_recherchesregionales209_8.pdf (**Mackert**).

Cesarani, David. *Eichmann: His Life and Crimes*. London: Heinemann, 2004 (**Dannecker**; **Eichmann**; **Wisliceny**).

Coleman, Fred. *The Marcel Network, How One French Couple Saved 527 Children from the Holocaust*. Washington, DC: Potomac Books, 2013 (**Mackert**).

Cornelius, Deborah S. *Hungary in World War II: Caught in the Cauldron*. 3rd ed. New York: Fordham University Press, 2011 (**Csatáry**).

Crowe, David M. *Oskar Schindler: The Untold Account of His Life, Wartime Activities, and the True Story Behind the List*. Cambridge, MA: Westview Press, 2004 (**Goeth**).

Curtis, Michael. *Verdict on Vichy: Power and Prejudice in the Vichy France Regime*. New York: Arcade, 2002 (**Lischka**; **Papon**).

Cymet, David. *History vs. Apologetics: The Holocaust, the Third Reich, and the Catholic Church*. Lanham, MD: Lexington Books, 2010 (**Hudal**).

Dahl, Hans Fredrik. *Quisling: A Study in Treachery*. Cambridge: Cambridge University Press, 1999 (**Quisling**; **Terboven**).

Dalin, David, and John Rothman. *Icon of Evil Hitler's Mufti and the Rise of Radical Islam*. New York: Random House, 2008 (**al-Husseini**).

Deichmann, Ute. *Biologists under Hitler*. Cambridge, MA: Harvard University Press, 1999 (**Blome**).

Deletant, Dennis. *Hitler's Forgotten Ally: Ion Antonescu and His Regime, Romania 1940–1944*. Basingstoke, UK: Palgrave Macmillan, 2006 (**Antonescu**).

De Mildt, Dick. *In the Name of the People: Perpetrators of Genocide in the Reflection of Their Post-War Prosecution in West Germany*. The Hague: Martinus Nijhoff Publishers, 1996 (**Koppe**).

Dicks, Henry V. *Licensed Mass Murder: A Social-Psychological Study of Some SS Killers*. New York: Basic Books, 1972.

Dillon, Christopher. *Dachau and the SS: A Schooling in Violence*. Oxford: Oxford University Press, 2015 (**Eicke**).

Dobroszycki, Lucjan (ed.). *The Chronicle of the Łódź Ghetto, 1941–1944*. New York: Vail-Ballou Press, 1984 (**Biebow**).

Dobroszycki, Lucjan, and Jeffrey S. Gurock (eds.). *The Holocaust in the Soviet Union: Studies and Sources on the Destruction of the Jews in the Nazi-Occupied Territories of the USSR, 1941–1945*. Armonk, NY: M. E. Sharpe, 1993 (**Strauch**).

Dwork, Debórah, and Robert Jan van Pelt. *Auschwitz: 1270 to the Present*. New York: Norton, 1996 (**Broad**).

Earl, Hilary. *The Nuremberg SS Einsatzgruppen Trial, 1945–1958: Atrocity, Law, and History*. Cambridge: Cambridge University Press, 2009 (**Blume**; **Six**; **Strauch**).

Epstein, Catherine. *Model Nazi: Arthur Greiser and the Occupation of Western Poland*. Oxford: Oxford University Press, 2012 (**Greiser**).

Evans, Richard. *The Coming of the Third Reich*. New York: Penguin, 2004 (**Frick**).

Ezergailis, Andrew. *The Holocaust in Latvia 1941–1944: The Missing Center*. Washington, DC: U.S. Holocaust Memorial Museum, 1996 (**Jeckeln**; **Lange, R.**; **Prützmann**; **Roschmann**).

Fénelon, Fania. *Playing for Time*. New York: Atheneum, 1977 (**Mandl**).

Fenyo, Mario D. *Hitler, Horthy and Hungary: German-Hungarian Relations, 1941–1944*. New Haven: Yale University Press, 1972 (**Veesenmayer**).

Fest, Joachim C. *The Face of the Third Reich: Portraits of the Nazi Leadership*. New York: Pantheon Books, 1970 (**Eichmann**; **Eicke**; **Goebbels**; **Heydrich**; **Himmler**; **Hoess**; **Rosenberg**; **Speer**; **Stangl**).

Frank, Niklas. *In the Shadow of the Reich*. New York: Alfred A. Knopf, 1991 (**Bühler**; **Frank**).

Friedlander, Henry. *The Origins of Nazi Genocide: From Euthanasia to the Final Solution*. Chapel Hill, NC: University of North Carolina Press, 1995 (**Bouhler**; **Fischer**; **Lange, H.**; **Stangl**; **Thomalla**).

Friedländer, Saul. *Nazi Germany and the Jews, 1939–1945: The Years of Extermination*. New York: HarperCollins, 2007 (**Stahlecker**).

Gellately, Robert. *Backing Hitler: Consent and Coercion in Nazi Germany*. New York: Oxford University Press, 2001 (**Nebe**).

Gellately, Robert. *The Gestapo and German Society: Enforcing Racial Policy, 1933–1945*. New York: Oxford University Press, 1992 (**Best**; **Müller**).

Gerwarth, Robert. *Hitler's Hangman: The Life of Heydrich*. New Haven: Yale University Press, 2011 (**Heydrich**; **Schöngarth**).

Golsan, Richard J. (ed.). *The Papon Affair: Memory and Justice on Trial*. New York: Routledge, 2000 (**Papon**).

Gutman, Yisrael, and Michael Berenbaum (eds.). *Anatomy of the Auschwitz Death Camp*. Bloomington, IN: Indiana University Press, 1994 (**Boger**).

Hale, Christopher. *Hitler's Foreign Executioners: Europe's Dirty Secret*. Stroud, UK: History Press, 2011 (**Klimaitis**; **Stahlecker**).

Harding, Thomas. *Hans and Rudolf: The True Story of the German Jew Who Tracked Down and Caught the Commandant of Auschwitz*. New York: Simon and Schuster, 2013 (**Hoess**).

Hayes, Peter. *From Cooperation to Complicity: Degussa in the Third Reich*. New York: Cambridge University Press, 2004 (**Tesch**).

Heberer, Patricia, and Jürgen Matthäus (eds.). *Atrocities on Trial: Historical Perspectives on the Politics of Prosecuting War Crimes*. Lincoln, NE: University of Nebraska Press, 2008 (**Gebhardt**).

Helm, Sarah. *If This Is a Woman: Inside Ravensbrück, Hitler's Concentration Camp for Women*. New York: Nan A. Talese/Doubleday, 2015 (**Binz**).

Hilberg, Raul. *Perpetrators, Victims, Bystanders: The Jewish Catastrophe, 1933–1945*. New York: HarperCollins, 1992 (**Klimaitis**).

Himmler, Katrin, and Michael Wildt (eds.). *The Private Heinrich Himmler: Letters of a Mass Murderer*. New York: St. Martin's Press, 2016 (**Himmler**).

Hirschfeld, Gerhard. *Nazi Rule and Dutch Collaboration: The Netherlands under German Occupation, 1940–1945*. New York: St. Martin's Press, 1988 (**Harster**; **Seyss-Inquart**).

Hitchins, Keith. *Rumania: 1866–1947*. Oxford: Oxford University Press, 1994 (**Antonescu**).

Hoess, Rudolf. *Commandant of Auschwitz: The Autobiography of Rudolf Hoess*. London: Weidenfeld and Nicolson, 1959 (**Hoess**).

Höhne, Heinz. *The Order of the Death's Head: The Story of Hitler's SS*. New York: Penguin Books, 1971.

Hoidal, Oddvar K. *Quisling: A Study in Treason*. Oxford: Oxford University Press, 1989 (**Quisling**).

Horwitz, Gordon J. *Ghettostadt: Łódź and the Making of a Nazi City*. Cambridge, MA: Belknap, 2008 (**Übelhör**).

Housden, Martyn. *Hans Frank, Lebensraum and the Holocaust*. New York: Palgrave Macmillan, 2004 (**Bühler**; **Frank**).

Ingrao, Christian. *Believe and Destroy: Intellectuals in the SS War Machine*. Cambridge, MA: Polity Press, 2013.

Ingrao, Christian. *The SS Dirlewanger Brigade: The History of the Black Hunters*. New York: Skyhorse, 2011 (**Dirlewanger**).

Jacobsen, Annie. *Operation Paperclip: The Secret Intelligence Program That Brought Nazi Scientists to America*. Boston: Little, Brown, 2014 (**Becker-Freyseng**).

Jacobson, Mark. *The Lampshade: A Holocaust Detective Story from Buchenwald to New Orleans*. New York: Simon and Schuster, 2011 (**Koch**).

Jasch, Hans-Christian. "Civil Service Lawyers and the Holocaust: The Case of Wilhelm Stuckart." In Steinweis Alan E. and Robert D. Rachlin (eds.). *The Law in Nazi Germany: Ideology, Opportunism, and the Perversion of Justice*, 37–61. New York: Berghahn, 2013 (**Stuckart**).

Jasch, Hans-Christian. *Staatssekretär Wilhelm Stuckart Und Die Judenpolitik: Der Mythos Von Der Sauberen Verwaltung*. Munich: Oldenbourg Wissenschaft Verlag, 2012 (**Stuckart**).

Jelinek, Yeshayahu A. *The Parish Republic: Hlinka's Slovak People's Party, 1939–1945*. New York: Columbia University Press, 1976 (**Tiso**).

Jensen, Olaf, and Claus-Christian W. Szejnmann (eds.). *Ordinary People as Mass Murderers: Perpetrators in Comparative Perspectives*. London: Palgrave Macmillan, 2008.

Jones, David H. *Moral Responsibility in the Holocaust: A Study in the Ethics of Character*. Lanham, MD: Rowman & Littlefield, 1999.

Kasten, Frederick H. "Unethical Nazi Medicine in Annexed Alsace-Lorraine: The Strange Case of Nazi Anatomist, Professor Dr. August Hirt." In George O. Kent (ed.). *Historians and Archivists: Essays in Modern German History and Archival Policy*, 173–208. Fairfax, VA: George Mason University Press, 1991 (**Hirt**).

Katz, Fred E. *Ordinary People and Extraordinary Evil: A Report on the Beguilings of Evil*. Albany, NY: State University of New York Press, 1993 (**Boger**).

Kay, Alex J. *The Making of an SS Killer: The Life of Colonel Alfred Filbert, 1905–1990*. Cambridge: Cambridge University Press, 2016 (**Bradfisch**).

Kay, Alex J., Jeff Rutherford, and David Stahel (eds.). *Nazi Policy on the Eastern Front, 1941: Total War, Genocide, and Radicalization*. Rochester, NY: University of Rochester Press, 2012 (**Bach-Zelewski**).

Kershaw, Ian. *Hitler, 1889–1936: Hubris*. New York: Norton, 1999 (**Hitler**).

Kershaw, Ian. *Hitler, 1936–1945: Nemesis*. New York: Norton, 2000 (**Hitler**).

Klee, Ernst. *Das Personenlexikon zum Dritten Reich. Wer war was vor und nach 1945*. Frankfurt am Main: Fischer-Taschenbuch-Verlag, 2007 (**Batz**).

Klee, Ernst, Willi Dressen, and Volker Riess. *"Those Were the Days": The Holocaust through the Eyes of the Perpetrators and Bystanders*. London: Hamish Hamilton, 1991 (**Bach-Zelewski**; **Bothmann**; **Eberl**; **Hering**).

Koch, H. W. *In the Name of the Volk: Political Justice in Hitler's Germany*. London: I. B. Tauris, 1997 (**Freisler**; **Gürtner**; **Rothenberger**; **Schlegelberger**).

Koehl, Robert Lewis. The *Black Corps: The Structure and Power Struggles of the Nazi SS*. Madison, WI: University of Wisconsin Press, 1983 (**Kaltenbrunner**).

Kogon, Eugen, Hermann Langbein, and Adalbert Rückerl. *Nazi Mass Murder: A Documentary History of the Use of Poison Gas*. New Haven: Yale University Press, 1993 (**Lambert**).

Kogon, Eugen. *The Theory and Practice of Hell: The German Concentration Camps and the System behind Them*. New York: Farrar, Straus and Giroux, 2006 (**Glücks**).

Kohl, Christiane. *The Maiden and the Jew: The Story of a Fatal Friendship in Nazi Germany*. Hanover, NH: Steerforth, 2004 (**Rothaug**).

Koonz, Claudia. *Mothers in the Fatherland: Women, the Family, and Nazi Politics*. New York: St. Martin's Press, 1987 (**Scholtz-Klink**).

Köster, Roman. "Hugo Boss, 1924–1945. A Clothing Factory during the Weimar Republic and Third Reich." Hugo Boss, http://group.hugoboss.com/files/Study_on_the_Companys_History_Abridged_Verson_en_final.pdf (**Boss**).

Krakowski, Shmuel. *Chelmno, A Small Village in Europe: The First Nazi Mass Extermination Camp*. Jerusalem: Yad Vashem, 2009 (**Bothmann**).

Kruk, Herman, and Benjamin Harshav. *The Last Days of the Jerusalem of Lithuania: Chronicles from the Vilna Ghetto and the Camps, 1939–1944*. New Haven: Yale University Press, 2002 (**Kittel**).

Kulish, Nicholas, and Souad Mekhennet. *The Eternal Nazi: From Mauthausen to Cairo, the Relentless Pursuit of SS Doctor Aribert Heim*. New York: Penguin Random House, 2014 (**Heim**).

Lagnado, Lucette Matalon. *Children of the Flames: Dr. Josef Mengele and the Untold Story of the Twins of Auschwitz*. New York: William Morrow, 1991 (**Mengele**).

Lampe, David. *Hitler's Savage Canary: A History of the Danish Resistance in World War II*. Barnsley, UK: Pen and Sword, 2014 (**Best**).

Lampe, David. *The Last Ditch: Britain's Secret Resistance and the Nazi Invasion Plan*. New York: Putnam, 1968 (**Six**).

Lang, Jochen von. *The Secretary. Martin Bormann: The Man Who Manipulated Hitler*. New York: Random House, 1979 (**Bormann, M.**; **Klopfer**).

Lang, Jochen von. *Top Nazi SS General Karl Wolff: The Man between Hitler and Himmler*. New York: Enigma Books, 2005 (**Wolff**).

Langbein, Hermann. *People in Auschwitz*. Chapel Hill, NC: University of North Carolina Press, 2003 (**Liebehenschel**).

Langer, Lawrence L. *Admitting the Holocaust: Collected Essays*. New York: Oxford University Press, 1995 (**Heissmeyer, K.**; **Strippel**).

Laub, Thomas J. *After the Fall: German Policy in Occupied France, 1940–1944*. Oxford: Oxford University Press, 2010 (**Hagen**).

Lehrer, Steven. *Wannsee House and the Holocaust*. Jefferson, NC: McFarland, 2000 (**Klopfer**).

Lewy, Guenter. *Perpetrators: The World of the Holocaust Killers*. New York: Oxford University Press, 2017.

Lidegaard, Bo. *Countrymen: The Untold Story of How Denmark's Jews Escaped the Nazis, of the Courage of Their Fellow Danes, and of the Extraordinary Role of the SS*. New York: Knopf, 2013 (**Best**).

Lifton, Robert Jay. *The Nazi Doctors: Medical Killing and the Psychology of Genocide*. New York: Basic Books, 2000 (**Becker-Freyseng**; **Blome**; **Conti**; **Gebhardt**; **Mengele**; **Oberheuser**; **Wirths**).

Lingen, Kerstin von. *Allen Dulles, the OSS, and Nazi War Criminals: The Dynamics of Selective Prosecution*. New York: Cambridge University Press, 2013 (**Wolff**).

Litvak, Meir, and Esther Webman. *Empathy to Denial: Arab Response to the Holocaust*. New York: Columbia University Press, 2009 (**al-Husseini**).

Longerich, Peter. *Goebbels: A Biography*. New York: Random House, 2015 (**Goebbels**; **Hippler**).

Longerich, Peter. *Heinrich Himmler*. Oxford: Oxford University Press, 2012 (**Berger**; **Dirlewanger**; **Frick**; **Himmler**; **Oberg**).

Lower, Wendy. *Hitler's Furies: German Women in the Nazi Killing Fields*. Boston: Houghton Mifflin Harcourt, 2013 (**Grese**; **Petri**).

Lower, Wendy. *Nazi Empire-Building and the Holocaust in Ukraine*. Chapel Hill, NC: University of North Carolina Press, 2005 (**Prützmann**).

Lozowick, Yaacov. *Hitler's Bureaucrats: The Nazi Security Police and the Banality of Evil*. New York: Continuum, 2005 (**Müller**).

Lukas, Richard C., and Norman Davies. *Forgotten Holocaust: The Poles under German Occupation, 1939–1944*. Lexington, KY: University Press of Kentucky, 2011 (**Dirlewanger**).

Lumans, Valdis O. *Himmler's Auxiliaries*. Chapel Hill, NC: University of North Carolina Press, 1993 (**Greiser**).

Lumans, Valdis O. *Latvia in World War II*. New York: Fordham University Press, 2006 (**Arājs**; **Lange, R.**).

MacLean, French. *The Field Men: The SS Officers Who Led the Einsatzkommandos, the Nazi Mobile Killing Units*. Atglen, PA: Schiffer, 1999 (**Schöngarth**).

Mallmann, Klaus-Michael, and Martin Cüppers. *Nazi Palestine: The Plans for the Extermination of the Jews in Palestine*. New York: Enigma Books, 2010 (**Rauff**).

Mann, Michael. "Were the Perpetrators of Genocide 'Ordinary Men' or 'Real Nazis'? Results from Fifteen Hundred Biographies." *Holocaust and Genocide Studies*, vol. 14, no. 3 (Winter 2000): 331–66.

Manvell, Roger, and Heinrich Fraenkel. *Goering: The Rise and Fall of the Notorious Nazi Leader*. London: William Heinemann, 1962 (**Göring**).

Mauthner, Martin. *Otto Abetz and His Paris Acolytes: French Writers Who Flirted with Fascism, 1930–1945*. Brighton, UK: Sussex Academic Press, 2016 (**Abetz**).

Mazower, Mark. *Hitler's Empire: How the Nazis Ruled Europe*. New York: Penguin, 2008 (**Höppner**).

Mazower, Mark. *Inside Hitler's Greece: The Experience of Occupation, 1941–44*. New Haven: Yale University Press, 1993 (**Blume**).

McGovern, James. *Martin Bormann*. New York: William Morrow, 1968 (**Bormann, M.**).

McKale, Donald M. *The Nazi Party Courts: Hitler's Management of Conflict in His Movement, 1921–1945*. Lawrence, KS: University Press of Kansas, 1974 (**Buch**; **Freisler**; **Gürtner**).

Miller, Richard M. *Nazi Justiz: Law of the Holocaust*. Westport, CT: Praeger, 1995 (**Freisler**; **Gürtner**; **Rothenberger**; **Schlegelberger**; **Thierack**).

Mitchell, Allan. *Nazi Paris: The History of an Occupation, 1940–1944*. New York: Berghahn Books, 2008 (**Dannecker**).

Moczarski, Kazimierz. *Conversations with an Executioner*. Englewood Cliffs, NJ: Prentice-Hall, 1981 (**Stroop**).

Moeller, Felix. *The Film Minister: Goebbels and the Cinema in the Third Reich*. Stuttgart and London: Edition Axel Menges, 2000 (**Hippler**).

Montague, Patrick. *Chelmno and the Holocaust: The History of Hitler's First Death Camp*. London: I. B. Tauris, 2012 (**Bothmann**; **Lange, H.**).

Moore, Bob. *Victims and Survivors: The Nazi Persecution of the Jews in the Netherlands 1940–1945*. London: Hodder Education, 1997 (**Harster**).

Mosley, Leonard. *The Reich Marshal: A Biography of Hermann Goering*. New York: Doubleday, 1974 (**Göring**).

Muller, Ingo. *Hitler's Justice: The Courts of the Third Reich*. Cambridge, MA: Harvard University Press, 1991 (**Rothenberger**; **Schlegelberger**).

Müller-Hill, Benno. *Murderous Science: Elimination by Scientific Selection of Jews, Gypsies, and Others, Germany 1933–1945*. Oxford: Oxford University Press, 1988 (**Fischer**).

Murphy, Brendan. *The Butcher of Lyon: The Story of Infamous Nazi Klaus Barbie*. New York: Empire Books, 1983 (**Barbie**).

Nathans, Eli. "Legal Order as Motive and Mask: Franz Schlegelberger and the Nazi Administration of Justice." *Law and History Review*, vol. 18, no. 2 (Summer 2000): 281–304 (**Schlegelberger**).

Newman, Richard, and Karen Kirtley. *Alma Rosé: Vienna to Auschwitz*. Pompton Plains, NJ: Amadeus Press, 2000 (**Mandl**).

O'Connor, Garry. *The Butcher of Poland: Hitler's Lawyer Hans Frank*. Stroud, UK: Spellmount Publishers, 2014 (**Bühler**; **Frank**).

Orth, Karin. *Die Konzentrationslager-SS. Sozialstrukturelle Analysen und biographische Studien*. Göttingen: Wallstein, 2000 (**Hoppe**).

Overy, Richard. *Goering: Hitler's Iron Knight*. London: I. B. Tauris, 2011 (**Göring**).

Paris, Edmond. *Genocide in Satellite Croatia, 1941–1945: A Record of Racial and Religious Persecutions and Massacres*. Chicago: American Institute for Balkan Affairs, 1962 (**Pavelić**).

Pateman, Colin. *Beheaded by Hitler: Cruelty of the Nazis, Civilian Executions and Judicial Terror 1933–1945*. Oxford: Fonthill Media, 2014 (**Gürtner**).

Patterson, David. *A Genealogy of Evil: Antisemitism from Nazism to Islamic Jihad*. New York: Cambridge University Press, 2011 (**al-Husseini**).

Pauley, Bruce F. *Hitler and the Forgotten Nazis: A History of Austrian National Socialism*. London: Macmillan, 1981 (**Seyss-Inquart**).

Paxton, Robert O. *Vichy France: Old Guard and New Order, 1940–1944*. New York: Columbia University Press, 2001 (**Laval**).

Payne, Robert. *The Life and Death of Adolf Hitler*. New York: Henry Holt, 1973 (**Hitler**).

Petropoulos, Jonathan. *Art as Politics in the Third Reich*. Chapel Hill, NC: University of North Carolina Press, 1996 (**Abetz**).

Petrow, Richard. *The Bitter Years: The Invasion and Occupation of Denmark and Norway, April 1940–May 1945*. New York: William Morrow, 1974 (**Terboven**).

Pohl, Dieter. *Nationalsozialistische Judenverfolgung in Ostgalizien, 1941–1944*. Munich: Oldenbourg Verlag, 1997 (**Wächter**).

Pollock, Benjamin (ed.). *The Philosopher as Witness: Fackenheim and Responses to the Holocaust*. Albany, NY: State University of New York Press, 2008 (**Dolp**).

Poprzeczny, Joseph. *Odilo Globocnik: Hitler's Man in the East*. Jefferson, NC: McFarland & Company, 2004 (**Globocnik**).

Porat, Dan. *The Boy: A Holocaust Story*. New York: Hill and Wang, 2010 (**Stroop**).

Priemel, Kim C., and Alexa Stiller (eds.). *Reassessing the Nuremberg Military Tribunals: Transitional Justice, Trial Narratives, and Historiography*. New York: Berghahn, 2012 (**Rothaug**).

Pringle, Heather. *The Master Plan: Himmler's Scholars and the Holocaust*. New York: Hyperion, 2006 (**Hirt**).

Proctor, Robert. *Racial Hygiene: Medicine under the Nazis*. Cambridge, MA: Harvard University Press, 1988 (**Becker-Freyseng; Fischer**).

Rashke, Richard. *Escape from Sobibor*. London: Michael Joseph, 1983 (**Bauer**; **Wagner**).

Rawson, Andrew, *Schindler's Krakow: The City under the Nazis*. Barnsley, UK: Pen and Sword, 2015 (**Goeth**).

Read, Anthony. *The Devil's Disciples: Hitler's Inner Circle*. New York: Norton, 2005 (**Speer**).

Reicher, Harry. "Evading Responsibility for Crimes against Humanity: Murderous Lawyers at Nuremberg." In Alan E. Steinweis and Robert D. Rachlin (eds.). *The Law in Nazi Germany: Ideology, Opportunism and the Perversion of Justice*, 137–59. New York: Berghahn Books, 2013 (**Rothaug**).

Reitlinger, Gerald. *The Final Solution*. London: Vallentine Mitchell, 1953 (**Ohlendorf**).

Reitlinger, Gerald. *The SS: Alibi of a Nation, 1922–1945*. London: William Heinemann, 1956 (**Prützmann**; **Streckenbach**).

Reitter, Ekkehard. *Franz Gürtner, politische Biographie eines deutschen Juristen, 1881–1941*. Berlin: Duncker und Humblot, 1976 (**Gürtner**).

Rentschler, Eric. *The Ministry of Illusion: Nazi Cinema and Its Afterlife*. Cambridge, MA: Harvard University Press, 1996 (**Hippler**).

Rhodes, Richard. *Masters of Death: The SS-Einsatzgruppen and the Invention of the Holocaust*. New York: Knopf, 2002 (**Batz**; **Blobel**; **Bradfisch**; **Ohlendorf**; **Rasch**; **Thomas**).

Rieger, Berndt. *Creator of Nazi Death Camps. The Life of Odilo Globocnik*. London: Vallentine Mitchell, 2007 (**Dolp**; **Franz**; **Globocnik**).

Roland, Paul. *Nazi Women: The Attraction of Evil*. London: Arcturus, 2014 (**Bormann, J.**).

Roseman, Mark. *The Wannsee Conference and the Final Solution: A Reconsideration*. New York: Metropolitan Books, 2002 (**Stuckart**).

Safrian, Hans. *Eichmann's Men*. Cambridge: Cambridge University Press, 2009 (**Dannecker**; **Wisliceny**).

Sarti, Wendy Adele-Marie. *Women and Nazis: Perpetrators of Genocide and Other Crimes during Hitler's Regime, 1933–1945*, Palo Alto, CA: Academica Press, 2011 (**Bothe**; **Koch**).

Schelvis, Jules. *Sobibor: A History of a Nazi Death Camp*. London: Bloomsbury Academic, 2007 (**Bauer**; **Reichleitner**).

Schmidt, Ulf. *Karl Brandt, the Nazi Doctor: Medicine and Power in the Third Reich*. London: Bloomsbury, 2008 (**Bouhler**).

Schwarberg, Gunther. *Bullenhuser Damm: The SS Doctor and the Children*. Bloomington, IN: Indiana University Press, 1984 (**Heissmeyer, K.**; **Strippel**).

Segev, Tom. *Soldiers of Evil: The Commandants of the Nazi Concentration Camps*. New York: McGraw Hill, 1987 (**Hoppe**; **Liebehenschel**).

Seibel, Wolfgang. *Persecution and Rescue: The Politics of the "Final Solution" in France, 1940–1944*. Ann Arbor, MI: University of Michigan Press, 2016 (**Dannecker**; **Lischka**; **Thomas**).

Sereny, Gitta. *Into That Darkness: From Mercy Killing to Mass Murder*. New York: McGraw-Hill, 1974 (**Hirtreiter**; **Stangl**).

Shelley, Lore (ed.). *Secretaries of Death: Accounts by Former Prisoners Who Worked in the Gestapo of Auschwitz*. New York: Shengold, 1986.

Shephard, Ben. *After Daybreak: The Liberation of Bergen-Belsen, 1945*. New York: Schocken Books, 2005 (**Kramer**).

Showalter, Dennis E. *Little Man What Now? Der Stürmer in the Weimar Republic*. Hamden, CT: Archon Books, 1982 (**Streicher**).

Silberklang, David. "Wilful Murder in the Lublin District of Poland." In Michael L. Morgan and Benjamin Pollock (eds.). *The Philosopher as Witness: Fackenheim and Responses to the Holocaust*. Albany (NY): SUNY Press, 2008, pp. 185–205 (**Freisler**; **Thierack**).

Snyder, Louis L. *Hitler's Elite*. New York: Brinkley Books, 1990 (**Kramer**).

Speer, Albert. *Inside the Third Reich: Memoirs by Albert Speer*. New York: Macmillan, 1970 (**Speer**).

Spitz, Vivien. *Doctors from Hell: The Horrific Account of Nazi Experiments on Humans*. Boulder, CO: Sentient Publications, 2005 (**Mengele**).

Stangneth, Bettina. *Eichmann before Jerusalem: The Unexamined Life of a Mass Murderer*. New York: Knopf, 2014 (**Eichmann**).

Steinacher, Gerald. *Nazis on the Run: How Hitler's Henchmen Fled Justice*. Oxford: Oxford University Press, 2011 (**Hudal**; **Wagner**).

Steinhart, Eric C. *The Holocaust and the Germanization of Ukraine*. Cambridge: Cambridge University Press, 2015 (**Bierkamp**).

Steinweis, Alan E., and Robert D. Rachlin. *The Law in Nazi Germany: Ideology, Opportunism and the Perversion of Justice*. New York: Berghahn, 2013.

Stephenson, Jill. *The Nazi Organization of Women*. New York: Routledge, 2013 (**Scholtz-Klink**).

Stroop, Jürgen. *The Stroop Report: The Jewish Quarter of Warsaw Is No More!* New York: Pantheon Books, 1979 (**Stroop**).

Sweet, William. "The Volksgerichtshof: 1934–45." *Journal of Modern History*, vol. 46, no. 2 (June 1974): 314–29 (**Freisler**).

Szegedy-Maszák, Marianne. *I Kiss Your Hands Many Times: Hearts, Souls and Wars in Hungary*. New York: Spiegel and Graf, 2013 (**Becher**).
Temple, Mark. "The Politicization of History: Marshal Antonescu and Romania." *East European Politics and Societies*, vol. 10, no. 3 (1996): 457–503 (**Antonescu**).
Teschke, John P. *Hitler's Legacy: West Germany Confronts the Aftermath of the Third Reich*. New York: Peter Lang, 1999 (**Globke**).
Tetens, T. H. *The New Germany and the Old Nazis*. New York: Random House/Marzani & Munsel, 1961 (**Globke**).
Toland, John. *Adolf Hitler*. New York: Doubleday, 1976 (**Hitler**).
Vági, Zoltán, Csősz László, and Kádár Gábor. *The Holocaust in Hungary: Evolution of a Genocide*. Lanham, MD: AltaMira Press, 2013 (**Szálasi**).
Ventresca, Robert A. *Soldier of Christ: The Life of Pope Pius XII*. Cambridge, MA: Harvard University Press, 2013 (**Hudal**).
Vigness, Paul Gerhardt. *The German Occupation of Norway*. New York: Vantage Press, 1970 (**Terboven**).
Wachsmann, Nikolaus. "The Dynamics of Destruction." In Jane Caplan and Nikolaus Wachsmann (eds.). *Concentration Camps in Nazi Germany: The New Histories*, 17–43. New York: Routledge, 2010 (**Glücks**).
Wachsmann, Nikolaus. *KL: A History of the Nazi Concentration Camps*. New York: Farrar, Straus and Giroux, 2015 (**Eicke**; **Glücks**).
Waller, James. *Becoming Evil: How Ordinary People Commit Genocide and Mass Killing*. New York: Oxford University Press, 2002.
Ward, James Mace. *Priest, Politician, Collaborator: Jozef Tiso and the Making of Fascist Slovakia*. Ithaca, NY: Cornell University Press, 2013 (**Tiso**).
Warner, Geoffrey. *Pierre Laval and the Eclipse of France, 1931–1945*. New York: Macmillan, 1968 (**Laval**).
Weale, Adrian. *Army of Evil: A History of the SS*. New York: NAL Caliber, 2012 (**Berger**; **Heissmeyer, A.**; **Krüger**; **Wolff**).
Webb, Chris, and Michal Chocholatý. *The Treblinka Death Camp: History, Biographies, Remembrance*. Stuttgart: Ibidem Press, 2014 (**Miete**).
Weitz, John. *Hitler's Diplomat: The Life and Times of Joachim von Ribbentrop*. New York: Ticknor & Fields, 1992 (**Ribbentrop**).
Wells, Leon Weliczker. *The Janowska Road*. London: Macmillan, 1963 (**Katzmann**).
Westermann, Edward B. *Hitler's Police Battalions: Enforcing Racial War in the East*. Lawrence, KS: University of Kansas Press, 2005 (**Daluege**).
Wiesenthal, Simon. *The Murderers among Us*. New York: McGraw-Hill, 1967 (**Wächter**).
Wildt, Michael. *An Uncompromising Generation: The Nazi Leadership of the Reich Security Main Office*. Madison, WI: University of Wisconsin Press, 2009 (**Best**; **Sandberger**; **Scheel**).
Winstone, Martin. *The Dark Heart of Hitler's Europe: Nazi Rule in Poland under the General Government*. London: I. B. Tauris, 2014 (**Bühler**; **Frank**; **Krüger**).
Wistrich, Robert S. *Who's Who in Nazi Germany*. London: Routledge, 1995 (**Glücks**).
Wünschmann, Kim. *Before Auschwitz: Jewish Prisoners in the Prewar Concentration Camps*. Cambridge, MA: Harvard University Press, 2015.
Yeomans, Rory. *Visions of Annihilation: The Ustasha Regime and the Cultural Politics of Fascism, 1941–1945*. Pittsburgh, PA: University of Pittsburgh Press, 2013 (**Pavelić**).

Yerger, Mark C. *Allgemeine-SS: Commands, Units and Leaders of the General SS*. Atglen, PA: Schiffer Publishing, 1997 (**Heissmeyer, A.**; **Oberg**).

Zuccarelli, T. "The Time of Justice and Punishment: The Red Panther." *Ergot*, May 1946, https://translate.google.com.au/translate?hl=en&sl=fr&u=http://judaisme.sdv.fr/histoire/shh/htrhin/Laurenti.html&prev=search (**Mackert**).

Index

Page numbers in **bold** indicate the location of main entries. Page numbers in *italics* indicate photos.

About the Authors

Paul R. Bartrop is a multiple award-winning scholar of the Holocaust and genocide. He is a professor of history and the director of the Center for Judaic, Holocaust, and Genocide Studies at Florida Gulf Coast University, Fort Myers, Florida. Across an extensive academic career, he has taught at the Richard Stockton College of New Jersey, Virginia Commonwealth University, Deakin University, the University of South Australia, and Monash University. The author, editor, or coeditor of 18 books, his published works with ABC-CLIO include *The Holocaust: An Encyclopedia and Document Collection* (2017); *Resisting the Holocaust: Upstanders, Partisans, and Survivors* (2016); *Bosnian Genocide: The Essential Reference Guide* (2016); *Modern Genocide: The Definitive Resource and Document Collection* (2015); *Encountering Genocide: Personal Accounts from Victims, Perpetrators, and Witnesses* (2014); and *An Encyclopedia of Contemporary Genocide Biography: Portraits of Evil and Good* (2012). He is currently vice president of the Midwest Jewish Studies Association and is a past president of the Australian Association of Jewish Studies.

Eve E. Grimm is an Australian lawyer with advanced qualifications in law. After a working life in government service as a senior attorney, she has written about the German legal profession during the Nazi period and the Holocaust. Having formerly taught in the School of Law at Monash University, Melbourne, she was one of the legal team that provided comment on the State of Victoria's racial vilification legislation and was for many years a member of the B'nai B'rith Anti-Defamation Commission in Australia, during which she prepared numerous briefs relating to antisemitism. Her published work has appeared in the journal *Without Prejudice*, and she was a key contributor to *The Holocaust: An Encyclopedia and Document Collection* (2017). She now serves as a senior adviser to the Center for Judaic, Holocaust, and Genocide Studies at Florida Gulf Coast University, Fort Myers, Florida.

[redacted]
3 0080 10096592 6 R 940.53 BAR
Perpetrating the Holocaust :